*Politics and
Social Structure*

Talcott Parsons

Politics and Social Structure

THE FREE PRESS · NEW YORK
COLLIER-MACMILLAN LIMITED · LONDON

Contents

Foreword

*P*olitical scientists will welcome this collection of essays on politics and political theory by one of America's most distinguished sociologists—Talcott Parsons. While Professor Parsons has long been known as a leading sociological theorist, his work on politics has, perhaps, been less well-known among both sociologists and political scientists. This anthology, consisting of some seventeen papers, is but a small sample of his politically relevant work; yet it amply conveys its author's concerns and modes of analysis. While several of these essays have been previously reprinted, their juxtaposition here, in a single volume of political writings, is fortunate. They complement one another and illustrate the gradual evolution of Parsons' thinking about politics.

Readers of these essays cannot help but note certain persistent themes in the Parsonian treatment of political life and theory. As every social scientist knows, his has been a powerful voice for the development of macrosociological theory and more generally for a theory of action cast in systems terms. The relevance of this aspect of his work for political theory is evidenced in Parts I and IV.

This collection also points up Parsons' persistent, although not always recognized, concern for practical matters of public policy, a concern only now being revived within political science itself. The essays in Part II, entitled "Historical Interpretation," not only manifest Parsons' profound interest in history but also illustrate a strong policy orientation. The same is true of Chapters 11 and 12 in Part III on "Full Citizenship for the Negro American?" and "The Problem of International Community." Somewhat less directly policy-oriented are Chapters 7–9 in Part III, "Interpretations of American Politics," but even these diagnostic and analytical essays all have policy implications, a few of which are spelled out. But I should also note a much earlier and less well-known essay (originally published in two parts), "Max Weber and the Contemporary Political Crisis." This essay (Chapter 5), published in 1942, analyzing the rise of Fascism through the sympathetic use of Weberian ideas is particularly welcomed, not only because it has never before been reprinted, but also because it offers a splendid early interpretation of Weber's political theory. At the same time it conveys some of Parsons' own views of the doom of the nineteen thirties and war period.

What seems so remarkable about these many essays in Parts II and III is the persistent desire to construct and use general social theory in the interpretation of some of the great events of our times. Parsons rarely, if ever, interprets without explicit theoretical guide lines. The real world becomes, as it did for Weber, real within the categories of abstract analysis. Notable, too, is the practice of broad comparative, historical inquiry. Interpretation means nothing if it is done without a fine appreciation of comparative variations through time and space, as the essays on pre-Nazi Germany and Japan so vividly illustrate. As one might expect from a sociologist, Parsons is vitally and primarily concerned with the impact of social structure on politics, and secondarily with the reverse set of relationships. Politics in this perspective can become dangerously close to epiphenomena, but Parsons avoids this serious error. He treats politics, and especially so today, as a concrete system, in its own right, and having reciprocal relationals with other cognate subsystems.

Some of Parsons' more recent and more purely theoretical formulations are found in Parts I and IV. In these papers he attempts to supply cornerstones for a highly original conception of political systems. Much of this work is already widely known in political science, but this is the first time the various essays have been pulled together and the theory synthesized as it has in Chapter 17. Much of this work is, necessarily, conceptual, in which definitions are provided, problems defined, and only broad generalizations attempted. But the end result clearly portends a most startling and potentially fruitful work, based as it is on sociology, economics, and political science. While this formulation of a theory of politics is still in process, its major components are clear and not likely to change greatly in the near future. Political scientists have already employed a great many of Parsons' earlier formulations, approaches, and terms. I have in mind such basic ideas as suggested by "systems," "equilibrium," "exchanges," and the conditions of stability and change. Much of the work now being done by political scientists on developing areas and more broadly in the revitalized comparative politics area is deeply indebted to Parsons. Needless to say, Parsons has not been the only figure in advancing systems analysis, but he has been a pioneer and a major one. Rarely has a single theorist from one discipline contributed so much to the work of another discipline.

Finally, I should like to express my personal appreciation to The Free Press for publishing this most convenient and handsome edition of Parsons' political writings. This volume will be much used by future students of Parsons' work, as well as by students of political theory.

WILLIAM C. MITCHELL
University of Oregon

Introduction

*t*his volume has been put together at the suggestion of Professor William C. Mitchell, who has kindly written a foreword to it. After he had completed his *Sociological Analysis and Politics,* which discussed in considerable detail the bearing of the author's work on the interests of political science, he suggested that it would be useful to political scientists, and to some others, to have a selection of my principal essays bearing on political subjects made available between two covers, even though most of them would also be available in other volumes of my collected papers—i.e., in book form rather than in scattered journals and symposia only. The Free Press has kindly accepted the suggestion, with the result herewith presented.

This interest on the part of a well-known political scientist in the work of a man known primarily as a sociologist, as evidenced by both Professor Mitchell's book and his suggestion for the present one, is not only personally gratifying to me, but is to some significant degree a sign of the intellectual times. Though Alfred Marshall had, before the end of the last century, declared the independence of economics by publishing his *Principles of Economics,* rather than of "Political Economy," as had been usual up to that time, the concept of political economy was very prominent for a long time after that, and indeed to some extent still is. "Political Sociology," however, was scarcely heard of before the middle of this century, but now has become a prominent conception giving a title to the interests and work of a considerable number of people on both sides of the disciplinary line. Indeed this trend has gone far enough to suggest that, if political science has not shifted its principal partnership among related disciplines from economics to sociology, at least its allegiance has tended to become more nearly "bigamous."*

* As an exceedingly rough index of the prominence of the field which sociologists call "political

The shift is connected with the relative rise of sociology. When I entered the field, sociology was, compared to economics and political science, a "poor relation" within the orbit of social science disciplines. In turn, the development of sociology requires explanation in terms of the "times." Linking with political science, Max Weber, a figure identified mainly as a sociologist, had substantial influence, eclipsing that of Pareto, who was prominent earlier. But the Weberian influence was perhaps as much a symptom of a change as cause, indeed in part *because* rather than in spite of his very central concern with economic problems.

There was a very real sense in which the "economic interpretation of history" was not so much invented by Marx and Engels as by the English Utilitarians. In many respects it was common to both the predominantly socialist intellectual "left" of the later nineteenth century and to the predominantly capitalist, but not in the older sense "conservative," center. From these points of view the basic political problems seemed to be more than anything else the consequences of self-generating developments in the burgeoning industrial economy of the Western world. There was, to be sure, rather more autonomy accorded to the political process in other than revolutionary phases in the tradition of Bentham and John Stuart Mill than in that of Marx.

The relative, but highly significant, stability and sense of security of the "Victorian" nineteenth century, in some senses going back to Waterloo, was rudely shaken by World War I, which not only was itself a socio-political convulsion of the first order of magnitude, but ushered in a period of turbulence which has lasted ever since—as we have just been reminded by the fiftieth anniversary of the end of that war.

In a certain sense, which will be enlarged upon in the new final chapter of this book, the focal problems of the "post-Victorian" era have been political. In the earlier era, however, it was generally assumed that their primary "substratum" was economic. Gradually, and against much resistance, the conviction has gained headway that this substratum was more "social" than economic. In this often relatively vague reference of

sociology" and political scientists do not yet have a stable term for—the nearest perhaps being the "behavioral" orientation in political science—I made a quick canvass of names familiar to me—without attempting any further check—who could reasonably be classified in these categories. On the political science side, the list includes, in alphabetical order and without implication of relative merit, Gabriel Almond, David Apter, Samuel Beer, Karl Deutsch, David Easton, Harry Eckstein, Samuel Huntington, Robert Lane, William Mitchell, Lucien Pye, Ithiel Pool, Stein Rokkan, Sidney Verba, and Myron Wiener. On the sociological side, it includes Raymond Aron, Reinhard Bendix, Bernard Berelson, Francois Bourricault, Ralf Dahrendorf, S. N. Eisenstadt, Alex Inkeles, Morris Janowitz, William Kornhauser, Paul F. Lazarsfeld, Seymour Martin Lipset, C. Wright Mills, Arnold Rose, and Edward Shils. It would also be quite logical to include theorists of "organization" such as Herbert Simon or James March on the political side, Peter Blau, Michel Crozier, or Philip Selznick on the sociological side. These citations of names, I repeat, are in no sense exhaustive and may well turn out to involve some glaring omissions, but I hope serve my purpose. Clearly, what we are dealing with is an "interstitial" discipline in some ways comparable to social psychology.

the term social lay the opportunity for a discipline which was not altogether new, but which had the potential of explanatory power in the new
situation which was necessary at least to supplement economic preoccupations, though by no means necessarily to supplant them.

In relatively contemporary terminology, the trend was toward increasing attention to the problems of the integration of societies and social
groups. The earlier sociologists had become alert to symptoms of malintegration by and even before the turn of the century. Perhaps the most
salient example was Durkheim's analysis of the relation of high rates of
suicide to the more "progressive" aspects of the processes of modern
social change (1897). In a sphere of outstanding political importance,
however, perhaps the most important single focus of attention was the
rise of the Fascist movements in the period following World War I.
There were, of course, brave attempts to treat these movements as the
simple reflex of self-generating disturbances of the economy, operating
through the ensuing frustrations. But it could be just as plausibly argued
that the economic difficulties were generated in the political system as the
other way round. Indeed, to take a famous "tract" of that time, what
Keynes, in *The Economic Consequences of the Peace,* stigmatized as the sheer
economic foolishness and shortsightedness of the victorious powers,
could not be very well explained in terms of the shrewd pursuit of their
national economic interests.

From my own perspective as a young sociologist with strong interests
in the relation of economics to political and "social" phenomena, the
experience of Fascism, as documented in the papers brought together in
Part II, was decisive. I hope it can be claimed that my own experience was
shared by a good many others in defining problems of the interpretation
of political events in terms which were at least three-way, not only
economic and political, but sociological as well. Whether still other dimensions would be needed may remain here an open question.

A set of problems which were conceived to be both political and sociological at the same time, could not be only empirical—though, of course,
they were very much that—but were also theoretical in a very broad sense.
The early phase of my own development as a social theorist was very
centrally concerned with the problem of the status of economic theory, as
that concern was documented in *The Structure of Social Action.* The problem of the corresponding status of the theory, as I called it later (Chapter
13), of the "political aspect" of the social system, in its relations both to
the economic and the sociological aspect, was very much on my mind,
indeed increasingly so through the "middle years" of my career as a theorist. Indeed I made a serious attempt to deal with it as late as *The Social
System* (1951), which I now recognize to have been quite unsatisfactory.

In the meantime, as documented in Part III of this book, the political
aspect of a variety of *empirical*-theoretical problems with which I became

engaged, such as McCarthyism, the concentration of power, the patterning of voting behavior, the role of mass media, the inclusion of the Negro American, and the bases of international order, not only continued to be unmistakably prominent, but increasingly cried for a better theoretical solution.

As I shall recount in a little more detail in the introduction to Part IV, a break came in the developments following the writing of the *Social System* book, interestingly first coming to a head in a reconsideration of the problem of the status of economic theory. This restatement, however, arrived at collaboratively by Neil Smelser and myself, proved capable of generalization to the case of the "polity," in a sense in which the previous conception of the place of economic theory did not. Part IV is essentially concerned with the theoretical fruits of this reorientation. The two fullest and most cogent statements on the political side are those of Chapter 13 and 14. The first of these is an attempt at a general outline of the nature of the "polity" as a primary functional subsystem of a highly differentiated society, whereas the second takes up the very central conception of power which is redefined within the new frame of reference, above all with a view to working out its theoretical relation to money, on the one hand, and the other two generalized societal media, influence and value-commitments, on the other. These two chapters, plus the new concluding one, fragmentary as they are, constitute the core of such contribution as this book is able to make to more abstractly technical "political theory."

The remainder of a rather large book is not, however, mere "padding" as compared with these three chapters. The considerable amount of material which comprises Parts II and III has been called empirical-theoretical, to stress the fact that there is a great deal of theoretical material included in them. Though clearly these papers are predominantly essays rather than technical research reports, they do, I think, serve at least as a beginning of the "operationalizing" of a theoretical scheme, which, however, has been in course of development rather than being simply given from the beginning. Conversely, of course, theoretical development has been greatly influenced by the kinds of empirical facts presented and the struggle to give many of them generalized meaning rather than immediate *ad hoc* interpretations.

Theoretically, however, the analysis of the "political aspect," as I cautiously called it in the title of Chapter 13, is obviously involved with a broader theoretical context. This is the rationale for including here the two chapters which comprise Part I, since they constitute, on two different levels, recent attempts to outline the conception of a society as a total social system. Among other things, they provide a framework within which the political aspect, as well as the aspect of economic production and societal community, may find an intelligible place.

Secondly, the inclusion of the essays on influence and on value-commitments in Part IV are meant to emphasize the theoretical relations between the polity and the other primary functional subsystems of a society. Indeed such clarification of theoretical problems concerning the polity as has occurred since the writing of Chapters 13 and 14, and is partially documented in Chapter 17, has to a large extent been a product of clarification of the theory of the nonpolitical aspects of the social system, notably what I have recently been calling the societal community, which I conceive to be the focus of sociology as a theoretical discipline.

I have followed the policy of introducing each of the four Parts of the book with a rather brief commentary on the papers included and the rationale of their inclusion. Such general synthetic considerations as seem to be appropriate are stated in the concluding section of the last chapter.

PART *I*

Theoretical Perspectives

art I is the only part of this volume which does not deal explicitly with political subject matter. Its raison d'être, *however, is rather simple, namely that such contributions as the author may have made to the political field have throughout been directly concerned with a more general theoretical scheme, the "theory of action," of which a central part has been the more general theory of social systems. Such claim as the essays included in the rest of this volume may have to originality thus derive from continual interplay between the problems and theoretical heritage of political theory and other parts of the theory of action—as well, of course, as from concern with a variety of different empirical political problem areas and evidence available for dealing with them.*

The problem has been how to give the reader the most useful introduction to the more general theory which could be presented within a relatively short space. For this purpose I have selected two theoretical statements which are relatively recent and hence up to date, and which were written for a readership which consists primarily of nonspecialists. These are the theoretical chapters of each of my two contributions to the series The Foundations of Modern Sociology *(Alex Inkeles, editor, Prentice-Hall). These contributions are each concerned with the analysis of total societies, namely* Societies: Comparative and Evolutionary Perspectives *(1966) and* The System of Modern Societies *(forthcoming, 1969).*

The two chapters overlap somewhat, because the two small volumes for which they were written were designed to be comprehensible independently of each other. The emphasis, however, is substantially different in the two cases. Since the first was designed to introduce an analysis of an exceedingly wide range of different types of society, it is couched in very general terms, being concerned essentially with the concept of a society as a special type of social system, its principal relations to its environments, which are not only physical, but also organic, psychological, and cultural, and the main lines of organization of the internal structure of societies, of their "routine" processes and their patterns and processes of structural change. The latter, as indicated in the subtitle of the book, were particularly considered in the perspective of the conception of social evolution.

Chapter 2 of the present volume has a narrower focus, namely on the theoretical background for the analysis of modern *societies. These problems are considered within the assumption that the type of society we call modern has had a unique origin, namely in the modern "West", and that therefore the relevant empirical field of concern was European society from the seventeenth century on, including of course its "offshoots" overseas and eastward in the Soviet system, and such cases of modernization, overwhelmingly influenced by the West, as Japan.*

The primary point of reference here, even more strongly emphasized than in Chapter 1, is the concept of societal community, *defined as the analytically distinguished integrative system of a society in a sense parallel to the conceptions of economy and polity. This conception has become increasingly salient as the prime focus in the structure of societies of sociology as a theoretically oriented discipline. This I understand in a sense in which the economy is the focus of the discipline of economics and the polity—as will be rather fully discussed in Chapters 13 and 14—is the structural focus of political science.*

Chapter 2, however, does not simply discuss and outline the structure of the societal community, but attempts to sketch some of its main relations to the other primary functional subsystems of the society, which are, as a characteristic of modern societies, so much more fully differentiated from each other than in societies at lower evolutionary levels.

An especially important reference here, which will become salient again later on, is to the principal "evolutionary universals" which have characterized modern societal development.* The market, with its special relation to

---

* Cf. Talcott Parsons, "Evolutionary Universals in Society," *American Sociological Review*, June 1964. Chapter 2 will be found to differ considerably from the version formally appearing in *The System of Modern Societies* because exigencies of space limitation for the latter volume necessitated substantial abbreviation and some rewriting.

money as a generalized medium of exchange, is surely one of them, and the one which of course is central to the theoretical concerns of economics. I should argue similarly that the phenomenon usually called bureaucratic organization has had a similar place in the modern phase of development of the polity, as analytically defined. This in turn is articulated with power as a generalized medium of interchange, as we have attempted to delineate that concept in Chapter 14. The comparable structural focus of the societal community is the normative system, as embodied above all in law, but extending well beyond that. Such a community must, however, also have an underpinning which directly articulates with the motivational orientations of individuals. It is this underpinning which is the focus of the sociological conception of solidarity, especially as that has come to be understood since the work of Durkheim.

There is a complex difficulty, extending deep into intellectual history, in defining the boundary of analytical concerns between political and sociological theory. One primary focus of this is in the conception of a legal system. It has broadly been conventional to allocate law to the political domain, but this is a convention I wish to question. I should rather treat law as an interstitial, connecting structure between the two analytical spheres. Clearly the criterion of bindingness in the sense which carries with it enforceability by public authority is a primarily political aspect, which also implies that courts of law and of course judicial office must have publicly political status. But both courts and judges are, traditionally, semi-independent from the executive and legislative branches of government, and law, as a normative system, links up with complex "traditions," with solidary loyalties, and with legitimation in moral terms.

The other most important problematic area concerns the associational structure of politically organized communities or collectivities of various sorts. This of course becomes of prime significance in modern "democratic" systems where so much political power derives from electoral constituencies. The view I take is that all collectivities are in the first instance political in function so far as they are oriented to "action in concert" in the service of collective goals and by processes which include binding the members of the collectivity. The democratic association, then, both as underlying the authority of governments and in the private sectors, is a political entity, but it is not only that. It is grounded in the solidarities of various kinds and levels of associational "communities" which, with their institutionally normative "definitions of the situation," function in ways which are at least to a considerable degree independent of collective decision-making and enforcement mechanisms. This problem will come to a head in Chapter 14, in relation *to the concept of power and its relations to that of influence, both in the technical sense of this discussion.* *

There is an illuminating parallel between polity and economy in the fact that the relation of holders of political power through office to their constituencies in certain respects resembles that of economic producers to the customers who constitute their ultimate markets. It is through the spending of income that consumers give producers control of the monetary resources necessary to carry on the productive process. Similarly, it is through the support of constituents that officeholders acquire the power to be effective in assuming leadership in the shaping of collectively binding decisions and implementing them. Consuming units—ideal-typically households—are not, however, in the first instance part of the structure of the economy. In a parallel sense I should maintain that the solidary groupings of constituency structure are not as such part of the political system, always considered strictly in an analytical sense.*

The above are samples of the far-reaching theoretical problems which inevitably emerge in any attempt, such as runs through these essays, to treat what are concretely "political" problems at the level of a more generalized type of analytical theory than has usually been the case on either side of the line between political science and sociology. Since this is a collection of essays written at various times and for various occasions, a fully systematic, connected analysis of these problems cannot be presented in the chapters which follow. A few summary remarks will, however, be attempted in the final chapter.†

---

* It is more than anything else the problem of how to draw the analytical boundaries of a political system which has formed the principal focus of difference of opinion between myself and David Easton in his stimulating attempts at theoretical systematization. Cf. Easton, *A Systems Analysis of Political Life* (Englewood Cliffs, N.J.: Prentice-Hall, 1965).

† An exceedingly valuable guide to the reader whose background is more in political science is of course the book by William C. Mitchell, *Sociological Analysis and Politics* (Englewood Cliffs, N.J.: Prentice-Hall, 1967).

Chapter **1**

The Concept
of Society:
The Components
and Their
Interrelations

*t*he society is a special kind of social system. We treat the social system as one of the primary subsystems of the human *action* system, the others being the behavioral organism, the personality of the individual, and the cultural system.[1]

THE GENERAL CONCEPTUAL SCHEME
OF ACTION

Action consists of the structures and processes by which human beings form meaningful intentions and, more or less successfully, implement them in concrete situations. The word "meaningful" implies the symbolic

---

[1] The reader may find it helpful in following this discussion to refer to Tables 1 and 2, appended to this chapter, for graphic representation of the interrelations between these systems.

Reprinted from Talcott Parsons, Societies: Evolutionary and Comparative Perspectives, *Chapter 2, copyright* © *1966, by permission of Prentice Hall, Inc., Englewood Cliffs, N.J.*

or cultural level of representation and reference. Intentions and implementation taken together imply a disposition of the action system—individual or collective—to modify its relation to its situation or environment in an intended direction.

We prefer the term "action" to "behavior" because we are interested not in the physical events of behavior for their own sake, but in their patterning, their patterned meaningful products (physical, cultural, and other) ranging from implements to works of art, and the mechanisms and processes that control such patterning.

Human action is "cultural" in that meanings and intentions concerning acts are formed in terms of *symbolic* systems (including the codes through which they operate in patterns) that focus most generally about the universal of human societies, language.

There is a sense in which all action is the action of individuals. However, both the organism and the cultural system involve essential elements which cannot be investigated at the individual level.

For the organism, the primary structural reference is not the anatomy of the particular organism, but the *species-type*.[2] To be sure, this type does not actualize itself, but works through the genetic constitutions of unique individual organisms, which involve both varying combinations of the genetic materials characteristic of the species and the effects of different environmental conditions. But however important individual variations may be in determining concrete action, it is the common patterns of large human groups—including their differentiation into two sexes—which constitute the massive organic sub-stratum of action.

It would not be correct to say that the genetic constitution of an organism is modified by environmental influence. Rather, the genetic constitution comprises a general "orientation" which develops into specific anatomical structures, physiological mechanisms, and behavioral patternings as it interacts with environmental factors during the life of the organism. The environmental factors can be analyzed into two categories: first, those responsible for the non-hereditary elements of the physical organism; second, those responsible for the *learned* elements of behavioral systems, which is the category upon which we must focus. Although an organism may certainly be capable of learning in immediate environments devoid of other behaving organisms, the theory of action is primarily concerned with learning in which other organisms of the same species constitute the most important feature of the general environment.

Symbolically *organized* cultural patterns, like all other components of living systems, certainly emerged through evolution. Yet, the human linguistic *level* of their development is a phenomenon entirely unique to

---

[2] Good modern reviews of evolutionary biology are *The Meaning of Evolution* by George Gaylord Simpson (New Haven: Yale University Press, 1950); and *Animal Species and Evolution* by Ernst Mayr (Cambridge: Harvard University Press, 1963).

man. The capacity to learn and use language clearly depends on man's special genetic constitution, as the failure of attempts to teach it to other species (especially the primates and "talking" birds) has shown.[3] But only this general capacity is genetically determined, *not* the specific symbolic systems which are actually learned, used, and developed by specific human groups.

Furthermore, despite the great capacity of human organisms for learning and, indeed, for creating cultural elements, no individual can create a cultural system. The *main* patternings of cultural systems change only over periods of many generations and are *always* shared by relatively large groups; they are never special to one or a few individuals. Therefore, they are always learned by the individual, who can make only rather marginal creative (or destructive) contributions to their change. Thus the more general cultural patterns provide action systems with a highly stable structural anchorage quite analogous to that provided by the genetic materials of the species-type, focusing on the learned elements of action just as the genes focus upon the inheritable elements.[4]

Within the limits imposed by the genetic species-type on the one hand, and the patterning of the culture on the other, lies the opportunity for given individuals and groups to develop independently structured behavioral systems. Because an actor is genetically human, and because his learning occurs in the context of a particular cultural system, his learned behavioral system (which I shall call his personality) shares certain broad features with other personalities—e.g., the language he habitually speaks. At the same time, his organism and its environment—physical, social, and cultural—are always in certain respects unique. Hence his own behavioral system will be a *unique variant* of the culture and its particular patterns of action. It is therefore essential to consider the personality system as not reducible to either the organism or the culture—*what* is learned is part of neither the "structure" of the organism in the usual sense nor a feature of the cultural system. It comprises an *analytically independent system*.[5]

Though intimately intertwined with the personalities of the interacting individuals and the patterns of the cultural system, the process of social interaction forms a fourth system that is analytically independent of both personal and cultural systems, as well as of the organism.[6] This independ-

---

[3] See Chap. V in *Words and Things* by Roger Brown (New York: The Free Press, 1958).

[4] This point has been clearly stated by Alfred Emerson in "Homeostasis and Comparison of Systems" in Roy Grinker (ed.), *Toward a Unified Theory of Human Behavior* (New York: Basic Books, 1956), pp. 147–162, especially p. 152.

[5] A more detailed discussion of the relations of the personality to the other subsystems of action is contained in Jesse R. Pitts, "Introduction" to Part Three of *Theories of Society*; Talcott Parsons, Edward A. Shils, Kasper D. Naegele, and Jesse R. Pitts (eds.) (New York: The Free Press, 1961).

[6] "Some Fundamental Categories of the Theory of Action," the general collaborative essay, and "Values, Motives and Systems of Action," the contribution of Talcott Parsons and Edward A. Shils in *Toward a General Theory of Action* (Cambridge: Harvard University Press, 1951).

ence becomes most evident in regard to the requirements for integration that impinge upon systems of social relationships because of their inherent potential for conflict and disorganization. This is sometimes known as the *problem of order* in society, posed in classic form by Thomas Hobbes.[7] The system of interaction constitutes the social system, the subsystem of action with which this book is primarily concerned.

The above classification of four highly general subsystems of human action—the organism, personality, social system, and cultural system—is an application of a general paradigm which can be used throughout the field of action, and which I shall use below to analyze social systems. This paradigm analyzes *any* action *system* in terms of the following four functional categories: (1) that concerned with the maintenance of the highest "governing" or controlling patterns of the system; (2) the internal integration of the system; (3) its orientation to the attainment of goals in relation to its environment; (4) its more generalized adaptation to the broad conditions of the environment—e.g., the non-action, physical environment. Within action systems, cultural systems are specialized around the function of pattern-maintenance, social systems around the integration of acting units (human individuals or, more precisely, personalities engaged in roles), personality systems around goal-attainment, and the behavioral organism around adaptation (see Table 1).

THE CONCEPT OF THE
SOCIAL SYSTEM

Since the social system is made up of the interaction of human individuals, each member is *both actor* (having goals, ideas, attitudes, etc.) *and object* of orientation for *both* other actors and himself. The interaction system, then, is an *analytical aspect abstractable* from the total action processes of its participants. At the same time, these "individuals" are also organisms, personalities, and participants in cultural systems.

Because of such interpenetration, each of the other three action systems (Culture, Personality, Behavioral Organism) constitutes a part of the environment—or, we may say *an* environment—of a social system. Beyond these systems are the environments of action itself, standing above and below the general hierarchy of factors that control action in the world of life. These relationships are depicted in Table 1.

Below action in the hierarchy stands the physical-organic environment, including the sub-human species of organisms and the "nonbehavioral"

[7] I used Hobbes' statement as a major point of departure for my own treatment of the theory of the social system in *Structure of Social Action* (New York: McGraw-Hill, 1937).

Also see Talcott Parsons, "Interaction," in the *International Encyclopedia of the Social Sciences* (New York: Macmillan, 1968).

components of human organisms. This is a particularly important boundary of action because, as humans, we know the physical world *only* through the organism. Our minds have no direct experience of an external physical object unless we perceive it through physical processes and the brain "processes" information about it. In their psychologically known sense, however, physical objects are aspects of action.

In principle, similar considerations apply to the environment above action—the "ultimate reality" with which we are ultimately concerned in grappling with what Weber called the "problems of meaning"—e.g. evil and suffering, the temporal limitations of human life, and the like. "Ideas" in this area, as cultural objects, are in some sense symbolic "representations" (e.g., conceptions of gods, totems, the supernatural) of the ultimate realities, but are not themselves such realities.

A fundamental principle about the organization of living systems is that their structures are differentiated in regard to the various exigencies imposed upon them by their environments. Thus the biological functions of respiration, nutrition-elimination, locomotion, and information-processing are bases of differentiated organ-systems, each of which is specialized about the exigencies of certain relations between the organism and its environment. We will use this principle to organize our analysis of social systems.

We will consider social systems in their relations to their most important environments. I will contend that the functional differentiations among the three subsystems of action other than the social—the cultural system, the personality system, and the behavioral organism—and the articulation of two of them with the two environments of the entire action system, constitute very major references for analyzing the differences among social systems. That is, my analysis will be developed on the basis of the fundamental system-and-environment relations of Table 1.

In the functional terms of our paradigm, the social system is the *integrative* subsystem of action in general. The other three subsystems of action constitute principal environments in relation to it. In the analysis of societies or other social systems, then, the above principle can be applied. We will see that three of the primary sub-systems of the society (Table 2, column III) are functionally specialized around their interrelations with the three principal environments of a social system (Table 2, column IV), each relating most directly to one of these environments. Each of these three societal subsystems may also be considered a distinct environment of the subsystem which is the society's integrative core (Table 2, column II). We will employ this *dual* application of the functional paradigm throughout the exposition of our general theoretical scheme, and in the analysis of particular societies in the body of the book.[8]

[8] Cf. Talcott Parsons, "Social Systems and Subsystems," in the *International Encyclopedia of the Social Sciences*.

THE CONCEPT OF SOCIETY

In defining a society, we may use a criterion which goes back at least to Aristotle. A society is a type of social system, in any universe of social systems, which attains the highest level of self-sufficiency as a system in relation to its environments.

This definition refers to an abstracted system, of which the other, similarly abstracted subsystems of action are the primary environments. This view contrasts sharply with our common-sense notion of society as being composed of concrete human individuals. Organisms and the personalities of members of the society would then be internal to the society, not part of its environment. We cannot argue the merits of these two views of societies here. But the reader must be clear about the usage in this book.

With this understanding, the criterion of self-sufficiency can be divided into five sub-criteria, each relating to one of the five environments of social systems—Ultimate Reality, Cultural Systems, Personality Systems, Behavioral Organisms, the Physical-Organic Environment. The self-sufficiency of a society is a function of the balanced *combination* of its controls over its relations with these five environments and of its own state of internal integration.

We have referred to a hierarchy of control which organizes the interrelations of the analytically distinguished systems. This includes the *cybernetic* aspect of control by which systems high in information but low in energy regulate other systems higher in energy but lower in information (Table 1, column V).[9] Thus, a programed sequence of mechanical operations (e.g., in a washing machine) can be controlled by a timing switch using very little energy compared with the energy actually operating the machine's moving parts or heating its water. Another example is the gene and its control over protein synthesis and other aspects of cell metabolism.

The cultural system structures commitments vis-à-vis ultimate reality into meaningful orientations toward the rest of the environment and the system of action, the physical world, organisms, personalities, and social systems. In the cybernetic sense, it is highest within the action system, the social system ranking next, and personality and organism falling respectively below that. The physical environment is ultimate in the *conditional*, as distinguished from the organizational, sense. Insofar as physical factors are not controllable by the cybernetically higher-order systems, we must adapt to them or human life will disappear. Human

[9] The theory of cybernetics was first developed by Norbert Wiener in *Cybernetics* (Cambridge: The M.I.T. Press, 1948, second edition, 1961) and was applied to social problems in his *The Human Use of Human Beings* (Garden City, N.Y.: Anchor Books, 1954). A good introductory statement for the social scientist will be found in Karl W. Deutsch, *The Nerves of Government* (New York: Free Press, 1963).

dependence on oxygen, food, tolerable temperatures, and so on, are very familiar examples.

Because of our wide evolutionary perspective, our major concern among the non-social subsystems of action will be with the cultural system. Because they develop over long periods and under widely varying circumstances, forms of social organization emerge which have increasingly broad adaptive capacities. In their broad characteristics, they tend to become decreasingly subject to major change from narrow, particularized, conditional causes operating through specific physical circumstances or individual organic or personality differences. In the more advanced societies, the range of individual personalities may even broaden whereas the structure and processes of the society become less dependent on individual idiosyncracies. Thus we must focus on the cybernetically higher-order structures—the cultural system among the environments of the society—in order to examine the major sources of large-scale change.

THE SOCIETAL COMMUNITY AND ITS ENVIRONMENTS[10]

The core of a society, as a system, is the patterned normative order through which the life of a population is collectively organized. As an order, it contains values and differentiated and particularized norms and rules, all of which require cultural references in order to be meaningful and legitimate. As a collectivity, it displays a patterned conception of membership which distinguishes between those individuals who do and do not belong. Problems involving the "jurisdiction" of the normative system may make impossible an exact coincidence between the status of "coming under" normative obligations and the status of membership, because the enforcement of a normative system seems inherently linked to the control (e.g., through the "police function") of sanctions exercised by and against the people actually residing within a territory.[11] Unless these problems become critical, the societal collectivity can act effectively as a unit when required, and so can various of its sub-collectivities.

We will call this one entity of the society, in its collective aspect, the societal community. As such, it is constituted both as a normative system of order *and* by statuses, rights, and obligations pertaining to membership which may vary for different sub-groups within the community. To survive and develop, the social community must maintain the integrity of a common cultural orientation, broadly (though not necessarily uniformly

[10] This section concerns the relations between columns II and columns III and IV in Table 2.

[11] Talcott Parsons, "Some Reflections on the Place of Force in Social Process," in Harry Eckstein (ed.), *Internal War: Basic Problems and Approaches* (New York: The Free Press, 1964) reprinted in my collection, *Sociological Theory & Modern Society* (New York: The Free Press, 1968).

or unanimously) shared by its membership, as the basis of its societal identity. This problem concerns its connection with the superordinate cultural system. However, it must also meet systematically the conditional exigencies regarding the integration of members' organisms (and their relations to the physical environment) and personalities. All these factors are complexly interdependent, yet each is a focus for the crystallization of a distinctive type of social mechanism.

The Cultural System as Environment to Society[12]

The central functional exigency of the interrelations between a society and a cultural system is the *legitimation* of the society's normative order. Legitimation systems define the reasons for members' rights and for the prohibitions incumbent upon them. Above all, but not exclusively, the use of power requires legitimation. The present concept of legitimation need not imply the adjective "moral" in a modern sense. But it does imply that it is in some sense "right" that things be done in accord with the institutionalized order.

The function of legitimation is independent of the *operative* functions of a social system. No normative order is ever *self*-legitimating in the sense that the approved or prohibited way of life *is* right or wrong and admits of no questions. Nor is it ever adequately legitimized by necessities imposed at lower levels of the hierarchy of control—e.g., that things *must* be done in a *specific* way because the stability or even survival of the system is at stake.

However, the *extent* of the culturally-grounded independence between the bases of legitimation and specific lower-order operative mechanisms (*e.g.,* bureaucratic organization and economic markets) is highly variable among societies. By and large, an increase in this independence is a main trend of the evolutionary process, involving differentiation between cultural and societal structures and processes. Whatever its position on this line of development, however, a legitimation system is always related to, and meaningfully dependent on, a grounding in ordered relations to ultimate reality. That is, its grounding is always in some sense religious. In quite primitive societies, there actually is little differentiation between the general structures of a society and its religious organization. In more advanced societies, the interrelation of social and cultural systems in the religious and legitimation contexts involves highly specialized and complicated structures.

Cultural value patterns provide the most direct link between the social and cultural systems in legitimizing the normative order of the society. The mode of legitimation in turn is grounded in religious orientations. As

[12] The following three sections concern relations obtaining between columns III and IV in Table 2.

cultural systems become more differentiated, however, other cultural structures assume increasing independent importance, particularly the arts, which have special relations to the autonomy of personalities, and empirical cognitive knowledge, which at an advanced level becomes science.

Personality as Environment to Society

A society's relation to the personality system differs radically from its relation to the cultural system, because the personality (like the behavioral organism and the physical-organic environment) stands *below* the social system in the cybernetic hierarchy. The society as a system, and *each* of its constituent units, is subject to constraining conditions—which are also opportunities to be utilized—in each of these three contexts. Behavior, of which social systems comprise one analytical aspect, is always in another aspect the behavior *of* living human organisms. Every such organism has at any given moment a given location in physical space which can be changed only through physical motion. Hence, the ecological aspect of the relations among individuals and their actions is never safely neglected. Similar considerations apply to organic processes and to personality functioning and development, both of which are also constantly present as factors of concrete action. Exigencies relating to personalities, behavioral organisms, and the physical-organic environment account for many of the complex, cross-cutting dimensions of the actual organization and functioning of social systems, which require careful analysis and which constantly raise difficulties for social scientists.

The major functional problem concerning the social system's relation to the personality system involves learning, developing, and maintaining through the life cycle adequate motivation for participating in socially valued and controlled patterns of action. Reciprocally, a society must also adequately satisfy or reward its members through such patterns of action, if it is continually to draw upon their performances for its functioning as a system. This relationship constitutes "socialization," the whole complex of processes by which persons become members of the societal community and maintain that status.

Since personality is the *learned organization* of the behaving individual, the socialization process is always critical to its formation and functioning. Successful socialization requires that social and cultural learning be strongly motivated through the engagement of the pleasure mechanisms of the organism. Hence, it depends on relatively stable intimate relations between young children and adults, whose own erotic motives and relations tend to be deeply engaged too. This complex of exigencies, which we have come to understand much more fully since Freud, is an essential aspect of the functioning of kinship systems in all human societies. Kinship always involves an ordering of the erotic relations of adults, of their statuses in relation to presumptive parenthood, of the statuses of the new generation, and of the socialization process itself.[13] It is an evolutionary universal found in *all* societies, though its forms and relations to other structural complexes vary enormously.

A kinship system requires some stable arrangements for day-to-day living which involve organic and psychological as well as social factors. Hence it is a zone of interpenetration among behavioral, personality, and social systems and the physical environment. The latter reference involves the institutionalization of *residence* with respect to location and the constitution of the social unit we call the *household*. The household members are the people who live together as a unit. They share a definite location with physical arrangements, such as a hut or house, or in temporary settlements, a "camp." In most societies, people normally sleep, prepare and eat most of their food, and carry on at least most formally approved sexual activity in that physical and social setting. The household unit is, with all its variations, perhaps the primordial unit of solidarity in social systems.

Although its forms vary greatly, adult status involves the assumption of a certain amount of autonomous responsibility in all societies. The individual performs *services* in some context of collective organization. As a product of a long evolutionary process, these performances become institutionalized in modern societies primarily around the occupational role in a specific-function collectivity, or bureaucratic organization. In any case, the *primary* functional relation between adult individuals and their societies concerns the contributions adults make through performing services and the satisfactions or rewards they derive from them. In sufficiently differentiated societies, capacity for service becomes a mobile resource of the society, mobilizable through the market. When this stage is reached, we can speak of services as an output of the economic process, available for "consumption" in non-economic connections.

For most people in most societies, the places of residence and work are not differentiated. Where this differentiation does occur (mainly in advanced urban communities), these *two* locations constitute the locational axis of the individual's more routine life. Furthermore, the two places must be mutually accessible, a functional requirement about which the major ecological structure of modern cities is generally formed.

A variety of functional relations between personalities and their environments must be treated in other contexts relative to the social system. An individual's value-commitments and their maintenance link primarily with the cultural system, especially as it interrelates with the society through religion. The maintenance of adequate levels of motivations involves mainly the social structures concerned with socialization, particularly kinship. Although physical health is another matter, it shades

[13] Cf. Talcott Parsons and Robert F. Bales, *Family, Socialization, and Interaction Process* (New York: The Free Press, 1955).

complexly into the important but vague areas of mental health and the will of the sick to regain health. It seems that *no* society is without motivation-maintenance mechanisms that operate through some kind of "therapeutic" procedures.[14] In many societies these procedures are predominantly religious or magical, but in modern societies they have been emerging into an applied science. Yet, in no case are they radically dissociated from kinship on a society-wide basis—rather, therapy generally supplements kinship, which is the focal support for the security of personalities.

Surprising as it may seem, the relation between personality and social system, socially structured through what we have called *service*, provides the basic unit for the *political* aspect of societies.[15] Political structures are concerned with organizing collective action for the attainment of collectively significant goals, whether on a society-wide basis or on more narrow bases, either territorially or functionally defined. Advanced political development requires status-differentiation within the adult population on some combination of two bases. The first involves levels of responsibility for coordinated collective action and grounds the institutions of leadership and authority. The second concerns levels of competence, based on knowledge, skill and the like, and assigns greater influence in collective deliberations to the more competent. A political system's differentiation from the matrix of the societal community involves institutionalizing higher-order statuses in both these contexts, often in very complex combinations. The relation of such statuses to religious leadership, particularly the degree of differentiation between leadership in religious and in political contexts, may also present major complications. The imperative of legitimation, not only of the societal order, but also of political authority in particular, indicates a main context of such complications.

Lower in the cybernetic hierarchy is another basis of complication. As we mentioned earlier, the maintenance of a normative order requires that it be implemented in a variety of respects; there must be very considerable —even if often quite incomplete—compliance with the behavioral expectations established by the values and norms. The most basic condition of such compliance is the internationalization of a society's values and norms by its members, for such socialization underlies the consensual basis of a societal community. In turn, socialization to the grounds of consensus is reinforced at various points by interlocking interests, notably economic and political. However, no society can maintain stability in the face of varying exigencies and strains unless the interest constellations of

[14] Cf. Benjamin Nelson, "Self-Images and Systems of Spiritual Direction in the History of European Civilization," in S. Z. Klausner (ed.), *The Quest for Self-Control* (New York: The Free Press, 1965).

[15] Talcott Parsons, "The Political Aspect of Social Structure and Process," in David Easton (ed.), *Varieties of Political Theory* (Englewood Cliffs, N.J.: Prentice-Hall, 1966), Chapter 13, in this volume.

its members are grounded in solidarity and internalized loyalties and obligations.

Beyond consensus and the intermeshing of interests, there is still need for some machinery of *enforcement*. This need links in turn with the necessity for an authoritative interpretation of the institutionalized normative obligations. Hence, all societies have some type of "legal" procedures by which rights and wrongs can be decided without recourse to violence, and by which parties deemed in the wrong can be constrained from acting upon their interpretations, interests, or sentiments at the expense of others.

Because of the indicated territorial involvements of residence, work, religious activities, political organization, and various other factors, the maintenance of a normative order cannot be dissociated from control over activities within territorial areas. The function of government must include responsibility for preserving the *territorial integrity* of the society's normative order. This imperative has both an internal and an external reference. The first concerns the conditions of enforcing general norms and facilitating the performance of essential functions by the various units of the society. The second concerns the prevention of disruptive interference by non-members of the community. By virtue of the organic-locational exigencies we have discussed, the two references have one thing in common: The *ultimate preventive* of disruptive action is the use of physical force.[16] The use of force takes many forms, notably defense vis-à-vis outside territory and deprivation of liberty (imprisonment) within. The control or neutralization of the organized use of force is one functional necessity of maintaining a societal community. In more highly differentiated societies, this always involves some degree of governmental monopolization of socially organized force.

Thus a society's *primary* exigency vis-à-vis the personalities of its members is the motivation of their participation, including their compliance with the demands of its normative order. This exigency may be divided into three levels. First is the highly generalized commitment to the central value patterns that relate directly to the religious orientations. Second is the "sub-stratum" of the personality which, stemming from early socialization, links with the erotic complex and the motivational significance of kinship and other intimate relations. Third is the level more directly involved with services and the instrumental activities which vary with particular goals and situations. These levels of the personality correspond roughly to the superego, id, and ego in Freud's classification.

Secondarily, the linkage of the personality with the organism and the organism's involvement with the physical world operates in two relevant contexts which we have noted here. The first concerns the generalized

[16] Parsons, "Some Reflections on the Place of Force in Social Process." *op. cit.*

organic processes that condition adequate personality functioning, especially in relation to the complexes of kinship, residence, and health. Second is the relation between coercion by physical force and the problem of maintaining the integrity of a societal normative order throughout a varied territory.

Organism and Physical Setting as Environment to Society

Consideration of the social system's relation to its organic base and, through that, to the physical world must begin with the physical requirements of organic life. Here the primordial problems concern the provision of food and shelter, but many other factors are also problematic in all known societies. Ramifying from the relatively simple tools and skills of primitive peoples to the very complex systems of modernity, technology is the socially organized capacity for actively controlling and altering objects of the physical environment in the interest of some human want or need. In limiting cases, the social organization may involve simply teaching skills to individual craftsmen who produce by themselves. But even in such cases, if the technology is important, the craftsman is unlikely to remain totally insulated from practitioners of his craft other than the master who taught him. Furthermore, if his work is specialized, he *must* have some organized relations with consumers of his product and, very likely, with sources of his materials and equipment. Truly, there can be no craft wholly divorced from social organization.

Technological processes obviously serve to meet human needs and wants. They depend on the cultural system for their *techniques*[17]—one person's addition to the total technical lore of his society is always an increment rather than an entirely "new system." Furthermore, technological tasks in this sense are always performed in a socially defined *role*. Products are very generally, though by no means always, the outcome of *collectively* organized processes, not the work of one individual. Thus some executive or coordinating functions must be performed in a broad variety of social relations with consumers, suppliers, workers, researchers, and the like.

Technology, then, is the primarily physical reference of the complex which includes the *economy* as its primary social system reference. The economy is the aspect of the societal system which functions not just to order technological procedures socially, but more importantly to fit them into the social system and control them in the interests of social units, whether individual or collective.[18] The institutional complexes of property, contract, and the regulation of terms of employment are important integrating elements here. The more strictly economic aspects of the

[17] *Skill* is essentially the internalization of certain elements of culture in the *organism*.
[18] Talcott Parsons and Neil J. Smelser, *Economy and Society* (New York: The Free Press, 1956).

complex are, in primitive and archaic societies, embedded in diffuse structures where kinship, religion, or political interests are paramount. Under certain circumstances, however, markets develop, along with money as a medium of exchange.

Technological organization, then, should be regarded as a boundary-structure between the society as a system and the organic-physical environment. On the societal side of the boundary, the economy is the focal structure, providing linkage with the societal community. Here, as the traditions of economic theory strongly emphasize, the function of *allocation* is central. Resources must be allocated toward the satisfaction of the vast variety of wants present in *any* society, and opportunities for satisfying wants must be allocated among different categories of the population. As socially organized, technological considerations also apply to the utilization of services. As the services of individuals become a truly mobile and *allocable* resource, they comprise an economic category, as their bracketing with physical goods in the economists' formula "goods and services" makes clear. Once involved (through employment) in an operating organization, however, they become enagaged in what is in analytical terms political functioning—organizational processes oriented toward attaining the specific goals of the society or a relevant sub-collectivity.

These considerations imply that technology involves a complex of territorial references parallel to residence. In fact, it differentiates from the residence complex only late in social evolution.[19] Its major concern is the location of "industry." Insofar as personnel perform differentiated occupational or service roles, they must work *where* their services are needed, though this location must be coordinated with residential factors. However, location must also depend on access to materials and equipment and on distribution of output. Industry in the strict sense represents the case in which such economic considerations take primacy. But the location problems of governmental administration or of specialized religious personnel can be analyzed in somewhat similar terms.

THE SOCIETAL COMMUNITY
AND SELF-SUFFICIENCY

Certain priorities of control are inherent in the linkages between the societal subsystems that relate the society to its environments and the societal community itself. The societal community is dependent on a superordinate *cultural* orientation system which is, above all, the primary source of legitimation for its normative order. This order then constitutes

[19] Neil J. Smelser, *Social Change in the Industrial Revolution* (Chicago: University of Chicago Press, 1957).

the most essential higher-order reference for the political and economic subsystems, which connect most directly with the personality and organic-physical environments, respectively. In the political sphere, the priority of the societal normative order is highlighted most sharply in the function of enforcement[20] and in the need for agencies of the society to have some final control over sanctioning by physical force—not because physical force is the cybernetic controller, but because it must *be* controlled in order for the higher-order controls to operate. In the economic sphere, the parallel is that economic processes in the society (e.g., of allocation) must be institutionally controlled. Both cases also indicate the functional importance of *normative control* over the organism and the physical environment. When used as sanctions, force and other physical-organic factors contribute much more to the security of collective processes than they can as mere "conditional exigencies." Similarly, the priority of economic over technological considerations—questions of *what* is to be produced (and *for whom*) take precedence over questions of *how* things are to be produced—is a basic requirement for making technology actually useful.[21]

We may now sum up the ramifications of the self-sufficiency criterion we used in defining the concept of a society. A society must constitute a societal *community* that has an adequate level of integration or solidarity and a distinctive membership status. This does not preclude relations of control or symbiosis with population elements only partially integrated into the societal community, such as the Jews in the Diaspora, but there must be a core of more fully integrated members.

This community must be the "bearer" of a cultural system sufficiently generalized and integrated to legitimize normative order. Such legitimation requires a system of constitutive symbolism which grounds the identity and solidarity of the community, as well as beliefs, rituals, and other cultural components which embody such symbolism. Cultural systems are usually broader than any one society and its community organization, although in areas containing many societies distinct cultural systems may indeed shade into one another. A society's self-sufficiency in this context, then, involves its institutionalizing a sufficient range of cultural components to meet its *societal* exigencies tolerably well. Of course, the relations among societies having the same or closely related cultural systems present special problems, some of which will be discussed later.

[20] The emphasis on enforcement here is concerned with the conditions of security of a normative order. Where collective goal-attainment, as discussed above, is at issue, the corresponding emphasis will be on the effective mobilization of services and non-human resources. They are linked by the fact that adequate normative order in the political system is a condition of effective mobilization for goal-attainment.

[21] Clearly, such priorities do not preclude two-way relations between the levels involved. Certainly a technological innovation leading to a new product can "stimulate" a demand for that product. But such a change always raises a new problem of allocation at the economic level. Is it justified in terms of alternative ways the relevant resources may be used?

The element of collective organization imposes additional criteria of self-sufficiency. Self-sufficiency by no means requires that *all* the role-involvements of all members be carried on within the society. However, a society does have to provide a repertoire of role-opportunities sufficient for individuals to meet their fundamental personal exigencies at all stages of the life cycle, without going outside the society, and for the society itself to meet its own exigencies. A celibate monastic order does not meet this criterion, because it cannot recruit new members by birth without violating its fundamental norms.

We have shown that the implementation of a normative order in a collectively organized population entails control over a territorial area. This is a very fundamental imperative regarding the integrity of governmental institutions. Furthermore, it is a major reason why no functionally specific collectivity such as a church or a business firm can be called a society. In relation to members as individuals, then, societal self-sufficiency requires—perhaps this is most fundamental—adequate control of motivational commitments. With exceptions which are inherently limiting (such as the establishment of new colonies), this requires that membership be recruited by birth and socialization, initially and primarily through a kinship system, however much it may be supplemented by formal education and other mechanisms. The recruitment complex may be considered a mechanism of social control over the personality structures of the membership.

Finally, self-sufficiency implies adequate control over the economic-technological complex so that the physical environment can be utilized as a resource base in a purposeful and balanced way. This control is intertwined with political control of territory and with control of membership in relation to the residence-kinship complex.

No one of these sub-criteria of self-sufficiency is paramount, except in regard to their generalized relations in the cybernetic and conditional hierarchies. Severe deficiency in any one or any combination of these criteria may be sufficient to destroy a society, or to create chronic instability or rigidity that prevent its further evolution. Hence this scheme will prove particularly useful in explaining breakdowns in the process of social evolution.

THE STRUCTURAL COMPONENTS OF SOCIETIES

The foregoing exposition of the relations between a society and its environment has employed a relatively systematic classification of structural components. It is important to make this scheme explicit because it underlies a great deal of the analysis in this book.

Our initial definition of the societal community focused on the inter-relatedness of two factors—namely, a *normative order* and a *collectively* organized population. For most general purposes in analyzing societies, we need not extend our classification of components beyond a single distinction within each of these factors. We will distinguish between the aspects of each factor which are primarily internal to the societal community and those which primarily connect it with environing systems.

On the normative side, we can distinguish between *norms* and *values*. Values—in the pattern sense[22]—we regard as the primary connecting element between the social and cultural systems. Norms, however, are primarily social. They have regulatory significance for social processes and relationships but do not embody "principles" which are applicable beyond *social* organization, or often even a particular social system. In more advanced societies, the structural focus of norms is the legal system.

On the side of organized population, the *collectivity* is the category of intra-social structure and the *role* is the category of boundary-structure. The relevant boundary relation is with the personality of the individual member of the social system of reference. The boundary with the organic-physical complex is of an order that does not require distinct conceptualization in this context, although outputs from both personalities and the cultural system converge upon the organism in socialization processes, in the operation of skills, and in various other ways.

These four structural categories—values, norms, collectivities, roles—may be related to our general functional paradigm.[23] Values take primacy in the pattern maintenance functioning of a social system. Norms are primarily integrative; they regulate the great variety of processes that contribute to the implementation of patterned value commitments. The primary functioning of the collectivity concerns actual goal attainment on behalf of the social system. Where individuals perform *societally* important functions, it is in their capacity as collectivity members. Finally, the primary function of the role in the social system is adaptive. This is particularly clear for the category of service, as the capacity to fulfill valued role-performances is the most basic generalized adaptive resource of any society, though it must be coordinated with cultural, organic and physical resources.

Any concrete structural unit of a social system is always a combination of all four components—the present classification involves *components, not types*. We often speak of a role or collectivity as if it were a concrete entity, but this is, strictly speaking, elliptical. There is no collectivity without member roles and, vice-versa, no role which is not part of a

[22] It is important not to confuse this usage with the one referring to *valued objects*, which has been maintained by such theorists as Thomas and Znaniecki, Lasswell, Easton, and Homans.
[23] Cf. Talcott Parsons, "General Theory in Sociology," in Robert K. Merton, Leonard Broom, and Leonard S. Cottrell, Jr. (eds.), *Sociology Today* (New York: Basic Books, 1959, and Harper Torchbooks, 1965).

collectivity. Nor is there a role or collectivity which is not "regulated" by norms and characterized by a commitment to value patterns. For analytical purposes we can, for example, abstract the value components from a structure and describe them as *cultural* objects, but when they are employed technically as categories of social structure they *always* refer to components of social systems which *also* contain all three of the other types of components.

Nevertheless, the four categories of components are, in the nature of the case, independently variable. Knowing the value pattern of a collectivity does not, for example, make it possible to deduce its role-composition. Cases in which the contents of two or more types of components vary together so that the content of one can be deduced directly from another are special and limiting, not general, cases.

Thus, the *same* value patterns generally form structural parts of a wide variety of different units or sub-systems in a society and are frequently found at many levels in structural hierarchies. Furthermore, the *same* norms are often essential to the functioning of a variety of kinds of operative units. Thus, the legal rights of property entail common normative elements whether the holder of such rights is a family, a religious body, or a commercial firm. Of course, norms are differentiated by situation and function, but the bases of their differentiation are never the same as those of collectivities and roles. Within limits, then, it appears that *any* collectivity involved in a certain situation or performing a certain function will be regulated by a certain norm *regardless* of its other features. Finally, such independent variation is also characteristic of roles. For example, executive or managerial roles and certain types of professional roles are common to many types of collectivity, not just one.

The same basic principle of independent variation applies to the relations between the social-system and its environing systems. It is the person in role, not the total concrete individual, who is the member of a collectivity, even the societal community. For example, I am a member of certain international collectivities which are not parts of the American societal community. The plural character of the roles assumed by one personality is a major foundation of sociological theory and must be kept in mind continually. As a society evolves, role pluralism becomes more rather than less important, but it characterizes *any* society.

PROCESS AND CHANGE

The phrase "Evolutionary and Comparative Perspectives" constitutes the subtitle of this book. The scheme of structural categories just outlined will provide the key references for the comparative aspect of our empirical analysis. Evolution, however, is a summary generalization standing for a type of process of change. Before proceeding to empirical matters, we must briefly consider the treatment of process, change and the conception of societal evolution.

The type of process characteristic of social systems is what we call *interaction*.[24] To comprise action in our sense, such process must focus on *symbolic* levels. This means, essentially, the linguistic *level* of expression and communication—the conception of a broad level is justifiable because the factors we call speech and writing mesh with many other meaningful events, such as "gestures," physical "implementations" of goals, and so on. Furthermore, there are symbolic media of interaction other than language, such as money, which are probably better regarded as specialized languages than as essentially different orders of communication.

A language is not merely an aggregation of symbols which have been used in the past; it is a *system* of symbols which have meaning relative to a *code*.[25] A linguistic code is a *normative* structure parallel to that composed of societal values and norms—indeed, it is properly considered a special case of the norm if one allows for its cultural, as distinguished from a social, focus.

Processes of communication generally affect the recipients of messages, although the degree to which the effects are ones intended by the communicators is always problematical. The input of a message may stimulate an output which is in some sense a response. However, failure to respond is also an alternative, particularly if some messages are "broadcast" (e.g., printed in a newspaper), so that "anyone" may or may not notice and may or many not respond.

The process which leads to a response that is somehow related to one or more communicative inputs we may call a "decision." This process occurs inside that "black box," the personality of the actor. Insofar as the communication is part of a social process, the personality is acting *in a role*, the nature of which depends on his relations with the actual and potential recipients of the message and with sources from which communicative inputs are relayed to him.

Though a decision may ostensibly be a response to a particular message, it is elliptical to consider it the consequences of a single stimulus. A decision is *always* a consequence of a *combination* of factors, among which an immediate input is only one. All social processes must be conceived as the combination and re-combination of variable, communicable factors.

For example, the use of power can be conceived as the communication of a decision to the requisite parties, the implications of which bind a collectivity and the actions of its relevant members. Thus, in ordering his

[24] Parsons, "Interaction," *op. cit.*
[25] See Roman Jacobson and Morris Halle, *Fundamentals of Language* (The Hague: Mouton, 1956); and Noam Chomsky, *Syntactic Structures* (The Hague: Mouton, 1957).

unit to carry out an attack, an officer merely gives the command, thereby activating a complex behavioral system on the part of his men. Clearly, however, such cybernetic *communicative processes* can operate effectively *only* in contexts in which *institutional structures* exercise tight cybernetic control over the various factors we discussed earlier.[26]

More detail on social processes will be introduced when particular examples in particular societies, or classes and systems of them, are discussed in subsequent chapters. The special type of process with which this book is concerned, however, is *change*. Though all processes change something, it is useful for our purposes to distinguish from others the processes which change social structures. Here, it is evident that many complex processes are necessary to *maintain* the functioning of any societal system; if its members never did anything, a society would very soon cease to exist.

At the most general theoretical levels, there is no difference between processes which serve to maintain a system and those which serve to change it. The difference lies in the intensity, distribution, and organization of the "elementary" components of particular processes relative to the states of the structures they affect. However, when we describe a charismatic revolution or the development of a bureaucratic system as processes, we are not speaking at such elementary levels, but are generalizing about very complex combinations of elementary processes. Of course, we will have to do this at many points, partly because space limitations preclude more detail, and partly because we lack knowledge about the finer composition of many of the processes in question.

A PARADIGM OF EVOLUTIONARY CHANGE

Among change processes, the type most important to the evolutionary perspective is the *enhancement of adaptive capacity*, either within the society originating a new type of structure or, through cultural diffusion and the involvement of other factors in combination with the new type of structure, within other societies and perhaps at later periods. Some societies have been seedbeds of developments that became crucially important only long after the societies themselves ceased to exist. Ancient Israel and Classical Greece did not endure long as distinct politically independent societies, yet they contributed essential ingredients to the system of modern societies.

---

[26] In two papers, I have developed this position to handle some much more complex problems in the conceptualization of social process; see "On the Concept of Influence," in *Public Opinion Quarterly* (Spring 1963) and "On the Concept of Political Power," in *Proceedings of the American Philosophical Society* (June 1963), Chapters 14 and 15 in this volume.

Nevertheless, both seedbed developments and cases of more immediate adaptive enhancement (such as the emergence of large-scale bureaucratic organizations in certain empires) seem capable of being analyzed in terms of a common paradigm, which I will simply sketch here, but elaborate further in subsequent chapters.

First is the process of *differentiation*. A unit, subsystem, or category of units or subsystems having a single, relatively well-defined place in the society divided into units or systems (usually two) which differ in *both* structure and functional significance for the wider system. To take a familiar example already mentioned, the kinship-organized household in predominantly peasant societies is *both* the unit of residence and the primary unit of agricultural production. In certain societies, however, most productive work is performed in specialized units, such as workshops, factories, or offices manned by people who are *also* members of family households. Thus two sets of roles and collectivities have become differentiated, and their functions separated. There must also be some differentiation at the level of norms and some specification of common value patterns to the different situations.

If differentiation is to yield a balanced, more evolved system, each newly differentiated sub-structure (e.g., the producing organization in the above case) must have increased adaptive capacity for performing its *primary* function, as compared to the performance of *that* function in the previous, more diffuse structure. Thus economic production is typically more efficient in factories than in households. We may call this process the *adaptive upgrading* aspect of the evolutionary change cycle. It applies to both role and collectivity levels; the participating people, as well as the collectivity as a whole, must become more productive than before, as measured by some kind of output-cost relationship. These changes do not imply that the older "residual" unit will have "lost function" in all contexts of its operations. The household is no longer an important economic producer, but it may well perform its other functions better than in its earlier form.

Differentiation processes also pose new problems of *integration* for the system. The operations of two (or more) categories of structural units must be coordinated where only one category existed before. Thus, in employment-occupational systems, the father of the household can no longer supervise production *in his kinship role*. Therefore, the producing organization must develop an authority system which is *not* embedded in kinship, and the producing and household collectivities must be co-ordinated within the broader system—e.g., through changes in the structure of the local community.

Adaptive upgrading thus requires that specialized functional capacities be freed from ascription within more diffuse structural units. There is, then, a reliance upon more *generalized* resources that are independent of their ascriptive sources. For these reasons, differentiation and upgrading processes may require the *inclusion* in a status of full membership in the relevant general community system of previously excluded groups which have developed legitimate capacities to "contribute" to the functioning of the system.[27] Perhaps the most common case concerns systems which have been divided into superior and inferior classes, and in which the upper class has monopolized the status of "real" membership, treating the lower class, so far as it is conceived to belong at all, as a second-class citizenry. The processes of differentiation and upgrading make it increasingly difficult to maintain such simple dichotomies. Differentiation, particularly, produces cases in which the necessities for integrating newly differentiated sub-systems strongly indicate including otherwise excluded elements.

The final component of the change process pertains to its relation with the value system of the society. Any given value system is characterized by a particular type of *pattern,* so that, when it is institutionalized, it establishes the desirability of a *general type of social system.* By what we have called specification, such a general valuation is "spelled out" in its implications for the various differentiated subsystems and the various segmental units. Hence, the value orientation appropriate to a particular collectivity, role, or norm-complex is not the general pattern of the system, but an adjusted, specialized "application" of it.

A system or subsystem undergoing a process of differentiation, however, encounters a functional problem which is the opposite of specification: the establishment of a version of the value pattern appropriate to the new *type* of system which is emerging. Since this type is generally more complex than its predecessor, its value pattern must be couched at a higher level of *generality* in order to legitimize the wider variety of goals and functions of its sub-units. The process of generalization, however, often encounters severe resistance because commitment to the value pattern is often experienced by various groups as commitment to its particular content at the previous, lower level of generality. Such resistance may be called "fundamentalism." To the fundamentalist, the demand for greater generality in evaluative standards appears to be a demand to abandon the "real" commitments. Very severe conflicts often crystallize about such issues.[28]

The state of any given society and, still more, of a system of related societies (such as that comprised of the Middle and Near Eastern city-state societies in antiquity) is a complex resultant of progressive cycles involving these (and other) processes of change. Such a resultant will, at any broad

[27] This may be a case of extending the scope of community to avoid the expulsion of newly differentiated elements—e.g., cadet lineages with new residential locations.

[28] This analysis of the processes of evolutionary change is a revision of the schema set forth in "Some Considerations on the Theory of Social Change," in *Rural Sociology* (September 1961), 219–239.

stage of a more general process, tend to produce a fan-like spectrum of types that vary according to their different situations, degrees of integration, and functional locations in the broader system.

Some variants within a class of societies having broadly similar characteristics will, more than others, favor additional evolutionary steps. Some of the others may, indeed, be so beset with internal conflicts or other handicaps that they can barely maintain themselves, or will even deteriorate. But among these may be, as we mentioned, some of the the most creative societies from the viewpoint of originating components of great long-run importance.

When somewhere in a variegated population of societies there emerges a developmental "breakthrough," the ensuing process of innovation will, I suggest, always approximate our paradigm of evolutionary change. Such a breakthrough endows its society with a new level of adaptive capacity in some vital respect, thereby changing the terms of its competitive relations with other societies in the system. Broadly, this kind of situation opens four possibilities for the societies not immediately sharing the innovation. The innovation can simply be destroyed by more powerful, even if less advanced, rivals. If the innovation is cultural, though, it is difficult to destroy completely, and may assume great importance even after its society of origin has been destroyed. Second, the terms of competition may be evened through adoption of the innovations. The present drive to "modernization" among underdeveloped societies is an obvious and important case in point. A third alternative is the establishment of an insulated niche in which the society can continue to maintain its old structure, relatively undisturbed. The final possibility is the loss of societal identity through disintegration or absorption by some larger societal system. These possibilities are type concepts, and many complex combinations and shadings of them may occur.

THE DIFFERENTIATION OF
THE SUBSYSTEMS OF SOCIETY

We must now consider the broad lines along which societal differentiation is likely to proceed. Given the cybernetic nature of social systems, these lines must be *functional*. The increasing complexity of systems, insofar as it is not due only to segmentation, involves the development of subsystems specialized about more specific functions in the operation of the system as a whole, and of integrative mechanisms which interrelate the functionally differentiated subsystems.

For our purposes, it has been essential to analyze function on two principal levels, the general action system and the social system. Each level has the potential to increase the degree of its differentiation into subsystems, along the lines of the four functional references we have outlined.

The most conspicuous processes of evolution out of primitive social conditions concern the general action level, particularly the relation between social and cultural systems. However, the special relations of the organism to technology, and of the personality system to political organization, indicate that the other two primary sub-systems of action are also involved very fundamentally.

The next chapter (in the volume *Societies*) will argue that a very low level of differentiation among these four subsystems—perhaps approaching the minimum level that is congruent with human modes of action—is the major distinctive criterion of the most primitive type of society.

The differentiation between cultural and societal systems is, in its earlier stages, most conspicuous in the field of religion, becoming evident as greater "distance" emerges between the gods and the human condition.[29] This first develops in more advanced primitive societies, becomes much more marked in archaic societies, and reached a crucial new level in what Bellah calls the "historic" religions.[30] A parallel process of differentiation can be traced between personality and society concerning the degree of autonomy of individuals. Between the organism and society, differentiation emerges between the level of physical technology and the level of economic processes that is concerned with the allocation of mobile resources, the consumable goods which are "appropriated" or produced, and the factors of production.

As the above outline of inter-system relations shows, we would expect this process of differentiation at the level of the general action system to stimulate, and be stimulated by, similar processes internal to the society as a system.

What we call the pattern-maintenance system of the society has *cultural* primacy in that it is the locus of direct relationship with the cultural system. It first becomes clearly differentiated from the other societal subsystems as the latter establish themselves as clearly "secular" spheres which, though legitimized in religious terms, are not directly part of the religious system. This process leads to the differentiation of "church and state," which was not fully achieved until the post-Roman phases of Christianity.

The development of autonomous legal systems is perhaps the most important indicator of differentiation between the societal integrative system, focusing about the societal community, and the polity, which is concerned with the selection, ordering, and attainment of collective goals rather than the maintenance of solidarity (including order) as such. Of all premodern

[29] Henri Hubert and Marcel Mauss, *Sacrifice: Its Nature and Function* (Chicago: University of Chicago Press, 1964).

[30] See below, Chaps. IV and V, and Robert N. Bellah, "Religious Evolution," in *American Sociological Review* (June 1964).

systems, Roman society made the greatest progress in this direction.

Finally, the economy tends to become differentiated, not only from technology, but also from the polity and those aspects of pattern-maintenance associated with kinship. Money and markets are among the most important institutional complexes involved in the differentiation of the economy. Perhaps the differences between Mesopotamian and Greek society mark the most crucial earlier steps in this institutional development, but many additional developments occurred in the transition to modern systems.

The master scheme of four functions and our analysis of the tendency of societal systems to differentiate into four *primary* subsystems will constitute major guidelines for our whole analysis.[31] Where there appear to be more than four important subsystems, we will treat this in one or a combination of three ways. First, the essential phenomenon may be due to segmentation rather than differentiation. Second, more than one level of system-reference may be involved. For example, kinship institutions involve a special integration between societal components located in the pattern-maintenance subsystem and personality, and are hence functionally less differentiated than such structures as modern universities or churches. Third, there are different distributions of primacy among functionally significant components, so that important typological distinctions must be made *within* a relatively highly differentiated subsystem—e.g., an economy or polity. Often these differences result from interpenetrations with elements at other system levels or other subsystems at the same level.

Hence, it should be clear that the grounding of the above classification is analytical, not concrete.[32] Any particular subsystem of a society may involve all three types of complication in a special combination. It is, however, important for theoretical purposes to disentangle them analytically. Although the concrete specifics will vary considerably (and complexly) according to the type of system we are analyzing, the reference points of the societal subsystems—pattern-maintenance, integration, polity, and economy—will comprise a major analytical tool of our entire analysis.

STAGES IN THE EVOLUTION
OF SOCIETIES

An evolutionary perspective implies both a criterion of evolutionary direction and an evolutionary scheme of stages. We have formulated the directional factor as an increase in generalized adaptive capacity

---

[31] Cf. Parsons, Part II of the "General Introduction" to *Theories of Society, op. cit.*

[32] That is, it follows from the theoretical relations depicted in Table 2, especially in columns I, II, III.

consciously adapting it from the theory of organic evolution.

Here it remains to address the problem of stages. We do not conceive societal evolution to be either a continuous or a simple linear process, but we can distinguish between broad levels of advancement without overlooking the considerable variability found in each. For the limited purposes of this book and its sequel, we will distinguish three very broad evolutionary levels, which we will call *primitive, intermediate,* and *modern.* This book will focus upon the first two categories, leaving the third for the sequel. There is some arbitrariness in any particular scheme of stages, and within the two broad categories to be treated below, we will find it essential to make a major sub-division within each.[33]

The dividing criteria, or watersheds, between the major stages in our classification center about critical developments in the code elements of the normative structures. For the transition from primitive to intermediate society, the focal development is in language, which is primarily part of the cultural system. In the transition from intermediate to modern society, it is in the institutionalized codes of normative order internal to the societal structure and centers in the legal system.

In both cases, the criterion stated is merely a catch-word indicating a complex subject matter. *Written language,* the focus of the fateful development out of primitiveness, increases the basic differentiation between the social and cultural systems and vastly extends the range and power of the latter. The principal symbolic contents of a culture can, with writing, be embodied in forms which are independent of concrete interaction contexts. This makes possible an immensely wider and more intensive cultural diffusion, both in space (e.g., relative to populations) and in time. It initiates the phenomenon of "broadcasting"—i.e. the orientation of messages to undefined audiences, to whomever is literate in the language and comes across the document. Furthermore, there is no inherent time limitation on the relevance of a message. Only literate cultures can have a *history* in the sense of an awareness, based on documentary evidence, of past events which are beyond the memories of living persons and the vague hearsay of oral traditions.

There are many aspects and stages of the development and institutionalization of written language and literacy.[34] The early stages, particularly prominent in what we call archaic societies, generally confined writing to the "craft" literacy of small groups using it for specialized purposes, often esoterically religious and magical. A second important development, probably a criterion of the advanced intermediate society, is the

---

[33] Bellah, in his notable article, "Religious Evolution," uses a scheme of five major stages, which does not exactly correspond with the present scheme. Partly, we have different perspectives, Bellah's being more specifically upon cultural than societal factors. But I think our differing schemes also involve a difference of theoretical opinion.

[34] Cf. Jack Goody and Ian Watt, "The Consequences of Literacy," in *Comparative Studies in Society and History* (April 1963).

institutionalization of full literacy for the adult males of an upper class. Such societies usually organize their cultures about a set of especially important, usually sacred, writings, knowledge of which is expected of all "educated" men. Only modern societies approach institutionalizing literacy for the whole adult population, which indeed may signalize a second major stage of modernity.

Written language and the availability of documents act to stabilize a great many social relations. For example, the terms of a contractual agreement need not depend on the fallible memories of the parties or witnesses but can be written and made available for verification as need arises. The importance of such stability should not be underestimated. Undoubtedly, it is a major condition for increasing the extent and complexity of many components of social organization.

At the same time, writing is also a source of flexibility and an opportunity for innovation. However frequently "classical" documents have provided the basis for a rigid traditionalism, the availability of officially correct documents makes possible a much more far-reaching and deep-going critical analysis of relevant cultural issues. If the document is normative for some sphere of action, it poses quite acutely the problem of how, in practical situations, its injunctions may actually be fulfilled. Above all, written documents form a basis for a *cumulative* cultural development; they permit the *differences* introduced by an innovation to be defined far more precisely than by oral tradition alone.

While written language furthers the *independence* of the cultural system from the more conditional exigencies of the society, law, when developed to the requisite level, furthers the independence of the normative components of the societal structure from the exigencies of political and economic interests and from the personal, organic, and physical-environmental factors operating through them.

The problem concerning the kind of law, the institutionalization of which marks the transition from intermediate to modern societies, is highly complex. Clearly, its organization must be highly generalized according to universalistic principles. It is this factor, above all, that precludes such imposing systems as the Talmudic law, or that of traditional Islam, from being classed as "modern" law. They lack the level of generality which Weber called *formal rationality*.[35] Modern legal systems must also strongly emphasize the factor of *procedure*, as distinguished from substantive precepts and standards. Only on the basis of procedural primacy can the system cope with a wide variety of changing circumstances and types of cases without prior commitment to specific solutions.

As we shall see, Roman law of the Imperial period came by far the closest, among premodern systems, to meeting the more "formal" aspects of

[35] Cf. Max Rheinstein (ed.), *Max Weber on Law in Economy and Society* (Cambridge: Harvard University Press, 1954), especially Chap. 8.

these requirements—and, of course, it made essential contributions to the later emergence of fully modern systems. However, it was not a sufficient framework for developing "modern" structures in the Roman Empire itself. We will suggest that this was primarily due to the level of institutionalization of law in Roman society. The Roman Empire did not develop a sufficiently integrated societal community, and failed to integrate all the major ethnic, territorial, and religious groups with reference to a single primary normative order standing for the whole society and above the authority of Roman government.

Table 1—Subsystems of Action

I Functions in General Action Systems	II	III Intra-Action Environments of Social Systems	IV Environments of Action	V Cybernetic Relations
			"Ultimate Reality"	High Information (Controls)
Pattern Maintenance		Cultural System		
Integration	Social System			Hierarchy of Conditioning Factors Hierarchy of Controlling Factors
Goal Attainment		Personality System		
Adaptation		Behavioral Organism		
			Physical-Organic Environment	High Energy (Conditions)

Table 1 presents the main relations between the social system and its total system of environments in terms of the functional scheme we have used. Column I lists the functional categories, interpreted here at the general action level. Column II singles out the social system from the others according to its integrative functions within the action system. Column III, corresponding to Column IV of Table 2, lists the other three primary subsystems of action as immediate (i.e., as intra-action) environments of the social system. Column IV presents the two environments within which action systems function—at least so far as they are distinguished here—namely, the physical-organic environment, relations with which are mediated in the first instance through the behavioral organism, and the environment we have called "ultimate reality," relations with which are mediated through the constitutive symbol systems (i.e., religious components) of the cultural system. Finally, Column V indicates the two directions in which factors exert their effect on these systems. The upward-pointed arrow indicates the hierarchy of conditions, which at any given cumulative level in the upward series is, in the common formula, "necessary but not sufficient." The downward-pointed arrow designates the hierarchy of controlling factors, in the cybernetic sense. As we move downward, control of more and more necessary conditions makes the implementation of patterns, plans, or programs possible. Systems higher in the order are relatively high in information while those lower down are relatively high in energy.

Table 2—The Societal Community and Its Environments

I Intra-Societal Functions	II	III Intra-Social Environments of Societal Community	IV Extra-Social Environments of Societal Community	V Function in General Action System
Pattern Maintenance		Maintenance of Institutionalized Cultural Patterns	Cultural System	Pattern Maintenance
Integration	Societal Community			Integration
Goal Attainment		Polity	Personality System	Goal Attainment
Adaptation		Economy	Behavioral Organism	Adaptation

Table 2 presents schematically the set of relationships which have been outlined in the text concerning the primary structure of the society as a system, centering on the place of the societal community. Column I lists the four primary functional categories according to their place in the cybernetic hierarchy of control. In relation to Column I, Column II identifies the societal community as the integrative subsystem of the society—i.e., that *analytically* defined subsystem characterized by the primacy of integrative function in the larger system. Column III designates the other three primary analytical subsystems (the functions of which are also given in relation to Column I) as constituting environments of the societal community which are *internal* to the society as a social system. It both carries on processes of input-output interchange and shares certain zones of interpenetration with them. Column IV details in the cognate order the primary subsystems of action other than the social system itself, showing them as in turn constituting environments for the social system, presuming the same order of interchange and interpretation, but with different specific content. The slanting dashed lines indicate that the *entire* societal system, not each of its subsystems, is involved in these interchanges with the action environments. Finally, Column V lists the functional categories in terms of which action systems are differentiated, this time in the context of the general action system rather than, as in Column I, of the social system.

Chapter **2**

Theoretical Orientations on Modern Societies

ACTION SYSTEMS AND
SOCIAL SYSTEMS

*W*e consider social systems[1] to be constituents of more general systems of action, the other primary constituents being cultural systems, personality systems, and behavioral organisms, all four being abstractly defined relative to the concrete behavior of social interaction. We treat the three subsystems of actions other than the social system as constituents of its

[1] See Chapter II of *Societies: Evolutionary and Comparative Perspectives,* (Englewood Cliffs, N.J.: Prentice Hall, 1966), Chapter 1 in this volume; also my articles "Social Systems and Subsystems" and "Interaction" in the *International Encyclopedia of the Social Sciences* (New York: Macmillan, 1968) and the introductory materials in T. Parsons, E. Shils, J. Pitts, and K. Naegele, (eds.) *Theories of Society* (New York: Free Press, 1961).

environment. This usage is somewhat unfamiliar, especially for the case of the personalities of individuals. It is justified fully elsewhere, but to understand what follows it is essential to keep in mind that neither social nor personality systems are here conceived as concrete entities.

The distinctions among the four subsystems of action are functional. We draw them in terms of the four primary functions which we impute to all systems of action, namely pattern-maintenance, integration, goal-attainment, and adaptation.[2]

An action system's primary integrative problem is the harmonization and coordination of the attributes and actions of its constituent units, in the first instance human individuals, though for certain purposes collectivities may be treated as actors. Hence, we attribute primacy of integrative function to the social system.

We attribute primacy of pattern-maintenance—and of creative pattern change—to the cultural system. Whereas social systems are organized with primary reference to the articulation in systems of social relationships as such, cultural systems are organized about the characteristics of complexes of symbolic meaning, the codes in terms of which they are structured, the particular clusters of symbols they employ, and the conditions of their utilization, maintenance, and change as parts of action systems. We attribute primacy of goal-attainment function to the personality of the individual. The personality system is the primary *agency* of action processes, hence of the implementation of cultural principles and requirements. On the level of reward in the motivational sense, the optimization of gratification or satisfaction to personalities is the primary goal-output of action systems. The behavioral organism is conceived as the adaptive subsystem of action, being the locus of the primary generalized facilities which underlie the other systems. It embodies a set of conditions to which action must adapt and comprises the primary mechanism of interrelation with the physical environment, especially through the input and processing of information in the central nervous system and through motor activity in coping with exigencies of the physical environment.

There are two systems of reality which are environmental to action in general and not constituents of action in our analytical sense. The first is the physical environment, including not only phenomena as understandable in terms of physics and chemistry, but also the world of living organisms so far as they are not integrated into action systems. The second, which we conceive to be independent of the physical environment as well as action systems as such, we will call "ultimate reality," in a sense derived from traditions of philosophy. It concerns what Weber[3] called "problem of meaning" for human action and is mediated into action primarily by

---

[2] The four-function theory is presented in my introductory essay, "An Outline of the Social System," in *Theories of Society (op. cit.)*, and more briefly in *Societies (op. cit.)*.

[3] Max Weber, *The Sociology of Religion* (Boston: Beacon Press, 1963).

the cultural system's structuring of meaningful orientations that include, but are not exhausted by, cognitive "answers."[4]

In analyzing the interrelations among the four subsystems of action—and between these systems and the environments of action—it is essential to keep in mind the phenomenon of *interpenetration*. Perhaps the best-known case of interpenetration is the *internalization* of social objects and cultural norms into the personality of the individual. Learned content of experience, organized and stored in the memory apparatus of the organism, is another example, as is the *institutionalization* of normative components of cultural systems as constitutive structures of social systems. We hold that the boundary between any pair of action systems involves a "zone" of structured components or patterns which must be treated theoretically as *common* to *both* systems, not simply allocated to one system or the other. For example, it is untenable to say that norms of conduct derived from social experience, which both Freud (in the concept of the Superego) and Durkheim (in the concept of collective representations) treated as parts of the personality of the individual, must be *either* that *or* part of the social system.[5]

It is by virtue of the zones of interpenetration that processes of interchange among systems can take place. This is especially true at the levels of symbolic meaning and generalized motivation. In order to "communicate" symbolically, individuals must have culturally organized common codes, such as those of language, which are also integrated into systems of their social interaction. In order to make information stored in the central nervous system utilizable for the personality, the behavioral organism must have mobilization and retrieval mechanisms which, through interpenetration, subserve motives organized at the personality level.

Thus, we conceive social systems to be "open," engaged in continual interchange of inputs and outputs with their environments. Moreover, we conceive them to be internally differentiated into various orders of subsystems which are also continually involved in processes of interchange.

Social systems are the subsystems of action constituted by states and processes of social interaction among acting units. If the properties of interaction were derivable from properties of the acting units, social systems would be epiphenomenal, as much "individualistic" social theory has contended. Our position is sharply in disagreement: it derives particularly from Durkheim's statement that society—and other social systems—is a "reality *sui generis*."

The structural aspect of social systems may be analyzed in terms of four types of independently variable components, which we call values,

---

[4] Cf. Clifford Geertz, "Religion as a Cultural System" in Michael Banton, ed., *Anthropological Approaches to the Study of Religion* (New York: Praeger, 1966).
[5] Talcott Parsons, "The Superego and the Theory of Social Systems" in *Social Structure and Personality* (New York: Free Press, 1964).

norms, collectivities, and roles.[6] Values take primacy in the pattern maintenance functioning of social systems, for they are conceptions of desirable types of social systems that regulate the making of commitments by
social units. Norms, which function primarily to integrate social systems,
are specific to particular social functions and types of social situations.
They include not only value components specified to appropriate levels
in the structure of a social system, but also specific modes of orientation for acting under the functional and situational conditions of particular
collectivities and roles. Collectivities are the type of structural component
having goal-attainment primacy. Putting aside the many instances of
highly fluid group systems, such as crowds, we speak of a collectivity
only where two specific criteria are fulfilled. First, there must be definite
statuses of membership so that a useful distinction between members and
nonmembers can generally be drawn, a criterion fulfilled by cases that
vary from nuclear families to political communities. Second, there must be
some differentiation among members in relation to their statuses and functions within the collectivity, so that some categories of members are expected to do certain things which are not expected of other members.
A role, the type of structural component that has primacy of adaptive
function for a social system, we conceive as the sector of the action system
of a definable class of individuals which, through reciprocal expectations,
is involved in a particular collectivity. Hence, roles comprise the primary
zones of interpenetration between the social system and the personality
of the individual. A role is never idiosyncratic to a particular individual,
however. A father is specific to his children in his fatherhood, but is a
father in terms of the role-structure of his society. At the same time, he
also participates in various other contexts of interaction, occupying, for
example, an occupational role.

The reality *sui generis* of social systems may involve the independent
variability of each of these types of structural components relative to the
others. A generalized value-pattern does not legitimize the same norms,
collectivities, or roles under all conditions, for example. Similarly, many
norms regulate the action of indefinite numbers of collectivities and roles,
but only specific sectors of their action. Hence a collectivity generally
functions under the control of a large number of particular norms.
It always involves a plurality of roles, although almost any major category of role is performed in a plurality of particular collectivities. Nevertheless, social systems are comprised of *combinations* of these structural
components. To be institutionalized in a stable fashion, collectivities and
roles must be "governed" by specific values and norms, whereas values
and norms are themselves institutionalized only insofar as they are "implemented" by particular collectivities and roles.

[6] Cf. Talcott Parsons, "General Theory in Sociology" in R. K. Merton, L. Broom, and L. S.
Cottrell, Jr., *Sociology Today* (New York: Basic Books, 1959, and Harper: Torch Books, 1965).

THE CONCEPT OF SOCIETY

We define society as the type of social system which is characterized by the highest level of self-sufficiency relative to its environments, including other social systems.[7] Total self-sufficiency would be incompatible with the status of society as a subsystem of action. Any society depends for its continuation as a system on the inputs it receives through interchanges from its environing systems. Self-sufficiency in relation to environments, then, means stability of interchange relationships and capacity to control interchanges in the interest of societal functioning. Such control may vary from capacity to forestall or "cope with" disturbances to capacity to shape environmental relations favorably.

The physical environment has an adaptive significance for a society in that it is the direct source of the physical resources which the society can exploit through its technological and economic mechanisms of production. The allocation of access to physical resources, in order to be linked with the division of labor through the ecological aspect of society, requires a territorial distribution of residental locations and economic interests among the various subgroupings of the population. The physical environment has a second significance for societies in that, because of the importance of physical force as a preventive of undesired action, effective societal goal-attainment requires control of actions within a territorial area. Hence, there are two contexts of societal self-sufficiency that concern, respectively, economic and political functioning in relation to the physical environment, through technology and through the organized use of force in the military and police functions.

A third context of societal self-sufficiency concerns the personalities of individual members in a special mode of interpenetration with the organisms involved. The organism links directly to the territorial complex through the importance of the physical location of actions. But its main link with the social system involves the personality; this primary zone of interpenetration concerns the status of *membership*. A society can be self-sufficient only in so far as it is generally able to "count on" its members' performances to "contribute" adequately to societal functioning. No more than in the other interchanges involved in self-sufficiency, need this integration between personality and society be absolute. Yet, one could not speak of a society as self-sufficient if the overwhelming majority of its members were radically "alienated."

The integration of members into a society involves the zone of interpenetration between the social and personality systems. The relation is basically tripartite, however, because parts of the cultural system as well as parts of the social structure are internalized in personalities, and because parts of the cultural system are institutionalized in the society.

[7] Chapter 1 in this volume.

At the social level, the institutionalized patterns of *value* are collective representations (in Durkheim's sense) that define the *desirable types* of social system. These representations are correlative with the conceptions of types of social systems by which individual personalities orient themselves in their capacities as members. It is the members' consensus on value-orientation with respect to their own society, then, which defines the institutionalization of value-patterns. Consensus in this respect is certainly a matter of degree. Hence self-sufficiency in this context concerns the degree to which the institutions of a society have been *legitimized* by the consensual value-commitments of its members.[8]

At the cultural level, social values comprise only part of the content of wider systems of value, since all other classes of objects of the orientation of action must be evaluated too. Values are also related to other components of a cultural system, which include empirical knowledge, expressive symbol systems, and the constitutive symbolic structures that compose the core of religious systems.[9] Above all, values, as institutionalized in societies, are ultimately legitimized in religious terms. In the context of cultural legitimation, then, a society is self-sufficient in proportion as its institutions are legitimized by values which its members hold with relative consensus *and* which are in turn legitimized by their congruence with other components of the cultural system, especially its constitutive symbolism.

It is essential to remember that cultural systems do not correspond exactly with social systems, including societies. The more important cultural systems generally become institutionalized, in varying patterns, in a number of societies, though there are also "subcultures" within societies. For example, the cultural system centering on Western Christianity has, with certain qualifications and many variations, been common to the whole European system of modernizing societies. Two modes of the relation of one society to other societies must be discussed in a book entitled *The System of Modern Societies*. First, all societies we speak of as "politically organized" are involved with various other societies in "international relations" of various types, friendly or hostile. We shall extend this conception and regard these relations as themselves constituting a social system which can be analyzed with the same general concepts as other types of social system. Second, a social system may be involved with the social structure and/or the members and/or the culture of two or more societies. Such social systems are numerous and of many different kinds. American immigrant families often retain effective kinship relations with people in the "old country," so that their kinship systems have both American and foreign "branches." Something similar can be said of

[8] Cf. "An Outline of the Social System," *op. cit.*
[9] See Talcott Parsons, "Introduction" to the section "Culture and the Social System" in *Theories of Society (op. cit.).*

many business firms, professional associations, and religious collectivities. Although the Roman Catholic Church, for example, is a social system, it clearly is not a society since its self-sufficiency is very low by our criteria. Its control of economic resources through the organization of production is minimal; it lacks autonomous political control of territorial areas; in many societies, its members constitute a minority. Thus we must take account of both social systems which are "supersocietal" in being comprised of a plurality of societies and social systems that are "cross-societal" in that their members belong to a plurality of different societies.

THE SUBSYSTEMS OF SOCIETY

In accord with our four-function scheme for analyzing systems of action, we treat a society as being analytically divisible into four *primary* subsystems. Thus, the pattern-maintenance subsystem is particularly concerned with the relations of the society to the cultural system and, through it, ultimate reality; the goal-attainment subsystem or the polity to the personalities of individual members; the adaptive subsystem, or the economy, to the behavioral organism and, through it, the physical world. These divisions are clearest and most important for societies advanced on the scale of modernity. However, the complexity of the relationships, both among subsystems of action and among subsystems of society, prevent these divisions from ever being very neat. For example, kinship structures must be located in all three of the above-mentioned subsystems. Through their relation to food, sex, biological descent, and residence, they are involved with the organism and the physical environment. As the individual's primary source of early learning of values, norms, and modes of communication, they are very much involved with the pattern-maintenance system. As the primary source of socialized services, they are involved with the polity.

Within this framework, the core of a society as a social system is its integrative subsystem. Since we treat the social system as integrative for action systems generally, we must pay special attention to the ways in which it achieves—or fails to achieve—various kinds and levels of integration itself. We will call the integrative subsystem of a society the *societal community*.

Perhaps the most general function of a society community is to articulate a *system* of norms with a collective organization that has unity and cohesiveness. Following Weber, we call the normative aspect the system of legitimate order,[10] the collective aspect is the societal community as a single, bounded collectivity. Societal order requires definiteness and

[10] Max Weber: *The Theory of Social and Economic Organization* (New York: Oxford University Press, 1947).

clarity of integration in the sense, on the one hand, of normative coherence and, on the other hand, of societal "harmony" and "coordination." Moreover, normatively-defined obligations must on the whole be accepted while conversely collectivities must have normative sanction in performing their functions and promoting their legitimate interests. Thus, normative order at the societal level contains a "solution" of the problem posed by Hobbes, of how human relations can be prevented from degenerating into a "war of all against all."

THE CORE OF THE SOCIETAL COMMUNITY

It is important not to treat a societal structure of norms as a monolithic entity. Hence we distinguish four components analytically, even though they overlap greatly in specific content. Our distinctions concern the grounds of obligations and rights as well as the nature of sanctioning noncompliance and rewarding compliance or unusual levels of performance.

Our core category is perhaps relatively unfamiliar, probably because discussion has generally focused upon religious and political references. It is the component centering about the definition of obligations of *loyalty* to the societal collectivity, both in the capacity of membership as such and in various categories of differentiated status and role within the society— thus in most modern societies willingness to perform military service is not a test of loyalty for women, but is so for men. Loyalty is a readiness to respond to properly "justified" appeals to the collective or "public" interest or need. The normative problem concerns the definition of occasions when such a response constitutes an obligation. In principle any collectivity requires loyalty, but it has a special importance for the societal community. Organs of government are generally the agents of appeals to societal loyalty and of the implementation of the associated norms. However, there are many types of cases in which government and justified community agency do not directly coincide.

Particularly important are the relations between sub-groups' and individual's loyalties to the societal collectivity and their loyalties to other collectivities of which they are members. *Role-pluralism*, the involvement of the same persons in roles in several collectivities, is a fundamental feature of all human societies. On the whole, an increase in role-pluralism is a major feature of the differentiation processes leading toward modern types of society. Therefore, the regulation of the loyalties of members, to the community itself and to various other collectivities, is a major problem for the integration of a societal community.

Individualistic social theory has persistently exaggerated the significance of individual "self-interest" in a psychological sense as an obstacle to the integration of social systems. The self-interested motives of individuals are, on the whole, effectively channeled into the functioning of social systems through a variety of memberships and loyalties to collectivities. The more immediate problem for most individuals is the adjustment of obligations among the competing loyalties in cases of conflict. For example, the normal adult male in modern societies is both employed and a member of a family household. Although the demands of these two roles often conflict, most men have a heavy stake in fulfilling loyalties to *both*.

A societal community is a complex network of interpenetrating collectivities and collective loyalties, a system of units characterized by both functional differentiation and segmentation. Thus, kinship-household units, business firms, churches, governmental units, educational collectivities, and the like will be differentiated from each other. Moreover, there will be a plurality of each type of collective unit. For example, there will be a very large number of households, each comprised of only a few persons, and many local communities.

Loyalty to the societal community must occupy a high position in any stable hierarchy of loyalties and is a primary focus of societal concern as such. In the general order obtaining among the elements of action systems, however, it does not occupy the highest place in the hierarchy. We have stressed the importance of cultural legitimation of a society's normative order because it occupies a superordinate position. It operates in the first instance through the institutionalization of a value-system, which is part of both the societal and the cultural systems. Then its sub-values, which are specifications of general value patterns, become parts of every concrete norm that is integrated into the legitimate order. The system of norms governing loyalties, then, must integrate the rights and obligations of various collectivities and their memberships not only with each other, but also with the bases of legitimation of the order as a whole.[11]

In its hierarchical aspect, the normative ordering of the societal community in terms of memberships comprises its *stratification* scale, the scale of the accepted—and, so far as values and norms are integrated, legitimized—*prestige* of sub-collectivities, statuses, and roles and of persons as societal members. It must articulate both with the universal components of the normative ordering of the status of membership and with the elements of differentiation among the functions of subcollectivities, statuses, and roles, which do not as such imply hierarchical differences. The concrete stratification system, then, is a complex function of all these components.

Role-pluralism renders the problem of the status of individuals in a

[11] On these matters, see Robert N. Bellah, "Epilogue," in *Religion and Progress in Modern Asia* (New York: Free Press, 1965).

stratification system especially complex. Stratification mechanisms have generally treated individuals as diffusely integrated in large collective systems, membership in which defines their status. Lineages, ethnic groups, "estates," and social classes have operated in this way. However modern society requires a differentiation of individual statuses from diffuse background solidarities, giving modern systems of stratification a distinctive character.[12]

The position of a subcollectivity or individual in the stratification system is measured by the level of its or his *prestige* or capacity to exercise *influence*. Influence we conceive to be a generalized symbolic medium of societal interchange, in the same general class as money and power. It consists in capacity to bring about desired decisions on the part of other social units without directly offering them a valued *quid pro quo* as an inducement or threatening them with deleterious consequences. It must operate through persuasion, however, in that its object must be convinced that to decide as the influencer suggests is to act in the interest of a collective system with which both are solidary. Its primary appeal is to the collective interest, but generally on the assumption that the parties involved have particular interests in promoting the collective interest and their mutual solidarity. Typical uses of influence are persuasion to enter into a contractual relation "in good faith" or to vote for a specific political candidate. Influence may be exchanged for *ad hoc* benefits or for other forms of influence, in a sense parallel to that in which monetary resources may either be used to obtain goods or pooled or exchanged. Influence may also be exchanged for other generalized media such as money or power.[13]

SOCIETAL COMMUNITY
AND PATTERN-MAINTENANCE

The bases of cultural legitimation transcend direct contingencies of influence, interests, and solidarity, being grounded at the societal level in *value-commitments*. By contrast with loyalty to collectivities, the hallmark of a value-commitment is greater independence from considerations of cost, relative advantage or disadvantage, and social or environmental exigency in the meeting of obligations. The violation of a commitment is defined as illegitimate; its fulfillment is a matter of honor or conscience which may not be comprised without dishonor and/or guilt.

Although this may sound very restrictive, as indeed such commitments often are, the degree and kind of restrictiveness involved depends on a

[12] Talcott Parsons, "A Revised Analytical Approach to the Theory of Stratification" in *Essays in Sociological Theory* (New York: Free Press, 1954).
[13] Talcott Parsons, "On the Concept of Influence," Chapter 15 in this volume.

variety of factors. Commitment to values in general implies the assumption of an obligation to help implement them in concrete action. Especially where the value system is "activistic," as it generally is in modern societies, this implies realistic acceptance of certain conditions of collective action. Thus, value *systems* contain a category of commitments to "valued association," solidarity with legitimate collective relationships and enterprises. What associations are valued is a matter that varies widely among societies. It is almost impossible to ensure the legitimacy of association by restricting legitimation to quite specifically defined acts, however, because actors need scope for considerable discretion if they are to implement their values under varying circumstances. One major factor in setting the breadth of this scope is the level of generality at which the legitimating values are couched. For example, an injunction not to exploit others in economic transactions is very different from a specific prohibition of lending money at interest. The generalization of value systems, so that they can effectively regulate social action without relying upon particularistic prohibitions, has been a central factor in the modernization process.

At the cultural level, the relevant aspect of values is what we ordinarily call moral. It concerns the evaluation of the objects of experience in the context of social relationships. A moral act implements a cultural value in a social situation involving interaction with other actors. As a matter of interaction, it must involve standards which bind the interactors reciprocally.

Moral values comprise only one component of the value-content of a cultural system, others being, for example, aesthetic, technical, or specifically religious values. Cultures also become differentiated on bases other than the moral, so that religion, art, as expressive symbolization, and empirical knowledge, eventually science, also become independent, differentiated cultural systems. A highly differentiated cultural system is a hallmark of modern societies, along with complex modes of the articulation of the differentiated aspects of culture in the society.[14]

SOCIETAL COMMUNITY
AND THE POLITY

Besides the aspects of a societal normative order centering about membership and loyalty and about cultural legitimation, we must consider a third. Influence and value-commitments operate voluntarily, through persuasion and appeal to honor or conscience. However, no large and complex social system can endure unless compliance with large parts of its normative order is *binding* in that negative situational sanctions attach

[14] Talcott Parsons, "Introduction" to "Culture and the Social System" in *Theories of Society, op. cit.*

to noncompliance. Such sanctions both deter noncompliance—in part by "reminding" the good citizen of his obligations—and punish infraction if, as, and when it occurs. The socially organized and regulated exercise of negative sanctions, including threats of using them when intentions of noncompliance are suspected, we call the function of *enforcement*. The more highly differentiated a society, the more likely enforcement is to be performed by specialized agencies such as police forces and military establishments.[15]

Regulated enforcement requires some mode of determining the actual fact, agency, and circumstances of the infraction of norms. Among the specialized agencies that operate in this connection are courts of law and the legal profession. A complex normative order requires not only enforcement, however, but also authoritative interpretation. Court systems have very generally come to combine the determination of obligations, penalties, and the like for specific cases with interpretation of the meaning of norms, often a very general problem.[16] Less developed societies tend to reserve the latter function to religious agencies, but modern societies entrust it increasingly to secular courts.

These problems raise questions about the relation between a societal community and the political subsystem of society. In our analytical terms, the concept *political* includes the primary functions of government, in its relation to a societal community, but also corresponding aspects of any collectivity.[17] We treat a phenomenon as political in so far as it involves the organization and mobilization of resources for the attainment of the goals of the collectivity of reference. Thus, business firms, universities, and churches have political aspects. In the development of modern societies, however, government has increasingly become differentiated as a specialized organ of the society that is at the core of the polity and is distinct from the societal community.

As it has become differentiated, government has tended to center on two primary sets of functions. The first concerns responsibility for maintaining the integrity of the societal community against generalized threats, with special but not exclusive reference to its legitimate normative order. This includes the function of enforcement and a share in the function of interpretation, at least. Moreover, the general process of governmental differentiation creates spheres within which it becomes admissible explicitly to formulate and promulgate new norms, making legislation part of this function also. The second primary function, the executive,

---

[15] Talcott Parsons, "Some Reflections on the Place of Force in Social Process" in *Sociological Theory and Modern Society, op. cit.*

[16] Extremely suggestive in this regard is Lon Fuller, *The Morality of Law* (New Haven: Yale University Press, 1964).

[17] Talcott Parsons, "The Political Aspect of Social Structure and Process" in David Easton, ed., *Varieties of Political Theory* (Englewood Cliffs, N.J.: Prentice-Hall, 1966), Chapter 13 in this volume.

concerns collective action in whatever situations indicate that relatively specific measures should be undertaken in the "public" interest. This involves certain inherently essential matters, such as defense of territorial control and maintenance of public order. Otherwise, the content of executive responsibility may include almost any issue deemed to be "affected with a public interest."[18]

The basic relations between government and the societal community may be ascribed. Even early modern societies defined the common people as simply "subjects" of a monarch, ascriptively obligated to obey his authority. Fully modern levels of differentiation, however, have tended to make the power of political leadership contingent on the support of very extensive proportions of the population. In so far as this is true, we shall distinguish roles of political leadership from positions of authority more generally.

Differentiation between leadership and authority necessitates special generalization of the medium we call power.[19] We define power as capacity to make—and "make stick"—decisions which are *binding* on the collectivity of reference and on its member units in so far as their statuses carry obligations under the decisions. Power must be distinguished from influence since the promulgation of binding decisions differs importantly from attempts to persuade. By our definition, a citizen exercises power when he casts his vote because the aggregate of votes bindingly determines the electoral outcome. Only a little power is still power, just as one dollar, though only a little money, very definitely is money.

SOCIETAL COMMUNITY
AND THE ECONOMY

A fourth component of the normative order concerns matters of practicality. Its most obvious fields of application are the economic and technological; its governing principle is the desirability of efficient management of resources. Even where issues of collective loyalty, binding obligations, and morality are not involved, the action of an individual or collectivity will be disapproved if it is unnecessarily wasteful or careless. In modern societies, the normative aspect of these considerations is especially clear in the regulation of the use of labor as a factor of production in the economic sense. Commitment to the labor force involves an obligation to work effectively within the legitimate conditions of employment.[20] As Weber noted, there is a crucial moral element in this obligation. But short of the

---

[18] *Ibid*; see also Gabriel A. Almond and G. Bingham Powell, *Comparative Politics; A Developmental Approach* (Boston: Little, Brown, 1966).

[19] Talcott Parsons, "On the Concept of Political Power," Chapter 14 in this volume.

[20] Neil J. Smelser, *The Sociology of Economic Life* (Englewood Cliffs, N.J.: Prentice-Hall, 1963).

moral emphasis, rational economic and technological action is very generally approved, while deviation from the relevant standards of rationality is disapproved.

The differentiation of autonomous structures necessitates the development of a generalized monetary medium in association with a market system. Money and markets operate where there is a sufficiently complex division of labor and where spheres of action are sufficiently differentiated from political, communal, or moral imperatives.[21] Of the generalized mechanisms of societal interchange, money and markets is the least directly involved with the normative order as it centers in the societal community. Hence, practical rationality is regulated mainly by institutional norms, above all the institutions of property and contract which have other bases of sanction.[22]

THE LEGAL SYSTEM

What we have been treating as the societal normative order comes very close to what is generally meant by the concept of law. Much discussion of the law stresses the criteria of bindingness and enforceability and associates law primarily with government and the state. Other lines of analysis stress the consensual elements in the normative validity of law, a theme which permits emphasis on the importance of its moral legitimation. We treat law as the general normative code regulating action of, and defining the situation for, the member units of a society.[23] It is comprised of the components just reviewed, but as integrated into a single system.

Very generally, modern legal systems contain constitutional components, whether written as in the United States or unwritten as in Britain. In the zone of interpenetration between the pattern-maintenance system and the societal community, the constitutional element defines the main outline of the normative framework governing societal relationships in general—as in the American Bill of Rights. On modern levels of differentiation, such content is clearly not religious, since its normative validity is framed for the societal system, not the full range of action in general. Indeed, there has been a modern tendency to dissociate specific religious commitment from the constitutional rights and obligations of citizenship. Because religious affiliation generally involves the formation of collectivities, it must always be articulated in the societal community. However, the two need not be coextensive.

The constitutional element is also not "purely moral," for moral con-

[21] *Ibid*; also Talcott Parsons and Neil J. Smelser, *Economy and Society* (New York: Free Press, 1956).

[22] The classic analysis of the significance of property and contract for social systems was developed by Emile Durkheim in *The Division of Labor in Society* (New York: Macmillan, 1933).

[23] Cf. Fuller, *op. cit.* Also his *Anatomy of the Law* (New York: Praeger, 1968).

siderations too extend over a wider range than the implementation of societal values. Constitutional norms articulate with the societal community and involve the component of societal loyalty in the form of valued association; law concerns the morality of citizenship, but not necessarily all morality. Furthermore, the moral context can provide the grounds for legitimized revolts against a societal normative order, varying from minor civil disobedience to revolution.

Although the constitutional element is presumptively enforceable, enforcement always raises a question of whether the organs of government are legitimately acting in a constitutional—and back of that a moral —sense. Hence, a second aspect of the constitutional element is the normative definition of the broad functions of government, including the powers and limitations on powers of the various governmental agencies. Constitutional law in this sense becomes increasingly important as the societal community comes to be differentiated from its government. The powers of government then need specific justification, for the societal community would not be adequately protected from arbitrary uses of power if it were to grant blanket legitimacy to its "rulers" to act upon their own interpretations of the public interest.[24]

It is crucial that "executive" authority comes to be differentiated from the governmental functions which have direct constitutional relevance. It is well known that, in premodern societies, a differentiated function of explicit legislation is minimal, since the normative order is mainly *given* in a tradition or founding revelation. Hence, the legitimation of a continuing legislative function is a distinctively modern development. With a good many qualifying complications, it has tended to require that the legislative process should actively involve the societal community through a system of representation. The trend has been to make the power to legislate contingent upon the legislators' interaction with the interested elements of the community, ultimately the total electorate in most modern societies.[25] Indeed, a similar contingency generally applies to occupants of executive authority. The changeability of the law, which has resulted from these developments, has made it particularly important to have differentiated provision for concern with the "constitutionality" of law. Although the American system of judicial review is special in various respects, modern constitutions have very generally established some agency which is not purely governmental, especially in the executive sense, to pass judgment on constitutional issues.

It is under this broad constitutional framework, that the lower order functioning of the legal system proceeds. It consists in the making of

[24] On our usage of the concept of legitimation, compare Weber, *The Theory of Social and Economic Organization, op. cit.*

[25] Cf. Parsons, "The Political Aspect of Social Structure and Process" in *Varieties of Political Theory, op. cit.*

binding decisions, for the most part by officially "authorized" agencies, usually courts of law, and in various processes of their implementation by administrative procedures. It is particularly important that the extra-constitutional content of law is not confined to specific acts of legislation, nor to publicly binding decisions of executive agencies. It also includes both elements of legal tradition generated in court decisions that stand as precedents and the "administrative law" of generalized "rulings," rather than particular case decisions, promulgated by administrative agencies, but subject to legislative and judicial review.

Our whole discussion of normative order and its relation to the polity applies in principle to *any* social system, although the relation between government and the societal community is of principal importance. One source of this importance is that in general only government is authorized to use socially organized physical force as an instrument of compulsion. Indeed an effective governmental monopoly of force is a major criterion of integration in a highly differentiated society.[26] Moreover, only government is entitled to act for the societal collectivity as a whole in contexts of collective goal-attainment. Any other agency that directly presumes to do so commits a revolutionary act *ipso facto*.

MEMBERSHIP IN
THE SOCIETAL COMMUNITY

In discussing the legitimate order of society, we have made many references to the collectivity aspect of the societal community. Our multiple criteria of a society indicate that the relation between these two primary aspects must be complex, especially in that the jurisdiction of the norms cannot neatly coincide with community membership. The most obvious discrepancy derives from the territorial basis of societies. Territorial jurisdiction requires that normative control apply to some extent independently of actual membership in the societal community. For example, temporary visitors and long term "resident aliens," as well as the property holdings of "foreign" interests, must be regulated.

These considerations indicate that a particularly important part of the relation between the normative and the collective aspects of a societal community concerns their mutual relations to government. Government cannot simply "rule," but must be legitimized in governing a relatively bounded community by taking responsibility for the maintenance of its normative order. At one extreme, the principal content of the normative order may be considered more or less universal to all men. However, this raises acute problems of how far such highly universalistic norms can be effectively institutionalized in the actual operations of so extensive a

[26] Weber, *The Theory of Social and Economic Organization, op. cit.*

community. At the other extreme, both government and the normative order may apply only to a particular small community. Within the broad range of variation between these extremes, modern societal communities have generally taken a form based upon nationalism. The development of this form has involved both a process of differentiation between societal community and government and a reform in the nature of societal community, especially with respect to membership.

The immediate background for the development was, for the most part, a more or less "absolute" monarchy in which the individual was considered a "subject" of his king. It was important that this "direct" relation of subject to sovereign replaced the tangle of particularistic solidarities which characterized feudal society. However, the "subject" pattern of societal membership was in turn replaced by a citizenship pattern.

The first phase in the development of the citizenship complex involved the creation of a legal or civic framework that fundamentally redefined the boundary-relations between the societal community and the government or "state."[27] A critical aspect of the new boundaries was the definition of "rights" of the citizen, the protection of which became an important obligation of government. In the early phase, the protection of rights probably went farthest in English Common Law of the 17th century. However, it was a pan-European development that also produced the German conception of the *Rechtsstaat*. The process was simplified in Protestant areas because the citizens had to deal with only one main focus, the political authority, which organizationally controlled the church as well as the state.[28] In England the first phases of religious toleration within Protestantism comprised an essential part of the broader process of establishing citizen rights.

The second main phase in the development of citizenship concerned participation in public affairs. Although the legal rights of the first phase did protect attempts to influence government, especially through rights of assembly and freedom of the press, the next phase institutionalized positive rights to participate in the selection of governmental leadership through the franchise. The spread of the franchise "downward" in the class structure has often been gradual, yet there has been a conspicuous common trend toward universal adult suffrage, the principle of one citizen, one vote, and secrecy of the ballot.[29]

A third main component of citizenship is "social," concerned with the "welfare" of citizens, treated as a public responsibility.[30] Whereas legal

---

[27] Our entire discussion of citizenship is heavily in debt to T. H. Marshall's *Class, Citizenship, and Social Development* (Garden City, N.Y.: Anchor Books, 1965).

[28] Cf. Seymour Martin Lipset and Stein Rokkan, "Introduction" to *Party Systems and Voter Alignment* (New York: Free Press, 1968).

[29] Stein Rokkan, "Mass Suffrage, Secret Voting, and Political Participation" in *European Journal of Sociology*, II (1961), pp. 132–152.

[30] Marshall, *op. cit.*

rights and the franchise support capacities to act autonomously in the status of citizenship, the social component concerns the provision of realistic opportunities to make good use of such rights. Hence, it attempts to ensure that adequate minimum standards of "living," health care, and education are available to the masses of the population. It is particularly notable that the spread of education to ever wider circles of the population, as well as an upgrading of the levels of education, has been closely connected with the development of the citizenship complex.

The development of modern institutions of citizenship has made possible broad changes in the pattern of nationality as a basis of the solidarity of the societal community, In early modern society, the strongest foundation of solidarity was found where the three factors of religion, ethnicity, and territoriality coincided with nationality. In fully modern societies however, there can be diversity on each basis, religious, ethnic, and territorial, because the common status of citizenship provides a sufficient foundation for national solidarity.

The institutions of citizenship and nationality can nevertheless render the societal community vulnerable if the bases of pluralism are exacerbated into sharply structured cleavages. Since the typical modern community unifies a large population over a large territory, for example, its solidarity may be severely strained by regional cleavages. This is particularly true where the regional cleavages coincide with ethnic and/or religious divisions. Many modern societies have disintegrated before varying combinations of these bases of cleavage.

SOCIETAL COMMUNITY, MARKET SYSTEMS, AND BUREAUCRATIC ORGANIZATION

Where societal solidarity is emancipated from the more primordial bases of religion, ethnicity, and territorially, it tends to foster other types of internal differentiation and pluralization. The most important of these are upon functional bases, economic, political, and associational (or integrative). Hence the economic category refers above all to the development of markets and the monetary instruments essential to their functioning, which, we have noted, presuppose the institutionalization in new forms of contract and property relations. Thus, they rest on the "rights" component of citizenship, for an economy that is purely "administered" by agencies of central government would violate the freedoms of private groups to engage in market transactions autonomously. Once the market system of an economy is highly developed, however, it becomes very important to government as a channel for the mobilization of resources.

In the earlier phases of modernization, markets are primarily commercial, involving trade in physical commodities, and secondarily financial, involving operations of lending and borrowing. The large scale entrance of the primary factors of production into the market system is the principal hallmark of the "industrial" phase of economic development. Besides the advances in technology, this centered on the social *organization* of the productive process, involving new forms of the utilization of manpower in bureaucratic contexts.[31]

In discussing the political aspect of societies above, we were rather selective. We dealt primarily with the relation of government to the total societal community, stressing the direct articulation between them in the "support" system. This system concerns primarily the interaction of leadership elements, both within and aspiring to governmental positions, with elements of the social structure which are not directly involved in the governmental system as such. The processes of interaction comprise both the interchange of political support and leadership initiative, and the interchange of governmental decisions and "demands" from various interest groups. These interchanges constitute a system requiring a certain equilibration if the polity is to be stably integrated with the societal community.

The other principal operative structure of government is the administrative organization, including military establishment, through which policy decisions are implemented. In general, bureaucratization experienced its most important, though not exclusive, early development in governments. Among its primary features is the institutionalization of roles as *offices* that have relatively well defined spheres of official function, authority, and "powers" which are separated from the incumbent's private affairs. Offices are differentiated on two bases, function performed for the organization and position in the hierarchy or "line" authority.[32]

The development of bureaucratic organization in general necessitates that the relevant form of office be an *occupational* role, an incumbent being "appointed" through some kind of "contract of employment." Hence, his family's subsistence generally depends on his salary or wage remuneration. In turn, this requires a "labor market" for the allocation of human services in terms of negotiations over employment opportunities and conditions.

A very major feature of an industrial economy is the bureaucratic organization of production and, correspondingly, the mobilization of manpower through labor markets. By a complex progression through a number of phases, it has produced an immense proliferation of bureaucratic organization outside the governmental sphere. A principal stage was based upon the "family firm" of early industrial "capitalism," which

---

[31] Smelser, *op. cit.*
[32] Talcott Parsons, *Structure and Process in Modern Societies* (New York: Free Press, 1960), Chapters 1–5.

was bureaucratized at the "labor" level, but not the managerial level.

We consider bureaucratic organization to be primarily political because it is oriented in the first instance to collective goal-attainment. In the case of the business firm the collectivity of reference is a private group within the societal community; in the case of government it is the whole community organized for collective goal-attainment. Nevertheless we treat employment as a form of collectivity membership, leaving aside the problem of its relations to membership through other modes of participation in economic enterprise. Of course, private bureaucracy is not confined to economic production, but is found in churches, universities, and many other types of collectivity.

The market systems we have discussed are involved in interchange between the economy and the pattern-maintenance system, on the one hand, and the economy and the polity, on the other hand. They do not directly involve the societal community since its functions vis-à-vis these subsystems are regulative through the general normative order more than directly constitutive. We must also emphasize the distinction between the "commercial" markets, dealing with physical commodities, and the "labor" markets, dealing with human services, including those at high levels of competence and responsibility. From a sociological point of view, we find confusing the economists' common practice of treating "goods and services" together as *the* primary output of the economy.

ASSOCIATIONAL ORGANIZATION

A third main type of structuring which modern societal collectivities make possible is the "associational." Perhaps the prototype of an association is the societal collectivity itself, considered as a corporate body of citizens holding primarily consensual relations to its normative order and to the authority of its leadership. A major trend of modern associations has been toward a certain egalitarianism, manifested most clearly and importantly in the three aspects of citizenship which we have discussed.

A second main trend of associational structure is toward voluntariness. Of course, this principle can never apply quite strictly to compliance with a normative order or collective decisions, since an element of bindingness is essential to all collectivities. However, it often applies almost literally to decisions to accept and retain membership, an alternative to compliance always being resignation. In the case of the societal community, however, there are special circumstances that derive from its articulation with government. Other associations exist under a general governmental and societal protection, but the very basis of security itself rests on this fundamental combination. Hence, elements of compulsion and coercion are present in the enforcement of the societal normative order which are absent in other cases. The equivalent of "resignation," which is emigration, entails a far heavier cost than does the relinquishment of other associational memberships. In principle, it also entails accepting another societal-governmental order, whereas in the case of divorce, one need not remarry.

A third major characteristic of associational organization, which very definitely applies to the societal collectivity and to governmental agencies, is the importance of procedural institutions.[33] Although particularly significant in the legal system, they also permeate the processes of associational decision-making, both at the level of representative bodies and at the level of membership participation. In general, procedural systems consist of two levels, each governed by a code of rules. The first level regulates the discussions by which interested parties may attempt to persuade the participants in the making of binding decisions. It has many forms, but generally meetings are conducted according to rules of order which a presiding officer is responsible for implementing. Discussion within associations is a primary sphere of the operation of influence as a medium for facilitating social process. From the viewpoint of an interested party, discussion serves to improve the chances of having his view prevail; from the viewpoint of the collectivity, it facilitates an approach to consensus.

The second level concerns the actual process of deciding itself. In courts of law, the deciding agency is a jury, judge, or panel of judges. Otherwise, by far the most common procedure is voting—as it also is within juries and judicial panels—with its general tendencies toward the principles of one member, one vote, and the equal weighting of votes, the logical consequence of which is majority rule. In any case, decision by voting must follow rules fixed in advance, including the expectation that decisions arrived at by correct observance of the procedural rules will be accepted by all defeated elements. In such cases as the election of governmental leadership this may be a focus of very severe strain; implementing this requirement is a paramount test of the institutionalization of "democratic" solidarity.

Concurrent with the development of associationalism in government, there has been a vast proliferation of associations in other sectors of society. Political parties articulate with governmental process, but also with many sorts of associated "interest groups," most of which represent a variety of operative collectivities. There are also associations organized about innumerable "causes," as well as interests of diverse sorts, for example, recreational, artistic, etc.

In two broad contexts, highly important operative functions of modern societies are performed almost entirely by associational structures. The

[33] Compare Weber's concept of formal rationality in *Max Weber on Law and Society,* Max Rheinstein, ed. (Cambridge: Harvard University Press, 1954).

first is the involvement of "fiduciary" boards in the larger-scale sectors of business enterprise and in many other types of "corporate" organizations. In relation to "executive management," they somewhat parallel the relation of the legislature to the executive organs of a modern government. Sometimes the members of such boards are in some sense elected, e.g. by stockholders, but often not. In any case, they have largely replaced the kinship element as the "nonbureaucratic" top of the predominantly bureaucratic structures of business.[34] In the "private nonprofit" sector, too, ultimate control, especially in regard to financial responsibility, tends in some sense to be held by fiduciary boards.

The second very large associational development concerns the professions.[35] Though much professional function has traditionally been performed in the framework of individual "private practice," professionals have long tended to associate in order to advance their common interests, including the maintenance of professional standards of competence and integrity. Higher education has gained increasing prominence in this complex, not least in the training of practicing professionals. Hence, the profession of higher education, and of scholarly research, has also been acquiring greater relative importance. It is notable that the core structure of the academic profession, the faculty, is basically associational.

All three of the main types of operative organization (markets, bureaucracy and associational structures) have been growing increasingly prominent in the processes of differentiation and pluralization of modern societal communities.

PROCESSES OF
EVOLUTIONARY CHANGE

Although it has been the most prominent in the foregoing discussion, we consider differentiation to be one of *four* main processes of structural change which, interacting together, constitute "progressive" evolution to higher system levels. We call the other three processes adaptive upgrading, inclusion, and value-generalization (in application to social systems).[36]

Differentiation occurs when a unit or structure in a social system divides into two or more units or structures that differ in their characteristics and functional significance for the system. We have already discussed a complex instance of differentiation: the emergence of both the modern family-household and the modern employing organization from the more

---

[34] Weber in *The Theory of Social and Economic Organization, op. cit.,* emphasizes that all bureaucracies must be headed non-bureaucratically.

[35] Talcott Parsons, "Professions" in the *International Encyclopedia of the Social Sciences, op. cit.*

[36] This paradigm was originally presented in Talcott Parsons, "Some Considerations on the Theory of Social Change" in *Rural Sociology*, September 1961, pp. 219–239. It is also discussed in somewhat more detail with some revisions in Chapter 1, above.

diffusely functioning peasant family-household involved changes in many roles, collectivities, and norms. A process of differentiation results in a more evolved social system, however, only if each newly differentiated component has greater adaptive capacity than the component that previously performed its primary function. Adaptive upgrading is the process by which more generalized resources are made available to social units, so that their functioning can be freed from some of the restrictions of previous conditions. Modern factories, as compared to peasant households, require much more generalized commitments to render service from those who engage in production, but can produce a greater variety of goods much more economically. The enhanced complexity of a system undergoing differentiation and upgrading necessarily raises problems of integration. In general, these problems can be met only by the inclusion of the new units, structures, and mechanisms within the normative framework of the societal community. For example, when employing organizations become differentiated from the family-household, the authority systems of both types of collectivity must gain articulation within the society's structure of norms. Finally, the foregoing processes must be complemented by value-generalization if the various units in the society are to gain appropriate legitimation and modes of orientation for their new patterns of action. We noted above that the general value patterns of a society must be specified to the great variety of situations in which action is socially structured. We are now stating an obverse point, namely that when the network of socially structured situations becomes more complex, the value-pattern itself must be couched at a higher level of generality in order to provide the basis of social stability.

We also wish to call attention to one further aspect of processes of evolutionary development. In discussing the generalized media of interchange among units of a social system, namely influence, political power, money, and value-commitments, we have attended primarily to their most obvious function of facilitating routine interchange among the differentiated units of social system. However, they may also facilitate creative increases in the extent and level of operations within social systems. Modern economists have shown that money, through the process of lending and investment, can be a primary instrumentality for increasing the level of economic production as well as for facilitating exchange in a system of division of labor. We have argued elsewhere that this fundamental property of money, i.e., its capacity for expanding economic productivity through the credit mechanism, has analogues in the operations of the other generalized media, above all power and influence.[37] Thus, the power mechanism can operate to increase the long-run effectiveness of the polity and influence can be used to enhance the capacity for solidarity of the societal community.

[37] Cf. "On the Concept of Political Power" (*op. cit.*) and "On the Concept of Influence" (*op. cit.*).

Briefly, anchorage in a higher-order subsystem of action is the basic condition of the upgrading effects of a generalized medium of interchange. On a very broad basis, therefore, cultural development is essential for the evolutionary advance of social systems. For example, religious developments underlie all major processes of value-generalization and the advancement of empirical knowledge underlies the institutionalization of new technologies. Within the society as a system, sufficient levels of value-generalization, implemented above all through the legal system, are prerequisite to major steps of inclusion in the structure of a societal community. A consensual base that promotes adequately extensive operation of the influence mechanism is necessary for major developments in the system of political power. Certain degrees of heightened political integration are prerequisite to the expansion of monetary economies beyond relatively simple levels.

PART *II*

Historical
Interpretations

*art II is one of the two relatively em-
pirical sections of this volume. It
differs from the other, Part III, in
two major respects. One is the time of writing, which in the case of Part II
was the early 1940's, and of Part III, ranging from the mid 1950's to the
'60's. Secondly, with respect to subject matter, Part II is entirely concerned
with developments in Europe in the relevant period, with special reference
to Germany and the Nazi movement, where Part III is concerned with
various aspects of American society in the period following World War II.
It is perhaps significant that, for the author, his own society had, in the
intervening years, become at least relatively more problematical.*

*The autobiographical background of the concerns of Part II lies in the
fact that, following a year of graduate study in England, I went (in 1925) to
Germany as one of the first group of postwar German-American exchange
fellows. I was assigned to the University of Heidelberg where, without having
planned to do so in advance, I took my Ph.D. degree in 1927. This study
in Germany was a crucial experience in my life, in the first instance because
of it bringing me into contact with the work of Max Weber—I had not even
heard his name before arriving in Heidelberg—but also because of the impact
on me of the problems of German society.*

At Heidelberg I came into contact with what most would regard as the very best of German culture in the early part of this century, building on the great traditions of the German universities of the nineteenth century. This, combined with the evidence of German industrial achievement and the high level of general civilization, made a strong positive impression on a young American intellectual who, like many of his contemporaries, had reacted rather strongly against the pervasive and often crude American antipathy to things German which had developed during the war.

With the Weimar regime and the economic stabilization which had occurred very shortly before my going to Germany, the country seemed to have gotten onto an even keel such as had not existed since the best days of Bismarck. Like many others, and following the lead of Keynes, I was also disposed to assign a great deal of the blame for Germany's, and Europe's, postwar troubles to the Allies, particularly the French under the leadership of Poincaré. But even this situation seemed greatly ameliorated—thus the Locarno Treaty was negotiated by Briand and Stresemann in 1926 during my stay in Germany.

The dangers which eventuated in the Nazi movement were simply not evident at that time. The Munich Putsch *of 1923 had definitively "failed" and Hitler was in jail—of course busily writing* Mein Kampf. *The Nazis were very generally dismissed by liberal Germans—who were the ones I knew—as a tiny band of extremists who did not need to be taken seriously.*

By the time of my last visit to Germany prior to World War II, in the summer of 1930, much had changed. The Nazi movement was in full swing. It was in the election which took place in September of that year that Nazi representation in the Reichstag jumped from 12 to 109, a move from 2.4% of the chamber's 421 seats to 21.8%; the latter total advanced them from the smallest to the second largest party represented. The mounting tension was only too evident to a visitor who knew something of Germany, and it could no longer be drastically surprising that by early 1933, Hitler would assume power.

For all observers of social and political processes in the Western world of the time, the Nazi movement presented not only intellectual, but also profoundly moral, problems. Perhaps I can say that these were somewhat more poignant for me than for most other American intellectuals, not only because of my German experience, owing to the fact that I had come to love and respect that aspect of Germany which I had known. The critical question was, Why and how could this happen in what from so many points of view should be evaluated as a "good society"?

It is obvious that there are at least two ways of reacting to such disturbing phenomena: to try to "do" something about them, and to try to understand them. As an academic man, in a situation heading toward the danger and eventual outbreak of a new world war, I became relatively active as an anti-Nazi, but as a sociologist, particularly in view of the limited opportunities for action, I came under very strong "internal" pressure to try to contribute both to my own and to others' understanding of what had gone on.

I have selected for this volume the four most important essays, all written during the war, which bear in different ways on the topic. The first to be written and at the same time the most comprehensive and focused was "Democracy and Social Structure in Pre-Nazi Germany," which was published in the then extant Journal of Legal and Political Sociology *in 1942. The essay was concerned very directly with the problem of explanation, namely, what combination of factors and circumstances could explain the fact that the Nazi movement had in fact gained ascendancy over the German nation and polity so soon after the apparent stabilization of the Weimar Republic.*

Since my approach was primarily sociological, I did not attempt to follow out the complex series of political maneuverings which took place either on the German political scene itself, or in the international area. I confined my treatment of these matters to very broad sketches of main political groups and their interests and orientations, but concentrated attention on the one hand on a series of features of the social structure which had been inherited in Germany from the imperial period and on the other hand on some of the tension which existed between her pre-Weimar political system, including loyalties to it, and those of the victorious Western democracies. I was at least satisfied that there was a cogent case for the intelligibility of the genesis and victory of Nazism, which of course is something very different from its justification.

The second paper in Part II should be regarded as an attempt to generalize the analytical basis of the first paper to a level which could comprehend the Fascist movements generally in their place in the processes of development of Western society. "Some Sociological Aspects of the Fascist Movements" was written as my presidential address to the Eastern Sociological Society for its 1942 meeting and was published initially in Social Forces. *The analysis at least opened up the question of why the Fascist movement had been so prominent in Italy, Germany, and Spain and why other parts of the Western world, including Great Britain, the Low Countries, Scandinavia, to a large degree France, and of course the United States, were at least relatively immune to it. The case of Germany, contrasted with these others, at least made clear that Fascism was not in any simple sense a product of "capitalism."*

The third essay in Part II, "Max Weber and the Current Political Crisis," is at the same time somewhat different and part of the same complex. It was written in response to a request from the editor of the then extant Journal of Politics, *and published there in two installments (Vol. 4, pp. 68–76, 155–172) but has never before been reprinted. Weber of course was not only by far the most eminent theoretical social scientist in Germany in his generation, but he had throughout his life been passionately concerned with politics and a prolific commentator on political developments and events. Hence the question was, Had Weber lived to experience the events in his own Germany from his early death (at fifty-six) in 1920 to the early 1940's, what would his attitudes towards them have been? This, though an "iffy" question, was an eminently reasonable one. My essay was an attempt to answer that question in terms not only of Weber's personal character and expressed political opinions, but of the nature of his broad sociological analysis of modern society.*

My answer was that it was inconceivable that Weber could have been, to say nothing of a Nazi himself, anything closely resembling a sympathizer with the movement. Though in certain important respects a German nationalist, in a deeper sense he was, like the overwhelming majority of Western intellectuals concerned with social and political problems in this century, basically a liberal. *Among many other considerations Weber's very sharp critical attitude toward all the more extreme manifestations of German "Romanticism" would make it inconceivable that he would have been "carried away" by Hitler's charisma.*

These considerations do not directly deal with the question, which has become salient in recent years in Germany, whether in some sense Weber's nationalism may have contributed to a cultural climate relatively favorable to Nazism. The merits of different views on the strictly historical question cannot be gone into here. The question, however, has gotten involved in the politics of the New Left in Germany, and in those quarters Weber's influence has suffered severely. This was evident even so early as the special meeting of the German Sociological Association which was held in Heidelberg in April 1964 to celebrate the centenary of Weber's birth. The problem of Weber's significance to the politics, both of his own time and of the more recent era, in my opinion figured so prominently as seriously to mar an occasion which should have been far more concerned with Weber's contributions as social scientist.* However these complex questions may stand, this

---

* In the background is the important, though I think partly mistaken, book of Wolfgang Mommsen, *Max Weber und die Deutsche Politik*. The proceedings of the conference have been published as Otto Stammer, editor, *Max Weber und die Soziologie Heute*. A judicious and insightful discussion of the intellectual currents involved is given in Guenther Roth, "Political *history constituted one of my own motives for including my 1942 essay on Weber in the present collection, since, relative to the complex intellectual and emotional tensions of recent years, it can be claimed to be a "disinterested" discussion of Weber's relations to Nazism, and since, with the disappearance of the journal in which it was originally published, it has been read by very few contemporaries.*

The last of the four chapters of Part II is in a quite different vein. It came out of a "Conference on Germany After the War" which was essentially an attempt of psychoanalytically oriented psychiatrists and a few social scientists to understand both the German problem and each other, in an atmosphere where it was evident that the war would end relatively soon with Hitler's defeat. What then were the responsibilities of the victors, centering on the question of how to prevent a repetition of the holocaust, the full extent of which, in the form of the "final solution," was not yet widely known?

A good deal of attention has been attracted in psychiatric and "culture and personality" circles by the thesis of the "authoritarian personality" as the key to German national character, and the special German form of family structure as the agency of its genesis. I was considerably attracted by these ideas, in the context of a more general concern with the relevance of psychoanalytic theory to social science and especially sociology. Perhaps the tone of the paper, however, is one of emphasizing caution in expecting that "instant" applications of such insights, e.g., by psychiatrically oriented "teams" attempting to educate German parents to change their ways, so as to produce nonauthoritarian personalities in their children, would transform German society. The general theme concerned the embeddedness of child-training practices in a larger social structure in such a way that persuasion concentrated in this area was unlikely to have major socio-political effects unless other things could also be changed.

Critiques of Max Weber: Some Implications for Political Sociology," *American Sociological Review*, Vol. 30 (April 1965), pp. 213–23.

Chapter 3

Democracy and Social Structure in Pre-Nazi Germany

*f*rom a sociological point of view, the "democratic," or better "liberal-democratic" type of society, which has reached its highest degree of large-scale realization in such countries as England and the United States, has developed from a complex combination of structural elements. Some of these elements have been common to the Western world as a whole, while others have played a part particularly in these two countries. By contrast Germany presents a rather bewildering array both of similarities and of differences. This comparison will provide the main starting point of the present analysis of German social structure.[1]

On a common-sense level, perhaps Germany's most conspicuous

[1] In broad historical perspective, of course, France has a strong claim to be considered at least as important to "democracy" as the modern Anglo-Saxon countries. There are, however, notable differences the discussion of which would introduce too many complications to be dealt with in the limited space available. On another level, many of the smaller European countries and the British Dominions must be neglected for the same reason.

Reprinted from Journal of Legal and Political Sociology, I (*1942*), *96–114*, and *Talcott Parsons* Essays in Sociological Theory, *Free Press, 1954, 104–124.*

similarity, especially with the United States, lies in the high development of industrialism, under the aegis of "big business." In particular this involves in the economy a high development of large scale organization, with a large, propertyless industrial class, a high concentration of executive authority and control of industrial property, and an important element of highly trained technical personnel, especially in engineering, but also in relation to legal and administrative functions. Certainly in no other country except the United States has the economy been so highly "bureaucratized" as in Germany.

In Germany, as in other industrial countries, this structure of modern industrial enterprise has been imbedded in a complex of other institutional features which in many ways are very similar. It has had a highly developed money economy. Only a relatively small fraction of the population has even approached self-sufficiency. The great majority, on the contrary, have been mainly dependent on money income from salaries, wages or the profits of enterprise or disposal of services. To a high degree occupational status has been institutionally segregated from other not strictly functional bases of total status, though in this important respect there has certainly been a notable difference of degree, especially from the United States. We have had no landed nobility, hardly an important class closely approaching the European peasantry, and a considerably smaller class of independent artisans and shopkeepers, whose status has in certain respects been similar to that of peasants.

Pre-Nazi Germany was also notable for the high development of the one-price system with its consequent restriction of the bargaining process to the larger-scale, hence often relatively highly organized, market situations. Indeed, by means of the development of cartels and collective bargaining through trade unions, Germany went further, at an earlier time, than any other country in the regulation of the exchange process. All this was backed by a firm and, on the whole, technically and impartially administered legal system in the fields of contract, monetary transactions and the like.

The similarity, in spite of certain differences, between Roman and Common Law, extends to the basic structure of the institution of property, especially by contrast with the feudal background of European society. There was full institutional segregation between ownership and either political authority or social status in other respects, combined with full alienability and centralization of all property rights in a single ownership —a condition which is an essential prerequisite of "capitalism" as well as of certain elements of personal freedom and of the mobility of resources, both human and non-human, which underlie the "liberal" type of industrial economy.

These similarities in the structure of the economy and of its more immediate institutional penumbra go so far that many writers, especially those inclined to Marxism, have strongly tended to treat the social structures of Germany and the United States as for most practical purposes identical. For them the appearance and political success of the Nazi movement in Germany would then indicate only relatively superficial differences perhaps of external conditions, or of the constitution in the formal, legal sense. It will, by contrast with that view, be the thesis of the present analysis that a divergence of political orientation so fundamental as that at present developing between the fascist and the liberal-democratic societies must go back to deeper structural sources than this view would indicate. On subtler institutional levels, important differences can be discerned even in the economy, but they can be more clearly brought out by noting their association with elements which contrast more obviously with our own.

It has thus long been clear to competent scholars that the German state differed markedly from its British or American counterparts. This difference may in the main be characterized in terms of its interdependent "feudal," militaristic, bureaucratic, and authoritarian features. The predominant impress of these elements came from Prussia, but the position of Prussia was sufficiently central strongly to color the whole of Germany.

Prussia, like England, has had a well-established "ruling class" even though the two have developed radically different patterns of life. In Prussia it has been a landed nobility with families settled on ancestral estates. Their status has involved complete local dominance over a subordinated rural population, with control of local government, with the lower classes kept in a state of economic dependency, and the enjoyment of a position of high social prestige enforced by rigid conventions. In the state itself, however, the primary mode of participation of this class has not been in the civil administration but in the armed forces. Members of the Prussian *Junker* families have, over a considerable period, set the "tone" of the officers' corps even though a majority of its members in recent times have not come from these families. The status of officer was that of maximum social prestige although not of impressive wealth or political influence in ordinary times—indeed there was a strong tradition of neutrality in ordinary political affairs.

Thus by virtue of its connection with the *Junker* nobility the German, especially the Prussian, officers' corps did not constitute an ordinary "professional" military force in the sense in which that is true of our regular army. This situation was further bolstered by two other circumstances. In the first place, the armed forces under the old German constitution were not under the control of the civil administration but were responsible directly to the Kaiser. This fact was not merely of constitutional significance but was indicative of the solidarity of social status between nobility and royalty, the two elements of the traditional "ruling class." The reciprocal solidarity is strongly indicated by the tendency of

European royalty to emphasize their status as military commanders, for instance by making most public appearances in uniform, even in peace time. Secondly, the officers' corps, in continuity with the whole *Junker* class, carried on a highly distinctive "style of life" which was in sharp contrast with everything "bourgeois," involving a strong contempt of industry and trade, of the bourgeois virtues, even of liberal and humane culture. Perhaps the most conspicuous symbol of this difference is the part played by the duel and its attendant code of honor. The most important criterion of eligibility to belong as a social equal was *Satisfaktionsfaehigkeit*, acceptability as an adversary in an "affair of honor." To be an officer one had also to be a "gentleman" in a technical sense which hardly included many elements of the population which we would consider high up in the middle class.

It has been remarked that toward the time of the first World War considerable bourgeois elements had penetrated into the officers' corps. They were, however, in Germany, predominantly what was called the "feudalized" bourgeoisie. That is, though sons of civil servants, professional men, even on occasion bankers or industrialists, they tended to take on the style of life of the *Junker* group rather than vice versa, and to be acceptable in proportion as they did so. One conspicuous phenomenon in this category was the place of the duelling "corps" in the universities.

Thus the "feudal-militaristic" elements have played a prominent role in the structure of the German state. Though not in any simple sense involved in "politics," they have been integral to the structure especially through their close connection with the monarchy and their position at the top of the scale of social prestige. The deposition of the monarchy and great reduction of the peace-time army after 1918 went far to remove this element from its central position on the formal level, but the process was not sufficiently thorough to break up its social identity nor to destroy its traditional prestige, especially in view of its close integration with other "conservative" elements in the social structure.

Along with the position of the *Junker* military element, the German state has been famous for the high development of its civilian administrative bureaucracy. As in the case of the *Junkers* the main outlines of this structural element ante-date, and are independent of, the development of industrialism in Germany. The bureaucracy does not, however, have the same continuity with "feudal" traditions, but developed as an aspect of the growth of centralized territorial monarchies in post-mediaeval times. It has been closely integrated with the adoption of Roman law and its teaching in the universities so that the bulk of administrative civil servants have had a university legal training. The judiciary has also, although a special branch, still been much more closely involved with this tradition than in the Anglo-Saxon countries. Indeed in Germany the legal profession as a whole has been far less independent of the state.

This famous German civil service has constituted a highly professionalized group, with a very high degree of formalization of status and of the operation of the organization. Specificity of status and powers in terms of formal legal definition have been carried very far. Impartiality and scrupulous precision in application of the law in meticulous detail has been the keynote. Again not only has impartial application of the law been called for, but there has been a strong tradition of aloofness from politics, of duty to carry out the legislation and decrees of the supreme authority without question.

Generally speaking the civil service has constituted for Prussia in particular the highest prestige element in the bourgeoisie. At court and in other "social" respects they have not been the equals of the nobility, but their sons could often become officers and even intermarriages with the nobility were not uncommon. A very strong sense of social superiority to most other bourgeois elements, particularly of a "capitalistic" tenor, except for the old "patricians" of the Hanseatic and other free cities, and latterly the most prominent business magnates, were conspicuous. University professors and the highest reaches of the independent liberal professions, as medicine and law, would be the closest below them in social prestige.

Unlike the *Junker* military element, the higher civil service was not, in the Weimar Republic, displaced from formal participation in the operation of Government. If anything their power was probably on the whole increased because short of really radical revolution their knowledge and competence in administrative affairs was indispensable for keeping the essential governmental services in operation in a time of crisis.

These two elements which were most closely involved in power and responsibility in the structure of the old German state were for the most part integrated together by the ideology which is perhaps best called "Prussian conservatism." It might be characterized as a combination of a patriarchial type of authoritarianism with a highly developed formal legalism. Government has constituted an *Obrigkeit*. Its role was by no means defined as "absolutism" in the sense of an unlimited right of those in authority to promote their own self-interest or indulge their personal whims. On the contrary, the pattern of "duty" as classically formulated by Kant was one of its keynotes. But this devotion to duty was combined with a strong sense of prerogative and authority which would not brook the "democratic" type of control by persons without authority, or any presumption, of elements not authorized by their formal status to interfere in the functions of duly constituted authority. Legitimacy and order were very strongly emphasized. At the same time it was a system of authority under law, and one principal keynote of the pattern of duty was scrupulous adherence to the law. The obverse of what seems to many Anglo-Saxons the petty proliferation of minor regulations, the ubiquitous notice that such and such is *Verboten*, was the meticulous incorruptibility of the administration.

Perhaps the master complex of ideological symbols of this system lay in Lutheranism. The ultimate legitimation of authority was the divine ordination of government and princes. Organizationally the Lutheran church and clergy were more closely bound up with the regime than perhaps any other major branch of Christianity in modern times—not only was it in Prussia the established church, but the pastor was directly a civil servant and the principal supervisor of the system of public education. But more on the ideological level, the realm of idealism and genuine wish-fulfillment is for the Lutheran exclusively subjective and spiritual. This world is dominated by sin, mitigated only by the restraining influence of ordained authority. Society is not and can never be a Kingdom of God on Earth, but is fundamentally a vale of tears. In its application to the role of authority, this pattern favors a certain realism, for instance with respect to the advisability of adequate military protection of one's territory, but its benevolent patriarchalism readily slips over into a kind of harsh authoritarianism and even into a cynical pursuit of power in defiance of the welfare of the masses of people. Government is to it a grim business, of which war is a very typical and essential part.

It should not, of course, be forgotten that parliamentary government had developed in Imperial Germany to a considerable degree. But it is the above two elements in the state which were distinctive of Germany by contrast with the Western democracies, and which very greatly limited the decisiveness of the influence of the parliamentary element. This situation would seem to have a good deal to do with the tendency of German parliamentarianism, certainly more conspicuously than in either England or the United States, to become structured as a system of representation of rather specific interest groups such as agrarian interests, big business, labor unions, the Catholic Church, a tendency which came to full flower under the Weimar Republic and had a good deal to do with its instability.

The fact that a modern industrial economy developed in Germany in a society already to a large extent structured about the Prussian state and in the context of the pervasive configurational patterns of Prussian conservatism, undoubtedly colored the total development in many different respects. In the first place, "economic individualism" was never so prominent as in the Anglo-Saxon countries. Greater government participation in the affairs of the economy was taken for granted or not resisted, whether it was a question of government ownership and operation of the railways, or the fact that it was Germany which first introduced a comprehensive system of social insurance. It is undoubtedly significant that the "classical economics" never took real root in the German universities; for since it was never only a technical discipline but was also an ideology, it expressed an ideal of independence of "business" from the state and other "social" interests which was on the whole uncongenial to German mentality.

The same circumstances, however, favored the rapid growth of large-scale organization in the German economy, and its relatively close assimilation to the pattern of government bureaucracy. Particularly conspicuous in this respect is what to Anglo-Saxons appears to be a peculiar tendency towards the formalization of status in Germany, both in the economy and in other aspects of the society. Perhaps the best indication of this is the ubiquity of the use of titles. We give titles to high government officials, and various other persons in positions of dignity such as physicians, ministers and priests, sometimes officials of large organizations. But at least three differences are conspicuous as compared with pre-Nazi Germany. First, the system of titles is far less extensive. One could almost say that the prominence of formal rank and titles which we feel to be appropriate to armed services applies in Germany to the whole occupational world, reaching down even to statuses on the skilled labor level such as *Eisenbahneamter*, etc. The number of people who are plain Herr Braun or Herr Schmidt is relatively small. Secondly, titles are continuously used, so that in addressing a letter, or even in personal addresses it is a definite discourtesy to omit the full title. Thus anyone with any kind of a doctor's degree is always addressed as *Herr Doktor*—or so referred to—while we reserve this usage almost entirely for physicians. We often refer to, and even address titled people without the title—it would in Germany be disrespectful to refer to the Chancellor as Herr . . ., whereas speaking of "Mr. Roosevelt" instead of President Roosevelt is certainly not disrespectful. In Germany it would have had to be Herr Reichskanzler Dr. Bruening, or at least *Reichskanzler* Bruening. Closely related is the German tendency to use an accumulation of titles. Thus where on a letter we would write Professor John Smith, there it would have to be Herr Professor Doktor Johann Schmidt. Our tendency to ignore titles on occasion is related to the usage with other symbols of formal status such as uniforms. In peace time a military officer generally appears in civilian clothes, even at work, unless he is on military post or, for a naval officer, on shipboard. Even when the nation was imminently threatened by war we had the spectacle of the Army's Chief of Staff on an eminently official occasion, testifying before a Senate Committee, in civilian clothes. That would be completely unthinkable in Germany. Even in war time the President, though he is commander-in-chief of the armed forces, *never* wears a uniform. Finally, German titles are far more highly differentiated, both with respect to rank and to field of competence, than are ours. We have the one honorific title of "honorable" for high government officials; in Germany there are many graduations. The honorific title of *Rat* is differentiated into an indefinite number of subclasses according to the particular occupation of the incumbent *Kommerzienrat, Justizrat, Sanitaetsrat, Rechnungsrat,* etc. Finally there is, in general, a far greater insistence on meticulous observance of correct titles.[2]

Except for the status of nobility—including the title "von"—the primary content of this formalized status system in Germany was occupational. But the tendency to emphasize titles and other aspects of formal status even on what we would treat as "informal" occasions seems to indicate a difference from the predominant American pattern. With us, occupational status is to a relatively high degree segregated from the individual's "private life," while in Germany this seems to be considerably less the case; his specific formal status as it were follows him everywhere he goes. In social life generally he is less significant as a person, as John Smith, than he is as the incumbent of a formal status, as an official, an officer, a physician, a professor, or a worker.

Another aspect of this formalism is worthy of note. To an American the continual German insistence on titles connotes not only emphasis on formal status rather than individuality, it connotes also "formality" in the sense which is antithetical to the informality of intimacy or of friendship. To an American it is surprising that German students may associate for months and never speak to each other at all, or when they do, address each other as *Herr* and *Fraeulein*, when their American counterparts would be addressing each other by their first names. Similarly with us, colleagues of about the same age, especially if relatively young, almost always address each other by their first names; they do so in Germany only if they have a specifically intimate friendship. These differences of usage may be said to symbolize that to American sentiments, at all close association in common activities should include an element of friendship—he is not only my fellow student or colleague, but also my friend—while in Germany occupational association and friendship are specifically segregated. It is most untactful to "presume" a level of intimacy to which one is not entitled.[3]

[2] To relate an amusing instance: as an official exchange student at a German university, I was formally received by the Rector of the University. After the interview a German student friend said, "I hope you addressed him correctly as *Euer Magnifizenz*." When the reply was, "No, I said *Herr Professor*," my student friend was genuinely shocked. To an American, however, the idea of addressing a rather seedy-looking elderly professor as "Your Magnificence" seemed more than a little ridiculous.

[3] From a superficial point of view the above two points might seem to be contradictory. This, however, is not the case. The German pattern seems to extend assimilation of other elements of status to formal occupational status considerably farther than ours does, and hence greatly to narrow down the sphere of private individuality relative to the American pattern. But then a point is reached where matters concern a restricted sphere which is highly "private"—one's relations to one's true "friends." When this point is reached the segregation is far sharper than in the American case. The American pattern, on the other hand, does not go so far in extending the pattern of formal status beyond the immediate occupational context. Indeed, it minimizes it even there by admitting elements of "informality" which are structurally related to the friendship pattern in a way which would seem improper and undignified to most Germans. But there is a gradual transition, not marked by symbols of rigid distinction, between casual acquaintance with an occupational colleague through various degrees of intimacy to the most intimate friendship, which may or may not be with

The above considerations suggest that differences which are perhaps most conspicuous to the social scientist in terms of the broader status-groupings of the state and the economy can be followed into the realm of the more intimate personal relationships. It surely would be remarkable if the order of difference which has been discussed did not extend into the realm of family structure, of the definition of sex roles, and the patterning of the relations of the sexes, within marriage and outside it.

In the first place, there would clearly seem to be in Germany a pattern of masculine superiority and a tendency to assume authority and prerogatives on the part of husbands and fathers which is much less pronounced in the United States. From the American point of view, particularly of women, German men tend to be dominating and authoritarian, and, conversely, to expect submissiveness and dependency on the part of their wives. This is perhaps particularly true in the middle classes. The "typical" German woman, especially if married, is thought of as a *Hausfrau*—significantly a word taken over untranslated into English to denote a social type, while "housewife" suggests rather a census classification. The Hausfrau is, perhaps, the antithesis of the "emancipated" woman—emancipated in any one of several directions. To the former applies the old adage of the three K's *Kinder, Kirche, Kueche*. Her life is concentrated on the home, on husband and children, and she participates little in the outside world, in community affairs, or even in cultural life. She tends to lack both "sex appeal" and other elements of "attractiveness." From the American point of view she does not dress well but is more "dowdy" than is accountable for in terms of lack of financial resources.

The difference is, of course, relative. Solid, conservative domesticity is very much a live ideal in the United States, but relatively less prominent. In Germany there has been "high society" with a great deal of aristocratic emancipation from moralistic domesticity, but one can say confidently that it has never been capable of really competing with its French counterpart. In the upper middle classes there have, especially in recent times, been many highly educated and cultured women, many of them leaders in the *Frauenbewegung*. Finally, gainful employment of married women outside the home has been as conspicuous in Germany as in other industrial countries, and has greatly modified this pattern for the working classes. But the quantitative difference of emphasis remains: more German women are Hausfrauen than American, and even the American woman who has no career or job, has on the average a different style of life, is more concerned with her personal appearance, with men other than her husband

---

occupational associates, but certainly are not structurally required to be. In a sense the German system is more favorable to strict universalistic impartiality and less open to nepotism and other clique-like disturbances, but at the same time probably involves other elements of instability.

and with impersonal interests outside her home. Above all on the ideological level there is, perhaps outside Catholic circles, a considerably more
favorable attitude toward the non-domestic virtues in women. There is
less tendency to encourage submissiveness and psychological dependency,
less resentment at women "intruding" in the world of masculine affairs.
The principal exception is probably in the areas of greatest intellectual,
cultural, and "bohemian" emancipation which have probably been more
extreme in Europe generally, including Germany, than in the United
States at least until quite recently.

Closely related to this difference in feminine roles is a far lower development in Germany of the "romantic love" pattern. The love relationships
of youth have been as it were "sentimentalized" in Germany to a considerable extent, but with a different emphasis. The *Maedchen* is more simple,
sweet, and submissive, and less glamorous than her American counterpart. It is less a relation of equality. She is more apt, in the middle classes,
to marry an established, somewhat older man. Related to this is another
usage of titles, the fact that the German married woman takes not only
her husband's surname, as with us, but also his title. She is addressed as
Frau Doktor, Frau Justizrat, or *Frau Professor.* Would it not be legitimate
to infer that while with us the primary emphasis is put on marriage to a
particular man as an individual, in Germany it is put rather on his formal
status? The significant thing is not that she is the wife of John Smith,
but of *a* professor. The impression further is that the marriage relationship
typically involves more impersonal attitudes, less emphasis on being "in
love," as well as greater inequality so that to a certain extent the wife is
classed with her children by contrast with the authority of the husband.

Rather generally speaking, there seems to be in Germany a good deal
sharper segregation of the roles of the sexes than in the United States.
With this, however, goes as a significant counterpart a strong tendency
to emphasize, indeed to romanticize, the relationship of men to one
another. On one level *Bruederschaft,* with its ritual oath and its symbolic
use of *Du* as the form of address, is much more sharply emphasized than
any particular form of masculine friendship with us, and seems to be
invested with a very intense emotional significance. On another, comrade-
ship, of which the relation of soldiers in the field is perhaps the prototype,
is particularly idealized. Thus the main emphasis in the German Youth
Movement was a romantic idealization of solidary groups of young men—
sometimes with at least an undercurrent of homosexuality. The closest
counterpart in our society is the romantization of the cross-sex love
relationship.

The reader may quite reasonably ask what is gained by dwelling at
such length on all these features of pre-Nazi Germany social structure,
all of which are very well known, and a good many of which seem to have
little to do with the issue of Germany's relation to democracy. The justi-

fication lies in the fact that they need to be brought to mind because of their bearing on what is doubtless still to many a very puzzling problem. We have seen that in many fundamental respects of the social structure of Germany has been very similar to that of other Western industrial societies. Until 1918, to be sure, it did not have a democratic constitution politically, but surely it has become a commonplace of social science that the mere formal provisions of the constitution are quite secondary to the deeper-lying social structure. In that respect perhaps the most important feature of the German state, its administrative bureaucracy, was very far from being in radical conflict with at least liberal if not democratic patterns. Indeed, by contrast particularly with the American spoils system of the same era it might be considered to be in closer line with our own idealistic values because of its scrupulous adherence to the impartial "rule of law." Moreover, the collectivistic, if somewhat paternalistic, social welfare tendencies of the German state could go far to mitigate the more extreme consequences of rampant individualistic capitalism as it was found particularly in the United States. Then the one important thing would seem to have been the removal from power of the "feudal" elements of the old regime, an end which for all practical purposes was achieved with the revolution of 1918. The question is, why did this solution fail to stick, why did not Germany continue in what many have thought to be the main line of the evolution of Western society, the progressive approach to the realization of "liberal-democratic" patterns and values?

There can be no doubt that various kinds of external factors such as the treatment of Germany by the Allies after the last war, economic difficulties both in international trade and finance and internally to Germany and the like, played an important part. Perhaps these factors were even decisive in the sense that a more favorable set of circumstances in these respects would have tipped the total balance of forces so as to permit the democratic trend of evolution to continue uninterrupted. No doubt also the development of the relations of capital and labor, in the sense in which that tension is structurally inherent in all capitalistic industrial economies, played an important part. The Weimar regime put the Trade Unions and the parties of the left in a position of greatly enhanced power; wages were continually pushed up; and undoubtedly many business people became frightened and were ready to accept almost anything which would protect them from the danger of expropriation. Their fear was greatly enhanced by the ideological appeal to the danger of Communism which has been to a considerable degree effective in all the capitalistic countries.

But German National Socialism is a grand scale movement of a very particular type. It is, to be sure, nationalistic in opposition to the national humiliation and alleged submission to the enemies of Germany for which it purports to hold the men of Versailles and Weimar responsible. It is also anti-Communistic in that it purports to lead a great crusade against Bolshevism and to purge Europe forever from this "disease." But it is more than either or both of these. It is a revolutionary movement which, both in ideology and in actual policy, has already done much to alter fundamentally the broader social structure not only of the Weimar Republic but of the Germany which preceded and underlay it. National Socialism arose in a situation which quite understandably could have produced a strong nationalistic and conservative reaction, a reaction toward social patterns which, though in conflict with the leftward elements of the "liberal-democratic" tradition of the Western world, need not have removed Germany from the general sphere of Western civilization. But Nazi Germany is even today not a strong, national community with conservative leanings, as distinguished from the leftward leanings of British Labor or of the American New Deal. It is a radically new type of society which, if not interfered with, promises to depart progressively more radically from the main line of Western social development since the Renaissance. It is in the sources of this element of revolutionary radicalism in the Nazi movement that the interest of the present analysis is focussed.

In our common-sense thinking about social matters we probably tend greatly to exaggerate the integration of social systems, to think of them as neatly "exemplifying" a pattern type. For purposes of sheer comparative structural study this need not lead to serious difficulty, but when dynamic problems of directions and processes of change are at issue, it is essential to give specific attention to the elements of malintegration, tension, and strain in the social structure.

In the first place, all Western societies have been subjected in their recent history to the disorganizing effects of many kinds of rapid social change. It has been a period of rapid technological change, industrialization, urbanization, migration of population, occupational mobility, cultural, political, and religious change. As a function of sheer rapidity of change which does not allow sufficient time to "settle down," the result is the widespread insecurity—in the psychological, not only the economic sense—of a large proportion of the population, with the well-known consequences of anxiety, a good deal of free-floating aggression, a tendency to unstable emotionalism and susceptibility to emotionalized propaganda appeals and mobilization of affect around various kinds of symbols. If anything, this factor has been more prominent in Germany than elsewhere in that the processes of industrialization and urbanization were particularly rapid there. In addition, the strain and social upset of the last war were probably more severe than in the case of any other belligerent except Russia. On top of that came the political difficulties after 1918 and the inflation, finally exceedingly severe economic depression in the early thirties. Such a situation predisposes to radical emotional dissociation from the principal institutional statuses and roles of the existing order, but does not of itself give any clue to the direction which the structuring of definitions will take.

A second element of the situation is also common to all Western countries, but also perhaps somewhat more intense in Germany than elsewhere. A major aspect of the dynamic process of development in Western society ever since the Middle Ages has been a particular form of what Max Weber called the "process of rationalization." One of its central foci has been the continual development of science and the technologies derived from it in industry, in medicine, and in other fields. Closely related has been the development of bureaucratic organization, of economic exchange, and of the orientation of economic activity to capitalistic monetary calculation. Various aspects of the cultural tradition have also been affected in the form of the secularization of religious values, emancipation from traditional patterns of morality, especially in Christian form, and the general tendency of rational criticism to undermine traditional and conservative systems of symbols.

This process, looked at from the point of view of its dynamic impact on the social system, rather than the absolute significance of rationalistic patterns, has an uneven incidence on different elements in the social structure. In the first place, it tends to divide elements of the population according to whether they tend toward what are, in rationalistic terms, the more "progressive" or "emancipated" values of patterns of conduct, or the more conservative "backward," or traditional patterns. This introduces a basis of fundamental structuring in the differentiation of attitudes. It is a basis which also tends to coincide with other bases of strain in the structuring of interests, especially in that "capitalism" tends to be predominantly a phenomenon of emancipation which grows up at the expense of the "good old ways" and sound established values.

But not only does the process of rationalization structure attitudes. It is precisely the further effects of the dynamic process of change which are most important in this connection. In part this process is a principal source of the disorganization and insecurity discussed above as involved in *anomie*. In so far, however, as such disorganization is not specifically structured in other ways, it and its behavioral manifestations tend to become structured in terms of their relation to this process. Hence manifestations of these polar attitude patterns tend to bear the marks of psychological insecurity, to be "overdetermined." This is true on both sides: on the emancipated side in the form of a tendency to a compulsive "debunking" and denial of any elements of legitimacy to all traditional patterns, on the traditional side of a "fundamentalist" obstruction to all progress, a traditionalist literalism with strongly emotional attitudes.[4]

Though general to the Western world, this situation has probably been

4 This is, in the sense of Bateson, a particularly good example of the process of "Schismogenesis." See Gregory Bateson, *Naven*.

more extreme in Germany because, relative to Western Europe and the United States, it has been more "conservative." Hence the impact of science, industrialism, and such phenomena has been more unsettling and has led to more drastic extremes of attitudes. One significant symptom of this fact is to be found in the conspicuously greater tendency of German social thought to repudiate the primary rationalistic and emancipated ideological structures which have dominated the intellectual traditions of France and England. There has been conspicuously less intellectual "liberalism" in Germany—the obverse of the predominant "conservative" tendencies being the extreme of rationalistic radicalism found in Marxism.

One conspicuous tendency in this connection is for "fundamentalist" sentiments to crystallize about phenomena symbolic of the extremer forms of emancipation in defining what was dangerous to society. The coincidence in Nazi ideology of the Jews, capitalism, bolshevism, anti-religious secularism, internationalism, moral laxity, and emancipation of women as a single class of things to be energetically combatted is strongly indicative of this structuring.

In combination with certain peculiaries of the German cultural tradition, this situation helps to account for the fact that the German labor movement was considerably more extreme in the radical rationalistic direction than its counterparts in the Anglo-Saxon countries. Long before the British movement it was committed to a political socialist program, and this came to be formulated in terms of the strict Marxist ideology which, above all, required drastic repudiation of traditional religious values. This undoubtedly made it easier for the labor movement to be defined as "dangerously radical" to the rest of the population, even apart from the growth of the Communist element during the later Weimar years.

One of the most important reactions to elements of strain of the sort just discussed, and certain more specific ones which will be taken up presently, is the formation of patterns of wishes or idealized hopes which, in the majority of cases, the established institutional patterns and their attendant situations do not permit to be fully realized. They hence tend to be projected outside the immediate social situation into some form of "idealized" life or existence. Since they are the results of certain emotional tensions which develop only in so far as people are imperfectly integrated with an institutionalised situation, they tend to involve a conspicuous element of "irrealism." They are associated with a negative valuation of the existing situation and, instead of a "realistic" orientation to its altera-tion in the direction of greater conformity with an ideal, involve an element of "escape." This phenomenon may be called "romanticism"—its essence is the dissociation of the strongest emotional values from established life situations—in the past or the future or altogether outside ordinary social life.[5] A most important question about any social system is that of its

[5] Perhaps only when the content of the "dream pattern" is secular should the term "romantic-

general predisposition to romanticism, and of the specific ways in which this tendency is structured.

In the Anglo-Saxon world it is probably true that there is on the whole a smaller predisposition to romanticism than in Germany because patterns which, in important respects, go back to Puritanism, canalize the orientation of action more in the direction of taking active responsibility for translating ideal patterns into reality. Associated with this, however, is a marked tendency to a kind of "utopianism," an attraction for many sorts of unrealistic blueprints for the "ideal society" where there will be perpetual peace, an elimination of all inequalities, of all irrationality or superstition, etc. This is a kind of romanticism which helps explain the appeal of the rationalistic movements of the left in these countries. In addition to that, however, there are two very important patterns of "individualistic" romanticism, the romanticism of personal "success" and romantive love. A very prevalent theme of American fiction is the boy whose abilities were such that he was *bound* to succeed. Its prevalence suggests a very high level of emotional investment in occupational functions. It is a pattern which, by contrast with the German, is also associated with the relative lack of formalism in our occupational system. Occupational functions are treated—however unrealistically—more as a matter of ability and achievement, and less as a matter of status for its own sake. The prominence of the pattern of romantic love, again however unrealistic it is, seems to indicate a particularly strong emphasis on the fusion of the sex relationship with the strongest bonds of personal intimacy and loyalty. That this is made the dominant ideal precisely of marriage, again relatively disregarding status as such, is striking. Both these romantic tendencies of American society, it may be noted, are not closely related to any form of political radicalism but tend, except in so far as their lack of realism leads to disillusionment, to reinforce the dominant institutional structure—or at least not to undermine it in a political direction.

The element of formalism in the patterning of the basic institutional system of Germany, which was discussed at some length above, seems to indicate a stronger general tendency to romanticism than exists in the Anglo-Saxon countries, in that institutionalized status tends to absorb less of the individual's emotional attachment. It is as if it were said: status is *only* formal; after all the most important things lie elsewhere. This impression is confirmed by the fact that Germany, precisely in the time when she was not dominated by a radical political movement, was known as the land of poets, philosophers and dreamers, of religious mysticism, of music. It has also been a land of peculiarly strong reaction against "bourgeois" values, an attitude which socialists and radicals,

---

ism" be used. Certain elements of other-wordly religious ideals are, however, closely related in psychological significance.

bohemian artists and intellectuals, and the Youth Movement have all had in common. Surely in recent times precisely the world of formal status structure has been the core of these bourgeois values.[6]

At the same time there were important structural reasons why two of the most important manifestations of romanticism in the Anglo-Saxon world could not be so important in Germany. A dominance of the personal success ideal was in conflict with the formalism of the status structure, as well as with the dominant position in the prestige scale of hereditary status groups. A corresponding role of the romantic love pattern was in part blocked by the connection of marriage with the formal status system, in part by the related difference in the definition of sex roles which made it difficult for a man and woman to be treated as equals in respect to the most profound emotional commitments of life. The kind of attachment to a woman which we idealize in the romantic pattern would, to most Germans, seem possible only to a soft, effeminate type of man, certainly not to the heroic type.

By virtue of its industrialization and urbanization, however, and of the impact in other respects of the rationalization process, the actual social life of Germany had developed for much of its population to a point where the older conservative patterns, especially in defining the role of youth, of sex relationships, and of women, could not serve as an adequate basis of institutional integration. "Leftist" radicalism appealed to organized industrial labor and to some intellectuals, but it had too narrow a base in the social structure to be stable. Sheer "emancipation," as practiced in bohemian circles, was not adequate and was too unstable, apart from the fact that both these phenomena inflamed conservative sentiment. At the same time among the middle class youth, among large numbers of women, and elsewhere in the society there were acute strains which strongly predisposed to romantic forms of expression.

The other side of the picture lies in the fact that the German situation presented possibilities for a structuring of these elements in a radically different direction from that predominant in most democratic societies. The traditions of national glory were bound up with conservative tendencies which were generally speaking stronger in the German social structure than elsewhere. An aspect of this was the appeal of military values with a strong tradition behind them which could become romanti-

[6] Though there is no space available here to develop the point, it may be noted that there is strong evidence of a close connection between this combination of formalism and a tendency to romanticism, and the heritage of Lutheran Protestantism, precisely as distinguished from Calvinistic. For the Lutheran the true spiritual values could not be embodied in secular life, but only in the individual's completely intimate and personal communion with God. Secular duties were divinely ordained and conscientiously to be performed, above all the duty of submission to authority, but secular achievement was in no sense the real business of life, even in the service of the most exalted ideals. The world was essentially evil and could not be made a "Kingdom of God on Earth."

cized in terms of a "heroic" ideal[7] of the fighting man who could be propagandistically contrasted with the money-grabbing capitalist of the "plutocracies." The whole appeal of nationalism could be mobilized in the same direction and combined with the reaction against all forms of dangerous radicalism. The military ideal forms in the nature of the case a strong contrast to the bourgeois stuffiness and safetymindedness against which young people tended to react. Finally from the point of view of German women, a heroic ideal could mobilize their romantic idealization of men in a pattern which adequately fitted the German segregation of the sex roles, as the man in the role to which, of all roles, women were by tradition least suited, that of fighter.

To recapitulate: The Revolution of 1918 had the immediate effect of "Democratizing" Germany, of removing the "feudal" element and apparently bringing Germany at last into line with the other "progressive" industrial nations of the Western world. Why this result proved to be so unstable, so abruptly to overturn in favor of the most radical anti-liberal and anti-democratic movement of modern history, is certainly one of the most critical questions of the interpretation of social events of our time. Certainly political pressures on defeated Germany, economic dislocation, and such factors as the class struggle must be conceded to be highly important. The above analysis has, however, attempted to indicate, if only in a highly schematic way, that an equally important part has probably been played by factors distinctive to the social structure of Germany, in dynamic interrelation with the general processes of social development in Western civilization. From this point of view at least one critically important aspect of the National Socialist movement lies in the fact that it constitutes a mobilization of the extremely deep-seated romantic tendencies of German society in the service of a violently aggressive political movement, incorporating a "fundamentalist" revolt against the whole tendency of rationalization in the Western world, and at the same time against its deepest institutionalized foundations. The existence of such romantic elements is inherent in the nature of modern society. That, however, their manifestations should become structured in such a pattern and placed in the service of such a movement is understandable only in terms of specific features of the social structure of Pre-Nazi Germany which differentiated it from that of other Western countries.

[7] Dr. E. Y. Hartshorne has particularly called my attention to the possibility that romantization among Nazi Youth of the heroic life—and of the *Fuehrer*—might have functions similar to those of the pattern of romantic love in the United States.

4

Some Sociological Aspects of the Fascist Movements

*t*he older type, especially of European, social theory was, very largely, oriented to the understanding, in broad terms, of the social situation of the writer's own time. Whatever was sound in these older attempts, as of a Comte, a Spencer or a Marx, tended to be so intimately bound up with scientifically dubious elements of grandiose speculative construction and methodological assumption and dogma that the whole genus of analysis has tended to become discredited as a result of the general reaction against speculative thories.

In the course of such reactions, it is not uncommon for the baby to be thrown out with the bath, for elements of sound insight and analysis to be lost sight of through their seemingly inseparable involvement with these other elements. Perhaps in the last few years more strongly than at any other time there have been signs that warrant the hope of an ability in the social sciences to apply generalized theoretical analysis to such problems in a thoroughly empirical, tentative spirit which will make possible a cumulative development of understanding, relatively unmarred by scientifically

Originally published in Social Forces, *21, 138–147 (written as the presidential address to the Eastern Sociological Society at its 1942 meeting). Reprinted in Talcott Parsons,* Essays in Sociological Theory, *Chapter 6, Copyright© 1954, Free Press, New York, N.Y.*

irrelevant or untenable elements. The very breadth of the problem of diagnosis of the state of a great civilization creates a strong demand for such a method.

Perhaps the most dramatic single development in the society of the Western world in its most recent phase has been the emergence of the great political movements usually referred to as "Fascist." In spite of their uneven incidence, with Germany and Italy by far the most prominent centers, and their varying character in different countries, there is sufficient similarity to justify the hypothesis that the broad phenomenon is deeply rooted in the structure of Western society as a whole and its internal strains and conflicts. However much my own approach may turn out to differ from the Marxian, this much must certainly be granted the latter— that it does relate Fascism to fundamental and generalized aspects of Western society.

As a starting point for the present analysis perhaps the common formula of characterization as the "radicalism of the right" is as satisfactory as any. It has at least the virtue of calling attention to two important points. In the first place Fascism is not "old conservatism" of the sort especially familiar before 1914, although elements which were once conservative in that sense have often been drawn into the Fascist movements. Secondly, it is definitely of the "right" in that it is specifically oriented in opposition to the political movements of the "left," notably of course communism.

Perhaps the most important reason why we are justified in speaking of "radicalism" lies in the existence of a popular mass movement in which large masses of the "common people" have become imbued with a highly emotional, indeed often fanatical, zeal for a cause. These mass movements, which are in an important sense revolutionary movements, are above all what distinguishes Fascism from ordinary conservatism. They are movements which, though their primary orientation is political, have many features in common with great religious movements in history, a fact which may serve as a guide to the sociological analysis of their origins and character.

A second important feature is the role played by privileged elite groups, groups with a "vested interest" in their position. While from some points of view the combination of these two elements in the same movement is paradoxical, it will be argued here that it is of the very essence of the phenomenon and perhaps more than anything else throws light on the social forces at work.

It has come to be a well-known fact that movements of religious proselytism tend to develop in situations involving a certain type of social disorganization, primarily that early thought only roughly characterized by Durkheim as "anomie." Anomie may perhaps most briefly be characterized as the state where large numbers of individuals are to a serious degree lacking in the kind of integration with stable institutional patterns

which is essential to their own personal stability and to the smooth functioning of the social system. Of this there are in turn perhaps two principal
aspects. In the first place there seems to be a deep-seated need for a relative
stability of the expectations to which action is oriented. The aspect of
this on which Durkheim lays primary stress is the sufficiently clear definition of the goals of action—there can, he says, be no sense of achievement
in progress toward the realization of an infinite goal. But goals are, to a
very large extent, defined by institutionalized expectations. This Durkheim
illustrated by the inability of indefinite increase of wealth, once cut loose
from definite standards, to satisfy ambition.

Similar considerations apply to other aspects of conduct. Expectations
cannot be stable if the standards with which conformity is demanded are
left so vague as not to be a real guide, or if the individual is subjected, in
the same situation, to two or more conflicting expectations each of which
advances claims to legitimacy which cannot be ignored.

The second, it would seem somewhat more difficult and complex
aspect, lies in the need for a sufficiently concrete and stable system of
symbols around which the sentiments of the individual can crystallize.
In many different aspects of life highly concrete associations are formed
which perhaps in many cases have no great intrinsic importance in themselves, but in that they become stabilized and perpetuated through a living
social tradition perform a highly important function in integrating social
groups and in stabilizing the orientation of individuals within them.

The general character of the typical reaction of the individual to anomie
is that usually referred to in psychological terms as a state of insecurity.
The personality is not stably organized about a coherent system of values,
goals, and expectations. Attitudes tend to vacillate between indecision
which paralyzes action—and all manner of scruples and inhibitions—
and on the other hand compulsively "overdetermined" reactions which
endow particular goals and symbols with an excess of hatred, devotion
or enthusiasm over what is appropriate to the given situation. Generalized
insecurity is commonly associated with high levels of anxiety and aggression, both of which are to an important extent "free-floating" in that they
are not merely aroused in appropriate form and intensity by fear or anger-
provoking situations but may be displaced onto situations or symbols
only remotely connected with their original sources.

The present formulation of the psychological correlates of anomie
has consciously adhered to the level closest to the more general character
of social situations—lack of definition of goals and standards, conflicting
expectations, inadequately concrete and stable symbolization. I am well
aware that many psychologists find the deepest sources of insecurity
to lie in the relations of the individual to his parents and others in the
family in early childhood. The two approaches are by no means necessarily
in conflict. There is much evidence that insecurity developed in adults

from the sources here indicated affects their relations to their children and in turn the character formation of the latter, so that a cumulative vicious circle may work itself out.

An increase in anomie may be a consequence of almost any change in the social situation which upsets previous established definitions of the situation, or routines of life, or symbolic associations. To be sure, the members of some societies have average character types which are better able to withstand and to adapt to rapid changes than are others—but in any case there is a limit to the extent and rapidity of change which can take place without engendering anomie on a large scale. There is ample evidence that the period immediately preceding our own time was, throughout the Western world, one of such rapid and fundamental change as to make this inevitable.

It was, in the first place, the period of the Industrial Revolution which, though going much farther back in history, tended cumulatively to gain in force throughout the nineteenth century and well into the twentieth. Though in widely differing degrees, most Western countries changed from predominantly agricultural to industrial and commercial societies, a change impinging not only on occupation but on the life of very large numbers of the population in many different aspects, especially in the tremendous growth of cities and the continual introduction of new elements into the standard of living.

Secondly, and intimately connected with this, the society has been subjected to many other influences adversely affecting situational stability. Migration of population from the rural areas to the growing urban concentrations has been only one phase of a tremendous and complex migration process which has necessitated the complex process of adaptation to new social environments—sometimes, as in the great bulk of immigration into the United States, assimilation to a drastically different cultural tradition with exposure to conflicting expectations and discrimination on ethnic lines. A somewhat different source of strain lies in the instability of the new economy—the exposure to cyclical fluctuations with unemployment and rapid and drastic changes in the standard of living. Inflation and many of the social and economic effects of war fit into the same general pattern.

Though it is perhaps more significant as a consequence of than as a causal factor in anomie, the fact is relevant that not only in women's dress but in any number of other fields our society is to a very high degree subject to rapid and violent changes of fad and fashion. No sooner have we become attached to a pattern than its social prestige melts away leaving the necessity to form a new orientation. This is especially true in the recreational and other expressional fields, but applies also to political and cultural ideas, and to many fields of consumption patterns.

Finally, the cultural development of the period has been preeminently one to undermine simplicity and stability of orientation. It has been to an extraordinary extent a period of the "debunking" of traditional values and ideas, and one in which for previously stable cultural patterns in such fields as religion, ethics, and philosophy, no comparably stable substitutes have appeared—rather a conspicuously unstable factionalism and tendency to faddistic fluctuation. Part of the situation is an inevitable consequence of the enormous development of popular education, and of the development of mass means of communication so that cultural influences which in an earlier time reached only relatively small "sophisticated" minorities now impinge upon a very large proportion of the total population.

Returning for a moment to the psychological level of consideration, one of the most conspicuous features of the present situation lies in the extent to which patterns of orientation which the individual can be expected to take completely for granted have disappeared. The complexity of the influences which impinge upon him has increased enormously, in many or most situations the society does not provide him with only one socially sanctioned definition of the situation and approved pattern of behavior but with a considerable number of possible alternatives, the order of preference between which is by no means clear. The "burden of decision" is enormously great. In such a situation it is not surprising that large numbers of people should, to quote a recent unpublished study,[1] be attracted to movements which can offer them "membership in a group with a vigorous *esprit de corps* with submission to some strong authority and rigid system of belief, the individual thus finding a measure of escape from painful perplexities or from a situation of *anomie*."

Thus the large-scale incidence of anomie in Western society in recent times is hardly open to doubt. This fact alone, however, demonstrates only susceptibility to the appeal of movements of the general sociological type of fascism but it is far from being adequate to the explanation of the actual appearance of such movements or above all the specific patterns in terms of which they have become structured. It is this latter problem which must next be approached.

The state of anomie in Western society is not primarily a consequence of the impingement on it of structurally fortuitous disorganizing forces though these have certainly contributed. It has rather, involved a very central dynamic process of its own about which a crucially important complex of factors of change may be grouped, what, following Max Weber, may be called the "process of rationalization." The main outline of its character and influence is too familiar to need to be discussed in detail—but it must be kept clearly in mind as a basis for the subsequent analysis.

[1] Theodore W. Sprague, "Jehova's Witnesses: a Study in Group Integration." Dissertation, Harvard University, 1942.

Undoubtedly the most convenient single point of reference is to be found in the patterns of science. The development of science is of course inherently dynamic and has a certain immediate effect in progressively modifying traditional conceptions of the empirical world. It is, however, its application in technology which provides the most striking source of cumulative social change, profoundly affecting the concrete circumstances of men's lives in a multitude of ways. Again it is not only that the explicit formal content of occupational roles is affected—this is the center from which many complex ramifications of change radiate into the informal and symbolic areas of men's working lives, and into their private lives through changes in their patterns of consumption, recreation, etc. Whatever the positive value of the changes, they always involve an abandonment of traditional orientation patterns, circumstances, and definitions of the situation which necessitates a process of readjustment.

Though by no means simply an aspect of science and its application in technology, a second dynamic complex is intimately related to it. It may be characterized as the treatment of a wide range of action patterns and contexts of human relationship in terms of orientation to relatively specific and limited goals. Perhaps the classic center of the complex is the field of "contractual" relationships, and its formulation at the hands of such theorists as Spencer and Tönnies provides the classic sociological characterization. Contractualism overlaps widely with the use of money and the wide extension of market relationships. This involves the enormous extension of the mobility of elements essential to co-ordinated human action and the extension of the possibility of focussing elements from many sources on the realization of a single goal. Codification and systematization of personal rights and individual liberties is another essential aspect as is the clear development of the modern institution of ownership in the sphere of property. The question of where ownership is lodged is not the primary issue—but rather the concentration of the various rights which taken together we call ownership into a single bundle rather than their dispersion; and by the same token their segregation from the other elements of the status of their holder.

By no means the least important element of this complex is the patterning of functional roles primarily about their functional content itself with clear segregation from other elements of the total social status of the individual—in kinship, local ties, even to a considerable extent social class and ethnic adherence. Though prominent in the case of independent roles such as those of private professional practice, this patterning of functional roles is most prominent in the field of large-scale organization; indeed without it the latter as we know it would scarcely be conceivable at all.

The interdependence between the complex of science and technology on the one hand, and that just discussed on the other is exceedingly close.

Some schools of thought, as of Veblen and Ogburn, give the former unquestioned primacy. This is at least open to serious question since it is only in relatively highly developed stages of the patterning of functionally specialized roles that the most favorable situation for the functioning of scientific investigation and technological application is attained. Less directly the mobility of resources through property and market relations, and the institutions of personal freedom all greatly facilitate the influence of science on social life.

Finally, science itself is a central part of the cultural tradition of our society. As such it is perhaps the most conspicuous embodiment of the more general pattern which may be called that of "critical rationality," differing from others primarily in the place accorded to the canons of empirical observation and verification. This same spirit of critical rationality has to an increasing extent ramified into many or even most other areas of the cultural tradition.

Notably of course it has permeated philosophical thought and the religious traditions of the various branches of Christianity. In this direction two consequences above all have appeared—the questioning of the cognitive status of the "non-empirical" elements of philosophical and religious thought, and the tendency to eliminate patterns and entities of primarily symbolic significance. The use of the categories of "ignorance" and "superstition" as sufficient characterizations of all thought not in conformity with the particular rational or pseudo-rational standards of the moment is an indication of the basic attitude.

The present concern is not whether the patterns of rationality in these different areas are in some sense superior to those they have tended to supplant, but rather the relation of their relatively rapid process of development to the functioning of the social system. It should be clear that their development is in itself the most important single source of anomie. Its significance in this respect is by no means simple and cannot be adequately analyzed here. It is partly a matter of the sheer rapidity of the process, which does not provide an opportunity for stable reorientation. Another aspect is the unevenness and incompleteness of its incidence so that it engenders conflicts in the social pressures impinging on the same groups and as between different groups. There is also the question whether, to balance its underminding effect on traditional patterns and values, it succeeds in providing even for the groups most thoroughly permeated, functionally adequate substitutes.

But beyond the significance as a source of temporary or permanent anomie, the process of rationalization has a further significance of crucial interest here. It is to it that we must look for the primary explanation of the structuring of attitudes and social organization so far as it can be treated as a response to the generalized condition of anomie. This question will have to be discussed on two primary levels, first that of the cognitive definition of the situation, second that of the differential affective appeal of the competing definitions of the situation which have come to be available.

The process of rationalization would scarcely have been of profound social importance if it had not affected large numbers of people in the immediate circumstances of their daily lives. But as an essential part of the same general cultural movement there has developed a tradition of "social thought" which, in a sufficiently broad perspective, can be seen to be highly distinctive in spite of its internal complexity. It has provided, above all, two interrelated things, a diagnosis of the status of the society—particularly in relation to the traditional patterns and structures with which the process of rationalization has stood in conflict, and a frame of reference for determining the proper attitudes of "reasonable" men toward the social problems of the day. Its functioning as the "ideology" of social and political movements is a natural consequence. In a very broad sense it is the ideological patterns of the movements of the "left" which are in question.

Such a tradition of thought is inevitably compounded of various different elements which today we find it convenient to distinguish. In the first place, there are certain elements of genuine scientific insight which by contrast with previous stages may be considered new. Undoubtedly the "utilitarian" pattern of analysis of the division of labor and exchange and the corresponding analysis of the functioning of a system of competitive market relationships—in short the "classical economics"—is largely in this category. With the shift on this level from "economic individualism" in the direction of socialism, especially Marxism, certain changes of emphasis on different factors have occurred, but a fundamental constancy of cognitive pattern, the "utilitarian," has remained.

From the perspective of a later vantage point we can now see that in spite of the undoubtedly sound elements there have from a scientific point of view been certain shortcomings in this scheme of thought. Attention has been concentrated on one sector of the total structure of a social system—that of contract, exchange, monetary transactions—and others such as family life have been neglected. But even within the area of focussed attention the "fallacy of misplaced concreteness" has, understandably enough, played a prominent role. The prominent patterns of thought have, that is, been inadequately placed in perspective and integrated with other elements of a total social system.

The scientifically relevant element has, at the same time, been closely related to certain patterns of value orientation—with both a positive and a negative aspect. In one connection the new social thought expressed a revolt against the old order and a rationalization or justification of the changes introduced by the process of rationalization. Its primary targets of attack have been traditionally established statuses of prestige, authority, and privilege and the traditionalized patterns themselves which have been integrated with these. Positively, the rights of the individual both as against other human agencies and as against tradition itself have provided the main focus. A fundamental trend towards egalitarianism has also been prominent. Broadly the pattern can be described as one of "emancipation" from the control of forces without rational sanction, from unjust authority, from monopoly and competitive privilege, from the "tyranny" of ignorance and superstition.

Finally, apart both from questions of science and of ethical value the tendency has, it has been noted, been to extend patterns of rationality into the metaphysical realm. Science has been taken as the prototype of all sound cognitive orientation and all elements of tradition not scientifically defensible have tended to be "debunked." Here of course traditional religion has been the primary object of attack.

In the earlier phases of its development this scheme of thought overwhelmingly embodied positive value attitudes. It defined the situation for the emergence and establishment of a new and magnificent social order, for freedom against tyranny, for enlightenment against ignorance and superstition, for equality and justice against privilege, for free enterprise against monopoly and the irrational restrictions of custom.

Gradually, however, with the growing ascendancy of the associated patterns, in certain directions certain elements of the scheme of thought have with altered emphasis and formulation come to be built into a pattern embodying quite different value attitudes. This has centered primarily on the developed system of emancipated and rationalized economic organization. The liberation of free enterprise from the tyranny of monopoly and custom has, it is said, led only to the system of capitalistic exploitation. The "profit motive" has become the object of deep reproach. Inequality, unemployment, and new forms of unjust privilege have been brought into the limelight. Political liberation from the tyrannical Bourbons has led only to a new enslavement under the "executive Committee of the Bourgeoisie."

This new negative orientation to certain primary aspects of the maturing modern social order has above all centered on the symbol of "capitalism," which is certain circles has come to be considered as all-embracing a key to the understanding of all human ills as Original Sin once was. But it is important to note that the main intellectual movements within which this has developed have retained, even in an extreme form, the rationalized patterns in other connections, particularly in attitudes toward ignorance and superstition—lurking behind which economic interests are often seen—and many other symbolic and unrationalized patterns of thought and social behavior. What in terms of the recent situation is "leftist" social thought is overwhelmingly "positivistic" as well as utilitarian.

With the wisdom of hindsight, it can now be clearly seen that this rationalistic scheme of thought has not been adequate to provide a stably institutionalized diagnosis of even a "modern" social system as a whole, nor has it been adequate to formulate all of the important values of our society, nor its cognitive orientation to the world. It has been guilty of the fallacy of misplaced concreteness in neglecting or underestimating the role of what Pareto has called the "non-logical" aspects of human behavior in society, of the sentiments and traditions of family and informal social relationships, of the refinements of social stratification, of the peculiarities of regional, ethnic or national culture—perhaps above all of religion. On this level it has indeed helped to provoke a most important "anti-intellectualist" reaction.

On another level it has "debunked" many of the older values of our cultural tradition, and above all the cognitive patterns of religion, to a point well beyond that to which common values and symbols in the society had moved. Even apart from questions of its metaphysical validity it cannot be said adequately to have expressed the common orientations of the members of the society.

But on top of these inherent strains a crucial role has been played by the emergence within the rationalized cultural tradition itself of a definition of the situation which has thoroughly "debunked" many of the institutionalized products of the process of rationalization itself. Surely the stage was set for a combination of this definition of the situation with a reassertion of all the patterns which the utilitarian scheme had omitted or slighted—an acceptance of its own indictment but a generalization of the diagnosis to make "capitalism" appear a logical outcome of the whole process of rationalization itself, not merely of its perversion, and the fact that in certain directions it had not been carried far enough. By the same token it is possible to treat both capitalism and its leftist antagonists, especially communism, not as genuine antagonists but as brothers under the skin, the common enemy. The Jew serves as a convenient symbolic link between them.

This reaction against the "ideology" of the rationalization of society is one principal aspect at least of the ideology of fascism. It characteristically accepts in essentials the socialist indictment of the existing order described as capitalism, but extends it to include leftist radicalism and the whole penumbra of scientific and philosophical rationalism.[2]

The ideological definition of the situation in terms of which the orientation of a social movement becomes structured is of great importance but it never stands alone. It is necessarily in the closest interdependence with the psychological states and the social situations of the people to whom

[2] I am aware of the importance of other aspects of the total fascist pattern such as its romanticism and a tendency to ethical nihilism, but cannot stop to analyze them here.

it appeals. We must now turn to the analysis of certain effects of the process of rationalization on this level.

The fundamental fact is that the incidence of the process within the social structure is highly uneven—different elements of a population become "rationalized" in different degrees, at different rates, and in different aspects of their personalities and orientations.

It may be said that both traditional and rationalized patterns are, to a high degree, genuinely institutionalized in our society. Indeed the distinction is itself largely relative and dynamic rather than absolute, and both are functionally essential to an even relatively stable society. Some elements of the population are relatively securely integrated but with varying emphasis in one direction or the other. Thus the best integrated professional groups would lean in the rational direction, certain rural elements in the traditional.

This difference of incidence has important consequences on both the structural and the psychological levels. Structurally it differentiates the social system broadly along a continuum of variation from the most highly traditionalized areas which have been least touched by the more recent phases of the process of rationalization to the most "emancipated" areas which tend at least partly to institutionalize the most "advanced" of the rationalized patterns or those which are otherwise most thoroughly emancipated from the traditional background.

For these and other reasons certain areas of the social structure have come to stand out conspicuously. In the first place is the area of "intellectualism" emancipated from the patterns and symbols of traditional thought, secondly of urbanism particularly on the metropolitan scale with its freedom from particularistic controls, its cosmopolitanism and general disrespect for traditional ties. Third is the area of economic, technological, and administrative rationalization in the market system and large-scale organization, especially toward the top, with its responsiveness to *ad hoc* situations and its relation to conflicting codes. Fourth is the area of "cultural" emancipation in literature and the arts with its high susceptibility to unstable faddism, and its association with bohemianism. Finally there is the moral emancipation of "Society" with its partial permeation of the upper middle class, the adoption of manners and folkways not in keeping with various traditional canons of respectability, all the way from women smoking to polite adultery.

The uneven incidence of these various forms of emancipation results in an imperfect structural integration with latent or overt elements of conflict and antagonism. These conflicts in turn readily become associated with the tensions involved in other structural strains in the society. In particular may be mentioned here first, the difficult competitive position of the lower middle class, near enough to the realization of success goals to feel their attraction keenly but the great majority, by the sheer relation of their numbers to the relatively few prizes, doomed to frustration. Secondly, the particular strains in the situation of youth engendered by the necessity of emancipation from the family of orientation and exposure to the insecurities of competitive occupational adjustment at about the same stage of the life cycle, and third, the insecurity of the adult feminine role in our urban society.[3]

An element of at least latent antagonism between relatively emancipated and relatively traditionalized elements of the society would exist even if all its members were perfectly integrated with institutional patterns, if there were no anomie. But we have seen that anomie exists on a large scale. In relation to the above discussion, however, two principal foci, each with a tendency to a different structuring of attitudes, need to be distinguished. On the one hand certain of the population elements involved in the spearheads of the processes of emancipation and rationalization are subject to a high incidence of it with its attendant insecurity. These elements tend to find the main points of reference of their orientations in the relatively well institutionalized rational and emancipated patterns—in science, liberalism, democracy, humanitarianism, individual freedom. But being insecure they tend to "overreact" and both positively and negatively to be susceptible to symbolizations and definitions of the situation which are more or less distorted caricatures of reality and which are overloaded with affect. Thus negatively the traditional order from which emancipation has been taking place is characterized overwhelmingly as embodying ignorance, superstition, narrow-mindedness, privilege, or in the later stages, acquisitive capitalistic exploitation. On the positive side there has been not only a marked abstractness but also some form of naive rationalistic utopianism. The pattern tends to bear conspicuous marks of the psychology of compulsion. It is held that if only certain symbolic sources of evil, superstition, or privilege or capitalism were removed "everything would be all right" automatically and for all ime. Indeed there is every reason to believe that the psychology of this type of insecurity has had much to do with the cognitive biases and inadequacies of utilitarian thought as sketched above. It has contributed largely to the currency of a definition of the situation which contains conspicuous elements of utopianism and of distorted caricature.

The other type of reaction has been prominent in those areas of the society where traditional elements have formed the institutionalized points of reference for orientation. There the principal sources of anomie have often been derived from situational factors such as technological

[3] A colleague (E. Y. Hartshorne in an unpublished paper) has noted that in Germany the most conspicuous support of the Nazis came from the lower middle class, from youth, and from women. On the two latter factors see the author's paper "Age and Sex in the Social Structure of the United States," (*American Sociological Review*, Vol. 7, October, 1942) reprinted in this volume.

change, mobility, and ethnic assimilation, with relatively little direct relation to rationalized ideological patterns. There insecurity has tended to be structured in terms of a felt threat to the traditionalized values. The typical reaction has been of an over-determined "fundamentalist" type. Aggression has turned toward symbols of the rationalizing and emancipated areas which are felt to be "subversive" of the values. Naturally there has at the same time been an exaggerated assertion of and loyalty . to those traditional values. The availability of ready-made caricatured definitions of the situation and extreme symbols has of course greatly facilitated this structuring. The use of such slogans as "capitalism," has made it possible to exaggerate the "rottenness" of the whole modern society so far as it has departed from the good old values.

In the complex process of interaction in Western society between imperfectly integrated institutional structures, ideological definitions of the situation, and the psychological reaction patterns typical of anomie, at a certain stage in the dynamic process of its development this newly structured mass movement has come upon the scene and at certain points in the Western world has gained ascendancy. It is perhaps safe to conclude from the above analysis that its possibility is at least as deeply rooted in the social structure and dynamics of our society as was socialism at an earlier stage.

Before turning to another phase of the problem a word may be said about the role of nationalism in the present context. Though not, in terms of the "old regime," itself strictly a traditional value, the complex of sentiments focussing on national cultures has involved many of these traditionalistic elements—varying in specific content from one case to another. Ever since the French Revolution a functional relationship between the rise of nationalism and the process of rationalization has been evident—they have developed concurrently.

For a variety of reasons nationalistic sentiment has been perhaps the readiest channel for the fundamentalist reaction to flow into. The national state assumed great actual importance. The actual or potential enemy in the power system of states, differing in national tradition, has formed a convenient target for the projection of many aggressive effects. At the same time many of the emancipated areas of the social structure have been defined as "international" and could be regarded as subversive of national interest, honor, and solidarity. Finally, nationalism has been a kind of lowest common denominator of traditionalistic sentiments. Above all, the humblest insecure citizen, whatever his frustrations in other connections, could not be deprived of his sense of "belonging" to the great national community.

Undoubtedly one of the most important reasons for the different degrees of success in the fascist movement in different countries has lain in the differing degrees in which national traditions and with them pride and honor, have been integrated with the symbols of the rationalized patterns of Western culture. In the United States, on the one hand, the great national tradition stems from the Enlightenment of the eighteenth century —liberty, democracy, the rights of the individual are our great slogans. A radically fundamentalist revolt would have to overcome the enormous power of these symbols. In Germany on the other hand the political symbols of a liberal democratic regime could be treated as having been ruthlessly imposed on a defeated and humiliated Germany by the alien enemy. National sentiments instead of being closely integrated with the existing regime could readily be mobilized against it.

The second important element of the fascist movements, that of "vested interests" can be much more briefly treated. It is one of the most fundamental theorems of the theory of institutions that in proportion to the institutionalization of any pattern a self-interest in conformity with it develops. Self-interest and moral sentiments are not necessarily antithetical, but may, and often do motivate conduct in the same direction. Though this is true generally, it has a particularly important application to statuses involving prestige and authority in the social system. There, on top of the broader meaning of an interest in conformity, there is an interest in defending higher status and its perquisites against challenge from less privileged elements. For this reason the reaction of privileged elements to insecurity is almost inevitably structured in the direction of an attitude of defense of their privileges against challenge. For the same reason any movement which undermines the legitimacy of an established order tends to become particularly structured about an overt or implied challenge to the legitimacy of privileged statuses within it.

Western society has in all its recent history been relatively highly stratified, involving institutionalized positions of power, privilege, and prestige for certain elements. In the nature of the case the sentiments and symbols associated with these prestige elements have been integrated with those institutionalized in the society as a whole. In so far, then, as the process of rationalization and other disorganizing forces have undermined the security of traditional patterns the status and the bases of the legitimacy of privileged elements have inevitably been involved. But in addition to this they have been affected by threats to the legitimacy and security of their own position in the social structure. This situation tends to be particularly acute since the process of more general change is regularly accompanied by a process of the "circulation of the elite."

It is in the nature of a highly differentiated social structure that such privileged elements should be in a position to exercise influence on the power relations of the society through channels other than those open to the masses, through political intrigue, financial influence, and so on. Hence, with the progressive increase in the acuteness of a generalized state of anomie it is to be expected that such elements, which have been privileged in relation to a traditional social order should, within the limits provided by the particular situation, develop forms of activity, sometimes approaching conspiratorial patterns, which in these terms may be regarded as a defense of their vested interests. Exactly what groups are involved in this phenomenon is a matter of the particular structural situation in the society in question.

The general phenomenon would seem to be clear enough. It is also not difficult to understand the tendency for elite elements whose main patterns go far back into the older traditional society to become susceptible to the fascist type of appeal—such as the landed nobility and higher clergy in Spain, or the Junker class in Germany. But there is a further complication which requires some comment.

The process of institutional change in the recent history of our society has brought to the fore elite elements whose position has been institutionalized primarily about the newer rationalized patterns. The most important are the business and professional elites. The latter are, except where radical fascist movements have immediately threatened to gain the ascendancy, perhaps the securest elite elements in the modern West.

The position of the business elite has, however, been much more complex. It gained for a time a position of great ascendancy, but for various reasons this rested on insecure foundations. With the "leftward" turn in the movement of ideology its position came under strong attack as the key element of capitalism. With its position thus threatened by the leftward sweep of the process of rationalization the legitimacy, the moral validity of its position was under attack, and its actual vested interests became less and less secure. From this point of view Fascism has constituted in one respect a continuation, even an intensification of the same threat. The threat has been made concrete by the rise to power of a new political elite with the means in hand to implement their threat.

At the same time fascism has seemed to stand, in the logic of the sentiments, for "sound" traditional values and to constitute a bulwark against subversive radicalism. Very concretely it has been instrumental in breaking the power of organized labor. At the same time on the level of power politics there has been a distinct area of potential mutual usefulness as between a political movement of the fascist type and entrenched business interests. This has been especially true because of the fascist tendency immediately to mobilize the economy in preparation for war.

The relation between fascism and vested interests in general may thus be regarded as a constant. In the case of the older traditional interests it is relatively unequivocal, but in that of business it is highly ambivalent. Especially where, as in Germany, business interests have not been closely integrated with strong liberal institutions the relationship has tended to be very close. But even there the movement can by no means by considered a simple expression of these vested interests and there are elements in the Nazi movement which may, in a certain state of the internal balance of power, turn out to be highly subversive of business.

In such brief space it has been possible to analyze only a few aspects of the very complex sociological problem presented by the fascist movement—the analysis is in no sense complete. But perhaps it will serve in a humble way to illustrate a direction in which it seems possible to utilize the conceptual tools of sociology in orienting ourselves, at least intellectually, to some of the larger aspects of the tragic social world we live in. To consider the possibility of going farther, of predicting the probable social consequences, of possible outcomes of the war and considering what we can do about fascism in other than a strictly military sense would raise such complex issues even on the scientific level, that it is better not even to attempt to touch upon them here.

Chapter

5

Max Weber and the Contemporary Political Crisis

THE SOCIOLOGICAL ANALYSIS OF POWER AND AUTHORITY STRUCTURES

*W*e are living in a time when men most urgently feel the need of intellectual clarification of the social and political situation in which they stand. By no means all the great masters of social thought who have made important potential contributions to such clarification are sufficiently well known, even among social and political scientists. One of these is Max Weber who, in the English-speaking world, is known more as a sociologist of religion and a methodologist of social science than as an interpreter of the political scene. Weber's scope of interest in institutional problems, with specific reference to the modern Western world, was, however, exceedingly broad, and a substantial part of his work was centered on the field of political institutions, particularly in their relations to the economic order and to other aspects of the social structure.

Weber died in 1920, so the question may be asked, of what relevance could his work be to a situation arising twenty years after his death? There can of course be no question of his having predicted the present

---

Reprinted from Review of Politics, *VIII (1942), 66–71 (Part I), 155–172 (Part II).*

situation in exact detail, nor having predicted its outcome. He did, how-ever, have certain striking ideas about the situation in his own time,[1] which held many of the roots from which that of the present has grown. Certainly far less than most social scientists would Weber have been surprised by the course developments have taken, had he lived to see them. But still more, Weber developed an original generalized analysis of the social structure of political relationships[2] which is, in many different connections, applicable to the present situation. This body of generalized analysis is very far from having become assimilated into the kit of working conceptual tools of the majority of people claiming appreciable technical competence in the field.

In a certain sense, Weber's primary interest as a social scientist lay in what are ordinarily considered the economic aspects of social life. But he treated economic phenomena in terms of a frame of reference far broader than that usual to the economist. He was more interested in economic institutions than he was in the equilibrium relationships of economic quantities as such. In what is perhaps the best known part of his empirical work, Weber was directly concerned with the relation of religious movements to the basic attitudes and institutional patterns involved in economic activities.[3] His attention was, however, by no means confined to this field. He was, throughout his career, profoundly impressed with the importance of the interrelations of the structure of authority and the economic order and devoted a major part of his work to this range of problems. He also, throughout his life, had a passionate personal interest in the political situation of his own country, both internally and in international affairs, and continually linked this up with his scientific work.

Authority, Power, and Political Systems

To Weber, a fundamental feature of all complex systems of human relationships was the element of authority, the fact that a minority of men are put in a position of ability to control the action, to an appreciable degree and in a variety of respects, of the great majority. To him the most important generalized type of group structure is the *Verband*.[4] This may

---

[1] Most directly documented in the volume *Gesammelte Politische Schriften*.

[2] Most fully developed in *Wirtschaft und Gesellschaft*, Part I, Chapter III and Part III, both under the title "Typen der Herrschaft." An English translation of the entire work, edited by Guenther Roth, has recently been published under the title *Economy and Society* (New York: Bedminster Press, 1968).

[3] See especially the three volumes of *Gesammelte Aufsätze zur Religionssoziologie*. A fairly full secondary account of this phase of Weber's work is given in the present writer's *Structure of Social Action*, Chapters XIV and XV.

[4] *Wirtschaft und Gesellschaft*, Part I, Chapter I, Sec. 12.

have any conceivable content of interests or of function in the social system, but cutting across this is a basic uniformity in structure with respect to authority. There is normally an individual, a chief (*Leiter*), at the top of the structure, and a group of persons under him who have the function of administering the policies of the chief, and thereby exercise authority over the mass of the members, the "administrative staff." Groups where the element of authority is minimized, or altogether absent, are by no means unknown, but are definitely the exception, particularly in large-scale organization under settled routine conditions. Where they exist they are apt to be unstable and to depend upon circumstances, such as the active phase of a movement of religious enthusiasm, which are in the nature of the case temporary.

The role of authority and its basic structure run through all fields of human relationship, and are by no means peculiar to the political. The political aspect Weber distinguishes in terms of two further criteria, the use of physical force and the exercise, as an organized function of the group, of control with a specific territorial area.[5] This is not to be understood to mean that political groups use only physical force as a means of control or even that they use it more than other means. It is rather that the use of force is structurally specific to them; they are organized about the use of force in a sense in which this is not true of other types of groups. But it is only in combination with the orientation of control to a territorial area as such that Weber speaks of the use of force as political. The political structure of human societies is a phase of their organization relative to the territorial environment of action. In defining the category of political in this way, Weber specifically repudiates its definition in terms of any specific type of "end" or value which political bodies in general, or the state in particular, serve. The content of their goals in this sense may be widely variable.

It is an essential aspect of the structure of authority in human groups that it necessarily becomes the primary focus of the power relationships within a social system. Indeed, in a sense, the structure of authority in a given group may be said to constitute the principal way in which power relationships are institutionalized. Though this is true of all systems of authority, it is preeminently so of the political. This is so because of the peculiar potency of the combination of elements which characterize political authority. The use of force is, of course, on a certain immediate though fundamental level, the *ultima ratio* in the control of human action, the last resort when others fail. Above all, it is effective as a negative instrument of control, as a means of preventing others from doing things which the wielder of force does not want done. The use of force in turn is intrinsically linked to territoriality. For to exercise force it is necessary to

---

[5] *Ibid.* Part I, Chapter I, Sec. 17.

get at the person to be controlled, that is, it is necessary to have him within range of the instruments of force. Conversely, he who commands the instruments of force with a given range of effectiveness at a given territorial location, thereby has a certain kind and degree of potential control over all the persons acting within that range.

Thus within an exceedingly wide range of human interests and goals, the relation of the corresponding activity to the structure of political authority is functionally crucial. To be able to attain almost any goal it is necessary as a fundamental condition, either to have a degree of control over the exercise of political power within the relevant area, or to be able to assume that those in possession of political power will not use it to interfere with the action in question—the political element has either to be controlled or to be neutralized.

Thus from a very wide range of potential motives on other levels, the behavior of and control of political power and authority becomes an object of immediate concern, of, as Weber would say, the orientation of action. Political behavior as such, Weber thus defines as that which is oriented to the attainment and use of political power, or to the exercise of influence on the holders of political power. It is thus fundamentally a matter of action oriented to the power structure of the society, to maintaining or altering the balance of power between individuals and groups, through political means, and in relation to consequences affecting the holding and use of political power. The "political" in this sense is an aspect of a system of social relationships. The political aspect sometimes becomes of primary significance for particular classes of actions and for particular differentiated structures, but it is always, in the nature of the case, closely interwoven with the other aspects of the same social system, and interdependent with them.

The Three Types of Authority

Though Weber held that there was a basic tendency to uniformity in the authority structure of groups, it does not follow that there are no important variations within it. This variation, which is in certain respects the key to Weber's dynamic analysis, he analyzed in terms of a classification of three basic types of structure of authority, what he called "rational-legal" authority, "traditional" authority, and "charismatic" authority. The basis of the classification lies in the first instance in variation in the nature of the claim to "legitimacy" that is made for the holders of a position of authority, that is of their having a "right" to exercise authority over others and claim obedience as a duty, as distinguished from merely compelling it by *force majeur*. It is this claim which distinguishes "authority" (*legitime Herrschaft*) from *Herrschaft* in general.[6]

Rational-legal authority[7] is the form which is most characteristic of the modern Western world, including, though not confined to the state. In it, authority is exercised legitimately by virtue of holding an "office" under a generalized system of rules of law. The source of legitimacy does not lie in a personal prerogative of the individual incumbent of the office, but in the "legality" of his action as defined by his legal competence under the rules—that is, it is the system of rules which defines the powers of his office, not the person of the incumbent. The rules themselves in turn are legitimized by having been enacted or imposed by a agency which has legitimate authority to do so—a monarch, a legislature, etc., and when this has been done by the legally correct procedure. The rules are generalized and impersonal, applying "impartially" to all persons and cases falling within the generalized definitions of their scope without regard to personal loyalties or privileges. In the extreme type case they claim to cover all possible exigencies which fall within the scope of the system of authority.

The incumbent of office has authority only within the scope defined by the legal order—it is in the nature of the case specifically limited to this sphere. This in turn implies a clear distinction between the property over which the incumbent has powers by virtue of his office, and whatever personal property interests outside that he may have. The former is treated as the property of the corporate body in which he holds office.

Finally, administrative functions, under a system of rational-legal authority, tend to be organized in bureaucratic form. The administrative staff is organized in a hierarchy of offices such that the lower levels are subject to the control of the higher. Incumbency is by appointment, not by election, and higher authorities have powers not only of appointment, but of promotion, demotion and dismissal. Fitness for appointment is in general according to criteria of individual competence, not according to any particularistic criteria and in the most rational case is tested by examination. Remuneration is in the form of fixed money salary entirely separated from the "means of administration."

What has been outlined is what Weber calls an "ideal type" rather than a description of any concrete system of authority. The organization of authority in the modern Western world has, however, more closely approached this type than any other large-scale example in history and, for broad comparative purposes, it serves to characterize that system. Perhaps the most important general exception which Weber made was the observa-

[6] For the definitions of these types see *Wirtschaft und Gesellschaft* Part I, Chapter III, Sec. 2. They are also briefly characterized in "Politik als Beruf" in *Gesammelte Politische Schriften*, pp. 398–399.
[7] *Wirtschaft und Gesellschaft*, Part I, Chapter III, Sec. 3–5. The fullest secondary discussion is in Goldhamer and Shils, "Types of Power and Status," American Journal of Sociology, Sept. 1939.

tion that in a bureaucratic system of administration it was seldom that the top authority was of a purely bureaucratic nature. It could belong to a radically different type, as in the case of a traditional monarch or a charismatic leader, or it could belong to a variant within the rational-legal type, as in the case of an elected official, who still held an office. Thus the American President is not himself a bureaucratic official, though he has supreme authority over the administrative branches of the government. Also cabinet ministers, though appointed, are selected by quite different criteria from even the highest civil servants.

The second basic type Weber calls that of "traditional" authority.[8] In it a position of authority is not an "office" but rather a "status." It involved subjection to a system of concrete rules, to a greater or less degree generalized, but these are binding because they have "always existed," not because of the legality of their enactment. New legislation is in principle excluded—there can only be the fiction of ancient validity to cover actual innovations. But besides this, the traditional order legitimizes an authority-bearing status, or rather a system of them. Each incumbent is limited by the concrete traditional precepts, and by the prerogatives of others above him in the hierarchy or in other spheres of jurisdiction which have become traditionally defined. But within these limitations he enjoys a sphere of arbitrary personal prerogative in which he is free to make decisions and to take action according to considerations of utility, of *raison d'état*, of substantive justice, or even of mere personal whim.

When a status is thus defined, obedience is due to the person of the holder of authority, and the relation becomes one of personal loyalty. Those subject to authority can of course be absolved from their obligations if the incumbent violates the traditional code too seriously or infringes their traditionally defined rights, but these are negative rather than positive limits. Correspondingly there is no clear-cut differentiation between the status of authority and the sphere of personal affairs, and none between the "means of administration" and personal property. Authority over others is not limited to a defined sphere of official function but can extend to any aspect of the concrete social relationship which is not excluded by one of the above types of limitation. Thus authority in political or other spheres is often associated with relations of personal dependency through such ties as kinship, the client relationship, and feudal fealty.

One of the key features of Weber's concept of traditional authority is the place he gives to the sphere of arbitrary personal prerogative of the chief. There is, however, an important range of variation in this respect. It is subject to two main types of limitation. On the one hand there is a type of "primary" gerontocracy or patriarchalism where the chief does not have any independent command over an administrative staff, where the persons on whom he is dependent for carrying out his authority all

[8] *Wirtschaft und Gesellschaft*, Part I, Chapter III, Sec. 6–9.

occupy traditional statuses in the social structure with the attendant rights which he is traditionally obligated to respect. On the other hand, an administrative staff each member of which has, in some important respect, authority the legitimacy of which is associated with the status of the chief, may still impose important limitations on the prerogative of the chief to control them. This usually takes the form of some kind of "appropriation" of status as a member of the administrative staff, the enjoyment of recognized rights in this status beyond the control of the chief. This appropriation may touch a variety of different aspects of the relationship—thus the incumbency of the position of authority as such, for instance through heredity, the definition of its powers, control over the means of administration which are treated as the personal property of the incumbent, and control over the sources of remuneration. This situation is, historically, usually in an important degree the outcome of a struggle for power between the chief and the members of the administrative staff in the course of which the latter have succeeded in imposing limitations on the former's power and getting them institutionally established.

The third major type Weber calls "charismatic authority."[9] It is sharply distinguished from the other two in that it cannot, in the nature of the case, be a form of the organization of authority under routine, settled conditions. A charismatic source of authority always legitimizes opposition to, or defiance of, the established institutional order in some important respect. As Weber treats it, this focuses in the claim of an individual person, a "leader," to obedience from a group of followers. Though it is a personal claim, in the sense that it is put forward by the individual on his own responsibility and not by virtue either of an office or of a traditionally legitimized status, it is a moral authority, which claims obedience as a duty, not merely as conformity with the leader's personal wishes as such.

Where such a charismatic leader builds up an administrative staff, their positions cannot be regulated in terms of the other two types. They are typically engaged in *ad hoc* "missions" by personal designation of their chief, and their status varies with his personal decisions and the exigencies of the particular situation. There is no fixed hierarchy of offices or of traditionalized status. The closest analogy in the other types is to the "favorites" of a traditional chief.

Perhaps an even more fundamental difference from the other two types lie in the modes of provision of the "movement" with the means of administration and remuneration for the administrative staff. Routine provision is out of the question. There are two typical forms, free gifts, and "booty," that is, economically significant goods which are secured by coercion and force. This distinction corresponds roughly to the two main directions which, according to Weber, such charismatic movements take,

[9] In *Wirtschaft und Gesellschaft*, Part I, Chapter III, Sec. 10-12.

namely an otherworldly religious orientation, or an imposition of their pattern at least in part by force. The particular relevance of the latter alternative to the political field is clear.

It is a fundamental theorem of Weber's that the charismatic type is inherently unstable and temporary. Hence in the course of time it will inevitably become "routinized," and particular importance attaches to the ways in which this process develops. Fundamentally it must lead in the direction either of a rational-legal or a traditional type of organization. Which it will be depends on a variety of factors which can play a part in the course of the process. One of the most crucial of the points at which these factors can operate is that of the disappearance of the original leader, when the problem of succession must be faced. For precisely insofar as the position of authority of the founder of the movement was personal, this cannot be true of his successor, who must be legitimized at second hand as legitimately *carrying on* what another has begun. There are in turn two interdependent aspects of the modes in which this situation can be met: on the one hand, the pattern according to which a successor is legitimized, that is, in what his authority consists and on the other hand, the criteria for selection of an appropriate successor as an individual. Thus both in the Roman and in the modern western states political authority has, with the exception of monarchs, been held only by virtue of election or appointment of office, not as the personal or private prerogative of any non-official status. It is clear that according to the patterns employed there will be a tendency to treat the incumbency of the succession more as an office with impersonally defined powers, or as the prerogative of an individual as such, by heredity, personal designation, etc., which becomes crystallized into a traditionalized status such as that of monarch or hereditary priesthood. Essentially the same considerations apply to the routinization of the status of members of the administrative staff after they can no longer be treated simply as followers of the leader to whom they are personally devoted, and after they secure a settle status in relation to the established institutions of the society.

Closely interdependent with these questions of personal status are those concerning the relation of the movement to the property system of the society. During the charismatic phase it is possible for both the means of administration and the remuneration of the administrative staff to be provided, out of resources which are placed at the disposal of the movement or of the leader personally, and which he in turn dispenses to his followers according to *ad hoc* exigencies, or which they acquire independently in the course of their activities. But such a system is, in the long run, impossible both from the point of view of internal relations within the administrative staff, and of its relations with the general population, both members of the corporate body and others with whom they stand in relationship. Here again the same basic alternatives of development are open. Provision may tend to take the form of regularized systems of taxation with the proceeds becoming the property of the organized group as such, not of any individuals within it. Then the means of administration remain its property, and at the disposal of members of the administrative staff, including the chief, only in their official capacity. Their remuneration then consists in salaries, fees, etc. On the other hand, especially where provision originates in contributions and compulsory levies, these can be very readily become "appropriated" by the members of the administrative staff who are closest to their sources, and, along with the authority over the sources which is involved, as their "private" property, that is, as perquisites of their status within the group. Weber would call this general type of organization that of "benefices" or "fiefs." The essential difference from the rational-legal type lies in the breakdown of the distinction between the areas of personal and official capacities, property and status, and correspondingly, the "tieing" of a great number of elements which in our institutional system are segregated together in a single status.

It may be said that a charismatic movement is particularly subject to the struggle for power between a chief and the members of his administrative staff, which can play such an important part in determining the structural outcome of the process of routinization. This is because, relative to the structural background, it is a movement of innovation. The patterns themselves which govern the regulation of relationships are very generally not clearly crystallized and definite, thus leaving scope for differing claims to legitimacy on many points. At the same time the status of the members of the administrative staff, and of the various modes of provision and remuneration is unsettled and unstable, hence subject to influence by all kinds of pressures. Finally, the actual situation of such a movement is rapidly changing, making it difficult for the problems to be readily settled in a permanent way. Though on account of the dominant status of the original leader there is a tendency for charismatic movements in their early stages to show a highly centralized structure, it may be said that this very easily breaks down later on into a system of appropriated rights at various levels in the structure with which the nominally supreme authority is powerless to interfere.

In formulating these three basic types of the institutional structure of authority, it should be clear that Weber was treating only one aspect of complex social systems. He himself treated explicitly various of their relations to other aspects of the same societies, notably the economic order[10] and the systems of sentiments and value-attitudes associated with the great religious movements. Certain of these will have to be briefly mentioned at appropriate points in the subsequent discussion. Authority

[10] In especially, *Wirtschaft und Gesellschaft*, Part I, Chapter II, "Die Soziologischen Grundkategorien des Wirtschaftens", as well as various other parts of the work.

is a phenomenon common to all fields of social activity. The aspect of peculiar interest to the present discussion is, however, a somewhat specialized one, namely political authority. One particularly important consequence of this needs to be mentioned briefly, namely the fact that the development and change of authority patterns in the political field goes on in the closest connection with the development and interrelationships of political power systems.[11] It is the organization in terms of legitimate authority of the population of a territorial area which constitutes, from the internal point of view, the essential basis of political power. Only when a political entity is relatively well-integrated, in this sense, is it in a position to exercise a formidable influence in the interrelations of different power-systems, such as the modern "world powers" have been. This includes, but is by no means confined to, the command over military force. In all his comparative institutional investigations Weber paid far greater attention than most social, or even political, scientists to the social structure of military organization.[12]

The system of types which has just been outlined Weber treats as a scaffolding with which he can analyze empirical problems. No case would be likely to meet exactly all the criteria of the pure type of any one of the three, and each case is to varying degrees unstable, subject to change under the pressure of forces unfavorable to its maintenance. With this qualification Weber saw the modern Western political system as in a peculiarly high degree approaching the type of a rational-legal system of authority. Of this, we may say, there have been two primary, interdependent aspects, the supremacy of law,[13] and the high development of bureaucratic administration. Law, as exemplified in the two great systems of continental Roman Law and Anglo-Saxon Common Law, has not only regulated the relationships of citizens under the political authority, but above all has defined the status of authority itself, and the institutional forms within which it has been exercised. This has, to a relatively high degree, been a rationalized system of law which has defined authority as that of a system of offices in Weber's sense. In its dealing with those subject to authority again, the modern systems of law have strongly tended to universalistic forms. All men have had formal "equality before the law," have been protected in certain basic liberties, in their contracts, and in the possession and disposal of legitimately acquired property. Our legal systems have tended either to combat or to ignore most of the traditional class and status discriminations inherited from our earlier history which

[11] On power-systems see especially "Deutschland unter den Europäischen Weltmächten." *Politische Schriften*, pp. 73–93.

[12] In particular see his "Agrarverhältnisse im Altertum" in *Gesammelte Aufsätze zur Sozial und Wirtschaftsgeschichte.*

[13] On Weber's view of the modern legal system see especially his "Rechtssoziologie," *Wirtschaft und Gesellschaft*, Part II, Chapter VII. English translation *Max Weber on Law, Economy and Society*, ed. by Max Rheinstein, (Cambridge: Harvard University Press, 1968).

have, for the most part, gradually tended to disappear. Of bureaucratic administration under such a system of law, perhaps the above brief discussion suffices. Naturally these two primary aspects of modern political organization have not developed, and do not subsist, in a social vacuum. They have been closely interdependent with developments in the field of economic organization, and with the cultural developments affecting our sentiments and value-attitudes.

The Instability of Rational-Legal Authority

The modern system has, however, never been a purely rational-legal-bureaucratic one. Though there has been a good deal of variation in different parts of the Western world, one may perhaps say that structurally there have been two most important limitations on the realization of the pure type. In the first place, at a number of key points structural elements originating in historically important traditional and charismatic patterns have survived—particularly perhaps in the institutions of monarchy. Secondly, though not so much at variance with the rational-legal type, there have been various elements which did not fit the bureaucratic type but either derived authority in different ways or tended to be anti-authoritarian in general. In this category belong certain of the "democratic" elements in the modern political systems, above all as found in the institutions of elective office.

These elements have stood in a delicate balance with the rational bureaucratic structure, such that important changes in the situation could with relative readiness set cumulative tendencies to change into motion. In addition to this lack of full structural integration in the modern political situation there have been numerous other sources of instability, notably the strains that are inherent in the enforcement of such a system of order to a high degree, and those which have impinged on the political system from elsewhere in the social system.

As a combined result of these various elements of malintegration the modern political system has been subject to important tendencies to change. Some of these have led directly toward a traditional organization of authority, while others have favored the rise of charismatic movements which, in turn may readily, in the process of routinization, lead in a traditionalistic direction.

Perhaps the most important of the points of strain of the first type are concerned with the maintenance of the functional specificity and the universalism required by rational-legal patterns. It is very difficult for those in authority in their relations to those under them to observe the limitations of the sphere of office sufficiently meticulously and to avoid letting considerations belonging to the "private" sphere influence the relationship. This difficulty is by no means confined to the tendency of persons in authority, especially for a long time, to regard their status as something of a personal prerogative and hence not strictly bound by the limitations of office. It is essential to a rational-legal system that there is a process of competitive struggle for position in the administrative staff, and for advancement. It is essential to a bureaucratic system that office is secured by appointment of superiors. Where there are any loopholes in the rationally universalistic criteria of fitness for appointment and promotion, as there inevitably are, there may develop a competition to influence the appointing authority through what are, in terms of the rational-legal pattern, illegitimate means. One of the most important classes of such means consist in appealing to the interests and sentiments of such authorities in respects which are not directly relevant to the criteria of office. As Weber was well aware, no system of authority works perfectly without strain.

The other principal source of strain is closely related. It is essential to a rational-legal system that persons are treated according to "impersonal," universalistic criteria, such as competence, and the like. But this is inherently difficult to maintain. The concrete relationships of persons are never confined to such a level, and it is very easy for particularistic consideration to acquire a decisive role. Thus on the part of persons in authority we hear a great deal about favoritism, nepotism, etc., on the part of persons in a dependent position, about seeking favors by "pull."

The consequence of any considerable development of these two tendencies is to bring about a radical structural alteration in the organization of authority. Though not inherently traditionalistic, it brings about a situation which is in many respects closely related to Weber's type of traditional authority. Perhaps the best example in the American political scene is the development of the urban "party machine" with its control over access to many public offices, both elective and appointive. It is usual to interpret this as an example of the victory of mercenary self-interest on the part of politicians over the disinterested devotion to the public interest which is prescribed in the dominant pattern. It may, however, be suggested that this is at least a seriously incomplete diagnosis. What is probably a much more important aspect of it lies in a shift in loyalties—from that to the functionally specific and universalistic standards of "office" in a rational-legal system, to the diffuse and particularistic set of obligations to the party organization, and to the "boss" as an individual. It is noteworthy how great an emphasis in our party politics is laid on "loyalty," both on the part of followers to the organization and its leadership, and on the part of the leadership to the loyal party workers and members. The unforgiveable sin on the part of a party boss is to "let his people down."

This direct shift from the rational-legal to the traditionalistic pattern is, however, not the only, and probably not the most important pattern of change. At least considerably more dramatic is that by way of charismatic movements. Weber had relatively little to say about the kind of social conditions which favor the emergence of large-scale charismatic movements—he was more interested in their nature, their patterns of development and their consequences. There is, however, a great deal of evidence available to show that modern Western society provides particularly fruitful soil for this kind of development. It is a society in which there are important social stresses and strains, and which shows a great deal of relatively diffuse "social disorganization" or "anomie." Certain strains are inherent in any large-scale complex society, such as elements of antagonism between different social classes, tendencies to differentiation of wealth, resistance to the exercise of power and of authority which is only imperfectly legitimized. But the source of strain which is specific to our society, at least in quantitative importance, is the consequence of the rapidity of the process of "rationalization" as Weber called it, the undermining of traditional patterns, symbols, by rational or pseudo-rational criticism, and the development of rationalized patterns. This is found in science, technology, and economic life, in government and administration, in philosophical and religious thought, in cultural fields and the arts. The result, along with rapid mobility and change in other respects, is to make it particularly difficult for large numbers of people to have sufficiently settled routines, and modes of orientation—to have enough which they can "take for granted." The accompaniment of this in turn is widespread psychological "insecurity" and anxiety. Charismatic movements of various sorts seem to function in this situation as mechanisms of "reintegration" which give large numbers of disorganized, insecure people a definite orientation, give "meaning" to their lives.[14]

The incidence of this sort of phenomena is clear in many different fields. In spite, for instance, of the high development of rationalism in religious matters, our society is notable for the proliferation of religious cults of many different sorts—to mention only a few of the most prominent, Christian Science, Buchmanism, Father Divine, Jehovah's Witnesses, etc. The prevalence of unstable faddism is another symptom of the same situation. In the political field similar phenomena are to be found, on a minor scale in this country in such movements as Technocracy, Townsendism, the Huey Long "Share the Wealth" movements, etc. But of course the grand scale examples are Communism and German National Socialism, or more broadly, Fascism.

[14] This field is one which is only lately taking full shape. There is considerable evidence of the relation of social disorganization to religious movements in anthropological studies of the impact of white culture on primitive societies, and on the background of various important historical religious movements such as certain aspects of Early Christianity, Hazidism, Methodism. See A. D. Nock, *Conversion*, Israel Kazis', *Hazidism* (unpublished Ph.D. dissertation, Harvard University), E. K. Nottingham, *Methodism and the Frontier*. Also an as yet incomplete doctor's dissertation (Harvard University) by Theodore Sprague on Jehovah's Witnesses.

II. THE POLITICAL SITUATION
OF WESTERN SOCIETY

Democracy and the Party System

Max Weber died in 1920, when communism was in its beginnings and Fascism had not appeared on the scene at all. There can be no question of his having predicted anything like the exact nature of these movements. But he did develop a line of thought which, in connection with his broader analysis of authority, has an important bearing on the understanding of the process by which they came into prominence, and some of the possible consequences of their dominance.

There is an inherent connection between a rational-legal system of authority and democracy. In the first place this is because the former both depends on conditions, and in turn favors their intensification, which are incompatible with a stably traditionalized system, which usually, in a complex society, involves a system of established formal distinctions of social rank and status. The inherent tendency of bureaucracy on the other hand is a leveling tendency,[15] to treat persons indiscriminately according to objective criteria, and to select for office according to individual qualities, not established status. Much the same features have been true of the modern market economy.

With the progressive development of these tendencies the majority of the population tend for many purposes to constitute a relatively undifferentiated mass, without fixed status or loyalties. Though a certain role must be assigned to specifically anti-authoritarian ideologies in the "revolutionary era," Weber lays stress on the fact that all systems of authority are dependent on legitimation, on some form of recognition by the great majority of those subject to them. Bureaucratic administration as such does not secure this for basic policy, and the form which the search for legitimation has taken in the modern Western state has involved the development of the party system.[16] In its earlier stages of development the most influential elements in parties in Europe have tended to be various sorts of "magnates" (*Honoratioren*), persons of established prestige whose lead the masses of humbler people could be expected to follow. Thus in England in the Tory party it was more than any other the class of the landed gentry. But with the development of the process of leveling, these elements have tended to lose their power and be replaced by another type, the personal party leader. Weber sees this first developing in England in the Liberal Party, with Gladstone as the first figure occupying this status in unequivocal form. While in England such leaders have been public

---

[15] *Wirtschaft und Gesellschaft*, p. 129.
[16] See especially *Politik als Beruf*, in *Gesammelte Politische Schriften*. Also *Wirtschaft und Gesellschaft*, Part I, Ch. III, Sec. 18ff.

figures who directly strove to secure the highest office, in the United States part of the function came to be in the hands of another type, the party "boss," who typically has worked behind the scenes and avoided high office.

The basis of party power, along with patronage, lies in command over votes in the electorate, and the political struggle becomes one over votes, thus involving an appeal to the sentiments of the masses. This, then, is the fundamental combination, the dependence, of any group wishing to secure power, on an individual party leader with a mass popular appeal, and the basing of his power on an ability to command support by a direct appeal to the masses, apart from the influence of the traditionally or otherwise established prestige or interest groups. Of course in the traditional party system a party leader has been one among several competitors, and the legitimation of access to power has lain in the winning of majorities. Occasionally, however, in the past it has shifted over to a dictatorial pattern, as in the case of the two Napoleons in France. But even there certain elements of the previous pattern have remained present; the leader who has gained power is not, to be sure, legitimized by having "won" an election in the usual sense, but he claims mass popular support, evidenced by the plebiscite. However "unfair" the conditions under which this is achieved, Weber lays stress on the importance of the plebiscite as a symbol of popular support.

Even where there is a free competition of rival party leaders it is not uncommon for tendencies to develop which shift the basis of appeal from that which is ordinarily thought of as democratic, in a charismatic direction. Perhaps the best criterion of the distinction is that on an ordinary democratic basis what the electors are expressing is their "preference," either or any of the competitors can *legitimately* hold power if he is preferred, and the others must accept defeat in good grace. There is no one objectively *right* cause which it is a duty of the electorate as a whole to support. But in a charismatic pattern this is precisely the case—for those who fall within the range of his claims, it is delinquency in duty not to heed the call of the leader. Any competitor is by definition intolerable—there must be a decision as to which is *the* legitimate leader. The leader is not legitimized by incorporating the preferences of the electorate, but by their "recognition" of the rightness of his position. When, as has happened in the United States, one party claims that it alone is "fit" to govern the country and that the policies of its rival are "Unamerican," it is closely approaching the charismatic pattern.

This may be said to be the setting and the essential process, in certain respects, by which the Fascist dictatorships have developed. The dictators were originally party leaders taking part in the competitive struggle for power with other parties. But their resort to other than "orthodox" methods of rallying support before attaining power is already a symptom of their changed character. Thus the Nazis in their party rallies would never permit discussion and would forcibly eject all hecklers, implying that *only* their position was legitimate. This is certainly "undemocratic," but in the other crucial aspect, the appeal for mass support, they have remained close to democratic patterns. Hitler's use of the plebiscite to legitimize so many of his decisive steps of policy fits admirably into Weber's analysis.[17]

The Probable Consequences of the Permanent Consolidation of National Socialist Power

What then, in terms of Weber's analysis, are the probable consequences of permanent consolidation of the political power of such a movement over a wide area of Western civilization? This may be said to depend primarily on two sets of considerations. In the first place there is the question of the specific content of the ideal patterns in terms of which the movement has put forth whatever claim to legitimacy it has, in the second, those factors general to the process of routinization of a charismatic movement in application to the circumstances of this particular case.

[17] When it is said that a man in some sense predicted a political development, there is usually danger of people assuming that he therefore favored it. Exactly what Weber's personal attitude toward National Socialism would have been, had he lived to see it, cannot of course be determined, but it seems pretty certain it would have been overwhelmingly negative. He was certainly, in his personal values, deeply attached to the rational-legal pattern, and could not have approved the Nazi attack upon it. He was also deeply contemptuous of demagogic tactics in politics, as comes out at numerous points in his political writings.

He was, however, as will appear below, in a certain sense very much of a realist in politics, and hence held that these elements must be taken account of. In the discussion over the Weimar constitution he urged that the President of the *Reich* be given a strong "plebiscitary" basis for his position, that is that he be elected by universal popular vote, definitely not, like the French president, by the legislature. But his other most important single proposal was that the Parliament be given a central position in the government, above all one of high responsibility. He felt that one of the most serious defects in the monarchical constitution of Germany was that the Parliament was deprived of responsibility. Hence he could not have approved Hitler's centering of all power in the party, and reduction of the *Reichstag* to the position of a mere sounding board for his speeches.

In another specifically political connection Weber would almost certainly have fundamentally disapproved National Socialism. He had a deep antipathy to a wildly "adventurous" foreign policy. He very sharply criticized the annexationist elements in Germany in his time, and thought of Germany as *one* of the great units in a European power system, not as having hegemony over Europe. He argued that the destruction of Germany as such a unit could not in the long run succeed, but by the same token, in the present situation he would probably have argued that the destruction of the other great powers, namely France, Russia and England by Germany could not conduce to German welfare.

These are two specifically political contexts in which it is relevant to cite Weber's position. His ethical attitude to such things as Nazi Anti-Semitism and political repression generally, or his attitude toward the long-run consequences of predominance of the Nazi movement for social institutions and structure, lie upon a different plane. Something will be said about the latter in what follows. On Weber's personal attitudes see Marianne Weber, *Max Weber Ein Lebensbild* and Eric Voegelin, *"Max Weber," Kölner Vierteljahrshefte für Soziologie*, Vol. 9, No. 1-2.

The first set of questions Weber does not go into in his political writings or in his analysis of the institutionalization of authority. However, from his analysis of the role of ideas in his sociology of religion,[18] and from certain other sources a rough appraisal on this level is possible. For Weber "ideas" do not directly determine action in the sense of becoming the immediate "motives" of action. Their function is rather to "define the situation," that is to orient the actor to his situation in such a way as to tell him what courses of action are "meaningful" in the realization of his "interests," material or immaterial. It is, says Weber, "interests, not ideas, which are the motive forces of action."[19] But interests alone, religious or economic, in hedonic satisfaction or in power, do not suffice to tell people *what* to do. For this a system of ideas is, implicitly or explicitly, essential.

Now in certain essential respects the still rather vague and imperfectly crystallized system of ideas of the National Socialist movement, stands in drastic conflict with those which have held the dominant position in the Western world and become institutionalised as part of its social structure. Thus for instance, "race" membership in the "mystical body" of the German people, in all cases supersedes any considerations of individual quality or competence.[20] This constitutes a fundamental break with the ethical significance of universalistic standards, in a variety of fields of application, such as rational knowledge, the personal rights and liberties of a human individual as such, technical competence and the like. In place of these, in its racial and party particularism, and in its emphasis on unlimited loyalty to the *Führer*, it puts patterns that are much more appropriate to a traditionalistic organization of authority than a rational-legal one.

There are deeper functional reasons for this—it is not merely a matter of the arbitrary inventions of Hitler and the other party leaders. Precisely the "rational" patterns of modern Western society which are most important to its system of rational-legal authority have, in many respects, been an important source of strain in its development. For these patterns have been able to develop as far as they have only by virtue of undermining many of the values which have played an important part in our past history, especially in the informal, traditionalized social structures. Thus loyalties to neighbourhood locality, extended family tradition, social class tradition, and to a large extent traditional religion have been undermined. There has been a process of "emancipation" from these ties and the associated sentiments which is one of the most important sources of widespread insecurity.

[18] See his *Religionssoziologie*. Also the present writer's "Role of Ideas in Social Action," *American Sociological Review*, April 1939.
[19] *Protestant Ethic and the Spirit of Capitalism.*
[20] See Eric Voegelin, *Rasse und Staat.*

This process, however, has by no means led to the complete destruction of the traditionalistic elements in our society. What it has done is to leave a very considerable residue so that the actual situation is one of considerable tension, partly between different groups in the population, partly within the personalities of the same individuals who participate in both elements at the same time without fully integrating them. Thus we still have a great deal of adherence to traditional religion, to peculiarities of local tradition, to "prejudices" about social class and ethnic origin.

When such elements in a culture are associated in a solution of unresolved tension, it is natural that many of the elements which feel the tension, consciously or not, most acutely, should react in terms of a distorted appraisal of the other side of the tension. Thus among insecure and "touchy" people in the emancipated areas of our society there has been a prevalent "debunking" attitude which has tended to undermine traditional values and attitudes, especially those which are relatively "non-logical," considerably farther than the intrinsic facts or the basic rationalized patterns justify. This has taken the form both of denying the positive social functions we know to be associated with those structures and attitudes, and of imputing to their holders negative qualities such as stupidity which they do not, at least in the same measure, deserve. Thus, to many "emancipated" persons, anyone who adheres to one of the traditional Christian denominations is "childishly stupid and ignorant."

Conversely, insecure people associated with the traditionalist elements of our social structure tend to react in a "fundamentalist" pattern, to attribute to these values an absoluteness and literalness which is untenable, to treat every slight departure from the formalistic letter of tradition as an indication of the most fundamental immorality, etc. The term "fundamentalism" is taken from the field of religion, but the same kind of pattern of reaction is observable in many fields, that of morality, of devotion to the Constitution, of patriotism, and many others.

Among the forms which such "distorted" reaction patterns take, is that of ideas. Either type of distortion is, in such a situation, with different groups, a favorable source of symbols and of ideological definitions of the situation for charismatic movements, since both groups inevitably feel important dissatisfaction with certain aspects of the existing established order.[21] In this connection it is noteworthy that the political movements of the "left" have, with varying emphasis, been bound up with the elements of "emancipation" in our society. Some of the extremer

[21] It is interesting to note that Weber, in his sociology of religion, strongly emphasized that *no* institutionally established order was ever fully integrated, and hence free from strain. Hence there is always, to a greater or less degree, an opportunity for a charismatic leader to take a stand which, in opposing some elements of the established order, will have an appeal to some elements of the population who feel a strain in relation to these points. Quantitatively, however, modern Western society contains much more of these strains than many others. See "Religionssoziologie," *Wirtschaft und Gesellschaft*, Part II, Chapter IV.

versions have incorporated important elements of emancipated distortion which could easily provoke or strengthen the fundamentalist type of reaction among their opponents. For understandable reasons these movements of the left for long tended to monopolize the popular appeal since they have been in principle "democratic," while their opponents have relied upon and been identified with the more traditional status groups, and mass support has been derived more through the prestige of these groups than directly. With, however, the weakening of these groups and the progressively increasing leveling, the way has been opened to a demagogic appeal to fundamentalist sentiments. This, undoubtedly, is a most prominent aspect of National Socialism, as is shown by the fact that most of its negative symbols are chosen to represent the phenomena and groups of emancipation, the capitalist, the internationalist, the Jew (not the "orthodox," but the metropolitan, emancipated Jew), the political radical. Along with this go the imputation to their opponents of immorality (night club life), corruption, irreligion, and "subversive" cultural tendencies, the Nazi *Kulturbolschewismus*.

In so far as this diagnosis is correct one would expect the Nazi movement (and more generally Fascism) to develop a system of ideas which overwhelmingly favored a traditionalistic type of institutionalization, and which undermined the ideological foundation of the rational-legal system of authority in favor of a traditional. In this connection it may be noted that this is an excellent example of a basic conflict about which Weber had much to say: that between "Formal" and "Substantive" rationality.[22] By formal rationality Weber meant the adherence to certain formal criteria in action and decision relatively regardless of the consequences in other respects. Thus in the economic field there are the rules of capital accounting, the tendency to reduce all elements of the situation to calculability in money terms as far as possible. A tendency to order in this sense often, and Weber held, necessarily, comes into conflict with the requirements of a substantive ethical code, no matter what its content. Similarly in law and bureaucratic administration there is the formalism of adherence to generalized rules relatively regardless of the ethical quality of the particular result in any given case. In this sense the modern institutional order is dependent for its functioning on a relatively high level of formal rationality in various fields, but for this to be possible, those acting under it must somehow be effectively capable of "taking" a considerable amount of violation of their sentiments of "substantive" rationality and justice. The Nazi movement precisely mobilizes a great deal of this outraged sentiment in opposition. What to the supporters of the system are its "abuses" become to the opponents its essence.

Thus on one set of grounds there is a strong presumption that long-

---

[22] See, for instance, *Wirtschaft und Gesellschaft*, Part I, Chapter II, Sec. 9. The same theme is developed in the *Rechtssoziologie*, Sec. 5.

term predominance of National Socialism would strongly favor a traditionalistic rather than a rational-legal outcome of the process of routinization. This is greatly strengthened by the fact that, by its revolutionary activity, the movement everywhere goes far directly to destroy the institutions which are most essential to rational-legal authority. Thus, for instance, the inviolability of the regular system of courts from interference is fundamental to a system of the "rule of law." In Nazi territory the secret police is above the courts and need give them no accounting for its actions. Beyond that, every person with authority in the party hierarchy is in an important sense above the law. Any of the regular state system of law-enforcement agencies which tried to touch him, unless he were delivered to them by his party superiors, would do so at their peril. But what of the specific process of routinization of the movement as Weber analyzed it in this treatment of the structure of systems of authority?

The evidence concerning the pattern of succession is indecisive. The type most favorable to traditionalization, heredity, is, at least for the first succession, excluded. Hitler seems to favor personal designation, which could conceivably develop into a pattern of office, but need not. The other most important problems concern the status of members of the administrative staff, provision with means of administration, and remuneration. The party organization seems to have been a mixture of a purely charismatic and a bureaucratic type,[23] but with the charismatic elements of great prominence, particularly at the most important points, toward the top. There has been some "division of labor" according to different functional fields, but the primary principle seems to be hierarchy of leaders and sub-leaders, in the most important part, organized in terms of territorial jurisdiction (the *Gauleiter*), though again subdivided according to organizations such as the Labor Front, the Hitler Youth etc. The most important norm is that of loyalty to the immediate superior, on whom one is personally dependent, and who is in turn responsible to his superior. As is typical, a higher functionary, when he is present, supersedes a lower even in the latter's own jusrisdiction.

At present the most prominent feature of the party hierarchy is its high degree of centralization, the extreme dependence of the whole mechanism on the will of the supreme leader. But there is also evidence that a struggle for power has been going on within the party almost from the very beginning, as evidenced most dramatically by the blood purge of June, 1934. There are also persistent stories of bitter personal rivalries, such as that between Goering and Goebbels. There seems, therefore, to be a high probability that important elements of the upper circles would be in a position to establish a high degree of independence of the Führer, to appropriate rights to status in the organization, to the

---

[23] See Hans Gerth, "The Nazi Party: It's Leadership and Composition," *American Journal of Sociology*, Jan. 1940.

patronage under them, etc. This is particularly likely to occur after the passing of the original leader, unless he should be succeeded by an unusually strong personality. Above all it should be remembered that the party has broken the state's monopoly of the use of physical force—various organizations within the party structure exercise force in their own right, notably the *Gestapo* and the *S.S.* It is quite possible that those who control these organizations can establish a high degree of independence of the central party leadership. Hence the following seems likely: The system has gone far to break down the restrictions on arbitrary power which were constitutionally established in the old regime. In its place immediately has come a charismatic absolutism of the dictator. But in the longer run the break-up of the hierarchy into a variety of different elements which jealously guard their own rights, territorially or functionally segregated from the whole, is probable. This might well lead to a situation akin to feudalism except that the relation to land would presumably be different. There is good ground for believing that a great political empire built up by this movement would, in the second and third generations, prove as unstable as other imposing structures built up by charismatic and patrimonial conquerors in the past, such as Kublai Khan or Charlemagne. But such instability would not necessarily mean that its long-run social consequences would be anything but profound.

In its economic provision for its functional goals and for the remuneration of the administrative staff the Nazi movement has to a large extent conformed with charismatic patterns. On the assumption of power it has, of course, taken over the taxation system of the state and used it to its own ends, principally to promote armaments. But before and since the party organization as such has lived principally by Weber's two classic forms of charismatic provision, gifts and booty. Gifts range all the way from the small weekly dues of party members to the subsidies of industrial magnates. Booty has consisted, internally, in the processes of acknowledged or concealed confiscation at the expense of all kinds of established interests. This has included the "Aryanizing" of Jewish business, and various forms of "protection" accorded to non-Nazi elements, etc., whereby enormous resources have been appropriated by the party and elements of it. In addition many funds, such as those of Trade Unions, have been formally confiscated. Externally, since the War, and before that in Austria and Czechoslovakia, there has been a systematic process of expropriation going on, only part of the proceeds of which have gone to the German "state." We can be sure that already the distinction between "party" resources and those private to people with power in the party has not been very scrupulously observed. Functionaries in the party have feathered their own nests very thoroughly, no doubt, and above all, have systematically, and, from a rational-legal point of view, shamelessly used the power of their party positions to do so.

But, as Weber insisted, this mode of provision is inherently temporary. If the party escapes collapse it will have to evolve gradually to a routine basis. The party has, in a sense, been living off capital—in time it will have to establish settled sources of steady income. It is conceivable that this might happen with a return to the rational-legal form—taxation according to universalistic norms by the state for the support of state functions, with the only difference that Nazis would be the office-holders paid out of taxation—and the meeting of strictly "party" needs by genuinely voluntary contributions—as in the United States (to a considerable extent). But this is very unlikely. What is much more likely is that these various sources of income, especially those associated with "protection," should develop into kinds of benefices which would be treated as the private property of the various party functionaries, from which, without distinction as to source of income, they would both meet the costs of their political functions and secure their personal remuneration. Such an outcome is the more likely the more the members of the administrative staff are in a position to assert their independence of centralized control. In addition to the above evidence it is relevant that the Nazi mentality is very definitely one which sees no sense in segregating political authority from other aspects of the same concrete social relationships. One of the most conspicuous consequences of the movement has been the "politicizing" of a whole range of relationships which otherwise could be treated as non-political, that is, in which the potential problems of political influences and power could be treated as neutralized. Thus to do business under Nazi auspices one must be properly "in" with the party authorities who might be in a position to intervene.

When considerations of the ideological content of National Socialism are combined with those of the dynamics of routinization of the charismatic movement the evidence seems to be overwhelming. The consequence of its political predominance for a considerable period would with a very high degree of probability be the transformation of the area concerned into a system of institutional patterns of a strongly traditionalistic character. Other elements of the social system which in the Western world have been realtively independent of the political organization as such, such as the dominant forms of private property and economic enterprise, market relationships, education, and cultural activities, could hardly avoid being drawn into the same basic course of change. That the most distinctive cultural features of our civilization could not long survive, such a change, would scarcely seem to need to be pointed out.

The Outcome of War and the Development of Institutions

The above analysis has been mainly confined to the political aspect of social structure. If space permitted it could readily be supplemented by considerations touching other aspects of our modern Western institutional system, which point in the same general direction. But Weber's "sociology of authority" alone, when applied to the present situation, can make a most important contribution to the understanding of the deeper nature of the crisis in which we have become involved. Building on that understanding, it can go farther to contribute, with a high degree of probability, to an understanding of the probable consequences, on a very broad scale, of either of the two main possible decisive outcomes of the present armed struggle. It is interesting to point out the analogy of the present situation to another to which Weber, in a discussion with Eduard Meyer, devoted considerable attention, that of classical Greece at the time when the outcome of the Persian Wars hung in the balance.[24]

Weber argues that on their outcome, especially as determined by the battles of Marathon and Salamis, hung, in all probability, the entire fate of Western civilization. This is because a decisive Persian victory, with long-term political control of the Greek peninsula, would have checked and probably destroyed the process of rationalization and secularization which made possible the distinctive Greek contributions to our cultural heritage (not only directly but through Rome): Greek philosophy and science, humanistic Greek literature and art. Without these influences the distinctive cultural development of the Western world, which distinguishes it from the Orient and the Near East, could not have taken place.

But why would the outcome of a mere war[25] have checked it—is not Greece forever Greece? Because Persian political control would probably have resulted in a rigid traditionalistic stereotyping, strongly aided by the predominance in social prestige and power of a ritualistic priestly class. It is well known that Greece was deeply divided at the time. Important elements, such as the oracle of Delphi, tended to favor the Persian cause and counseled non-resistance. Perhaps these were the "fascists" of the time. The effect of Persian political occupation would have been to alter the internal balance of power in Greece. The free autonomous city states, which were the carriers of the secularizing civic cults, and the associated cultural developments, would have been destroyed. Further, in the interests of their own power, the Persians would undoubtedly have favored the religious elements which stood outside this structure, the priesthoods of the oracles, and perhaps certain otherworldly religious tendencies. This is, indeed, precisely what they did in the nearest comparable case, their conquest of Judea, and this policy contributed greatly to the ritualistic stereotyping of Judaism, hence of all subsequent Jewish culture. There must have been many good people in Greece even as early as the sixth century who shook their head at the excesses of the turbulent *demos* and

[24] Talcott Parsons, *Structure of Social Action*, Chapter XVI, pp. 611 ff. A. von Schelting, *Max Webers Wissenschaftslehre*, pp. 280 ff.
[25] We are told in some quarters that "war never settles anything."

longed for a "strong authoritarian regime," to paraphrase Marshal Pétain. And who promised more in this respect than the Persians?

Today religion as such is not so prominently involved. But it is safe to say that the reaction of the oracle of Delphi was a "fundamentalist" reaction in the sense of the above discussion. And most of the basic analysis which Weber applied to the Persian wars seems applicable today. It is altogether possible that we now stand at another equally critical point of decision for the course of history as a whole. There are those who feel that the rationalized liberal culture of the Western world has played itself out, that it has no further creative potentialities. Who in sober realism would, however, dare to presume such a judgement? But whatever its potentialities are, in following the further unfolding of its main historic course, it seems as certain as conclusions of such scope can be, that their realization depends on the prevention of domination over the principal Western cultural area by such a movement as National Socialism.

Moral Responsibility in Politics

In closing, a few brief remarks may be made about Weber's approach to the problems of political action. Weber himself would not have considered the question of the ultimate values to be embodied in a policy to lie within the province of science. There are, however, two sets of considerations which fall legitimately within the field of social science as such.

The first touches the question of the possibility of the accomplishment of decisive results by political action. Today a very considerable influence is exerted over men's minds by "deterministic" theories of history according to which there is an inevitable process of unfolding of the historic pattern, and what men may or may not "do about it" by their decision and character and effort, cannot in the nature of the case be important.[26] Weber's position, as he developed it both in his empirical studies and in his methodological work, is sharply opposed to this view. No one was more empirically realistic than he; no one better realized the limitations placed upon action by the conditions of the situation which are beyond the actor's control. But at the same time, to him, human choice and decision were fundamental factors in the determination of events. Above all, in many sitations, there is a relatively delicate balance between the forces working in radically opposed directions, so that the *difference* made by a war, a political movement, or even the influence of a single man may be of very far-reaching consequences in determining which of the different potentialities of the situation is realized. It is not that such a factor "creates" the result. It is rather that, in addition to the other forces working

[26] Oswald Spengler, *The Decline of the West*, and P. A. Sorokin, *Social and Cultural Dynamics*, may be cited as prominent recent examples of this attitude.

in that direction, it is sufficient to throw the total balance in favor of the one possible outcome rather than the other.

Weber's general view of the social process, then, was such as to fit in with a high sense of responsibility. Very great consequences for what are, in terms of the values a man happens to adhere to, good or evil, may well hang on his particular action. He repudiates both what may be called the optimistic and the pessimistic versions of "determinism." For these, in the former case there is no need to worry or take responsibility, in the latter there is no sense in it, since the worst is bound to happen no matter what one does. It is relevant to this problem that, to Weber, social systems were notably unstable and inherently involved in tension and conflict. His "activism" was by no means based on an optimistic bias which saw the desired outcome as easy and simple.

On the background of this general position, Weber developed a theory of two possible, radically opposed types of attitude toward action, that is, toward the problem of moralres ponsibility. These he called *Gesinnungsethik*, the "ethic of absolute value" and *Verantwortungsethik*, the "ethic of responsibility."[27] By the former he meant the type of attitude according to which a given value—such as religious salvation—is pursued without relation either to the cost in blocking the realization of other values, or to the consequences in injury to other persons or values. The individual's duty is to "do what is right" (however that be specifically defined). If the consequences of this procedure are in any respect unfortuate or worse, he is not responsible—the responsibility can be turned over to God, who created the world that way. To Weber, undoubtedly, action in terms of *Gesinnungsethik*, especially in charismatic movements, has been a force of the greatest importance in history.[28]

It was not, however, his personal choice, which fell rather to the

---

[27] See *Politik als Beruf* and von Schelting, op. cit.

[28] It is plain that the very way Max Weber approaches these ethical problems is determined by a background of secularized Calvinism. The Thomistic theory of morality (Sum. Theol. I–II, 6–21), the Thomistic notion of prudence (I–II, 5 and II–II, 47–52), finally the Thomistic conception of the natural law (I–II, 94) eliminate any radical (and essentially insoluble) antinomy between "Gesinnung" and "Verantwortung." The opposition between Gesinnungsethik and Verantwortungsethik would assume at most a psychological meaning. Max Weber's views on the irrational character of the acceptance of the supreme values has also a decidedly Calvinistic flavor. Thomists would say that reason, even unaided by revelation, can know something about the supreme values. Of course, the ultimate end which is really (or existentially) that of man can be known only by revelation and faith. But even in regard to supernatural faith, it should not be spoken of as irrational adherence, since the credibility of the objects of faith can be rationally manifested. Supra-rationality, rather than irrationality, would be the proper expression.

For a thoroughly Thomistic discussion of the relationship between ethics and political activities see J. Maritain, "End of Machiavellianism," *The Review of Politics*, January, 1942; for a good exposition of "Nature and Functions of Authority," the Aquinas Lecture, 1940, by Yves R. Simon, Milwaukee, 1940. A general criticism of Max Weber's fundamental concepts can be found in Gustav Gundlach, S.J., *Zur Sociologie der katholischen Ideenwelt und des Jesuitenordens* (Herder, Freiburg, 1927).

other type. What is characteristic of this is the broadest possible extension of the field of rational understanding of action, and the use of this understanding in particular ways. Namely, in weighing the possible ways of attaining a desirable goal, one must take specific account of the cost of its attainment, of the fact that other goals will have to be sacrificed in its favor—perhaps to such an extent as to counsel its abandonment altogether. Moreover, the consequences of a course of action are by no means confined to its direct bearing on the realization of the immediate goal. It also has indirect consequences, in many directions perhaps, affecting many interests. To the actor in terms of *Verantwortungsethik* it is an ethical obligation to be aware of these indirect consequences as far as possible, and to take responsibility for them. Since, to Weber, ethical conflict was, from the point of view of any system of substantive values whatever, inevitable, inherent in the structure of the world of action, taking responsibility for consequences meant the assumption of guilt for things which were, in themselves, unethical.

One may say that Weber thoroughly respected the *Gesinnungsethiker* if he was sincere and courageous enough to follow the implications of his position through to the bitter end, to the conclusion that it meant bitter renunciation of most of the accepted "good things of life" of ordinary society, as well as stringent control of many of the most "natural" of human impulses—it is really only possible of fulfillment through a heroic pattern of conduct. In *Politik als Beruf* he illustrated this by the example of absolute pacifism. Absolute Pacifism, if taken seriously must be consistently applied—in particular it was not tenable, as many "leftists" of his time were doing, to argue the inadmissibility of international war on grounds of the ethical principle that the use of force was inherently evil, and not apply it to the revolution internally. One either repudiates resistance to evil by force in all fields, or the use of force becomes a "strategic" question, not one of fundamental ethical principle as such.

Though respecting the heroic type of *Gesinnungsethik*, Weber felt that in most cases, particularly in his own time, it conduced to wishful thinking and irresponsibility. Thus he says "In reality we find that the *Gesinnungsethiker* repeatedly becomes suddenly transformed into the chiliastic prophet, of the type for instance, of those who, having preached the doctrine of love against that of force, in the next moment rally their followers for a struggle by force, which they assure them will be the last time force will ever have to be used, since it will lead to the permanent elimination of force. The *Gesinnungsethiker* cannot bear the ethical irrationality of the world. He is a 'cosmic-ethical rationalist'."[29] That is, the adherence to *Gesinnungsethik* readily degenerates into utopianism, to wishful thinking which refuses to face the depth of tragedy and conflict which is inherent in the world. To Weber this utopianism was an object of deep personal

[29] *Politische Schriften*, p. 443.

antipathy. To him intellectual honesty demanded the facing of unpleasant reality. If one could do this and honestly accept the consequences of a system of absolute values, as in a genuine Christian pacifism, well and good. But if not, the only honest procedure was that of *Verantwortungs-ethik*, which refused to judge any act, any means, any situation, as absolutely good or bad, which was as clear-headed as possible as to the complex ramifications of action, and which, above all, was not afraid to assume responsibility with its inevitable accompaniment of guilt, responsibility for being instrumental in bringing about things which, for their own sake, must without hesitation be judged to be evil.

Along with this personal feeling for the extreme difficulty of combining *Gesinnungsethik* with clear-headed honesty, there is another aspect of the matter in Weber's analysis. It was, to him, one of the prime characteristics of this position, that it absolved the individual from responsibility for a whole range of the inevitable consequences of his own actions. But in absolving him from responsibility it at the same time deprived him of a powerful motive for acting rationally, for the hard work of securing information and thinking the problems of conduct through to the point where these consequences are known. There can be no doubt that, to Weber, not only was *Gesinnungsethik* "irrational" in the sense that he held all orientation to ultimate values to lie beyond the competence of rational analysis, but also that it was a force which inhibited what possibilities of rational orientation to problems of conduct exist. The relative predominance of the two types of orientation would, then, be an important factor in the ability of a social system to maintain rational patterns on the institutional level, and not to fall into traditionalism, either directly or through charismatic movements.

To a considerable extent the movements which, today, mobilize the forces which threaten the basic modern Western institutional system, are such as appeal to the *Gesinnungsethik* type of orientation, particularly in its weakened "chiliastic" form. This is true of National Socialism, in spite of its apparent extraordinary political "realism," since it purports, in its propaganda appeal, to end the sources of difficulty and frustration for the German people "once and for all" and to usher in a completely utopian society of indefinite duration. Conversely there can be little doubt that an ability to assume the burdens of responsible action in Weber's particular sense constitutes one of the most important conditions for the successful preservstion of a rational-legal system of authority and its related institutional forms in other aspects of the society, and for keeping open the potentialities of human development which our Western "great society" holds.

Chapter 6

The Problem of
Controlled
Institutional Change

*t*he members of the Conference[1] reached definite agreement on the important conclusion that the sources of German aggressive expansionism are not merely a matter of the particular recent situation in which the German nation has been placed, or of the character and policies of a particular régime which can be expected to vanish with the fall of the régime. Although drawn out and accentuated by these factors, the more important sources lie deeper and would not necessarily be seriously affected by changes at these levels.

The principal emphasis of the Conference was on the existence of a typical German character structure which predisposes people to define all human relations in terms of dominance, submission, and romantic revolt. It was, however, also agreed that such a typical character structure, although probably an independent factor[2] of great significance, is sup-

---

[1] For the setting in which this paper was written see Introduction to Part II.

[2] Exactly how far it is an independent factor is exceedingly difficult to judge since only actual uniformities of behavior are available as direct evidence. Hence, for certain purposes character structure and institutional structure may be treated as different abstractions from the same facts. Even so far as they are actually independent permanent change of character structure is dependent upon institutional change.

Reprinted from Psychiatry, *VIII (1945), 79–101. Also reprinted in* Essays in Sociological Theory, *The Free Press, 1954.* |

ported by, and closely interdependent with, an institutional structure of German society. The interdependence is such that on the one hand any permanent and far-reaching change in the orientation of the German people probably cannot rest on a change of character structure alone, but must also involve institutional change; otherwise, institutional conditions would continue to breed the same type of character structure in new generations. On the other hand, it may prove that a direct attack on character structure as such is less promising than one through other forces that operate on the institutional system and which, through changes in that, may serve to create conditions favorable to a change in character structure.

ANALYTICAL INTRODUCTION

Institutions in the Social System

The institutional structure of a society must be regarded as a special aspect of the total social system. Especially for purposes of considering the possibilities of dynamic change in institutions it is essential to treat them systematically and explicitly in terms of their interdependence with the other principal elements of the system.

Institutions are those patterns which define the essentials of the legitimately expected behavior of persons insofar as they perform *structurally important roles* in the social system. There are, of course, many degrees of conformity or lack of it, but a pattern is "institutionalized" only insofar as at least a minimum degree of conformity is legitimately expected— thus its absence treated with sanctions at least of strong disapproval—*and* a sufficient degree of conformity on the part of a sufficient proportion of the relevant population exists so that this pattern defines the *dominant* structural outline of the relevant system of concrete social relationships. It is the *structurally* significant elements of the total concrete relationship pattern which are institutionally relevant. What these are cannot be decided in terms of the subjective sentiments of participant observers, but only in the perspective of structural analysis of the social system.

Institutional patterns are the "backbone" of the social system. But they are by no means absolutely rigid entities, and certainly have no mysteriously "substantial" nature. They are only relatively stable uniform resultants of the processes of behavior of the members of the society, and hence of the forces which determine that behavior. Their relative stability results from the particular structure of interdependence of those forces, and institutional structure is subject to change as a function of any one of many different kinds of change in the underlying system of forces. Their relatively stable role in social systems, however, indicates that institutionalized patterns do in fact mobilize a combination of forces in support of their maintenance which is of primary significance in the total equilibrium of a social system. Analysis of the nature and principal components of this combination is the first requisite of an approach to the problem of institutional change.

Furthermore, institutionalization is a *general* phenomenon of all extensive and permanent social systems. Hence, the broad outline of the problem concerns elements which are universal to all societies and does not depend upon specialized knowledge of the particular society in question. A general analysis of the problem can be presented first[3] and then applied to the particular facts and circumstances of the case.

The uniformities of human behavior must be analyzed in terms of the structure of motivational forces, on the one hand, and of the situation in which they have to operate, on the other. In looking for the structure of forces underlying institutions, it is important to keep in mind that *both* elements of the determination of human behavior are involved in a peculiar kind of interdependence. For in social relationships it is the *expected* and actual behavior and manifestation of the sentiments of others which is the most important component of the situation in which any one person acts. Hence, to a very large extent, the structure of the situation is dependent on the stability of the motivational structure of the members of the society at large. So long as a stable structure is maintained this accounts for the interlocking of so many motivational elements in support of the same goals and standards. It above all accounts for the cardinal fact of institutional behavior: that in an integrated system "self-interested" elements of motivation and disinterested moral sentiments of duty tend to motivate the *same* concrete goals.

Such an interlocking is, however, never complete. There are important elements of the situation of action of different classes of persons which are not primarily dependent on the crystallized sentiments of others. Conversely, there are unstable elements in the motivation structure of persons. It is at these two points that the principal openings for institutional change are to be sought. It is a further implication of the general character of institutions that the consequences of changes at these points may be more important than would appear at first sight because any change at these points will *interact* with the other elements of the system and may well set up cumulative tendencies to change.

Before exploring these possibilities further, however, it is necessary to develop a somewhat clearer picture of the main elements of stability in an institutional system. It is these which have to be modified to achieve fundamental changes.

[3] This analysis is of course generalized from the study of many empirical cases—not simply deduced from general considerations.

FACTORS OF RIGIDITY:

"VESTED INTERESTS"

It is inherent in the nature of an institutional system that it should create, and is in part supported by, a complex system of vested interests. Even on occasion in conflict with very deep-rooted moral sentiments, people will often be powerfully motivated by considerations of interest. There is no question of the importance of interests, but only of the perspective in which they are seen in the total social system and of the nature of the structure of motivational elements referred to as an interest.

Among "interests" in general those which may be called "vested" are distinguished by the fact that they are oriented to the maintenance of objects of interest which have already become established. This means that to a greater or less degree the status and situations and their perquisites to which such interests are attached already involve some element of legitimacy or claim to it. To attempt to deprive a person or a group of something in which they enjoy a vested interest thus involves not only imposing the frustrations attendant to the deprivation as such but also to a greater or less degree outrages the moral sentiments surrounding the claim of legitimacy. The resistance of the people or groups affected is thus strengthened by their sense of injustice. Furthermore, the same fact enables them to rally support for their claims from people who do not share the same interests. The obverse of this, finally, is the fact that among those who oppose a vested-interest group there is likely to be an element of sense of guilt arising from the fact that they share the same patterns of value. This introduces an element of ambivalence which in an important sense weakens the position of the attacker. If the guilt is repressed, however, it may make the actual attack more extreme that it would otherwise have been. But in such cases the attacker may be highly vulnerable to the proper kind of attempt to change his attitudes.

The structure of interests in a group is a function both of the structure of the realistic situations in which people act and of the "definitions" of those situations which are institutionalized in the society. It is this latter fundamental aspect which is most likely to be misunderstood in common sense thinking, since one is prone to assume that what people want to "get out of" a realistic situation, or avoid in it, is universal, a matter of "human nature." The actual tendency is to project one's own definitions of situations onto the action of other people and societies. A actor thinks of what he would want in such a situation.

The consequence of the role of institutionalized definitions of situations in the structuring of interests is at some points to introduce elements of rigidity, which would not otherwise exist, of flexibility at others. In the first case it delays or altogether blocks what might otherwise be felt to be a "natural" reaction to a change in the realistic situation.[4] It is, therefore, never safe to count on the effect of changing a situation on the structure of interests without specifically investigating the definitions of situations within the groups involved.

The effect of a change in the realistic situation while an institutionalized definition remains unchanged is to create a strain. The line of least resistance in reaction to this strain will usually be to attempt more aggressively than before to reassert the old definition of the situation and to shape the realistic situation in conformity with it. This total reaction involving above all the appropriate emotional components is what is generally meant by talking about the behavior of "the vested interests." For constructive change to take place it is therefore not only necessary to provide realistic opportunities which can be utilized to satisfy the interests of groups. It is also necessary to have some mechanism for coping with these other aspects of the problem. Two things are above all important: first, to provide new alternative definitions of the situation which give the new realistic opportunities positive meaning. It is particularly important that these should not be too far removed from the symbols and prestige standards previously current. Secondly, the emotionally aggressive defensiveness must be dealt with. This is to a large extent a reaction to a sense of insecurity, and requires some kind of measures of reassurance.

Of course, there are occasions where it is not possible to redefine the situation so that an interest group will fit into a new situation. Then its compulsory repression is the only way. But here, besides the question of adequate means of compulsion, a most important consideration is that of the moral position of the compelling agent. For the moral sentiments which legitimize an interest are shared by, and shade into, those of other groups. For the long run effect the moral isolation and insulation of a group which has to be frustrated is at least as important as the physical capacity to carry it through.

The converse of this difficulty lies in the fact that rational adaptation to realistic situations *is* a fundamental component of human social behavior. Hence, change of situation plus sheer cognitive enlightenment about its possibilities can often effect important changes. It must, however, to exploit this possibility, operate so as to avoid too serious conflict with the forces just discussed. Above all the change must be such as not to be interpreted—psychologically, not intellectually alone—as threatening security in those things in which members of the group have important emotional investment.

The phenomenon of vested interests thus proves to be a special case

[4] A dramatic example is the "suicidal mania" of Japanese soldiers. To the Occidental a hopeless situation where no further contribution to the cause is possible is an occasion for honorable surrender. To most Japanese, apparently, surrender under any circumstances is an intolerable disgrace. This is a matter of differences in the *definition* of the situation, not of the *realistic* situations themselves.

of the general integration of diverse motivational forces about an institutional structure. It is exceedingly difficult to say that the elements of self-interest are *the* decisive factors in most cases. It is the mutual reenforcement of the different elements which is the principal source of rigidity—interest taken alone is probably one of the factors most accessible to change.

A particularly important class of cases of this mutual reenforcement is that where group solidarities are involved. In a functionally differentiated society like that of the modern Occident, in perhaps a majority of groups solidarity is secondary to the functional significance of the roles of the members. But even here, sentiments of solidarity readily acquire a prominent place. Insofar as this happens the security of their members becomes associated with the status of the group as such, rather than fulfillment of the functional norms which ideally govern its role; and sanctions come to be applied to what is interpreted as loyalty to the group rather than functionally adequate achievement. Once such patterns of group solidarity are firmly established a serious obstacle to change is introduced. Appeals to a group in terms of functional values may be ineffective unless they can also carry the sentiments of group solidarity with them. Such sentiments are particularly difficult to deal with when the members of the group feel insecure,[5] because this creates a "defensive" attitude system.

The concept of "vested interest" thus serves as a key to the problem of rigidity in an institutional system because it is the most conspicuous pattern of behavior which appears in particular groups in resistance to change or threats of it. As such, however, it applies to particular groups. It is a mode of focusing all the principal components of motivation on such resistance. But any one group is structurally interdependent with others in the same social system. Moreover, the same persons play a variety of different roles as members of different groups.

It is a cardinal fact of social change that it impinges unevenly on the different parts of the society it affects. It alters the status and role of some groups but not directly of others. Or it may alter the situation or definition of it of the members of a group in *one* of their roles—for example, occupational; but not directly in another—for example, kinship. But it is in the nature of this structural interdependence of groups and roles in a social system that alteration in any one will set up waves of repercussion in many others. The different structural elements of a social system are "geared in" to one another. The factors of stability or rigidity just discussed are present in each one. Change at one point sets up a strain in

---

[5] Guilt may be an important element in this insecurity. Where people are really uneasy about the moral justification of their position, they may defend it with all the emotional intensity of fanaticism. In this case the "ethics" of group loyalty is often used to rationalize away the deeper moral conflict.

neighboring parts of the system. One fundamental and immediate possibility of reaction to the strain is the vested-interest reaction—to activate an emotionally defensive resistance to the change. After the problem of overcoming this pattern of reaction at the points where the forces of change impinge most immediately on the system itself, the next problem is that of preventing the development of this barrier to its structurally necessary repercussions beyond these points.

This is a basically important consideration since if the defensive reaction becomes sufficiently firmly consolidated, one of two things must happen. Either the reaction will be so powerful as to eliminate the change and, if not restore the previous balance, lead to a quite different direction of change. Or, short of this, there will be a permanent state of malintegration and tension which will prevent stable institutionalization of the new patterns even within their primary area of application. Not only will there be elements of group conflict but, perhaps even more important, a large number of persons will be caught in a pattern of conflicting pressures and ambivalent attitudes as "marginal men." For the patterns dominant in one set of roles a person plays will conflict more or less seriously with those in others. The resulting situation of insecurity for many produces a high degree of instability of overt attitudes and behavior.

An example of fundamental significance in modern Western society is the tension between occupational and family roles. The occupational system has, through the inherently dynamic character of modern technology and of the development of large-scale organization, been a focus of continual change, profoundly altering the pattern of the occupational role. On the whole the forces for change operating *directly* on the family have not been so strong and have been of a different, largely an ideological, character. Hence, the defensive reaction pattern has been particularly strong in the family and in those agencies which, like the churches, have assumed the role of guardians of the integrity of its traditional patterns. As so often happens, only a very vague insight into the real sources of the changes has existed, so the hostility generated has largely been discharged upon scapegoats, prominent among which has been the "younger generation."

Two further features of the "psychological" structure of social systems are of very general significance for the present discussion. First, psychologists have strongly emphasized the importance of emotional attitudes toward those objects which impinge directly upon the everyday emotional life of a person, particularly those concrete persons with whom he is placed in immediate contact: his own parents, siblings, spouse, or "boss." It is readily understandable that he should have strong and often complicated emotional feelings toward them. But it is also true that people have very strong feelings about objects, patterns, and symbols which are relatively remote from their personal experiences and interests. Indeed, for most of a population most of the time the majority of those objects which are essential to the structuring and behavior of large-scale social units are in this category. Thus, in time of peace a potential national enemy, the ideal of equality of opportunity, or the flag can arouse very powerful reactions. Of course, reflection and analysis shows that even people's immediate interests are in fact dependent on these things and what they symbolize. But the intellectual complexity of the relation is too great for it to account adequately for the emotional reaction. This must depend on non-rational mechanisms to an even higher degree than reactions to immediate objects. The nature of these mechanisms is a problem of great importance.

It is clear that the connection may be relatively loose between these two basic levels and that attitudes toward the remoter objects may be subject to change by psychological techniques which would not operate successfully to change a man's attitude toward his mother or his "boss." It is essential to keep this in mind in discussing problems of ideology, political attitudes, and the like.

The second important fact is that the conception of a completely integrated social system is a limiting case. Every at all complex society contains very important elements of internal conflict and tension. In some respects this is an impediment to change, since patterns of defensive vested-interest behavior already exist in important cases as responses to conflict with other internal elements. But it also almost certainly means that there are "allies" within the social system itself which can be enlisted on the side of change in any given direction.

In particular, Germany is not, relatively to the rest of the Western world, a completely "sealed off" unique society. Many of its most important culture patterns and structural elements shade imperceptibly into those on the democratic side of the conflict. They are genuinely institutionalized in Germany or have been very incompletely eradicated under the Nazi régime. They constitute fundamentally important avenues of approach to change in the other, the conflicting, elements.

This lack of full integration has a further consequence; it means that the underlying institutional foundations of national behavior are not as firm as they would be in a better integrated system. Indeed, one factor in the violence of these manifestations in the case of Germany lies in the conflict; part of the energy has the function of repressing the sentiments and patterns opposed to the recent course. The expectation may then be that not too radical an alteration in the *balance* of forces could have "disproportionately" great effects on immediate behavior. This is, indeed, what happened in the shift from Weimar to the Nazi régime. The Germany of Weimar was not spurious—a "deceitful mask" as many are now inclined to feel. That would be as serious an error as the previous one of supposing that it was the one "true Germany" once the "bad" monarchy had been eliminated.

But of course merely shifting the balance till the scale tips is not a radical cure—it would take too little to shift it back again. But it can be an early phase of a farther-reaching process—the obverse of what the Nazi régime has hoped it was accomplishing.

CHANNELS OF INFLUENCE

To recall a previous starting point: human behavior may be influenced either through the situations in which people must act, or through "subjective" elements—their sentiments, goals, attitudes, definitions of situations. This classification may serve for orientation to the analysis of the elements of flexibility, hence possible openings for control, of a social system.

The first must be differentiated according to whether it is the situation external to the social system as a whole, which is independent of its internal institutional structure, or the immediate situations in which large classes of people act—of which institutional patterns themselves constitute a crucial element—which is to be deliberately controlled. In the latter case only certain elements of situations are subject to control as a *means* of bringing about institutional change; others must be a result of it.

A second essential discrimination is between using control of the situation to suppress a structural element or manifestation, and using it to alter it by making available new channels of expression for the same basic sentiments and goals—so that the sense of continuity need not be lost.

Turning to the subjective side, it is possible to attempt through "education" and "propaganda" to affect mass sentiments through influencing various of their manifestations. The phenomena in this field are exceedingly complex and in an elementary stage of analysis. The most important thing to be said is that the chances of successful influence do not depend mainly on the apparent "reasonableness" of what is transmitted, but on its relation to the functional equilibrium of the system on which it impinges. This in turn depends on at least three factors: the functional significance of the manifestations it attempts to displace, the potential functions of the new patterns which are put forward, and the appropriateness of the source and manner of influence, that is, the definition of the situation of "being influenced" from the point of view of the recipients.

Again it is important to discriminate sentiments and their manifestations touching remoter objects concerning the society at large, from those touching the immediate interests of its members.

Just as actual situations deviate from institutionally sanctioned definitions of the same situations, so ideological and symbolic patterns associated with the sentiment system do not stand in a simple relation of correspondence with the sentiments manifested. Ideological patterns are inevitably highly selective if not distorted relative to the system of sentiments which support institutions. These and other patterns often involve psychological reactions to strain and thus contain elements of projection and displacement on "culture heroes" or scapegoats. Finally, symbolism plays a very prominent part in this field.

These considerations, combined with the others already discussed, show that it is not to be expected that the "logical" consequences of ideas will be automatically "acted out." What will happen is rather the resultant of the interaction of verbal patterns with a variety of other elements in the total social system.

THE CASE OF GERMANY

The Problem: Objectives of a Program

The members of the Conference agreed that the dominant character structure of modern Germany has been distinguished by a striking dualism between "*A*: an emotional, idealistic, active, romantic component which may be constructive or destructive and anti-social," and "*B*: an orderly, hard-working, hierarchy-preoccupied, methodical, submissive, gregarious, materialistic" component.[6]

In the traditional pre-Nazi German society it is overwhelmingly the *B* component which has become institutionalized. The *A* component arises from two principal interdependent sources: certain features of the socialization process in the German family, and the tensions arising from life in that type of institutional order. It is expressed in romantic, unrealistic emotionalism and yearnings. Under other circumstances the dissociation has historically been radical—the romantic yearning has found an outlet in religion, art, music, and other-worldly, particularly a-political, forms.

The peculiarity of the Nazi movement is that it has harnessed this romantic dynamism to an aggressive, expansionist, nationalistic political goal—and an internal revolution—and has utilized and subordinated all the motives behind the *B* component as well. In both cases the synthesis has been dependent at the same time on certain features of the situation and on a meaningful definition of the situation and system of symbols. The first task of a program of institutional change is to disrupt this synthesis and create a situation in which the romantic element will again find an a-political form of expression. This will not, however, "cure" the basic difficulty but only its most virulent and, to the United Nations, dangerous manifestation. Its importance, however, should not be underestimated.

---

[6] Quoted from Report of the Conference, Appendix 3, p. 10. Compare Erikson, Erik Homburger, "Hitler's Imagery and German Youth," *Psychiatry, V* (1942), 475–493.

This may be referred to as a semi-institutionalized feature of the German system.

The second problematical set of features of the German institutional system comprises certain traits associated with the *B* components of her character structure.[7] Orderliness, industry, and methodicality are not "trouble-making" traits if they are stable. Even these, however, are skewed by their relation to the dominance-submission element which finds its institutional counterpart in a rigidly hierarchical status system where the superiority-inferiority aspect of roles tends to be emphasized to the exclusion of their positive functional significance, and in a peculiar prominence of relations of authority.

A second conspicuous general trait of German institutions is their "formalism." In part this serves to emphasize status and authority as such. But there is also what to Americans seems a peculiar kind of dissociation between the status system and the "inner" emotional interest and character of persons. This is both a determinant and a consequence of the dualism of German character. Goals *within* the status system fail to satisfy the romantic longings of component *A* as previously defined. Germans are much more preoccupied with status than Americans, but there has been little romantization of *success* in Germany. Americans are prone to romanticize attainment *within* the institutionalized status system; while Germans have a greater romantic interest in goals *outside* it.

Both these traits permeate the whole role and group structure of German society. But their special incidence varies in the different parts of the social structure. The Prussian state has remained the center of both these patterns. For, long before industrialization, in its civil service it developed a highly formalized hierarchical and authoritarian structure which, with the waning of feudalism, came to hold a position of high prestige in the society. Much the same was true of the other main structure, the military establishment, which shared the same traits, but in the officers' corps, with even greater emphasis on a prestige status, and with this, a highly favorable situation for the dominance of "militaristic" values.

Another important pre-industrial component of the German institutional system was the "conservative" structure of the peasantry and the older artisan and middle-class groups. Above all, these lower groups could readily integrate their status in the occupational system with a patriarchal-authoritarian family structure. For the most part the significant occupational unit was a family, not an individual person as such. The father was, as a peasant, for instance, the actual head of a producing organization in which his familial and productive roles coincided.

The third fundamental aspect of German society is a structural tension

[7] For a somewhat fuller analysis of these institutional traits than space allows here, see Parsons, Talcott, "Democracy and Social Structure in Pre-Nazi Germany," *J. Legal and Political Sociol.* Nov. 1942, Chapter 3 above.

which in a very broad sense may be described as that between the firmly institutionalized patterns of this older pre-industrial structure and the structure of situations and—in part—sentiments resulting from the impact of modern industrialism and its principal social accompaniments, notably large-scale urbanization. It is a case of partial integration and partial conflict. Industrialism would never have had the spectacular development which, by contrast with all the Latin countries, it had in Germany unless the previous institutional structure had been favorable to it. But in part the result was an industrial system with a different emphasis from that in the United States. The state has played a much more prominent role. Within industry itself there has been more emphasis on hierarchy, authority, formalism, status-consciousness.

But at the same time there has been a very serious tension. One point of tension is between the status system and the patterns of individual, technical achievement. The enormous German sensitivity to "proletarization" has something to do with the definition of all but the highest statuses in organization as involving subordination and limitation to a strictly formal definition of role. Another most important consequence is the change in the kinship situation. Where the role of father and head of a small economic unit were combined they reenforced each other. But where a man is an authoritarian father in the family, but a subordinate whose subordination is continually symbolically rubbed in outside, it creates a serious ambivalence in his own attitudes and in his significance to his wife and children. The result has been to break down a relatively well-integrated patriarchal pattern.

The result of this major internal tension was to arouse intensely defensive vested-interest behavior on the part of the groups most closely identified with these conservative patterns and to introduce a very large element of insecurity into the lives of large numbers who were torn between conflicting patterns. This situation played a large part in the instability of the Weimar régime and accounted for much of the susceptibility of large elements of the population to the appeal of Nazi propaganda.

The problem of control of German institutional structure may be put, therefore, in terms of the following three major objectives:

> To eliminate the specific Nazi synthesis of the two major components of German character, or to divert it from its recent distinctive channels of expression, if this is possible.
> To eliminate, or at least seriously reduce, the structural role of the hierarchical, authoritarian, and formalistic elements in the "conservative" German institutional structure—in particular its focus on the army and the military class should be broken.
> To displace the conservative pattern and to reduce the tension by systematically fostering those elements of the pattern of modern Germany, especially of industrialism, which are closest to their counterparts in the democratic countries.

Representative Control of the Situation

It is clear that the first task, now nearing completion, is to break down the German military effort against the United Nations. Victory for the United Nations can, in combination with other things, have a profound effect on the internal institutional structure of Germany as well as on its immediate power to make war. This is particularly true since the Nazi movement, as an anti-traditional "charismatic" movement, is peculiarly dependent on success to maintain its internal prestige. It is irrevocably committed to success in this war and can scarcely survive a really thorough defeat. Defeat should, if properly managed, not only realistically disrupt the Nazi organization but be the most important factor in permanently eliminating the "Hitler myth" as the primary focus of the romantic elements in German national psychology. For this to happen it is, however, essential that the *moral* prestige of the victorious powers in *Germany* should be maintained. The German propaganda line will surely be that it is an "unfair" victory of material force alone. However stern the victors should be, they should never lose sight of the importance of getting across a sense of the justice of their cause—not of impulsive and arbitrary revenge.

The logical "follow-up" of military victory is to place Germany in a position where it is quite clear that a repetition of her aggression will not be tolerated and cannot be successful. There are many possible ways in which this objective can be achieved. There is no point in trying to decide between them; it is necessary only to indicate that once chosen, they should fulfill three principal conditions:

The control must be effective. To the German type of mentality the idea that objectively it is possible to "get away" with a repetition of aggressive aggrandizement is a direct invitation to attempt it. The security system *must* be strong. This means above all solidarity among those responsible for its enforcement.

It must be such as to maintain the moral position of those who impose it. It is not necessary to be bound by Nazi ideologists' definitions of German rights nor to avoid all just punishment for past derelictions of duty to the community of nations—but the attendant severity must not be such as to be construed, in the long run, as dictated simply by the victors' self-interest or revenge—using main force to hold Germany down. The Germans must be given "a chance" to play a role of honor and dignity in the world.

It must not be such as to interfere with any of the other vital measures to be proposed in following paragraphs. This applies above all to the widely current proposals for deindustrialization of Germany which, while depriving her immediately of the power to make war, would almost certainly confirm the patterns which it is desirable should be changed. Much the same objections apply to most of the proposals for partition of Germany, which would be very likely to arouse an irredentist nationalism such as dominated the early nineteenth century there, only more intense.

The effect of these measures should be to eliminate the Nazi synthesis and perhaps accomplish even more. But to accomplish this permanently, it is necessary to think well beyond the problem of German military power as such, toward coping with the psychological repercussions of its collapse. It is here that the combination of effective firmness with a strong *moral* position is so crucial, as is also non-interference with other measures.

The Nazi pattern of aggrandizement is an extreme manifestation of a more general German tendency to be fascinated with power. The flourishing of this tendency is in part dependent on the German nation functioning as a unit of power in a system of competitive politico-military power relationships, where the definition of success consists in achieving a position of ascendancy *over* its competitors. The fundamental remedy for such a sitation is so to define the situation that the international order is a *cooperative* order and Germany is not primarily a competitive unit. The moral foundations for such a definition exist but have been overlaid by the competitive power pattern. They must be brought again to the fore.

Successful fulfillment of the conditions just enumerated would force the romantic element into a-political channels, or into internal revolution.[8] By thoroughly discrediting certain crucial elements of the conservative structure—which are already vulnerable because of having "played ball" with the Nazis—it can go farther to facilitate the weakening of this deeper stratum of German institutions. This is particularly true of the military class and tradition.

In the internal structure of Germany the two obvious cases for compulsory suppression are the Nazi party and all its subsidiary organizations and the Junker class. The greater the extent to which both these measures are accomplished by spontaneous internal German movements or agencies, the better, for the principal danger to be avoided is the saddling of the victorious foreigner with responsibility for destroying "legitimate" German institutions. The collapse of the Party should be an almost automatic consequence of thorough military defeat. Allied Military Government will simply have to step into the resulting organizational vacuum.

The case of the Junker class is more difficult because of its deeper-seated status of legitimacy. First, however, it is important that it has been considerably weakened during the events of recent years. The further the Party-Army conflict goes in this direction before final collapse the better. The considerable element which has been closely identified with Nazism should be a victim of the collapse of the Party while another is destroyed in conflict with it.

It may well be that the bulk of what is left will be adequately cared for by Russian occupation of Northeastern Germany. Since the Soviets

[8] This is a case of attitudes toward a "remote" object which, because of their loose connection with the experience of persons, can be relatively easily transferred to another object.

have not the same tradition of respect for established property rights as Americans, the moral dilemma for them of direct expropriation of Junker estates would not be nearly so serious.

Should this combination of factors prove insufficient, it is probably best to attack the Junkers at their most vulnerable point—their economic basis. Their system of estates had notoriously long rested on an unsound economic basis and could be maintained even in Weimar times only by an elaborate system of agricultural tariffs and subsidies. These should be swept away and "nature" allowed to take its course.

The main point is to destroy the principal symbolic focus of the historic military tradition in Germany. This is vulnerable because it is out of keeping with "modern" patterns and structures—it can above all be attacked as a case of exclusive *class* privilege. But it is essential to avoid the boomerang effect of the sufferings of the Junkers being defined as the symbol of the "unfair persecution" of Germany.

There are two other structural elements of conservative Germany which raise serious problems because of their previous association with Nazism, and more broadly, militarism. These are the traditional higher civil service groups and the big industrialists. In the situation which led to Nazism both tended to behave as typical vested-interest groups and largely threw in their lot with the Nazis although, for most of their members, probably mainly as a choice of what they felt to be the lesser evil.

The two groups are by no means identical in their significance. The higher civil service has had strong pre-industrial traditions which, with its ideal of disinterested service to the state, has made it peculiarly susceptible to an anti-capitalist ideological appeal—a susceptibility which the Nazis have exploited to the full. But it is overwhelmingly a *conservative* anti-capitalism which can be readily mobilized against all movements of the left. In some respects it is the main citadel of the conservative German patterns which are the source of most trouble: hierarchy, authoritarianism, formalism, and status-consciousness. Hence, it is a potentially dangerous focusing point second only to the military.

At the same time, however, it is much more difficult for the Democracies to cope with. The military ideal has little appeal to the Democratic peoples—but an honest, highly trained, technically competent civil service does, largely because Americans are so acutely conscious of their own shortcoming in this respect.[9] Hence, a policy of direct liquidation could scarcely fail to be attended by very formidable guilt feelings. This, and the importance of this group to order and stability in a transitional period in Germany suggests the advisability of an indirect attack. Probably the most important single defense of the old conservative pat-

---

[9] Dr. Margaret Mead points out—in a private communication—that the appeal of a good civil service to Americans and to the British is very different and that, on this point, it may prove difficult to devise a policy satisfactory to both countries.

terns here is the *class* basis of recruitment of the higher personnel. Nazism itself involved a revolt against the class aspect of the older German society and the general process may be expected to continue after its fall, with a leftward emphasis. The most important policy then is to facilitate *effective*, not merely formal, equality of opportunity in the civil service.[10] It is to be hoped that the stage will have been set for such a development by the disorganization of this class produced during the Nazi régime.

The case of the industrial groups is somewhat different. Part of their orientation has, of course, been determined by the internal capital- or management-labor tension—but only part. In Germany industry has developed within a conservative pre-industrial social structure. This has meant that the higher business groups were in a more insecure position than in this country because in a highly status-conscious society the highest prestige statuses were not their own. They have thus tended to become "feudalized" by imitating and attempting to amalgamate with the old upper classes. In the situation which led up to Nazism this tendency was accentuated by the common polarization against the left.

It has also been accentuated by the very prominence of the state in the German economy—for the power of the state has meant in this connection prominence of the role relative to business of the old, conservative, administrative civil service. The same has been true of the close relations of the army to those industries important to war.

Hence, it may be concluded that it is largely by virtue of its close fusion with and dependence on the traditional conservative upper structure of Germany—and more recently with elements of the Nazi party organization—for example, Goering—that German industry has developed institutional tendencies dangerous to the United Nations, and not by virtue of the intrinsic characteristics of industrialism. It is above all its integration with a militaristic state and conservative class structure which is the source of this danger.

For other reasons the deindustrialization for Germany seems most undesirable. But unless the character of the state is greatly changed, socialization would not improve the situation—by giving more power to the conservative bureaucracy it might make it worse. So long as free enterprise is permitted a prominent place in the American and the British economies, an attempt at radical suppression of its German counterpart would arouse a powerful guilt reaction. Hence, it is a reorientation of German business in the direction of a liberal industrialism which seems most desirable.

[10] A key strategic point here is entrance to the Law faculties of the universities, the most important channel of access to the higher civil service. In the Weimar days there was a striking difference between the Philosophical faculties, which leaned on the whole to the left—with students drawn from the middle classes—and the Law faculties, which were rightist, with students mainly from the Conservative upper groups. The system of student *Verbindungen* played an important part in this situation.

The cases just discussed have been those of the principal élite groups in pre-Nazi and Nazi Germany. Other groups, such as the lower middle class and in certain respects the peasantry, have played a very important part in the background of Nazism. But there is little to be said for their compulsory suppression. It is to alterations in the situation and sentiments of their members, and in the remote objects upon which their sentiments become projected, that one must look for any important change in their characters and attitudes.

The case for compulsory suppression in relation to Germany may then be summarized. Both in the case of her power to make war and of the most important élite groups contributing to her aggressive disposition, the United Nations will soon have the physical opportunity to go as far as they deem wise. In using this power two dangers must be avoided. On the one hand certain forms of ruthlessness, while effective, would conflict so radically with democratic values that their repercussions in the society of the victors would be devastating. On the other hand, certain ways of exercising their power would probably arouse a powerful boomerang reaction and thus fail of their purpose. It is not in any simple sense a question of a "hard" or a "soft" peace. It is rather a *technical* question of the measures which will attain the goal on which the members of the Conference were agreed—a reintegration of Germany into the community of Western nations. The technical problem is largely that of protecting security interests but at the same time minimizing the defensive vested-interest reaction to change, the importance of which the whole weight of modern social science emphasizes.

Permissive Control of the Situation

As in the case of compulsory suppression, use of control of the situation to open new avenues of action can have consequences at more than one level. It is probably advisable to avoid *all* use of this for the immediate future for the German nation as a whole. But the prospect of future full membership in a cooperative international organization should be offered. The danger is that of making this offer too patronizing. It is essential to safeguard the moral position of those dispensing favors.

With respect to the internal situation in which the various groups of people act, the first problem is that of order and security. The evidence is very strong that the rapid change, the mobility, and the complex tensions of an industrial society will in any case produce a high level of psychologically significant insecurity among the masses of the population. The reaction to this state contains an important element of aggression, which has in part been displaced upon the foreign enemy. In addition to this, the German people have been subjected to an extraordinary variety of influences making for still greater insecurity. Some of these are consequences of war as such.

But the character of the Nazi régime has a special place in this connection. On the remote level it undoubtedly gave a temporary basis for a greatly enhanced sense of security—although this will be devastatingly shattered by defeat. But on the immediate level in at least two respects, it operated the other way. It subjected millions to an essentially arbitrary hazard to status, property, freedom, and life itself, which must have stood in terrific contrast to the old, orderly German system. Fear and anxiety as to what may come next must play a tremendous role among almost all Germans. In addition to this the Nazis have pursued a systematic policy of breaking up virtually all the independent groupings in the society— from the great Trade Union movement to the family. They have "atomized" the society wherever its older groupings conflicted with the Party, which involved an exceedingly wide area. Since the importance of attachment to such groupings for the security of the individual citizen is known, their disruption must have been attended by an immense heightening of the level of insecurity.[11]

Hence, it can be inferred that the fundamental immediate need of the German people is for order and security—as an essential condition of almost anything else. It seems clear that the immediate agency for providing this will be Allied Military Government, and its role will be crucially important.

There is a most important basis in German tradition for a favorable response to such a change: in the old pattern of meticulous order, of security of property and of status, and strictly legal procedure. In this circumstance it is inevitable that important vestiges of the old conservative pattern should re-emerge, including hierarchy, authoritarianism, and formalism. Indeed, the role of the AMG authorities will itself be defined in terms of these *German* patterns, more rigidly authoritarian and more formalistic than would be the case in an Anglo-Saxon country. To be effective in the present sense, it is essential that AMG should accept this role.

But it is none the less important to avoid two closely interdependent dangers: One is, as the path of least resistance to quick restoration of order, lending too strong a sanction to the older conservative patterns and the social elements which symbolize them. Above all it is essential that the occupying authority should not "identify" with the old, upper classes, but should remain aloof from them.[12] There is presumably a very tangible limit to the extent to which such an authority can permit any pattern of order it once allows to be established to be displaced by violence. But it can do much by refraining from lending its positive sanction and pres-

---

[11] Though emotional enthusiasm for Nazism has compensated for this—to how great an extent no one can say. In any case, this source of security will be gone after the war.

[12] It is probable that the extent to which the Allies confirmed the legitimacy of the position of the conservative elements after the last war was an important impediment to the strengthening of more liberal forces within Germany.

tige to an order and thereby handicapping other groups and patterns. It should assiduously cultivate as fluid a situation as the basis requirements of order will permit.

The second danger arises from the fact that in a state of pronounced insecurity spontaneous groupings tend to be largely "defensive" in orientation. There will be a strong tendency to rally around old traditional patterns. But, in addition, there is ample evidence that the patterns governing such defensive orientation to security tend, when seen in relation to the main institutional trends of modern Western civilization, to be "regressive" in character. In particular, the elements of universalism in relation to functional efficiency, and the orientation to functionally specialized roles tend to distintegrate in favor of particularistic group solidarities. This is a particularly serious danger for Germany, both because of the high level of insecurity and because the Nazis have already gone very far to destroy these patterns in the older German society.

A certain amount of this tendency is a "healthy" reaction in the circumstances. But it should not be allowed to become too firmly consolidated. It may be necessary to take positive steps to eliminate some of its more extreme manifestations. But more important ways of mitigating it are to reduce the need for it by improving the level of security, and opening opportunities for alternative patterns of institutionalization.

This type of group formation is a danger for two main reasons. The importance of conservative, militaristic, nationalistic patterns in recent German history is so great that it would be exceedingly difficult to avoid a very close connection and hence a tendency to resurgence. But secondly, if Western civilization is to survive at all, it must be as a relatively mobile, "individualistic," industrial society where such universalistic values as those of science, modern technology, and the rights of the individual citizen play a prominent part. No major unit like Germany in this "Great Society" can be successfully insulated from these patterns. But a great block of the social structure which is institutionalized in a conflicting pattern is a source of serious internal conflict and tension in the society as a whole. It is precisely from such a conflict that, in large measure, the Nazi movement has grown. A policy which would consolidate such tendencies would not conduce to less tension than existed in pre-war European society. It would be laying the foundations of a repetition of the disturbance through which the Western world has lived.

Security, and measures to counteract the above tendencies, important as they are, are probably not enough to start a strong movement of positive institutional change in the right direction. There is, however, a possibility of using control of the situation of action at least to encourage this. In selecting points at which to exert such control three primary considerations are most important: first, accessibility to effective influence; second, strategic significance in the total system of the structure affected; and third, vulnerability to serious boomerang repercussions which might nullify the desired effect. There are four principal structures which have been widely discussed as possibilities—the family, the educational system, the state itself and economic or, more in sociological terms, occupational situations.

There is little doubt that in terms of strategic significance the family is the most important structure because of its paramount influence on the socialization of the younger generation. It is, however, by far the least accessible to direct influence, since it belongs so much to the sphere of private life which is protected from interference. Probably, by far the most important ways of influencing the family are by *indirect* influence. It is to be expected that any substantial change in the occupational structure would profoundly influence the roles of husband and father. Greater security and a removal of the emphasis on hierarchy and relations of authority would greatly reduce the need of a man to "take it out" by being a petty tyrant over his wife and children. This would be a primary objective of the economic policy suggested hereafter.

The second major point touches the position of women. This has been a major source of difficulty in German society because of the deep ambivalence in the child's relation to his mother it has fostered. Any change which can enhance the dignity and position of independent responsibility of women, so that they can successfully "stand up" to men, will operate in the right direction. But here also it is probable that occupational changes offer the most important possibilities. The opening of further occupational opportunities for women is only one phase of it. Making domestic service more expensive and servants less submissive would have an important effect in throwing more responsibility on middle-class women. But most important would be a shift in the definition of the masculine occupational role. Germany has been a rather extreme case of status consciousness. This has meant that the position of the married woman has, to a far greater extent than with the democracies, been defined by the status of her husband[13]—and hence her scope for independent development has been very narrowly circumscribed. A change of emphasis in the direction of functional role rather than status would alter this and give a wider scope for feminine independence. The use of this freedom need not take any one direction—it does not do so in the United States. But it would go far to emancipate women from a dependency relationship to particular men.

The case of the educational system is a peculiarly difficult one. To the psychologically minded, it offers a very tempting opening. This is particularly true of the naive "rationalists" who think of the German problem as one of simple indoctrination with the proper attitudes and values.

[13] Symbolized by the fact that a married woman takes not only the name, but the *title* of her husband; for example, *Frau Oberst, Frau Professor*.

But it is quite positively known, both on the level of psychology and of social structure, that this is not the case. The problem is that of making the desired patterns "stick." The attitudes fostered in democratic schools are not the product of teachers and text books alone—These influences are reinforced by many others, such as those of home, play group, and the general social atmosphere. If all these could be controlled at the same time, the case of the educational system would be less difficult. But they almost certainly cannot, as the case of the family shows.

Even if it were possible to mold the school system rather completely to the desired pattern, it is very questionable whether it would be desirable to attempt it, since in the absence of control over the other elements of the situation there would be an especially strong likelihood of a powerful boomerang reaction which would more than nullify the direct effect. The German type of mentality is, with its paranoid characteristics, more than usually likely to resent what it interprets—often irrationally—as gratuitously patronizing "interference." Any United Nations agency or policy which was in the position of "dictating" the education of Germans would be an ideal scapegoat around which to rally all the resentments which will inevitably be produced by the humiliation of defeat. Not only would this produce serious difficulties in the behavior of adults, but it would react so powerfully on the younger generation that it would probably completely destroy the educational program. This is particularly true if it has not proved possible through the family to lay appropriate foundations in character structure for a "democratic" education.

Even more in this field than in many others, any fundamental change ought to *appear* to come from spontaneous German sources. And should attempts to alter the institutional balance by other measures succeed, an educational reorientation would automatically follow. But to use imposed educational reform—even with the cooperation of Democratic Germans— as a main direct avenue of change is one of the most dangerous suggestions under discussion.

This does not, of course, by any means preclude a certain amount of negative control of education. But even here, the more it can be a spontaneous result of the revulsion incident to the collapse of the Nazi régime, the better.

Somewhat the same considerations apply to proposals for the direct control of government, for this is a critical symbolic focus of the ideological and sentimental structure of a nation. The fate of the Weimar régime in this regard is instructive. It was, in fact, by no means simply imposed by the victorious allies. But the Nazis fully succeeded in getting it defined as such by a large fraction of the German masses—as an "alien" régime which should be replaced by something "truly German." In general it is much better to attempt to control the patterns of government through control of the *situation* in which it has to act. If that is properly handled, the "form" of government can safely be allowed to care for itself. Attempts to influence that directly are in grave danger of boomerang effect.

These two cases suggest two further, rather general maxims which should govern United Nations behavior towards Germany. The first is that a quick, easy turning of the German people to patterns and forms closely in accord with democratic values should be regarded with serious suspicion and not too readily and joyfully accepted. This is not so much because it is likely to be "insincere," masking a plot, as because of the ambivalence and instability of the structure of sentiments underlying it. It is likely to represent the dominance of one potentiality of an ambivalent structure. It is after all the major premise of this analysis that basic changes of institutions and character structure are necessary before a stable, permanent re-orientation of the German people can take place. It is impossible that such changes should have been completed within a brief period after the war.

Secondly, American functionaries dealing with Germans in any capacity should be on their guard against using those who on a naive level "make a good impression" on them personally. For the probability is that they will be people congenial to American patterns and hence incapable of exercising leadership over those Germans whose attitudes are different and hence most need to be changed. The *first* question to ask about a person, an organization, or a group is, What is its position in the *German* social system? Is it in a sufficiently strategic position to exert an important influence in the right direction? Only when this question can be answered in the affirmative does it become even relevant to ask, How can we get along with him or them?

There are two specific directions in which this danger is particularly acute. First, attraction to Germans with good democratic ideas and attitudes is likely. But this very fact may so define their status in their own society as to preclude their effectiveness in doing what is desired. Second, there is an inclination to have a strong predilection for people of the old, established, upper classes—they are "educated," and have good manners, for example. But in a revolutionary situation, identifying with them may directly block the forces which could accomplish the most desirable changes in a larger context.

These considerations suggest one aspect of a policy. It seems unlikely that after the collapse of the Nazi régime there will be anything like a government of Germany. Although a difficult situation in many respects, this will have the great advantage of relieving the occupying forces of the obligation to work with any particular group. In such a situation it would, within the requirements of order, seem highly advisable to allow as much freedom as possible for the spontaneous formation of groups and emergence of leaders. Such a policy could do much to prevent the serious error of premature commitment to people who later prove unable to carry their own followers with them. The basic principle applies all the way from a national government down to the smallest groups.

The fourth major structure to be considered here is the economic-occupational structure. This seems to be much the most promising as a lever of institutional change according to all three of the criteria previously set forth.

First, it is undoubtedly a higher strategic point in the total structure. It is one in which the great bulk of the adult male population, and a considerable fraction of the female, spend nearly half their waking hours. The situation and definition or role in the occupational sphere is of profound, direct significance. But through its close structural interdependence with kinship and the class structure an important change there would have major repercussions in these neighboring areas.

The desirable direction of change is in the first place a quantitative spread in the incidence of functionally differentiated roles where functional achievement is the principal emphasis and value. In proportion to this spread, roles in which an established status was the main emphasis, as in large sections of the peasantry, the old *Mittelstand* and the older élite groups, would be correspondingly weakened.

The second aspect of change is one of altered emphasis, away from hierarchy, authority and formalism, in the direction of functional achievement as the dominant value, and status as the reflection of this, not vice versa.

The probable effect on the family has already been indicated—mitigation of the authoritarianism of the husband-father role and opportunity for a more dignified feminine role to develop. On the class structure the principal effect would be to weaken the rigid formalism of the status hierarchy.

Secondly, it is a point of departure which is much less likely than the others to arouse defensive reactions which might be strong enough to defeat its purpose. In the first place, it is, as such, fairly close to ideological neutrality. Most of the required changes, so far as they need advertisement at all, can be justified simply as measures to open opportunities and contribute to the welfare of Germans. Many can be so unobtrusive as to arouse little attention beyond the limited groups most immediately affected. So far as the context is mainly commercial and technical the democratic peoples are used to treating these problems more objectively than others. Above all the status of the German nation need not be dramatically involved.

There is a very solid common basis of shared value here in the admiration for technical and organizational efficiency and achievement. Few Americans will deny the Germans a high rating in these respects and vice versa.

There seems to be one major point at which trouble is likely; namely, German oversensitiveness to alleged American "materialism," and "money-consciousness." For this reason the emphasis should probably be placed on technical—including scientific—development rather than directly on trade and commercial development.

In the field of indirect repercussions there is one major risk, and one factor which might block the process. In the nature of the case the German tendency to military aggression could only be gradually eliminated. It is possible that a policy which increased German industrial power before the deeper structural change had gone far enough would play into the hands of a nationalistically aggressive resurgence. The answer to this objection lies in other features of the control structure. If the latter is strong, no tendency to militarization of the German economy could get well started, however great her industrial potential. Even after Hitler's advent to power, it was the *weakness* of the Allies, who could not bring themselves to intervene before it was too late, not the strength of Germany *before* her rearmament was far advanced, which made it possible for Germany to become a military threat. It is to a better system of international control, not to de-industrialization of Germany, that one must look for a solution of this problem.[14]

The possible block lies in the question of capacity to accept the repercussions of such a policy. The probable consequence is German industrial expansion. In view of Germany's economic position, this would be possible only with considerable expansion of her foreign trade. Protectionism has been a growing tendency all over the world and has not been least prominent in the United States. If the automatic reaction to German trade expansion everywhere were the progressive raising of trade barriers, this would bring the process to a halt or force it into a nationalistic-aggressive pattern.

It has not been possible to consider here the probable repercussions of the opposite policy—the drastic de-industrialization of Germany. Suffice it to say that from the point of view of Western institutional stability they would appear to be even more serious.

But apart from these questions of repercussions, is a control through economic-occupational channels, on a scale large enough to be effective, realistically feasible? If it is seriously meant, it should be.

The essential thing is that there should be a policy of fostering a highly productive, full-employment, expanding economy for Germany. The inherent tendencies of the modern industrial economy are such that if this is achieved its influence on institutional change will be automatically in the right direction. Conversely, tendencies to particularism, the breakdown of functional specialization, and over-emphasis on group solidarity

---

[14] This paper was written before the public discussion of the so-called "Morgenthau Plan." That discussion has not caused me to alter my fundamental opinion.

are overwhelmingly defensive reactions to the insecurity attendant on a contracting field of opportunity. It is not modern industrialism as such, but its pathology and the incompleteness of its development which fosters these phenomena.

Specific means are various: One is relative freedom for trade expansion. Another is fostering fiscal and monetary stability and the measures economists advocate to stimulate high production.

Apart from this type of measures there is another possibility. It has been indicated that the principal area of common value is technical and organization achievement. It is, therefore, suggested that the first major steps in the reintegration of Germany into the Western community should be the admission of the professional representatives of these values into the community of their Allied "opposite numbers." This should be true of technologists, trade groups, scientific societies, professional groups, university exchange. The professionally specialized character of their role would do much to reduce their vulnerability to being defined as "traitors selling out" to the enemy, in the German view. At the same time, these groups have a key influence in defining crucially important patterns in democratic society. Genuine integration of the German counterparts would do much to set a right tone for the corresponding development in Germany. It would also help to avoid defining the situation in terms of corrupting German "idealism" with Western commercialism and "materialism," since science, technology, and the professions are relatively immune to this charge.

Direct Control of Subjective Factors

Whatever may be true of the long-run influence of "ideas" in shaping social structures and culture patterns, it is one of the most important results of modern psychological and social science that, except in certain particular areas, ideas and sentiments, both on the individual and the mass levels, are more dependent manifestations of deeper lying structures—character structure and institutional structure, as they have been called here—than independent determinants of behavior. They are, however, *inter*dependent with the other elements of the system, and there is always the possibility that in particular instances they may be highly strategic factors. Hence, the problems on this level should be explicitly considered as an integral part of an analysis like the present.

The most obviously important of the mass manifestations in this field is the ideological definition of the situation. The Nazi movement has succeeded in winning acceptance by a large portion of the German people —in varying degrees of intensity and completeness—for a relatively well-integrated, complex ideological system. Its principal component elements have been "endemic" in Western society, although part of the combination has been peculiarly German in a pre-Nazi sense. But it is the intensity of affective fixation and the particular combination which are unique.

The most important components, familiar as they are, had best be summarized as follows: first, perhaps, is the conception of the German national community, the *Volksgemeinschaft*, pseudo-biologically defined as a "race," as having a special historic role, a mission to purge the world of the great evils and impurities of the time—of "materialism," "corruption," plutocracy, bolshevism. This purge is to usher in an eschatological millennium, the New Order or *Tausendjaehriges Reich* in which all men will be blissfully happy and noble.

A major aspect of the corrupt world which is to be purged is capitalistic materialism, commercial-mindedness. Over against this is set the "heroic" ideal which serves to rationalize a conspicuous readiness to resort to force in order to execute the providential mission—and thus to idealize "militarism."

The sense of a special mission is also closely associated with the "master race" idea. Since the Germans are the heroic people, it is to be expected that their superiority should be manifested in a position of dominance attained by force and perpetuated that way. All other peoples are thus inferior and to be subordinated—for their own good, of course. The development of democracy, capitalism, and bolshevism among the most important of these other peoples demonstrates their decadence and unfitness to perform a role of leadership in the world.

The Jew has of course served as the master symbol of the adversary of the German people and their mission. One of his most important functions is to unify the different evils which beset them in a single tangible symbol—above all to bring capitalism and bolshevism together. The Jew is not only a group enemy but is also a semi-magical source of "infection." So far as the Nazis attack anything, it becomes "Jewish," in sovereign disregard of the alleged biological race doctrine. Thus both American capitalism and Russian communism are essentially Jewish, although J. P. Morgan and Henry Ford, like Lenin and Stalin, would appear to have no Jewish antecedents whatever. Even the British people as a whole have become "white Jews" to certain radical Nazi circles.

The relation of an ideological system to the social system in which it takes root is highly complex, and subject to a great deal of variation in different circumstances. In a well-integrated society the dominant ideology in large measure reflects and interprets a large part of the system of actually institutionalized patterns. But even in the most stable societies the ideological patterns are selective relative to the institutional. Ideological formulation often reflects a need to justify, which may imply a sense of insecurity. Hence, those patterns which are most completely taken for granted are likely to play a small role, if any, in explicit ideology. The system is thus "skewed" in the direction of emphasizing elements which are felt to be "problematical." Consciousness of contrast with other societies is one major factor in this.

Every society has important elements of conflict. Hence, an ideology which has unifying functions will tend to "play down" the elements of internal conflict and thus be "skewed" in another way. In the United States, for example, from the "official" ideology one could get little insight into the actual divergences and conflicts between religious, ethnic, and class groups.

Finally, the objects of ideological formulation are mainly in the "remote" category to most persons—or are high-level abstractions with a similar significance. Hence, they are less fully controlled by realistic considerations and constitute particularly favorable opportunities for the operation of such nonrational and irrational mechanisms as projection, displacement, identification. Where there are severe and definitely structured tensions in a society there are almost certain to be ideological patterns which contain conspicuous elements of unrealism, romantic idealization, and distortion.

All these considerations apply in full measure to the various levels of German ideology. The nearest thing to an official ideology of the older Germany was what may be called "Prussian conservatism." This went far toward directly reflecting the institutionalization of the conservative patterns previously discussed. It took relatively little account of the A component of German character. To some extent, however, this was expressed in religious form, and in the valuation of various forms of a-political romanticism—in the arts and philosophy. Germany as a land of poets and idealistic dreamers fits into this situation.

Perhaps the most important aspect of this underlying conservative ideology for the present problem is its bearing on the readiness with which Germans respond to an "anti-capitalistic" appeal. The basis value and prestige symbols of this pattern are *pre*-industrial, centering on class traditions, the enormous dignity of the state, a *noblesse oblige* code of honor, and an ideal of disinterested service and duty. This made it easy to define profit-making business as a form of corruption of these high ideals, and the countries particularly marked by its prominence, such as England and the United States, became very vulnerable to the stigma of "materialism"; for example, England as the "nation of shopkeepers" and the United States as ruled by the "Almighty Dollar." The Anglo-Saxon "business ideology" has served to make these countries all the more vulnerable. The German devil could only too easily find scripture to quote.

It may be assumed that the sentiments expressed in this ideological complex are still very powerful in Germany and that their definition of Anglo-Saxon character as materialistic by contrast with their own noble idealism is a very serious impediment to the Allies acquiring a role of moral prestige relative to Germany. It is also one primary foundation of the appeal of the symbol "socialism" there.[15]

This background is important to understanding the role of the ideology of the "left" in Germany also. This took over the patterns of rationalism and the Enlightenment, and of course opposed German conservatism. But *it too* was, although from a very different point of view, anti-capitalistic. It may even be suggested that the latent anticapitalism of the conservative background, plus the prestige of the state, were important positive factors in the wide appeal of Marxian socialism in Germany—which gave it the largest socialist party in Europe. At any rate, "liberalism" tended to be ground down between these two millstones and was far weaker than elsewhere in the Western world.

From an ideological view Nazism is a kind of synthesis of these two basic currents plus a highly emotionalized nationalistic-political expression of the *A* component of German character as an eschatological political romanticism. It has presented an extraordinarily wide combination of symbolic appeals calculated to catch virtually every main strain of German sentiment with which it is difficult for Anglo-Saxons to cope.

What are the prospects and possibilities following the collapse of Nazism? First, the immediate collapse is likely to be devastatinnly thorough and to give rise to a profound convulsion of sentiment and thought. The Germans are likely to be the most badly disoriented people of modern history for a considerable period. This is, in part, because in accepting emotional adherence to such a drastically romantic doctrine as Nazism, they have gone extraordinarily far to isolate themselves both from the reality and from the moral community of Western civilization. Hence, the awakening from their "hypnotic self-intoxication" will produce a very severe national "hangover." But it is also in part because of a fundamental factor in instability. As a charismatic movement par excellence Nazism has lacked the security given by an established basis of legitimacy. Lacking this, it has to be legitimized by success and is overwhelmingly dependent on this. Hitler has unequivocally committed the movement to the definition of this war as the ultimate test by ordeal of his mission. Its definitive loss cannot but result in the deflation of the whole Nazi myth and an acute crisis of confidence.[16]

But though the Nazi ideological structure may, except for a group of fanatical die-hards who will go underground, be expected to disintegrate,

---

[15] For an expression of this antithesis on a very high level, see Troeltsch, Ernest, *Deutscher Geist und Westeuropa*, Tübingen, Mohr, von Hansbaron, 1925 (ix and 268 pp.). A much more vulgar version is that of Sombart, Werner, *Händler und Helden*, Munchen, Duncker and Humbolt, 1915 (vii and 145 pp.). Both are *pre*-Nazi.

[16] These considerations remind one of the importance of insuring that in every *symbolic* as well as realistic respect it is a *definitive* victory of Allied arms. It seems quite possible that a major motive of the tenacity of German resistance at certain conspicuous points—as in Italy and at Brest—is to preserve the myth that a German force is not "really" beaten. It is only eventually "unfairly" overwhelmed by superior force. It has won a moral victory.

its components will remain "endemic" in the German situation. What are the prospects of restructuring?

The selectivity of ideologies is such that in the German case it is highly probable that there are more favorable starting points for integration with American—and British—patterns on the institutional level than on the ideological. Institutionally German society has been rather conspicuously unintegrated. A dominant national ideology tends to concentrate on defining the situation for the nation as a unit; it has to unify and therefore to play down actual structural elements which do not fit well. Furthermore, orientation to other national units plays a very prominent role with a need to feel a strong contrast and assert a "real" superiority to those which seem to enjoy the dominant external position in the world.

Given the forces underlying the formation of ideology in Germany on the character structure and institutional levels, it seems most unlikely that before these are greatly changed there is any prospect of stimulating the formation and dominance of a national ideology which could be closely integrated with those of the democratic countries and also be made to "stick." A repetition of the 1918–1919 romantic-utopian enthusiasm for Wilsonian democracy seems unlikely. But if it should appear, it should be regarded with even more skepticism than the study of this experience would suggest. For a firm basis for it almost certainly could not exist.

It is more likely that a revolutionary situation may develop in Germany which would bring a communist ideology to a commanding position. By interpreting the defeat as a victory for the working classes and the revolution, and thoroughly liquidating the old upper classes, this could do much to eradicate the humiliation of defeat.[17] But it is scarcely likely that Britain and the United States will wish actively to promote this solution, although they may adapt to it more or less gracefully if it should happen spontaneously or through Russian influence.

These considerations play an important part in determining the emphasis placed in foregoing paragraphs upon approach to the German problem through situational factors. Above all the view so common among Americans that it is "conversion" to democratic values which is the key to bringing Germany "around" is one of the most dangerous misconceptions currently in the air. To attempt to do so by propaganda or other means of indoctrination would almost certainly intensify a tendency to ideological reaction which would give the Germans the unique role they so desperately feel they need and deserve.

The main conclusion from the foregoing analysis is that the ideological problem needs to be handled with especial care, and most important, an attempt to define the situation for the German *nation* as a unit in

[17] This possibility was suggested to me by Dr. Robert Waelder—unpublished correspondence.

"democratic" terms is dangerous. But before considering what can be done, it is necessary to discuss one possibility of spontaneous development.

One of the keynotes of German attitude structure for a very long time has been dualism. Although the best-institutionalized, the conservative pattern has never had the sanction of more than *one* side of this duality. This fact has been fundamental to the "formalism" of German institutions. There has been a strong feeling that somehow the fulfillment of institutionalized roles did not provide a field of expression of the "real" inner personality. It was rather a set of duties and obligations laid down by Providence—or "fate"—which merely demonstrated the tragic element in life. In earlier times this "inner" life was predominantly defined in religious terms, with a specific Lutheran slant. More recently it has been in artistic or philosophical terms.

But this romanticism has not remained individualistic. It has in later times gotten linked to a conception of the "real" life—that is, mission—of the German people, which was not to remain a prosaically conservative system of order. The ability to mobilize the romantic urge was one of the most important sources of strength of the Nazi movement.

This dualism goes to the very roots of the German structure. It will not and cannot be overcome until the long process of fundamental change is nearly complete. Furthermore, the romantic element cannot be permitted political expression in terms of national power. The immediate effect of suppressing this expression will be to bring the conservative component back to a dominant position. But the romantic component will not disappear—it will have to find expression in some other form.

It is of course possible that the link with the mission of the German nation will be broken and a purely individualistic romanticism reappear. But particularly in a world where nationalistic feelings run high everywhere, this seems unlikely. It is more likely that it will take another direction. The element of aggression may well be turned inward upon themselves. The defeat may be interpreted masochistically as just punishment for their own derelictions—surely there must be an enormous reservoir of guilt available for this purpose.[18]

But if this happens it is likely to be associated with a new expression rather than an elimination of the national sense of mission as a specially chosen people. If this can be completely sublimated into a cultural mission perhaps, well and good. But it is more likely to contain an undercurrent of a sense of persecution and an orientation to the day of fulfillment when revenge can be taken.

The analogy to the Jewish people in the time of the Prophets is striking. Acceptance of the same order of deposition from all immediate hopes of

---

[18] The existence of this reservoir has been questioned by Dr. Margaret Mead. A good deal of evidence, however, seems to indicate its great importance. This is surely one of the most important problems for further research about Germany.

worldly glory as a judgement of God would solve the immediate problem of German aggression. But it would not insure against its eventual revival, and it would preserve a basis for it because it would consolidate the separateness of the German people instead of assimilating them into the larger community of Western civilization. It would probably favor alteration of their institutional structure in a direction different from that envisaged here.

Whether or not such a development will take place is probably considerably more dependent on processes on the situational and institutional levels, and thus the direct influence on them of Allied policies, than on those on the ideological level as such. But Allied ideological policy can at least avoid measures which would favor it—or the perpetuation of Nazism—and can exert some pressure toward influencing a balance of forces if it is at all close.

The most fundamental consideration is that of the moral position of the victorious Western powers. This is a field where actions speak louder than words and a propaganda deliberately emphasizing a strong moral case would probably be interpreted as self-righteous cant. But the Western Allies are rather unlikely to indulge in this. A more serious danger is succumbing to a wave of guilt and self-depreciation. This could hardly fail to have a serious effect on Germany, since it would confirm their own arrogance. To regain moral self-confidence without "protesting too much" is one of the most important conditions of exerting the right influence.

Western civilization as a whole has been a moral community historically—although never anywhere nearly perfectly integrated. This has been based on the values of Christianity and certain derived or closely related secular values—such as those of science, and free inquiry, the dignity and freedom of the person, even equality of opportunity. Despite differentiated versions, distortions, and contradictory values there, these values are by no means dead in Germany. Their wholesale violation must have produced much guilt-feeling however deeply repressed it may now be.

A cautious propaganda appeal to these sentiments may be considered —by word and deed. In doing so, two especial precautions should be observed. First, the appeal should as far as possible be *dissociated* from anything to do with the status of the German nation as a unit. It should be made to the rights and duties of persons or citizens and groups as such, not as Germans, and to impersonal patterns such as truth or freedom. The obviousness of the inclusion of Germans under the universality of such values should be the main context.

Second, the form in which they are expressed should so far as possible avoid association with or suggestion of those aspects of Western societies which have served as widespread negative symbols in Germany. Thus, expressions of the values of freedom should not emphasize freedom to make profits, or even, in many contexts, of trade. Similarly suggestion of a direct connection of adherence to such values with the British or American position of power in the world should be avoided.

Although major effects cannot be expected from positive propaganda of this sort, it is undoubtedly worth promoting on the principle that "every little bit helps." But in the field of ideology and sentiments the most important conclusions from sociological and psychological analysis are those concerning the dangers to avoid.

One general methodological point may be emphasized in conclusion. A complex social system like the German is composed of many variable elements which are interdependent in complex ways. It is highly unlikely that there is any one sovereign "key" to the practical solution of the German problem. The Germans do not suffer from a unified disease syndrome for which a specific remedy is known. Confronted with this kind of problem the basic orientation of policy is clear. Although some openings for control are far more strategic than others, in general there are two fundamental maxims:

> Utilize every opening for control which is practicable and can be shown to influence the system in the right direction, but
> Analyze the repercussions of such change throughout the system as carefully as possible.

Where there is reason to believe that these, as will frequently be the case, include processes which tend to neutralize or nullify the change, make sure that one or more of the following conditions is fulfilled; that the counteracting force is of sufficiently small magnitude so that the net gain is substantial; that measures are feasible which can be expected effectively to neutralize it; or, that the proposal for change is abandoned.

PART III

Interpretations of American Politics

*a*s noted in the "Headnotes" to Part II, Part III is the second of the two parts of this volume which have a strong empirical orientation, but the papers which comprise it come from a substantially later period in the author's development, and shift their focus of attention from the Europe of the between-the-wars period to the United States of the postwar (II) period. There is, however, a certain continuity in concern with the problems of the bases of stability and factors of instability in the political systems of the modern world and the background of these political phenomena in the structure of the societies.

In view of the concern of the essays of Part II with the phenomena of Fascism in Europe, it has seemed appropriate to begin Part III with a paper dealing with the most important resurgence of right-wing extremism during the later period in the United States—barring the possible further growth of the current Wallace movement—namely (Joseph) "McCarthyism." This is the only essay in the volume which was not written in response to a particular request; hence the circumstances of its "spontaneous generation" may be of interest, especially in relation to the essays of Part II. In addition to sharing in the general concern of liberals about the rampages of the then

*senator from Wisconsin and the resonance they were finding, I had been
personally rather involved in the attempt of the academic community to fend
off his (and others' related) depredations—especially at Harvard in the
spring of 1953—and somewhat later found myself denied governmental
clearance for a considerable time, in part because of such activities. In the
midst of this I went as a visiting professor to the University of Cambridge
for the year 1953-54 and, in addition to my general concerns as an American,
found myself in the position of having to react to the attitudes of my English
friends, many of whom were intellectuals, more or less on the left, with anti-
American inclinations. The obvious question was whether McCarthy was
the American Hitler, and whether Fascism was really taking hold in the
United States. Basically the essay was written as a device for clarifying the
problem in my own mind. On my return to the United States, I "peddled"
the manuscript, succeeding in placing it in the* Yale Review. *It was then
picked up by Daniel Bell and included in the volume he edited,* The New
American Right. *Several years later (1962), Professor Bell arranged a new
edition of this volume for which each author was invited to present new
materials dealing with developments bearing on his estimate of changes in
the place of the political right in American society since the original
contributions were written. This was the genesis of the "Postcript" which
is appended, in the present volume also, to the original article. (The new
volume was titled* The Radical Right.)

*The conclusion was that, while many of the ingredients which had gone into
the Fascist movements in Europe in the previous period were present in the
United States, the total balance of forces made it unlikely that the main
trend here would be the ascendancy of such elements and the consolidation of
that ascendancy. Indeed, before the article could be published, the peak of
the crisis of "McCarthyism" had passed, with the impact of the Army-
McCarthy hearings and the final censure of the senator by the vote of his own
membership body, the Senate itself.*

*It was, perhaps, natural to choose for the next selection an essay which,
in the form of a review article, discussed one major position in the diagnosis
of the relation of state and society in America, a conceptualization that
attempted to specify certain conditions which seemed to imply a chronic
susceptibility to Fascism. This was the book of the late C. Wright Mills,*
The Power Elite, *which, almost immediately on its publication, had a
substantial impact on intellectual opinion, ranging from high social science
expertise to more diffuse intellectual circles.*

*The article was written in response to a request from the editor of a
proposed new journal which was never published, but it was then accepted by*

World Politics *and first published in the latter. The attempt was to appraise the soundness of Mills's thesis about the nearly monolithic concentration of power in the American society of the 1950's. I tried to state the case for the view that Mills's emphases were highly selective, in particular that he underestimated the importance, not so much of the competitive "market" components of the system, as of the pluralistic and, in certain contexts, "associational" components. Among these I gave relatively high rank to the independence of the legal system, which Mills drastically derogated. It also seemed to me that underlying Mills's analysis was the uncriticized assumption that power was inherently a zero-sum phenomenon.**

Mills was certainly one of the most important precursors of the orientation —it is probably insufficiently rationalized to justify calling it an "ideology" —of the "New Left" in American politics, to which the relatively monolithic character of the "power structure" (which, with a certain penumbra added, becomes the "Establishment") is a cardinal tenet of faith. Indeed, this view is the primary cognitive basis of the claim that there is an essentially evil "system" which must, by ethical imperative, be combated. There are, of course, important resemblances of this position—though also important differences—to the older Left allegation of the control not only of American society, but of other "capitalist" ones, by the "ruling circles," as Soviet ideology has tended to call them, of "late monopoly capitalism." A major difference, however, seems to be that the Communist societies, the Soviet Union in particular, are now held to be guilty of being dominated by a "power elite" which is considered not much less objectionable than the capitalist version.

In my own development, it has been an important step to move from the kind of critique of Fascism involved in Part II to a revised version of a defense, not specifically of "capitalism," but of pluralistic-democratic society. It is in this context that the evaluative aspect of the critique of Mills is to be understood. The issue, however, was not the simple counter-assertion to Mills's assertion that democratic pluralism was a good thing, but of the actual empirical importance, and probable future viability, of this type of sociopolitical organization. The vulnerability of the Mills exposition, among other things, contributed importantly to my own confidence in the soundness of the alternative interpretation on which I had been working, and, in the face of the recent resurgence of the "power elite" thesis, this confidence has not been diminished.

---

* It was a matter of considerable satisfaction that some years later there appeared an extensive study of the American power system which, with much fuller empirical grounding than my own, characterized it as mainly decentralized and pluralistic. Cf. Arnold Rose, *The Power Structure* (New York: Oxford University Press, 1967).

There is a sense in which the next essay, on voting, belongs in the same series. It was written in response to a request, from Burdick and Brodbeck, to attempt an empirical-theoretical assessment of the spate of studies of voting behavior in the American system which had appeared over a period of years. After reviewing the principal contributions to the literature, I found myself concentrating on the one study, that by Berelson, Lazarsfeld, and McPhee, on the 1948 presidential election as seen in Elmira, New York, the findings of which were published, some years after the empirical field work, in 1954. In spite of the narrowness of its empirical scope, this study itself, especially in the final chapter, went considerably farther in analyzing the sociological significance, both of the background of the processes which the data reflected and of the data themselves, than other empirical studies in the field. It therefore proved to be an appropriate vehicle for discussing a range of questions about the American political system at the governmental level involved in presidential elections, and which were continuous with the problems involved in the two preceding essays.

The 1948 election with its surprise outcome caught the American political system in the midst of an important turn which may be characterized as that from the Roosevelt era to the Eisenhower era, and the study, Voting, was able to capture important aspects of the attendant processes at work. The evidence presented seemed to be interpretable in terms, on the one hand, of some of the bases of the two-party system in the structure of the American polity, and on the other hand of some of that system's functions in making transitions of such magnitude possible without greater disturbance than in fact has generally occurred; in this case, it should be remembered, however, that the peak of McCarthyism came in the early years of the Eisenhower administration, and was considerably foreshadowed in the Truman era. It was surely a manifestation of the strains of transition.

These considerations should make clear that the article was concerned with the understanding of political mechanisms which could be interpreted as having a stabilizing effect in American society precisely in situations where major social changes had been going on and where internal tensions were high. Thus in one sense it provided part of the answer to the question of how the disturbance which was McCarthyism could be absorbed. From a longer-run and less obvious point of view, it could give part of the framework within which the often-claimed disequilibrating consequences of inequality, especially of what is often called "economic power," are somewhat counterbalanced in the political process, a view which assumes that the concentration is not as sharp and monolithic as Mills alleged, and that the electoral process does in fact provide counterbalancing mechanisms which among other things give a genuine voice to what Mills called the "mass." The paper was written for and originally published in the volume edited by Eugene Burdick and Arthur Brodbeck, American Voting Behavior (*The Free Press, 1959*). *It was reprinted in my collection of essays,* Sociological Theory and Modern Society (*The Free Press, 1967*).

Chapter 10, on the relation of mass media to the structure of American society, was written, in collaboration with Winston White, in response to a request of the editor of the Journal of Social Issues *to comment on a study by Raymond and Alice Bauer of the available empirical studies of the determinants and effects of mass media.* This paper, by White and myself, might appropriately have been placed in Part IV, because it deals with the role of influence as a generalized medium of societal interchange (cf. Chapter 15). The more general topic of the role of such media, with special reference to that of political power conceived as one of them, figures prominently in that section. It seemed, however, more appropriate to include the paper on mass media in the present section, because its substantive topic is continuous with the others, as a contribution to the understanding of the functioning of American society in respects which, while including much which is not primarily political, are very important to the political system. Since the Bauers had, in their monograph, strongly emphasized the prominence of the conceptions of "mass" society in the interpretations of the mass media which they reviewed, my co-author and I thought we could throw some analytical light on the problems of the soundness of the "mass society" hypothesis— thereby reinforcing the Bauers' skepticism about it. In planning the present volume there seemed to be an important continuity between the critique, in Chapter 8, of Mills's use of the concept of mass, the theme of the role of pluralistic solidary groups in the determination of voting behavior, as analyzed in Chapter 9, and the corresponding features of pluralistic social structure as impinging on the role of mass media. Though there is much about mass media which we do not know, it seems highly unlikely that the "mass culture" interpretation, as that prevailed in the late 1950's, will prove to be adequate. White and I were particularly pleased to be able to show the formal similarities between the "pathologies" which are alleged to dominate the mass communication system and those which have figured so prominently in the discussions of the economy, as well as the political system.*

Chapter 12 turns to a somewhat more specific problem area, that of the conditions and changes of full "inclusion" of the Negro American in the American societal community. Not only has this problem become far more

---

* Raymond A. Bauer and Alice H. Bauer, "America, 'Mass Society' and Mass Media " *Journal of Social Issues,* Vol. 16, No. 2 (1960), pp. 3–66.

salient in public awareness since the paper was written, but it forms a particularly important test case, both practically and theoretically, for the problem of the mode of integration of the American system and the trends of its development.

While granting the many respects in which the Negro case is unique, the paper still attempts to explore the parallels to the processes of inclusion of other "minority" ethnic or religious groups, notably the Catholic and the Jewish. It could certainly be predicted, as of the time of writing (1965), both that the tension over the problem would be likely to grow, and that the storm center would move from the South to the northern urban communities. The intensification of conflict, however, does not itself invalidate the view that in time a high level of inclusion will be reached. Though perspective in such a matter is difficult, I am of the opinion that, though the tension at present, and for some time to come, is more severe than in the cases of the non-Anglo-Saxon Catholic groups, that an outcome similar in pattern to that of the inclusion of the latter is probable. The theme then is that of the integrative resources of the American societal community as exemplified by the study of a particularly salient—partly because exceedingly difficult—case.

The paper grew out of the conferences sponsored by Daedalus *on the Negro American. It was first published in that journal (Fall 1965), and reprinted in the hard-cover volume,* The Negro American, *in the Daedalus Library Series, of which I was privileged to serve as co-editor with Kenneth Clark.*

Finally, Chapter 12 moves to another dimension of political concerns, the international. It has, of course, been implicit in all of this volume that the classical "problem of order" is central to both the political and the sociological perspectives on social systems. In fact, it may be put that the central problem area concerns the relations between "polity" and societal community in our analytical senses, both in promoting societal order and in generating disturbances of it. The international field may be considered to be a test case of the view, central to my own theoretical orientation, that normative components are essential to the stability of any social system. The international system is today, to a greater extent than ever before, definitely a social system. The precariousness of its order is not, as such, a negation of this proposition. The paper is thus an attempt to bring out some of the elements of normative order in international systems and the modes of their interlocking with interests. The paper was written for and published in the symposium, International Politics and Foreign Policy, *edited by James N. Rosenau (The Free Press, 1961).*

7

Chapter

Social Strains in
America

*t*o the relatively objective observer,
whether American or foreign, it
seems clear that the complex of phenomena that have come to be known as
"McCarthyism" must be symptoms of a process in American society of
some deep and general significance. Some interpret it simply as political
reaction, even as a kind of neofascism. Some think of it as simply a manifestation of nationalism. The present paper proposes to bring to bear some
theoretical perspectives of sociology in an attempt to work out an interpretation which goes beyond catchwords of this order.

McCarthyism can be understood as a relatively acute symptom of the
strains which accompany a major change in the situation and structure
of American society, a change which in this instance consists in the
development of the attitudes and institutional machinery required to
implement a greatly enhanced level of national political responsibility.
The necessity for this development arises both from our own growth to
an enormous potential of power, and from the changed relation to the rest
of the world which this growth in itself, and other changes extraneous to
American development, have entailed. The strains to which I refer derive

Yale Review, *Winter, 1955, 226–45 as "McCarthyism and American Social Tension: A Sociologist's
View." Reprinted in Talcott Parsons,* Structure and Process in Modern Societies, *Chapter 7,
Copyright* © *1960, Free Press, New York, N.Y., plus* Postscript, *1963, from Daniel Bell, editor,*
The Radical Right, *1963, Doubleday, Garden City, N.Y.*

primarily from conflicts between the demands imposed by the new situation and the inertia of those elements of our social structure which are most resistant to the necessary changes.

The situation I have in mind centers on the American position in international affairs. The main facts are familiar to all. It is not something that has come about suddenly, but the impact of its pressures has been cumulative.

The starting point is the relative geographical isolation of the United States in the "formative" period of its national history, down to, let us say, about the opening of the present century. The Spanish-American war extended our involvements into the Spanish-speaking areas of the Caribbean and to the Philippines, and the Boxer episode in China and our mediation of the Russo-Japanese war indicated rapidly growing interests in the Orient. Then the First World War brought us in as one of the major belligerents, with a brief possibility of taking a role of world leadership. From this advanced degree of international involvement, however, we recoiled with a violent reaction, repudiating the Treaty of Versailles and the League of Nations.

In the ensuing period of "normalcy," until the shock of Pearl Harbor settled the question, it could still be held that the "quarrels" of foreign powers beyond the Americas were none of our concern, unless some "arbitrary" disturbance impinged too closely on our national interests. By the end of the Second World War, however, this attitude could not again be revived by any body of opinion which pretended to depend upon a realistic appraisal of our situation. Our own strength, in spite of our massive disarmament and demobilization, had grown too great; the defeat of France and the disorganization of Germany destroyed such continental European balance of power as had existed; Britain, though victorious, was greatly weakened in the face of world-wide commitments; and Soviet Russia emerged as a victorious and expanding power, leading with a revolutionary ideology a movement which could readily destroy such elements of stability favorable to such of our own national values and interests as still remained in the world. Along with all this have come developments in military technology that have drastically neutralized the protections formerly conferred by geographical distance, so that even the elementary military security of the United States cannot now be taken for granted apart from world-wide political order.

The vicissitudes of American foreign policy and its relations to domestic politics over this period show the disturbing effect of this developing situation on our society. We have twice intervened militarily on a grand scale. With a notable difference of degree, we have both times recoiled from the implications of our intervention. In the second case the recoil did not last long, since the beginnings of the Cold War about 1947 made it clear that only American action was able to prevent Soviet domination of the whole continent of Europe. It can, however, be argued that this early and grand-scale resumption of responsibility imposed serious internal strains because it did not allow time for "digesting" the implications of our role in the war.

The outstanding characteristic of the society on which this greatly changed situation has impinged is that it had come to be the industrial society par excellence—partly because the settlement of the continental area coincided with the later industrial revolution, partly because of the immense area and natural resources of the country, but partly too because of certain important differences between American and European society. Since the United States did not have a class structure tightly integrated with a political organization that had developed its main forms before the industrial revolution, the economy has had a freedom to develop and to set the tone for the whole society in a way markedly different from any European country or Japan.

All highly industrialized societies exhibit many features in common which are independent of the particular historical paths by which their developments have taken place. These include the bureaucratic organization of the productive process itself, in the sense that the roles of individuals are of the occupational type and the organizations in which they are grouped are mainly "specific function" organizations. Under this arrangement the peasant type of agricultural holding, where farming is very closely bound up with a kinship unit, is minimized. So too are small family businesses; people tend to look to their productive function and to profit as a measure of success and hence of emancipation from conflicting ties and claims. The rights of property ownership are centered primarily in the organization which carries functional responsibility, and hence permits a high degree of segregation between private life and occupational roles for production purposes. Contract plays a central part in the system of exchange, and para-economic elements tend to be reduced in importance.

Outside the sphere which touches the organization of the economy itself, industrialism means above all that the structures which would interfere with the free functioning of the economy, and of their adaptation to it, are minimized. The first of these is family and kinship. The American family system, chiefly characterized by the isolation of the nuclear or conjugal family, has gone farther than in any European society toward removing all interferences with the occupational roles of the breadwinning members, and with occupational mobility. A second field is religion. The American combination of federalism and the separation of church and state has resulted in a system of "denominational pluralism" which prevents organized religion from constituting a monolithic structure standing in the way of secular social developments. The third field concerns the matter of social stratification. The United States of course has a class structure, but it is one which has its primary roots in the system of occupational roles, and in contrast to the typical European situation it acts as no more than a brake on the processes of social mobility which are most important to an industrial type of occupational system. Under an effective family system there must be some continuity of class status from generation to generation, and there cannot be complete "equality of opportunity." In America, however, it is clearly the occupational system rather than kinship continuity that prevails.

Linked to this situation is our system of formal education. The United States was among the pioneers in developing publicly supported education; but this has taken place in a notably decentralized way. Not only is there no Department of Education in the Federal government, but even the various state departments are to a large extent service organizations for the locally controlled school systems. Higher education further has been considerably more independent of class standards which equate the "scholar" with the "gentleman" (in a class sense) than has been the case in Europe. Also a far larger proportion of each age-group attend institutions of higher education than in European countries.

Politically the most important fact about American industrialism is that it has developed overwhelmingly under the aegis of free enterprise. Historically the center of gravity of the integration of American society has not rested in the political field. There came to be established a kind of "burden of proof" expectation that responsibilities should not be undertaken by government unless, first, the necessity for their being undertaken at all was clearly established, and second, there was no other obviously adequate way to get the job done. It is therefore not surprising that the opening up of vast new fields of governmental responsibility should meet with considerable resistance and conflict.

The impact of this problem on our orientation to foreign relations has been complicated by an important set of internal circumstances. It is a commonplace that industrialism creates on a large scale two sets of problems which uniformly in all industrialized countries have required modifications of any doctrinaire "laissez-faire" policy: the problems of controlling the processes of the economy itself, and of dealing with certain social repercussions of industrialization.

As the process of industrialization has proceeded in America there has been a steady increase in the amount of public control imposed on the economy, with the initiative mainly in the hands of the Federal government. This trend was accelerated in the latter years of the nineteenth century, and has continued, with interruptions, through the New Deal. The New Deal, however, was more concerned with the social repercussions of industrialization, rather than with more narrowly economic problems. The introduction of a national system of social security and legislation more favorable to labor are perhaps the most typical developments. This internal process of government intervention has not gone far enough to satisfy European socialists, but it certainly constitutes a great modification of the earlier situation. Moreover, in broad lines it can be regarded as firmly established. It is significant that the major political parties now tend to vie with each other in promoting the extension of social security benefits, that there is no likelihood of repeal of the Federal Reserve Act, and that there is no strong movement to place the unions under really severe legal restraints.

On the whole, business groups have accepted the new situation and cooperated to make it work with considerably more good faith than in Continental Europe. Nevertheless, these internal changes have been sufficiently recent and far-reaching to keep the strains attendant on them from being fully resolved. Moreover they have created an important part of the problems with which this examination is chiefly concerned, problems touching the composition of the higher strata of the society, where the primary burden of responsibility must fall.

By contrast with European countries, perhaps in some ways particularly Britain, the United States has been conspicuous for the absence or relative weakness of two types of elite elements. The first of these is a hereditary upper class with a status continuous from pre-industrial times, closely integrated with politics and public service. The second is an occupational elite whose roots are essentially independent of the business world—in the independent professions, the universities, the church, or government, including civil and military services.

In America the businessmen have tended to be the natural leaders of the general community. But, both for the reasons just reviewed and for certain others, this leadership has not remained undisputed. On the whole the business community has, step by step, resisted the processes of internal change necessitated by industrialization rather than taken the leadership in introducing them. The leadership that has emerged has been miscellaneous in social origin, including professional politicians, especially those in touch with the urban political machines, leaders in the labor union movement, and elements in close touch with them. An important part has been played by men and women who may be said to exhibit a more or less "aristocratic" tinge, particularly in the Eastern cities, President Roosevelt, of course, having been among them. An important part has been played by lawyers who have made themselves more independent of the business connection than the typical corporation lawyer of a generation ago. Under the pressure of emergency, there has been a tendency for high military officers to play important roles in public life.

Another important group has been composed of "intellectuals"—again a rather miscellaneous assembly including writers, newspapermen, and members of university faculties. In general the importance of the universities has been steadily enhanced by the increasingly technical character of the operations of the economy; businessmen themselves have had to be more highly educated than their predecessors, and have become increasingly dependent on still more highly trained technicians of various kinds.

The important point is that the "natural" tendency for a relatively unequivocal business leadership of the general community has been frustrated, and the business group has had to give way at many points. Nevertheless, a clearly defined non-business component of the elite has not yet crystallized. In my opinion, the striking feature of the American elite is not what Soviet propaganda contends that it is—the clearcut dominance by "capitalists"—but rather its fluid and relatively unstructured character. In particular, there is no clear determination of where political leadership, in the sense including both "politics" and "administration," is to center.

A further feature of the structure of American society is intimately related to the residual strains left by recent social changes. There is a continuing tendency for earlier economic developments to leave a "precipitate" of upper groups, the position of whose members is founded in the achievements of their ancestors, in this case relatively recent ones. By historical necessity these groups are strongest in the older parts of the country. Hence the cities of the Eastern seaboard have tended to develop groups that are the closest approach we have—though still different from their European equivalent—to an aristocracy. They have generally originated in business interests, but have taken on a form somewhat similar to the mercantile aristocracies of some earlier European societies, such as the Hanseatic cities. In the perspective of popular democratic sentiments, these groups have tended to symbolize at the same time capitalistic interests and social snobbery. In certain circumstances they may be identified with "bohemianism" and related phenomena which are sources of uneasiness to traditional morality.

As the American social and economic center has shifted westward, such groups in the great Middle Western area and beyond have been progressively less prominent. There the elites have consisted of new men. In the nature of the case the proportional contribution to the economy and the society in general from the older and the newer parts of the country has shifted, with the newer progressively increasing their share. But at the same time there is the sense among them of having had to fight for this share against the "dominance" of the East. A similar feeling permeates the lower levels of the class structure. A major theme of the populist type of agrarian and other radicalism had combined class and sectional elements, locating the source of people's troubles in the bankers and railway magnates of the East and in Wall Street. It must not be forgotten that the isolationism of the between-the-wars period was intimately connected with this sectional and class sentiment. The elder La Follette, who was one of the principal destroyers of the League of Nations, was not a "conservative" or in any usual sense a reactionary, but a principal leader of the popular revolt against "the interests."

It also must not be forgotten that a large proportion of the American population are descendants of relatively recent immigrants whose cultural origins are different from the dominant Protestant Anglo-Saxon elements. A generation and more ago the bulk of the new immigration constituted an urban proletariat largely dominated by the political machines of the great cities. By now a great change has taken place. The children of these immigrants have been very much Americanized, but to a considerable degree they are still sensitive about their full acceptance. This sensitivity is, if anything, heightened by the fact that on the whole most of these elements have risen rapidly in the economic and social scale. They are no longer the inhabitants of the scandalous slums; many have climbed to lower middle class status and higher. They have a certain susceptibility to "democratic" appeals which are directed against the alleged snobbery of the older dominant elements.

Finally, the effect of the great depression of the 1930's on the leading business groups must not be forgotten. Such a collapse of the economy could not fail to be felt as a major failure of the expectation that business leaders should bear the major responsibility for the welfare of the economy as a whole and thus of the community. In general it was not the business-men but the government, under leadership which was broadly antagon-istic to business, which came to the rescue. Similarly, the other great class of American proprietors, the farmers, had to accept governmental help of a sort that entailed controls, which in turn inevitably entailed severe conflicts with the individualistic traditions of their history. The fact that the strains of the war and postwar periods have been piled so immediately on those of depression has much to do with the severity of the tensions with which this analysis is concerned.

My thesis, then, is that the strains of the international situation have impinged on a society undergoing important internal changes which have themselves been sources of strain, with the effect of superimposing one kind of strain on another. What responses to this compound strain are to be expected?

It is a generalization well established in social science that neither individuals nor societies can undergo major structural changes without the likelihood of producing a considerable element of "irrational" behavior. There will tend to be conspicuous distortions of the patterns of value and of the normal beliefs about the facts of situations. These distorted beliefs and promptings to irrational action will also tend to be heavily weighted with emotion, to be "over-determined" as the psychologists say.

The psychology of such reactions is complex, but for present purposes it will suffice to distinguish two main components. On the negative side, there will tend to be high levels of anxiety and aggression, focused on what rightly or wrongly are felt to be the sources of strain and difficulty. On the positive side there will tend to be wishful patterns of belief with a strong "regressive" flavor, whose chief function is to wish away the disturbing situation and establish a situation in phantasy where "everything will be all right," preferably as it was before the disturbing situation came about. Very generally then, the psychological formula tends to prescribe a set of beliefs that certain specific, symbolic agencies are responsible for the present state of distress; they have "arbitrarily" upset a satisfactory state of affairs. If only they could be eliminated the trouble would disappear and a satisfactory state restored. The role of this type of mechanism in primitive magic is quite well known.

In a normal process of learning in the individual, or of developmental change in the social system, such irrational phenomena are temporary, and tend to subside as capacity to deal with the new situation grows. This may be more or less easily achieved, of course, and resolution of the conflicts and strains may fail to be achieved for a long period or may even be permanently unsuccessful. But under favorable circumstances these reactions are superseded by an increasingly realistic facing of the situation by institutionalized means.

Our present problem therefore centers on the need to mobilize American society to cope with a dangerous and threatening situation which is also intrinsically difficult. It clearly can only be coped with at the governmental level; and hence the problem is in essence a matter of political action, involving both questions of leadership—of who, promoting what policies, shall take the primary responsibility—and of the commitment of the many heterogeneous elements of our population to the national interest.

Consequently there has come to be an enormous increase in pressure to subordinate private interests to the public interest, and this in a society where the presumptions have been more strongly in favor of the private interest than in most. Readiness to make commitments to a collective interest is the focus of what we ordinarily mean by "loyalty." It seems to me that the problem of loyalty at its core is a genuine and realistic one; but attitudes toward it shade all the way from a reasonable concern with getting the necessary degree of loyal cooperation by legitimate appeals, to a grossly irrational set of anxieties about the prevalence of disloyalty, and a readiness to vent the accompanying aggression on innocent scapegoats.

Underlying the concern for loyalty in general, and explaining a good deal of the reaction to it, is the ambivalence of our approach to the situation: The people in the most "exposed" positions are on the one hand pulled by patriotic motives toward fulfillment of the expectations inherent in the new situation; they want to "do their bit." But at the same time

their established attitudes and orientations resist fulfillment of the obligation. In the conflict of motives which ensues it is a natural consequence for
resistance to be displaced or projected onto other objects which function
as scapegoats. In the present situation it is precisely those parts of our
population where individualistic traditions are strongest that are placed
under the greatest strain, and that produce the severest resistance to
accepting the obligations of our situation. Such resistances, however,
conflict with equally strong patriotic motives. In such a situation, when
one's own resistance to loyal acceptance of unpalatable obligations, such
as paying high taxes, are particularly strong, it is easy to impute disloyal
intentions to others.

Our present emotional preoccupation with the problem of loyalty
indicates above all that the crisis is not, as some tend to think, primarily
concerned with fundamental values, but rather with their implementation.
It is true that certain features of the pattern of reaction, such as tendencies
to aggressive nationalism and to abdication of responsibilities, would, if
carried through, lead to severe conflict with our values. But the main
problem is not concerned with doubts about whether the stable political
order of a free world is a goal worth sacrificing for, but rather with the
question of how our population is rising, or failing to rise, to the challenge.

The primary symbol that connects the objective external problem and
its dangers with the internal strain and its structure is "Communism."
"World Communism" and its spread constitute the features of the world
situation on which the difficulty of our international problem clearly
centers. Internally it is felt that Communists and their "sympathizers"
constitute the primary focus of actual or potential disloyalty.

With respect to the external situation, the focus of the difficulty in the
current role of Soviet Russia is of course reasonable enough. Problems
then arise mainly in connection with certain elements of "obsessiveness"
in the way in which the situation is approached, manifested, for instance,
in a tendency to subordinate all other approaches to the situation exclusively to the military, and in the extreme violence of reaction in some
circles to the Chinese situation, in contrast to the relative tolerance with
which Jugoslavia is regarded.

Internally, the realistic difficulty resides mainly in the fact that there
has indeed been a considerable amount of Communist infiltration in the
United States, particularly in the 1930's. It is true that the Communist
Party itself has never achieved great electoral success, but for a time
Communist influence was paramount in a number of important labor
unions, and a considerable number of the associations Americans so like
to join were revealed to be Communist-front organizations, with effective
Communist control behind the public participation of many non-Com-
munists. Perhaps most important was the fact that considerable numbers
of eth intellectuals became fellow-travelers. In the days of the rise of

Nazism and of the popular front, many of them felt that only Soviet Russia was sincere in its commitment to collective security; that there was a Franco-British "plot" to get Germany and Russia embroiled with each other, etc. The shock of the Nazi-Soviet pact woke up many fellow-travelers, but by no means all; and the cause was considerably retrieved by Hitler's attack on Russia.

Two other features of the Communist movement which make it an ideal negative symbol in the context of the present loyalty problem are the combination of conspiratorial methods and foreign control with the progressive component of its ideological system. On the one hand, the party has drastically repudiated the procedures of constitutional democracy, and on this issue has broken with all the democratic socialist parties of Europe; it claims the protection of democratic procedures and civil liberties, but does not hestitate to abuse them when this seems to be advantageous. There further has never been any question of the American party determining its own policies by democratic procedures. Perhaps in fact the knowledge of the extent to which the "front" organizations have been manipulated from behind the scenes has been the most disillusioning aspect for liberal Americans of their experience with Communism at home.

At the same time the movement had a large content of professed idealism, which may be taken to account for the appeal of Communism before the Cold War era for such large elements of liberal opinion in the United States, as in other Western countries. Marx was, after all, himself a child of the Enlightenment, and the Communist movement has incorporated in its ideology many of the doctrines of human rights that have formed a part of our general inheritance. However grossly the symbols of democracy, of the rights of men, of peace and brotherhood, have been abused by the Communists, they are powerful symbols in our tradition, and their appeal is understandable.

Hence the symbol "Communism" is one to which a special order of ambivalence readily attaches. It has powerful sources of appeal to the liberal tradition, but those who are out of sympathy with the main tradition of American liberalism can find a powerful target for their objections in the totalitarian tactics of Communism and can readily stigmatize it as "un-American." Then, by extending their objections to the liberal component of Communist ideology, they can attack liberalism in general, on the grounds that association with Communist totalitarianism makes anything liberal suspect.

These considerations account for the anti-Communist's readiness to carry over a stereotype from those who have really been party members or advanced fellow-travelers to large elements of the intellectuals, the labor movement, etc., who have been essentially democratic liberals of various shades of opinion. Since by and large the Democratic Party has more of this liberalism than has the Republican, it is not surprising that a tendency to label it as "sympathizing" with or "soft toward" Communism has appeared. Such a label has also been extended, though not very seriously, to the Protestant clergy.

But there is one further extension of the association that is not accounted for in these terms, nor is the failure to include certain plausible targets so accountable. The extension I have in mind is that which leads to the inclusion as "pro-Communist" of certain men or institutions that have been associated with political responsibility in the international field. Two symbols stand out here. The first is Dean Acheson. Mr. Acheson has for years served the Democratic Party. But he has belonged to the conservative, not the New Deal wing of the party. Furthermore, the coupling of General Marshall with him, though only in connection with China, and only by extremists, clearly precludes political radicalism as the primary objection, since Marshall has never in any way been identified with New Deal views. The other case is that of Harvard University as an alleged "hot-bed" of Communism and fellow-traveling. The relevant point is that Mr. Acheson typifies the "aristocrat" in public service; he came of a wealthy family, he went to a select private school (Groton) and to Yale and Harvard Law School. He represents symbolically those Eastern vested interests, against whom antagonism has existed among the new men of the Middle West and the populist movement, including the descendents of recent immigrants. Similarly, among American universities Harvard has been particularly identified as educating a social elite, the members of which are thought of as "just the type," in their striped trousers and morning coats, to sell out the country to the social snobs of European capitals. It is the combination of aristocratic associations— through the Boston Brahmins—and a kind of urban-bohemian sophistication along with its devotion to intellectual and cultural values, including precisely its high intellectual standards, which makes Harvard a vulnerable symbol in this context.

The symbol "Communism," then, from its area of legitimate application, tends to be generalized to include groups in the population who have been associated with political liberalism of many shades and with intellectual values in general and to include the Eastern upper-class groups who have tended to be relatively internationalist in their outlook.

A second underlying ambivalent attitude-structure is discernible in addition to that concerning the relation between the totalitarian and the progressive aspects of Communism. On the one hand, Communism very obviously symbolizes what is anathema to the individualistic tradition of a business economy—the feared attempt to destroy private enterprise and with it the great tradition of individual freedom. But on the other hand, in order to rise to the challenge of the current political situation, it is necessary for the older balance between a free economy and the power of government to be considerably shifted in favor of the latter. We must have a stronger government than we have traditionally been accustomed to, and we must come to trust it more fully. It has had in recent times to assume very substantial regulatory functions in relation to the economy, and now vastly enhanced responsibilities in relation to international affairs.

But, on the basis of a philosophy which, in a very different way from our individualistic tradition, gives primacy to "economic interests," namely the Marxist philosophy, the Communist movement asserts the unqualified, the totalitarian supremacy of government over the economy. It is precisely an actual change in our own system in what, in one sense is clearly in this direction, that emerges as the primary focus of the frustrations to which the older American system has been subjected. The leaders of the economy, the businessmen, have been forced to accept far more "interference" from government with what they have considered "their affairs" than they have liked. And now they must, like everyone else, pay unprecedentedly high taxes to support an enormous military establishment, and give the government in other respects unprecedentedly great powers over the population. The result of this situation is an ambivalaence of attitude that on the one hand demands a stringent display of loyalty going to lengths far beyond our tradition of individual liberty, and on the other hand is ready to blame elements which by ordinary logic have little or nothing to do with Communism, for working in league with the Communist movement to create this horrible situation.

Generally speaking, the indefensible aspect of this tendency, in a realistic assessment, appears in a readiness to question the loyalty of all those who have assumed responsibility for leadership in meeting the exigencies of the new situation. These include many who have helped to solve the internal problems of the control of the economy, those who in the uneasy latter 'thirties and the first phase of the war tried to get American policy and public opinion to face the dangers of the international situation, and those who since the war have tried to take responsibility in relation to the difficult postwar situation. Roughly, these are the presumptively disloyal elements who are also presumptively tainted with Communism. Here again, admittedly, certain features of our historical record and attitudes provide some realistic basis for this tendency. In fact many elements in both parties have failed lamentably to assess correctly the dangers of the situation, both internally and externally. New Dealers have stigmatized even the most responsible elements of the business world as economic royalists and the like, while many elements in business have clung long past a reasonable time to an outmoded belief in the possibility of a society with only a "night watchman" government. In foreign affairs, some members of the Democratic Party have been slow to learn how formidable a danger was presented by totalitarian Communism, but this is matched by the utopianism of many Republicans about the consequences of American withdrawal from international responsibilities, through high tariffs as well as political isolationism. The necessity to learn the hard realities of a complex world and the difficulty of the process is not a task to be imposed on only part of the body politic. No party or group can claim a monopoly either of patriotic motive or of competent understanding of affairs.

In a double sense, then, Communism symbolizes "the intruder." Externally the world Communist movement is the obvious source of the most serious difficulties we have to face. On the other hand, although Communism has constituted to some degree a realistic internal danger, it has above all come to symbolize those factors that have disturbed the beneficent natural state of an American society which allegedly and in phantasy existed before the urgent problems of control of the economy and greatly enhanced responsibility in international affairs had to be tackled.

Against this background it can perhaps be made clear why the description of McCarthyism as simply a political reactionary movement is inadequate. In the first place, it is clearly not simply a cloak for the "vested interests," but rather a movement that profoundly splits the previously dominant groups. This is evident in the split, particularly conspicuous since about 1952, within the Republican Party. An important part of the business elite, especially in the Middle West and in Texas, the "newest" area of all, have tended in varying degrees to be attracted by the McCarthy appeal. But other important groups, notably in the East, have shied away from it and apparently have come to be more and more consolidated against it. Very broadly, these can be identified with the business element among the Eisenhower Republicans.

But at the same time the McCarthy following is by no means confined to the vested-interest groups. There has been an important popular following of very miscellaneous composition. It has comprised an important part of those who aspire to full status in the American system but have, realistically or not, felt discriminated against in various ways, especially the Mid-Western lower and lower middle classes and much of the population of recent immigrant origin. The elements of continuity between Western agrarian populism and McCarthyism are not by any means purely fortuitous. At the levels of both leadership and popular following, the division of American political opinion over this issue *cuts clean across the traditional lines of distinction between "conservatives" and "progressives,"* especially where that tends to be defined, as it so often is, in terms of the capitalistic or moneyed interests as against those who seek to bring them under more stringent control. McCarthyism is *both* a movement supported by certain vested-interest elements *and* a popular revolt against the upper classes.

Another striking characteristic of McCarthyism is that it is highly selective in the liberal causes it attacks. Apart from the issue of Communism in the labor unions, now largely solved, there has been no concerted attack on the general position of the labor movement. Further, the social program aimed toward the reduction of racial discrimination has continued to be pressed, to which fact the recent decision of the Supreme Court outlawing segregation in public education and its calm reception provide dramatic evidence. Nevertheless, so far as I am aware there has been no outcry from McCarthyite quarters to the effect that this decision is further evidence of Communist influence in high circles—in spite of the fact that eight out of nine members of the present court were appointed by Roosevelt and Truman.

Perhaps even more notable is the fact that, unlike the 1930's when Father Coughlin and others were preaching a vicious anti-Semitism, anti-Semitism as a public issue has since the war been very nearly absent from the American scene. This is of course associated with full employment. But particularly in view of the rather large and conspicuous participation of Jewish intellectuals in the fellow-traveling of the 1930's, it is notable that Jewishness has not been singled out as a symbolic focus for the questioning of loyalty. A critical difference from German Nazism is evident here. To the Nazis the Jew was the *primary* negative symbol, the Communist the most prominent secondary one. But it must also be remembered that capitalism was symbolically involved. One of the functions of the Jew was to *link* Communism and capitalism together. This trio were the "intruders" to the Nazis. They symbolized different aspects of the disturbance created by the rapid development of industrialism to the older pre-industrial *Gemeinschaft* of German political romanticism. It was the obverse of the American case—a new economy destroying an old political system, not new political responsibilities interfering with the accustomed ways of economic life.

Negatively, then, the use of the symbol "Communism" as the focus of anxiety and aggression is associated with a high order of selectivity among possibly vulnerable targets. This selectivity is, I submit, consistent with the hypothesis that the focus of the strain expressed by McCarthyism lies in the area of political responsibility—not, as Marxists would hold, in the structure of the economy as such, nor in the class structure in any simple, Marxian-tinged sense.

The same interpretation is confirmed by the evidence on the positive side. The broadcast formula for what the McCarthyites positively "want" —besides the elimination of all Communist influence, real or alleged—is perhaps "isolationism." The dominant note is, I think, the regressive one. It is the wishful preservation of an old order, which allegedly need never have been disturbed but for the wilful interference of malevolent elements: Communists and their sympathizers. The nationalistic overtones center on a phantasy of a happy "American way" where everything used to be all right. Naturally it is tinged with the ideology of traditional laissez-faire, but not perhaps unduly so. Also it tends to spill over into a kind of irritated activism. On the one hand we want to keep out of trouble; but on the other hand, having identified an enemy, we want to smash him forthwith. The connection between the two can be seen, for example, in relation to China, where the phantasy seems to be that by drastic action it would be possible to "clean up" the Chinese situation quickly and then our troubles would be over.

The main contention of these pages has been that McCarthyism is best understood as a symptom of the strains attendant on a deep-seated process of change in our society, rather than as a "movement" presenting a policy or set of values for the American people to act on. Its content is overwhelmingly negative, not positive. It advocates "getting rid" of undesirable influences, and has amazingly little to say about what should be done.

This negativism is primarily the expression of fear, secondarily of anger, the aggression which is a product of frustration. The solution, which is both realistically feasible and within the great American tradition, is to regain our national self-confidence and to take active steps to cope with the situation with which we are faced.

On the popular level the crisis is primarily a crisis of confidence. We are baffled and anxious, and tend to seek relief in hunting scapegoats. We must improve our understanding and come to realize our strength and trust in it. But this cannot be done simply by wishing it to be done. I have consistently argued that the changed situation in which we are placed demands a far-reaching change in the structure of our society. It demands policies, and confidence, but it demands more than these. It demands above all three things: The first is a revision of our conception of citizenship to encourage the ordinary man to accept greater responsibility. The second is the development of the necessary implementing machinery. The third is national political leadership, not only in the sense of individual candidates for office or appointment, but in the sense of social strata where a traditional political responsibility is ingrained.

The most important of these requirements is the third. Under American conditions, a politically leading stratum must be made up of a combination of business and nonbusiness elements. The role of the economy in American society and of the business element in it is such that political leadership without prominent business participation is doomed to ineffectiveness and to the perpetuation of dangerous internal conflict. It is not possible to lead the American people *against* the leaders of the business world. But at the same time, so varied now are the national elements which make a legitimate claim to be represented, the business element cannot monopolize or dominate political leadership and responsibility. Broadly, I think, a political elite in the two main aspects of "politicians" whose specialties consist in the management of public opinion, and of "administrators" in both civil and military services, must be greatly strengthened. It is here that the practical consequences of McCarthyism run most directly counter to the realistic needs of the time. But along with such a specifically political elite there must also be close alliance with other, predominantly "cultural" elements, notably perhaps in the universities, but also in the churches.

In the final sense, then, the solution of the problem of McCarthyism lies in the successful accomplishment of the social changes to which we are called by our position in the world and by our own domestic requirements. We have already made notable progress toward this objective; the current flare-up of stress in the form of McCarthyism can be taken simply as evidence that the process is not complete.

Social Strains in
America:
A Postscript—1962

I think that the diagnosis I put forward originally can stand. McCarthyism was essentially a crisis of national solidarity in the face of what, for us as a nation, were accumulating and unprecedented political demands and responsibilities. The precipitating factor was the Korean War, which, acting as a "last straw," frustrated the expectations of relaxation that many Americans held after the end of the big war, a war that itself was entered into only after serious internal division and conflict. The focus of the strain was the problem of national loyalty. But the very insistence on national loyalty created a paradox that Edward Shils, in his *The Torment of Secrecy*, has highlighted more clearly than anyone else, in that the very demand for nearly absolute national loyalty undermined our national capacities for effective action.

One of the most striking features of the McCarthy movement was its intensity while it lasted, and the rapidity with which it subsided when the "bubble" finally burst. Though more deep-rooted and underlying strains may have been involved—and may still be—McCarthyism as a social threat was more clearly analogous to a financial panic, say, than to a long-drawn-out depression. Putting the situation in terms of that analogy may help to clarify the ways in which the strain operated. When there is a run on the bank by depositors the tendency is, in a cumulative regression, to more and more "elementary" monetary transactions. In the ordinary course of business "cash" is only a minor convenience, for most transactions are carried out essentially by exchange of deposits within a credit system. But if too many depositors want payment all at once, these demands cannot be honored and the credit system maintained. "Logically" the end of the line of monetary deflation, of course, is a return to species payments, or the use of metal, the toting of which would make any commercial transaction quite weighty. Such a downward spin can only be checked by a restoration of "confidence," which means willingness to accept payment other than "hard" cash—the return to credit. In short, there has to be a foundation of trust for the credit system to operate.

McCarthyism was such a "deflationary spiral." The "credit" repudiated was the ordinary level of commitment of the citizen to the national interest, which in a pluralistic society is virtually never total. What the McCarthyites demanded of those who claimed to be "trustworthy" was not fulfillment of ordinary obligations, but an absolute guarantee that no other commitment could conceivably compete with what *they* called "loyalty" to the government.

Obviously this pressure generated a special kind of conflict in American society. We have a tradition that the claims of government on the individual are relatively minimal, and the presumptive morality is one of defense of individual rights against government. In the 1950s we were made acutely aware of the serious threats to national security and of the necessity of strengthening the government in ways that, in some sense, involved a sacrifice of private rights.

In such a situation there will necessarily be widespread ambivalence, and it was to be expected that the phenomenon of scapegoating would be prominent. It was my view, as stated in the original paper, that the most prominent scourgers would be those who had a strong—moral as well as "material"—vested interest in limiting the powers of government, and that the victims would be those who had on the whole taken the initiative in realistic attempts to meet the situation. From this point of view it was not unintelligible that the men who had entered government service were the ones most victimized. (This is perhaps analogous to the banker who, having taken the responsibility for lending "other people's money" is then, by populistic demand, subjected to the most rigorous checking, so that even any minor loss through error of judgment comes to be attributed to his bad faith.)

The question may now be raised whether the most recent phase of development of the radical right is a repetition of McCarthyism or something different. There is, it seems to me, a common substratum, but in many respects the current flare-up has markedly different features.

The common substratum seems to lie in the tendency to polarization that derives from the main pattern of developmental change in American society. In the broadest sense—which can be made to correspond only approximately to political-party divisions—the "right" is the protest against the fact that American society is changing, and against the direction of change. The United States is a society that has been evolving toward increasing complexities and scale of its organization and functions; a greater concentration of population and activities in complex communities; increasing responsibility in the world political system; and a higher order of technology, knowledge, sophistication, and the like. The conservatives are the rearguard resistance to this trend.

Common to all the multifarious aspects of the right wing is a certain type of "individualism." It has such facets as the individualism of the small unit as against the large—the independent entrepreneur versus the large corporation, and similarly the rural and small town versus the city and the metropolis. As regards international relations, this individualism romanticizes our earlier lack of involvement in the complex world of power relations, when America could be left to work out its own destiny. Most generally perhaps this individualism is the idealization of pristine simplicity as against organizational and other complexity.

In the general picture, the current right seems to be the more regressive of the two, and for that very reason possibly less threatening, since the radical wing of conservatism is likely to be excluded from power. In understanding its salience it should also be remembered that while McCarthyism started during the latter part of the Truman administration, it came to a head under a Republican administration. The so-called "resurgence" of the right in the past year is, in part, undoubtedly a simple function of the Republican Party's again going into opposition.

In spite of this common substratum, in an important sense the current rightist preoccupations, typified perhaps by the John Birch Society, are the obverse of the McCarthyites. The right of the 1960s shares, of course, the symbol of Communism as the source of all evil, but its meaning has been shifted in a way that brings to the fore the other side of an ambivalent motivational complex.

An important symptom of the difference between McCarthyism and Birchism is the shift in the geographical center of gravity.[1] This is a move from the Middle West to the Southwest. (Texas, to be sure, is the common sector in both movements, and to some extent the same is true of that perennial hothouse of the exotic, Southern California.) This is no accident; the Southwest is the nearest thing left to a frontier, or, more specifically, Texas and Southern California are the sections that, despite a rapidly burgeoning urban civilization, still cherish the illusion that the old frontier is alive.

[1] For emphasizing this point, as well as considerable contribution to the general pattern of analysis outlined here, I am indebted to Dr. Winston White.

The essential point about the frontier is that it was the situation—in legend at least—of the predominance of self-help. Here a man—who was allegedly *really* a man—was most obviously "on his own." If "bad" men were about, he had to defend himself—and of course the good women—with his bare fists or his six-shooter. He made his living "honestly"—by wrestling with nature in the form of recalcitrant soils, drought, storm, and "ornery" beasts—so that no one could say when he won that it was because he was dependent on anyone.[2]

It seems to me that it is this fierce and hence "defensive" independence which is the hallmark of the most recent right.[3] The good life is to be completely untamed by the disciplines of complex society. From the point of view of this individualism, the income tax is a "tribute" exacted by a "foreign" usurper; namely, the urban, and more or less European, America. The income tax—attacks on which were by no means absent from the ideology of the McCarthy era (cf. the views of the late Representative Carroll Reece)—has been upgraded to become almost the central symbol of evil; i.e., the first entering wedge of "Communism." The reason why it is unexceptionably "Communist" is simply that it presumes to assert the authority of government. By taking away what "belongs to" the taxpayer, it symbolizes the arbitrariness in almost any regulation of the complete freedom of the individual to "do what he will with his own," and defend himself against all comers who challenge his rights.

This is the essential structure of the ambivalence. The McCarthyites demanded absolute subordination of all private rights to the government. McCarthy was in effect the most drastically radical "Socialist" imaginable. The Bircher demands nearly absolute immunity from any type of public control over his independence.

In this regard, the image of Communism is somewhat different in the two cases. In the original paper I argued that for the McCarthyites the aggression against the source that called for the development of government was the key to its pattern. To meet the threat of real Communism, there was a strengthening of responsible government and more centralized authority. To fight "Communism," which stands for the total state, McCarthy demanded even more centralized government. This is a motivational mechanism operating analogously to the normal oedipal situation—the resentment against the "father" as the symbolic source of the pressure to grow up, but also an identification with him. The McCarthyites, by demanding absolute loyalty, were in fact promoting a kind of distorted identification with government. The identification was carried out in a destructive way so as to threaten the many altogether

---

[2] A paradigmatic case of this frontier mentality is described in E. Z. Vogt, Jr., *Modern Homesteaders* (Harvard University Press), a study of "Texan" migrants into a semi-arid section of New Mexico.

[3] Another interesting manifestation of this complex is the part it plays in the opposition to the fluoridation of water supplies.

legitimate pluralistic loyalties and associations, to subordinate them altogether too drastically to the one national loyalty, and in the process to attack large numbers of completely innocent persons and in general spread an atmosphere of unwarranted distrust.

Except for the readiness in quick anger to deal summarily with sources of frustration, and hence to demand total victory over international Communism, the new right movements seem to lack this element of identification. Hence they are more regressive than McCarthy, in that they apparently seek, without qualification, to preserve the socially "infantile" state of everything "little." Their influence is even more drastically "deflationary" than the McCarthyite, in the constriction of commitments to the more highly organized sectors of society. This includes the extensive functions of government, but it also goes beyond them. Even the large corporation is in some sense felt to be vaguely "Socialistic," in that it interferes with the complete independence of the small man.

In this sense, the Birchers are the extreme wing of a much more ramified complex. The central focus of it seems to be the political rear-guard action (and its roots in the social structure) of the rural and small-town elements in the society, which have been able to "dig in," above all through legislative refusal to redistrict, first for the House of Representatives, but even more for the state legislatures. In this connection, the question of "equal protection of the laws" through fair representation is slowly building up to becoming the most important internal political question of the society, a question that crosscuts many of the older bases of political differentiation and segmentation, most conspicuously, of course, underlying the coalition of Republicans and Southern Democrats.[4]

But one must see, too, that "individualism" is by no means confined to a complex of what I have here called "regressive" attitudes. There is an opposite group whose orientation, though "ideological," presents a very different case from that of the reactionary individualists. These are the intellectuals whom Winston White has called the Moralizers.[5] Regarding themselves as liberals, or left of center, they deplore many of the features of contemporary society, in particular what they hold to be the increasing pressures to "conformity," but they also stress the importance of the responsibility of the individual, not for "self-help," but for the welfare of the society, and hence for the collective interest of the nation as a whole. They stand in an obverse relation to the Birchers, but in a quite different direction from that of the McCarthyites. The element of acceptance of the developing social order, of "identification" with it, as described above, is stronger for them than for the McCarthyites. It does not, however, involve a coerced loyalty, but the opposite—a free acceptance of individual

---

[4] The decision of the Supreme Court to restrict the legislatures' freedom to avoid redistricting may prove to be a highly important factor in this situation.

[5] *Beyond Conformity* (Free Press, 1961).

responsibility to the point of often being utopian about the necessity for formal organization and for authority that can implement important collective goals. Whereas the Birchers are drastically "deflationary" with respect to any sort of social responsibility, the Moralizers are "inflationary," in that they seem to hold that full commitment of the individual is enough —the practical organization and know-how are secondary.

But there is a third, and indeed a very different type of individualism that is focal to the whole American pattern of values and attitudes—the strong emphasis on freedom and responsibility of the individual *within* a framework of both normative order and collective organization. This is what on occasion I have called "institutionalized individualism," using Durkheim's famous analysis of the relation between contractual agreements and the "non-contractual" institutional elements of contract as a prototype.[6] In this point of view, we can see society as providing for more complex, more technical, and more "professional" jobs; allowing for more variety of choices, in occupation and in culture, and providing greater diversity within the framework of organization. It is my strong conviction that the main trend of development in the society is individualistic in *this* sense. [7]

The regressive individualism of which the Birchers are the extreme examples is very different from this. Regressive individualism resists the processes of institutional change by virtue of which a more complex and hence more effective division of labor or differentiation has been developing, by which there has developed an increasingly ramified system of pluralistic collective solidarities and enterprises (including, of course, the enterprises of government, but by no means confined to them[8]), and, finally, by which there has been developing a more generalized and elaborated system of norms, especially at the level of law, through which the inevitably complex relations of such a society come to be regulated. Seen in this perspective, the Birchers are the generic type of the true "reactionary." The phrase that has already been rather widely applied to them and to groups like them—that they want to "repeal the twentieth century"—seems to sum them up very well indeed.

[6] Cf. Emile Durkheim, *The Division of Labor in Society*, Bk. I, Ch. 7.

[7] Perhaps the fullest statement of the sense in which this is the case yet published is Parsons and White, "The Link Between Character and Society," in Lipset and Lowenthal, editors, *Culture and Social Character* (New York: The Free Press, 1961), reprinted in my collection, *Social Structure and Personality* (New York: The Free Press, 1964).

[8] Durkheim was one of the few to see clearly that the "division of labor" in the private sector must proceed concomitantly with increasing elaboration of the functions of government. Cf. Durkheim, *op. cit.*

Chapter 8

The Distribution of
Power in American
Society

*i*t has been remarked that it is relatively rare, in the United States at least, for social scientists to attempt interpretive analyses of major aspects of the total society in which they live. This is particularly true of sociologists, unlike economists, who have made notable attempts in recent years to interpret their societies—for example, Schumpeter's *Capitalism, Socialism and Democracy* and Galbraith's *American Capitalism*. The main exception is Robin M. Williams, whose *American Society* is excellent. If for this reason alone, Professor Mills's book, *The Power Elite*, which must be understood as one of a series as yet far from complete, would be worthy of serious attention.

In the nature of the case, to produce such a study is a very difficult enterprise. However operationally useful precise data may be—and Mills makes copious and, with some exceptions, relatively good use of them—they cannot suffice for a full empirical grounding of interpretive conclusions, not only because on their own level they are fragmentary and

Reprinted from World Politics, *vol. 10, 123–43. Reprinted in Talcott Parsons,* Structure and Process in Modern Societies, *Chapter 6, Copyright* © *1960, Free Press, New York, N.Y.*

incomplete, but because many of the crucial empirical questions arise on a level at which available operational procedures are not of much or any use. This is not in the least to say that observation is not feasible, but rather that it cannot be precise observation in the usual operational sense.

I am referring to questions of the type which are central to Mills' argument, as to whether and in what sense a relatively small group of the occupants of "command posts" in the society has acquired a paramount position of power, as to whether the relative power of such a group has greatly increased in the last twenty years, as to how unified such a group is, and the like.

There are technical ways of reducing the element of arbitrariness in such judgments and protecting them against at least the grosser sorts of ideological distortion. Checking against all the available precise data is one such method; viewing the problem from the perspective given by wide and deep knowledge, not only of our own society but of others, is another. But I think the most important is exercising control through the use of a relatively well-integrated and technical theoretical scheme. Undertaking as a professional sociologist to review Mills' book, I am motivated largely by the opportunity to test some of his main conclusions against expectations derived from a type of technical theory that is at best only partially shared by the author of the book. In these terms I wish to take serious issue with Mills' position on a number of very important points and to outline an alternative interpretation of what I take to be the salient facts of the situation. There are some points at which I differ from Mills on simple questions of fact, but for the most part my criticisms will deal with empirical generalizations and their theoretical background.[1] These generalizations concern not only the facts he chooses to state and emphasize but others he omits or treats as unimportant.

What is the gist of Mills' argument? I am able here to give only a very brief summary. The reader should not depend on this review alone for his information about the contents of the book itself, but should go directly to Mills' own statement of his case.

Mills' central theme is the contention—in contrast to what he refers to as the traditional view of the political pluralism of American society—that there has developed to an unprecedented degree, in the last generation or so, a concentration of power in the hands of a small, relatively tightly integrated group of people. These are defined as the people occupying the institutional "command posts" of the society, the places where the decisions are made that have the greatest immediate and direct

---

[1] Mills is clearly writing only partly for an audience of technical social scientists. Though my own argument will be largely based on considerations of technical theory, I shall not introduce explicit justification of my theoretical judgments into this review, but will try to state my case in relatively non-technical terms.

influence on the course of events in the society and on the shaping of its future and that of the rest of the world, so far as that future is dependent on what happens in the United States. Mills argues that the power of this group has grown disproportionately to the growth in size and power of the society as a whole.

The "command posts" in question are centered in large-scale organizations, which are certainly a prominent feature of American society. The power elite are in general those who occupy the main decision-making positions in these large organizations. Mills identifies these in only two basic areas, business and government—although for his purposes the field of government is subdivided into the military and the political sectors; indeed, he almost tends to treat the military as independent of the rest of government. He clearly is thinking of the centralized type of organization where a few "top executives" exercise the main immediate decision-making power, in contrast to the democratic association with a somewhat more decentralized structure of authority and influence. It seems to be largely on this ground that he contends that the executive branch of the federal government has gained a pronounced ascendancy over the legislative. He relegates Congress—even the most influential group of Senators—to what he calls the "middle level" of the power structure; such people do not belong to the "power elite."

Mills broadly identifies the power elite with the "upper class." But he does not agree with Lloyd Warner and his group that the primary element of this upper class is a hereditary group of families or lineages; its position clearly depends on occupational status, though there is also emphasis on the importance within it of the "very rich," the majority of whom have inherited their wealth. Contrary to most sociological usage, Mills restricts the term "class" to an economic meaning, so that by "upper class" he means, essentially, the rich. But this still leaves open the question of the substantive relations between inherited and newly acquired wealth, family status relatively independent of at least very large wealth, occupational status within various income ranges, and similar problems.

Generally, Mills is rather vague on the relations between the power elite and other elements which in some sense enjoy rather high prestige. He emphasizes the prominence of lawyers among the "political directorate," but there is no clear analysis of the role of professional groups in the occupational structure generally; one presumes that except for a few lawyers who are successful in politics or business, and perhaps some engineers, professional people do not belong to the power elite. Similarly he emphasizes that members of the power elite have more than the average amount of education, and in particular he stresses the proportion who have been to select private schools and to "Ivy League" colleges. In general, he is greatly concerned about the fact that the power elite are not "representative" of the population as a whole in the sense of constituting a random sample by socio-economic origin, by education, by ethnic group, etc. This is a point to which I shall return.

Neither the "higher circles" generally nor the component of the "very rich" (Mills' term) are a leisure class in Veblen's sense; many, if not most of them, "work" in various fields of business and financial management. Furthermore, the processes of recruitment are about what social scientists have come to expect. Mills does not give any exact criteria for what he considers to be "upper class" as a category of social origin, but I have the impression that he puts the line somewhat lower than most sociologists would. But, however that may be, it is clear that there is a considerable element of stability from generation to generation in the higher-status groups in American society. Thus if, to employ a pattern used by Mills, we take a group of prominent persons, the family origin of from two-thirds to three-fourths of them will be the upper third of the American status structure. It is not these essential facts but the interpretation placed upon them which raises questions for us. The only point of fact I would question is whether the recruitment of the very rich has shown a sharper increase through the process of inheritance than through self-earning. It is possible that this is so, but I am inclined to doubt it, and in any case their position does not depend only on the process which Mills calls "cumulative advantage."

Mills radically denies that the group he calls the "very rich" and the "corporate rich" are distinct "classes," in his sense. He explicitly lumps them together and on the whole gives the very rich a greater position of influence than they are usually accorded or than, I think, they actually enjoy. This is in line with his thesis that there is a single, unified power elite. Clearly, it is his contention that the base of the (business) group as a whole lies in command of the very large business enterprises—somewhat erroneously, or at least ambiguously, he puts the primary emphasis on control of property in accounting for this power.

Of the three main subgroups, Mills treats the "political directorate" as by far the weakest. It has, according to him, been greatly infiltrated by the business element, so that it can scarcely be treated as independent. Hence virtually the only element independent of what might be called the business oligarchy is the military—and this, he holds, is coming increasingly to fuse with the business group, or at least to form a close community of interest with it.

The pluralistic components of our older political traditions, Mills feels, are rooted primarily in local groupings—partly, of course, through the constitutional provisions which establish federalism and make Congressional representation dependent on local constituencies. But the operations of the big organizations have become national in scope, and often international. Hence structures rooted in localism have simply been pushed into a secondary position.

But at the same time Mills contends that the structural base of authentic localism has been progressively atrophied through the development of what he calls the "mass society." The most conspicuous phenomena of the mass society are the prevalence and characteristics of the media of mass communication, which tend to serve as instruments of the power elite out of the reach of locally based "publics" and influential elements in them. The theory of the mass society is only very sketchily presented in one chapter near the end of the book, but is clearly meant to provide one of the main components of the total picture of American society which Mills is presenting.

In terms of recent history, one of Mills' main contentions is that the New Deal period did not represent a turning point in social development, but rather a superficial flurry which only momentarily disturbed the process of emergence of the power elite and the dominance of the business contingent within it. Thus Mills speaks of the economic elite as in due course coming "to control and to use for their own purposes the New Deal institutions whose creation they had so bitterly denounced" (pp. 272–73).

Mills repeatedly disavows any intention of presenting a "conspiratorial" interpretation of American social and political development. He stresses the institutional positions occupied by his elite rather than their personalities and conspiratorial activities. Nevertheless he often comes very close to this implication because of the special theory that a peculiar irresponsibility attaches to the elite and their actions. By this he seems to mean the absence or relative ineffectiveness of formal legal restraints or of a system of "checks and balances" of the sort which has traditionally been associated with our political system. His contention, thus, is that the power elite has been freed from the historic restraints of our society and uses its power in terms of what he calls a "higher immorality"—a conception which is not very clearly explained.

Finally, it should be mentioned that in this, as in some of his previous writings, Mills' general tone toward both men and institutions is sharply caustic. *The Power Elite* certainly purports to be an exposition and an explanation of what has been happening in American society, but it is equally an indictment. There is no pretense of even trying to maintain a scientific neutrality; the book is a fiery and sarcastic attack on the pretensions of the "higher circles" in America, either to competence in exercise of their responsibilities, or to moral legitimation of their position. In such a case, the critic must ascertain the moral position from which the indictment is formulated; I shall have something to say about this later. In his combination of often insightful exposition and analysis, empirical one-sidedness and distortion, and moral indictment and sarcasm, Mills reminds one more of Veblen than of any other figure; that he has attained the stature of Veblen I question, but the role he is cutting out for himself is similar.

As I have said, the Mills analysis presents what, to me, is a subtle and complex combination of acceptable and unacceptable elements. Let me now attempt, at some of the most important points, to unravel these elements from each other. I want to try this first on the level of empirical generalization and then to raise one or two more strictly theoretical problems. I shall do so more in my own terms than in those employed by Mills.

In my opinion, two salient sets of processes have been going on in American society during the past half-century, the combination of which encompasses the main facts which are essential to our problem. The first of these is the dynamic of a maturing industrial society, including not only the highly industrialized economy itself but its setting in the society as a whole—notably, its political system and class structure (in a wider sense of the term "class" than Mills')—and the repercussions of the industrial development on the rest of the society. The second concerns the altered position of the United States in world society, which is a consequence in part of our own economic growth, in part of a variety of exogenous changes, including the relative decline of the Western European powers, the rise of Soviet Russia, and the break-up of the "colonial" organization of much of the non-white world. The enormous enhancement of American power and responsibility in the world has taken place in a relatively short time and was bound to have profound repercussions on the characteristics of our own society. Our old political isolation has disappeared and given way to the deepest of involvements.

My first thesis is that these two processes *both* work in the direction of increasing the relative importance of government in our society and, with it, of political power. But their impact has been all the greater because of the extent to which the United States has been an almost specifically non-political society. This has been evidenced above all in the institutions and tradition of political decentralization already mentioned, one aspect of which is the localism which Mills discusses. A second, however, has been a cultural tradition which has emphasized economic values—an emphasis on enterprise and production in an activist sense, not a merely passive hedonistic valuation of the enjoyment of material well-being. Moreover, the virtually unimpeded process of settlement of a continent in political isolation from the main system of world powers has favored maintenance of this emphasis to a greater extent than would otherwise have readily been possible.

At some points in his discussion, Mills seems to look back to the Jeffersonian picture of a system of economic production consisting mainly of small farmers and artisans, with presumably a small mercantile class mediating between them and consumers. Clearly this is not a situation compatible with high industrial development, in either of two respects. First, the order of decentralization of production, where the standard unit is a family-size one, is incompatible with either the organization or the technology necessary for high industrialism. Second, the "Jeffersonian" economy is not one in which economic production is differentiated from other social functions in specialized organizations; instead, the typical productive unit is at the same time a kinship unit and a unit of citizenship in the community.

In all salient respects, the modern economy has moved very far from the Jeffersonian ideal. The pace-setting units have become both large and specialized. Their development has been part of a general process of structural differentiation in the society which has led to greater specialization in many fields. An essential aspect of the process of development of the economy as a system in *both* these senses is greater specialization on at least three levels: first, the specialization of organizations in the functions of economic production as distinguished from other functions; second, the specialization of functions within the economy; and third, the specialization of the roles of classes of individuals within the organization.

Leadership is an essential function in all social systems which, with their increase of scale and their functional differentiation, tend to become more specialized. I think we can, within considerable limits, regard the emergence of the large firm with operations on a nation-wide basis as a "normal" outcome of the process of growth and differentiation of the economy. Similarly, the rise to prominence within the firm of specialized executive functions is also a normal outcome of a process of growth in size and in structural differentiation. The question then arises whether the process of concentration of firms, and of executive power within firms, has "gone too far" because it has been greatly influenced by factors extraneous to the process of economic development itself.

Mills makes the assertion that the size of the large firm has exceeded the limits of economic efficiency. He presents no evidence, and I think most competent persons would regard this as an exceedingly difficult question. There is, however, one line of evidence not cited by Mills which has a bearing on it. It is true that the absolute size of firms has steadily increased —General Motors today is larger than any firm of the 1920's. But the *relative* share of the largest firms in the production of the economy has remained essentially stable for more than a generation, a fact which points to some kind of equilibrium condition with respect to the degree of concentration in the system as a whole.

A cognate question is whether the power of the executive or managerial class within industry, and particularly within the large firms, has increased inordinately, which, if true, would indicate that factors other than the functional needs of the productive process were operating to skew the internal power structure of firms in favor of the executive groups.

Generally speaking, Mills' argument is that the power of the very rich and the corporate rich *within* the economy is inordinately great and, by virtue of the factor of cumulative advantage, is becoming continually greater. At the very least, I think, it can be said that his case is not proved and that there is equally good, if not better, evidence for an alternative view, particularly with reference to the trend.

First, I am not able to accept Mills' close identification of the very rich (i.e., the holders of "great fortunes") with the "corporate rich" (the primary holders of executive power in business organizations) as a single class in any very useful sense. Certainly, in the "heroic age" of American capitalism, from the Civil War to just after the turn of the century, the dominant figures were the entrepreneurs who, mainly as the founders of great enterprises and as the bankers and promoters concerned with mergers and reorganizations and the like, came to control these great organizations. But the dominant sociological fact of the outcome of that era was that these owning groups did not, as a group, succeed in consolidating their position precisely *within* their own enterprises and in the economy. It is a notorious fact that the *very* large enterprise, still largely under family control through property holdings, is much more the exception than the rule. Instead, the control has passed—by no means fully, but for the most part—to professional career executives, who have not reached their positions through the exercise of *property* rights but through some sort of process of appointment and promotion.

Mills concedes the main facts of this situation but fails, in my opinion, to evaluate them properly. It seems to be clear that the original "captains of industry," the makers of the great fortunes, *failed* to achieve or to exercise sufficient cumulative advantages to consolidate control of the enterprises in their families and their class ("class" in a sociological, not an economic, sense). This came about essentially because there were factors operating contrary to that of cumulative advantage, which Mills stresses so heavily. The main factor was the pressure to link executive responsibility with competence in such a way that the ascriptive rights of property ownership have tended to give way to the occupational functions of "professionals."

There are, above all, two ways in which Mills' treatment obscures the importance and nature of this shift. First, he continues to speak of power *within* the economy as based on property. To a considerable degree, of course, this is legally true, since the legal control of enterprise rests with stockholders. But, as Berle and Means first made abundantly clear, very generally it is not substantively true. In the old-style family enterprise, still predominant in the small-business sector of the economy, the functions of management and ownership are fused in the same people. In the larger enterprise they have by and large become differentiated. The fact that executives receive large salaries and bonuses is not to be twisted into an assumption that they control, so far as they do, through their property rights. Paradoxical as it may seem, a relatively backward industrial economy like that of France is far more *property*-based than is the case with the United States. In general, property holdings have not, of course, been expropriated, except for their diminution through inheritance and income taxes, which are not as negligible as Mills maintains. What has happened is that their relation to the *power* structure of the economy has been greatly altered. Mills almost entirely passes over this change.

The second problem concerns the process of recruitment in the higher occupational reaches of the economy. It is entirely clear that the process operates in the higher reaches overwhelmingly by appointment, i.e., the decisions of superiors as individuals or in small groups as to who should occupy certain positions. It is also true that the process is relatively un-formalized—e.g., there are no competitive examinations and few, if any, formal qualifications of training. But from these facts Mills concludes, and again and again reiterates, that executive competence has very little, if anything, to do with the selection, that it is an overwhelmingly arbitrary process of choosing those who are congenial to the selectors, presumably because they can be counted upon to be "yes men." At the very least this contention is unproved, and I seriously doubt its correctness. There are certainly many difficulties and imperfections in the selection process. But I think it almost certain that higher levels of competence are selected than would on the average be the case through kinship ascription, and that, as such processes go, the levels selected are relatively high.

One final point in this field. It does seem probable that the factor of cumulative advantage has a good deal to do with the high levels of financial remuneration of the higher executive groups and with the discrepancies between their incomes and those of governmental and professional people on comparable levels of competence and responsibility. But this is very far from the great fortune level of the founding entrepreneur type, and the evidence seems to be that the discrepancy has not been cumulatively increasing to an appreciable degree, particularly relative to wages at the labor levels; cases like that of the academic profession are somewhat special.

So far I have been speaking about the nature and power position of the elite *within* the economy. The general tenor of my argument has been that, given the nature of an industrial society, a relatively well-defined elite or leadership group *should be expected to develop* in the business world; it is out of the question that power should be diffused equally among an indefinite number of very small units, as the ideal of pure competition and a good deal of the ideology of business itself would have it. But first I question whether the position of power of the business leadership groups is such that a heavy operation of the factor of cumulative advantage must be invoked to account for it. Secondly, I must stress that the business elite is no longer primarily an elite of *property*-owners, but that its center of gravity has shifted to occupationally professional executives or managers. Differential advantages of family origin, etc., are about the same for admission to this group as to other groups requiring educational and other qualifications. Again the evidence is that the proportion of its members recruited from the upper economic and social groups is and remains relatively high, but it has not, in recent times, been increasing, as the theory of cumulative advantage would lead us to expect.

The problem of an elite within the economy must, however, be clearly distinguished from that of an elite in the society as a whole and the power position occupied by such an elite. There are two main orders of questions bearing on the transition from one to the other. Though a thorough consideration of this transition would lead into very far-reaching questions, for present purposes one can be treated rather briefly. Mills gives us the impression that "eliteness" in any society, including our own, is overwhelmingly a question of the power that an individual or a group can command. By this, he means (I shall further discuss his concept of power presently) influence on the "big" decisions directly affecting what happens in the society in the short run. But there are many elements in the society which are relatively powerless in this sense, but nevertheless of the greatest functional importance. Our society has almost divested kinship units as such of important power in this sense. But this does not mean at all that the family has ceased to be important. Closely linked with this is the question of the feminine role. Women *qua* women by and large do not have a position of power comparable to that of men; but this is not to say that they are unimportant—otherwise how can we account for the extent of our national preoccupations with questions of sexuality? Finally, there is a *distinct* difference between the rank-order of occupations—which, relative to other role-types, are closely involved with decision-making in a society like ours—by power and by prestige. The most striking case is the relatively high position of the professions relative to executive roles in business, as revealed by the famous North-Hatt data. Physicians as a group do not exercise great power, but there is no reason to question their very high prestige, which has been demonstrated in study after study.

The second main context, however, directly concerns the question of power. In a complex society the primary locus of power lies in the political system. There are many subtle analytical problems involved in the delineation of this system and its functions in the society which cannot be gone into here; this formula will have to suffice. Two questions are, however, primary for our purposes: the degree of differentiation of the political system from other systems; and its own internal structure. These two problems, it will be noted, parallel those raised with reference to the economy.

For historical reasons, it seems clear that the development of the

American political system, since the breakdown of the first synthesis associated with the "founders of the Republic," has lagged behind that of the economy. This is a function primarily of the two factors already noted—the economic emphasis inherent in our system of values, and the relative lack of urgency of certain political problems because of our especially protected and favored national position. Relative to the economic structure, which had by that time grown enormously, the political was at its weakest in the period from the Civil War to the end of the century; this situation is sketched by Mills in broadly correct terms. Since then, both internal exigencies and the exigencies of our international position have been stimuli for major changes.

Internally, beyond the more elementary provisions for law and order and essential minimum services—much of this, of course, on a local basis —the main focus of the development of our political system has been *control* of economic organization and processes, and coping with some of the social consequences of economic growth and industrialization. The process started well before the turn of the century with the Interstate Commerce legislation and the Anti-Trust Act and continued through the New Deal era, not steadily but with waves of new measures and levels of political control.

A major problem in relation to Mills' analysis is whether this is "genuine" control. His view seems to be that at times it has been, but that on balance it is the business powerholders who control government, not vice versa. In my opinion this is a misinterpretation. If genuine and, in some sense, effective controls had not been imposed, the results would surely have been disastrous and thus I find it impossible to understand the bitter and continuing opposition on the part of business to the measures which have been taken. Even some of those most completely taken for granted now, like the Federal Reserve system, were bitterly fought at the time. It therefore seems to me to be the sounder interpretation that there has been a genuine growth of autonomous governmental power— apart from the military aspect, which will be discussed presently—and that one major aspect of this has been relatively effective control of the business system. This control and the growth of "big government" have been generally accepted in the society as a whole. The participation of big-business men in governmental processes is by no means to be interpreted as a simple index of their power to dominate government in their own interests, as Mills often seems to maintain.

To me, another indication of Mills' biased view of the governmental situation is his almost complete failure even to mention the political parties, or to analyze their differences. It seems to me broadly true that the Republican party, though a coalition, is more than any other single thing the party of the bigger sector of business. Four years of a Republican administration—two of them without control of Congress—is certainly not enough to indicate that big business, through its favorite party organ, controls the government on a long-run basis. So Mills is practically forced to the view that the alleged control operates above and beyond the party system. This seems to be connected with his relegation of the legislative branch to the "middle level" of power. I have strong reservations about this, but also it must not be forgotten that the presidency is the biggest prize of all in party politics, and it is its importance which forms the primary integrating focus of our particular type of party system. Surely the presidency is not simply the football of an inner clique which manipulates the executive branch independently of the party.

Mills, of course, recognizes that the aftermath of two world wars, the rise of Communist power, and the relative decline of the older Western Great Powers provide the occasion for the increasing prominence of the military group in our governmental system. Before these changes—and, indeed, to a remarkable extent, as late as the 1930's—the military played a far smaller role in this country than in any other society of comparable scale and organizational and technological development. Part of the change may be interpreted as simply the redressing of a balance. But it seems to me correct to say that for the last ten years there has been a special situation attributable to the extremely unsettled condition of the world at large and to the difficulties entailed for the American system, given its background, in meeting the problem on its own terms. There is thus a sense in which it is true that the higher military officers have tended to fill a vacuum in the field of national decision-making. There are two main points to be made about Mills' treatment of the matter. First, more in this field than perhaps any other, Mills' discussion is marred by a hasty tendency to generalize from very recent short-run developments to the long-run prospects of the structure of the society. Even here he fails to mention that in certain crucial questions the recommendations of the military have been overruled by civilian authority, although the President is a former military man. Secondly, the tone of indictment, particularly evidenced by the quite unnecessary and, I think, inappropriate parading of the term "warlord," is stronger in his discussion of this area than in any any other, except perhaps the "mass society."

Related to the position of the higher military officers is what Mills calls the "military metaphysic," meaning the definition of international problems in terms of the primacy of military force. That there has been such a tendency, and that it has gone beyond the objective requirements of the situation, seem to be unquestionable. But I very much doubt whether it is as absolute as many of Mills' statements make it appear, and a swing in another direction is discernible. This seems to be another case of Mills' tendency to make large generalizations about major trends from short-run experience.

Finally, let us say a word about what Mills calls the "political direcntate"—that is, the non-military component in the groups most influential in the affairs of government and politics. Again I think there is a certain correctness in his contention that a definite weakness exists here, and that the high participation both of business and of military elements in the exercise of power is related to this. But a difficulty arises in terms of the perspective on American society which I have been emphasizing throughout. Both the non-political stress in American social structure and values generally, and the recency and intensity of the pressures to build up this aspect of our structure, would lead one to predict that it would be a major focus of strain. American society has not developed a well-integrated political-government elite, in the sense that it has developed a relatively well-integrated business-executive group. For this reason responsibility has been carried—imperfectly, of course—by a very miscellaneous group which includes members of the business and military groups, as would be expected, but also "politicians," in the usual sense of people making an at least partial career out of elective office and the influencing of elections; professional people, particularly lawyers but also economists, political scientists, and even natural scientists (e.g., John von Neumann as Atomic Energy Commissioner); journalists; and, a very important element, upper-class people in more than the purely economic sense that Mills employs, of whom Franklin Roosevelt was one and Adlai Stevenson, though also a lawyer, is another. In my opinion, the structure of the American political leadership group is far from a settled thing. It certainly is not settled in terms of the long-run dominance of a business-military coalition.

Mills holds that the United States has no higher civil service at all, in the European sense, and seems to imply that we should have. There is relative truth in his empirical contention, though I think he tends to underestimate the real influence of "non-political" government officials on longer-run policy. Good examples are the Department of Agriculture and the Reclamation Service of the Department of the Interior—and now, increasingly, the Public Health Service. I think that this is even true of the Foreign Service, and that Mills here, as in so many other connections, seriously exaggerates the probable long-run consequences of the McCarthyites' intervention in the affairs of the State Department.

At least it seems highly probable that, in the nature of the case, the tendency will be toward a strengthening of the element of professional governmental officials who are essentially independent both of short-run "politics" and of elements extraneous to the structure of government and its responsibilities. In fact, the military officer is a special case of this type, and though his role is not stabilized, it presumably must come to be more important than it traditionally has been. However, it is questionable how far the specific models of civil service organization either of Britain or of Continental Europe—particularly, certain of their special connections with the class structure and the educational system—are appropriate to American conditions. Such connections in the American case would accentuate rather than mitigate the prominence of the Ivy League element to which Mills so seriously objects. I think it correct to say that five years of Labour government in Britain, far from lessening the prominence of Oxford and Cambridge educations as qualifications for the civil service, in fact increased their relative importance, by increasing the national importance of the civil service itself.

Above all, I do not think that Mills has made a convincing case for his contention that the power structure impinging directly on American government is in process of crystallizing into a top business-military coalition with a much weaker political "junior partner" whose main function presumably is, by manipulation of the mass media and the political process in the narrower sense, to keep the great majority of Americans from protesting too loudly or even from awakening to what allegedly is "really" going on. On a number of counts which have been reviewed, there is a case on a short-run basis for part of his interpretation. But I think that the kinds of factors brought out in the previous discussion make it extremely dubious that even the partial correctness of his interpretation of a current situation will prove to be a sound indicator of what is to be expected over such longer periods as a generation or more.

My conviction on this point is strengthened by a variety of other considerations which, for reasons of space, cannot be discussed here, but may be mentioned. First, I am extremely skeptical of Mills' interpretation of what he calls the "mass society," which includes the structural position of the great majority of the American population. In this he ignores both kinship and friendship, and the whole mass of associational activities and relationships. One example is the spread of church membership—which I suppose Mills would dismiss as simply an escape from the boredom of white-collar life, but in my opinion is of considerable positive significance.

Another very important complex which Mills either treats cavalierly or ignores completely involves education at the various levels, and with it the enormous development, over a century, of science and learning and the professions resting upon them. It is true that the people rooted in these areas of the social structure are not prominent in the power elite, and are even subject to some conflicts with it; but they would not be expected to be prominent in this way—their functions in the society are different. Nonetheless, they must be taken very seriously into account in a diagnosis of what has been happening to the society as a whole. One of the most important sets of facts concerns the ways in which the services of technical professional groups have come to penetrate the structures both of business and of government, a circumstance which over a period of time has greatly enhanced the role of the universities as custodians of learning and sources of trained personnel.

Finally, there is one special case of a professional group whose role Mills treats with serious inadequacy—namely, lawyers. First, he dismisses the judicial branch of governmnent as just "trailing along," with the implication that with a slight lag it simply does the bidding of the "real" holders of power. This seems to be a most biased appraisal of the role of the courts. Not to speak of the longer-run record, the initiative taken by the courts in the matter of racial segregation and in the reassertion of civil liberties after the miasma of McCarthyism does not appear to me to be compatible with Mills' views. Similar considerations seem to apply to various aspects of the role of the private legal profession, notably with respect to the *control* of processes in the business world. Mills tends to assume that the relation between law and business is an overwhelmingly one-way relation; lawyers are there to serve the interests of businessmen and essentially have no independent influence. This, I think, is an illusion stemming largely from Mills' preoccupation with a certain kind of power. His implicit reasoning seems to be that since lawyers have less power than businessmen, they do not really "count."

III

The last problem I wish to raise, therefore, concerns Mills' conception of power and its use as a category of social analysis. Unfortunately, the concept of power is not a settled one in the social sciences, either in political science or in sociology. Mills, however, adopts one main version of the concept without attempting to justify it. This is what may be called the "zero-sum" concept; power, that is to say, is power *over* others. The power A has in a system is, necessarily and by definition, at the expense of B. This conception of power then is generalized to the whole conception of the political process when Mills says that "Politics is a struggle for power."

Within limits, every student of social affairs is free to define important concepts the way he prefers; there is no canonically "correct" definition. But choosing one alternative will have consequences which differ from those implied in another, and this is the case with Mills' conception of power. The essential point at present is that, to Mills, power is not a facility for the performance of function in, and on behalf of, the society as a system, but is interpreted exclusively as a facility for getting what one group, the holders of power, wants by preventing another group, the "outs," from getting what it wants.

What this conception does is to elevate a secondary and derived aspect of a total phenomenon into the central place. A comparison may help to make this clear. There is obviously a distributive aspect of wealth and it is in a sense true that the wealth of one person or group by definition cannot also be possessed by another group. Thus the *distribution* of wealth is, in the nature of the case, a focus of conflicts of interest in a society. But what of the positive functions of wealth and of the conditions of its production? It has become fully established that the wealth available for distribution can only come about through the processes of production, and that these processes require the "co-operation" or integration of a variety of different agencies—what economists call the "factors of production." Wealth, in turn, is a generalized class of facilities available to units of the society—individuals and various types and levels of collectivities—for whatever uses may be important to them. But even apart from the question of what share each gets, the fact that there should be wealth to divide, and how much, cannot be taken for granted as given except within a very limited context.

Very similar things can be said about power in a political sense. Power is a generalized facility or resource in the society. It has to be divided or allocated, but it also has to be produced and it has collective as well as distributive functions. It is the capacity to mobilize the resources of the society for the attainment of goals for which a general "public" commitment has been made, or may be made. It is mobilization, above all, of the action of persons and groups, which is *binding* on them by virtue of their position in the society. Thus within a much larger complex Mills concentrates almost exclusively on the distributive aspect of power. He is interested only in *who* has power and what *sectoral* interests he is serving with his power, not in how power comes to be generated or in what communal rather than sectoral interests are served.

The result is a highly selective treatment of the whole complex of the power problem. There is, in the first place, a tendency to exaggerate the empirical importance of power by alleging that it is only power which "really" determines what happens in a society. Against this, I would place the view that power is only one of several cognate factors in the determination of social events. This bias of Mills is particularly evident in his tendency to foreshorten social processes and emphasize overwhelmingly short-run factors. There is, secondly, the tendency to think of power as presumptively illegitimate; if people exercise considerable power, it must be because they have somehow usurped it where they had no right and they intend to use it to the detriment of others. This comes out most conspicuously in Mills' imputation of irresponsibility to his "power elite" and the allegation, vaguely conceived and presented with very little evidence, that they are characterized by a "higher immorality." It is notable that as he approaches the climax indicated by the title of his final chapter the tone of indictment becomes shriller and shriller and the atmosphere of objective analysis recedes.

Back of all this lies, I am sure, an only partly manifest "metaphysical" position which Mills shares with Veblen and a long line of indicters of modern industrial society. I would call it a utopian conception of an ideal society in which power does not play a part at all.

This is a philosophical and ethical background which is common both to utopian liberalism and socialism in our society and to a good deal of "capitalist" ideology. They have in common an underlying "individualism" of a certain type. This is not primarily individualism in the sense that the welfare and rights of the individual constitute fundamental moral values, but rather that *both* individual and collective rights are alleged to be promoted only by *minimizing* the positive organization of social groups. Social organization as such is presumptively bad because, on a limited, short-run basis, it always and necessarily limits the freedom of the individual to do exactly what he may happen to want. The question of the deeper and longer-run dependence of the goals and capacities of individuals themselves on social organization is simply shoved into the background. From this point of view, both power in the individual enterprise and power in the larger society are presumptively evil in themselves, because they represent the primary visible focus of the capacity of somebody to see to it that somebody else acts or does not act in certain ways, whether at the moment he wants to or not.

There are, in contemporary society, three main versions of this individualistic utopianism, which may be called "liberal" and "capitalist" and "socialist"—I place all three terms in quotation marks deliberately. The liberal version is mainly "humanistically" oriented to the *total* welfare of the individual as a person, and in American terms it is very likely to assume a Jeffersonian cast, to hold up the vision of a simpler and hence almost by definition "better" society against the inhumanities and impersonalities of large-scale modern industrialism and all its concomitants.

The capitalist version is, with all the qualifications which such an assertion must occasion, *primarily* production-oriented. Essentially it says that, whatever the cost to individuals—including even businessmen themselves, or especially so—production must be achieved, carried on, and so far as possible increased. This is the focus of what has been called the "business creed." Understandably it has been highly sensitive to "interferences" on both fronts, from liberal sources which would sacrifice productivity to humanistic values, and from governmentalist sources which would "interfere" with the businessman's primary responsibility for production. Social organization beyond the level of the firm is thus presumptively a limitation of its freedom.

The socialist version has been a secondary theme in American ideology largely because of the a-political character of American society, which, as I have noted, has been prominent historically. The opposition to capitalism has centered on two fronts: the control of the economy in the interests of preventing abuses of power, and the steering of the benefits of productivity in the humanistic direction of "welfare." But the socialist questions whether *control* of the abuses of private enterprise is possible at all; to him, for the state to take over production directly is the only way. From this perspective, furthermore, the "Jeffersonian" version of romantic utopianism seems particularly unrealistic and unacceptable.

From one point of view, the socialist romanticizes the state and the political process. Whereas he distrusts private interests almost totally and feels that they cannot be entrusted with any responsibility, he romantically believes that if public authority alone is entrusted with all responsibilities, all will be well—because some mystical "popular will" or "public interest" controls it—forgetting that public authority, like other forms of social organization, is administered by human beings. And that he does not fundamentally trust even public authority is evidenced by his ultimate ideal that the state should "wither away" and the spontaneous co-operation of institutionally unorganized human beings should take over. The socialist has been put in a particularly difficult position in the contemporary world by the development of Communism which, while still paying lip service to the eventual withering-away of the state, carries the enforcement of its predominance over all private interests, including the liberties of its citizens, to the totalitarian extreme.

Mills does not make his own position explicit in this book. As noted, at times he speaks like a nostalgic Jeffersonian liberal. I understand, however, that he professes to be a socialist—non-Communist, of course. But a basic strain of his thinking is consistent with both wings of the liberal-socialist dilemma on the basically *individualistic* premises that I have outlined: either that social organization beyond the level of the family and the local community is a bad thing *in toto*, or that is is instrumentally justified only to get society over a particular hump, the threat of the capitalist evil.

Mills seems to be suggesting that the development of the power elite is bringing that capitalist evil to a climax, to a situation which is intolerable to liberals and socialists alike. I suggest an alternative view: that, though of course accompanied by a whole range of "abuses," the main lines of social development in America are essentially acceptable to a humanistic ethic which in my case is closer to the liberal than to either of the other two outlined here. But it differs in not being in the older sense an individualistic liberalism. If the individualistic assumptions are modified in favor of a set which not only admit the necessity but assert the desirability of positive social organization, much of the ideological conflict between the three positions as total "systems" evaporates. Above all, it can be positively asserted that power, while of course subject to abuses and in need of many controls, is an essential and desirable component of a highly organized society. This position, in asserting and justifying the increased importance of government, thus grants that there is a grain of truth in the "socialist" theme. There is, however, also some justification for the existence of "capitalism," if by that is meant the institutionalization of responsibility for the larger part of economic production in the hands of a variety of private, non-governmental agencies. To my mind, there is no more reason why all important economic production should be controlled by government than why all scientific research should be.

Hence, in my opinion, many of the difficulties of Mills' analysis of a crucial problem in American society arise from his failure to transcend the dilemmas inherent in much of the individualistic tradition in American and, more broadly, in Western thought. It seems to me that he is clearly and, in the degree to which he pushes this position, unjustifiably anti-capitalist. He is partly pro-liberal and probably even more pro-socialist. But in the American scene a choice between these old alternatives of ideological orientation is no longer enough. It is necessary not only to criticize existing conditions from the older philosophical or ideological points of view, but to take serious stock of the ideological assumptions underlying the bulk of American political discussion of such problems as power.

Chapter 9

"Voting" and the Equilibrium of the American Political System

*t*his chapter[1] concerns certain *theoretical* issues raised by the research studies that the volume *American Voting Behavior* as a whole discusses in a broader framework. There are two broad types of problem involved in the studies as a whole, namely (1) why a given *individual* votes as he does, and (2) how the voting process functions as part of the *social system* in which it operates. I shall focus my attention on the latter, the sociological, as distinct from the psychological problem. The two are, however, so closely interwoven in the studies that some discussion of the relation between the two problems will prove necessary. I shall also, like the studies themselves, be concerned with recent presidential elections in the United States.

Because of the compactness with which *Voting*[2] presents a set of findings and interpretations that throw a great deal of light on political

[1] I am indebted to Samuel A. Stouffer, John W. and Matilda Riley, and Charles Drekmeier for a number of stimulating suggestions.
[2] B. R. Berelson, P. F. Lazarsfeld, and W. N. McPhee, *Voting* (Chicago: University of Chicago Press, 1954).

Reprinted from American Voting Behavior, *ed. Eugene Burdick and Arthur Brodbeck. Copyright* © *1959 by The Free Press.*

process in a society like ours and on the whole fit very well with a generalized analysis in terms of the theory of social systems, I shall concentrate my attention on it. To show the relation between such an analysis and the findings will be my main theme. Naturally, critical questions will be raised at certain points, but I shall not anticipate them.

A framework of broad analysis of certain aspects of the structure, processes, and functional problems of the American political system will be developed, and then applied to the principal findings of the study.

A THEORETICAL MODEL OF A TWO-PARTY SYSTEM

The political aspect of a social system may be thought of as centered on the generation and distribution of power. Power may, for the present purposes, be conceived as the capacity of the society to mobilize its resources in the interest of goals, defined as positively rather than permissively sanctioned by the system as a whole—goals that are "affected with a public interest." The amount of its power is an attribute of the total system and is a function of several variables. These, as I conceive them, are the *support* that can be mobilized by those exercising power, the *facilities* they have access to (notably the control of the productivity of the economy), the *legitimation* that can be accorded to the positions of the holders of power, and the relatively *unconditional loyalties* of the population to the society in its politically organized aspects. It is above all the factor of support which will be the center of concern here. In a modern, differentiated society the most important "producers" of power on the collectivity level, though by no means the sole ones, are those who hold responsible positions in what we call the structure of government—here, of course, the federal government.

An old question about power needs to be mentioned. One school of thought emphasizes power as power *over* others, with the implication that in a larger system the power held by different units must cancel out. My own emphasis is on power as capacity to get things done. Whether there is opposition or not is an empirically very important but theoretically secondary matter. My point of reference will be the *capacity of a social system to get things done in its collective interest.* Hence power involves a special problem of the *integration* of the system, including the binding of its units, individual and collective, to the necessary commitments.

Looked at in this way, the capacity to act focuses on the capacity for an agency or system of organization to make decisions responsibly, that is, with relative assurance that they can be effectively carried out. Power is essentially the basis of responsible action in this sense. The variables just mentioned are the "ingredients" of power—which can vary in quantity and combination; on them capacity for responsible action depends.

I have defined power as the capacity of a social system to mobilize resources to attain collective goals. A total society's paramount "goal" must be conceived on a very high level of abstraction. It is a function primarily of two sets of factors: the institutionalized value system of the society, and the exigencies of the situation. Together they define states of affairs that need to be changed in the interest of a higher level of value-implementation. The specificity of a societal goal will vary greatly for different societies, but in any case there will be many subgoals that vary as functions of a societal development and the manifold relations of the society to the situation.

The value system of the contemporary United States centers on what may be called "instrumental activism." It is oriented to control the action situation in the interest of range and quality of adaptation, but with more economic than political emphasis. In goal definition it is highly indefinite and pluralistic, being committed to a rather general direction of progress or improvement, without any clearly defined terminal goal. Economic production is highly valued as the most immediate focus of adaptive capacity. Beyond that, however, we particularly value technology and science as means to productivity, and the maximization of opportunity for individuals and subcollectivities (manifested above all in concern with health and education). Moreover, we have a special set of attitudes toward organization and authority which might be summed up as involving, on the one hand, a pragmatic acceptance of authority in the interest of limited, specifically approved goals, but, on the other hand, an objection to any pretensions of generalized superiority of status.

The over-all goal of American society (in a special technical sense) may then be tentatively defined as the *facilitation* of effective adaptive development of the society and of the societal conditions associated with it. It centers on economic development, but definitely includes the integrative conditions that are relevant. At the next lower level of specification, American society stresses the more immediate facilitation of production and the development of productivity, the effective ordering of political organization itself, the furthering of effective integration of the social system, and the promoting of conditions on the level of opportunity for operation of the system and adjustment of personalities.

The generation and allocation of power in a society occurs through a set of structures and processes, a subsystem parallel to the economy which we may call the "polity." It is essentially a functional-relational system, controlled by institutional patterns and controlling collectivities and roles.[3] The relevant institutional patterns are those governing the hierarchical

---

[3] The concept of the economy used here is fully discussed in Talcott Parsons and N. J. Smelser, *Economy and Society* (New York: The Free Press, 1956). The parallel concept of the polity has

ordering of social statuses, authority, and the compulsory regulation of "private" activities. The focus of the collectivity structure is clearly government, though there is a political as well as economic component in all collectivities in the society. Government is that complex of collectivities which have political *primacy*. This means that governmental organizations primarily, in their relations to the rest of the society, generate power and make it available to the rest of the society.

Like the economy, the polity is an analytically distinct subsystem of the society. It too is conceived to stand in relations to other parts of the society which involve the interchange of inputs and outputs over its boundaries. Of these interchanges, one is of primary importance for present purposes. It may be characterized through a comparison between the functions of government and those of the polity. On the federal level, which alone will concern us here, the main functions of government are relatively clearly set forth in the Constitution itself. The most important concern the conduct of foreign relations, the regulation of commerce between the states, the enforcement of rights (personal freedom, opportunity, property), the ensuring of justice and internal order, and the promotion of the "general welfare." Broadly, this constitutional mandate is to implement within a certain framework the goals of the society as sketched above.

The functions of the polity, as contrasted with those of government, I conceive to center in creating the conditions necessary if those assuming responsibility in government are to be able to assume and discharge this responsibility. Given the American value system these may be said to be (1) the legitimation of the powers of government and the statuses of its various subcollectivities and offices; (2) the requisite share in the control of the basic facilities available in the society, especially control of the productivity of the economy through the establishment of "rights to intervene"; and (3) the mobilization of "support" for the assumption, by office holders in government, of leadership roles and the corresponding responsibilities for formulation of more specific goals and their implementation.[4]

The theoretical analysis of this chapter concerns the third of these conditions of responsible leadership. I shall call this the "goal-attainment" process of the polity as a system. *Its* goal, which must be distinguished from that of the society as a whole as sketched above, is to generate power in the political sense, that is, to mobilize "resources" that can be used to

---

[4] The reader will note that these are the variables introduced above.

not previously been discussed in print, except sketchily in the above publication. Unfortunately limitations of space make it impossible to present it here, also, except in very sketchy form. A brief discussion of these and related concepts in formal theoretical terms appears in the Technical Note appended to this chapter. Cf. also my paper "The Political Aspect of Social Structure and Process" in David Easton (ed.), *Varieties of Political Theory* (Englewood Cliffs, N.J.: Prentice-Hall, 1966). (Reprinted as Chapter 13 in the present volume: ed.)

implement societal goals. There are two main levels on which this goal is (more or less effectively) achieved. The more general is the provision of effective *leadership* in the goal-specification and goal-implementation processes on the requisite collective level. The more specific is arriving at *decisions* which are binding on the society as a politically organized collectivity. For present purposes the subsystem that functions as recipient of these outputs of the polity may be referred to as the "public."

We are, however, speaking of a boundary-interchange process and must be concerned not only with outputs from the polity but also with the inputs to the polity from the public—which on the one hand are essential factors in its functioning, on the other are in certain ways contingent on its performance. I should like to suggest that support (point 3) is the appropriate input category (from public to polity) which matches the outputs of provision of leadership and making of decisions. At the more general level, the support that is exchanged with and contingent upon leadership is *generalized*. It takes the form of broadly based confidence in those assuming responsibility for leadership in governmental affairs which is necessary to enable them to act with real power, that is, to make necessary and far-reaching decisions responsibly in the sense that elements of the population affected will accept the consequences. Such consequences inevitably include burdens and obligations that affect some elements adversely and bear unevenly on different groups. On the lower level of generality, the relevant type of support which corresponds to decision-making may be said to be the *advocacy of policies*. By this I mean an accepting attitude on a level more general than that of specific decisions but less general than that of an "Administration" in the American or a "Government" in the British sense (which is a term of generalized support).

In the above formulation I am thinking self-consciously in terms of a parallel with the corresponding boundary-interchange of the economy, the one involved vis-à-vis the household with labor as a factor of production and the production of consumers' goods. On the higher level of generalization the primary output of the economy to the household is the production of *income* in the monetary sense—in the labor case, wage income. On the lower level it is the production of specific commodities made available to consumers. The corresponding inputs to the economy from the household are, on the high level, labor in the factor sense and, on the lower level, consumers' spending.

These relations of interchange of inputs and outputs—on the one hand, between the economy and the household—may be represented diagrammatically in a simple way as follows:[5]

---

[5] The paradigm for this boundary-interchange of the economy (with the household in the empirically primary case) is set forth in Parsons and Smelser, *op. cit.,* Chap. 2. Cf. especially Fig. 5, p. 11. A simplified version of the general interchange paradigm is presented in the Technical Note.

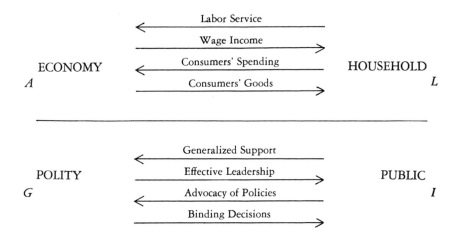

* For an explanation of the notation, *A, G, I, L,* see final section of this chapter entitled, Technical Note.

I shall have this parallel in mind throughout the following analysis. It should be clearly understood, however, that it is a parallel—in the strict sense an analogy—and not an identity. Power as an output is not income in the economic sense, decisions are not commodities, support is not labor, and consumers' spending is not advocacy of policies. In an analytical sense the "public," as the source of support and advocacy of policies, is altogether different from the household, as the source of labor and consumers' spending, though members of households are at the same time parts of the public. I shall delineate the relevant characteristics of the public as we go along.[6]

Let us now attempt to apply this abstract analytical scheme to some familiar facts of American political structure. I have stated that the focus of political organization on the collectivity level is government, in our case the federal government. The boundary-interchange just outlined is that set of processes by which control of the federal government is decided, its major policies are worked out, and public attitudes toward them are influenced and brought to bear. The focus of the mechanisms by which the processes work out is what we call the party system. At the support level the most important single process on the side of the public is voting because, under our constitutional system, this decides who is to assume the primary roles of responsible leadership.

There are, of course, many other influences on leadership: media of opinion, behind-the-scenes persuasion and threats, financial interests, and the like. But voting is the central focus of the process of selection of

[6] In technical analytical terms I conceive the public in this sense as an aspect of the integrative subsystem of the society. See Parsons and Smelser, *op. cit.,* pp. 51–70 and Fig. 4, p. 68.

leadership, and hence in one sense all other influences must channel their effects *through* the voting process.

The most important fact about the American situation is the existence on the national level of the *two*-party system which, with some interruptions, has proved stable over a long period. This means that the presidency must at any given time be occupied by the candidate of one of the two parties, and that the majority party in each house of Congress has the opportunity to "organize" its house through the speakership (in the case of the House of Representatives) and chairmanships and majorities of committees. In spite of the looseness of party discipline there can be no doubt of the overwhelming importance of this two-party structure.

Within the complex of operation of the two-party system this analysis, in line with the empirical studies with which it is concerned, will be confined to the voting processes that determine the incumbency of the presidency. It is, of course, vital to realize that the process of electing the President, considered as a system, is only part of a larger one. It has been noted that a variety of influences operate to determine the decisions of voters. But even where the voting mechanism itself is concerned, voting for presidential candidates is only part of the voter's function and opportunity. The separation of powers means that he also votes for congressional candidates and for state and local offices.

A salient fact of American politics is that there is only a rough correlation between party votes for President and for these other offices. The looseness of party discipline and the plural voting opportunities provided in the American system mean that in no sense can the determination of the presidency be considered a *closed* system. For example, tensions generated by being forced to choose between only two candidates for President may be expressed in supporting for other offices candidates not in sympathy with the presidential candidate, or candidates of the opposing party. Empirical statements made in the following analysis should always be qualified with these considerations in mind.

Nevertheless, I think it is legitimate to consider the voting process by which Presidents are elected as authentically a *social system*. It is a set of processes of action and interaction which may be treated in terms of specific modes of interdependence which can be analytically separated from other influences. Furthermore, in our system, the Presidency is the focus of integration of the political system as a whole. Of course, the concrete data that will be reviewed are affected by factors emanating from outside this particular system—including the other voting processes in other subsystems of the political structure. But in principle this is true of any social system that is a subsystem of a larger one, that is, less than the total society.

To return to the substantive discussion, the main function of political organization is the facilitation of effective action on collective levels. The two-party system may be regarded as a mechanism that makes possible a certain balance between effectiveness through relative centralization of power, and mobilization of support from different sources in such a way that there is genuine contingency—the supporter is offered a real alternative.[7] Dictatorships naturally are different; their concern is to avoid losing support lest the opposition become dangerous, and there is a strong tendency to use coercive measures in coping with actual or feared opposition. But the two-party system, as has often been pointed out, makes it possible for the holders of power to be changed without upsetting the system. Naturally this depends on definite institutional conditions, notably the acceptance of electoral results by the losing side without impairment of basic loyalties, and the restraint of winners from using their power to suppress opposition. It depends overwhelmingly on the firm institutionalization of such "rules of the game."

All this I take for granted. The point of present interest is that the two-party system, as distinguished from a many-party system or one of an indefinite number of shifting factions, has certain implications for the structure of support in its relation to leadership. This way of structuring the situation forces a high level of *generalization* of support on the one side, of responsibility on the other. This is particularly true in a society with a social structure as diverse as the American, in economic, class, occupational, regional, ethnic, religious, and other terms. Support, focusing on the presidency, must be given to one of two party candidates: the alternative is a "protest" vote for a minority-party candidate, or non-participation altogether. Many votes are motivated by more particularized considerations having to do with specific interest groups, and the like. But *whatever* their motivation on lower levels of generality, all the votes have to be *counted* as support for the party candidate and his administration, and on some level for the power of the party in Congress. This point brings out in one context very sharply the difference in significance between the problem of the *motivation* of the individual voter, and of the *consequences* of his vote for the political system.

A word may now be said about the line of differentiation between the two major parties. This line is less one of ideological "principle," and more pragmatic, than is the case in European politics. A broad line can, however, be discerned. I would like to characterize this distinction as that between "right" and "left" in a sense appropriate to American conditions. The focus of the American right in this sense is the organization of the free-enterprise economy. This is by no means "conservative" in a general social sense; it is in fact the main center of dynamic development in the society. But it is *politically* conservative, because the economy is

[7] There is not, of course, at any given time a wide range of alternatives, but if the analysis of the direction of party orientation given later in this chapter is correct, it is highly important, and a wide range would be incompatible with effective political integration.

institutionalized on a private-enterprise basis in such a way that positive political action can readily be defined as threatening to interfere with the conditions of operation of this type of economy.[8] Connected with the "business" interest in this sense are various other elements with a tendency to fear innovative change, notably in our recent history the rural small-town elements of a large part of the country.

The "left," on the other hand, has been the focus of those elements predisposed to favor positive action on the political level, who have been favorable to "reform" of various sorts, to control of the economy, to promotion of "welfare," and not least to "interventionism" in foreign affairs.[9] On a broad basis this distinction adequately characterizes the *main* line of distinction between Republican and Democratic tendencies. Of course the Solid South has been a special case, and at the present time major processes of realignment seem to be going on. It is my judgment, however, that the realignments will result, not in substituting a new major axis, but in reshuffling the elements involved in the support groups about the present axis. Business will continue to be the major focus of the more conservative party.

In our system the party leader, as candidate and as President, must appeal to a variety of diverse groups and interests for the support necessary to elect. He must come up with some balance involving compromises and creative syntheses. The general meaning of the aggregate of the support he receives cannot be more than the endorsement of a broad *direction* of action for the polity. More specific interests can be endorsed only as they fit the general direction; they always stand in competition with others. There can never be any "absolute" commitment to a particular interest—economic, ideological, religious, or other—because this would lead to burning of bridges connecting with other elements necessary for an effective support-coalition, elements that would not "go along" with such a commitment. For example, in pre-Nazi Germany the Center party was definitely committed to represent the interests of the Catholic Church. It had considerable range for maneuver, but was prevented by this commitment from becoming a genuine national party in a religiously divided society. Similarly, an American Catholic party under our system could not conceivably become one of the two general parties.

Let us return to the parallel with the input-output boundary of the economy. What I have called the generalization of support is parallel to the "mobility of labor," the readiness to cooperate in the production of goods and services that do not themselves satisfy one's own personal needs or those of one's family. The individual worker must in an important

---

[8] This is by no means to say either that "business" has taken a consistently laissez-faire attitude— on many occasions it has sought help from government. But clearly the *main* trend is the one stated.

[9] This is a type of intervention which is often characteristic of the right. Cf. footnote 41 this chapter.

sense relinquish control of the product of his labor. Similarly the political supporter, in our case the voter, must not claim direct control of the consequences of his vote; if he did, political support would be reduced to a "barter" basis and the political integration of a complex social system would become impossible. What then does the voter receive that is analogous to the money income of the worker? He receives the expectation that many *kinds* of measures that he approves will be implemented if his candidate wins, but without exact specification of particular policies. The directional orientation of a party candidate is a kind of political "currency" which, if he wins, will improve the probabilities that a *kind* of direct political action, over which the voter does not have direct control but which *in general* he favors, will be taken. In taking money wages for his work and relinquishing control of the product, the worker evidences "faith" that by spending the money he will be able to get something he values as much or more than the product of his work. Similarly the voter evidences faith that, if his candidate wins, the "way things will go" will be relatively in accord with his wishes, but he cannot directly control the specific decisions that will be taken.

This generalized support is, I have noted, a fundamental ingredient of power. It, along with the other ingredients, is used to help produce concrete decisions, binding on the collectivity, which are analogous to specific goods. The support is necessary because without it the decisions could not be responsible, that is, could not be made to "stick." But if the support is to be of any "use," its consequences must eventuate in concrete decisions that deal effectively with the real problems of the collectivity. The quality and quantity of these decisions and of their consequences in turn justify the acts of faith involved in giving political support. But it is the *aggregate value* of such decisions, not their particularities, which is the basis of the community's political "income" from its commitments of support.

Perhaps it is worthwhile to carry the parallel between the economic and the political one step further. The keynote of economic organization has rightly been said to be the division of labor. Through it the individual "producer" makes a sacrifice and receives a gain. The sacrifice is essentially one of self-contained independence; he can no longer meet his own needs from his own efforts and resources. The gain is one of "efficiency." He gets more by pooling competence and resources with others than if each operated alone on a self-sufficient basis. In the political case the axis is the differentiation of responsibility. The giver of support makes a sacrifice—loss of immediate control of collective decisions that affect his own interest; he "delegates" this control to the holders of power. But he also receives a gain, which is his share in the benefits of the *effectiveness* with which collective action can be taken. If the responsibility of every voter, including the President, for collective action were exactly equal, in effect *no* collective action would be taken at all.

But in exchange for this gain the voter has to take his chances that the *particular* decisions in which he is most directly interested will be forthcoming.[10]

A built-in element of the conflict of interest is always present in any system of the economic division of labor—for example, the terms of the contract of employment. But this is greatly accentuated in the political case because of the commitment of the collectivity as a whole which is involved. At the leadership-support level this is, in our system, dramatized by the duality of the parties and the fact that in an immediate presidential election, what is gained by one—namely electoral victory—is by definition lost by the other. Hence there are inherently divisive potentialities in political "competition" which are not present to the same degree in economic competition. The control of such divisive potentialities is, in our society, attained through the institutionalization of the two-party system referred to above.

So far we have attempted to do two things. The first was to outline a general model of the relation between the organization of leadership and the mobilization of support in a political system. The second was to apply this to the main facts of the American two-party system so far as it involved the processes of election to the presidency. It is clear that the operation of such a system is dependent on the firm institutionalization of the "rules of the game" by which certain standards of fairness are insured, by which the losing party accepts the legitimacy of electoral victory of the winner, and by which in turn the winners do not use the power of the state to make it impossible for the losers to have a real chance of winning in future elections.

In addition to this condition of general institutionalization, it follows, I think, from the above analysis that there are certain further conditions necessary to the successful operation of a democratic two-party system. These conditions may be stated in the following four propositions:

1) There must be mechanisms by which the average voter can come to a responsible decision that is meaningful to him. He must not, in too many cases, withdraw to nonvoting, nor be too susceptible to appeals that would be grossly disruptive of the stability of the system. Since the intellectual problems involved in a rational solution are not practicably soluble, my thesis is that the mechanisms are typically nonrational. They involve stabilization of political attitudes *in terms of association with other members of the principal solidary groups in which the voter is involved.* In terms of party affiliation this may be called "traditionalism." The traditionalistic operation of nonrational mechanisms is a condition of the stability of the system. That they root in the solidary groupings of the society follows from

---

[10] Realistically, of course, neither the worker nor the voter *could* be self-sufficient. The argument is analytical, not a discussion of concrete alternatives.

the fact that support is mobilized from the integrative subsystem of the society.[11]

2) Pure traditionalism, however, would result in a rigidity of the system which would be incompatible both with the shift of conditions under which problems of public goal-specification and attainment must be posed and with the necessity, for a two-party system, that there be realistic opportunities for each party to win in its bid for leadership through the election of a President. A certain proportion of voters must shift from time to time in party allegiance, if a flexible balance is to be maintained. The data show that this takes place mainly through what has been called above the "indifference" reaction—the voting change of people under cross-pressures who show relatively low levels of interest in the campaign and have difficulty in making their decisions. This finding will be interpreted as in line with the importance of solidary groupings as foci of political loyalties. It is a mechanism which on the whole minimizes the dangers of instability, inherent in political shifting. But it is primarily a condition of effective attainment of *new* goals as they become salient.

3) Under two-party conditions a limited polarization of the electorate is essential—a choice between only two realistic alternatives is offered. This means that the inherently divisive potentialities of political power-struggle are increased. There must clearly be mechanisms which prevent this polarization from producing a progressively deepening rift in the electorate. In the subsequent discussion, it will be shown that there are two main foci of such mechanisms. First, there is the supraparty consensus referred to above, which institutionalizes the duality of party organization, prescribing rules of political fair play. Second, there is the involvement of voting with the solidary groups in the society in such a way that, though there is a correlation, there is no *exact* correspondence between political polarization and other bases of differentiation. Hence, pushing the implications of political difference too far activates the

[11] The necessity for the operation of nonrational mechanisms may be further illustrated as follows: I have emphasized that the focusing of the decision of the electorate on two candidates forces a very high level of the generalization of support. A voter cannot, in effect, decide on highly concrete grounds, using his vote as a specific means to a specific end. However important such specific considerations may be for a given voter, the *effect* of his vote must be to contribute to the pool of general support for the candidate and party, and he cannot fail to be aware that on some level he is thrown, with respect to this pool, together with strange bedfellows who have quite different specific ends in view than his.

At the same time, to judge rationally in terms of the "welfare of the country" is an intellectual task of a very high level of complexity and difficulty. Since even the most competent technical experts in such matters, political and social scientists, are far from being agreed on the better direction in a given case, how can the average voter have a competent and well-grounded opinion? This is a classic type of situation in which non-rational psychological mechanisms can be expected to operate. The voter is faced with problems to which a rational solution in the usual sense is impossible; he must fall back on mechanisms that are psychologically possible for him. But at the same time there must be some type of regulation of these mechanisms, lest voters' behavior prove to be too unsettling to the society.

solidarities between adherents of the two parties which exist on other, nonpolitical, bases so that members of the political majority come to defend those who share other of their interests but differ from them politically. These mechanisms serve the effective integration of the system.

4) American society is not static, but dynamically evolving. The political system must be adapted to this fact and must include mechanisms of adjustment to social change. Under American conditions the main autonomous processes of social change do not operate through government, but largely through the development of the economy. The business element, which is the core of this process of change, tends to be politically conservative because positive use of the powers of government has been felt, since the early thirties, to imply interference with the process. The left, on the other hand, is relatively residual, tending to gather together those elements in the society on whom the problems and difficulties arising from the dynamic process impinge, and who see in governmental action an opportunity to remedy their situations. There must be mechanisms in the political system which mediate the balance between right and left without running the risk that either set of elements will be oppressively overwhelmed by the other. They are mechanisms that are essential to adapt the system to *changes in the structure of the society.*

The reader will note that, with some differences, these four conditions bear a close relation to the balances on which the functioning of the system depends, as formulated by the authors of *Voting* in their final chapter. The authors speak of the balances between "involvement and indifference" and between "stability and flexibility." Both of these balances are related to each of my first two statements about conditions of functioning of the system. The relations between involvement and indifference are highly pertinent to the nature of the nonrational mechanisms on which the stability of the system depends and to the anchorage of the voter in the solidarity groupings of the society. But the same nonrational mechanisms operate in maintaining the type of flexibility that is most important in what may be called "normal" functioning. Hence, in my more detailed review of the findings of the studies, especially *Voting*, I shall treat these two together in connection with my own first two statements of conditions.

A further balance discussed by the authors is that between "consensus and cleavage." This directly concerns my third condition, that of the integrative basis of the voting system, and will be discussed under that heading. Finally, the fourth of their balances is that between "progress and conservation," as they call it. It is clear that this is essentially the same as my fourth condition, which concerns adaptation to changes in the structure of the society. The fifth of their balances, that between "individualism and collectivism," seems to me to stand on a different level from the other four. It is very close to what I have called the balance between leadership responsibility and the necessity of support. This has already been discussed and will be a continuing theme throughout the remainder of the chapter.

Under the three rubrics just indicated I would now like to attempt to spell out the implications of the above analysis and relate them to some of the more detailed findings of the studies. This will both show the degree of goodness of fit between their findings and my model, and lead to a few theoretical conclusions that are not explicitly stated by the authors.

STABILITY, FLEXIBILITY, AND THE SHIFT OF POLITICAL ALLEGIANCE

Perhaps the most striking group of findings come in the first of the three main areas: stability, flexibility, and level of interest in the campaign. These concern in a sense the status of the "independent voter"; and, from the point of view of some of the ideologies dear to intellectuals, the findings may seem rather shocking. The fact seems to be that the groups most likely to escape from the traditionalism of habitual and inherited voting patterns are those least intensely interested in the issues of the campaign. They are not particularly well informed and, indeed, often are on the margin of not voting at all. These are the groups that provide the main element of flexibility in the system, the main source of the shifters from one party to the other.[12] It is also important that these are the same kind of people who, as they report their recollection of previous votes, are most likely to have shifted allegiance between campaigns. Furthermore, intensification of the campaign tends to drive them back to their previous habits of voting.

A second very important and closely related finding is that a large proportion of the voters susceptible to shifting are people subject to "cross-pressures."[13] These are people who, in the cross-cutting status structure of our complex society, belong simultaneously to solidary groups membership in which would predispose them to vote in both of the two major directions, so that they are exposed to a role conflict. An example would be the well-to-do businessman of Irish-Catholic origin. The evidence seems to be that a considerable proportion of the people thus exposed to cross-pressures resolve their conflict by not voting at all. In any case, those who do vote make up their minds later than those not so exposed, and shift from previous allegiances more frequently.[14]

Another primary fact, of course, is that the great majority of voters are settled in their party allegiances and will not be influenced to vote for

[12] Berelson, Lazarsfeld, and McPhee, *op. cit.*, Chap. 1, especially propositions stated on pp. 33–34.   [13] *Ibid.*, p. 33, Proposition 6.   [14] *Ibid.*, pp. 148–49.

the opposing party by either the personality of the candidate or the discussion of issues. These in general include those who feel most intensely about the outcome and take the most active part in politics at all levels.[15] This evidence, combined with other facts, seems to make clear a fundamental connection between the psychology of voting behavior and the mechanisms by which the balance of stability and flexibility are maintained which is of great interest here.

On one level we may say that the nonshifters vote "from habit" or that they are "traditionalists," but these statements do not carry us very far. Fortunately data are presented which enable us to look considerably deeper for the bases of these habits and traditions. These data show that there is a marked tendency to agree in voting preferences with certain categories of others. This is so true of the family that the authors say the family rather than the individual perhaps ought to be taken as the unit of voting behavior. The tendency to agreement then extends to friends, and somewhat less intensely to occupational associates, fellow members of ethnic and religious groups, and class associates—this last the more so in proportion to the individual's class identification.[16]

In considering the implications of these findings, let us again note that when a rational decision is not possible, but at the same time there is pressure to make commitments, there has to be some stable set of reference points so that beliefs can give meaning to the commitment and people can feel "comfortable" about it. The "issues" are in general too numerous and specific to provide a focus, the individual can directly "care" about only a minority of them, and the chances are good he will disapprove of his candidate's stand on some. Furthermore, his own action can have little decisive effect on the outcome—he casts only one of millions of votes—and the direct effect of the immediate outcome on his own personal interests is usually slight.

In this situation the individual seems to vote, other things being equal, with the people whom he most directly feels to be "his own kind," who are in social status and group memberships like, and hence like-minded with, himself. It may be said that the question is not so much, on the levels of psychological determination, *for what* he is voting as it is *with whom* he is associating himself in voting. There are many questions about the specific psychological mechanisms involved in this behavior, especially because it is largely unconscious in a considerable proportion of cases. Presumably processes akin to those of natural selection have been at work. One point, however, of congruence with the social situation can be brought out. As outlined above, the relationship of political leadership and support must be in some sense one of mutual trust. The leader is dependent on the stability of his support in order to carry out the responsibilities he has assumed, and supporters have per-

[15] *Ibid.,* pp. 27, 34.   [16] *Ibid.,* Chap. 6, especially p. 116.

formed an implicit act of faith in the necessary relinquishment of control of their affairs to leadership.

Broadly, the solidary groupings of a social structure are those on whose members' political developments will have some sort of common impact. Probably the tightest solidary grouping in our society is the family, and this seems to show the greatest cohesiveness in voting. Certainly the members of this grouping share to a high degree a "common fate" in the face of whatever vicissitudes may come and go. Occupational, ethnic, religious, class, local, and regional groupings have similar characteristics to lesser and varying degrees. I suggest that it is symbolically appropriate that, in performing an "act of faith" which establishes a relation of trust the consequences of which, however, cannot be directly controlled, a person should feel most secure in associating himself with persons who, by virtue of their real solidary relationship to him, are the ones he feels most naturally can be trusted.

In any case, whatever the more specific psychological mechanisms, the *effect* of the "pull" of the solidary groupings of the social structure on individuals, as a result of which they vote with their fellow members of such groups, is to contribute greatly to what I have called the generalization of support. As the authors of *Voting* state several times, the individual tends to vote as a group member. But it is precisely as a structure of groups that a society is stable and integrated. If people vote as members of the stably important groups of the society, this provides an element of stability in the structure of political alignments itself which matches and is a consequence of the stability of the social structure.

It was noted above that the primary problem of the generation of power was the requisite integration, in a political action context, of the social system in which it occurs. At the top, this integration is organized around the two-party alternative within the institutional framework of a constitutionally guaranteed set of alternatives and the opportunity for the losing side to try again. But at the bottom, the process is dependent on the statistical outcome of millions of individual acts. I have argued that the direct rational determination of those acts without intermediary "nonrational" mechanisms is out of the question. The attachment of the individual to his solidary associations as a voting reference builds the society up in a series of graduated steps from the more elementary units of the society to units that can be meaningfully related to the important issues of the day, the realistic alternatives facing the political system as a system. As a structure of political integration, the top of this structure is constituted by the two national parties. That there should be such a structure of integrations is directly deducible from general theory.[17] The clarity with which the studies have provided empirical evidence of its existence and concrete nature is impressive.

[17] Some technical aspects of this deduction are discussed in the Technical Note.

This line of argument does not, however, account for flexibility, which is also necessary to such a system. It is here that the findings about the changers and shifters and their relation to relative political indifference and to cross-pressures are so interesting and significant. In spite of the empirical difference, it can be said that the basic theme is the same. The phenomenon of cross-pressures means that many people are involved in solidary groupings which politically, and certainly in other ways, are not well integrated with each other. The potential voter is, by his solidary associations, being pulled two ways at once.

Of course the fact that these are the main sources of the shift in votes, both between elections and during campaigns, brings out the importance of group attachments for those whose voting orientation is more stable. But there are two other particularly important aspects. The first is the psychological reference: the "cross-pressure" people are the more indifferent (many on the margin of not voting at all) and make up their minds later than others.[18] Psychologically this is an understandable reaction to conflict, namely vacillation and the postponement of decision, and the tendency to withdraw from a difficult dilemma by avoiding decision altogether. These tendencies are of course facilitated by the fact that generally in American society there is little strong sanction brought to bear on nonvoters, and the ballot is secret.

There is also, secondly, an important social aspect of the phenomenon. It is through the mobility of individuals between groups and the formation of new groups (and correspondingly the weakening and eventual disappearance of old ones) that the social structure itself changes. It therefore seems legitimate to conclude that on the whole the people exposed to cross-pressures are, in terms of social structure, among those most directly involved in processes of social change. Thus, for example, the upward mobility of immigrant populations produces the Catholic of high socio-economic status who is a type case of involvement in cross-pressures. Surely the result of this process in the long run will be to split the Catholic vote far more evenly between the parties than was true in the New Deal era. In the other direction, we may cite the large-scale process of migration of rural people to the industrial areas and their eventual incorporation into trade unions, a process which occurred a little earlier. The Republican predilection of many rural people thus was crossed with the Democratic predilection of many union members. On the whole one would expect the concomitant growth of industry and of unionism to produce a relatively stable increment to Democratic strength—though particularly in the light of the 1956 results, and also of facts cited in *Voting*, there must be some qualifications of this generalization. In any case, however, the cross-pressure element in its relation to social change provides the primary

[18] Berelson, Lazarsfeld, and McPhee, *op. cit.*, p. 33.

element of flexibility in a system which, were the factor of group solidarity too strong, might well be unduly rigid.

These facts about solidarity and its loosening through cross-pressures provide an empirical setting for the theoretical problem I posed above about the nature and significance of the levels of generalization of support.[19] This problem is very much involved in the distinction the authors of *Voting* make between what they call "position" issues and "style" issues.[20] Position issues are close to the level of what I have called binding decisions and advocacy of policies—typical examples from the 1948 campaign being revision of the Taft-Hartley Act and price control. Style issues, on the other hand, are closer to the ideological level and to that of "generalized support" which requires broad bases of justification—communism in government would be such an issue, though it was not yet very prominent in 1948. My essential point is that these types of issues correspond to a distinction between levels at which people are integrated in the solidary group structure of the society. Promotion of what is ordinarily called an "interest" involves acting with people who feel they have a common interest, sometimes in opposition to others.[21] It is usually thought of at a level which can be coped with by relatively specific "policies." But at this level interests are too diverse and sometimes too conflicting to serve to integrate the electorate at the level of generalized support. Hence we would expect to find symbolizations at higher levels of generalization which can come closer to setting off the two parties against each other as a whole.[22]

CONSENSUS AND CLEAVAGE

Let us now turn to the problem of "polarization," or what Berelson *et al.* speak of as the balance between consensus and cleavage. It is important that the studies provide direct evidence of the underlying consensus that is essential if a party system is to work at all without disrupting the community, that is, polarizing it in a radical sense. This centers on the recognition that there are common "rules of the game"

[19] Clear insight into this problem is shown by Berelson, Lazarsfeld, and McPhee, *op. cit.*, chap. 4, with special reference to the functioning of position.

[20] *Ibid.*, pp. 184–185.

[21] It is interesting to note the systematic attempts of totalitarian governments to destroy the solidary groupings that mediate between individual and state.

[22] There is a possible confusion in classifying religion as a "style" issue, if the ditinction between it and position issues is meant to be more than a rather *ad hoc* empirical one. Religious groups constitute bases of solidarity just as do "economic" or local groups. They can become, especially in a system of denominational pluralism like the American, the focus of highly specific position issues. But, for reasons having to do with the integration of the society, there are strong pressures against making religion an *explicit* focus of political controversy. It hence tends to become one of the things nearly everyone is "in favor of," with careful avoidance of mentioning the differences of interest between different denominational groups.

binding on all participants. But consensus seems to go beyond this. Though some distortion in perception of candidates and issues can be detected, it seems fair to say the notable thing is not that distortion exists, but that it is relatively small. Thus there seems to be fair agreement across party lines on the characteristics of the candidates and the relevant criteria to judge them, on what the major issues of the campaign are, on various expectations for the future, and on expectations of the voting tendencies of various blocs of voters. There is, to a fair degree, a common framework both of institutional norms and of cognitive definition of the situation.[23]

This supraparty consensus should, I think, be regarded as the top of the more general hierarchy of politically relevant solidarities. Its existence and continual reinforcement through symbolic expression should be regarded as the essential condition of the tolerance of division at the next lower level, which is the division between the major parties as such. For sociological reasons, if this division is to be considered as "tolerable," it must be based on a genuine *differentiation* of function with reference to the system as a whole. The line of division between right and left in American politics suggests a framework in which our main party structure may be interpreted. The chief problem here concerns the balance of conservation and progress, but certain problems with respect to the nature of the cleavage and the limitations on it need to be taken up. My broad thesis is that divisive tendencies are controlled by being placed in the context of the hierarchy of solidarities which I have outlined, so that the cleavages that develop tend to be toned down and muted on their own level and referred to higher orders of integration for resolution.

We have had a prominent recent example of the operation of this mechanism. One can scent a certain danger to this higher level consensus when, particularly in the heat of campaigns, spokesmen for the parties go beyond stating their differences from their opponents as differences of desirable directions and policies, and raise doubts about the "fitness to govern" of the opposite party and its candidates. Almost inevitably there is some of this in every campaign. On occasion it may go further, as it did in the 1952–54 period. The theme of the threat of communism was played up by the Republican extremists until it began to be applied, by inference if not explicitly, not just to certain limited allegedly subversive elements, but to the Democratic party as a whole. This culminated in McCarthy's slogan of "twenty years of treason." For a moment it seemed as though this would be taken up by the Republican moderates; a few speeches by such spokesmen as Attorney-General Brownell and Governor Dewey were couched very nearly in this vein. But this provoked a strong reaction from specifically *conservative* Democrats, such as Sam Rayburn, and in general the Republican moderates, after a brief "flirtation" with

---

[23] Berelson, Lazarsfeld, and McPhee, *op. cit.,* especially chap. 9 summarized on p. 212 [of that work: ed.]

the idea, drew back sharply from it. Essentially what happened is that the vicious circle of divisive cleavage began to activate the sentiments clustering around the higher-order solidarity of the national supraparty consensus. To accuse a person of disloyalty or treason is to place him outside that consensus. To extend this accusation to one of the two major parties as such is to break national solidarity at a most critical point. It gradually became clear that at most a small fanatical minority really "meant it" in this radical sense. The anxieties aroused by this really radical implication probably had a great deal to do with making the final resolution of the McCarthy episode possible. Though this was not an explicit item in the Senate indictment, it was fundamentally McCarthy's challenge to the higher-order consensus that was the underlying basis of his censure.

Only once in our national history has such a cleavage been driven to a really disastrous point. In the events that led to the Civil War, the question of loyalty to the Union could be related to a whole series of issues and ideological symbols on which the two regional sectors of the society could divide. There were in fact real and deep differences of social structure underlying the symbols and slogans, differences that divided the population into two sufficiently equal parts. McCarthyism could not split the country in this way because it did not reflect any clear-cut *structural* division, but cut across the main structural divisions. The most generalized "style" issue of the Communist threat could not split the more differentiated structural solidarities. No clear-cut line could be drawn between elements that could be activated pro and con around the Communist symbol as they were around slavery and secession. Later in this chapter I will say a little more about the nature of the disturbance that made it possible for McCarthyism to get as far as it did.

The level where the problem of cleavage and consensus next arises involves bases of solidarity not in the *first instance* political. The broad picture has already been sketched and is clearly delineated in *Voting* and the other studies. The general relationships between party alignment and socio-economic status, occupation, ethnicity, and religion are by now well established.

Almost equally important, however, is the looseness of this relation. Shifts in the alignment are continually occurring, largely reflecting processes of change in the social structure, but with an important feedback from political action.

The very looseness of the relation between structural solidarities other than political party and the party structure itself can be said to constitute an important protection against the divisive potentialities of cleavage. The essential fact here is that most structurally important groupings in the society will contain considerable proportions of adherents of *both* parties.[24] To an important degree, therefore, the structural ties that bind

[24] *Ibid.,* chap. 4.

them together on nonpolitical bases cut across their political allegiances. Hence the tendency to political cleavage will tend to be checked by a set of mechanisms that operate *below* the level of party division as well as by the more general national consensus that operates above that level. The pressure of political cleavage—by activating ties of solidarity at the more differentiated structural levels that cut across the line of cleavage—tends automatically to bring countervailing forces into play. The point of view of an individual voter is likely to be, "My fellow union member (lodge member, coreligionist, office colleague, and so forth) who is intending to vote Republican (Democratic) is in general a pretty decent guy. I just can't see how all people who hold his views can be as bad as they're made out to be." Awareness that this type of sentiment will be activated may put a certain restraint on extremism in the campaign.

This mechanism may be said to be the obverse of what the authors of *Voting* and of *The People's Choice* call "activation."[25] In the case just described, the activation of essentially nonpolitical sentiments of solidarity acts as a brake on processes leading to divisive cleavage. Activation in the meaning of the studies, on the other hand, works as a stabilizing mechanism with reference to party alignments. It is clear that the pluralistic nature of the general social structure is so important that if nonpolitical solidarities were too strong, the necessary generalization of support that the party system requires could not be assured. The evidence from the studies seems to show that the principal direct effect of the political campaign itself on vacillating voters is to reactivate the voting preferences that predominate in the individual's past history and predominate in the solidary groups to which he is currently attached.[26]

At the psychological level this process is related to nonrational mechanisms. The very conception of rationality implies a certain ordered responsiveness to changes and shifts in the external situation. There is hence an inherent connection between nonrationality and the relative absence of such flexible *responsiveness*. If the nonrational reaction, however, is to be *ordered*, it must, I think, lead inherently to a conservative response. In its impact on the individual voter the effect of the campaign is to intensify the urgency of situational stimuli. Insofar as the response is an orderly one, it has to be in terms of established patterns of voting behavior, that is, a "traditionalistic" response.

There are two main alternatives to this traditionalistic pattern of response. One is clearly delineated by the authors, the other not. The first has already been discussed as the response to cross-pressures—namely, low intensity of political interest, relative indifference, and readiness to shift

[25] Cf. especially P. F. Lazarsfeld, B. R. Berelson, and Hazel Gaudet, *The People's Choice* (2d ed.; New York: Columbia University Press, 1948), Introduction.

[26] Berelson, Lazarsfeld, and McPhee, *op. cit.,* pp. 262–72, in connection with the "Fair Deal Rally."

political allegiance. The other, illustrated by McCarthyism, is openness to a certain type of "charismatic" appeal, to extremism and emotionalism.[27] The first is well integrated in the political system and may be said to be the normal mechanism that mediates shifts in the political balance. It is, I think, an example of what Durkheim called an "egoistic" response to strain. The second is perhaps the major type of "pathology" of our system and, if not controlled, may have highly disruptive consequences. In Durkheim's term, it is the "anomic" response. Let us discuss each of these briefly in turn.[28]

The "indifference" reaction results when the individual, faced with a difficult conflict situation, reacts with conservative caution. Typically, he is playing with the idea of taking a new venture, of voting contrary to the voting traditions he himself has observed and/or which are observed by many of the people with whom he has important solidary ties—his relatives, friends, or associates. He hesitates, and is slow to make up his mind. If he actually does make the shift, he is likely to have been considering it since before the campaign began. But if the pressure on him is intensified through the campaign, his tendency is to retreat from his tentative overtures to the safer haven of his own accustomed pattern or that of his older and more tried associates. Finally the steps he takes are, typically, not radical ones, but from the more conservative side of the Democratic spectrum to the liberal side of the Republican or vice versa. These findings are of the first importance to the understanding of how the system functions.

By this process the voter is moving cautiously into unknown territory. He feels his way and does not actually move until sure he "has a place to go," assured that he will be accepted into the solidary groups with whom he newly identifies himself by his vote. Furthermore there is another important finding, namely that called by the authors the "breakage" effect. When the solidary groups in the voter's immediate personal environment are badly split, he is more likely to vote with the prevailing majority in the larger local community—he shifts his solidarity identification to a higher-order grouping.[29]

It is true that these tactics of the voter do not correspond to the stereotype of the classical independent voter with his sophisticated rational choice. But this newly discovered changeable voter has one trait consistent with that stereotype: he shows a kind of (albeit negative) sense of

[27] This problem is discussed at greater length in the two essays on naziism in Talcott Parsons, *Essays in Sociological Theory* (2d ed.; New York: The Free Press, 1954). [Reprinted as Chapters 3 and 4 in the present volume: ed.]

[28] These terms were used by Emile Durkheim in *Suicide* (New York: The Free Press, 1951), but can be generalized to include modes of reaction to strain in other fields. A third type of response illustrated by Eisenhower's special popularity will be commented on briefly later in this chapter.

[29] Berelson, Lazarsfeld, and McPhee, *op. cit.,* pp. 116–17.

responsibility. He does not jump or panic lightly into extreme shifts of allegiance. When he does move it is cautiously and not very far. When pressed he tends to retreat to safe ground. By and large he does not rock the boat. But he is the primary agent in shifting the balance of political forces. In favorable circumstances this shift is accomplished without any deep or lasting cleavage.

In addition to the considerations already brought forward it is perhaps relevant to note that voting is marginal and peripheral for the average citizen. He has many role-involvements in his sphere of private affairs and simply cannot be a sophisticated political expert. When the various factors playing on the "average voter" are combined, they add up to a relatively well-adapted set of mechanisms that facilitate shifts of balance without activating seriously divisive cleavages—as the authors of *Voting* clearly point out.

The mechanism *can* get seriously out of order, however, and then the types of "secondary defense" just discussed become necessary. The most recent example is the McCarthyism episode; hence a few further remarks about it may be in order.[30]

By and large the people to whom McCarthyism appealed were people subject to cross-pressures, for example, members of ethnic groups of recently low but rising status, and members of other ethnic groups, such as people of German origin in the Midwest who in World War II felt a conflict between their patriotism and their German traditions.[31] It seems very likely that many of them were members of solidary groups that were severely split.[32]

It may not be amiss to suggest that they represented a second sort of "breakage effect," not into the safe haven of the majority position in the community, but in response to a violently emotional symbolic appeal, sharply dissociated from the realities of the domestic scene. The central symbol—"communism"—represented a magical danger. Behind the scenes a treasonous conspiracy allegedly threatened the security of everything American. In this context communism can be interpreted as a symbol to which many of the relatively free-floating anxieties of our society could be transferred. Above all it was anxiety-generated. Associated with it was regression to a romantically nostalgic fantasied "Americanism" from which many of the realities of the modern world were pleasantly absent—not only Communists in a literal sense, but bureaucrats, intel-

[30] See Talcott Parsons, "McCarthyism and American Social Tensions," *Yale Review*, Winter, 1955. Reprinted under the title "Social Strains in America," chap. 5, in Daniel Bell (ed.), *The New American Right* (New York: Criterion Books, 1955). [Reprinted as Chapter 7, in the present volume: ed.] See also the other essays in the Bell volume.

[31] This and other cross-pressure situations are discussed in S. A. Lubell, *The Future of American Politics* (New York: Harper & Row, 1952).

[32] See S. A. Stouffer, *Communism, Conformity, and Civil Liberties* (New York: Doubleday, 1955) for some evidence on these points. See also Bell, *op. cit.*

lectuals, and various others, in the wilder flights even the income tax itself. This anomic response was not the "rational" alternative to the indifference response, but was wildly aggressive scapegoating and irresponsible withdrawal from disturbing reality. I suggest that too serious disturbance of the conservatism of the indifference response is likely to activate the McCarthyite type—which in content might be a "radical" rather than a "reactionary" Populism next time.[33]

In this connection it may be appropriate to make a few remarks about the phenomenon of Eisenhower popularity. This also is something of a departure from the main normal type called above the indifference pattern. Eisenhower, that is, seems to have exercised a kind of "charismatic" appeal that has shaken a certain proportion of voters out of their normal allegiances. The appeal seems to run in a "conservative" direction and may be likened to a "breakage effect," which the authors of *Voting* discussed on the level of the local community. At the present moment the country may have at the presidential level a *small* Republican majority. The mood of the country may be relatively conservative, more concerned with stability and integration than with positive action—though it is by no means certain that this is true, and even less certain that this will still be true in 1960. In any event, the Eisenhower margin of 1956 substantially exceeded such a "normal" Republican majority if it existed then.[34]

One further aspect of consensus and its relation to political balance may be discussed briefly. The authors of *Voting* seem to show some uncertainties in their assessment of the effects of the campaign. It is, of course, striking how few votes it seems to change and how it tends to drive the vacillators back into their traditional allegiances. It is further

---

[33] On the historical and analytical associations of McCarthyism and Populism, see E. A. Shils, *The Torment of Secrecy* (New York: The Free Press, 1956).

[34] Three types of evidence may be cited in favor of this interpretation. The first is the unusual amount of ballot-splitting of 1956 which led to the selection of a slightly Democratic Congress in the same election that produced a Republican landslide for the presidency. This strongly suggests that it is not conservatism in the party sense which alone accounts for the result. The second point is the unusual margin by which the vote of the sexes differed; when other factors are held constant, there was something like a 5 per cent excess of women's votes for Eisenhower. Generally speaking, political attitudes of women tend to be more conservative than those of men, for good sociological reasons. [See S. A. Stouffer, *op. cit.,* for evidence that women's attitudes toward radicalism or nonconformity are markedly more conservative than are those of men.] But the difference was, particularly in the second Eisenhower election, substantially greater than normal. Finally, the third bit of evidence is the magnitude of the shift to Eisenhower occasioned by the international crises over Egypt and Hungary. It is authoritatively estimated that about 5 per cent of Eisenhower's vote was attributable to this shift. Hence if the international situation had been calm and if women had divided in the same ratio as men, there is a probability that Stevenson would have been elected by a small margin.

The Republican slogan of "Peace and Prosperity" expresses well the basis of the Eisenhower appeal. [In Durkheim's terms this may be said to be an "altruistic" pattern of response; a flight into identification with a national symbol relatively independent of party.] It seems to rest above all in a need to find a base of security through national solidarity in a world felt to be full of uncertainties and threats. There seems to have been a general feeling that with "Ike" in the White House things would be safer than otherwise.

true that, in the classical theory, the function of the campaign is to "persuade" the voter to adopt the "reasonable" position. Though it clearly does not have this effect (as it should according to the classical formula), may it not be possible that there are certain other consequences of importance?

A few straws of evidence in the findings suggest this may be true. First, it is noted that in the course of the campaign *political* bases of solidarity are strengthened at the expense of *social* bases.[35] Secondly, it was found that opinion leaders support the party position on subsidiary issues more strongly than do voters who are not opinion leaders.[36] It is also true that opinion leaders are politically more interested than others and, though dispersed throughout the social structure, are slightly higher in status than those they lead.[37] Finally, it is noted that exposure to the mass media increases interest in the campaign and strength of feeling about it, but also that voters select media matter to confirm their presuppositions.[38]

From the point of view of bringing about the main shift of political allegiances, the campaign seems relatively "functionless"; it is a "ritual." But from another point of view, if I interpret this evidence correctly, it seems to serve a very important function. This is, essentially, *to reinforce the generalization of support*, which has been shown above to be an essential condition of the functioning of a two-party democratic system.[39] Thus, first, the "social" bases of solidarity are, from the point of view of *political* integration of the society, more particularlized than the political. The greater emphases on the political solidarities may thus be interpreted as a shift in the direction of generalization.

Second, the opinion leaders seem to be agents of this process in that, through supporting the party position on subsidiary issues, they serve to integrate the levels of generalization—what appeals to the more particularistic "interests" of special solidary groups, with what appeals to the more generalized level of the party. That the sources of such influence should be of somewhat higher social status than its objects is sociologically understandable. Generally the higher the status, the higher the level of political responsibility.

Third (and it would seem to fit the same context), the influence of the mass media works in the direction of increasing interest and strength of feeling. Interest and strength of feeling in this case concern the *outcome*

---

[35] Berelson, Lazarsfeld, and McPhee, *op. cit.*, pp. 34, 252. By political is clearly meant party bases.
[36] *Ibid.,* p. 117.
[37] *Ibid.,* pp. 116–117.
[38] *Ibid.,* p. 251. The studies point out that the mass media are not so directly influential in getting the voter to change his political allegiance as is commonly supposed. Voters generally select campaign materials to confirm the position they hold regarding candidates and issues.
[39] This is in accord with the theory of the function of ritual advanced by Emile Durkheim in *The Elementary Forms of the Religious Life* (New York: The Free Press, 1947).

of the campaign, which cannot be other than victory for one of the two major party candidates. Hence the interest and feeling become less concerned with the lower level interest-issues and more with the generalized question of which *party* is to win. Essentially this is to say that the effect of the campaign is to increase motivational commitment to the generalized support of the party, and thus to inhibit tendencies to particularistic fragmentation of the political system. The importance of this set of mechanisms is the more evident when it is considered that "when the chips are down" there is a strong tendency for people to revert to the more unproblematical loyalties. In a pluralistic, that is, highly differentiated, society like ours, this means loyalties closer to the "social" than to the "political" level of solidarity. In the major hierarchy of solidary integrations in a political reference, it means the decisions of voters are shifted closer to the "top" level of general societal integration than would otherwise happen.

PROGRESS AND CONSERVATION

Finally, I would like to discuss briefly the balance between what the authors of *Voting* call "progress" and "conservation."

They emphasize the conservative tendencies activated by the campaign to reinforce established patterns of voting in different population groups. Yet, in the more "relaxed" periods between campaigns the newer trends, which almost by definition involve "deviance" from established patterns, establish a foothold. Usually the main question is whether this footfold is solid enough to withstand the stress of the campaign itself. In 1948 the Republican trend was not quite solid enough, but by 1952 it had become so. With all this I entirely agree.

There is, however, another aspect of the conservation-progress problem clearly brought out by the authors in one connection, though there are other important bits of evidence bearing on it in their findings which deserve further comment. This is its relation to the right-left balance of the two-party system discussed briefly above. One way of putting it is to say that (in one sense and on one level) the two-party system is a relatively "symmetrical" system, more or less evenly balanced between two trends on the most generalized level of support. From this point of view the political process has an oscillatory character, a swinging from relative predominance of one trend to that of the other and back again.

But looked at in the perspective of the dynamic development of the society, there is another aspect of this process, namely a structured relation to the general process of social change, which introduces a factor of *asymmetry* into the party structure. This aspect is, as noted above, structured in the form of division into a relatively "conservative" party in the political sense (the Republican, of course) and a relatively "liberal" party (the Democratic). I have stressed above that the conservatism of the Republican party is a conservatism in the field of *political* action; it is reluctant to sponsor too much *positive* use of governmental power for collective goals, particularly the *extension* of governmental power into areas where traditionally it has not been exercised. The Democratic party, on the other hand, has been more hospitable to positive political innovation, particularly in the fields of control of the economy, of welfare legislation, and of new commitments in foreign affairs. The traditional attitudes of the two parties in the field of government spending and fiscal policy reflect this difference.

The first bit of evidence that bears on this asymmetry is the authors' account of the type of appeal put forward by the two candidates in the 1948 campaign. As they say, Dewey stressed "style" issues that emphasized general consensus and tended to avoid controversial particularities. Truman, on the other hand, stressed "position" issues on which he advocated positive action. Dewey on the whole suggested that his election would have a quieting, unifying effect on the state of affairs, but did not stress positive new measures that needed to be taken; Truman did stress such measures, including repeal of the Taft-Hartley Act as a "new measure."[40]

The authors interpret this as the difference between a strategy appropriate to a candidate expecting to win, who hence does not wish to antagonize any important groups by advocating things they may oppose, and the strategy of one anticipating a struggle, who has to mobilize what support he can in order to come up from behind. This may well be an important factor in the difference, but I feel confident that there is another aspect equally important. This is that the *conservative* party, in the sense just outlined, has broadly an interest in quieting things down politically, in damping the urgency of demands for specific and positive action. The *liberal* party, on the other hand, has an interest in arousing the public to the urgencies of action and tends to stress such action issues whenever they seem to be politically opportune.

Of course there are occasions when (rightly or wrongly) a threat to stability is felt to exist. Then there may be a demand for urgent action from the right. The "communism in government" and the "corruption" issues in 1952 are cases in point.[41] But by and large the policy of emphasizing consensus certainly has been the main Republican trend in the last three elections. Stevenson's attack on the (to him) too negative conception of the presidency by Eisenhower in the last election illustrates the point directly. Of course confirmation of this generalization would require a

[40] Berelson, Lazarsfeld, and McPhee, *op. cit.,* pp. 129, 251.
[41] This seems to be the most reasonable interpretation of the British-French intervention in Egypt in the fall of 1956 and indeed also, in one aspect at least, of the Soviet intervention in Hungary.

wider basis of fact, going back into earlier campaigns, which unfortunately has not been possible in connection with this chapter.

A second finding of the study illustrates a slightly different, though related, aspect of the right-left differentiation of the system. I have emphasized the central position of our business system in defining the relations of right and left. Differential wealth, particularly benefits to a conspicuously wealthy upper economic group, constitutes one of the most publicly salient consequences of situations favorable to the business system. This raises questions of the justice of the degree of inequality of wealth thus highlighted. Throughout our national history there has been partisan controversy about the justice and relation to national welfare of the financial rewards of the highest income groups, starting with the Jefferson-Hamilton differences. It is not surprising that the position of the wealthiest should be a target of attack from the left.

Republican voters held the view that a Republican electoral victory would benefit all classes of the society without exception, but the Democratic voters felt that a Democratic victory would benefit all classes except the wealthy.[42] This element of asymmetry in the views of adherents of the two parties is directly congruent with the interpretation of the nature of the difference between the parties, which has been put forward here. It is a special case of the general tendency of Republicans to emphasize high general consensus, of Democrats to emphasize more specific issues that demand positive action.

There is, finally, the interesting line of evidence bearing on the question of the right-left problem, which is presented directly in this light by the authors. They outline a very interesting conception of a time sequence in which issues come to and leave the center of political controversy. They speak of a "gateway" to political relevance.[43] Before the time is ripe, by approaching this gateway, an issue may be seen, particularly in hindsight, to be gaining in importance, but it is not politically resonant and somehow does not serve to create much interest or excitement in a campaign. Then there is an optimum time when taking up the issue pays handsome political dividends. Finally, the issue later fails to continue in the center of attention and gradually becomes "dead." It seems fair to say that "communism in government" could not have been made a central issue as early as 1948, that in 1952 it was moving into the "gateway," but that by 1956 it had become a dead issue. The Republicans not only did not, but could not, make important political capital of it as late as that—and not only because a Republican administration had been in office for four years.[44] It would be my prediction that though the issue of federal

[42] Berelson, Lazarsfeld, and McPhee, *op. cit.*, p. 87.

[43] *Ibid.*, pp. 206–12.

[44] The "gateway" theory thus, rightly in my opinion, throws strong doubt on the depth of the wisdom of the anonymous Republican pundit of early 1954 who is reported as having said, "We could stay in office indefinitely just by running against Joe Stalin and Dean Acheson."

aid to public education was in the 1956 election just approaching the "gateway" but not yet close enough to be a big issue, by 1960 it will be in the middle of the gateway.

This pattern applies, I think, to issues pressed by both sides, indeed I have used one from each side as examples. But, nonetheless, as the authors themselves suggest,[45] the basic asymmetry that has appeared in the other connections applies here. The Republican issues that come through the gateway tend to be "defensive" issues, namely they tend to concern real or alleged "dangers" to the system which must be warded off. Restriction of immigration, which came to a head in 1924, is an example, as are pressures for tariff increases. The Democratic issues, on the other hand, tend to be positive innovations that require political mobilization to be put through.

The gateway theory thus formulates a very important pattern of the history of American politics, of which the element of party asymmetry is the aspect in which I am primarily interested. The central phenomenon starts with the pressing of a policy by the party of the left, in recent times the Democrats. The policy is opposed by the right, that is, the Republicans, sometimes bitterly. There are many alarmist views expressed that the policy will ruin the country and destroy the unique virtues of the "American system." Then the measure, or a series of them, is enacted. Relatively quickly after enactment the excitement dies down, and the new situation comes to be accepted by its former opponents, for the most part with good grace, though there often is a little company of die-hards who remain irreconcilable for a long time. As the authors point out, there is a spectrum of relative enthusiasm from left to right. But when the next Republican administration comes along it does not try seriously to reverse the policy or restore the *status quo ante*. There may well be some modifications of what are felt to be "abuses," but on the whole the main phenomenon is acceptance; indeed there is probably as much modest extension as paring back. The main pattern introduced by the new policy thus becomes institutionalized and an essential part of the social structure of the country.

The more obvious examples come from the fields of control of business practices and social welfare legislation. Thus the Federal Reserve Act, the Securities and Exchange Act, the Wagner Act, and the Social Security Act were all Democratic measures—every one of which was strongly contested by the Republican party—not merely the "radical right," but the main party. Every one of them has come to be fundamentally accepted by that party with no attempt to undo the work. For example, the changes in the "charter of labor" introduced by the Taft-Hartley Act are on the whole secondary, and the present administration boasts of having extended the coverage of Social Security benefits, although their party predecessors of the 1930's widely predicted that the Act itself would

[45] Cf. Berelson, Lazarsfeld, and McPhee, *op. cit.*, pp. 207-9.

destroy the moral independence of the American working population.

I am not in a position to present here a careful appraisal over a long historical period, but I think it is safe to generalize, first, that in American history the considerable majority of policies judged to have resulted in major modifications of the social structure through government action have been sponsored by the party of the left and, at the time, opposed by the party of the right.[46] Secondly, however, the majority of these policies have resulted in fully institutionalized features of the society— their consequences have come to be accepted in the society as a whole, and we have "gone on from there."

The findings of *Voting* clearly indicate that the American two-party system is a mechanism by which, at any *given* time, a relative equilibrating balance in a pluralistic society is maintained, so that conflicts and tendencies are controlled and more or less fully resolved. It is also, seen over a period of time, a principal mechanism—though by no means the only one—by which the process of structural change in the society operates. The position of government in any modern society is such that it cannot be insulated from the broader process of social change. What happens at the governmental level both reflects these changes and is itself a major instrumentality in carrying them through. The main mechanism that adjusts the balance between the "reflection" aspect of the process and the "instrumentality" aspect is the raising and finally the resolution of issues through the operation of the party system. The essential point is that new things do "get done" and that the consequences do come to be accepted. In view of what sociologists now know of the intensity of the tensions and stresses generated by major processes of social change, the relative effectiveness of this set of mechanisms is impressive. Again, in view of the importance of this aspect for the whole process of political adjustment, the importance of the mechanisms involved in what has above been called the "conservative" or "indifference" pattern of the change of position of voters is again emphasized. There is a great deal of sociopolitical dynamite in the political process in a rapidly changing society. That it breaks over into charismatic "radicalism"—of right or left—so seldom, and that these "fires" have usually been so relatively quickly extinguished, is testimony to the power of the mechanisms of social control that operate in this area. The authors of *Voting* have given us notable insight into the way these mechanisms operate.

CONCLUSION

It has not been possible in this chapter to review more than a sample of the rich and suggestive findings presented in *Voting*, to say nothing of

---

[46] The administration of Theodore Roosevelt cannot be considered to have been a "typical" Republican administration in these terms.

the other related studies. My purpose, however, has not been to present a complete review, critical or otherwise, but to try to establish the relations between certain of these findings and a theoretical model of the operation of a two-party democratic political system. I have therefore selected for consideration the findings that seemed to be most directly relevant to the empirical problems involved in the model.

The model has been constructed essentially by extending a pattern of theoretical analysis which had been worked out in connection with the economy as a subsystem of the society, in interaction with other subsystems,[47] to the "polity" conceived as another subsystem of the society cognate with the economy. The polity in this sense is essentially the set of societal mechanisms that makes the generation of power in the political sense possible. In constructing this model I have, of course, leaned heavily on the literature of political theory.

It was possible to discuss here, as specifically relevant to the voting process, only part of an as yet incomplete model. This part, however, deals with a crucial aspect of the total system, the process by which the "goal-attainment" adjustments of the polity work out through interchange with another subsystem of the society, here vaguely referred to as the "public." The interchange in question is thought of as involving, at a high level of generalization, the interchange of "leadership" responsibility for "support," at a lower level, that of "binding decisions" for "advocacy of policies."

On the gross structural level the essential facts about the American system are that it is a constitutionally regulated, "democratic" two-party system operating in a society that is primarily oriented to growth of economic productivity and involved in a dynamic process of general internal social change, as well as a highly unstable international situation. Within this framework, if the political system is, in the relation between leadership and support, to be a relatively stable one that can integrate multifarious pluralistic interests and yet adapt to changing conditions, it must, within broadly specifiable limits, have certain characteristics. By applying the model to the general structure it was possible to identify four main areas in which to look for mechanisms relevant to these functional requirements.

These, the reader will remember, concerned (1) the relations between the nonrational psychological mechanisms that must be imputed to the "average voter" and the reference points of voting decisions in the structure of solidary groupings of the society that formed the main basis of stability of the system; (2) the element of flexibility necessary to allow sufficient shift of votes to permit a two-party system to function effectively without introducing unduly disruptive elements into the system; (3) mechanisms that will organize the limited polarization that a

[47] Presented in Parsons and Smelser, *op. cit.*

two-party system requires and yet protect the integration of the society against too deep-seated divisive forces; and (4) mechanisms that will mediate the processes of adaptation to structural change in a rapidly evolving society.

These requirements were found to correspond very closely with four of the balances formulated by the authors of *Voting* in their final chapter. The first two of my functional requirements were related to the balances of stability and flexibility and of involvement and indifference, the third to that between consensus and cleavage, and the fourth to that between progress and conservation. The fifth of the authors' balances, between individualism and collectivism, seemed to me to correspond to the more general need for balance between effective leadership and the generalization of support, which has formed the main analytical thread of the whole discussion. It hence seems to me to stand on a different level from the other four. For these reasons I organized my more detailed review of the relevant findings of *Voting* about the relation between my four propositions and the first four of the authors' balances just mentioned.

Particularly in their final chapter, but also at various points throughout the volume, the authors make generalizations from their findings which come halfway or more toward the generalizations that would have been generated deductively by use of the theoretical model with which I have been working. Hence it is not any originality of empirical insight into the workings of the American political system which I wish to claim; most of what is relevant is present and clearly stated in the book.

What is important in the present connection is rather the *fit* of these findings and conclusions with a more generalized conceptual scheme. This fit strengthens the impression from the authors' own exposition that there is an important *internal consistency* in the main structure of their findings and interpretations. In the light of the above discussion it seems to me inconceivable that the facts should be just a random collection of discrete items with no essential connection with each other. But beyond the question of internal consistency, such a fit strongly suggests the feasibility of extending a coherent analysis of the American political system in its connections with other aspects of the society, economic, institutional, and otherwise. Here I have stressed only that *theoretical* congruence exists with a part of a model for the analysis of the economy. But the political and the economic analyses are both parts of a still wider theoretical scheme that I may call a general theory of social systems.

I have attempted to take only a first step in the codification of the data of empirical studies of voting with this body of theory. These results, and of course other data, as noted, need to be fitted into other aspects of the problems of the polity. Only part of the American political system has been treated here. The American case needs to be treated in wider historical perspective and, comparatively, in relations of similarity and difference, with other political systems. Finally, of course, the political aspect of society needs to be much more systematically related to other aspects of the societies in which political systems function.

In spite of the modesty of the step here taken, it seems to me that it illustrates a kind of opportunity of which social scientists should take careful cognizance. If detailed empirical studies of the type of the voting studies can produce findings and empirical generalizations that fit as closely with deductions from highly general theory as seems to be true in this instance,[48] the prospects of a *cumulative* development of codified and systematic knowledge in this field seem to be better than they have often been thought to be. In my opinion this is not an isolated instance. Intensive work on both sides, and repeated attempts at codification, should produce important results.

TECHNICAL NOTE

As has several times been noted in this chapter, the main framework of the analysis it contains was not generated *ad hoc* in an attempt to interpret the results of the studies of voting behavior, but was developed independently and applied to these results. For the reader who may be interested in the technical aspects of the scheme employed, it seemed advisable to include a brief outline of the most important elements of the scheme, and their genesis.

The main background of the analysis is a generalized conceptual scheme for the analysis of social systems, which in turn is part of a still more generalized scheme for the analysis of action.[49] The basic outline of the social system scheme which is employed here was set forth first in

[48] It is, of course, extremely important to be clear about the sense in which I am and am not advancing a claim to a deductive anticipation of the findings of *Voting* and other studies. As I have stated above, "it was possible to identify four main areas in which to look for mechanisms relevant to these functional requirements." Given the "gross structural facts" of the American political system, ascertainment of which does not require technical research procedures, in terms of such a "functional" model it is possible to deduce that there must be mechanisms that operate in each of these areas, and that they must operate within certain limits if the degree of stability of the system which has historically obtained is to be accounted for. In addition to these and various other sociological considerations I have postulated certain simple psychological assumptions about the limitations of rational decision-making by the individual and the kinds of psychological mechanisms that can be expected to operate where rational decision-making is impossible.

This, however, is very different from deducing the *specific* findings of the empirical research. Of course this has not been done. I have only provided certain "theoretical boxes" into which these findings can be fitted and have tested the goodness of fit in a broad way. One of the main reasons why I could not possibly have deduced the specific findings is that they must in the nature of the case be functions of whole ranges of factors not considered in my model. The model itself is necessarily abstract and deals with only part of the specifically political aspects of the concrete phenomena.

[49] See Talcott Parsons and E. A. Shils, *Toward a General Theory of Action* (Cambridge, Mass.: Harvard University Press, 1951).

Working Papers in the Theory of Action.[50] The most essential feature of this latter formulation was the merging of a scheme of "pattern variables" put forward by Parsons and Shils with a scheme of the functional requirements of social systems originally put forward by Bales.[51]

The basis of this scheme is the idea that any social system may be analyzed in terms of four logically independent functional requirements, which we formulate as *adaptation, goal-attainment, integration,* and *latent pattern-maintenance.* For these we have, for convenience, adopted the notation *A, G, I, L.* These four functional requirements were interpreted as the *dimensions* along which variations in the state of a social system could be analyzed.[52]

Within the framework of this general scheme special attention has been paid to the fact that complex social systems should be conceived as differentiated into (hence made up of) a plurality of *subsystems.* Following the general lead of biological theory we have conceived that the most promising *initial* approach to the nature of the differentiation of such subsystems, and hence of their classification, lay in the concept of function as the basis of differentiation. Starting with the conception of a highly differentiated society, this conception was applied to the idea of the *economy,* as this has been used in economic theory, and it was found that the economists' conception fitted admirably with the specifications of an adaptive subsystem of a society as worked out in terms of this general theory of social systems.[53]

The whole conception of a social system which was delineated as distinct from "situation" or "environment" external to it, has implied the existence and importance of processes of interchange between system and environment which could be formulated in terms of the concepts of input and output. But further, if the system of reference is a subsystem of a larger system, these inputs and outputs would not likely, with respect to their sources and destinations, be randomly distributed over the environment as a whole, but would have relatively specific sources and destinations capable of theoretical identification.

Since we were operating with a theoretical scheme that involved four basic functional categories, and since we had been able to treat the economy as *primarily* (in an empirical sense *never* exclusively) identified with *one* of these categories (the adaptive), it seemed sensible to attempt to work out the logic of a system in which each of the four categories was the basis of a differentiated subsystem of the society. By elementary logic each such subsystem would have three boundaries internal to the system vis-à-vis each of the other three, and a fourth boundary in some sense

[50] Talcott Parsons, R. F. Bales, and E. A. Shils, *Working Papers in the Theory of Action* (New York: Free Press, 1953). See especially chaps. 3 and 5.
[51] R. F. Bales, *Interaction Process Analysis* (Reading, Mass.: Addison-Wesley, 1950).
[52] Parsons, Bales, and Shils, *op. cit.,* chap. 3.
[53] Cf. Parsons, Bales, and Shils, *op. cit.,* chap. 5, pp. 264 ff.

"external" to the system. Once seen in this light, the logical requirements of this reasoning corresponded with startling exactitude to the scheme, well established in economic theory, of classification of the factors of production and the shares of income. The factors of production, that is, could be treated as categories of input into the economy from "outside" and the shares of income as categories of output from the economy to the outside.

The next analytical problem was to identify the source-destination subsystems for each input-output and to determine which was the one "external" boundary. The key to this identification turned out to be the conception of the *goal* of the economy as *production* vis-à-vis the "consumer," identified as a member of the household. The output of production was conceived to be the goal-attainment output of the economy and to go to the household, which had already[54] been identified as belonging to the "pattern-maintenance" subsystem. With two further steps, which are detailed in *Economy and Society* and hence need not be repeated here, this type of reasoning led to setting up the following paradigm[55] of boundary-interchanges between four functionally primary subsystems of a society:

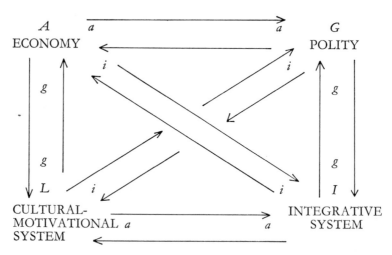

Three further implications, of special interest in the present context, followed from this. First, the category of "land" and its output cognate, "rent," clearly constituted the focus of the "external" boundary of the economy as a system. The sense in which land is a special case among the factors of production in economic theory corresponds directly with that in which the function of pattern-maintenance has been treated as a special case in general social system theory.[56]

[54] For the detailed argument see Parsons and Smelser, *op. cit.*
[55] Parsons and Smelser, *op. cit.*, Fig. 4, p. 68.
[56] See Parsons and Smelser, *op. cit.*

Second, as had already been well established in economic theory, it was, in a sufficiently differentiated society, not possible to limit consideration to a *single* interchange of inputs and outputs at any one boundary, but it was necessary to consider a *double* interchange. In the economy-household case this is a direct consequence of the division of labor and means that the source of wage income (the employing organization) is typically not the same as the producer of most consumers' goods purchased. Hence money, as income and as a medium of exchange for the purchase of desired goods, is a necessary intermediary mechanism in an economic *system*.

Third, it became clear that the boundary-interchange between a postulated polity, as the goal-attaining subsystem of the society, and the integrative system should be theoretically cognate with that between economy and household. To put it in the terms used above, the main output of the polity to the integrative system is effective leadership, which is a form of power, and the main input into the polity from the integrative system is generalized support. Or, to put it a little differently, the *goal* of the polity is the production or generation of effective leadership and, on the less general level, of binding decisions.

It was within this framework of analysis of input-and-output relations between primary functional subsystems of the society that a beginning has been made in the attempt to work out a conception of the polity as cognate with the economy and of its goal-attainment boundary interchange, which has been the main subject of this chapter.

Certain features of the adaptive boundary of the polity were already given, because it stood (in our scheme) vis-à-vis the economy. From the economic point of view it was the boundary concerned with the input of capital resources to the economy from the polity. But it proved to be a long and difficult task to formulate the categories relevant to the double boundary-interchange at the *goal-attaining* boundary of the polity which, according to the logic of our paradigm, stands vis-à-vis the integrative system and does not directly involve the economy at all. It was only here that the scheme used was fully worked out, though the categories of support and binding decisions had been worked with for some time. The scheme in its present form is obviously tentative.

The reader who has followed this rather involved theoretical argument (which he very likely cannot do without familiarity with the sources cited) may comprehend why it was so exciting to find that the results of the voting studies placed the primary basis of political support in the structure of solidary groups of the society: in our theoretical terms, *this is the integrative system* which, on the most general theoretical grounds, would be *predicted* to be the *primary* source. More generally, the deduced characteristics of a double level of interchange between polity and public turned out to fit the empirical findings of the studies with exciting exactitude.

One further technical point may finally be made: It should be clearly understood that, in terms of the technical paradigm I have used, this analysis does *not* deal with the polity as a system. The system of reference is the processes of input-output interchange between polity and integrative system (as "public"). In *Economy and Society* we dealt extensively with this type of system, the economically relevant prototype being a market. Thus we held that the interchange between economy and household may be treated as composed of two primary markets, the labor market and the market for consumers' goods. Similar logic was applied to the capital market and all of these were, in a strict sense, treated as social systems.[57]

Of course, empirically, the process of election of a President is most emphatically *not* a market in the economic sense. But in formal theoretical terms it was the paradigm worked out for the analysis of markets which proved most fruitful in analyzing the voting process. Seen in these terms, my first proposition about nonrational mechanisms in relation to solidary groupings concerned the "latent pattern-maintenance" basis of the system; the second about flexibility in pursuit of goals concerned its goal-attainment function; the third about control of divisive polarization concerned its integration; and the fourth dealing with its relation to the changing structure of the society concerned its adaptive function. These propositions are thus not arbitrary functional generalizations plucked "out of the air" and not dictated by the formal theoretical scheme, but are carefully formulated to meet the specifications of a specific generalized theoretical paradigm.

This demonstration that the voting process can be considered a social system in the fullest technical sense, and can be analyzed in terms of the analytical resources of social system theory, seems to me the important contribution of this chapter.

[57] Parsons and Smelser, *op. cit.,* chap. 3.

10

The Mass Media and the Structure of American Society

*R*aymond and Alice Bauer have made a careful and informative review of empirical research studies on the determinants and effects of the mass media.[1] Beyond this, the evidence they have adduced has led them into a critique of the so-called theory of mass society, which they speak of as the only available attempt at a generalized interpretation of the phenomena involved. Their findings indicate that there is not only a serious paucity of adequate research findings (which is one of the principal conclusions of this survey) but also an even greater lack of adequate theoretical analysis.

They note that in general the proponents of the theory of mass society operate both as commentators on the empirical state of the society and as evaluative critics of it. We think it extremely important, as do the Bauers, to distinguish between these two problems, and that by doing so it is possible to see the theory of mass society as an ideological position congenial to *certain groups* of intellectuals. The Bauers, for example, repeatedly point out the arbitrary ways in which these intellectuals place

---

[1] Raymond A. Bauer and Alice H. Bauer, "America, 'Mass Society' and Mass Media," *Journal of Social Issues,* Vol. 16, No. 2 (1960), pp. 3–66.

Reprinted from Journal of Social Issues, *XVI (1960), 67–77. Winston White, coauthor.*

one of several possible interpretations on items of evidence and tend further to ignore or often distort evidence—in ideological fashion—that does not support their evaluative strictures.

As an alternative to the position of the intellectuals, we wish to suggest a line of theoretical analysis that attempts to fit the evidence on the mass media (and on "mass culture") with that available on other aspects of the society, and that interprets this evidence in the larger context of some of the major features of American social structure and trends of its change. It is only through such a consideration of a wider range of evidence and of the larger social system, we feel, that steps can be taken to reduce the admittedly serious dangers of ideological selectivity and distortion.

Our discussion takes up three main topics. We will first analyze the assumptions underlying the intellectuals' conclusions, and then point out the relation between those assumptions and the elements of ideological selectivity that result from them.[2] We will then suggest that the problems involved in the field of communications are analytically similar to those in two other fields—the system of economic markets and the system of political power and influence. Finally, we will attempt to state a more generalized formula for the patterns of social structure and sociocultural change into which all three of these problem areas seem to us to fit.

THE STRUCTURE OF THE
INTELLECTUAL IDEOLOGY

In an effort to account for the intellectuals' position, the Bauers have suggested that they are at the same time both "cultural élitists" and "social democrats." These labels pinpoint for us two points of reference from which the authors' analysis might be carried further.

On the one hand, there is the problem of cultural values and taste —of cultural standards, if you will. On the other hand, there is the problem of the social structure in which these standards are institutionalized; or put another way, it is the problem of the extent to which a given social structure allows for the expression and development (or frustration and deterioration) of desirable standards. The intellectuals have contended that cultural standards have deteriorated and that social structure has tended to become an aggregate of mass men, alienated from the meaningful ties that would uphold standards. The authors have challenged both of these conclusions with evidence about the upgrading and extension of standards in many areas and with evidence about the viability of primary-group relations.

The intellectuals deplore the "mass man's" alleged vulnerability to

[2] This part of the discussion is developed at greater length in Winston White, *Beyond Conformity*, (New York: Free Press, 1961).

exploitation and his exposure to the mediocre. But underlying their discontent, the Bauers suggest, is their reluctance to let the guardianship of cultural standards slip out of their hands into those they consider less qualified. If the intellectuals do in fact hold both of these positions at once, how might one explain this seemingly inconsistent mixture of cultural conservatism and social liberalism?

We would agree with the Bauers that many intellectuals have explicitly or implicitly arrived at this conclusion. We do not feel, however, that all intellectuals have attempted to straddle the cultural and social fence in this manner; many have arrived at less ambiguous—although equally erroneous—conclusions. Behind these conclusions lie three distinct ideological sources, each with its own set of assumptions about social theory—about man's relation to society, to culture, and the like. These assumptions, as the authors point out, must be uncovered in order to understand and assess the intellectuals' positions. Tracing through these ideological patterns may clarify the problem. Two of them lie on the cultural side and one on the social side.

The ideology on the side of social structure assumes that man is essentially good and is only corrupted by social forces. Cultural standards are not seen as problematical but as epiphenomena of social conditions. Given a favorable social environment (e.g., the "right" economic-political institutions, the restoration of community ties, the elimination of "anonymous authority," etc.), desirable cultural standards will spring into efflorescence. But given the unfavorable conditions of a mass society, man is so alienated that he is unable to resist mass culture. He has, so to speak, no consumer sovereignty, and is compelled to "buy" whatever supply of culture is at hand. This point of view is more or less Marxian in its assumptions; Erich Fromm is one of its leading spokesmen.

The ideology on the cultural side assumes that man is conditionally good or evil and that his commitments to cultural standards cannot be taken for granted but must be vigilantly maintained. In this version, social structure is a non-problematical epiphenomenon of culture. Given the "right" cultural commitments, appropriate social institutions will follow along in due course. There are two ideological positions within this set of assumptions.

The élitist position, which the authors touch on, is that the highest cultural standards must be maintained by the agency of an élite and that high and folk culture alike should be borne by a gradation of classes. If standards are assured in this way (or, as we would put it, if they are ascribed to class and to region), then the social structure is safe. People know their place and what is expected of them. Without the guardianship of an élite, the demands of the untutored masses for a vulgarized cultural product will take over. T. S. Eliot and Ortega y Gasset have been spokesmen for this point of view.

Another important "cultural" ideology, however, is that held by those we will call the "moralizers." For them, social structure is even less problematical, in that buttressing by an elite and by a class structure is no longer felt to be necessary. The moralizers believe that standards must be maintained by individual responsibility. It is up to the individual to maintain his commitments to values, to hold the line on his own, as it were, against the seductions of mass society with its hedonistic flabbiness. It is in the hearts and minds of men that moral heroism (the intellectual's counterpart of the businessmen's rugged individualism) will shape the social fabric. Archibald MacLeish and Joseph Wood Krutch, for example, are notable spokesmen for this point of view. The élitists and the social-structure ideologists tend to regard the moralizers as hopelessly middle-brow, but it seems to us that any definition of "intellectuals" as social critics must include them.

Common to both types of "culture" ideologists—the élitists and moralizers alike—is the assumption that the individual does have "consumer sovereignty." The public gets what it wants (and deserves). Standards deteriorate because of the low quality of mass demand, not because of the low quality of supply.

Finally, those intellectuals whom the Bauers characterize as both cultural elitists and social democrats at the same time are, we suggest, ideologically analogous to, though of course not affiliated with, the Communist Party—an élite group that sets standards where, according to the ideology, there should be no need to. Further, the assertion of cultural autonomy by the mass of men, given favorable social conditions, is analogous to the withering away of the state. Either these intellectuals' beliefs are inconsistent in that they consider élite guidance necessary regardless of what kind of social conditions prevail, or they have embraced élitism as an intermediate means to hold the line until the proper social conditions can be attained, if ever.

None of these points of view is adequate, we believe, for analyzing the relationship between cultural standards and the social structure in which they are institutionalized. We have called them ideologies, for each in its own way is selective in its approach—tending to take for granted or to ignore factors that must be considered for proper analysis. As our further comments will spell out, we see the mass media as a mechanism operating in a "market" between the purveyors of cultural content and the public. And, as the Bauers have emphasized, it is not the only mechanism but one that operates in conjunction with others, such as informal primary-group relationships.

In such a "market,"[3] we maintain, both supply and demand operate without one always being subjected to the other. Our analysis has tried

---

[3] When we speak of market here in quotation marks we are generalizing the economic concept to cover several other related types. We hope no confusion results from this usage.

to show that the intellectuals are by no means in agreement on this issue. The élitists and moralizers believe that low-grade public demand lowers standards; the social-structure ideologists blame the quality of the supply, claiming that the public—or the masses, as they would say— cannot be expected to know better, social conditions being what they are.

It is with respect to standards that the issue comes to a head. The élitists regard standards as ascribed to class, with the highest standards maintained only through their agency. They are like parents who look on the public as their children, believing them incapable of acting responsibly without their surveillance.

The moralizers, on the other hand, tend to ignore the whole problem of the social context in which standards are defined. They believe that each individual, by exercising his autonomous "responsibility," can define his own standards independently of others, by means of "nonconformism" or "individualism." Standards, apparently, are given as in the utilitarian conception of "self-interest." Finally, for the social-structure ideologists, standards are taken for granted. Like autonomy and spontaneity, they spring full-born from the sane society.

Dwight MacDonald's metaphor of Gresham's law represents an interesting combination of the above. For him, the "market" is purely one of runaway inflation which cannot be checked because standards are continually falling. Low-grade demand stimulates low-grade supply, and vice versa—like a reciprocating engine, as he puts it. With no élite in charge of standards, he considers the situation hopeless.

ECONOMIC, POLITICAL, AND COMMUNICATIONS SYSTEMS

The context in which we wish to place our comparisons between mass communications and economic and political systems is that of the division of labor. Where the functions of units in a social system become sufficiently differentiated, it becomes impossible for the "producers" of an output— be it a commodity, an expression of political support, or a culturally significant message—to be ascriptively bound to the recipients, as would be the case, for example, for custom-made goods, feudal allegiance, or patronage of the arts. The offer of automobiles for sale or party appeals for votes are "broadcast" in a sense analogous to that of soap operas or symphony concerts. Their producers do not know in advance in detail who or how many the recipients will be, or what commitments they will be willing to make as a result of exposure, although market research can in all three cases narrow the range of uncertainty somewhat.

All such processes of differentiation lead to "alienation"—both for the producer from the ultimate use of his product and for the consumer from direct involvement with the source of his supply. Adam Smith's famous generalization about the economic efficiency of the division of labor can thus—with proper qualifications—be extended to these other two contexts: the "consumer" acquires degrees of freedom that would be impossible without such differentiation. At the same time, certain mechanisms of control become necessary if such a system is to be stable, and in fact bring about the degrees of freedom referred to. These controls center on *institutionalized* regulatory patterns—like contract and property in the economic sphere, leadership and authority in the political—and on institutionalized *media* such as money and political power (as exercised, for instance, through the franchise).

Let us consider first the degrees of freedom created by an economic market system, and then try to work out the parallels for political and communications systems. In so doing we hope to highlight those features of the latter that are analytically significant for the mass-media problem.

In contrast to a system of economic barter, the consumer who holds money funds in a highly differentiated market system has the following degrees of freedom: (1) in accepting money, e.g. in exchange for labor services, he is not *ipso facto* committed to buy what he wants to spend it for from any particular source of supply—he can "shop around"; (2) he is not committed to any particular composition of the "package" of items for which he spends it, but can select in terms of his wants at the time; (3) he is not committed to any particular terms of exchange but can shop and/or bargain over prices; and (4) he is not committed to any particular time of expenditure of his funds, but can extend his expenditures over time (indeed, the availability of interest puts a positive premium on delay).

This classification provides a convenient point of reference for identifying points of strain and certain possibilities of malfunctioning to which a market system is subject to a greater degree than one of ascriptive exchange or barter. All of these deviations have existed in fact in greater and less degree and in particular have figured prominently in critical discussions of "industrial" economies. Particularly prominent among these are the following: (1) Monopoly can restrict to varying degrees (and in the extreme case eliminate) the consumer's freedom of choice with respect to source of supply; indeed, one school of thought has alleged that its increase was an "inevitable" trend of a "capitalistic" economy. (2) Freedom to choose among a wide variety of products may be rendered valueless by an inherent process of product deterioration; the standards of handicraft excellence may give way to the shoddiness of mass-produced products, another point at which a prominent school of thought has alleged inevitability. (3) Freedom with respect to terms of exchange may be cancelled out by the inherently exploitative character of the market structure—a factor partly, but not necessarily wholly, deriving from monopoly. It has thus frequently been alleged that the "real" standards of living of consumers necessarily deteriorate at this point. Finally, (4) the freedom in time can be cancelled out by inflation, so that the longer one holds his dollar the greater the disadvantage of his position; inflation again has been held to be an inherent trend. The inference from this syndrome is that the economic welfare of some conceived "typical" individual is inevitably injured by the division of labor, markets, and industrialization—unless, as some think, it can be protected by socialism.

The broad answer, of course, is that, though all of these things can and do happen, such trends as have existed have not in general developed cumulatively to extremes in American society (to which present attention is confined). Thus to take one point, contrary to much opinion, it is impossible to prove that the degree of concentration in American manufacturing industry has increased appreciably over the past half century. If these trends have not gone to such extremes, there must be "countervailing" forces that lie in the mechanisms of control mentioned above. The prototypical problem statement here is Gresham's Law and both the Bauers and we must be grateful to Dwight MacDonald for having introduced this conception into the discussion. In the economic case it is simply not true empirically that, to paraphrase the Communist Manifesto, "the history of all market and currency systems is a history of galloping inflation"—nor of monopoly, nor of product deterioration, nor of exploitation.

Exactly parallel problems may be identified in the political field. Political differentiation, we suggest, creates degrees of freedom analogous to those of the market as follows: (1) The analogy of economic source of supply is leadership agency, e.g. a party as the agency taking responsibility for collective decision-making if given requisite political support. A "free electorate" has a choice between such agencies and is not ascriptively bound to any one by its legitimacy. (2) The political analogy of products is policies. By virtue of his position in a political system, the individual or group is neither ascriptively committed to favoring particular policies nor committed to them—except in a minority of cases—by "barter deals," but is free to allocate such influence as he has between a significant range of alternatives. (3) Economic price is essentially a determination of *cost*. The political analogy is the obligations entailed by commitment to a collective decision or policy. This means that there must be some balancing between the sharing of the benefits of what "gets done" and allocation of the burdens necessary to get it done, e.g. taxes. Finally, (4) in the political as in the economic case, differentiation makes it possible for leadership and followership both to enjoy greater flexibility with respect to time.

Elements of malfunctioning in such a differentiated political system which parallel those discussed in the economy can be identified as follows:

(1) Parallel to economic monopoly is the concentration of political power to the point where effectiveness of choice among leadership elements is eliminated. A typical case of this view is Mills' contention[4] of the existence of a single unified "power elite." (2) The parallel to economic product deterioration is the alleged cumulatively increasing predominance in the political system of special and group interests over the public interest. It is suggested that the public does not get acceptable policies but only the effects of the "selfish" utilization of positions of political advantage to further special group interests. (3) The parallel to economic exploitation through the price system is the conception of progressively increasing exploitation of the "little man" by the "interests." Mills' conception of "cumulative advantage" seems to be the most explicit recent formulation of this view. Finally, (4) there is a political parallel to economic inflation. This is a process of progressive deterioration in the worth of general public commitments to the effective functioning of the political system through leadership. Various elements, that is to say, make "sacrifices," such as military service, only to find that the polity they devoted themselves to is becoming progressively less effective, more interest-dominated, time-serving, and the like.

The question of the balance between these disorganizing trends and countervailing factors in the American political system over the last half century, for instance, is clearly a complicated one. There has always been a left-wing school of thought which has given overwhelming preponderance to the former factors, Mills being the most prominent recent exponent. The relative effectiveness in meeting the crises of two world wars and the great depression, however, seem to most observers to indicate the operation of important countervailing factors. It seems legitimate to consider the theorists of "late monopoly capitalism" and those of the "power elite" as exponents of an ideology in the same sense in which we have attributed this to the theorists of mass culture.

We would like to consider the system of mass communications as a differentiated social system in the same sense that economic and political systems are, and a necessary one in a highly differentiated society of the American type. It involves the same order of specialization of function between "producing" and "consuming" units, and—most importantly—between different kinds of communication output. It also involves relative concentration of resources in the hands of larger producers, though the question of the degree of monopoly is not a simple one. It of course involves "alienation" of the recipient from control over the sources of communications. And it goes without saying that it involves both formal and informal mechanisms of control, the most important of which are institutionalized.

[4] Cf. C. Wright Mills, *The Power Elite*. Oxford University Press, New York 1956.

Such a system could be expected to produce degrees of freedom for the typical recipient analogous to those of the economic consumer or the member of the political public.

These may be sketched as follows: (1) Contrasted with the ascriptiveness of tradition is the range of alternative sources of communication output, newspapers, magazines, books, broadcasting stations and programs. This is far from unlimited, but unless restricted by totalitarian types of policies, far wider than in any traditional system. (2) There is a wide range of choice with reference to content, both with reference to types of content and to levels of quality within types. (3) There are freedoms with respect to "cost"—a conception, however, in need of clarification when used in this context. One component, of course, is money cost. Another, which figures in the Bauer study, is time spent by the consumer. Still another is something like "receptivity" to the line of influence suggested. For advertising, purchases can be a measure of this; for political campaigning, actual voting; but where literary tastes are at stake, measures are more difficult. (4) There is freedom with respect to time, in the sense of receiving and not receiving communications, and allocation of time between particular kinds. Among the most important points here is the fact that, given storage facilities, the printed word can be preserved for reference at any future time.

It is now our suggestion that the main interpretive contentions of the theorists of mass culture can be fitted into this classification, as modes in which allegedly relevant standards fail to be met. Thus (1) with respect to source, there is much complaint about the concentration of sources, especially with reference to newspapers and broadcasting. This tends to play down the very wide variety available in some fields of communication, e.g. local newspapers and book publishing, especially recently of paperbacks. (2) Perhaps the most prominent single contention is the parallel of economic product deterioration, namely the notion that mass communication inevitably leads to the predominance of *kitsch* over quality items. (3) The analogue of economic exploitation and cumulative advantage in the power system is the idea of the "manipulative" exploitation of the irrational through the mass communication media; the portrayal of violence and its alleged relation to delinquency is a good case in point. Finally, (4) we might suggest that the theme of "apathy" is the analogue of economic inflation, namely the contention that the communication "market" is so flooded with inferior items, from whatever cause, that the standards of the recipient tend to become undermined, his responses becoming automatized and undiscriminating.

Again, as in the previous instances, these malfunctionings can and do occur. The evidence the Bauers have marshalled, however, does not support the contention that such has been the case in American society; at the very least, it compels serious consideration for the position we are advancing that countervailing forces, such as institutionalized standards and favorable "market" conditions, do in fact prevail, to a significant degree.

SUMMARY

In the field of communications, then, we suggest that structural changes have been occurring that are analytically similar to those more familiar in the economic and political systems and that these changes—in all three cases—have the consequences of what we call extension, differentiation, and upgrading.

With respect to communications in particular, fundamental to this process of change is the shaking up of older traditional ascriptions, among the most salient of which are those of stratification. The élitist system confined its audience, by and large, to its peers. It was not expected that the general public would, or could, in any way be interested—except perhaps for a diffuse admiration of the elegance of the upperclass way of life. One major consequence of the breaking down of ascriptive ties is the *extension* of accessibility to cultural content to ever wider circles of the population. In recent Western history, the most conspicuous example of this is the extension of education. Far wider groups than ever before are expected to appreciate elements of the great Western cultural heritage.

The second aspect of change is that of *differentiation*. The term "mass" media itself is misleading, suggesting that the media themselves are undifferentiated with respect to content and audience. Not only do different media (or often the same media) carry qualitatively different content and reach qualitatively different audiences, but the same individual, in many cases, uses a variety of media.

Just as economic and political systems—indeed, social structures in general—become more differentiated, so do the media themselves tend to differentiate. The news coverage, for example, of the news-magazine and the metropolitan newspaper enables the smaller community paper to specialize in local news. The advent of television has led to more specialization on the part of radio programming, witness the increase in musical programs.

With differentiation and specialization, one might expect, as in other systems, an increase of functional capacity in the communications system with the consequence of *upgrading*. If such is the case, one could expect a proportionately greater spread of the *higher* levels of culture than of the lower. Although the problems of evidence are formidable here, we would suggest, for example, that the advent of television has resulted in the upgrading of other "competing" media, itself coming in at the bottom of the qualitative ladder in certain respects (as successive waves of immigrants came in at the bottom of the occupational ladder, enabling previous arrivals to move up). Anyone watching old motion picture films on TV might well be impressed by their dismal mediocrity when compared with the contemporary films, a change that arises from something more than a mere shift in style. The growth of serious music programming on FM stations is also a case in point.

Perhaps one can suggest that both films and radio broadcasting have not only been "kicked upstairs" by TV competition, but that differentiation has led to an upgrading of taste. It is surely not too far-fetched to say that certain TV programs now fill a low-grade demand that previously turned to other media for satisfaction. This is not to say, however, that upgrading is *solely* a consequence of changes in the media of the "market" (the fallacy of a social-structure ideology). Upgrading is also dependent on raising the standards of the public in the sense of "building up" the level of their commitments to standards.[5] In addition to the extension of higher levels of education, this process is also effected through primary-group relations, where the individual learns not only to acquire new tastes but helps to define them as well. Even if his motivation arises purely from emulation or "status-seeking"—as some interpreters choose to suggest, brushing aside any realistic desire on the part of the individual to widen his range of experience—the *consequences* of this group interaction cannot be overlooked.

In conclusion, we hope that the combination of our treatment of the ideological problem with the parallel we have drawn between the selectivity of the mass-culture theorists and certain critics of the American economy and political system will serve to broaden the problem raised by the Bauers. By placing the mass-culture issue in a larger perspective, one can perhaps see that it is a special case of more general processes and that there is the same kind of problem in interpretation—not only of mass culture but of American society as a total system.

Most fundamental of the fallacies underlying the biases of the mass-culture theorists seems to us to be the assumption that this is an "atomized" mass society where the relations of one individual to another have become increasingly amorphous. Quite to the contrary, as Kornhauser[6] has pointed out, American society is one of the preeminent examples of a *pluralist* society in which—through the course of structural differentiation—an increasingly ramified network of criss-crossing solidarities has been developing. Nor is our conclusion to be taken as a defense of the status quo; American society has—in terms of our high expectations for it—many inadequacies. But, we believe, they cannot be "explained," much less confronted with any degree of sophistication, by the currently prominent theory of mass society.

[5] It is essential, in order to avoid ideological traps, to pay attention to both the "demand" and the "supply" sides, rather than explicitly or implicitly assuming that one determines the outcome of the other.

[6] Cf. William Kornhauser, *The Politics of Mass Society,* Free Press, 1960; and Parsons, "Social Structure and Political Orientation," *World Politics,* October 1960.

Chapter 11

Full Citizenship for the Negro American?

*t*he designation "second-class citizen" has often and with justice been used to describe the status of the Negro in American society. As the British sociologist T. H. Marshall has shown with particular clarity,[1] citizenship is a complicated matter that is by no means exhausted by the more literal meanings of the term "civil rights." I should like to begin this discussion with an analysis of the meaning of the concept of citizenship, leaning heavily on Marshall's work, though attempting to go beyond it in some respects. I shall then attempt to analyze some of the conditions which have been necessary to account for the progress which the Negro American has made so far toward gaining full citizenship—and which, at the same time, the society has made toward including the Negro in that status—and the further conditions which must be fulfilled if the process is to approach completion. In carrying out this analysis, I shall pay particular attention to comparing the status of the Negro with that of other groups that have in various analogous ways been discriminated against in American society. I hope that such an analysis will reveal a combination of similarities and differences which illuminates the salient features of the Negro case. Since the other groups have progressed

[1] T. M. Marshall, *Class, Citizenship, and Social Development* (Garden City, N.Y.: Doubleday, 1964), Chap. IV.

Reprinted from Daedalus (*November 1965*).

considerably further toward full inclusion than has the Negro so far, their experience may provide certain projective guide lines for considering the Negro case. The relation of the internal change of status of the Negro American to the color problem in world affairs will also be discussed.

The concept of citizenship, as used here, refers to full membership in what I shall call the *societal community*.[2] This term refers to that aspect of the total society as a system, which forms a *Gemeinschaft*, which is the focus of solidarity or mutual loyalty of its members, and which constitutes the consensual base underlying its political integration. This membership is central to what it means to be defined, in the case of our own nation, as "an American"—hence it gives a special justification for the word order used in the title of the present essay, that it is the Negro American, not vice versa. The Negro slave could have been, and certainly was called, an "American Negro"—he was resident in the United States and owned by American citizens, but was not part of the societal community in the present sense.

Perhaps John Rawls has formulated, in general philosophical terms, more clearly than anyone else the way in which full citizenship implies a fundamental equality of rights—not equality in *all* senses, but in the sense in which we refer to the rights of membership status in the societal community.[3]

From the unit viewpoint, societal community is a category of the commitment of members to the collectivity in which they are associated, and of the members to each other. It is the focus of loyalties which need not be absolute, indeed cannot be, but which require high priority among loyalties of the members.[4] To occupy this position the associational structure must be in accord with the common values of the society: members are committed to it because it both implements their values and organizes their interests in relation to other interests. In the latter context it is the basis for defining rules for the play of interests which make integration possible, preventing the inevitable elements of conflict from leading into vicious circles radically disruptive of the community. It is also the reference base of the standards for allocating available mobile resources in complex communities.

In all "advanced" societies, societal community is linked with political organization, but is also differentiated from it. Although all advanced societies are "politically organized," this aspect of their organization, what we ordinarily refer to, at the societal level, as government, is not identical with community in the present sense. It is precisely when the two are in some kind of conflict that revolutionary situations can arise.

[2] Cf. Talcott Parsons, *Societies: Comparative and Evolutionary Perspectives* (Englewood Cliffs, N.J.: Prentice-Hall, 1966).

[3] John Rawls, "Constitutional Liberty and the Concept of Justice," in C. J. Friedrich (ed.), *Justice (Nomos VI),* (New York: Atherton Press, 1963).

[4] Edward A. Shils, *The Torment of Secrecy* (New York: Free Press, 1956).

THE NATION AS
SOCIETAL COMMUNITY

In modern Western history, the focus of the differentiation of the societal community lay in the emergence of the nation, hence of "nationalism." Obviously, a similar process is now going on in many parts of the world in the formation of the "new nations." There are three aspects of the emergence of the nation which I should like to note and then briefly spell out for the American case.

The first is the differentiation of criteria for belonging to the nation in contrast to membership in the more "primordial" kinsnip-ethnic and, often, religious groupings. Here the change is toward the establishment of *associational* criteria. In the case of a total society, as politically organized, it is impossible for membership to be entirely voluntary for all, but it can move very far in this direction, that is, away from a purely ascriptive basis, and has done so. More importantly, the status of citizenship comes to be institutionalized in terms independent of the ascriptive criteria just cited, for it concerns above all the "natural rights" so fundamental to American tradition.

Second, the nation is differentiated from its government. This is *not* to say they are dissociated. Rather, this differentiation involves the development of political independence by the societal community so that it is no longer ascribed to any particular governmental leadership, such as hereditary monarchy with full executive authority. The obverse of this development is that government becomes structurally independent in that it is free to mobilize within the society those resources which are relatively fluid, for example, in establishing an appointive civil service free of more particularistic ties and in soliciting support from a range of different groups in the constituency.

Finally, the differentiation of the societal community as nation involves a shift of the integration of the three elements, community, ascriptive bases, and government, in the direction of a synthesis of citizenship and territoriality. This is necessary because the individual is anchored in residential ties, even though there is high residential mobility, because work as well as residence is located physically, and because the availability of resources is territorially anchored.[5]

For the United States, as for many other countries, the consolidation of nationhood was directly connected with a struggle for political independence. It may be said that there was sufficient ethnic and religious uniformity to make solidarity possible, but enough diversity to favor a major shift toward the associational basis of that solidarity, as compared

[5] Talcott Parsons, "The Principal Structures of Community," *Structure and Process in Modern Societies* (New York: Free Press, 1960).

with the European analogues. The core was surely white, Anglo-Saxon, and Protestant (WASP). The Negroes, most of whom were slaves, were not included, and the Catholic, Dutch, and Jewish minorities were so small as to be structurally almost negligible. However, one of the three components, the religious, had built-in diversity, in that there were many Protestant denominations.[6] And, in spite of the prominent involvement of the Anglican church in the colonies, the non-Anglican majority was understandably reluctant to countenance an Anglican Establishment, particularly because of the latter's relation to England.

On the side of values, two particularly important components were the influence of the Enlightenment, with its emphasis on assuring the rights of individuals independently of their ascriptive involvements, and the fact that the most important religious groups involved were in the same broad tradition, which we tend to call "liberal Protestantism" today. The Bill of Rights is the central institutional embodiment of these components.[7]

The new American Union was, however, a *federal* union of a special sort. Though the Constitution prescribed a Republican form of government as well as other universalistic patterns, especially through the Bill of Rights, the states could and did serve as a strong protector of the particularistic groups and institutions at many levels, from the South's "peculiar institution" before the Emancipation Proclamation and the Thirteenth Amendment to local power interests, police power, and the conservative interpretation of the Fourteenth Amendment.[8] Today we are acutely aware of how hard it has been to overcome the conception that the state was somehow "sovereign" and that we were only a confederation of states, not a federal state. In view of the difficulties of maintaining the Union, not only in the Civil War crisis, but also earlier,[9] it seems probable that this "concession" to state particularism was necessary in order to establish a union at all—*vide* the length of time it took Rhode Island to decide to join.

The essential consequence for our problem is that this version of federalism drastically limited the extent to which universalistic values and normative principles, formulated most conspicuously in the Bill of Rights, could be applied to the regulation of relations internal to a large variety of groups and collectivities. The extension of this jurisdiction has been a long process and is still far from complete. The most visible aspect of the process has been legal, based above all on the post-Civil War Amendments, the Fourteenth and Fifteenth. The legal process has been both cause and effect of a broader process of structural change in

[6] Richard Niebuhr, *The Social Sources of Denominationalism* (Cleveland: World, 1957).
[7] Cf. S. M. Lipset, *The First New Nation* (New York: Basic Books, 1963).
[8] Cf. Samuel Beer, "Liberalism and the National Idea," Public Affairs Conference Center. University of Chicago, 1965.
[9] S. M. Lipset, *The First New Nation, op. cit.*

the society, several aspects of which will figure in the following discussion. A major force in this process is further societal *differentiation* in many fields, such as property rights and the development of new institutions regulating marriage and education.

Some of the same circumstances established quite firmly the mutual independence of government and the national community. This was a phase which underlay another main source of American strains, namely, the suspicion between the private sector and government. This has had a long-run influence on the Negro problem by minimizing certain kinds of private business support for public action in favor of the Negro. On the whole, the differentiation proceeded faster and further here than in Europe, a fact which has, on balance, contributed positively to the inclusion of the Negro as well as other groups that were originally excluded. The reason for this judgment is that the relatively open and pluralistic situation, although it provided opportunity for much obstruction, has served as a structural base for challenging and overcoming the obstruction. Above all, such structural changes as industrialization and urbanization, which ultimately undermined the obstacles, were favored.

Finally, the new nation began with a unified, territorially based control of resources and of rights, a factor which eventually contributed to the integration of its societal community. The Constitution guaranteed economic unity by prohibiting tariffs between the states and by allowing no limitations on the movement of citizens. Inherent in this guarantee was a general bias against the consolidation of local and regional particularism, even though other powerful forces worked toward it. This was of special importance because it existed in the early phase of a unique opportunity—that of occupying a territorial area of continental scope. The integration of the pattern of citizenship with that of territory in all areas under American control created a relatively uniform standard of citizenship. This meant not the neglect of sectional interests, but the positive establishment of a pattern covering all regions. The special case of the South will, of course, occupy much of our attention.

As Lipset has pointed out,[10] the United States originated as a "new nation" in a way broadly similar to those that have been emerging in our own time. It achieved independence from colonial status. It approached the pattern of association of people who came to implement their own values and goals more closely than could older nations, but it had sufficient initial cultural homogeneity to achieve its initial integration, not without serious internal struggles, but still with a certain effectiveness. This "liberal" tradition, especially as expressed in the Bill of Rights, provided a basis for other groups, culturally and ethnically more distant from those predominant in the founding generations, to be included in the national community.

[10] *Ibid.*, Part I.

The consolidation of that community and the advancement of the process of differentiation of the society to the point that a strong national government could take precedence over local, state, and regional particularisms took a long time. Though the most serious crisis was settled by the outcome of the Civil War, as Samuel Beer has made clear, a new phase began in the period of the New Deal.[11] In part, this was a result of our wider sense of national responsibility in world affairs following our involvement in World War I. As we shall see, it was not unimportant that the process of inclusion of the "new immigration" reached its culmination at the same time that the Democratic party attained its new position of power in the New Deal era. It was not fortuitous that the same transitional period saw the predominant Negro political allegiance shift from the Republicans to the Democrats.

As not only the first, but probably by now the most "mature," of the "new" nations, the United States has, as Lipset emphasizes, a special opportunity to serve as a symbol of the movement of national "liberation" and to assume a role of leadership in this context. This role, in turn, has been intimately connected with the internal structure of the society with respect to liberty and equality. Of these internal standards, those of ethnicity and religion are particularly important. Unfortunately, the American role in international leadership has been severely compromised in the last generation by our competition and conflict with the Communist movement. Our hypersensitivity to the threat of internal subversion places us in danger of being identified internationally with the older European "colonial" powers and their imperialism. The relationship of these issues to race and color is patent. The suggestion will be made in this paper that the movement for inclusion of the Negro into full citizenship in the national community may prove to be a crucial aspect of this complex set of processes, and may present a great opportunity to claim a place of fuller leadership in this setting. This movement, as Rupert Emerson and Martin Kilson show in their paper,* has been stimulated largely by the rise of new nonwhite nations, particularly those of Africa. It is, however, my thesis that its *main* impetus has been internal to the development of American society itself. If the movement, and the forces that favor it in the white community, can succeed substantially, this may prove to have momentous international repercussions. I shall return to this theme at the end of the paper.

I shall conclude this introduction with a brief theoretical discussion. The process by which previously excluded groups attain full citizenship or membership in the societal community will, in this paper, be called *inclusion*. This is, as will be shown presently, a highly complex process. It will be argued that, at least under the conditions that have prevailed in American society, this has been intimately linked with the process of

[11] Samuel Beer, *op. cit.*   * [Another paper in the same issue of *Daedalus*, Fall 1965: ed.]

differentiation which has produced an increasingly *pluralistic* social structure. Not only are there many subcollectivities within the societal community, but the typical individual participates through membership in an increasingly wide variety. If interest is centered in *ethnic* groups, membership is necessarily by hereditary ascription.[12] In religious affiliation, a larger voluntary element is common, but most religious affiliations, at least to the larger groups, are *de facto* hereditary and often closely associated with ethnicity.

In a pluralistic social structure, membership in an ethnic or religious group does not determine *all* of the individual's social participations. His occupation, education, employing organization, and political affiliation may in varying degrees be independent of his ethnicity or religion. On the whole, the trend of American development has been toward increasing pluralism in this sense and, hence, increasing looseness in the connections among the components of total social status.

This trend has one particularly important implication for our purposes, namely, that it is essential to make a clear distinction between *inclusion* and *assimilation*. There may be pluralism of religious and ethnic groups among full citizens which cuts across many other involvements of the same people. The prototype was the original religious pluralism within the white Protestant group, which was built into the constitutional structure by the separation of Church and State and by religious toleration and freedom. It has subsequently been extended to include Jews and Catholics through what is usually called an "ecumenical" process.

However, because the United States was originally primarily a white Protestant society, it was often thought that inclusion was synonymous with becoming Protestant or as similar as possible to the Anglo-Saxon tradition. The developments that will be outlined below make it quite clear that this is not the case for the other white groups, and I shall argue that it need not and probably will not be so for the Negro. Full inclusion and multiple role participation are compatible with the maintenance of distinctive ethnic and/or religious identity, though not in the sense which is the obverse of exclusion, namely self-imposed isolation as in the case of extreme Jewish Orthodoxy.

THE COMPONENTS OF CITIZENSHIP

T. H. Marshall, in his discussion of the development of citizenship in Great Britain noted above, distinguished three components of the

---

[12] Qualifications must be made, for example, for interethnic marriages where, with or without formal "adoption," the couple functions primarily in one group and, hence, the "inmarrying" spouse may be said to have changed ethnic affiliation, especially if the children identify clearly with the one group.

status of citizenship, the *civil* (which in an American reference should perhaps be called legal), the *political*, concerned particularly with the democratic franchise, and the *social*, which refers essentially to the context we defined as "welfare" or, in the terms of our federal organization, health, education, and welfare.

Marshall establishes an important pattern of temporal sequence in the institutionalization of these three components as criteria of membership in the English national community: the civil came first, the political next, and the social last. In England, the establishment of civil rights in this relatively narrow sense was started at the time of Justice Coke in the early seventeenth century, with its consolidation of the independence of the Common Law vis-à-vis government, and extended in various phases through the eighteenth century. The political component began to emerge with the beginning of the development of the parliament's independence from the crown in the seventeenth century, which culminated in 1688. However, for the individual, its institutionalization centered in the franchise extensions of the nineteenth and twentieth centuries—from the Reform Bill of 1832 to the Women's Suffrage Act of 1918. The social component goes back to the factory acts of the nineteenth century, culminating in the enactment of the Beveridge Plan after World War II. With appropriate adaptations this pattern is applicable both to the American experience as a whole and to that of the Negro.

Before entering into this, further explanation of the meaning of these components is necessary. The civil or legal component concerns the *application* of the value system to the relevant context. This is what is particularly salient in the context of the term, *rights*. Rights indicate that members of the societal community in the normative sense "must" enjoy certain basic freedoms and securities in them. The catalogue is, of course, familiar. It involves security of each individual and of property, freedom of speech, religion, assembly, and association, and both substantive and procedural equality before the law—components formulated in our Constitutional tradition as "equal protection of the laws" and "due process of law." These rights are to take precedence over any particular political status or interest and over any social component such as wealth or poverty, prominence or obscurity.

It is a very long step from the constitutional and legal enactment of these rights to their effective implementation, and this process is still going on in many sectors of American society, even in some that are largely unrelated to the racial problem. But, the constitutional basis of these rights is firmly established and has served as the most important lever for exerting pressure during the earlier stages of the Negro inclusion movement. The special role of the N.A.A.C.P. has been to exploit this aspect of our citizenship structure in behalf of the Negro.

The political component concerns participation in collective goal-attainment, at the societal level in the process of government. The differentiation of government from the societal community, as noted above, implies that the average citizen is neither a governmental functionary in any usual sense nor a totally controlled subject of his government. He does, however, have rights of participation in the governmental process. These crystallize at two main points in modern politics. One is the franchise, basically the right of a formal voice in the selection of leadership —leadership being a more generalized and practicable focus than specific policies, which are decided by referendum. The other is the right to attempt to influence policy, starting with the rights of free speech and assembly, but extending to the sensitive area of "lobbying." As mediating structures, the party system and the institutionalization of mass media became involved here. The body of citizens needs "spokesmen," the potential influencer needs media for making his wishes and their gratifications known, and leaders need structural outlets for their opinions, appeals, and proposals.

The social component does not concern the opportunity to express and implement the rights derived from the societal values so much as the resources and capacities necessary for this implementation. In this connection the societal community defines and presents standards for the allocation of resources to the community as a whole and to its various subsectors. The obverse of this is the definition of the terms on which capacities, as matched with opportunities, can be involved in the process of inclusion. This is a special context of the problem of "qualifying" for inclusion.

There are two categories of resources which must be distinguished for our purposes. In our achievement-oriented society, one can scarcely imagine that justice would prevail if large classes of its members, through no fault of their own, were either denied opportunity for achievement (including the reaping of its rewards) or handicapped severely in gaining access to it. Given the formal status of equality in civil or legal rights and in basic political participation, these rights can be "empty" if opportunity is not equalized.

Of course, discrimination may be abolished or minimized across a whole range of opportunities, particularly in employment. But even absence of discrimination is "empty" if remediable handicaps continue to prevail. These handicaps may be randomly distributed among the categorial grouping with which this discussion is primarily concerned. But if they are linked to the status position of the excluded group, they raise the essential problem of the implementation of the rights of citizenship through the equalization of opportunity and the base from which that opportunity can be exploited.

This is where the distinction between the two categories of resources becomes essential. The first category is mainly financial. For an individual to be able to take advantage of available opportunities he must have not only the capacity but also the financial means to do so. This aspect of the social citizenship complex was paramount in the discussions and measures of public policy during the New Deal era. The second concerns the underlying capacity of the units, especially individuals and their families, to function effectively in the environment in which they are placed. At the level of the individual this concerns above all health and education. There has been so much discussion of all these themes that it is not necessary to spell them out further here. Suffice it to say that, first, increasing attention is being placed on education as the most decisive link between the individual's underlying levels of capacity and his relation to the opportunity structure.[13] Second, the concept of "welfare" is a diffuse one extending from the most elementary financial conditions of subsistence to the problem of the structure of the social environment in which disadvantaged groups are placed. This latter extension reflects the fact, firmly established by social science, that at the bottom of the social scale (as judged by the usual criteria of success, prestige, and so on) there is a vicious circle of cumulative *disadvantage*, the more marked the "competitiveness" of the society becomes. This broad tendency is inseparable from the development of individualism, the kinds of citizenship rights we have been talking about, and related matters. It almost goes without saying that the Negro in this country is very deeply caught up in this vicious circle and that Marshall's category of social citizenship is particularly important in the present context.[14]

The three principal components of the citizenship complex seem to constitute not only a rough temporal series, but also a type of hierarchy. With all the differences between British and American societies, they have very similar values. After all, with an important infusion from the French Enlightenment and the Revolutionary tradition, the origin of our own values lies mainly in our British heritage.

We can then say that it is the civil or legal rights which come closest to direct implementation of the values that Myrdal formulated in his famous summary of the "*American Creed.*"[15] In understanding what has been going on, it is crucial to remember that the societal commitment to this value pattern has exerted steady pressure toward its implementation in behavior and institutions, though this has often been counteracted in specific ways. These commitments, though they be genuine, cannot by themselves bring about a restructuring of the society. Attempts to implement them will inevitably encounter what Mayhew[16] has called

[13] Peter F. Drucker, "Automation is not the Villain," *The New York Times Magazine*, January 10, 1965.
[14] Considerable evidence on these points is presented in other papers in the *Daedalus* issue, notably those by Rashi Fein, Daniel P. Moynihan, and Thomas F. Pettigrew.
[15] Gunnar Myrdal, *An American Dilemma* (New York: Harper & Row, 1944).
[16] Leon Mayhew, *Law and Equal Opportunity* (Cambridge: Harvard University Press, 1968).

"structural discrimination," which can be overcome only if factors other than the assertion of commitments come into play. Without them, the outcome will be either a stalemate, as it was for so long in the United States, or a traditionalist revolution restoring the ascendancy of the contravalue orientation—a prototype being post-Reconstruction Southern society.

The spread and consolidation of the legal component through judicial process rather than legislation is particularly important in view of the present situation in America. This is a step well beyond a *moral* commitment to the relevant rights, because it places the power of government presumptively behind their implementation. In Little Rock, Governor Faubus was defying not only the "decent opinion of mankind," but also a specific order of a duly constituted federal court. This dramatizes the sense in which the 1954 decision on education was a decisive landmark —yet by itself it produced only a rather paltry "tokenism" in spite of being on the books for a full decade. Clearly something more was required, though this is not to belittle the enormous importance of the legal commitment. This Supreme Court decision was part of a much larger trend in the general development of judicial interpretation of the Constitution, of which more will be said later.

The two other principal factors are, on the one hand, the mobilization of political pressures designed to insure that the excluded group can enjoy both formal rights and actual participation in the political process and, on the other, the mobilization of the governmental apparatus to take the responsibility of implementing these rights. From this point of view, the step from the Supreme Court's espousal of Negro rights to the Civil Rights Acts of 1964 and 1965 was crucial, as has so often been remarked. Both, to be sure, obligate the government. But in the latter case the obligation has been enacted by the elected representatives of the people on the recommendation of a popularly elected President. Hence it can no longer be called the "whim" of nine men who, in the political as distinguished from the legal sense, do not "represent" anyone.[17] Of course there are still many steps which must be taken before effective implementation can be achieved, but the Civil Rights Acts clearly add a major set of social forces to the side of effective implementation.

Even if enforcement were effective, it would still be necessary to bring about the essential set of conditions concerned with qualifications for taking advantage of the opportunities offered. The newly included group must have the capacity to perform its role creditably. The mere statement that justice requires inclusion is not enough, because allegations of injustice must involve the capacity factor—namely, that the excluded group could make valuable contributions but is denied the opportunity to do so. Capacity must be asserted on the part of the excluded group, and, insofar as

[17] Even Arthur Krock, if my memory serves me, was impressed by this point.

it is not yet present, the larger community must take steps to help develop it.

The hierarchy to which we referred above concerns a relation between necessary and sufficient conditions. With reference to the Negro in the United States, I state broadly that although the institutionalization of both legal rights and political participation constitutes the necessary conditions of much further progress toward full inclusion in the societal community, this is not in itself sufficient. It also requires the implementation of the social component in such a way that the realistic handicaps, so conspicuous in the background, are reduced to the point that, though they cannot be expected to disappear in the short run, they become more or less manageable.

The constitution of a societal community is never static, but is continually changing over time. In my view, the main outline of the American community was established in the broad process of founding the new nation. This basic outline includes the Constitution as well as various aspects of the system as a total social process. At the same time, American society has been subject to major changes. The focus of the present essay is on changes in the composition of its membership through the inclusion of groups previously excluded, more or less unambiguously, from full membership. The Negro, both because of slavery and because of Southern regional isolation, was long kept insulated from the forces favoring inclusion. The groups with which I shall be concerned in the next section, those constituted by the "new immigration" of the turn of the century, were in a different situation.

I shall attempt to analyze the process of inclusion by using a model roughly similar to the "supply and demand" paradigm of economics. There are demands for inclusion—*both* from the excluded group and from certain elements who are already "in"—and there is a supply, which also operates on both sides of the exclusion line. Supply here refers, for the excluded groups, to their qualifications for membership, a matter of their cultural and social structures. Later I shall use the illustration that fully orthodox Judaism, with its rather strong insulation against all but the most instrumental contacts with Gentiles, constituted a formidable barrier to the inclusion of Jews in the American community. The presence of Reform Judaism in the German immigration that preceded that from Eastern Europe provided a focus for the general liberalization of the Jewish community structure. This made it far more amenable to inclusion than the Orthodox structure, as well as far more acceptable to its American hosts. On the side of the receiving community, "supply" consists in structural conditions that create institutionalized "slots" into which the newly received elements can fit, slots structured in accordance with the basic citizenship patterns of the developing community, not opportunities for crude "exploitation" by its members. Supply in this sense refers to a set of structural conditions on both sides of the "equation." This will be analyzed in terms of the factors necessary to extend and consolidate the societal community as such, that is, the commitment to association in a national community, the mobilization of political power and influence, and the establishment of the capacities that have been reviewed in the present section, as well as the underlying value-patterns that are assumed throughout.

The demand aspect concerns the *mobilization* of these factors and their consequences, again on both sides of the inclusion-exclusion boundary. It is a matter first of the existence of attitudes, in both the group "wanting in" and significant sectors of those already in, that the inclusion is normatively desirable and that it *should* be promoted, and then the transformation of these attitudes into various action programs and their implementation. Certainly, much of the actual process often occurs inconspicuously without much of a movement—this, for example, seems to have been the case for much of the inclusion of the new immigration, though by no means all of it. Nevertheless, as expression and implementation of demand in the present sense, the relevant *movements* have a very important place in our analysis.

Such movements tend to gather strength as the strain of conflict between the normative requirements for inclusion and the factual limitations on it are translated into pressures to act. Movements, however, not only express strain in this sense, but "stir things up" further. Thus, their consequences are often relatively unpredictable.[18] One tendency of this type of movement should be noted. The ultimate social grounding of the demand for inclusion lies in commitment to the values that legitimize it. The general reaction to increasing strain is to increase mobilization of such commitments. This in turn is often associated with a demand for direct, immediate, and complete action to implement the values in full. This tendency encounters a problem deriving from the fact that value-commitment, crucial as it is, is only one of the factors necessary for successful inclusion. Strengthening this factor without likewise strengthening the others may lead not to promotion of the "cause," but to a disproportionate activation of the *always-present* factors of resistance, and hence to setbacks. The activists in such movements are above all likely to become impatient with those who would pay attention to the importance of the other factors.[19]

This is the broad paradigm which the reader is requested to keep in mind in reading the sometimes involved discussion that follows.

[18] Neil J. Smelser, *Theory of Collective Behavior* (New York: Free Press, 1963).

[19] An almost classic instance of this is the recent impatience of the ministers, whose commitments to the values of racial equality have been impressively activated, with President Johnson, essentially because he wanted to mobilize strong political support for his more drastic proposals on voting rights before taking his own strong personal stand about the Selma crisis. The proposals were on the whole in favor of immediate and drastic federal compulsion in Alabama, regardless of the possible political costs.

THE AMERICAN RECORD ON
INCLUSION PROCESSES

The present crisis over the inclusion of the Negro in the American community has unique features besides its immediacy,[20] but it does not stand alone. A brief review of the larger context of related problems may prove illuminating. Two propositions willi ntroduce the discussion. First, as already noted, the core of the American community was basically white, Anglo-Saxon, and Protestant. These three terms, which have become so deeply embedded in the more popular culture, will serve as the axes of our analysis. Second, the United States, in sharp contrast to most of Europe, including our ancestral Britain, has been the proverbial land of open opportunity, welcoming all to join in building a new society in the "New World."

To be sure, this claim was never fully justified. Quite early it was made unmistakably clear that mass Oriental immigration would not be welcome (note the Chinese exclusion act of 1882). Indeed it may be argued that the Constitutional termination of the Slave Trade was as much an effort to limit the numbers of Negroes in the territorial United States as it was a reflection of hostility to slavery as such. Nevertheless, compared with other societies, especially of that time, the U.S. was notably liberal until the 1924 immigration laws. It placed more emphasis than any other nation of, or before, its time on the view that it was indeed a voluntary association. People were here because either they or their immediate forebears *wanted* to come. And, the proportion of those who came of their own volition was extremely high for quite a long time. The fact that many were escaping from what they felt to be oppressive conditions rather than coming to positive opportunities does not change this pattern. The Negro is the exception, because his forebears were typically *brought* here as slaves.

Though various early crises of the American nation may be related to this problem, the focus of this discussion will be on the aftermath of the great wave of free immigration of the generation ending with the First World War. This was perhaps, except for the Negro, *the* great test of the norms of freedom for all comers to associate in forming a new kind of nation.[21] Most of the immigrants were a part of the so-called new immigration from Eastern and Southern Europe, and as such they violated more sharply than previous large immigrations the older WASP formula for the societal community; they were not only non-Anglo-Saxon, but even non-Germanic in ethnic origin, being mostly from the

[20] Cf. T. F. Pettigrew, *A Profile of the Negro American* (Princeton, N.J.: Van Nostrand, 1964).
[21] Oscar Handlin, *The Uprooted* (Boston: Little, Brown, 1951).

Latin and Slavic countries (especially Italy and Poland). Also they were predominantly Roman Catholic, except for the very large influx of Jews from Eastern Europe. In addition, the Catholics were usually peasants. Earlier, there had been a small element of German Jews, who had become relatively fully included, and a larger group of English-speaking Catholics, the Irish, who were marked by a particularly sharp hostility to everything English. These two elements proved in the end to be very important mediators between the older elements and the larger masses of the new.

In this connection the WASP's generally succumbed to the temptation to define their own role on rather aristocratic terms, but on bases so tenuous that they must be considered only a pseudo-aristocracy. This occurred during the period immediately following World War I when economic prosperity was rampant and when "status-seeking" was certainly far more intensive than in the second postwar period. This is the period of the derogatory names like "wops," "polacks," and "kikes," and of the greatest prevalence of "snobbish" anti-Semitism, the deep feeling that having a Jew as a member of your club was totally unacceptable. (It is perhaps significant that such snobbishness was particularly prominent in the younger generation—in fraternities and sororities, and particularly in the Harvard Final Clubs.)

At the risk of typological oversimplification, I should like to deal with the problem of inclusion of the new immigration in terms of two categories, namely, the Jewish and the Catholic groups. It is clear that there is substantial ethnic diversity within both groups. There are not only East European Jews, who are not themselves homogenous, but also the earlier Germanic contingent and small numbers of Spanish-Portuguese origin. The Catholic group is still more diverse. The Irish were the earliest to arrive in large numbers and have been the most influential. They spoke English, a fact which is significant particularly because they discouraged and often as bishops forbade foreign-language parochial schools. Though bringing with them a strong hostility to things English, which was reflected for generations in their tense relations with the WASP's, their long association in Ireland with English Protestantism brought the Irish brand of Catholicism much closer to Protestantism than, for example, that of most parts of Southern Europe.

Furthermore, an important part of the earlier Catholic immigration was of German origin, which was ethnically closer to the WASP's than most of the new immigration, and therefore was more fully integrated earlier. In some regions of the country, particularly the Middle West, they have played a very important part. The other two largest groups were the Italians and the Poles, which are very different from each other. There were, of course, other Slavic groups, such as the Czechs and Croats, and the two Spanish-speaking groups in the Southwest—those taken over after the Mexican war and migrants from Mexico—and, more recently, the Puerto Ricans, who have begun to diffuse beyond New York City. There are also smaller numbers which are neither Jewish nor Catholic, such as the Greeks, the Armenians, and some other groups who adhere to Orthodox churches. Finally, Protestant immigration has continued, the largest being from the British Isles and still more from English-speaking Canada.

The problem of the absorption of Jews and Catholics resulted in a genuine crisis of the American community; it was probably one of the major foci of social tension and disturbance in this century. The Immigration Act of 1924, with its system of quotas based on the composition of the population by national origin in 1890, was one striking symptom of this strain; it is significant that only now is there a serious and widely supported proposal before Congress to eliminate that egregiously discriminatory policy. The very sagacious French observer of American society at that time, André Siegfried, spoke of the "two nations" and expressed sharp doubt whether they could ever be integrated.[22]

The substantial disturbances and anxieties over the presence of such large "foreign" groups in our midst and their relations to the fears of "un-American" influence and of Communism—from the Palmer Raids and the Sacco-Vanzetti case of the 1920's to the McCarthy episode of the early 1950's—must be understood in this context.[23] Until the crescendo of McCarthyism, the ogre of "Communism" as a danger of *internal* subversion rather than of external threat was increasingly of central concern. Nevertheless it can be claimed that the main crisis over full inclusion of these groups has now passed. I shall argue that the Catholic case was the more serious of the two, and that the election of John F. Kennedy as President, accentuated by the ritual significance of the public reaction to his assassination, put a final symbolic seal on the inclusion of all Roman Catholics, not only the Irish. Perhaps it was also symbolic that the first time Lyndon Johnson left Washington as President was to attend the funeral of a Jew in a Jewish temple, namely, that of former Senator Lehman of New York.

Neither civil rights in the legal sense nor political rights were seriously at issue in these inclusion problems. The Jewish ghetto and the status of Catholics in Britain before Catholic emancipation in the 1830's lay far in the background. The problem of acceptance lay more at the social level in the above classification than at either of the others. This we would define as the capacity and opportunity for full participation without informal discrimination, such as ineligibility for certain high political offices or relatively systematic "scapegoating." Nevertheless the problem

[22] André Siegfried, *America Comes of Age* (New York: Harcourt, Brace, & World, 1927).
[23] Talcott Parsons, "Social Strains in America" and "Postscript 1962" in Daniel Bell (ed.), *The Radical Right* (Garden City, N.Y.: Doubleday, 1964). [Reprinted as Chapter 7 in the present volume: ed.] Cf. also other essays in the Bell volume.

of discrimination has been serious and, though recently it has changed greatly for the better, pockets of such discrimination remain.

It is necessary to consider briefly a difference in emphasis and, hence, symbolic involvement of these two particularly important white groups, the Jews and the Catholics. Realistically, there has never been much question of Jewish motivation and capacity for achievement in terms of social mobility in America. This applies especially to mobility through educational channels. In any case, the Jewish group, despite having had to contend with serious discrimination, has had an extraordinary success story. From lowly origins in the overwhelming proportion of cases, it has, in general, risen very high in the American social scale in about two-thirds of a century.

The Jewish problem of inclusion has been almost purely one of "acceptance" on both sides. In comparative terms, there has been relatively little serious anti-Semitism, but the Jewish community itself has been concerned about how far "assimilation" should be allowed to progress. The symbolic focus of anti-Semitism has not questioned competence— the Jew has been a *dangerous* competitor. Irrational anxiety has centered about his observance of the rules, which is to say his acceptance of the obligations of solidarity in the national community. To the more discerning, his "unscrupulousness" has not involved a lack of moral discipline, but rather a higher loyalty to an alternative community, the Jewish. In this sense the Jew has often been considered "clannish."

The Jewish community has always been of a special type. It has been a "guest" community within a host society and, therefore, notably apolitical. Its contacts with Gentiles have historically been on the economic level, with strong Jewish emphasis on their own cultural traditions— including, of course, high valuation of learning which could be transferred to the modern professions. Strong solidarity and, in Orthodox Judaism, exclusiveness have been observed in kinship and, indeed, in all relations of intimacy. Jewish communities have been discrete and local, not organized on a national or international basis, and relatively egalitarian in their internal structure.

It seems that the conflict between Jewish and Gentile communities has been most acute where the former represented what could be interpreted as the exploitative aspect of urban society vis-à-vis the rural and parochial, as in the case of Jewish moneylenders or cattle dealers in relation to peasant communities or where, in urban settings, competition at the level of small business was most prominent.

The decline in the proportion of the American population engaged in agriculture and the development of large-scale corporate business have probably contributed to a climate favorable to inclusion. On this level the competition has not been very intense since Jewish business has centered in the small-scale proprietary fields of small business—notably the clothing industry—and certain fields of retail trade. It is very likely that the private practice professions, such as medicine and law, have been particularly congenial to the Jews who have sought higher education and that their late entry into the academic profession on a wide scale is not wholly the result of discriminatory exclusion, though that has certainly played a part.

The focus of the "problem" of anti-Semitism has been the conception of the foreignness of the Jews, of their solidarity in a community within the community, from which Gentiles could feel excluded. The pluralization of the general social structure, especially at occupational levels, and the diminishing global exclusiveness of the Jewish communities have set the stage for the progress of inclusion, since many of these groups have maintained their quite distinctive identities and considerable sense of solidarity, both among themselves and with the societies of their countries of origin.

The present essay cannot, however, attempt a generalized analysis of the ethnic and religious composition of American society, but is primarily focused on the problem of the status of the Negro American. It is my contention that, first, the Jewish group has had special significance because of its distinctive historic role and, second, the Catholic groups have been of great importance in spite of the internal ethnic diversity of the Catholic population. It is worth remarking in passing that the largest single "melting pot" in the society has probably operated within the Catholic population through extensive ethnic intermarriage, but much less so across religious lines. Within the Catholic group, the Irish have played a notable role for the reasons mentioned, with the result, among others, that there is a striking Irish predominance in the hierarchy of the American Catholic Church. For the limited purposes of this essay, I shall concentrate on these two considerations which have become the foci of two different problems and symbolic themes which can be contrasted with each other, as well as with the central issue of the Negro case.

The Jew could then be a good citizen, neighbor, business competitor, and occupational associate of the Protestant with neither relinquishing his religious identity. Religious pluralization—long under way in our society—opens the door to a conception of a basis of societal solidarity which makes all these nondiscriminatory relations possible. On the Jewish side, it should again be noted that a relaxation of the predominantly Orthodox separatism of the Jewish subcommunity has been a necessary condition. In America, the Reform movement, which stemmed from the older German-Jewish element, has been particularly important. Primarily by further development in the differentiation of roles, it has become increasingly possible for Jews to participate in more than the economic aspects of the Gentile community without having to relinquish their Jewishness. From a relatively total subsocietal community, the

Jewish group has tended to evolve toward becoming a denomination in the American Protestant sense.[24] Socially, American Jews have been included very fully, but have by no means been assimilated to the same extent.[25]

In the symbolism of discrimination, the Jew has tended to serve as the prototype of "foreignness," in the sense that he is diffusely attached to a community separate from and alien to the American, and therefore presumably untrustworthy in its commitment to the latter. Compared to certain European countries, notably Germany, but also those to the South and East, the United States has had only mild attacks of anti-Semitism. The most serious was in the 1930's (Father Coughlin) and was associated with a general contraction of economic opportunity, a state in which the theme of the dangerous competition of the outsider is more easily made prominent. The more important expression of this complex has perhaps been the diffuse anxiety about foreignness and un-Americanism. The prominence of this theme would seem to fit with an earlier phase of the development of the national community away from a restricted ethnic-religious basis of solidarity—the famous WASP—to a more cosmopolitan one which includes many elements not qualifying on the more traditional grounds.

The next phase of strain in the openness of the American community constituted a further development of the above. If "foreigners" in general —Jews in particular—are to be accepted, should they not conform to certain requirements? In the Jewish-Protestant case there seemed to be a kind of "fair exchange," involving the non-political stance of diffusely organized communal groups on each side. The idea of a Jewish conspiracy was a rather exotic extreme of anti-Semitic phantasy since the Jews were what they were precisely because of their withdrawal from politically significant organization. One might say much the same for the American brand of Protestantism, especially that part that advocated a radical separation of Church and State. On top of this was the pluralism of American political organization, the beginnings of which go back as far as the history of this nation.[26]

It is perhaps not surprising that *any* relatively or apparently monolithic organization should be a focus of anxiety. Compared with American Protestantism, the Catholic Church was relatively monolithic and in part both was and appeared to be so because of defensive attitudes about

---

[24] Will Herberg, *Protestant, Catholic, Jew* (Garden City, N.Y.: Doubleday, 1960).

[25] Thus, the rate of intermarriage with non-Jews is lower than corresponding rates for either Protestants or Catholics.

[26] It is notable that by contrast with German Nazism, American anti-Semitism has not strongly stressed the connection of Jewishness with Communism. Similarly, the anti-Communisim of this cold war period has dissociated itself from anti-Semitism. *Vide* the role of Cohn and Schine as lieutenants of McCarthy and the fact that the name Goldwater has not been a political liability in Rightist circles.

its minority position in American society. The problem for its members was not only how far they participated in the usual roles in the American community, but also whether, in doing so, they were under the explicit authoritative control of an organization, their church, which was pursuing its own goals and policies independently of, and possibly in conflict with, the interests of the American community. Put crudely, the Catholic Church could, particularly to non-Catholic Americans, appear to be a kind of state within the state. Sensitivity to this has been heightened by the individualistic cast of American society, with its suspicion of strong central government. Indeed, for special reasons, Catholics, particularly Irish, tended to gain their mobility through governmental channels, starting with the local ones, but extending to the others. Hence they tended to strengthen Protestant suspicion of them. For this reason the symbolic show-down in the election of a Catholic to the Presidency was particularly important.

Two additional facts, besides the nature and position of the Catholic Church, were essential here. First, as will be noted presently, the majority of the Catholic ex-peasants formed the urban lower class. In a sense they played symbolic "proletariat" to the WASP pretensions to privileged social status, a peculiar combination of the European traditions of aristocratic and "bourgeois." Second, the protection of local interests in our constitutional system opened the door, given the democratic franchise (reinforced by corruption), to organizing these new urban masses into the famous—or infamous—political machines of which New York's Tammany Hall was long a prototype. In the decisive period the leadership of these organizations, which tended to wrest immediate local political power away from the WASP element, was predominantly Irish and, of course, Catholic. Hence at a certain level—a highly salient one to the average "old" American—the Catholic Church as a state within a state seemed to have fused with an actual Catholic control of the most important systems of local politics of the nation, thus compounding the felony.

The general path of resolution here has been "pluralization" in a political sense. Generally we do not have monolithic or, as Rokkan and Lipset say, "columnar"[27] blocs as major units in our political system. By their continually increasing involvement in American society at all levels, Catholics have come to be widely represented in many different sectors. They are by no means always on the same side in political decision-making. In view of the European experience, it is striking that there has been no strong move to establish a Catholic political party in the United States at either the state or national level. Obversely, the non-Catholic community has been decreasingly apt to relate to Catholics as Catholics rather

[27] Stein Rokkan and Seymour Martin Lipset, "Cleavage Structures, Party Systems, and Voter Alignments: An Introduction," in *Party Systems and Voter Alignments* (New York: Free Press, 1967).

than on the various other grounds, especially personal competence in specific fields, which come to be so important in the allocation of personnel through the social structure.

Whereas the integration of the Jewish group seems to have been the "simplest," at least symbolically, in that it involved only the "capacity to accept membership," sometimes through renouncing but more importantly through transcending conflicting solidarities,[28] the present case involved a further complication, namely, that the group in question might have a propensity to organize within the community for its own special ends in a way subversive of the community's delicately balanced basis of consensus. This seems clearly to be related to the more general symbol of "Communism" as a source of vague danger. The Communist system is precisely characterized by maximal commitment to effectiveness through collective organization.

What I called the American hypersensitivity to the Communist danger is connected with the problem of inclusion of the Catholic groups. The link between them is highly integrated political organization, internally on a nationwide basis but with an international base centered outside the country. It is particularly significant that the fear in the United States has been primarily of internal subversion. This may have been somewhat plausible in the 1930's, but in the cold war period the strength of the American Communist party had been reduced to practically nothing, even among intellectuals. There is a discrepancy between this internal anxiety—firmly documented in Stouffer's study[29]—and the substantially smaller concern about the really serious conflict with Communist movements in foreign affairs. Communism, however, is a symbol, the latent meanings of which include various forms of collective authority which may be felt to threaten freedom—among which the Catholic Church has figured prominently. Therefore, we can infer that the fear of Communism includes a "displaced affect," the sources of which must be sought elsewhere.

[28] On the side of supply for the receiving community, another important consideration for the Jewish case may again be emphasized. This is that the rivalrous incompatibility of the two communities—Jewish and Protestant—seems to be at its height when both sides are constituted mainly of "independent proprietors," farmers, artisans, small businessmen, and private professional practitioners. The danger of acute anti-Semitism in the American system has probably been greatly mitigated by the fact that the central economic organization developed in the direction of a more highly differentiated corporate structure. In this, there is no "individual" proprietor whose interests can seem to be blocked by the competing Jew. Not unconnected with this development is that of a much broadened system of higher education, one that has changed the character of the general American elite, not least that of businessmen. Jews gradually gained access to this system and performed outstandingly in it, and, moreover, there were various structurally interstitial areas open to them, such as semi-monopolized areas of small business (for example, clothing) and, not least, the professions organized primarily on the basis of private practice.

[29] Samuel Stouffer *Communism, Conformity, and Civil Liberties* (Garden City, N.Y.: Doubleday, 1955).

Not only was there the problem of the Catholic Church, but the relevant period, from the New Deal on, was one of rapid increase in the size and functions of the federal government. It is notable that the main internal focus of this increase lay in the strengthening of the social component of citizenship that concerned the status of the largely immigrant urban lower classes. Externally, it derived, above all, from involvement in two world wars and the attendant changes in the level of American responsibility in world affairs.

In these circumstances, anti-Communism could serve as a unifying symbol for two important groups, namely the older "conservative" groups who stood in fear of and opposition to the general trend to "bigness," urbanization, and the like, and the upwardly mobile, largely Catholic, groups. The latter could claim to be more than one hundred per cent American and accuse the "liberal" elements among the WASP's of insufficient loyalty to their own country. The strongly anti-Communist stance of the Vatican before the Papacy of John XXIII presumably also strengthened this attitude.[30]

In spite of the complexities, I think it is justified to establish an equation that connects Communism symbolically with Catholicism, on the one hand, and with big government, on the other, as a focus of fears and anxieties of a large sector of the American public. It is significant that the relation to Catholicism seems to have eased greatly in the most recent period, especially since the Presidency of Kennedy. This is related to the new definition of the American Right (that is, rightward from Goldwater) as quite explicitly connecting the trend to big government and the danger of Communism. The mitigation of the anti-Communist feeling of the Catholic element—in spite of some lingerings in the South —was fundamental in Lyndon Johnson's ability to command a political consensus over such a wide band as he did in the 1964 election. The inclusion of the Catholic component in the anti-Communist syndrome seems to be parallel to the relation of anti-Semitism, again often latently, to the vaguely generalized anxiety about the "foreignness" of the new immigration as a whole, which was so prominent in the 1920's.

There is another aspect of the broadly "Catholic" inclusion problem which constitutes an important bridge to the Negro problem. The elements of the new immigration not only were different in cultural and national origin from most of their predecessors, but also occupied a different position in American society. Virtually all of them became the lower class of the large cities and industrial areas. The Jewish group escaped from this situation very rapidly, while the Catholic groups, most of whom were of peasant origin, did so more slowly. Indeed this circumstance sharply distinguished the United States from the European cases

[30] Cf. my paper "Social Strains in America," in Daniel Bell (ed.) *The Radical Right*, op. cit. [Reprinted as Chapter 7 in the present volume: ed.]

that were the prototypes for classical Marxian theory—there was hardly any indigenous "working class" here and the lower occupational roles were largely performed by immigrants whose eventual group status in the society was still very uncertain. Siegfried put great stress on this fact. With a good many qualifications, it can be said that the urban Negro has inherited this status as the immigrant has moved up. He, too, is by origin predominantly a "peasant," though from the rural South, and has had to undergo many similar processes of adaptation to the urban environment.

In the Jewish case we might speak of the "foreign" community as standing "beside" the main national one. It was difficult to assign it to a hierarchical position, and it was not highly stratified internally. In proportion as the situation just outlined applied to the Catholic group, it tended to bolster the WASP position as an aristocracy in the premodern sense. This tendency was of course most accentuated in the South, particularly vis-à-vis the Negro. But it was hardly unknown in the North. Indeed, the kind of anti-Semitism that has been manifested in the exclusion of Jews from select clubs, college fraternities, residential neighborhoods, and resorts is clearly an example of this. Precisely because the Jew has been such a capable achiever by American standards, he has been excluded in order to assert a claim to a status which is not only, or sometimes not at all, linked to achievement.

In the Catholic group, this has been overcome in part by their achieving admission on the most nearly aristocratic terms. The Kennedy story illustrates this dramatically. The elder Kennedy had great wealth which was linked to local political power by his marriage to the daughter of an Irish mayor of Boston. Then not only did his son achieve political success, ultimately the summit of the Presidency, but he partially joined the circle of the WASP aristocracy by attending Harvard College and developing, with his wife, a style of living which was anything but that of peasants.[31] This is an illustration of the process of pluralization. Increasingly the Catholic populations have diffused through the social structure so that there remains little in common among them but their religion and, of course, their Americanism. The great relative growth in the urban population has helped greatly in this by reducing the distinctiveness of a predominantly urban group. The same applies to the Jews.

It was noted above that, partly in reaction to the new immigration, but also to industrialization and urbanization, the tendency toward the turn of the century and well into the present one was for the WASP's to assume something of the position of an aristocracy—a trend related to "snobbish" anti-Semitism. The Jews did a great deal to discourage this through their striking record of upward mobility, especially in educational achievement, the professions, and latterly, science and the arts. There

[31] Further, the sister of the President's wife married into European aristocracy, taking the title of "Princess," while remaining very close to the whole Kennedy family.

have, however, been various symptoms of this, such as the conspicuous "Anglophilism" of the upper groups in this period, which has stood in strong contrast to the Anglophobia of earlier phases of our national existence. The England particularly emphasized was that of the "Establishment," the prestige of Oxford education being a prominent symptom. In this situation, it was natural in the North for there to be greater acceptance of the status of the Negro as belonging to a "service" class in a way not too different from the trends of English colonial practice.

The upward mobility of the new immigrant groups and their increasing inclusion in the national community tended to isolate the Negro in this capacity—the virtual disappearance of Irish domestic servants is an index. Such changes as the immense broadening of the pyramid of education—so that virtually the whole age cohort has received some secondary education and a rapidly increasing proportion has been going to college and beyond—have tended to alter this situation. Thus the brief tendency to crystallize a predominantly WASP upper class has increasingly given way to a new egalitarianism—one stressing equality of opportunity, rather than of final status, but definitely covering an ever-widening ethnic-religious range. This trend has made the recent status of the Negro even more anomalous, and is part of the setting of the recent phase of the inclusion process.

THE NEGRO CASE

If the predominantly Catholic part of the new immigration owed its primary status ascription in American society mainly to its lower-class status, for the Negro this has been almost wholly the case. For our purposes, color will be treated not as a direct component of the social status of the Negro—for in strict theoretical terms it is not that—but as a symbol. On relatively concrete levels, it is correct to say that individual Negroes are discriminated against in various ways solely because of their skin color. This statement is not, however, an explanation of the general phenomenon of color discrimination, as distinguished from individual cases. Unfortunately this vital distinction often is not kept firmly in mind. Our concern is with the general phenomenon.

In this context skin color symbolizes inferiority in the sense that it is purported to justify placing Negroes as a category so radically at the bottom of the scale as to be only equivocally inside the system at all. It will perhaps be illuminating to consider the problem first in connection with the difference between the South and the North.[32]

The Civil War broke out about the time of, and partly as a result of, the process of industrialization and urbanization in the North. This

---

[32] Color, in turn, symbolizes *parentage*, since of course the skin color of Negroes varies greatly. The social criterion is that a Negro is anyone, one or both of whose parents were socially classified as a Negro.

accentuated the difference in social structure of which slavery was a primary feature. The South was largely an agrarian society with a planter gentry at the top practicing an aristocratic style of life, and with the great mass of menial labor being done by Negro slaves. The principal class whose status was equivocal was the white group that could not pretend to gentry status, but that wanted above all to avoid being classified with the Negroes. It was something like a caste society. Though the slaves were formally emancipated as a result of the South's defeat in the war, the post-Reconstruction reaction confirmed this caste structure with the "Jim Crow" system.

Unlike the Jews and Catholics, the Southern Negro has generally had to start his rise by acquiring the most elementary components of legal and political citizenship. Through court decisions and now increasingly through legislation, this part of the task of inclusion has progressed a long way toward accomplishment. The social component is another matter—inclusion in this area is just beginning to develop, and there is no doubt that it will prove the most difficult of the three processes.

Until the First World War the Negro was scarcely a "problem" in the North, mainly because his numbers were so small. This was changed by the great migrations that began about that time, accelerated by the boll weevil havoc in Southern cotton growing. Of course, this process has now gone so far that less than half the Negro population is resident in the eleven states of the old Confederacy, and the proportion will continue to decline. Moreover, in the South there has been a great deal of migration to the cities, so that the category, Southern rural Negro—once the pre-dominant type—is now a distinct minority.

The upward mobility of the white urban lower groups, the new immigration, has contributed to the fact that, in both North and South, the Negro is predominantly urban and lower class. Today about half of the estimated 20 per cent of Americans who are "the poor" are Negroes.[33] This classifies about 50 per cent of the Negroes as poor, whereas no other group—Irish, Italian, and so forth—has nearly that large a proportion.

In a sense the South has "infected" the North with the virus of the Negro problem, even though its meaning has been deeply changed. It was hardly to have been expected that Southerners would get very much Northern political support for maintaining the Jim Crow system intact. Even the coalition of Southern Democrats and Northern conservative Republicans has been gradually eroded to the point that, with the mounting pressure and certain general changes, it has almost disappeared. However, the "problem" is now becoming much more uniform throughout the nation—it is becoming an urban class problem.[34]

[33] Cf. Pettigrew, *op. cit.*

[34] However dramatic, episodes like that in Selma are clearly coming into the category of "mopping-up operations."

As noted above, the Jewish inclusion would probably have been much more difficult had it not been for the type of differentiation process in the economy exemplified by the growth of corporate business, and for the great development of higher education, which opened the doors of the professions to considerable numbers of Jews. Similarly, the pluralization of the political system, the breakup of the city machines as the preserves of specific groups, and the decline of the corresponding "better element" sectors of the political structure have greatly facilitated the inclusion of the Catholic groups. I should like to suggest that the "host society" has been undergoing an important process of structural change which is creating essential conditions for the inclusion not only of the Negro, but of the whole lower class in the societal community.

In an important sense, American society has been protected against the urgency of the class problem by the fact that for so long such a large proportion of its lowest socio-economic groups has been of recent immigration status, especially in the crucially important cities which have increasingly become the structural focus of the newer society. As noted, upward mobility has greatly alleviated the potential class problems, but they are now being brought to an acute and symbolically appropriate focus by the Negro's becoming the prototypical disadvantaged category.

In the broadest terms the incipient inclusion process depends for its success on the much more effective institutionalization of Marshall's social component of citizenship. However, it comprises new movements with respect to all three of the components. It has, for example, been noted that a most important trend in the Supreme Court decisions of recent years is the extension of the Bill of Rights to the level of the states, especially through reinterpretation of the Fourteenth Amendment.[35] Many of these decisions, such as the school desegregation ruling of 1954, have most notably affected discrimination in the South. Others, however, such as the requirement that indigent defendants accused of crime be provided with counsel (the Gideon case), apply more generally. Furthermore, not only legal rights, in the narrower sense, but also political and social rights are affected. Thus the reapportionment cases profoundly affect the franchise and, with it, the distribution of political power; and the school cases impinge on the social component. They seem to imply that government is obligated to provide adequate educational facilities to the whole population—with discrimination by race being only one aspect of the present inadequacy.

Within this framework of legal rights, public policy is attempting to cope with the causes of *de facto* discrimination, not just by color but by any status of inferiority which cannot be fairly attributed to the individual himself. A certain religio-ideological grounding of this first emerged with

[35] Erwin N. Griswold, *Law and Lawyers in the United States* (Cambridge: Harvard University Press, 1964).

the prominent Social Gospel movement in American Protestantism in the latter part of the nineteenth century (which, incidentally, had much to do with the establishment of sociology as an academic discipline in this country) and with its role in the development of philanthropy concerned with the disadvantaged classes. The New Deal comprised a second main phase, with the beginning of comprehensive federal social welfare legislation, including the consolidation of the legal status of trade unionism through the Wagner Act and, particularly, unemployment, old age, and other benefits. The opposition of the Supreme Court to such legislation, especially by the states, was also ended in that period. The United States now seems to be well into a third phase. Perhaps its most important feature has been the shift in concern from welfare in the narrower sense to health, education, and the nature of the urban community, focusing most acutely so far upon housing.

By the narrower sense of welfare, I mean that concerned primarily with money income. The older conceptions of lower-class status emphasized lack of financial means as the central feature of being disadvantaged. Hence, stress was put on improvement in financial status. This was reasonable especially when, as in the Great Depression, massive unemployment was the most acute condition needing a remedy. However, there has been increasing insight that poverty is a function of other factors such as poor health, both physical and—as has been emphasized more recently—mental, and certain aspects of community structure and the like.

Education has become the most salient link with the occupational system, which is, in turn, the principal basis of financial independence for the individual and his immediate family. There has been a general upgrading of education. On the one hand, this means that larger proportions of the age cohort have been attaining higher levels of education, with the results that the disadvantaged minority, especially the well-known drop-outs, has been separated from the majority with increasing sharpness. On the other hand, educational requirements for good employment have been rising at the same time—most of the present unemployment is found among the poorly-qualified groups, and educational qualifications are becoming of increasing importance in holding jobs. It seems that not only formal opportunity for a relatively good education (that is, at least through high school), but also capacity to take advantage of it, both in individual ability and in motivation, is coming to be as much a requisite of full inclusion as civil and voting rights.

Behind this, as treated in much more detail elsewhere in this issue, is the problem of the social environment of the disadvantaged, the "slum." The central concern is the vicious circle of the factors in *actual* inferior capacity for valued performance, in which poverty, bad health, low educational standards, family disorganization, delinquency, and other anti-social phenomena are mutually reinforcing. This is where the structure of the urban community itself become a salient problem focus. The new concern centers on the residential community. In this connection attention has been called to the fact that the Negro is disadvantaged, even beyond other slum dwellers, in many senses besides the color of his skin. First and foremost, he has been peculiarly lacking in relatively strong family organization[36] which could give strong psychological support to the individual, especially as a child. Second, this has been connected in turn with a relative weakness in "community" institutions of mutual support and solidarity, for example, of the sort which have preeminently characterized Jewish groups even before they rose significantly from their initial low status in American society. Even as the victim of the most radical discrimination of any group, the Negro has not only been forced to be subservient, but has also failed to develop, or bring with him from his Southern rural past, sufficient ingredients for socially effective self-help —a question not merely of individual qualities and initiative, but of collective solidarity and mutual support at many levels, particularly the family and the local community. The strongest Negro institutions have centered in the churches, a vital complex which must be preserved carefully against some of the disintegrating tendencies of urban life. The role of the churches in the civil rights movement perhaps symbolizes this best and will be commented upon further below.

SOME HIGHLIGHTS OF THE INCLUSION PROCESS

It is reasonable to suggest that, whatever the extent and nature of the responsibility for the many previous failures, the time is ripe for a major advance. The broad tendency of modern society, one in which America has played a rather special role, has been egalitarian in the sense of institutionalizing the basic rights of citizenship in all three categories sketched here.[37] This tendency has become institutionalized over an increasingly broad front, the legal development noted above being prototypical. The basic types of inequality that have continued to be tolerated —in this context rather than that of recognition and reward of achievement—have been justified, when at all, primarily in terms of "paternalistic" immunities of a variety of sectoral types, the status of the child in the family being a kind of model. In case after case, these immunities have been whittled away, so that the universalistic norms of the society have applied more and more widely. This has been true of all the main bases of particularistic solidarity, ethnicity, religion, regionalism, state's rights,

[36] Cf. remarks of Clifford Geertz in the 1964 *Daedalus* planning conference.
[37] Contrary, of course, to the temporary trend to the establishment of a WASP aristocracy.

and class. The "sovereignty" of the individual American state has perhaps been the most important single bulwark of these particularisms, in the first instance those of WASP's, but potentially of every group. The inclusion of the Jewish and Catholic groups as outlined above fits this paradigm.

Today, more than ever before, we are witnessing an acceleration in the emancipation of individuals of all categories from these diffuse particularistic solidarities. This must be seen as a further *differentiation* of the role-set in which the individual is involved. By being included in larger community structures, the individual need not cease to be a member of the smaller ones, but the latter must relinquish certain of the controls over him which they previously exercised. This reasoning applies to aristocratic groups as much as it does to negatively privileged ones like the Negro. We have been witnessing major steps in the extension and consolidation of the societal community.

Let me emphasize again one particularly important aspect of the present phase, that the more general insistence on the basic equalities of citizenship, which is essential to the inclusion process, cuts across the status of Negro. In its deeper layers, it is a demand not for the inclusion of Negroes as such, but for the elimination of *any* category defined as inferior in itself. For a long time the status of the Negro was a peculiarly Southern problem. Then it became a national problem, but *qua* Negro. Now we are entering the phase in which it is no longer that, but the problem of eliminating status-inferiority as such, regardless of race, creed, or color. The Negro, in becoming only a "special case," even if a very salient one, loses a ground for special consideration which he has enjoyed. As the same time, he has established a position for tapping much wider bases of support than before. He can become the spokesman for the much broader category of the disadvantaged, those excluded on this egregious ground. The Negro movement, then, can become the American style "socialist" movement. This is to say that the basic demand is for full inclusion, not for domination or for equality on a basis of separateness.[38]

At the risk of repetition, I may note that the successful accomplishment of this goal of inclusion depends on a balanced mobilization of four categories of factors. The first is commitment to the values that underlie the assumption that the goal itself is desirable. This has a long history in American society and is clearly of the greatest importance. I have mentioned that it was invoked by Myrdal. Recently we have seen a notable "effervescence" (in Durkheim's sense) with respect to activation of these value-commitments at the requisite levels. Here the Negro movement has played the paramount part, but the activation has extended far beyond

---

[38] It could perhaps be said that the claim of Orthodox Judaism for a secure position in the host society is a case of the "separate but equal" principle. Similar things can be said of other ethnic and religious situations, for example the French minority in Canada.

the movement itself. Its incidence in religious circles is especially note-worthy, not least in the way it has brought all faiths of the white com-munity, Catholics and Jews as well as Protestants, together behind the Negro cause. The presence of Catholic nuns among the demonstrators in Selma was a new note having a significance scarcely to be overestimated.

Mere affirmation of the values is not enough. If a process of change is to be a new implementation of fundamental values, its basic direction must be articulated. This involves the development of a conception of the societal community in which all elements will be fully included in the sense of this discussion. In our own cultural background, quite different directions have also enjoyed powerful value-sanctions, even if rather insecurely. One example was the conception of the Negro as inherently inferior—indeed, in a certain version of older Calvinism now dominant in South Africa, as rightfully belonging in a subordinated status. It is the basic values, as applied to the developing conception of the American societal community, which together form the normative focus of the power of the movement.

This factor underlies the trend to implement the values by inclusion —the only tolerable solution to the enormous tensions lies in constituting a single societal community with full membership for all. This is a re-newal and reinterpretation of the concept of the Union that was so central for Lincoln. No other solution is tolerable from the American point of view—hence the Black Muslims cannot gain active support in the general community. And despite much ambivalence, it seems certain that the main Negro community is committed to this outlook. The continuing mobilization of these loyalties and commitments on both sides of the racial line seems to be the second crucial factor in the general inclusion process.

It has been very common to postulate and emphasize a primary differ-ence between the "idealists" who hope to achieve integration by asserting the values of, and a willingness for, acceptance, and the "realists" who say that *only* the mobilization of political power and economic interests will help. I should strongly repudiate this framing of alternatives. It is quite correct that the goal cannot be achieved *without* the mobilization of power and economic interests, but it does not follow that these factors are themselves sufficient. It is only a balanced combination of "ideal" and "real" factors which provides the formula for success.

In speaking of political power, I should like to conceive it here more broadly than is usual. Essential as government is, it does not stand alone in implementing major political changes. The political problems of inte-gration involve all fields of organizational decision-making, especially for business firms to accept Negroes in employment, for colleges and uni-versities to admit them for study, for trade unions to avoid discrimination. We have become acutely aware of the limitations of political power.

Against a recalcitrant group, attempts to *enforce* compliance are all-too-often ineffective. Nevertheless, at certain crucial points its mobilization is clearly an essential factor, a factor which includes making decisions affecting inclusion processes *binding* as obligations on all members of the requisite collectivity, whether governmental or private. It is particularly important to remember that the use of power has a double effect. First, it mobilizes sanctions against recalcitrants in such ways that they may no longer be able to afford previously feasible resistance. Second, it asserts on behalf of the relevant collectivity that the policy of inclusion must be taken seriously, and hence that noncompliance will not be allowed to proceed with impunity.

Of all the factors favoring integration, economic interests are the most neutral as far as normative obligations are concerned. They involve both the extent to which receiving elements can "afford" the risks involved in taking various steps and the development of realistic capacities to do so—a theme discussed above in connection with the whole complex of inferiority of status. Perhaps most important is that without support from the other three sets of factors, economic interests and capacity to exploit economic opportunities are weak reeds. This has been made vividly clear where state governments in the deep South, backed by what seems to have been a white consensus, have adamantly opposed steps toward integration. In such cases business men simply would not move. But where the balance of the other factors shifts toward integration, economic interests on both sides can provide a powerful reinforcement of the change. It is a question of "getting over the hump."[39]

A NOTE ON RESISTANCE TO INCLUSION

In American social thinking it is regarded almost as simple common sense to emphasize primarily, when speaking of the resistance to such developments as the Negro movement for inclusion, the material vested interests of the opponents, for example, the fear of loss of real-estate values or the view that "our customers would not like dealing with a Negro receptionist," so we would lose business. Such examples themselves suggest that another set of factors is involved. The structure of vested interests is a function of the structure of values and norms underlying the relevant sphere of social interaction. We are in the midst of a process of social change in which these components, and not only the interests, are changing.

Resistance has been strongest in the white South. This is because the structure of Southern society has been more "archaic" than that of the rest

---

[39] It must be understood that the economic factor here includes the whole opportunity-capacity complex, which is especially important for the Negro. For this reason *primary* reliance on economic interests is clearly inadequate.

of the country. It has, however, been changing very rapidly, and has tended more or less to polarize around its more advanced urban, industrial, and partly intellectual sectors, on the one hand, and its more traditional rural and small town sectors, on the other. This very broad polarization is by no means peculiar to the South, but is nationwide. Thus states' rights, the resistance to reapportionment on population bases, and many other issues mark a "conservative" reaction against many of the processes of change in the society at large.

Political developments in recent years bring this situation into sharp relief. The one-party system of the South has been breaking up rapidly, creating an opportunity for the Republican party to gain a major foothold in the South. This in turn relates to the tendency of a major—and the more activist—wing of Northern Republicanism to sympathize with the whole constellation of orientation of which the Southern resistance to desegregation has been a part. Hence that part associated with, or sympathizing with, the more radical Right has been particularly attracted by what has come to be known as the "Southern strategy," which was adopted by Goldwater and his advisers in the 1964 campaign.

Nothing could bring out more sharply the impact of changes in social structure in the last generation or so. The old isolation of South and North has largely broken down. The older Republican party was largely a sectional party, which on the whole opposed the New Deal, especially institutionalization of the social component of citizenship. Now, for the reasons sketched above and others, the Negro has come to the forefront all along the line of the process of social change feared by the "conservative" elements, North and South. Indeed it may be suggested that the affinity between the Goldwaterites and the segregationist Southerners was so strong that they became almost compulsive in their urge to unite. One may suspect that shrewd political calculation played a much smaller part than did this sense of affinity. Yet the outcome of the election makes crystal-clear how impossible it is for a national party that wishes to win nationwide elections to include endorsement of the segregation system in its major policies.

An important underlying aspect of this affinity is the great prominence of Protestant Fundamentalism on both sides of the political alignment. There is strong evidence that such religious orientations are particularly marked among the Radical Right, especially in its principal stronghold of the Southwest. Certainly this is true also of the South.

The alignment of the resistance to Negro inclusion, directly or through resistance to various measures essential to its success (such as federal support of education and the war against poverty), with a *generalized* political conservatism is a highly important development. Its obverse is the alignment of the society's more progressive political forces in support of the inclusion process, again both directly and by promoting policies which will provide or strengthen its major factors. Moreover, the more serious of the resistances seem to be located politically rather far on the right, so that it is unlikely that in the near future the opponents of inclusion of the Negro can reach far enough into the political center to mobilize very large political blocks at the national level. Many resistance groups will retain power at the more local levels, but the general trend of weakening parochial particularisms seems to be working in a favorable direction. The strengthening of federal power as such is only one aspect of a much more comprehensive process.

Finally, a further word should be said about the symbolization of the resistance to inclusion. I have stressed the theme of inferiority as the most central in defining the symbolic status of the Negro. If this is as important as has often been held, it follows that the main focus of anxiety involving resistance lies in the fear that the quality of the societal community will deteriorate if inferior members are admitted. Here the resemblance to fears of "debasing the currency" through irresponsible monetary management and banking is striking. Sometimes in our economic history such fears have proved justified, but over the long range the extension of credit systems and the like have contributed enormously to the productivity of the economy. The "sound money" people have on the whole fought a rearguard action against such extensions, one which would have contributed greatly to economic retardation had it prevailed.

The process under discussion here is that of a major extension of full membership in the societal community. If it is done imprudently—as, it might be said, was the completely free immigration before World War I —it may have effects analogous to inflation. But the fears of it are just as irrational as the fears of economic modernization have been, and they can be analyzed in closely parallel terms. The most important single condition of avoiding inflationary "debasement" is the general upgrading not only of the Negro but of all elements in the population falling below the minimum acceptable standards of full citizenship.

THE NEGRO MOVEMENT AND THE PROBLEM OF NEGRO IDENTITY

A particularly conspicuous feature of the recent phase in the changing status of the Negro has been the emergence of a strong movement which has had very extensive and important white support, but which has struck much deeper roots in the Negro community itself than have previous phases. The emergence of the movement is a function of several factors, such as the general social changes outlined above, the stimulus of the emergence of African states, the strengthening of the Negro middle classes, with their higher levels of education, and the concentration of Negro masses in the cities, primarily in the North. This essay cannot attempt a more detailed analysis of these developments. I should like rather to state a few of their implications, especially regarding the opportunities they present.

It has been remarked in several papers that the Negro group has generally had less solidarity and weaker organization than the other ethnic groups which have preceded it in gaining inclusion. The growth of the present movement seems to be both a symptom and a cause of a notable strengthening in this solidarity, which is beginning to create a more clearly defined group consciousness and sense of power and opportunity. It presents a new opportunity to shift the definition of Negro status away from its predominantly negative meaning as an oppressed group which is typically excluded and exposed to multifarious disadvantages. The problem is to develop a basis for a more positive conception of group identity in both American and world society. I should like to suggest that there is a most unusual opportunity inherent in the nature of the movement and its situation, the importance of which, however, is not yet widely appreciated.

One major point of reference is that the primary source of Negro grievance, exclusion on the basis of alleged *inherent* inferiority, is the most radical grievance entertained by any major non-WASP group, except possibly the American Indian's grievance of dispossession. It raises a clearer, more drastic *moral* issue than the other cases, one compounded by the status of the Negro's ancestors as slaves in America and by the injustice of using the "trivial" symbol of color as a primary basis of exclusion. Given the universalistic and egalitarian elements in our national traditions, both religious and Constitutional, it is difficult to find an issue which is morally more straightforward.

It has been possible to keep the issue relatively insulated for a long time, but recent social changes as well as the movement itself have made this progressively more problematic. Now, in a period of rising economic affluence, and, it may be said, moral ambivalence both about this and about the confusions over the American position in world affairs, the nation has been presented with a notable opportunity to define a clear and *simple* issue of conscience. By and large, the reverberation of the issue in many different groups has been extensive and impressive, in spite of the tenacious resistance just reviewed. Perhaps the issue also becomes more urgent precisely because of the progress made in resolving the other issues of inclusion which we have discussed, since this leaves the Negro even more conspicuously excluded.

It seems particularly significant that white involvement has come so definitely from two sources, the churches, especially the clergy, and the students.[40] Categorizing my examples of non-Negro inclusion problems

---

[40] There is no space here to go into the reasons that the mobilization of students in the civil rights movement is so significant. I do not accept Paul Goodman's suggestion that students are the

into Jews and Catholics, rather than the corresponding ethnic categories, was the result of deliberate theoretical choice, not simple convenience. I have long been convinced that the religious background of these problems has been—and remains—fundamental and that both the difficulties of inclusion and the opportunities for its success have been intimately involved with religion. One may say that, for the inclusion of the new immigrants, the problem centered in those elements of the relatively "liberal" Protestant community which were, in one way or another, involved in the tenuous WASP claim to aristocratic status.

I have noted that the processes of social change in the present century have tended increasingly to polarize the society along an axis which includes not only political conservatism in resistance to change but, closely related to this, what we call religious "fundamentalism." In the South the connection between militant segregationism and fundamentalism has been very clear,[41] and I have suggested that a broader connection was certainly evident in the Goldwater campaign.

Generally speaking, there are also important connections between lower-class status in industrial societies, social origins in more "primitive" or "underdeveloped" social settings, particularly of a peasant type, a certain general conservatism (or, as Lipset says, "authoritarianism"), and religious fundamentalism. Indeed, one may say that the predominant kind of Catholicism among the new immigrant urban masses was a form of fundamentalism and that the liberalization of American Catholicism in the last generation is partly a function of the upward mobility and inclusion of these masses. To a degree, the Orthodoxy of so many East European Jewish immigrants was also a form of fundamentalism.

The majority of Negro Americans have been and are, religiously speaking, fundamentalists. But, this fact does not have simple consequences. Undoubtedly, in their segregated and insulated status in the rural South, it helped to motivate acceptance of their lot, as the corre-

---

[41] Charles Campbell and Thomas Pettigrew, *Christians in Racial Crisis* (Washington, D.C., Public Affairs Press, 1959).

most exploited class in American society, but their position does have some similarities to that of an exploited class. Though their general prospects are good, as individuals they occupy a probationary status, being under rather strong control from their elders and their teachers. They have developed a strong subculture of their own, characterized by a "romantic" simplification of the general world—a part of the "youth culture." When politically activistic, they tend to be "radical," sometimes in a rightist as well as a leftist direction. Especially in "underdeveloped" societies, the violence of student nationalism is well known. This simplification makes them prone to a strongly moralistic stance—perhaps particularly emphasized because of the prevalence of various adult suspicions about their moral integrity. Hence, they tend to be kinds of "fundamentalists" to whom a simple moralistic issue can appeal greatly. But, by the same token, as representing the best of the future of the society, they can play an exceedingly important role in dramatizing really important moral issues. Cf. Eisenstadt, *From Generation to Generation* (New York: The Free Press, 1956), and my own article, "Youth in the Context of American Society," *Daedalus* (Winter 1961) reprinted in Erik H. Erikson ed., *Youth: Change and Challenge* (Garden City, N.Y.: Anchor Books, 1964), and my own *Social Structure and Personality* (New York: The Free Press, 1964) Chapter 7.

sponding features of Catholic and Jewish fundamentalism have done in both the peasant or ghetto circumstances of the "old countries" and in the difficult early stages of involvement in American society as first- and second-generation immigrants.

At the same time, there is the deep-seated Judeo-Christian tradition of religious motivation to preserve integrity, to assert autonomy, and eventually to seek justice through change in the structure of the situation. Here, what I am calling the more fundamentalist orientation has, in the course of history, repeatedly assumed moral leadership, in part facilitated by an unworldly lack of concern for the complexities of process in the highly differentiated societies. Fundamentalists in this sense—which includes such "secular religions" as Communism—tend to be direct-actionists, to see issues in *simple* moral terms; and about half the time they have the balance of long-run merit on their side.

However, Negro fundamentalism, like that of the previous immigrant masses, has come to be mobilized predominantly on the side of differentiation and inclusion, not of segregation and exclusion. The development of the movement has strongly activated the moral sentiments of the other groups, including very significant groups of non-Protestants. This process has quite directly *split* the fundamentalist element in American religion, with all its important *indirect* relations to politics and other contexts. The *moral* basis of opposition to change in the older and simpler order— so strongly emphasized by our latter-day conservatives—is thereby gravely undermined. There has developed, significantly, a strong and sometimes very sharp dialogue on the subject of moral justification between those camps. This brings the process of restructuring the social system to the highest normative level, a level already fully structured specifically in terms of religious and social pluralism. It raises, in a form difficult to evade, the question of the moral basis of the American type of "Free Society."

I should like to emphasize the subtle combination of similarities and differences between the processes of inclusion for the groups of the new immigration and for the Negro. All three have been in certain respects "foreign." They have also come with socio-cultural patterns which have been relatively "backward" by the main standards of the new society— to put it sharply, all except Jews have been "peasants," and they have been small-town bourgeois. All three have had religio-cultural orientations which can be called "fundamentalist." Environmentally, however, all three have been plunged into a converging set of integrating influences, as the most recently arrived lower-class group in the largest urban communities.

In the other context, the three are not only distinct from each other, but constitute a series. The Jews, curiously from some points of view, have proved the easiest to include. This was not the case in Germany, with its much more hierarchical social structure. But in "individualistic" America, the principal problem was that of defining the legitimacy of, and opportunity for, cultural pluralism without prejudicing the other, more instrumental bases of participation. The Catholics had to overcome high American sensitivity to tightly organized collectivities which might be accused of "conspiracy."

In this succession, the Negro stands at the "end of the line." His is the most serious (hence in some respects, the most plausible) basis of exclusion, namely, his inherent inferiority. The relatively satisfactory—it will not in our time ever be fully so—resolution of the problem of Negro inclusion will certainly be one of the greatest achievements of American society. Moreover, the record of the movement, even up to this point, makes it clear that a very major part of the credit will go to the Negro community itself; it will be *their* achievement, certainly in the sense of direct goal-orientation to a much greater degree than is true of the groups that have already gained inclusion.

This seems to me to constitute a crucially important focus for the future of the collective Negro identity. The Negro community has the opportunity to define itself as the spearhead of one of the most important improvements in the quality of American society in its history—and to do so not only in pursuit of its own obvious self-interest, but in the fulfillment of a *moral* imperative. It is a change in American society which is deeply consonant with our moral traditions, but also one which could not come about without systematically exerted pressures and strong leadership. The resistances are quite sufficient to explain these necessities.

This role of the Negro movement and the community behind it has significance far beyond the internal American scene. The whole world has now become more or less polarized between the developed and the underdeveloped nations. This polarization largely coincides with the freeing of large areas of the world from colonial status, a process which has moved with great rapidity in recent years, and with their emancipation from inferior status in terms of both political dependence and economic and educational development. Not least, this axis also relates very closely to a color line—the Asian and African new nations are largely nonwhite.

It has been stressed above that the American Revolutionary tradition has prepared this country for a position of leadership in the movement toward equality for the new nations of the extra-European world. The internal processes of inclusion of the Jewish and Catholic elements have strengthened the American position in this respect—the vaunted promises of equal treatment have not been wholly worthless. The opportunity, then, is for the Negro to symbolize the completion of this internal process (and to give symbolic promise of the solubility of the world-wide problems) as a massively large colored group which has found its rightful place in American society and has done so very largely by its own efforts.

It has been noted above that, earlier in this century, there was a tendency to define class lines in the United States as more or less equivalent to ethnic lines, with the new immigrants forming the core of the "working class." It is probably true that the heavy influx of immigrants contributed substantially to preventing the crystallization of class divisions in the older community along the European lines stressed by Marxists as typical of "capitalist" societies. In any case, American society has certainly evolved away from, rather than toward, this Marxian model, the inclusion of the earlier immigrant groups constituting a most important aspect of the development. However discriminated against the Negro has been, he has been too small a group to constitute a full "proletariat"—indeed, within the group itself, there has been very strong resistance to this definition of their role, in spite of intensive propaganda from Communist sources.

The whole trend of development in American society constitutes the sharpest challenge to the Communist diagnosis of the modern world, and, increasingly, Western Europe has also moved in many respects in the "American" direction. These trends cannot be explained on Marxist premises. The status of the Negro has been morally the most vulnerable feature of the American society. If, as there seems to be good hope, this can be dealt with effectively, it can have a most extensive effect on the larger world situation.

This is because the Communist trend has been to redefine the crucial "class struggle" as a struggle not between classes within societies, but between exploiting and exploited societies, with the famous theory of "imperialism." Just as successful Negro inclusion will put the seal on the Marxian error in diagnosing American society, so the United States, with strong Negro participation, indeed leadership, has the opportunity to present a true alternative to the Communist pattern on a world-wide basis, one which is not bound to the stereotype of "capitalism." Because of the immensely important role of race and color in the world situation, the strategic position of the Negro American is crucial. This subcommunity of our pluralistic society has the opportunity to be *the* main symbolic spokesman of the possibility of achieving a racially, as well as religiously, nationally, and otherwise, pluralistic world society in which some kind of integration among the racial groups can be developed without a loss of identity and in terms compatible with raising the previously inferior to the status of those fundamentally equal in world citizenship.

Near the beginning of this essay, the distinction between inclusion and assimilation was stressed. The purport of this latest phase of the analysis is to suggest that to identify non-discrimination (that is, inclusion) too strongly with complete "color-blindness" might be to throw away a very precious asset, not only for the Negro, but for American society

Table 1. Symbolic Groups in Relation to the Inclusion Problem

FOCUS OF ANXIETY	AMBIGUOUSLY, INCLUDED	PROJECTED UPON
Commitments outside the community High Achievement capacity plus "clannishness"	The Jews	Undefined Foreignness suspected of "un-Americanism"

      Common feature: diffuse foreignness.
      Dominant circa 1920's, but into 1930's.

Commitments to authoritarian, presumptively conspiratorial collectivities	Catholics	Communists

      Common feature: organization which might "take over."
      Dominant a little later, culminating in McCarthy era.

Incapacity for full participation	Fundamentalists	Negroes (Color as Symbol)

      Common feature: inclusion could debase the quality
      of citizenship. Dominant since about 1954.

Patterns for Inclusion

Jews—Foreigners: Fully differentiated participation with special reference to the occupational system—differentiating occupational status from ethnic belong-ingness—acceptance on one side, abandonment of "clannishness" on the other. Organic solidarity.

Catholics—Communists: Pluralization in the analytical-political sense. Movement from *altruisme* to *egoisme* in Durkheim's sense. Acceptance on both sides that citizenship is not ascribed to position in a "columnar" structure à la Rokkan and Lipset. Loyalty problem.

Fundamentalists—Negroes: Upgrading. The development of capacity for full participation after breaking the stigma of inferiority, as sinful reprobates or as biologically inferior. Symbolic animals and children.

as a whole. My own view is that the healthiest line of development will not be only the preservation, but the actual building up, of the solidarity of the Negro community and of the sense that being a Negro has positive value. In the process there is the danger of cultivating separatism, as most conspicuously exemplified by the Black Muslims. But the pluralistic solution, which has been stressed throughout this discussion, is neither one of separatism—with or without equality—nor of assimilation, but one of full participation combined with the preservation of identity. The American Jewish and Catholic groups have, by and large, been able to achieve this goal.

Quite clearly, the Negro's own associations with fellow Negroes who survive the inclusion process should no longer be compulsory.[42] Each individual Negro should be free to associate with any non-Negro

[42] Not only that, but the positive value of a Negro identity in the long run should not be used to justify failing to act to break up *discriminatory* segregation in the more immediate situation.

in any legal way he sees fit, and, if he so desires, to give up completely his identity as a Negro in the sense of belonging to a Negro community. But this does not mean that Negro identity should or will disappear. I should envision continuing predominance of marriages of Negroes with each other. I see no reason that some religious denominations should not be identified as "Negro churches," or that, as long as residence there is not compulsory, many neighborhoods should not continue to be mainly Negro, as many today are Jewish.

Once being a Negro loses the stigma of inferiority, I suggest, it is likely that these will cease to be salient issues. After, all, color is a *symbol* and, if the context of its historic meanings is sufficiently changed, the prospect is that it will cease to be the basis of a stigma. The schematic outline in Table 1 may be helpful to the reader in interpreting the preceding discussion.

Chapter *12*

Order and Community in the International Social System

*t*his brief paper must necessarily begin on a note of apology. It is an essay in a field in which the author is in no sense an expert. There has, in recent years, been an immense amount of work in this field which has produced an extensive literature, selections from which constitute the bulk of the present volume. My knowledge of this literature is fragmentary indeed, and it has not been possible to take time to familiarize myself with it to even a minimum degree of desirability. Under these limitations, the best that can be done is to attempt to mobilize concepts and propositions which have proved useful in the more general theory of social systems and its field of empirical application, with which I am more familiar, in order to throw light on this particularly important and urgent subject.

The problem of the basis of order in social systems has been a classic focus for theoretical analysis, and one which is of particular importance to sociology. Because of its evident centrality in the international field, this

Reprinted from International Politics and Foreign Policy *Revised Edition, ed. James A. Rosenau.* *Copyright* © *1961, The Free Press, New York, N.Y.*

seems to be a particularly appropriate point of reference for the present discussion.

In most current sociological theory, order is conceived as the existence of normative control over a range of the action of acting units, whether these be individuals or collectivities, so that, on the one hand, their action is kept within limits which are compatible with at least the minimum stability of the system as a whole and, on the other hand, there is a basis for at least certain types of concerted action when the occasion so requires. The essential normative components can be conceived as *values*, which concern the most general level of conception of the desirable type of social system, but without reference either to internal functional differentiation or to particularities of the situation, and *norms*, which are generalized formulations—more or less explicit—of expectations of proper action by differentiated units in relatively specific situations.

These normative components of a social system are also part of what, in analytical terms, we call the cultural system, but they become part of the social system insofar as they are *institutionalized*. Institutionalization, as that concept is used here, is a mode of integration of the appropriate cultural elements with the "interests" of acting units, whose action is oriented in terms of these normative components. Institutionalization is conceived as the phenomenon in social systems which is parallel to the internalization of values and social objects in the personality of the individual—a conception which has become relatively familiar to social scientists.

The crucial cultural component here is *evaluative orientation*. For full institutionalization, however, there must be three other components, namely, (a) an adequately precise cognitive conception of the nature of the desirable object (in this case the *type* of social system) in relation to its type of environment; (b) the goal-commitments of units of the system to "doing their part" in maintaining such a system (for the individual, "motivational" commitment); and (c) evaluative ideas concerning the conditions of operation of the system and the benefits and costs involved in the alternatives of success and failure (this is broadly the field of ideology in a nonpejorative sense).[1]

The basic consequence of the institutionalization of normative culture is to produce an area of *coincidence* of normative obligation, on the one hand, and "interest," on the other. That is to say, for acting units it comes to pass that it is to their interest to do what, in terms of the normative order, they *ought* to do. In this sense, institutionalization is not an either-or proposition, but a matter of degree. At one pole is the Hobbesian state of the war of all against all, whether the units of war be individuals or nation-

---

[1] Talcott Parsons, paper on "The Sociology of Knowledge," read at the Fifth World Congress of the International Sociological Association, 1959, reprinted in my collection, *Sociological Theory and Modern Society* (New York: The Free Press, 1969).

states. At the other pole is a state of complete integration, where any action which deviates from the normative order, which itself is presumed to be completely consistent and explicit, is unthinkable. Obviously *both* are theoretical limiting cases, and neither is descriptive of *any* empirical state of affairs. If international affairs were in fact a Hobbesian state of nature, none of us would be here to write about them, and we are all too painfully aware of the flaws in its state of integration. Here, however, it is relevant to remark that breakdown of order into war does not analytically imply that there are *no* forces which tend to support order, but rather that they have not proved strong enough to prevent a specific breakdown for the occasion in question. The very prevalence of ideological justifications for resorting to war may itself be regarded as evidence of the presence of the normative components under discussion.

The normative elements of a social system do not stand alone, of course. The reason for emphasizing them here is their involvement in the problem of order. Perhaps the best single term in general usage for the non-normative components is the term *interests*, of which, in turn, the most important subcategories are political and economic. Order as here conceived is order among interests. These may be conceived as related in one or a combination of the following ways: (a) as integrated in the sense in which a well-led collectivity, effectively achieving a well-defined goal, is integrated; (b) as competing when there is effective normative regulation of competitive relations without having a collective goal imposed on the regulated system (the market is the prototypical case); or (c) as conflicting when the lack of regulation tends toward a disequilibrium in the system, whether through polarization, or through various forms and levels of what may be called fragmentation.

It is essential to the treatment of the relations between components of normative order, on the one hand, and interests, on the other, to keep the relativity of this relation in mind continually. The distinction is analytical and does not represent a classification of concrete entities. It is primarily a matter of the level of system-reference at which analysis is carried out. Thus, religious ethics certainly constitute a component of normative order in one system reference, but at the same time a church, in its own conception of its position as a trustee of ethics, may also function as an "interest group," either positively integrated with others, competing with them, or in conflict with them. It is clearly the relation between the play of interests and the potential components of normative order which constitutes the core of our problem in this paper.

Of the two great categories of interests, the political category is most directly relevant to the present argument. For reasons which cannot be gone into here, political interests tend to come to focus in the problem of power as the generalized capacity to attain the goals of the unit in question. Where territorially organized political units are in question, the focus of the primary problem is, above all, the margin between a conflicting type of relation and one which can become competitive in the regulated sense. Economic interests are certainly important and will be mentioned at certain points, but there would probably be general agreement that the focus of the problem of international order lies in the regulation of the potential conflicts of political power interests. Given the political organization of territorial units, economic interests tend to be funneled, though not with uniform intensity, into competitive or conflicting power-interests.

Our central problem, then, may be defined as the need to identify the principal elements of normative order that are present in contemporary international relations, and to suggest their potentialities and limitations for being strengthened at cultural levels and for meeting the basic conditions of minimal institutionalization.

The concept of a society provides a convenient approach. In sociological tradition, this has tended to refer to the highest-order social system, one which fulfills the prerequisites of a level of order that permits a relatively complete and stable development, within its boundaries, of *all* the important types of structure and process with which the analyst of social systems is concerned. Perhaps the Aristotelian concept of self-sufficiency has served as the fundamental model.

One particular tendency evident in various treatments of the concept of society is especially important in the present context. This is the emphasis on the relation between a pattern of normative order and the effective control of action within a territorial area. In terms of the structure of complex societies, this refers to the relation between political organization, on the one hand, and a legal system, on the other. The legal system is the most explicit and formal aspect of the normative order. Not only to secure compliance, but also, as Durkheim noted, to assert the seriousness with which the normative order is taken, it is essential that there should be attempts at *enforcement* of the obligations defined in the order, and that some machinery should be entrusted with this enforcement function. In cases of resistance, the tendency is to resort to increasingly drastic measures. The element of territoriality becomes particularly crucial because, at least in the negative, preventive context, physical force becomes the ultimate sanction—the end of the line. Though it has crucial limitations as a stimulator of desired action, it is the ultimate preventive; sufficient force, properly applied, can prevent any human action, if only because dead men do not act. Hence, there can be no certainty of implementation of a normative order, unless the employment of physical force can be controlled—and controlled within a territorial area—because force must be applied to the object in the *place* where it is located. Of course, in many respects the threat of force, as a deterrent, is more important than is its actual application.

The same general idea of relativity that was applied to the distinction between elements of normative order and interests may be used here. The organization of order with regard to territorial jurisdictions is a common element of all societal organization. But the nation-state (or something like it), as seen in comparative perspective, is not an isolated and unique phenomenon. Organization of order on a territorial basis clearly continues to be important for many subunits of a politically organized society, including, of course, many units not ordinarily thought of as political; the relative immunity from interference within one's own residential premises—the famous "Englishman's castle"—is a case in point. This surely is one main reason why real estate is somewhat different from other objects of property rights. This becomes even more conspicuous with respect to what are explicitly considered units of local government as such, and is most fully institutionalized in the case of federal organization, where territorial units below the top level certainly have very important elements of institutionalized autonomy. With respect to the United States, the use of the word "state" for the federal unit rather than for the national government is surely significant. In certain respects, the importance of these autonomies, with territorial as well as other references, has necessarily increased as a result of the generally increasing differentiation of modern society, which carries with it an increasingly prominent pluralism of group structures.[2]

If this is true when one looks from the national state "downward" in the series of levels of organization, there is no reason why it should not also be true when one looks in the opposite direction. A relevant consideration here is the historical trend, very broadly conceived. With various important breaks and discontinuities, this is, of course, the progressive extension of the magnitude of territorial range of relatively stable political order. It would be hard to conceive of the process by which these extensions had taken place without reference to the prior existence of components of normative order that transcended the area of effective institutionalization at any given time. However important sheer conquest and forcible enforcement may have been in the extension process, the fact that many of the most important religious movements, for instance, have extended well beyond the political boundaries of any one society identified with them is surely relevant in this connection.

Thus, it can be seen that the strictures on the doctrine of absolute sovereignty, which were particularly emphasized by the late Professor Laski in his pre-Marxist period, should be interpreted as applying in both directions. The case of a "state" that is completely sovereign internally, in the sense that only the "top" political authority can make any decisions in case of conflict, is clearly a limiting case, incompatible not only with any genuine federalism, but also with a variety of other modes of more or less

[2] See William Kornhauser, *The Politics of Mass Society*, and my review article, *World Politics*, October, 1960.

pluralistic social organization. Similarly, whatever the level of centralization of the internal control of order, absolute sovereignty in the external sense (which postulates a state of war of all against all between such sovereign units) is a theoretical limiting case, which at most is only approximated in reality. At the very least there will be a component of competition mitigating conflict, and this implies some normative order.

These considerations are relevant to the question of how the concept of a social system should be understood in the present context. The essential point concerns the kind and degree of normative integration. I should regard the famous Hobbesian state of war as the limiting concept, the statement of the limit at which the concept of social system becomes meaningless. Short of this, there is an indefinite range of gradations in the direction of progressively higher levels of integration, with, of course, qualitative differences of type being involved as well. From this point of view, the national state represents a social system characterized by a relatively high level of integration in one respect, namely, capacity to control activity within a territorial area and to act concertedly as an "interest group" *vis-à-vis* other territorial units. But there is no implication either that its existence is incompatible with other elements of normative control over territorial areas, transcending those of its "sovereignty" (though the nature of such controls is, of course, problematic), or that elements of order that have other than primarily territorial-political references are negligible. On this basis I think we can quite legitimately consider an international order as a social system, however precarious the element of normative control may be. The problems of degree and conditions should be treated as empirical problems, not as problems of definition in an abstract theoretical sense.

Roscoe Pound's notion of the relation between law and "politically organized society" can, with proper qualifications, be taken as a central concept. It should not, however, be absolutized. With the development of the modern nation-state, the tightness of its control over the use of force within its boundaries has increased, partly because force has become more formidable, both technologically and organizationally, and hence more dangerous if not controlled. But the nation-state is, with some qualifications, the product of a process of social differentiation; hence it may be argued that by and large there are more—and more important— elements within a modern society that are essentially independent of the principal controllers of the use of force than there are in less differentiated societies. Thus, a military establishment that is predominantly professional and under civilian control, rather than fused with the higher echelons of government, as was recently the case in Imperial Germany and Japan, is one index.[3] Another is the structural independence of the legal

[3] See Morris Janowitz, *The Professional Soldier* (New York: The Free Press, 1960).

system from operative government. In such a situation, there is, in addition to government and law, the immense ramification of social structures and groups in cultural, economic, and other fields that are characteristic of highly differentiated societies; pluralism in this sense is a basic immanent trend.[4]

The most important exception is the modern more or less "totalitarian" state, which tries not merely to enforce a monopoly of force in the traditional political sense, but beyond this a basic subordination, in other respects, of potentially independent structural elements in the society. In spite of its prominence on the contemporary scene, I think it is legitimate to regard this as a special case, one which will have to be discussed further below.

All social systems, including societies (except for limiting cases), are *open* rather than closed systems. It would be expected that the trend of the process of differentiation just referred to would be to increase, rather than decrease, their openness. This is to say that the obverse of the independence of many internal structural elements from the political authority, which in one sense (but *only* one) "controls," would be both the permission and the encouragement of the establishment of connections that extend across national boundaries. A prototypical example, and one of very critical significance, is international trade.

The relations of international trade to the political actions and relations of governments have, of course, been very complex. It has sometimes been tempting to reduce them to such slogans as "trade follows the flag," and, in fact, there have been plenty of cases of "economic imperialism." Nevertheless, a certain level of independence of trade relations from the governments of the principals has existed for a long time and has probably been growing. The fact that governments, as well as business groups within their territories, have often had an interest in promoting trade, as well as in preventing or controlling competition, does not invalidate the preceding assertion. The essential question is whether this has been a field of activity in which there were components of *order* that were not a simple function of the political policies of governments. That this has in fact been the case is attested by the relatively extensive development of international law in this field.

Of course, this independence from governments should not be exaggerated. Very generally, governments have been in a position to limit, or even stop, their nationals in these activities, and have done so on occasion through tariffs, embargoes, and various other devices. But it would certainly be going too far to say that in no sense have governments respected international law and the interests of groups other than their own nationals in these fields; within certain limits it would be considered undesirable politically to go too far in these respects.

[4] Kornhauser, *op. cit.*, and my review article.

Closely connected with trade, but distinguishable from it, there has existed a normative order relative to freedom and security of persons and of communications as between political jurisdictions. One of the most important illustrations of this phenomenon is the code regulating conduct on the high seas where ships are out of range of national controls. Still another concerns freedom to travel, and with this the whole complex of norms regarding the rights of aliens present within the jurisdiction of a government, either as temporary visitors or as residents on various bases. Of course, the matters of passports and visas play a role here. It is significant that before World War I travel within the whole Western world was possible without passports or visas, and that this is now being revived. Another interesting tendency throughout much of Western Europe is to waive customs inspection in the matter of the personal belongings of travellers. Connected with these issues are such matters as international copyright conventions and, of course, freedom of communication through broadcasting, magazines, newspapers, etc.

All of these factors and many more involve elements of international order which, to be sure, are likely to break down under the stress of war, and sometimes during crises short of war, but which are very much present and not to be neglected. It is true that they are regulated by governments, but this does not mean that they are entirely the "creatures" of governments. It is also true that insofar as they do respect them or participate in their extensions, governments are by no means always wholly "disinterested"; they may well see a national interest involved in these procedures. But this is not the point. We have already noted that it is the hallmark of institutionalization that self-interest comes to be bound up with conformity with a normative order. Hence, the fact that a unit finds it to be in its self-interest to act in a certain way by itself says nothing one way or the other about whether the action is or is not in accord with a normative order. Only one point is certain, namely, that a normative order which laid down requirements which were in serious conflict with the self-interests of all the units related to it could not be upheld for very long.

Within frameworks such as these, there has developed a widely ramified system of private associations and solidarities across national boundaries. Those in the field of trade are probably on the largest scale. However, economic relations, because of the inherent competitive element, are perhaps in themselves more precarious with respect to order than some others. A very important category is that having to do with cultural interests. For example, almost all associations built around scientific disciplines have extensive international connections, hold frequent technical meetings and conferences, and, of course, engage in much exchange of information through publications that are mutually available.

Considering the fact that, historically, religion has been involved so prominently in social conflicts, not infrequently to the point of war, it is worthwhile to call attention to the extent to which religious adherence and, indeed, formal religious organization transcend national boundaries. In the Western world the largest single example is the Roman Catholic church, but on a smaller scale "international" Judaism and the various Protestant denominations have a similar character; for the latter group, the recent emergence of the World Council of Churches is a significant development.

Even in the nationalistically sensitive area of law there is one little-noted, but remarkable, phenomenon. Some Americans have taken delight in twisting the Lion's tail, but the legal profession in this country has quietly but consistently treated decisions in British courts, either current or made long after American independence, as providing valid precedents for American judicial process in areas not covered by legislation. Common Law is thus a common heritage of normative order, not merely in the sense that American law is historically derived from English law, but in the sense that today, in significant degree, Common Law is a *single* corpus which is treated as legally valid and subject to legal growth with little reference to national boundaries (at least in Great Britain itself, the United States, and the British Commonwealth). I am sure that similar statements can be made of Continental Roman Law.

Hence, my view is that there is already a very considerable scope of international normative order and of solidarities operating under it in private spheres, which, to be sure, are subject to governmental influence, but which are not in any sense simply agencies of governments. This is particularly important because the tendency toward pluralism of social structures, referred to above, creates a situation in which governments —and the political parties that compete for power in such governments and that seek support in this competition—tend to represent more or less integrated combinations of the various interest groups involved, to be dependent on them, and to try to further their interests. The long-run presumption is that the strengthening of private international solidarities should strengthen the interest of governments in protecting or even extending these solidarities. The essential point here is the existence, in the nature of modern societies, of a nexus of solidary relationships which cross-cut the divisions on the basis of "national" interest.

What now of the nation-state itself? The essential point, which has, of course, been made many times, is that it is by no means such a monolithic either-or unit as it has often been held to be. Just as there are many internal private groups with interests which cut across national lines, so the idea of the absolute sovereignty of governments is at best only an approximation of the truth. Since nationalism has been so prominent in the immediate historical background, there has been a strong ideological, and perhaps somewhat less a practical, sensitivity to any suggestion of surrendering elements of sovereignty. However, the boundary between international engagements that are "purely contractual" (in line with the usual interpretation of most treaties) and somewhat stronger bonds is difficult to draw.

Even in the purely contractual field, it is not irrelevant to point out that Durkheim's basic analysis of the conditions of functioning of a contractual system between individuals ought to apply as well in a system where national governments are the contracting parties. International relations in this field may appear to be highly unstable; but the important point here is that this is a *relative* matter. I, for one, do not believe that such stability as has existed would have been possible without a substantial "noncontractual element of contract,"[5] that is, a normative order regulating the content and procedures of contract. That this is so is indicated in the first instance by the immense body of tradition and protocol that governs the status of embassies and consulates and the conduct of diplomacy, but it clearly extends beyond this to values having to do with national independence and honor, with defining limits of legitimate pressures in securing assent to treaties, and the like.

Whether by formal contractual agreement or in various other ways, the international system is clearly not simply an aggregate of atomistic sovereign units; rather, these units are organized in complex ways into various kinds of "communities of interest" and the like. The British Commonwealth, the West European combinations (which, in certain respects, are now divided into the "six" and the "seven"), NATO, SEATO, and—by no means least—the Communist bloc, are familiar examples.

Perhaps the most crucial question here is the difficult one as to the extent to which such combinations are a simple function of "power" relations. It is my view that for ideological reasons the current tendency, perhaps particularly evident in the United States, is to exaggerate the extent to which this is the case. For example, there is the contention that the English-speaking community is not a genuine one at all, but that Britain and her dominions are attached to the United States *only* because of our predominant—in the last analysis, military—power position; in other words, that there is no alternative in the face of such power but to submit in the interests of elementary security. Similarly, on the side of the Communist bloc it is alleged that the dominant military power of the Soviet Union is the only significant factor. The alternative interpretation is that not only do the positions of the United States and the Soviet Union respectively contain elements of sheer power—which of course is there— but that they also contain elements of genuine *leadership*. Leadership in this sense exists only when there is political support for the position,

[5] Emile Durkheim, *The Division of Labor in Society*, Book I, Chapter VII.

backed by interests other than the most elementary security, and subject to an accepted (i.e., institutionalized) normative order. In my opinion, the element of sheer power is more prominent in the Communist case, but it is dangerous to assume that other elements are negligible. If this is so, the noncoercive elements on the "other" side are clearly of substantially greater weight. To take one well-known example, it seems very difficult to believe that the integrity of the British Commonwealth could be understood as a simple function of the predominant power of the United Kingdom.

It is also of particular importance to note that these solidarities that exist between formally "sovereign" states do not occur entirely in mutually exclusive groups, but that there are important cross-cutting elements. One of the most striking cases, of course, is that of Canada, which is a member of the Commonwealth, and which by virtue of geographical and power factors, but not these alone, also stands in a very special relation to the United States. The broad conclusion seems to be that, to a considerable extent, a *pluralistic* international system has been developing. This means that the most significant nearly "ultimate" units do not function simply as "individual" units, or as a "mass," but are involved in a complex network of solidary associations which, however, are not completely monolithic, but cross-cut each other in significant respects.[6]

Two further points about the international system should be made. The first is the very commonplace one that we *do* have a world-wide international organization in the United Nations. Quite obviously, this is not a "world government," with effective powers to legislate bindingly and to coerce the losing parties in disputes into acceptance of its decisions. However, these limitations do not mean that its presence in the situation is of negligible importance; it is a common fallacy of "liberals" to suppose that an element not strong enough to meet the most extreme stresses is so unimportant as scarcely to be there at all, (e.g., since civil rights are not completely and literally enforced in the United States in all contexts, the vaunted American commitment to civil rights is of no importance and, moreover, is sheer "hypocrisy"). Apart from its many unobtrusive "routine" operations, the role played by the United Nations in the Middle Eastern crisis in 1956, and more recently in the Congo crisis, shows that it can have a very appreciable effect, particularly in *legitimizing* the establishment of elementary political order under auspices *other* than those of the most powerful outside interests immediately involved.

The second focal phenomenon is the *polarization* of the world political system as between the Communist bloc and the "free world," with a substantial "uncommitted" contingent. This clearly is the focus of the danger of breakdown into general war. It has, however, another aspect, namely, the sense not only in which the whole world has come to be a

[6] Kornhauser, *op. cit.*

single political system, but also in which it is coming to be structured as something resembling, however remotely, a two-party system. A two-party system is clearly dangerous to order precisely because it polarizes allegiances, though not without residue in favorable cases. But on the other hand, there is the sharp focus on the *problem* of order, of creating a basis on which the conflict can be contained. Experience in relation to the two-party system within countries seems to indicate that two primary sets of conditions underlie the integrative stability of such a system.[7] One of these concerns the underlying structure of cross-cutting solidarities, referred to above under the heading of the problem of pluralism. The important point to note here is the asymmetry as between the free world and the communist bloc in this respect, the latter clearly being far more nearly "monolithic," both within itself and in its external relations. This, however, is a matter of degree; probably the infrastructure of pluralistic solidarities within the bloc is in fact far more ramified and important than the current image of the Communist system would readily indicate.

The more obvious—and more immediately acute—problem concerns another level, that of "constitutional" order standing "above" the party conflict. Here the question centers on the *legitimacy* of each major party group from the point of view of the other. The dominant public impression in the cold war period has undoubtedly been that on this level the conflict was absolute and irreconcilable, an impression documented by highly authoritative statements on both sides. The essential question is to what degree this represents an ideological and short-term set of positions, and, hence, whether it is possible that it is more in the nature of the internal partisan conflict in an electoral campaign than of a genuine "state of war." The most obvious indications that something of the sort may be involved concern the extent to which the "parties" are sensitive to the impact of not only their words, but of their actions, on "world opinion." Essentially, this constitutes an appeal beyond unit-interest to a basis for legitimacy common to both sides. From one point of view this is the instrumental exploitation of men's irrational "sentiments," but from another it is an index finger, pointing toward a set of normative factors of primary importance.

That there is some trend in this direction is the most plausible interpretation of a number of features of recent behavior across the line of the Iron Curtain. Two of these features are particularly noteworthy. One is the visits of prominent politicians from each side, including heads of state and of government, to neutral or semi-neutral territory. Examples would be the visits of Krushchev and Eisenhower to India, the interpretation of

---

[7] Talcott Parsons, "'Voting' and the Equilibrium of the American Political System," in Eugene Burdick and Arthur J. Brodbeck, eds., *American Voting Behavior* (Glencoe, 1959), Chapter 9, above.

which could surely be applied to the visits of two presidential candidates during a campaign to New York, for example. The other is the fact that, in spite of the debacle of the Summit meeting in May, 1960, the United Nations Assembly was used as a forum for debate, patently oriented to the influencing of "world opinion." Even though observance of the etiquette of parliamentary procedure is far from perfect, the Assembly is treated as a forum in which the point of view of one group is advocated within some sort of "constitutional" order, both of procedure and of definition of the rights of member states. Perhaps most important of all, conflict is fought out at the verbal level, rather than at the level of overt hostile acts.

This is the point at which the famous stalemate of mutual nuclear deterrence becomes most significant. We have stressed that, given the institutionalization of a normative order, it is to be expected that there will be a relative coincidence of the structure of interests in conformity with it. It would be most unlikely that this would be an entirely one-way relationship. It is therefore reasonable to hypothesize that if circumstances exist by virtue of which there is a realistic coincidence of interests over any important area, and given the presence of other essential factors, a relatively favorable situation will be created for the development of a normative order to govern these interests. A highly important historical example is the institutionalization of contract relative to economic exchange. Though by no means the only factor, it is certainly reasonable to suppose that one of the factors involved was the enhanced appreciation of the mutual advantage of exchange relationships, and with it, of course, appreciation of the mutual disadvantages, in a market of opportunities, of exploitation by some participants to gain at the expense of other parties (e.g., through fraud).[8]

The nuclear stalemate thus creates a situation in which, in highly dramatic form, there seems to be an element of mutual, *two*-sided interest in the stability of the system. The beneficial effect of polarization, along with its danger, is the tendency to dramatize the problem of stability, to focus responsibility for actions disturbing to it, and, with sufficient imaginativeness, to open up positive opportunities for formulating elements of normative order.

However, such elements of order are not likely to be created completely *ad hoc*, out of thin air; indeed, if they were not grounded in existing deeper-lying cultural traditions, it is unlikely that they could take hold. The next important question, therefore, is whether any *common* normative factors exist in the world situation which, by extension and further specification, might provide a basis for a stronger normative order, particularly at the "constitutional" level, as I have called it.

[8] See Max Weber's treatment of the English stock exchange, as discussed in Reinhard Bendix, *Max Weber: An Intellectual Portrait* (New York, 1960).

In the social sciences in the past generation, perhaps most particularly in anthropology, there has been a strong emphasis on cultural relativity which, however justified for certain purposes, has at times been interpreted to imply that there were no common factors at the value level. More recently there has been a reaction to this and a search for common elements, which, as will be evident, have to be our primary point of reference, and which are the subject of the present brief inquiry.

For the present paper, though by no means for all purposes, the keynote must, I think, be set in certain fundamental universal significances of Western culture.[9] In the present connection it is vital to note that, culturally, Communism is a product of Western civilization; after all, Karl Marx was a German Jew, who spent most of his productive life in England and who synthesized elements drawn primarily from English Utilitarianism and German Idealism. The adoption of Communism in Russia was certainly part of the westernization of Russia, the most important of the Christian areas that had been least touched by European developments dating from the Renaissance and the Reformation; further extension to China is even more obviously an aspect of "Westernization." But, of course, the impact of Western civilization at cultural levels has been far broader than the spread of the Communist movement; it has operated, in particular, through the role of the "intellectuals" in those non-Western societies that have had important literate traditions.[10]

With Weber as our principal guide, I think we can delineate those features of Western culture that are of primary significance in this context. They have to do with the development of normative institutional frameworks for the higher-order organization of secular society, whereas most of the important non-Western cultures had left a far greater sphere of "traditionalism" in these respects, as evidenced by predominantly peasant economies, by the special social position of hereditary aristocracies, by the relatively low level or complete absence of formal education of all but a very small elite group, etc.[11]

Whatever the deeper cultural bases of these emphases of Western values (and to me they are ultimately rooted in religious orientations), the primary consequence of present significance is an immense emphasis on the importance of the two primary levels of the *operative* organization of modern societies, of "modernization," namely, the political structure of the society and the economy. In the former case the drive is toward the development

---

[9] See Max Weber's remarks on this subject in his general introduction to his studies in the sociology of religion published in this country as the Introduction to the *Protestant Ethic and the Spirit of Capitalism*.

[10] See various papers by Edward Shils, especially "The Intellectuals and the Powers: Some Perspectives for Comparative Analysis," *Comparative Studies in Society and History* (October, 1958).

[11] On the concept of "traditional society" from the point of view of the process of economic development, see W. W. Rostow, *The Stages of Economic Growth* (Cambridge, 1960).

of a "modern state," with, above all, effective administrative organization of a "bureaucratic" character, which has meant the elimination or sharp reduction of the influence of "traditional" power groups. The involvement of anything approaching political democracy has, of course, been extremely uneven. The other main context is the modernization of the economy, which has meant a more or less close approach to industrialization as we understand it, with its use of bureaucratic organization, of a mobile and technically trained labor force, extension of monetary transactions and market organization, and various other familiar features.

Viewed in this context, and against the background of the conception of cultural relativity, there has emerged in the modern world the phenomenon of a remarkable world-wide consensus. For the sociologist this must be clearly understood in its societal relevance as located at the *value* level. Looked at in the twin perspectives of the development trend and a comparison with the advanced nations of the West, the primary "reference group," it may be called the valuation of *modernization*. It has in turn two primary foci, namely, the political—the development of a "strong" and viable political organization—and the economic, which has come to mean above all industrialization. Clearly, nationalism and its relation to political independence, particularly in respect to the history of Western "imperialism," is involved and is the aspect especially relevant to our present concern. Also, of course, one major basis of the interest in industrialization is its potential contribution to the power base of a strong national government.

Though precarious at many points and very unevenly diffused among populations, this is, in my opinion, a genuine value-consensus and one which runs deep. Its incompleteness lies not so much at this level as in the very serious problems involved in its integration with other components of the culture in two respects. One of these concerns the highest-level historic cultures of the various societies concerned. To take one example, in the considerable range of countries where Islam has figured prominently, there are acute problems in the threat of modernization to the traditional role of Islam, centering in the relations between new political and economic elites and the guardians of religious tradition and in the relationship of these new factors in the internal normative order to the traditions of religious law. Strains and potential conflicts of a similar order operate in very different ways, of course, in such countries as India and China.

The second major problem consists of the step in specification from values to what we have been calling norms. One of the main sources of difficulty in this field lies in the fact that in "traditional societies" norms are usually couched at rather low levels of generalization; they involve very detailed prescriptions. For the most part, the circumstances which originally made these details meaningful have been, or are in the course of being, radically changed by the modernization process itself. Such measures as the more or less wholesale adoption of Western law, which has happened to a considerable extent, create serious strains and difficulties which take a long time to resolve.

In my opinion, even the difference between the Communistic and the "liberal" versions of westernization lies primarily at these levels, not at the level of values, in the sense in which that concept is used here. In connection with the "cultural premises" of values, what Communism does is to shunt out the problems in this area altogether by making its special version of "materialism" a political religion. By becoming a Communist, a person renounces Islam, Confucianism, Hinduism, or Buddhism, *ipso facto*, to say nothing of Christianity, and pretends that the historic problems that cluster around such movements are pseudo-problems which enlightened modern men find unworthy of concern. It seems unlikely that in the very long run such problems will remain so conveniently dormant, but this complicated subject cannot be entered into here.

As to institutionalization of secular social norms, Communism introduces a similarly convenient truncation of the complexity of the problems involved. The essential point is the attempt to maximize, under the aegis of the semi-religious party, the centralization of political power and with it the *direct* political control of the society, particularly of the process of economic development. Above all, if it can harness the broad impetus we call "nationalism," this can in the short run (the shortness of which should not be overestimated) be a powerful combination, in that it can combine an impressive effectiveness with the channeling of very deep sentiments. The most formidable of these seem to be, on the one hand, the negative complex focusing about the resentments generated by the now rapidly passing political and economic ascendency of the Western powers; the primary ideological symbols here are colonialism and imperialism, both of which are considered as unequivocally evil. Social psychologists will see here an important case for application of the idea of relative deprivation; the very vehemence of the feelings expressed regarding colonialism is an index of lessened, rather than enhanced, subjection to it.

The other primary simplification centers about the ideological opposition between capitalism and socialism. Capitalism has come to symbolize a threat to the general integrity of the traditional community involved in the modernization process, and in particular to its economic aspects. It is questionable whether the actual strains are greater under politically controlled "socialistic" auspices or under those that allow a wider scope for "free enterprise," but that is not the point. Rather, the point is that the *symbol* of socialism permits the psychological security of belief in the continuity between the traditional community, which is conceived as coming into its own through national independence, and the emerging "modern" community; allegedly, there are no disruptive "self-interested" elements to threaten this integrity, above all, perhaps, to collaborate with the still dangerous "imperial" powers or those who, like Western businessmen, are symbolically identified with them, though they operate privately.

By virtue of the fact that, in its original Western core, economic modernization occurred largely under the aegis of free enterprise, and that this fact became ideologically crystallized as delineating the "right" way, the West has been saddled with the burden of vulnerability to the ideological derogation of being wickedly "capitalistic." The parallelism, as ideological symbols, of capitalism and socialism in the economic sphere, and imperialism and national independence in the political sphere, is patent. It is clearly the combination of the two contrasts that constitutes the primary ideological polarization in the world today.

If the above interpretation is correct, and I believe it is, the proposition that there exists a genuine value consensus underlying the various current differences, and *even* the ideological and interest-focused polarization of the cold war, is of the utmost importance in the present context. Equal importance must be attached to the assertion that there *is* a fundamental point of reference for the institutionalization of a system of normative order in the international field. There is a basis on which it is possible to recognize the *legitimacy* of the interests of various parties to conflicts and disputes, and to reduce the problems at issue to differences *within* a legitimized framework, rather than altogether outside it.

In visualizing this possibility, it is important to bear in mind that in situations of conflict there are tendencies both to ideological exaggeration and to what may be called overgeneralization. The first is perhaps most important in estimations of the "real" situation, e.g., estimates of the power and the drastic intentions of the opposition. Ambivalence in these fields is clearly indicated by oscillation between expressions of anxiety and boastfulness about one's own invincibility. ("Rocket-rattling," including the not-so-distant American threats of "massive retaliation," is very likely to involve at least an element of "whistling in the dark.") The second is clearly expressed in the tendency to insist on the absoluteness and inclusiveness of the conflict at the allegedly highest levels of "principle," which again has been prominent on both sides. From each point of view the other becomes the incarnation of an "absolute evil" with which no compromise of any sort is morally acceptable.

Members of democratic societies are familiar with the fact that in the heat of political campaigns (and under other conditions of strain), things are often said which imply an absolute condemnation of the opposition; such statements are usually forgotten in cooler moments.

It should be clear from the above that I contend that there can be value consensus which does not cover the *whole* range of social and cultural orientations. A good historical example of a relative resolution between bitterly opposed camps on such a basis is the religious conflicts in Europe following the Reformation. A *relative* order in the European system was in fact achieved, not by the definitive victory of either the Protestants or the Catholics, nor by their coming to terms on the level of theology. The reconciliation was on the level of *civil* polity, and it occurred in two main steps. The first invoked the famous formula of *cuius regio, eius religio*, thus permitting the enforcement of religious uniformity within the political unit, but not for the European *system* of units. Gradually, then, in varying degrees, religious toleration came to be institutionalized—although still in only rudimentary form in such countries as Spain—so that every such society became a religious mixture. It would be my view that there is a genuine prospect of attaining a resolution of the cold war conflict on this basis, which involves a genuine institutionalization of the valuation of the rights of individuals to religious freedom and of the role of law. There is no prospect whatever of a resolution of the conflict through the definitive victory of one side over the other, or through "demonstrating" the errors of Communism to the Communist world, or vice versa. If the conflict at this "politically religious" level is ever resolved, it will be because the *issues* have ceased to be significant, not because of the cultural "victory" of one side over the other.

One further point may be made in conclusion. I have argued that there exists a genuine consensus at a certain level of values. It should, however, be equally clear that the implications of this consensus are institutionalized at the level of norms only in the most fragmentary fashion, and that much further specification of these implications is necessary before even a moderately stable international order can be expected to emerge. It would lead us too far afield to attempt to go into these problems. However, it is perhaps correct to say that there are two main types of process by which the range of normative order has been extended to include wider participation. One of these is the establishment of "authority" which can, with varying degrees of consent on the part of the governed, undertake direct leadership and implement collective goals. The other is the process by which parties with conflicting interests in a situation have come to accept mediation (which may eventually develop into adjudication). The latter process has been associated historically with relatively autonomous legal developments. Often, though not necessarily, this has occurred under the "umbrella" of a political authority, although the important groups do not always act simply as agents of that authority.

A good deal of this type of institutionalization already exists in the various fields of international law and in a number of other contexts. Its extension is likely to be relatively slow and less dramatic than the policies of an international organization which is the center of world attention and the scene of confrontations of conflicting interests at the most explicit level. In the long run, however, this type of extension of order is potentially of great importance.

The above discussion has self-consciously stressed those elements in the current international situation that provide some basis for hope of the gradual evolution of a more stable international order. One major reason for this emphasis is that much of current discussion stresses the alternative —the absolute decisiveness of military power, the depth of the conflict of values, etc. There is very often a tendency for the factors stressed herein to be lost from sight or to be treated as of purely incidental significance. I do not, however, wish to state—or even imply—a concrete judgment of actual prospects in this area. This has been meant to be a *theoretical* essay on the analytical problems of international order. The assessment of empirical probabilities is another task, beyond the scope of this endeavor.

PART *IV*

Theory and the
Polity

art IV again, like Part I, becomes
explicitly and primarily theoretical.
To a large extent, because of the
fragmentary character of the work I have done in the political field, including
its theoretical aspect, the papers included are selective. The book is already
a long one and largely for this reason I have omitted several possible candidates
for inclusion; yet perhaps especially noteworthy are two of general theoretical
purport, namely, the paper on "The Place of Force in Social Process"
and the one on "Authority, Legitimation and Political Action." Both are
readily available in book form—in my own Sociological Theory and
Modern Society *and* Structure and Process in Modern Societies,
respectively. Furthermore, they both represent earlier stages in the develop-
ment of a pattern of theory which is more fully worked out in the five
papers that have been included. For the more than casual reader they may,
however, be recommended.

This pattern of theory first really began to crystallize in the reorientation
to the problems of the relation between economic theory and the rest of the
theory of social systems that was published in Economy and Society *in*
collaboration with Neil J. Smelser (1956). The two primary themes of
Part IV appear in that work with special reference to their economic rather
than political relevance. The first of these is the conception that the proper

theoretical subject matter, not only of economics, but of the other principal social science disciplines that are primarily theoretically oriented, should be the analytically defined functional subsystems of the larger systems involved. We think, thus, that we were able to clarify the concept of economy as developed in economic theory as a primary functional subsystem of a differentiated society. Other things equal, the more highly differentiated the society the more clearly would the analytical lines that were drawn on theoretical grounds match prominent features of the actual institutional structure of the society, including the economy as part of it. The economy, thus conceived, we identified as the subsystem differentiated from others in terms of adaptive function.

As soon as this conception of the place of the economy in a social system at the level of the highly differentiated society became clarified, the indications were very clear that, if it was sound, it should be capable of generalization to other cognate subsystems. Since then, a large proportion of my theoretical work has been devoted to the attempt to work out the implications of this presumption. As a sociologist, I would naturally have a special interest in the phase of the problem most directly concerned with the theoretical interests of sociology which, for reasons which cannot be fully discussed here, focus on the integrative problems of social systems.

For a considerable time, in the present century, economics and politics have been the closest "sister" disciplines, hence it was particularly tempting to make a try at fitting the latter into the paradigm. One important lead was the honored status of the term "polity" as linguistically the direct parallel of economy. At any rate, it proved possible, to my satisfaction at least, to work out a conception of the polity which fitted this theoretical model and which at the same time made sufficiently close contact with the historic themes of political theory, though the fit in this case has not, for reasons which I think can be explained, been as close as in the case of economic theory. The polity, in this framework, has been conceived as the "goal-attainment" subsystem of any social system, but in particularly important ways, of a society. In this context some contact with traditional usage is possible, in that the primary political system of a society becomes its "governmental" system in a sense parallel to that in which the primary economic system is its market system.

The functional paradigm within which this whole analysis has been couched distinguishes four primary functions of a social system, as of any system of action. If, then, the three primary theoretical disciplines in this field, economics, political science, and sociology, each focus at one of these four, there is an "empty cell" in the paradigm. This circumstance presents a problem with which I have been off and on concerned for a good many years. The "unclaimed" functional location, of course, is what I and various associates have called "pattern-maintenance." The logical occupant of this position is, in my opinion, anthropology, and indeed, it may be said to have moved halfway in. The reasons why the situation has not been fully clarified seem to me to have been particularly of two orders. In the first instance, both political science and sociology have seemed to lay claim to a good deal of the territory, the first above all through the strength of the emphasis on the problems of the legitimation of political systems, focusing of course on political obligation. Indeed, this normative concern has defined one of the principal dividing lines, with respect to intellectual type, between political science and economics. Sociology, on the other hand, has had difficulty in drawing clear theoretical lines between the analytical problems of integration and solidarity on the one hand, and values and their normative implications on the other. Secondly, anthropology has come to focus so much on the data of, if not wholly "primitive," predominantly nonliterate, societies that it has to a certain degree opted out of the competition. More recent anthropological concern, however, on the one hand for modern societies, on the other for the status of values and their position in cultural systems, suggests a moving in the indicated direction. Major progress along this line would, in my opinion, be salutary in relieving a heavy burden which has been resting, in different ways, on both political science and sociology.

The second major focus of theoretical interest growing out of the Economy and Society *stage, was that concerning the generalized media of societal interchange. The primary reference point here was the nature and functions of money, as this subject had become progressively worked out in the development of economic theory, in important respects culminating in the famous work of Keynes. In this connection it became increasingly clear that money should not be primarily tied to the "intrinsic" context of commodity values, especially of monetary metals, but should be regarded mainly as a medium of symbolic communication, in certain respects actually a language.*

This, of course, raised the question whether money was such a completely unique and theoretically isolated phenomenon as it had generally been conceived to be. If there is a parallel between economy and polity, why not between money, which has come to be so very central to economic theory, and a corresponding medium centered in the polity? The problem, of course, was put in the context of a presumption that, if there were more than one such medium, at comparable analytical levels, the number relevant to the social system as a whole should not be two, but four.

Within the theoretical tradition of political science there was obviously no close equivalent to the carefully codified place money held in economics. The leading candidate, however, was the concept of power, so I set to work to see what could be done with it in this framework. The preliminary result, which has stood up relatively well for several years, is Chapter 14. This was more a "spontaneous" rather than an "occasional" paper than any other in this volume except Chapter 7. It is traditional for a recently elected member of the American Philosophical Society to be asked to give a paper on any subject of his choice at one of the semiannual meetings of the Society, and I chose to speak on this topic—with twenty minutes allowed for oral presentation! Fortunately, however, there were no space limitations placed on the published version (Proceedings of the American Philosophical Society).

The attempt not to be left in the position either of isolating money as a totally unique phenomenon or of relating it only to power led me at about the same time to explore the question of mediation, by generalized symbolic mechanisms, in the integrative area of societal process. This was the genesis of an attempt to treat influence—*again taking a term in common usage and giving it a special meaning—as a generalized medium theoretically parallel to money and power as these media had been conceived. A particularly appropriate occasion for entering on this venture was an invitation to present a paper at the annual meeting of the American Association for Public Opinion Research, and the paper was first published in the* Public Opinion Quarterly (1963).

It is unlikely that any serious political scientist would overlook the importance, for concrete political phenomena, of the interplay between power —in almost any sense relevant to political theory, and hence not merely my special type of theory—and money. Similarly he would not be likely to ignore the importance of the relations between power and the phenomena of the general area I have referred to as involving influence. Indeed, a good many political scientists would include virtually the whole of this area in the domain of political science, though many fewer would in any strict theoretical sense treat money as a "form of power," and hence essentially a "political" phenomenon. However, my own endeavor has, as noted above, been to draw a rather strict analytical line, not only between polity and economy, but also between polity and societal community. Influence, therefore, has been treated as the generalized medium that is basically anchored in the societal community, not the polity, in a sense parallel to that in which money is anchored in the economy.

It is of crucial significance, however, that the generalized media, each anchored in one primary functional subsystem, serve to "mediate" the relations to each of the other three subsystems. Thus the kinship-centered household is not in a functional sense primarily economic, but through wage (and other) income and through consumer expenditures it serves to link households with the primary productive sectors of the economy. Similarly, money, as the primary mechanism of control of fluid marketable resources, serves to link economy and polity. Influence, then, I conceive not to be in the sense of analytical primacy a political phenomenon, but rather a "social" phenomenon which links societal community and polity, as power also does in the other direction.

It did not seem necessary to undertake a special exposition of the character of money as a generalized symbolic medium. There is, however, a fairly extensive and partly overlapping treatment of the subject in both the papers on power and influence. The completion of these two papers, about five years ago, substantially extended the range of application of the conception of such media. In particular, the concept of influence has rather extensively been used in substantive analysis, notably in a study of the modern academic profession,* but a revision and extension of the general theoretical statement has not yet been undertaken.

It will be evident that the extension of the discussion of money to encompass media within the polity and societal community still left a yawning gap with respect to the fourth generalized medium at the societal level. Considerable thought was devoted to its status and properties, but only very recently has a full-scale attempt to delineate these properties and the place of the medium in the general interchange system been made. Chapter 16 is that attempt. It was written within the last year for publication in the Spring 1968 issue (which actually appeared in November) of Sociological Inquiry. *I have, however, included in this volume a postscript to Chapter 15, the paper on influence, which seeks to bring the reader up to date on a few of the more important conceptual advances concerning influence as a generalized medium.*

The general structure of Part VI thus becomes evident. The first paper in it, Chapter 13, is meant to be a general exposition of the conception of the polity within the frame of reference outlined in this introduction. It was written for a meeting of the American Political Science Association in September 1963 and published in David Easton, editor, Varieties of Political Theory *(Prentice-Hall, 1966). The next three chapters all deal with the generalized media of interchange, one of which, power, is conceived to be directly anchored in the polity, to be "its" special medium, while the other two, and of course money as well, impinge very importantly on it. It is my conception that not only does this treatment of the generalized*

---

*See Talcott Parsons and Gerald M. Platt, "Considerations on the American Academic Profession," *Minerva*, Vol. VI, No. 4 (Summer 1968).

media constitute development of a technical problem area which is important for its own sake but that it is very central to the theory of social systems more generally, and, in particular, it provides perhaps the most important single link between the structural and the processual aspects of that theory. Furthermore, it seems to me that serious consideration of the media, their properties and their interrelations, provides a particularly important focus for stating the distinctions between the primary functional subsystems of a society and the complementary problem of the interrelations among them. In this judgment I am very mindful of the ways in which development of monetary theory has contributed to the more general advance of economic theory.

Finally, Chapter 17, which is the only chapter written especially for this volume, attempts to perform a synthetic function. It takes off from the outline of the polity presented in Chapter 13. It attempts, then, to stress not only the importance of, but some of the more specific characteristics of, the relations of the polity to the other three primary subsystems, particularly the societal community. This is a set of relations which, as just suggested, is greatly illuminated by some understanding of the generalized media and their operation. The attempt is then made to link these more strictly theoretical concerns with the more empirical ones discussed in the papers of Parts II and III. A central theme there is the nature and importance of the pluralistic character of the societal community in modern societies and the implications of this trend of development for their governmental and—indeed—political processes in the wider sense. The note on which it ends is to stress the overwhelming mutual interest of all the social sciences, and political science and sociology in particular, in the integration of their interests and theory in a wider "science of society"—which I do not treat as equivalent to sociology—or theory of social systems.

13

The Political Aspect of Social Structure and Process

*t*his paper[1] will present, in exceedingly condensed form, an approach to the theoretical analysis of political structure and process. The approach owes much to many analyses and discussions in the tradition of political theory; it is distinctive largely in that it places such materials in the context of a general theoretical analysis of the total society as a social system.

Our key orienting concept is the *polity*, defined as a primary functional subsystem of a society, strictly parallel in theoretical status to the *economy*, as that concept is broadly used in modern economic theory.[2] The term *functional* here means that the polity should not be identified either with any specific collectivity structure within the society, such as government

---

[1] In the preparation of this paper I am particularly indebted to Victor M. Lidz, who helped in shaping the argument itself through numerous discussions, mobilized reference material, edited the manuscript for style and clarity, and adapted the Technical Note from its previous, use. [See footnote 48 at the end of this chapter for an explanation of why this Technical Note is omitted there: ed.]

[2] See Talcott Parsons and N. J. Smelser, *Economy and Society* (New York: Free Press, 1956); N. J. Smelser, *The Sociology of Economic Life* (Englewood Cliffs, N.J.: Prentice-Hall, Inc., 1963); and P. A. Samuelson, *Economics: An Introductory Analysis*, 5th ed. (New York: McGraw-Hill Book Company, 1961).

(any more than the economy should be conceived as the aggregate of business firms), or with any concrete type of activity of individuals. It is conceived analytically as the aspect of all action concerned with the function of the collective pursuit of collective goals. The collectivity in question may be any system involving the coordinated action of a plurality of individuals oriented to the attainment of a collective goal or a system of collective goals. Collectivities in this sense range from very small groups to the political aspect of what Roscoe Pound called the "politically organized society,"[3] most notably the "state," and beyond that, to intersocietal organizations.

A *collective goal* here means a relatively optimal relation between the collectivity and some aspect of its intrasocietal situation (e.g., other collectivities) or its extrasocietal environment. It may concern relations not only to other collectivities, but also to personalities of individuals, cultural objects (e.g., as a result of change through research), and organic or physical objects. Especially for a collectivity continuing in time and holding multiple interests, a particular goal is not isolated; it is part of a system of goals. Any particular goal must, therefore, be fitted into a larger system of goals, according to its rank-order and timing with reference to other goals. A *goal* exists only if the desired state differs from the actual or expected state at the inception of action. Goals admit of degrees of attainment, all-or-none instances being special cases.

Committing a collectivity to attain a goal implies, in addition to an assertion of the desirability of the goal's attainment, a commitment to relatively specific measures designed to effect the desired goal-state. Hence, it involves the mobilization of resources at the collectivity's disposal, through authorized agencies. Thus, commitment to the attainment of a collective goal implies resource commitments which, under the pressure of conditions, themselves require further decision-making processes.

The attainment of its goal by a collectivity is, in the paradigmatic, integrated case, the performance of function to the social system, of which it is a part (the system includes structures other than goal-oriented collectivities). The proposition that such operations are "on behalf" of the larger system therefore assumed an "adequate" degree of integration of the larger system. Short of such integration, one must allow for structural dislocations which may cause a "success" from the viewpoint of the collectivity to constitute malfunction from the viewpoint of the system. Nevertheless, I wish to assert the fundamental proposition that collectivities are always the *agencies* of specific performances of societal function. Persons in roles perform functions in (and for) collectivities, but not directly in total social systems. The alleged performance of social goal-attainment function by an individual, e.g., an "independent" artisan or professional practitioner, is in fact the limiting, single-member case of a collectivity, a

[3] In seminars at Harvard University.

"corporation sole." The performance of societal function by "informal cooperation" without formal collectivities is another limiting case, one that minimizes the factor of "organization."

Like all other functional activities in social systems, political action must be regulated in terms of a value-standard.[4] The concept of *effectiveness* as used by Barnard fills the requirements of the value-standard very exactly.[5] It is directly parallel to *utility* as used in economic theory. If commitment to the collective goals may be considered as given, at the relevant levels, political judgment must concern the probability that implementive measures will in fact bring about the desired changes; that is, one must judge whether the available resources are adequate and the organization of their use competent. Here, effectiveness is the standard according to which the measures are evaluated. Insofar as the structures and processes of the polity are differentiated from those of the other societal subsystems, its value-standard will be also.

The distinction between effectiveness and utility involves complex questions which cannot be treated here. However, political effectiveness is parallel at the level of social organization to technological effectiveness at the level of physical production. Thus, cost in the economic sense is only one of several considerations involved in judgments of effectiveness. Whether or not resources devoted to a given collective goal might be better devoted to some alternative use cannot be determined on economic grounds. Such grounds are relevant to deciding whether or not to make commitments to a goal, but are irrelevant to evaluating the effectiveness vis-à-vis the situation and environment of measures undertaken to attain the goal. Cost, then, is not a political category itself, although it is relevant at the economic level and, as such, is conditional to political decisions. Cost is also relevant, at a cybernetically higher level, to the integration of the social system of which the political unit is a part, even if the unit comprises the total society in its political aspect. Here, cost is involved in choices among both the goals of a given collectivity and, for the wider system, the goals of its various collectivities. In this case, however, cost is integrative, not economic. It refers to the sacrifices in system-solidarity entailed by commitment to one collective goal as compared with the sacrifices entailed by commitments to alternative goals. In one context, this cost may be assessed in terms of the sacrifice of political support risked by those taking responsibility for collective decisions. In another context, it may be stated in terms of possible changes in the level of commitment to general collective action—that is, of loyalty to the social system in question.

[4] Talcott Parsons, "On the Concept of Political Power," *Proceedings of the American Philosophical Society*, CVII, No. 3 (1963), 232–62. [Reprinted as Chapter 14 in the present volume: ed.]

[5] C. I. Barnard, *The Functions of the Executive* (Cambridge: Harvard University Press, 1938), esp. pp. 236–39.

Before discussing the principal components of political structure and process, we must consider another central concept—*bindingness*, a quality of commitments and decisions which is both a condition of effective implementation of policies and a mode of specification of the value-standard of effectiveness.[6] As political process is a process of collective goal-attainment, it involves making decisions with regard to the implementation of the collectivity's values in relation to situational exigencies. For that implementation to be effective, the decisions regarding it must, to give assurance to the objects in the social situation,[7] be *binding* on the collectivity and, hence, on any member-units bearing responsibility for contribution to the implementation process. By virtue of membership, member-units may be regarded as having assumed certain very general commitments to contribute to collective processes. In the present context, decision making may be considered a process which specifies these generalized commitments so that, in a specific situation, specific units are expected to do or not to do specific things. *Bindingness* thus links these two levels of commitment.

The concept of *bindingness* is also central to the problem of sanctions.[8] If commitments or obligations exist and, as may be assumed for theoretical purposes, are acknowledged by the relevant members of a collectivity, questions will arise sooner or later about what consequences an obligated actor must face if he makes known his intention not to fulfill what the agent responsible for implementation considers his obligation. Whatever the extenuating circumstances, no system can be indifferent about the fulfillment of such an obligation. In cases of threatened noncompliance, the activator of the commitment may be expected to insist on compliance, as it indeed is generally his obligation to do. In cases of continuing noncompliance, insistence inevitably includes the threat of imposing negative sanctions as a consequence of noncompliance. Then their implementation becomes a commitment of the threatener.[9] As will be made clear later, this

[6] Parsons, "On the Concept of Political Power."

[7] This implies that in action systems, situational goal-objects are typically "social objects" having expectations in some sense complementary to those of the collectivity of reference. These social objects are either collectivities sharing membership in the same social systems or individuals in roles. In either case, attainment of the collective goal cannot be considered "secure" unless, in reciprocation with the social objects, binding obligations are assumed by the collectivity, for *its* interests are dependent on the objects' complementary performances. There are two principal limiting cases in which such complementarity fails to hold. First is the case of physical objects which by definition have no expectations in the action sense. A technologically oriented organization will be actuated in relation to physical materials and equipment by considerations of cost, not of obligation to the physical objects. Second is the "sovereign" collectivity which relates to other collectivities without any normative order. Clearly this is never the empirical state of affairs in an "international" system; it is a limiting concept.

[8] See Talcott Parsons, *The Social System* (New York: Free Press 1951), Chapter Seven, for a general discussion of the importance of sanctions.

[9] To take a simple case, most voluntary associations that require dues have a rule that those who persistently and intentionally fail to pay the dues will have rights of membership

in no way implies that fear of negative-sanctions is the principal motive for honoring collective commitments. But it does imply that contingent negative-sanctions are inherent components of the political system, because without them it would be senseless to insist on the bindingness of commitments.[10]

Like any social system, a political system is structurally composed of units and their relationship. As every political system is a collectivity, its units are always "members" which may be either individual persons *in roles*[11] or subcollectivities that themselves are ultimately reducible to individual persons in member roles. Member-units are characterized by four essential properties:

1. Generalized commitments to the specific values of the collectivity, i.e., their commitment to the collectivity's effectiveness, which may be called their loyalty;
2. Specified commitments consisting of rights and obligations to make certain types of decisions that integrate the collectivity's commitments with their own roles and statuses within it;
3. An integrative responsibility for implementing specified decisions and protecting certain interests of the collectivity, a responsibility which constitutes a normative context for particular roles or functions; and
4. A capacity to implement, through instrumental procedures, decisions constituting obligations in particular roles. Capacity includes both competence in the personal sense and control of resources adequate for specific purposes.

Since effectiveness is a value-pattern for a collectivity, ideally all members should be equally committed to it as a value on the generalized level. Empirically, however, there are both variations of intensity of commitment, and alienation in the sense of conflict over commitment, including complex ambivalences.

The operative functions of collective process tend to be structured primarily around the second and fourth of the above properties of membership roles. Specified commitment is very close to what is often called

[10] In the present context, any change in the situation that an enforcing agent can impose, and that is disadvantageous to the units from whom performance of commitments is expected, may serve as a negative sanction. Physical force has a strategic place in negative-sanction systems which is based on a special relation to territoriality; but that cannot be discussed here. See my "Some Reflections on the Place of Force in Social Process," in *The Problem of Internal War*, ed. Harry Eckstein (Princeton: Princeton University Press, 1963); reprinted in Talcott Parsons, *Sociological Theory and Modern Society*.

[11] The qualification *in roles* is essential, because no one, after early infancy, is ever a member of only one collectivity. The expression "*x* is a member of *y* association" is correct; but it is elliptical because it does not specify the other collectivities to which *x* also belongs. There have been spurious implications that the total person, not the "portion" of him involved in a specific role, is a member of a specific collectivity, often "society" almost personified.

revoked. The responsible officers cannot simply ignore intentional nonpayment indefinitely. At some time, they must honor their commitment to enforce the rules if the association is to function effectively in this respect.

the operative member's *sphere of responsibility*. Integrative responsibility, however, involves an additional component. It goes beyond responsibility in a clearly defined status to include a share of responsibility for defining the status.

THE CONCEPTS OF
AUTHORITY AND OFFICE

The primary institution carrying such relational responsibility in political function may be called *authority*. The unit-status associated with it may be called *incumbency of an office*.[12] Here I take the radical position that the concept of office should apply to *all* membership statuses in a collectivity. Thus, all such statuses are statuses of authority and, by that virtue, all members have some degree of power. Rather than differentiating between those having and those lacking authority and power, the more useful approach is to distinguish between those who have relatively more and those who have relatively less authority and power. Thus, to take an important case, voting membership in an association is here considered a position of authority, an office, and the franchise, though it has little power under the principle of one member, one vote, most definitely *is* power—just as a single dollar, though not much money, certainly *is* money.

Authority, then, is the legitimated right to make certain categories of decisions and bind a collectivity to them. Authority may be held not by an individual but by a collegial body, a subcollectivity such as a committee, in which individual members have only the authority to cast votes contributing to collective decisions.

There are two main kinds of authority, each of which is essential to collective functioning. The first, which is more purely political, regards the position of the office in a hierarchy of decision-making priorities. The second, which articulates with nonpolitical factors, concerns the "functional" areas within which authority operates.

Collective effectiveness depends on capacity to coordinate the actions of diverse contributing units and assure with bindingness that each will do its part. There must, then, be a priority scale among the *rights* to make decisions which, in a manner sufficiently differentiated to cope with the complexity of the organization, places those by which the collectivity is bound to specific policies above those by which various commitments are undertaken to effect policy implementation. Such an institutionalized priority scale of decision-making functions is the hierarchy of authority we have designated as an essential component of collectivity structure. Its struc-

---

[12] See Max Weber, *The Theory of Social and Economic Organization* (New York: The Free Press, 1947), pp. 329 ff.

tural principle seems to be a ratio scale. Thus, authority is arranged on a series of levels such that a status at a higher level of authority will take precedence, structured in the manner of proportion, over all lower statuses with reference to rights of decision-making over the allocation of available resources. A particular scale along which such precedence relations are structured is a line of authority in the classical sense.

Collective effectiveness, however, also depends on adaptation to the qualitative diverse exigencies to which collective operations are subject, both those exigencies situational to it and those involved in capacities and motives of member-units on whose contributions the collectivity relies. These exigencies are necessarily differentiated with respect to both their inherent properties and their functions in collective processes. The principle of hierarchy is, therefore, crosscut by the principle of functional differentiation as it has a bearing on implementive effectiveness. Thus, the collectivity must be divided into departments, divisions, etc., with each being assigned responsibility for a more-or-less differentiated aspect of operations.

Matters are further complicated because functional differentiation is not one-dimensional. It may be based on several different principles. For example, a collectivity with extensive operations may often be segmented territorially into branch offices with different locations; it may also be differentiated on such bases as specialization in particular technological processes. These are, of course, familiar complications regarding bureaucratic organization, which is one of the main types of structural complex in political systems, according to the present conception.[13]

The essential modifications of the hierarchical principle involved in bureaucratic (implementive) systems may be derived from the boundary exigencies of the system as expressed in qualities of the inputs necessary for collective processes. Here, one must distinguish the collective or political system from the technical system. The latter carries out technological processes and therefore is both the agency of manipulation of physical processes and the consumer of physical goods. The political system, however, controls the technical system.

This distinction greatly simplifies the definition of political exigencies bearing upon the implementive context, as it reduces them to the securing of financial resources and human services. Financial resources give access to *all* kinds of concrete resources accessible through the market. These concrete resources can be reduced to the two basic classes: goods and services.[14]

The critical problem here concerns the relation of resources to the

[13] Talcott Parsons, *Structure and Process in Modern Societies* (New York: The Free Press, 1960), Chapters 1 and 2.
[14] For present purposes, "cultural objects," as resources, can be assimilated into these two categories if we speak of the "embodiment" of cultural meanings in physical objects, such as books, or in services, such as copyrights, and their internalization in persons, as in the form of technical competence.

category of membership. Only human agents, individual or collective, can be *units in* a collective system. Money is a means of procuring services. In one context, by giving money to the performer of a service, the employing collectivity enables him to satisfy his wants, for example, in his capacity as family member. In another context, money constitutes the budget for facilities enhancing the performer's work within the collectivity, whether they are at the disposal of his role or whether higher echelons spend them for the benefit of his role. Such facilities constitute a primary component of the "opportunity for effectiveness" which the agent received in accepting employment in a collectivity instead of working on his own.

In return for this opportunity, the employee typically gives the collectivity rights to control his actions in the context of employment. The critical element to the collectivity is the right to ensure with binding power that his action contributes effectively to collective goal-attainment. A primary source of the power that the collectivity's leadership uses and allocates through the hierarchy of authority is the aggregate of commitments to service made by units who have accepted employment in the collectivity. Such commitments are initially generalized, defined only by the terms of the "job"; over time, they are continually specified to the many particular tasks undertaken and performed as occasions arise.

A crucial fact is that the authority of all offices stops at the boundary of the collectivity of reference. Therefore, in a sufficiently differentiated system, employment need not impair the freedom of the employee's personal actions outside the collectivity. In a free labor market, potential performers of service have, before actually accepting employment, no obligations of performance. Hence, the agent of the employer cannot insist that they perform, but may only negotiate to acquire their consent and, with that, their obligations to accept direction.[15] Hence, the labor market performs fundamental functions in setting the boundary of the authority-hierarchy, especially by defining certain limits within which that hierarchy is confined. Among the terms settled in a contract of employment is the position the employee will occupy in the hierarchy, including its risks and opportunities. His status may vary from the lowest menial position to chief executive.

This boundary makes an adjustment between grant of authority or power, and capacity and acceptance of responsibility for contribution. This boundary relation is thus governed, not by hierarchy of authority, but by opportunity to acquire positions in the hierarchy of authority, an opportunity which tends in turn to be governed by equality of units under universalistic standards of selection, the only principle maximizing collective effectiveness in the long run.

---

[15] This may, of course, be incompletely institutionalized, e.g. in transition periods, so that abuses may develop. See N. J. Smelser, *Social Change in the Industrial Revolution* (Chicago: University of Chicago Press, 1959).

THE CONCEPT OF POWER

I have used the term *power* a number of times. Now it is necessary to define it more explicitly and precisely.[16] I conceive *power* to be a generalized symbolic medium which circulates much like money, the possession and use of which enables the responsibilities of an office with authority in a collectivity to be more effectively discharged. *Authority* is the politically crucial quality of a status in a social structure. Power I conceive, in contrast, to be a primary instrumentality of effective performance *in* that position. To be effective, a unit must have an income of power, must be willing to spend it, and yet must be prudently rational in doing so. This may involve either transferring power to other units within a collectivity or transferring it over the collectivity's boundaries.

Power may be regarded as a medium for controlling action which, under certain conditions, is exchangeable for other such media operating in contexts from which power is excluded. The two other media we must now consider are money and influence. Money is a linear continuum which may be appropriately divided in terms of cardinal quantities; the question of "how much" is always essential in monetary contexts. For power, which is ordered in terms of a ratio scale, the question is not how *much* power does someone have, but what his position is *relative* to other foci of decision making. Furthermore, in a sense not necessarily applicable to money, the scale of positions with regard to power must be *particular* to the collectivity of reference and its boundaries. Universalistic principles, then, operate only in reference to access to power, influence on power, or standards governing the use of power.

Monetary resources can be allocated in a quantitative and distributive sense, as a pie can be divided into equal or unequal slices. Power-allocation, however, also involves questions of both the degree and the field of delegation. One does not divide power into numerically fractional shares, but one does decide which levels and spheres in a system are to be held by whom. Opportunity for effectiveness provides a distribution context for power, and is differentiated on the two axes, "level" in the power hierarchy, and functional type of unit-contribution.

Delegation of power or authority is performed as an exchange for something of value that consists of facilities for effective implementation of collective goals. A classification of types, then, must derive from the differentiation of the factors that enter into effective collective functioning. On the administrative or implementive side, the crucial factor is control of economic productivity, primarily through financial resources, which in turn is the basic condition for securing services. To attract services, however, the organization must, in addition to paying money, offer opportunity for effectiveness through position in both the hierarchi-

[16] See Parsons, "On the Concept of Political Power." [Reprinted as Chapter 14 in the present volume: ed.]

cal and qualitatively differentiated aspects of the power system. Although connected, these aspects vary independently. Indeed, freedom to alter the qualitative combinations "lower down" is a critical hierarchical feature of executive authority in this context. However, a primary condition of adequate integration of a collectivity is a good match in hierarchical position and functional location between the delegated power held by occupational members and the capacities that employed units bring to the organization.[17]

Because it relates to the bindingness of obligations, any use of power must, as noted, also relate to legitimized coercive sanctions. The free labor market, however, introduces a limiting factor which impinges primarily on higher authority. Not only acceptance of membership through employment, but also its continuation is voluntary in principle. Leaving the collectivity by resigning is always in principle a possibility. Thus the grant of power to the collectivity is conditional and can always be withdrawn. The consent of the employed to the discipline imposed upon him is hence a condition of retaining his services.[18]

This consensual condition of the attraction and retention of service relates to the functional significance of certain freedoms regarding the organizational role. Particularly important are roles that involve high levels of technical competence. Such competence is necessarily specialized, whereas high levels of authority in a collectivity necessarily involve responsibility for relatively wide ranges of problems. A person of high *technical* competence, therefore, is not likely to have an *organizational* superior who can competently judge the technical quality of many of his decisions—only his professional peers can do so. The specialist must, then, be given freedom from intervention by authority within his technical sphere. Yet, in order to be effective in attaining collectively desired outcomes, his specialized operations must be coordinated with other operations within a collective organization—hence he ordinarily has no interest in going it alone. The price of opportunity is acceptance of the organization's authority system within certain limits. Typically, the organization can effectively hold him responsible for satisfactory results, but not for the technical ways in which he achieves them. Collective responsibility for the technical and ethical standards governing such matters must lie predomi-

[17] Discussions in this context of *alienation* sometimes fail to make a critical distinction. In the economic context, the *alienation of labor* may be understood as the sacrifice of self-sufficiency in production in favor of advantages gained from the division of labor. In the political context, we may speak of the *alienation of services* which gives an employing collectivity *power* to control the manner of contribution to collective functioning. Perhaps the latter is the primary component of "alienation of labor" in the Marxian sense.

[18] There are important exceptions to this voluntary principle. Those in a deviant status, such as prisoners and the committed mentally ill, constitute one type. The closest to the occupational role is military service where, even when enlistment is voluntary, resignation at will is ordinarily not permitted.

nantly with a professional association which crosscuts the many types of operative organization employing its members.

By the nature of power systems, such expenditures of power by delegation must be balanced by incomes of power, essentially in the form of consent to accept organizational authority. The effective power, as distinguished from the authority, of an organizational status depends upon the aggregate of action commitments of organizational members to perform services within the sphere of the status-incumbent's responsibility. His possession of power typically depends on their voluntary continuance in their respective appointive positions.[19] The process complementing delegation of power may, then, be called its *aggregation*, in that a plurality of power "quanta" must be aggregated as the power income of a position. They will be differentiated according to both hierarchical level and the qualitative sphere of the assumed obligations.

SOME LIMITATIONS OF BUREAUCRATIC STRUCTURE

The aspect of political structures just outlined is usually called the *bureaucratic* or *administrative subsystem*, which is concerned primarily with the implementation of collective goals. For territorially organized societies, these goals typically include the maintenance of the basic internal order and the defense of territorial integrity, however gradually this may shade into aggression. They also include the mobilization of resources, in the case of government largely through taxation, for maintaining the administrative establishment as well as the differently structured components of the collective structure. Of course, there generally are various other goals, in the governmental case, especially the maintenance of such public functions as religious cults and priesthoods and welfare and economic policies.

One of Weber's famous dicta was that the top of a bureaucratic structure cannot itself be bureaucratic.[20] He specifically associated this with the problem of legitimation. Because it is a subsystem of a society, a polity can not be self-legitimating. It must depend for legitimacy on institutionalized values and agencies bearing primary responsibility for them, such as religious collectivities. Here the place of the valuation of collective effectiveness in the wider institutionalized value system is critical. In the American case, for example, it is far from having the highest priority. Generally, we favor autonomy of units over the subordination of units to collective interests. Hence, at the governmental level we emphasize the maintenance of limitations on the authority of government, e.g., through the Bill of

[19] Cf. Barnard's conception of efficiency of cooperation, in his *Functions of the Executive*, esp. pp. 253–55.
[20] Weber, *Theory of Social and Economic Organization*, p. 335.

Rights. The Soviet Union leans much further toward giving collective effectiveness top priority.

Legitimation, then, functions to define what political organization is for and, hence, to define the nature and scope of the agencies—collectivities and roles—which perform political functions. Correlative with these structural definitions are both authority for the implementation of the legitimate responsibilities, and access to power and the conditions of its use. In a sufficiently differentiated polity, we call this *the constitutional system*—with private as well as public collectivities having constitutions more or less formally specified. Where the political aspect of social structure is sufficiently differentiated from the others, *all* authority is "rational-legal" in Weber's sense.[21] His two other types of authority occur where structural differentiation is relatively incomplete. It is possible to link Weber's, or a more developed typology of authority, to a general typology of stages in the differentiation of the functional spheres of social systems.[22] Space limits my discussion to a few outstanding points.

A critical question here concerns the extent to which the constitutional definition of political authority is legally formulated and then institutionally interpreted by legal agencies essentially independent of executive and even legislative authorities, and of the trusteeship of the value-maintenance agencies.[23] Lack of differentiation from the sphere of value-maintenance is typical of systems of religious law, like those of Islamic societies, which give the civil normative system direct religious sanction. Lack of differentiation from the sphere of executive and legislative authorities is typical of early modern absolutism, in which the monarch claimed the prerogative to define the legal nature and limits of his own authority, subject only to religious sanction. Thus Justice Coke's ultimately successful assertion of the independence of the law from the royal prerogative in England was a landmark.[24] Such independence is, indeed, a major criterion of the polity's differentiation from other societal sybsystems, notably from what I call *the pattern-maintenance system*. For private collectivities, legal definition of authority and other rights is largely, though not entirely, imposed from outside. Clear reasons for this are abundant. For example, private corporations cannot simply arrogate to themselves rights and prerogatives that either conflict too drastically with those claimed by public authority or vary too greatly from those enjoyed by similar corporations. This is one reason that the universalistic character-

[21] Weber, *Theory of Social and Economic Organization*, p. 328.

[22] Talcott Parsons, "Evolutionary Universals in Society," *American Sociological Review*, XXIX (June, 1964), 339–57; Talcott Parsons, *Societies: Comparative and Evolutionary Perspectives* (Englewood Cliffs, N.J.: Prentice-Hall, Inc., 1966).

[23] Max Weber, *Max Weber on Law in Economy and Society* (Cambridge: Harvard University Press, 1954), esp. Chapter Eleven.

[24] See David Little, "The Logic of Order: An Examination of the Sources of Puritan-Anglican Controversy and of Their Relations to Prevailing Legal Conceptions of Corporation in the late 16th and Early 17th Century in England" (Doctoral thesis, Harvard University, 1963).

istics of advanced legal systems are most important—e.g., the American Constitution's prohibition of bills of attainder, or, especially prominent now, the doctrine of "equal protection of the laws."

In another context, the legitimation subsystem of large-scale political systems has been differentiated only recently from what I call the *support system*. The absolutist régimes ascribed the obligation of political support to the status of subject, as indeed modern totalitarian régimes do. Differentiation is marked by the development of legitimized procedures for expressing opposition to current leadership without impugning one's loyalty to the system. This implies that there are legitimized procedures for changing leadership, and that various constituent elements may try to bring about such change.

THE SUPPORT SYSTEM

In a differentiated support system, the leadership's "constituency" constitutes a democratic association. The franchise is the institutionalized instrumentality for giving support or nonsupport to specific leadership groups. Support systems are assumed to be hierarchical structures that are parallel to, and articulate with, the hierarchy of bureaucratic structures. There is an uneven distribution of the authority to make decisions that bind the association as a collectivity and, hence, its members in their respective roles. There is, to be sure, a theoretical limiting case where there is equally distributed power, but it requires that every decision be made by majority vote of the membership in order to be binding. This becomes more difficult to maintain as the scale, complexity, and urgency of collective business increase. Hence, parallel to the delegation of authority in bureaucratic systems, support systems, operating within constitutionally defined terms, grant authority and power to elected leadership subject to electoral defeat, i.e., withdrawal of support, as defined by procedural rules.[25]

Despite the many variations in the nature and extent of the franchise, there are certain relatively uniform tendencies in its institutionalization. A first essential is the establishment of procedural institutions which are reliably accepted across lines of internal conflict on policy matters. The severest test of these institutions comes when an incumbent leadership is expected to relinquish power after its electoral defeat. Since, in the case of the state, with its great control of resources and coercive machinery, this is a severe test indeed, it is not surprising that such institutions fail so often.

Aside from such reliance on formal procedural institutions, Rokkan[26]

[25] See Talcott Parsons, "'Voting' and the Equilibrium of the American Political System," in *American Voting Behavior*, eds. Eugene Burdick and Arthur Brodbeck (New York: The Free Press, 1959). [Reprinted as Chapter 9 in the present volume: ed.]

[26] Stein Rokkan, "Mass Suffrage, Secret Voting, and Political Participation," *European Journal of Sociology*, II (1961), 132–52.

has shown that three other elements of the franchise also tend to develop in democratic polities. First is universal adult suffrage. Thus, property and sex qualifications, to say nothing of religious ones, have generally been eliminated in Western electoral systems. Second is equality of the franchise. Class systems, in which votes are weighted unequally, tend to be eliminated; the last flagrant example of a class system was the Prussian one which was abolished at the end of World War I. In effect, however, markedly unequal apportionment of legislative seats relative to population often has some qualities of a class system. The Georgia county-unit system, invalidated by the U.S. Supreme Court in Gray v. Sanders in 1963, was an example. Third is secrecy of the ballot, which helps to differentiate the voting role from a member's other personal roles, thus protecting the freedom of his vote from pressures exerted by status superiors and peers.[27]

From the above, it is evident that a crucial characteristic of support systems, and hence democratic associations, is a relatively clear definition of membership status, especially of the boundary between membership and nonmembership. For the politically organized society, membership involves citizenship, the prerogative of which is the enjoyment of civil rights, including the franchise. There must therefore be distinctions between citizens and aliens, the latter enjoying fewer civil rights (e.g., being denied the franchise). The correlates of civil rights, of course, are such obligations as taxation and military service, and, in general, compliance with the policy decisions of duly constituted authority.

The franchise in a democratic association, public or private, is a form of authority, and its exercise is power because the decision of an electorate is strictly binding on the collectivity; defeated incumbents must relinquish their offices to new leaders. Election to office is a power input to the leadership of the polity, enabling it to exercise or spend power in making policy decisions that commit collective resources to specific uses and in delegating opportunity for effectiveness to members of the administrative system. Here, as in other contexts, power has an hierarchical aspect which stands in a complex and important relation to an egalitarian aspect. The hierarchical aspect takes an all-or-none form from the election. Just as one is, or is not, a citizen and endowed with power through the franchise, so one is, or is not, elected to office. The power of office is not divided among candidates according to the proportion of votes they received; all of it is given to the one elected.[28]

[27] I have recently argued elsewhere that both bureaucratic organization and democratic association are universals in social evolution in that their successful development generalizes adaptive capacity in degrees essential to the emergence of fully modern societies. These propositions are further explained in my "Evolutionary Universals in Society."

[28] Proportional representation systems are not an exception to this statement. Seats may be allocated according to proportions of party votes, but a given candidate is, or is not, elected. No proportional system goes so far as to elect candidates to represent their constituents on percentages of the issues coming before the legislature corresponding to the proportions of the votes they received.

Commonly, we think of democratic associations as inherently egalitarian and of power systems as inherently hierarchical, and so altogether dissociate membership and the franchise from power. This contradicts my view that the franchise is directly a form of authority and that its exercise is a form of power. The link between franchise and hierarchy lies in the aggregation of votes to determine electoral victory—that is, the difference between being in and out of office. Though the victor in an election becomes hierarchically superior to the loser, all the voters who determine the outcome may still be equal in regard to the power of their votes.

Power in a collectivity is a means of effectively mobilizing obligations in the interest of collective goals. Modifications of hierarchy involved in the employment of bureaucratic services are boundary-interchange conditions that differentiate the occupational role of the individual from his private concerns—a matter strongly stressed by Weber.[29] Unless that status of employment is either ascribed or coerced, it is necessary to offer inducements. In doing so, the employer cannot assert a hierarchical precedence based upon his internal authority. As stated in very general form above, he must use inducements consisting of opportunity for effectiveness and of monetary reward. Regarding the return for such inducements, the egalitarian element of equality of opportunity enters because the offer of concrete opportunity is conditioned on competence (that is, expected contribution to effectiveness).

We have emphasized that, as a function of the differentiated institutionalization of associational collectivities, the boundary between membership and nonmembership tends to become more clearly defined. There are, of course, various components of membership status, but the franchise seems to be crucial, since it is the component of the power of government of the association that is linked to membership as such. Subject then to such exceptions as minority and legal "incompetence" to manage one's own affairs, there tends to be a rigid distinction between members who enjoy franchise and nonmembers who do not, with a strong tendency to institutionalize the principle of one member, one vote.

The relevant all-or-none principle then extends to the selection of leadership in that, once a set of offices in an association has been set up, it is essential to know *who* the legitimate incumbent is, since he exercises power in a representative capacity on behalf of and *binding on the collectivity*. It is this functional exigency, representation of and bindingness for the collectivity as a whole, that explains the application of the all-or-none principle to election to office. If the powers of office were divided according to the strength of electoral support, as measured by votes, the representation would be that of "interests," not of the collectivity as a whole. For executive office the implication seems clear. For the legislature it is somewhat different, in that legislators are representatives of their constitu-

[29] Weber, *Theory of Social and Economic Organization.*

encies, in which some interest components will be, relative to the system as a whole, more salient than others. A legislator, however, at the same time has, by his vote in the legislature, a share of power to bind the total collectivity. In this connection he must, in order to make his action binding on a constituency as part of the whole, be in a position to legitimize the bindingness of the consequences of his vote on members of his constituency who were *not* of the predominant persuasion within it. The constituency is thus not only an "interest group," but also a genuine *segment* of the total political system.

The boundary distinction between membership and nonmembership is thus directly parallel in the case of citizenship status with that of employment in an "administrative" collectivity. In both cases one is either in or out; the cases of intermediate status are marginal. The same is true of the all-or-none principle as applying to what is usually called office within the collectivity, in the sense of the incumbent being given power to bind the collectivity as a whole, at the level and in the sphere of the "jurisdiction" of his office. The one essential difference lies in the procedure of access to office; in the administrative context it is appointive, while in the associational context it is elective.

In both cases there is an element of hierarchy in the structures of offices and their powers. Here again, it is common features of the exigencies of effectiveness in collective goal-attainment which account for the hierarchical component. The essential reference is again to bindingness for the collectivity as a whole. The diversity of interests which will somehow come to be involved in any complex collectivity is such that the "right" to make binding decisions cannot be dependent on any specific momentary and probably unstable combination of such interests, but must be independent of them. At the same time, the more "parochial" the level of operation of official authority, the more likely it is that interests particular to the subsystem of reference will exert strong pressure to decide "their way." If unitary responsibility is to be achieved, once the purely "populist" solution of deciding every issue by full membership vote has become impossible, there must be a hierarchy of offices in the sense that conflicts at lower levels must be resolvable by referring decisions to "higher authority." Of course it is the crucial feature of a democratic association that the highest elected official agency, president, or even legislature, is held responsible by the membership as a whole in that the power acquired by election is revocable through electoral defeat.

Power systems we conceive to be strictly bounded by membership status; the more so, the more differentiated is the polity from other societal subsystems. A society, however, consists of a large plurality of politically organized collective units, extending all the way from the societal community and its government to nuclear families. A crucial aspect of the pluralism of modern social structure lies in the fact that typical units, individuals and subcollectivities, have membership status in a considerable number of political collectivities. The mechanism of influence operates not only to help to persuade members and office-holders within any one collectivity of reference to make the decisions with reference to the use of power desired by the exerter of influence, but also to articulate the grounds for, and evaluation of, the consequences of particular decisions in particular units of the polity with the policies of other units in the broader system. Indeed, the use of influence within a politically organized collectivity may be said to be to an important degree a mechanism of adjustment of the relations of its subcollectivities with each other.

Thus government has tended to be a territorial focus of organization. But in the American system, as in other federal systems, there has been an important measure of autonomy institutionalised for territorial subunits. Insofar as states' rights have been institutionalized, coordination among the states has had to rely on influence at least as much as the direct use of power. The salience of conflicts in this area should not blind us to the importance of the positive possibilities of influencing the power-holders in states to "cooperate" in the national interest, even beyond the reach of the federal power in the literal sense. The same principles apply at the level of local autonomy and "home-rule" vis-à-vis both state and federal power.

Power as a generalized medium would not be necessary if the decisions of collectivities could be arrived at solely by the *quid pro quo* of political barter—"You vote for my measure, and I'll vote for yours." Power, we have argued, becomes necessary in giving representatives power vis-à-vis their constituencies—especially the minorities in them who are yet bound by their representatives' votes—and again giving the outcome of legislative votes binding character for the collectivity as a whole. Were the outcome a matter of pure political barter, there *could* be no dissident minorities whose cooperation either had to be "coerced" at the level of reaching the collective decision, or at least was made voluntary in part by their loyalty to the collectivity at a more general level.

At the next more general level of scope of interests and normative considerations, the integration of the many subcollectivities in a complex social system, notably a society, is achieved in a parallel sense by the mechanism of influence. Still less than in the power context would it be conceivable here for such integration to be achieved through barter alone, i.e., the trading of "interests" without their guarantee by binding authority. A very large part of the use of influence goes to persuading interest-spokesmen to accept binding obligations. In the context of government this refers us to the *consensus* aspect. It is probably the case that the more differentiated the society, the less possible it is for government to operate successfully without the backing of the informal consensus (or "loyalty") of most of the membership of the relevant societal community. Such loyalty, however, will only operate when it can be assumed that important elements are willing to trust leadership *beyond* the level of their formal commitments in terms of authority and power.

In its relation to the support system, hierarchy is still a function of the imperatives of collective effectiveness. The power output from the leadership elements of a collective organization to their constituencies consists of the responsibility those elements take for policy decisions. Within the constitutional framework, these decisions specify already established, highly generalized goals and establish priorities among various subgoals; thereby, collective commitments to specific subgoals and then measures for their implementation are made. A basic difference between the bureaucratic and associative contexts is that policies are open to decision making by associative leaders, whereas administrators are obliged to implement policies already established, even though they may also be expected to give "feedback" as to what future policies seem desirable from their viewpoint. Although, as is so generally the case, empirical lines are difficult to draw, this seems to be the crucial analytical distinction.[30]

Concretely, the process of policy decision has a dual character. It is the basis of the directives that policy-makers give to the administrative agencies responsible to them. It is a process internal to the polity. But it is also a process of power output from the polity to its constituencies through the support system. Thus, the power acquired from constituents in the electoral process is returned through another boundary interchange between the polity and the contiguous subsystem of the society, the integrative system.

We interpret this aspect of policy decision as an output of power to the community, which is conceived of as composing the constituencies of elective office. The crucial feature of this aspect of policy decision is the bindingness of policy decisions on all elements obligated to the collectivity as either associational or bureaucratic members. Policies, however, impinge differentially, not equally, on members. They generally favor certain interests over others and impose varying obligations so that they somewhat reallocate resources.

Such differential impingement must be justified with reference to the legitimation both of the paramount goals of the collectivity and of the rights of leadership to make such decisions.[31] Policy decisions essentially

---

[30] Concretely, of course, administrative agencies make policy, e.g., through administrative interpretation of a legislative act or executive order. Just as clearly, however, their primary function is not policy making; and the primary function of elected officials and their immediate advisers is not administration. It is a question of primacy.

[31] I include both executive and legislative elements here in the category of leadership. Like all such distinctions within our scheme, it is mainly functional in the last analysis. The legislative responsibility here is interpreted to be the formulation—or ratification—of the most general levels of policy and of the broad rules for their implementation. The executive function seems to center on modes and timing of implementation with, of course, responsibility for referring sufficiently broad problems to the legislative agency. The legislative function

spell out in more detail the primary goal commitments of a collectivity as specific situations develop and as their exigencies change. Unless the system is very undifferentiated, there must be mechanisms for justifying more particular decisions *within* the framework of the standards that provide legitimation. These I interpret as centering in the relations between power and influence as mechanisms for mediating social processes and the system's normative structure. In one context, justification refers to a consensual reference of the power system. When used to make policy decisions, power is presumptively justified as long as it remains within the limits of legitimate authority and adheres to the accepted norms. There is, however, a second, more specific aspect of justification, which has to do with the positions of the subgoals in the hierarchy that situationally specify the more general goals of the collectivity, and with the interests served by committing resources to those subgoals.

Here, however, inherent integrative problems arise. Resources are inherently scarce relative to demands for their use, and benefits and obligations are differentially distributed to interest groups. To resolve these grounds of conflict two basic factors are needed: persuasion that the relevant subgoal is urgent for the collectivity as a whole and persuasion that shifts in the benefit-burden balance implied by the decision are fair. For collective leadership, this involves exercising influence relative to the important elements of the constituency by "taking responsibility" for the implications of the decision, even at the risk of losing future political support. In a reasonably stable system, this output of influence may be conceived of as balancing the influence exercised by "interest groups" during the decision-making process.

These statements require support by a brief account of the concept of *influence*.[32] I conceive *influence* to be a generalized medium of social interaction that circulates among social units in the context of persuasion. It operates neither by offering situational inducements, such as economically valuable commodities, services, or money, nor by promulgating binding decisions backed by conditional, coercive sanctions, as in the use of power. Influence operates entirely on the intentions of the object of persuasion and through positive channels. It tries to convince him that acting as the persuader desires is in his own and the collective interest.

The major "intrinsic" means of persuasion is to declare firm intentions to act in ways favoring the particularistic interests or senses of solidarity held by specific segments of the constituency. Such persuasion is common and important, but it is theoretically analogous to barter in the case of

---

[32] Talcott Parsons, "On the Concept of Influence," *Public Opinion Quarterly*, XXVII (1963), 37–62. [Reprinted as Chapter 15 in the present volume: ed.]

in democratic states is concentrated in parliaments and congresses, but in less than fully democratic associations it is performed primarily by fiduciary boards to which the executive agencies are in some sense responsible.

economic exchange. It is insufficiently generalized to cover the vast gaps that arise in complex systems between the interests in ensuring support for policies and the necessity for decision-making that can cope with situational exigencies, when the constituencies are characterized by differentiation of functions, religious, ethnic, and social pluralism, and diversity of space-time locations.

If the declaration of specific intentions, the effect of which is to establish solidarity in some kind of a "coalition" with the object of persuasion, is the barter prototype of the exercise of influence, the medium itself operates at a higher level of generality, not the declaration of specific intentions, but rather of support for the more general "objectives" of the object of persuasion. Here the essential point is the establishment of solidarity and a contribution to its operation, without immediately specifying just *what* goals or interests are to be actively supported, e.g., the election of a particular candidate to a particular office, or the promulgation of a specific policy decision.

Influence is, of course, under certain circumstances, in institutionalized systems as defined by procedural rules, convertible for power. Thus when President Johnson and Vice-President Humphrey declared in favor of Comptroller Beame for Mayor of New York, they were exerting influence, which the Beame group hoped would be converted into power in the form of votes. Johnson and Humphrey did not in any clear sense "control" blocs of votes in the New York City election, but their general positions of prestige in the Democratic Party were hoped to serve as a generalized means of persuading Democratically inclined voters—however ineffectual it proved in the particular case.

Influence, then, I conceive of as the medium of persuasion that relies not on acceptance of the intrinsic argument presented, but on the prestige or reputation of the source of the argument. Like money and power, influence, to be sound, must ultimately be exchangeable for the intrinsically valuable inputs for which it is an appropriate medium. This fact, however, does not diminish the importance of its use *instead* of intrinsic means in many circumstances, for as we have noted, a complex polity could not operate on a basis of political barter. If support of leadership depended solely on deals regarding specific policy decisions, it would be very constricted. Unless support is ascribed to particular aspects of leadership status, such as hereditary class status, or to qualities of leadership transcending the political function, such as religious charisma, a generalized medium must be used to transcend barter and naked power in aggregating support.

It is also clear that in modern societies ascriptive bases of mutual obligation or expectation will operate constrictively. For the administration of a large-scale organization to be effective, the resources—especially the human resources—of the organization must be highly mobilizable. Inducements through the market can fill an important part of this need, but there are limits to the use of monetary advantage which cannot be transcended by the use of power. Here, influence may be utilized to persuade holders of resources, including their own services, that it is in their own long-run interests, financial and otherwise, to take certain actions, such as accepting a particular kind of occupational role. Political processes in modern totalitarian societies of the Soviet variety tend to blur the distinction between such uses of influence and appeal to the moral obligations involved in commitment to the régime. This moralism of expecting everything for the party and "building socialism" tends readily to become a basis for coercion.[33]

I will discuss influence with the other generalized media below in connection with some general problems of analyzing political process. Here, however, I will use this sketchy outline of its characteristics to examine Rokkan's conclusion that electoral systems inherently develop toward equality of the franchise. This problem is particularly salient because, if one holds that voting is an exercise of power, then the equality of the franchise strikingly contrasts with the hierarchical element in bureaucratic and leadership systems of power, the element very generally regarded as their defining characteristics. The solution of this problem may be found in the relations among power, influence, and the normative justifications of their use.

The value-premises of the relevant institutions concern the individualism in the value-system I have called *instrumental activism*.[34] According to this value-pattern, a ramified social system contains, rather than an over-all system goal, a set of standards for determining the social acceptability of goals of the system's units. From the viewpoint of the society, this is the value-basis of goal pluralism. From the individual's viewpoint, the basis is the valuation of both his autonomy and the absence of discriminations among individuals that are not justified by exigencies that the concrete system must meet in order to implement the values.

Such exigencies justify two basic gounds for limiting complete autonomy and nondiscrimination. First, the normative order must contain a compulsory element to protect the system from disruptions by force and fraud. Second, equal responsibility for policy decisions is incompatible with the conditions of collective effectiveness, for reasons stated above. Hence, power is concentrated in elective offices.

Subject to these two sets of conditions, the ideal patterns of the assumed value-premises are freedom of association, so that acceptance of membership obligations is as nearly voluntary as possible, and equality of the power of membership status as such, as distinguished from that of particu-

---

[33] See Gregory Grossman, "The Structure and Organization of the Soviet Economy," *Slavic Review*, XXI (1962), 203–22.

[34] I cannot take space here to explain fully these statements about values. For the American case, the fullest statement is Talcott Parsons and Winston White, "The Link Between Character and Society," in *Culture and Society*, eds. S. M. Lipset and Leo Lowenthal (New York: The Free Press, 1961). A much fuller analysis will be published later.

lar offices. The electoral system links these two patterns by aggregating the equal votes to determine the incumbency of offices and policy decisions on matters referred to the membership in referendum. Because the burden of proof falls on contentions that the goals of certain individual members will yield particularly valuable social contributions, there is no ground for discriminating among individuals regarding the amount of power inherent in membership.

However, it is manifestly impossible for all goals proposed by individuals or subgroups to have equal value and prospect for implementation. It is, then, as a mechanism for selecting and ordering the goals or interests of individual members and subcollectivities and the binding policies of the collectivity that influence is most significant politically. Individual members must be *persuaded* (not coerced or induced) to vote for candidates and policies; and office-holders must be *persuaded* to make policy decisions desired by their constituents. Justification of such decisions must be based on the more or less universalistically ordered normative system.

The institutions of franchise and elective office operate together to regulate, in broad accord with the paramount values, the distribution and use of power and the distribution of resources and obligations resulting from the use of power. In the long run, the quality of such regulation depends upon the solidity of the differentiation between power and influence. Here, problems focus about protecting voters from coercion as they exercise the franchise—they must be persuaded genuinely—and protecting office-holders from illegitimate pressure on the part of interest groups.

The conception, held by many eminent writers, that power is governed only by hierarchical principles clearly depends on the idea that the political system of reference is a closed system.[35] It is at the polity's two critical boundaries, however, that its most essential modifications appear. If, as I have argued, opportunity for effectiveness is power, then the principle of equality relative to competence governs a major access to power, however imperfectly this is realized in practice. It is crucial here to link the concept of service, as a category of the output of economic processes, to consideration of the bureaucratic or administrative aspect of collective organization. When freedom of the individual's choice has been institutionalized, the exigencies of procuring services necessitate the basic modification of hierarchical principles which is found at this boundary. At the boundary of membership (in the sense of the constituency of leadership), the hierarchical principle is modified even more radically by the principle of equality of the franchise. This, I have suggested, results from the exigencies of securing consent to the selection of leadership and to policy decisions.

[35] V. O. Key, *Politics, Parties, and Pressure Groups,* 4th ed. (New York: The Crowell-Collier Publishing Co., 1958); H. D. Lasswell and Abraham Kaplan, *Power and Society* (New Haven: Yale University Press, 1950); and R. A. Dahl, *Modern Political Analysis* (Englewood Cliffs, N.J.: Prentice-Hall, 1965).

DIFFERENTIATION OF
POLITICAL STRUCTURES

These considerations have an important bearing on the broad understanding of political structure; they refer particularly to the key concept of *collectivity*. The focus of the political aspect of a social system is organization oriented to the attainment of collective goals. This organization is subject to three primary sets of exigencies.

The first concerns the legitimation of collective goals and of the authority and power needed to implement them in terms of the values of the wider social system, not those of its political subsystem. The wider value-patterns must be specified as commitments in the context of collective action along the requisite lines and subject to the requisite limitations. The legitimation subsystem of a highly differentiated polity, therefore, centers around the constitutional system and the judicial agencies that interpret it. This subsystem is a major link between political and legal organization and thereby involves the integrative structures of the society. Any concrete collectivity depends on fulfillment of these functions, however rudimentary the agencies that implement them may be. The judicial branch of the U.S. government is a highly differentiated example.

Secondly, a political system is an agency for mobilizing resources from its intrasocietal environment and utilizing them to implement its policies. This is the function of the bureaucratic subsystem within which organization based on hierarchical "line authority" is most clearly differentiated. This principle, however, is sharply modified at the boundary where needed resources or capacities can be brought into the polity only by inducement and can be controlled by authority only through the intervention of influence.

Thirdly, there is the associational subsystem. This mobilizes not implementive resources, but rather constituent support and determination of the policies to be implemented. Such mobilization involves the interplay of power and influence between leadership and membership, the latter having dual roles as constituents and as interest groups.

This duality is, in a certain sense, parallel to the duality of roles of the members of households in relation to economic production through the market system. On the one hand, they are consumers, the source of primary market demand for goods. On the other hand, they are in the labor force and, as such, candidates for employment. Taken together, these two markets are the main boundary zones between the economy and its "final" production. Similarly, political leadership and the decision making of office have a dual relation to the publics which are associationally related to them. These publics constitute the sources of demands for particular policy decisions and, as such, function as interest groups. Some of the same people are also the sources of political support, above all, but not exclusively, through voting. The roles, however, must be distinguished, for where support is sufficiently generalized, it is not directly exchanged for particular policy decisions—that would be the political equivalent of barter. Another medium is needed to bridge the gap between the two "markets." This medium we conceive to be influence.

When the associational component dominates the others, we speak of *an association*, as in the case of a professional association of scientists. When the bureaucratic component is clearly primary, we generally do not call the collectivity *an association*. The typical manufacturing firm is such a case. Associational members have the passive role of stockholders, while their leaders, the boards of directors, are often almost assimilated into the top management. Authoritarian governments also approximate this type, although the top of the bureaucracy can never be purely bureaucratic. Independent collectivities giving clear primacy to the legitimation subsystem are far less prominent among political structures, although some types of religious organization do fit that category.

To conclude this sketch of the structure of political systems—which, one must remember, applies to both public and private collectivities—I will briefly discuss the principal ranges of their variability. So far I have emphasized the variability deriving from functional differentiation not only in the polity itself, but also in its relations to the other societal subsystems.

We have conceived the bureaucratic subsystem to be differentiated primarily in relation to economic exigencies, namely the procurement and management of the more-or-less fluid resources at the polity's disposal, and the corresponding outputs of political benefits. The critical resources are, first, financial, and, second, the services of individuals and collectivities. In a developed system, physical resources are mediated by these factors. The associative subsystem is differentiated with respect to problems of support, and outputs of policy decision are differentiated with respect to the management of influence inputs and outputs. Finally, the legitimation subsystem is differentiated with respect to relationship between the polity and the general normative structures (value-patterns and legal norms) of the society.

These external references of the polity's structural differentiation relate very closely to its internal differentiation, which I will treat here only briefly.[36] Very roughly, I will designate four primary internal subsystems of the polity.

In the analytical sense of this paper, a political system is by definition characterized by the primacy of commitment to the attainment of collective goals. Hence there should be a special primacy of the goal-attainment sub-

---

[36] The scheme I would present, were there space, would follow the model for the economy introduced by Smelser and myself in *Economy and Society*, Chapter Four, further developed by Smelser in *Social Change in the Industrial Revolution*.

system, which is not a quality of all types of social systems. In the broadest terms, this subsystem may be called the "leadership" subsystem, its spearhead—the more highly differentiated the system, the more so is the "politically responsible executive," whether, as in the American national system, a popularly elected president, or, in the parliamentary type, a prime minister and cabinet directly responsible to the legislature. This responsible executive is "flanked" within the leadership system on the one hand (the adaptive) by those who are mainly responsible for implementing executive policies, but not as such the highest order of decision-makers. These are the chief executive's "executive staff," which may involve cabinet members and administrative staff in varying combinations. On the other hand (the integrative) are those elements which constitute the principal liaison between executive and legislature, which is here conceived to involve the *dual* role of sponsors of the principal interest groups in the system, and direct involvement in the main system of collective responsibility. Legislative leadership stands most intimately in interchange with the executive in this sphere. The relatively "inert" pattern-maintenance subsystem of the leadership system is perhaps best described as the set of commitments of the whole leadership cohort to the values of the political system as a whole, to effectiveness, but effectiveness within the framework of the more general societal value-system and its political constitution. The very highest level function of the judiciary might be conceived to fit here.

Just as the executive component of leadership is "flanked" on two principal sides, it may be suggested that the leadership sector as a whole is similarly flanked. On the adaptive side is the administrative system which is ordinarily referred to as the "bureaucracy." The center of gravity here is in the elements that do not carry policy-making authority. Their functions are primarily implementive rather than originating. That no absolutely clean concrete line can be drawn does not change this general distinction.

On the integrative side, the leadership system as a whole must articulate with its basis in the integrative functions of the polity as a whole. In modern political systems, this seems to be broadly shared between legislative and judicial functions. The legislative gives relatively specific support, which takes the form of power, to the leadership—in parliamentary systems the whole position of the leadership depends directly on this. The judicial system gives a broader framework of justification and legitimation to the trends of leadership. Of course, on occasion, lack of judicial legitimation or justification may be very serious to leadership policies.

The legitimation of the whole political system as agency of the collectivity is the primary function of the pattern-maintenance subsystem of the polity. It rests in the first instance on its constitutional position and the constitutional framework within which its main orientations fit. The formal legal constitution, however, never stands alone, but has a background of more diffuse commitments in the societal community as a whole. Thus, the "American Creed," with reference to race relations, recently exerted pressure on the Constitution, in the first instance through the Supreme Court, rather than vice versa.

One range of variation among polities concerns the stage of differentiation of a given empirical polity with regard to both its differentiation from the other societal subsystems and its internal differentiation. Obviously, the two are closely interdependent.

The most primitive societies, as Lowie long ago made clear,[37] certainly have political functions, notably because of territorial exigencies. But they typically have no differentiated political structures that are not concurrently structures of kinship involving other primary functions. The early or "archaic" empires made no clear structural distinctions between the political and the religious components of their governmental structures. From such diffuse structures, bureaucratic aspects tend to be differentiated earliest; then comes some sort of independent legal system. A democratic electoral system finally emerges, but it remains the most difficult to institutionalize, with the problems involved varying considerably relative to its size.[38]

Another range of variation, though not as primary as that of differentiation, certainly needs to be mentioned. It concerns the levels at which given normative patterns are effectively institutionalized. For instance, British society seems not to carry certain aspects of differentiation between the polity and the other aspects of social structure as far as the United States does; thus, Britain has, for example, that aspect of social stratification known as the "Establishment." At least until recently, however, the British polity has probably been on its own terms more fully institutionalized than ours, so that phenomena like McCarthyism have been less likely to appear in Britain.[39]

SOME ASPECTS
OF POLITICAL PROCESS

From the present theoretical viewpoint, social process in sufficiently differentiated systems is centered in interactive exchanges involving the generalized symbolic media. In other words, the centrality of monetary transactions in economic analysis is used as a model for political and other sorts of analysis. For the political case, the focal medium is power. At various points in the societal system, power is exchanged both for other general-

[37] H. Lowie, *The Origin of the State* (New York: Harcourt, Brace & World, Inc., 1927).
[38] I cannot take space here to treat this enormous field any further. For a modest systematization of such material, see my *Societies, Comparative and Evolutionary Perspectives*.
[39] See my "Social Strains in America," [Reprinted as Chapter 7 in the present volume: ed.] and S. M. Lipset, "The Sources of the Radical Right," *The Radical Right* (Garden City, N.Y.: Doubleday & Company, Inc., 1963).

ized media, notably money and influence, and for intrinsically significant rewards (services and support) and factors of effectiveness. Factors of effectiveness, at levels where they are not primary symbolic media of social systems, include the technological means of effective coercion and administration, and the like, many of which must be mobilizable with money funds. At higher levels in the normative hierarchy of control, the intrinsic means of political process are commitments to collective loyalty and the value-commitments underlying them.

In analyzing processes involving the symbolic media, three types of process should be distinguished. Again following economic models, they may be called *circular flow*,[40] *growth*, and *structural change*.

Circular flow

No social system, perhaps least of all a polity, functions in a completely stable environment. Of the three components of the polity's intrasocietal situation, the legitimation system is presumably the most stable. It is difficult to generalize about the relative stability of the economic and integrative boundaries, but both are ordinarily less stable than the legitimation boundary. In other words, in any complex and differentiated political system, administrative and policy problems continually arise and change.

The primary function of power in *this* context is to stabilize the polity in the face of changes in its environment. Essentially, the process is always one of translating generalized expectations into more specific ones. Responsible leadership obviously cannot predict in advance the specific action that exigencies will require of their collectivity if its generalized effectiveness is to be maintained. Without precise knowledge of situational and environmental conditions, leadership cannot even define the goals that appear to be most attractive in terms of the generalized collective commitments. Hence it cannot impose situationally adapted obligations on its members far in advance of actual developments. But, lacking knowledge of what goals and means of implementation will be involved in future actions, responsible leadership can use its generalized power to allow for contingencies by holding open freedoms of choice which never emerge in ascriptive conditions, and which are exceedingly awkward to manage in barter conditions. Thus, the user of power can specify political obligations to levels of performance which were left undefined when the general undertaking began—e.g., in making an employment contract or in giving political support to a leadership element.

Without balancing mechanisms, however, such degrees of freedom would produce instability. The essential features of the balancing mechanisms is feed-back from the condition of resource scarcity. In the case of

[40] See Joseph Schumpeter, *The Theory of Economic Development* (Cambridge: Harvard University Press, 1936).

power, however, the scarcity element does not concern expenditure of a given fraction of a cardinal quantity, as it does with money, but the capacity to carry the day in establishing or implementing decisions as binding. The hazard of overspending is that losing important issues will impair after insisting upon some capacity to prevail in others. Such impairment, provided it is not so radical as to jeopardize legitimation, involves three primary factors.

The first is the risk that power inputs balancing such expenditures will not be forthcoming. Thus, failures in effective administration (through failure to procure or hold qualified services, for example) may lead to withdrawal of political support. Hence, there is a balance in the economy of power itself, a balance which is effected in quantum steps rather than in an even flow. Good administration and policy making should "make" power, as well as secure intrinsically significant results, just as production "makes" both goods and money for the producing unit.

Over the long run, the balance-of-power potential depends upon capacity to exchange power for the media of the societal subsystems adjacent to the polity. Hence, inadequate financial resources, whether procured through taxation, market transactions, or solicitation of voluntary contributions, comprise a second type of factor in the impairment of political processes. As Eisenstadt point out, when feudalism shrinks the base of mobilizable resources, e.g., taxes, the power of a centralized bureaucratic régime may be seriously impaired.[41] The third factor concerns influence. Here, problems focus on the risks to the leadership's prestige involved in pressing particular policies. Loss of influence may result in loss of support, and hence in a loss of power "income."

As Eisenstadt has shown, all three of these factors have been involved in the breakdown of higher-order political structures into some kind of feudalism. As a result, a generalized loyalty on the part of groups on whose support a régime depends—such as landowners, military officers, or civil servants—is replaced by relatively specific, more-or-less contractual relations in which loyalty is exchanged for specific perquisites and privileges. This is political barter. It is, however, noteworthy that the process of devolution usually continues further, because there is a strong tendency for the control of such resources to become hereditary and traditionalized. Hence, the devolution from generalized support to barter often proceeds to ascription of rights to resources and support. Broadly speaking, this is what happened in the breakdown of the political authority of the Roman Empire.

Thus, we may regard a polity as maintaining its power potential through continual interchanges with its environment. On the one hand, it "exports" power in the form of opportunity for effectiveness, and gets in return power in the form of commitment of services. On the other hand, it

41 S. N. Eisenstadt, *The Political Systems of Empires* (New York: The Free Press, 1963), esp. pp. 342 ff.

"exports" power in the form of policy decisions, and gets in return power in the form of political support.

Such interchanges function to ensure that needs for financial resources or influence will not drain the polity's allocable power potential more rapidly than they can be balanced by inputs into the polity. These considerations should make clear the vital importance of the *generalization* as media of both power and influence as well as of money. Without such generalized media, it is impossible to transcend the level of differentiation that uses what I have called *political barter*. Such barter, however, seems to be inherently unstable: without adequate generalization of both power and influence, ascriptive rigidity is almost inevitable.

In economic structures, a positive balance of the medium is maintained by regulating action with the standard of solvency—the requirement that monetary income balance monetary expenditures in market transactions. Units having political primacy, which must balance power outputs with power inputs, are governed by a parallel standard. With some trepidation, I will appropriate the old term *sovereignty* for this standard, though in a very non-Austinian sense. I mean to emphasize its implication of political independence, but in a sense applying to both governmental and private collectivities. Contrary to the Austinian conception, I assume a normative order superordinate to the "sovereignty" of any unit within a social system, including a national government. In these terms, a business firm is sovereign insofar as it maintains the authority of its offices and attracts both services and support without depending upon political subsidy, or the use of another collectivity's factors of effectiveness. Along with solvency, this is clearly the ideal of free enterprise.[42] Regarding territorial governments, the acceptance of a controlling normative order need not imply an impairment of sovereignty.

Units failing to maintain sovereignty must obtain inputs of power in addition to the "proceeds" of their own operations, or they must forego some of their capacity to command binding political obligations. This impairment of sovereignty regularly occurs in declining political systems, such as the declining empires Eisenstadt analyzes,[43] which distintegrate into components and/or become absorbed in other polities. Parallel considerations apply to various types of private collectivities, such as business firms and political parties.

Growth

The modes of losing strict sovereignty include, however, a special case connected with problems of growth. A collectivity may become com-

---

[42] See S. M. Lipset, *The First New Nation* (New York: The Free Press, 1963), for evidence that American businesses, however, have often been amenable to accepting political subsidy from government under certain circumstances.
[43] Eisenstadt, *Political Systems of Empires.*

mitted to the ambition to expand the system's power capacity to a degree that cannot be fulfilled by internal resources. It must then obtain an additional input of power which need not be immediately balanced by an output; in other words, power must be "borrowed." This is a political parallel to the extension of credit to an economic unit, which may then increase its productivity by proper investment, and eventually repay the loan, with interest, on terms compatible with its long-run solvency.

This raises the question of whether political power is subject to zero-sum conditions, as a majority of authorities on the subject seem to hold.[44] I suggest that political systems have mechanisms which are strictly parallel to credit-creation through banking, and which can also make net additions to the circulating medium. These mechanisms operate through a particular mode of relation between power and influence and involve the agencies using these media.

The generalization of political support, which precludes its being conditioned to particular policy decisions in *quid-pro-quo* fashion, is comparable to the deposit of money in a bank. Although elected leaders are, to be sure, responsible for safeguarding their constituents' interests, they are not obligated to use power only with specific authorization from their constituencies. Insofar as they make policy decisions without such particular authorization, they may bind the collectivity to commitments that can be jeopardized by a mass withdrawal of political support. Voters are no more obligated to re-elect leaders who have made commitments of which they disapprove than depositors are obligated to keep funds in a bank that makes loans which they believe to be economically unsound. It is, however, precisely through the lending of funds that depositors have a right to withdraw on demand that banks can make a net addition to the circulating medium through the *creation* of credit. Similarly, political leadership can make a net addition to the power in the system by taking responsibility for decisions which are not specifically authorized by the constituency. One consequence, however, is that a functioning political leadership, like a bank management, is always unable to meet all its formal obligations instantaneously; in this sense, the bank is insolvent, and the polity fails to guarantee its sovereignty.

Bank loans increase the amount of money in circulation by using power in the form of binding contractual commitments. The banker not only requires his borrowers to repay their loans at stated times, but he himself is bound not to demand early repayments even though his depositors may demand repayment of their funds at *any* time. Thus the banker takes the risk that a loss of confidence in the bank may touch off a run by de-

---

[44] H. Lasswell and A. Kaplan, *Power and Society*; C. W. Mills, *The Power Elite* (New York: Oxford University Press, 1956); Key, *Politics, Parties, and Pressure Groups*; R. A. Dahl, "The Concept of Power," *Behavioral Science*, II (1957), pp. 201–15, and Dahl, *Modern Political Analysis*, Chapter Five.

positors, catching him unable to pay. In monetary systems, of course, power is also explicitly used when the power of the government is put behind the stability of the banking system through, for example, a central banking system that is ultimately controlled by the government. Such added security may be an essential condition of a bank's capacity to expand credit without making the depositors' positions unduly insecure. Similarly, a political leader cannot guarantee that policy commitments obligating the collectivity for longer than his own term of office will be honored—the voters may throw him out in favor of a candidate pledged to repudiate his policy commitments. Yet, he "uses his influence" both to persuade those affected, whether inside or outside his collectivity, to regard such commitments as genuine and to persuade his electorate to support them. For example, the federal government carries long-term obligations to finance scientific research and development, even though Congress may legally terminate the whole program at nearly any time by refusing to appropriate the requisite funds.

The successful extension of binding commitments not specially authorized by the supporting constituencies can provide *net* additions to the power potential of the polity as a whole by making binding decisions stick despite costs in resources and leadership prestige. This comprises "prudent investment" in the increase of power if the conditions of long-run growth are met, so that the system's potential increases by degrees commensurate with the increase of commitments enforceable with power.

Detailed analyses of such processes are confronted by many complications. There is no space here to present even a few examples. I hope, however, that I have created sufficient presumption in favor of the two following propositions so that, when they are specified empirically, they will not simply be dismissed as absurd.

First, power is not a zero-sum resource: an increase in the amount of power held by one unit in a system does not necessarily involve a corresponding diminution in the power held by the other units in the same system. The crucial analogy is that, in accepting a bank loan, a unit does not normally diminish the money available to the bank's depositors. Similarly, the voters' power to select leadership is not impaired by the normal promulgation of commitments by their leaders.

An important difference between the two cases, however, affects the definition of conditions under which increments to the media are possible. Loans are pie slices which may vary in size on a continuous scale. But policy decisions are all-or-none commitments, competing with alternative commitments, with either prevail or fail, in many cases without possibility of compromise. This difference does not, however, invalidate the applicability of the general model of net increase through positive commitment despite risk factors.

Second, the leverage for increase in a given medium must come from the next-higher subsystem in the hierarchy of control. Credit creation is not possible through monetary manipulation alone—it requires the mobilization of power in the form of binding contractual obligations. Similarly, power cannot be increased simply by internal manipulation of power relations in the political system. It requires the mobilization of influence the use of which must be justified in terms of institutionalized norms. For specific agents, this means laying prestige and future potential for influence on the line in favor of the policy to which they wish to give the bindingness of power.[45]

Growth in a political system, as measured by changes in its power potential, may arise from exogenous sources, such as economic growth independent of political changes or improvements in the environment of the society. The growth process just outlined, however, is primarily endogenous. It requires articulation with the influence system, which is not, analytically, in the polity, although it can be oriented mainly to the polity or to relevant sectors of the polity.

Structural change

The third type of process to be discussed is institutional change in the structural components of the polity.[46] Here I will treat the problems of analyzing changes that contribute to evolutionary advancement, since I have remarked on devolutionary processes above. Modern examples are the development of the democratic franchise, as traced by Rokkan and his associates, or, in the private sphere, the transformation of family-firm entrepreneurship into corporate organization that differentiates the functions of ownership from those of active management.[47] From one point of view, the key aspect of such a process of structural development is differentiation—that is, the division of one previous structure into two, as when specialized units of economic production (firms) are differentiated from family households. At least three further processes must, however, take place if the outcome of a process of differentiation is to be stabilized. First, *both* units (or classes of units) must be included in a new level of

[45] This does not imply that concrete organizations cannot autonomously generate increases in their media. Firms ploughing back their profits into investment fuse the productive and banking functions in one concrete organization. Similarly a party in office may use both power and influence to invest in the increase of power.

[46] See Parsons and Smelser, *Economy and Society*; Talcott Parsons, "Some Considerations on the Theory of Social Change," *Rural Sociology*, XXVI (September, 1961), 217–39, for general discussions of problems in analyzing institutional change.

[47] Smelser and I used this example, roughly analyzed, to illustrate our paradigm of social change in *Economy and Society*, Chapter Five. The classical description and discussion of this example is in A. A. Berle and G. C. Means, *The Modern Corporation and Private Property* (New York: Commerce Clearing House, Inc., 1932). An excellent current example is the process leading toward full inclusion of the Negro in the American polity with full rights of participation and equal opportunity. For a particularly pertinent study of this process, see Leon Mayhew, *Law and Equal Opportunity*: Anti-Discrimination Law in Massachusetts (Harvard University Press, 1968).

collective organization—in this case, in a new type of local community that includes both units of residence and of employment. Second, norms must be generalized to the point where they can regulate action in both types of unit and the relations between them. Thus, property relations can no longer be regulated on the assumption that only households can hold property rights. Third, there must be an up-grading of the processes by which resources are made available to the newly differentiated operative units, so that their stricter exigencies can be met.

In such cases, not only must a need for the relevant change develop, but also any previously institutionalized norms that conflict with the newly emerging structure must be questioned. To legitimize a change of norms, it is necessary both to alter the constellation of interests and to invoke the value-system itself at requisite levels of specificity on behalf of the new norms. In the American race problem, this has been done by judicial declarations that the "separate but equal" doctrine is incompatible with the basic value-principle of "equal protection of the laws."

Legitimation of a change in norms, however, is not sufficient. It is necessary to deal with what Leon Mayhew, in the case of the race issue, calls "structural discrimination." Modes of action previously treated as acceptable and at least partially legitimate have to be coped with and changed. Examples are beliefs that only the community's "responsible" elements should be entrusted with the franchise, that the "impersonality" of corporate firms has destroyed the "paternalistic intimacy" of family firms having tangible, responsible bosses, and that people's rights to choose their own neighbors are violated by antidiscriminatory housing legislation.

Precisely because any normative system allows for alternative interpretations, the bearing that the new norms have on accepted values must be clarified. Concurrently, the definition of the situation with respect to practical interests must change enough so that an adequately large and strategically placed group develops an interest in actuating the new norms.

These three types of process involve a progressively widening circle of factors in the operation of a given political system. Circular-flow processes can be viewed as entirely intrapolitical in their processual mechanisms, though they involve responses to changes in the situation of the polity. Political growth, even when mainly endogenous, involves a specific mode of articulation with the next higher system in the hierarchy of control, which I call *the integrative system*, for which influence is the generalized medium. This mode is the mobilization of influence, a medium which is not (like power) primarily political, to increase the effectiveness of a political unit by "investing" in the increase of its power. Processes of change in the institutional structure of a political system require a still more complex process. They involve influence even more crucially because it must be used more broadly and must be backed by explicit references to generalized value-commitments in order to legitimize the changed norms that justify the given exercises of influence.

CONCLUSION

The above is a very sketchy, abstract outline of an approach to the analysis of what I deliberately call the political *aspect* of a society or other social system. I use this term to emphasize that the political system, or polity, is analytically defined and, hence, is an abstracted subsystem of a total social system which must systematically articulate with the other subsystems—the economy, the integrative system, and the pattern-maintenance system—abstracted at a comparable level.

While attempting to account for the many crucial substantive differences between polity and economy, I have tried throughout to follow the mode of analysis that Smelser and myself used to analyze the economy and its place in the society. Perhaps the main point of my analysis is the conception of political power as a generalized medium of political process that parallels the role of money in economic process.

Also paralleling the economic paradigm, I have stressed that the polity is not a closed system, but is engaged in continual interchanges with adjacent systems, the economic and the integrative. This crucial proposition seems to imply the disproof of two very important trends in recent literature on power. First is the idea that power is inherently hierarchical and necessarily dissociated from any egalitarian elements in social systems. Contrary to this, I have contended that equality of the franchise and the regulation of commitment to service by the equality-of-opportunity principle are authentic modes of institutionalizing power systems in relation to the boundary exigencies of the polity. Second is the assumption that zero-sum conditions always apply to power circulation. I have challenged this with the conception that influence may be used in certain circumstances to increase the power potential of a political system.

In this connection, a series of problems concerning the structure of political systems were discussed, notably in the fields of bureaucratic organization and democratic association, the latter with special regard to electoral systems. Then three types of process in political systems were sketchily outlined, with Schumpeter's analysis of economic process providing a principal model. These processes of circular flow, growth, and structural change were arranged according to the increasing factors exogenous to the polity that they involve and according to the complexity of the modes of such involvement that they require.

Whatever its limitations, I believe this to be a valuable approach to the systematic theoretical treatment of political systems. Though not developed very far, it is relatively systematic itself and relates systematically to both the conception of a society as a whole and the conception of a social system as part of a more general action system. These two latter points, indeed, I consider to be among its most important virtues.[48]

[48] [An appendix to this paper, a Technical Note that was in the original version, has been omitted because it was an adaptation of a similar note that is appended to Chapter 14 of the present volume. It would be redundant to include both: ed.]

Chapter 14

On the Concept of
Political Power

*P*ower is one of the key concepts in the great Western tradition of thought about political phenomena. It is at the same time a concept on which, in spite of its long history, there is, on analytical levels, a notable lack of agreement both about its specific definition, and about many features of the conceptual context in which it should be placed. There is, however, a core complex of its meaning, having to do with the capacity of persons or collectivities "to get things done" effectively, in particular when their goals are obstructed by some kind of human resistance or opposition. The problem of coping with resistance then leads into the question of the role of coercive measures, including the use of physical force, and the relation of coercion to the voluntary and consensual aspects of power systems.

The aim of this paper is to attempt to clarify this complex of meanings and relations by placing the concept of power in the context of a general conceptual scheme for the analysis of large-scale and complex social systems, that is, of societies. In doing so I speak as a sociologist rather than as a political scientist, but as one who believes that the interconnection of the principal social disciplines, including not only these two, but especially their relations to economics as well, are so close that on matters of general theory of this sort they cannot safely be treated in isolation; their interrelations must be made explicit and systematic. As a sociologist,

Reprinted from Proceedings of the American Philosophical Society, *CVII* (*June 1963*).

I thus treat a central concept of political theory by selecting among the elements that have figured prominently in political theory in terms of their fit with and significance for the general theoretical analysis of society as a whole.

There are three principal contexts in which it seems to me that the difficulties of the concept of power, as treated in the literature of the last generation, come to a head. The first of these concerns its conceptual diffuseness, the tendency, in the tradition of Hobbes, to treat power as simply the generalized capacity to attain ends or goals in social relations, independently of the media employed or of the status of "authorization" to make decisions or impose obligations.[1]

The effect of this diffuseness, as I call it, is to treat "influence" and sometimes money, as well as coercion in various aspects, as "forms" of power, thereby making it logically impossible to treat power as a *specific* mechanism operating to bring about changes in the action of other units, individual or collective, in the processes of social interaction. The latter is the line of thought I wish to pursue.

Secondly, there is the problem of the relation between the coercive and the consensual aspects. I am not aware of any treatment in the literature that presents a satisfactory solution of this problem. A major tendency is to hold that somehow "in the last analysis" power comes down to one or the other, i.e. to "rest on" command of coercive sanctions, *or* on consensus and the will to voluntary cooperation. If going to one or the other polar solution seems to be unacceptable, a way out, taken for example by Friedrich, is to speak of each of these as different "forms" of power. I shall propose a solution that maintains that both aspects are essential, but that neither of the above two ways of relating them is satisfactory, namely, subordinating either one to the other or treating them as discrete "forms."

Finally the third problem is what, since the Theory of Games, has widely come to be called the "zero-sum" problem. The dominant tendency in the literature, for example in Lasswell and C. Wright Mills, is to maintain explicitly or implicitly that power is a zero-sum phenomenon, which is to say that there is a fixed "quantity" of power in any relational system and hence any gain of power on the part of A must by definition occur by diminishing the power at the disposal of other units, B, C, D.... There are, of course, restricted contexts in which this condition holds, but I shall argue that it does not hold for total systems of a sufficient level of complexity.

[1] Thus E. C. Banfield, *Political Influence* (New York: The Free Press, 1962), p. 348, speaks of control as the ability to cause another to give or withhold action, and power as the ability to establish control over another. Similarly Robert Dahl, "The Concept of Power," *Behavioral Scientist* 2 (July, 1957), says that "*A* has power over *B* to the extent that he can get *B* to do something that *B* would not otherwise do." C. J. Friedrich takes a similar position in *Man and his Government; An Empirical Theory of Politics* (New York: McGraw-Hill, 1963).

SOME GENERAL ASSUMPTIONS

The initial assumption is that, within the conception of society as a system, there is an essential parallelism in theoretical structure between the conceptual schemes appropriate for the analysis of the economic and the political aspects of societies. There are four respects in which I wish to attempt to work out and build on this parallel, showing at the same time the crucial substantive differences between the two fields.

First, "political theory," as here interpreted, which is not simply to be identified with the meaning given the term by many political scientists, is thought of as an abstract analytical scheme in the same sense in which economic theory is abstract and analytical. It is not the conceptual interpretation of any concretely complete category of social phenomena, quite definitely not those of government, though government is the area in which the political element comes nearest to having clear primacy over others. Political theory thus conceived is a conceptual scheme which deals with a restricted set of primary variables and their interrelations that are to be found operating in all concrete parts of social systems. These variables are, however, subject to parametric conditions which constitute the values of other variables operating in the larger system that constitutes the society.

Secondly, following on this, I assume that the empirical system to which political theory in this sense applies is an analytically defined, a "functional" subsystem of a society, not, for example, a concrete type of collectivity. The conception of the economy of a society is relatively well defined.[2] I should propose the conception of the *polity* as the parallel empirical system of direct relevance to political theory as here advanced. The polity of a given society is composed of the ways in which the relevant components of the total system are organized with reference to one of its fundamental functions, namely effective collective action in the attainment of the goals of collectivities. Goal-attainment in this sense is the establishment of a satisfactory relation between a collectivity and certain objects in its environment, which include both other collectivities and categories of personalities, e.g., "citizens." A total society must in these terms be conceived, in one of its main aspects, as a collectivity, but it is also composed of an immense variety of subcollectivities, many of which are parts not only of this society but of others.[3]

A collectivity, seen in these terms, is thus clearly not a concrete "group,"

---

[2] Cf. Talcott Parsons and Neil J. Smelser, *Economy and Society* (New York: The Free Press, 1956), Chapter I, for a discussion of this conception.

[3] E.g., the American medical profession is part of American society, but also it is part of a wider medical profession which transcends this particular society, to some extent as collectivity. Interpenetration in membership is thus a feature of the relations among collectivities.

but the terms refers to groups, i.e. systematically related pluralities of persons, seen in the perspective of their interests in and capacities for effective collective action. The political process then is the process by which the necessary organization is built up and operated, the goals of action are determined and the resources requisite to it are mobilized.

These two parallels to economic theory can be extended to still a third. The parallel to collective action in the political case is, for the economic, production. This conception in turn must be understood in relation to three main operative contexts. The first is adjustment to the conditions of "demand" that are conceived to be external to the economy itself, to be located in the "consumers" of the economic process. Secondly, resources must be mobilized, also from the environment of the economy, the famous factors of production. Thirdly, the internal economic process is conceived as creatively combinatorial; it is, by the "combination" of factors of production in the light of the utility of outputs, a process of creating more valuable facilities to meet the needs of consuming units than would be available to them without this combinatorial process. I wish most definitely to postulate that the logic of "value added" applies to the political sphere in the present sense.[4]

In the political case, however, the value reference is not to utility in the economic sense but to effectiveness, very precisely, I think in the sense used by C. I. Barnard.[5] For the limited purposes of political analysis as such the givenness of the goal-demands of interest groups serves as the same order of factor in relation to the political system as has the corresponding givenness of consumers' wants for purposes of economic analysis —and of course the same order of qualifications on the empirical adequacy of such postulates.

Finally, fourth, political analysis as here conceived is parallel to economic in the sense that a central place in it is occupied by a generalized medium involved in the political interaction process, which is also a "measure" of the relevant values. I conceive power as such a generalized medium in a sense directly parallel in logical structure, though very different substantively, to money as the generalized medium of the economic process. It is essentially this conception of power as a generalized medium parallel to money that will, in the theoretical context sketched above, provide the thread for guiding the following analysis through the types of historic difficulty with reference to which the paper began.

---

[4] For discussions of the conception of "value-added" in spheres of application broader than the economic alone, cf. Neil J. Smelser, *Social Change in the Industrial Revolution* (New York: The Free Press of Glencoe, 1959), Chapter II, pp. 7–20, and Neil J. Smelser, *Theory of Collective Behaviour* (New York: The Free Press, 1963), Chapter II, pp. 23–47.

[5] C. I. Barnard, *The Functions of the Executive* (Cambridge: Harvard University Press, 1938), Chapter V, pp. 46–64.

THE OUTPUTS OF POLITICAL PROCESS
AND THE FACTORS OF EFFECTIVENESS

The logic of the combinatorial process which I hold to be common to economic theory and the type of political theory advanced here, involves a paradigm of inputs and outputs and their relations. Again, we will hold that the logic is strictly parallel to the economic case, i.e. that there should be a set of political categories strictly parallel to those of the factors of production (inputs) on the one hand, the shares of income (outputs) on the other.

In the economic case, with the exception of land, the remaining three factors must be regarded as inputs from the other three cognate functional subsystems of the society: labor from what we call the "pattern-maintenance" system; capital from the polity; and organization, in the sense of Alfred Marshall, from the integrative system.[6] Furthermore, it becomes clear that land is not, as a factor of production, simply the physical resource, but essentially the commitment, in value terms, of any resources to economic production in the system independent of price.

In the political case, similarly the equivalent of land is the commitment of resources to effective collective action, independent of any specifiable "pay-off" for the unit that controls them.[7] Parallel to labor is the demand or "need" for collective action as manifested in the "public," which in some sense is the constituency of the leadership of the collectivity in question—a conception which is relatively clear for the governmental or other electoral association, but needs clarification in other connections. Parallel to capital is the control of some part of the productivity of the economy for the goals of the collectivity, in a sufficiently developed economy through financial resources at the disposal of the collectivity, acquired by earnings, gift, or taxation. Finally, parallel to organization is the legitimation of the authority under which collective decisions are taken.

It is most important to note that none of these categories of input is conceived as a form of power. In so far as they involve media, it is the media rooted in contiguous functional systems, not power as that central to the polity—e.g., control of productivity may operate through money, and constituents' demands through what I call "influence." Power then is the *means* of acquiring control of the factors in effectiveness; it is not itself one of these factors, any more than in the economic case money is a factor of production; to suppose it was, was the ancient mercantilist fallacy.

[6] On the rationale of these attributions, *see Economy and Society, op. cit.*, Chapter II.
[7] "Pay-off" may be a deciding factor in choice between particular contexts of use, but not as to whether the resource shall be devoted to collective effectiveness at all.

Though the analytical context in which they are placed is perhaps unfamiliar in the light of traditional political analysis, I hope it is clear that the actual categories used are well established, though there remain a number of problems of exact definition. Thus control of productivity through financing of collective action is very familiar, and the concept of "demands" in the sense of what constituents want and press for, is also very familiar.[8] The concept legitimation is used in essentially the same sense in which I think Max Weber used it in a political context.[9]

The problem of what corresponds, for the political case, to the economist's "shares of income" is not very difficult, once the essential distinction, a very old one in economic tradition, between monetary and "real" income is clearly taken into account. Our concern is with the "real" outputs of the political process—the analogue of the monetary here is output of power.

There is, to us, one critically important revision of the traditional economic treatment of outputs that must be made, namely the bracketing together of "goods and services," which then would be treated as outputs to the household as, in our technical terms, a part of the "pattern-maintenance" system. The present position is that goods, i.e., more precisely property rights in the physical objects of possession, belong in this category, but that "services," the commitment of human role-performances to an "employer," or contracting agent constitute an output, not to the household, but to the polity, the type case (though not the only one) being an employing organization in which the role-incumbent commits himself to performance of an occupational role, a job,[10] as a contribution to the effective functioning of the collectivity.

There is, from this consideration, a conclusion which is somewhat surprising to economists, namely, that service is in the economic sense the "real" counterpart of interest as monetary income from the use of funds. What we suggest is that the political control of productivity makes it possible, through combinatorial gains in the political context, to produce a surplus above the monetary funds committed, by virtue of which under specified conditions a premium can be paid at the monetary level which, though a result of the combinatorial process as a whole, is most directly related to the output of available services as an economic phenomenon, i.e. as a "fluid resource." Seen a little differently, it becomes necessary to make a clear distinction between labor as a factor of produc-

[8] I have in fact adopted the term "demands" from the usage of David Easton, "An Approach to the Analysis of Political Systems," *World Politics*, 9 (1957), 383–400.

[9] Cf. Max Weber, *The Theory of Social and Economic Organization* (New York: Oxford University Press, 1947); translated by A. M. Henderson and Talcott Parsons; edited by Talcott Parsons, p. 124.

[10] The cases of services concretely rendered to a household should be considered as a limiting case where the roles of consumer and employer have not become differentiated from each other.

tion in the economic sense and service as an output of the economic process which is utilized in a political context, that is, one of organizational or collective effectiveness.

Service, however, is not a "factor" in effectiveness, in the sense in which labor is a factor of production, precisely because it is a category of power. It is the point at which the economic utility of the human factor is matched with its potential contribution to effective collective action. Since the consumer of services is in principle the employing collectivity, it is its effectiveness for collective goals, not its capacity to satisfy the "wants" of individuals, that is the vantage point from which the utility of the service is derived. The output of power that matches the input of services to the polity, I interpret to be the "opportunity for effectiveness" that employment confers on those employed or contract offers to partners. Capital in the economic sense is one form of this opportunity for effectiveness which is derived from providing, for certain types of performances, a framework of effective organization.[11]

The second, particularly important context of "real" output of the political process is the category that, in accord with much tradition, I should like to call capacity to assume leadership responsibility. This, as a category of "real" output also is not a form of power, but this time of influence.[12] This is an output, not to the economy, but to what I shall call the integrative system, which in its relevance to the present context is in the first instance the sector of the "public" that can be looked on as the "constituencies" of the collective processes under consideration. It is the group structure of the society looked at in terms of their structured interests in particular modes of effective collective action by particular collectivities. It is only through effective organization that genuine responsibility can be taken, hence the implementation of such interests demands responsibility for collective effectiveness.[13] Again it should be made quite clear that leadership responsibility is not here conceived as an output of power, though many political theorists (e.g. Friedrich) treat both leadership and, more broadly influence, as "forms" of power. The power category that regulated the output of leadership influence takes the form on the one side of binding policy decisions of the collectivity, on the other of political support from the constituency, in the type case

---

[11] In the cases treated as typical for economic analysis the collective element in capital is delegated through the *bindingness* of the contracts of loan of financial resources. To us this is a special case, employment being another, of the binding obligation assumed by an organization, whether it employs or loans, by virtue of which the recipient can be more effective than would otherwise be the case. It is not possible to go further into these complex problems here, but they will, perhaps, be somewhat illuminated by the later discussion of the place of the concept of bindingness in the theory of power.

[12] See my paper "On the Concept of Influence," in *Public Opinion Quarterly*, 27 (Spring, 1963). [Reprinted as Chapter 15 in the present volume: ed.]

[13] Here again Barnard's usage of the concept of responsibility seems to me the appropriate one. See Barnard, *op. cit.*

through the franchise. Policy decisions we would treat as a factor in integration of the system, not as a "consumable" output of the political process.[14]

Finally, a few words need to be said about what I have called the combinatorial process itself. It is of course assumed in economic theory that the "structures" of the factors of production on the one hand, and the "demand system" for real outputs on the other, are independent of each other. "Utility" of outputs can only be enhanced, to say nothing of maximized, by processes of transformation of the factors in the direction of providing what is wanted, as distinguished from what merely is available. The decision-making aspect of the transformative process, what is to be produced, how much, and how offered for consumption, is what is meant by economic production, whereas the physical processes are not economic but "technological"; they are controlled by economic considerations, but are not themselves in an analytical sense economic.

The consequence of successful adaptation of available resources to the want or demand is an increment in the value of the resource-stock conceived in terms of utility as a type of value. But this means recombination of the components of the resource-stock in order to adapt them to the various uses in question.

The same logic applies to the combinatorial process in the political sphere. Here the resources are not land, labor, capital, and organization, but valuation of effectiveness, control of productivity, structured demands and the patterning of legitimation. The "wants" are not for consumption in the economic sense, but for the solution of "interest" problems in the system, including both competitive problems in the allocative sense and conflict problems, as well as problems of enhancement of the total effectiveness of the system of collective organization. In this case also the "structure" of the available resources may not be assumed spontaneously to match the structure of the system of interest-demands. The increment of effectiveness in demand-satisfaction through the political process is, as in the economic case, arrived at through combinatorial decision-processes. The organizational "technology" involved is not in the analytical sense political. The demand-reference is not to discrete units of the system conceived in abstraction from the system as a whole—the "individual" consumer of the economist—but to the problem of the share of benefits and burdens to be allocated to subsystems of various orders. The "consumption" reference is to the interest-unit's place in the allocative system rather than to the independent merits of particular "needs."

---

[14] In order not to complicate things too much, I shall not enter into problems of the interchange system involving legitimation here. See my paper "Authority, Legitimation, and Political Process," in *Nomos* I, reprinted as Chapter V of my *Structure and Process in Modern Societies* (New York: The Free Press, 1960), pp. 170–198.

THE CONCEPT OF POWER

The above may seem a highly elaborate setting in which to place the formal introduction of the main subject of the paper, namely the concept of power. Condensed and cryptic as the exposition may have been, however, understanding of its main structure is an essential basis for the special way in which it will be proposed to combine the elements that have played a crucial part in the main intellectual traditions dealing with the problems of power.

Power is here conceived as a circulating medium, analogous to money, within what is called the political system, but notably over its boundaries into all three of the other neighboring functional subsystems of a society (as I conceive them): the economic, integrative, and pattern-maintenance systems. Specification of the properties of power can best be approached through an attempt to delineate very briefly the relevant properties of money as such a medium in the economy.

Money is, as the classical economists said, both a medium of exchange and a "measure of value." It is symbolic in that, though measuring and thus "standing for" economic value or utility, it does not itself possess utility in the primary consumption sense—it has no "value in use" but only "in exchange," that is, for possession of things having utility. The use of money is thus a mode of communication of offers, on the one hand to purchase, on the other to sell, things of utility, with and for money. It becomes an essential medium only when exchange is neither ascriptive, as exchange of gifts between assigned categories of kin, nor takes place on a basis of barter, one item of commodity or service directly for another.

In exchange for its lack of direct utility money gives the recipient four important degrees of freedom in his participation in the total exchange system: (1) He is free to spend his money for any item or combination of items available on the market that he can afford, (2) he is free to shop around among alternative sources of supply for desired items, (3) he can choose his own time to purchase, and (4) he is free to consider terms which, because of freedom of time and source, he can accept or reject or attempt to influence in the particular case. By contrast, in the case of barter, the negotiator is bound to what his particular partner has or wants in relation to what he has and will part with at the particular time. The other side of the gain in degrees of freedom is, of course, the risk involved in the probabilities of the acceptance of money by others and of the stability of its value.

Primitive money is a medium which is still very close to a commodity, the commonest case being precious metal, and many still feel that the value of money is "really" grounded in the commodity value of the metallic base. On this base, however, in developed monetary systems, there is erected a complex structure of credit instruments, so that only a tiny fraction of actual transactions is conducted in terms of the metal —it becomes a "reserve" available for certain contingencies, and is actually used mainly in the settlement of international balances. I shall discuss the nature of credit further in another connection later. For the moment suffice it to say that, however important in certain contingencies the availability of metallic reserves may be, no modern monetary system operates primarily with metal as the actual medium, but uses "valueless" money. Moreover, the acceptance of this "valueless" money rests on a certain institutionalized confidence in the monetary system. If the security of monetary commitments rested only on their convertibility into metal, then the overwhelming majority of them would be worthless, for the simple reason that the total quantity of metal is far too small to redeem more than a few.

One final point is that money is "good," that is works as a medium only within a relatively defined network of market relationships which, to be sure, now has become world-wide, but the maintenance of which requires special measures to maintain mutual convertibility of national currencies. Such a system is on the one hand a range of exchange-potential within which money may be spent, but on the other hand, one within which certain conditions affecting the protection and management of the unit are maintained, both by law and by responsible agencies under the law.

The first focus of the concept of an institutionalized power system is, analogously, a relational system within which certain categories of commitments and obligations, ascriptive or voluntarily assumed—e.g. by contract—are treated as binding, i.e. under normatively defined conditions their fulfillment may be insisted upon by the appropriate role-reciprocal agencies. Furthermore, in case of actual or threatened resistance to "compliance," i.e. to fulfilment of such obligations when invoked, they will be "enforced" by the threat or actual imposition of situational negative sanctions, in the former case having the function of deterrence, in the latter of punishment. These are events in the situation of the factor of reference which intentionally alter his situation (or threaten to) to his disadvantage, whatever in specific content these alterations may be.

Power, then, is generalized capacity to secure the performance of binding obligations by units in a system of collective organization when the obligations are legitimized with reference to their bearing on collective goals and where in case of recalcitrance there is a presumption of enforcement by negative situational sanctions—whatever the actual agency of that enforcement.

It will be noted that I have used the conceptions of generalization and of legitimation in defining power. Securing possession of an object of utility by bartering another object for it is not a monetary transaction. Similarly, by my definition, securing compliance with a wish, whether it be defined as an obligation of the object or not, simply by threat of superior force, is not an exercise of power. I am well aware that most political theorists would draw the line differently and classify this as power (e.g. Dahl's definition), but I wish to stick to my chosen line and explore its implications. The capacity to secure compliance must, if it is to be called power in my sense, be generalized and not solely a function of one particular sanctioning act that the user is in a position to impose,[15] and the medium used must be "symbolic."

Secondly, I have spoken of power as involving legitimation. This is, in the present context, the necessary consequence of conceiving power as "symbolic," which therefore, if it is exchanged for something intrinsically valuable for collective effectiveness, namely compliance with an obligation, leaves the recipient, the performer of the obligation, with "nothing of value." This is to say, that he has "nothing" but a set of expectations, namely that in other contexts and on other occasions, he can invoke certain obligations of the part of other units. Legitimation is, therefore, in power systems, the factor that is parallel to confidence in mutual acceptability and stability of the monetary unit in monetary systems.

The two criteria are connected, in that questioning the legitimacy of the possession and use of power leads to resort to progressively more "secure" means of gaining compliance. These must be progressively more effective "intrinsically," hence more tailored to the particular situations of the objects and less general. Furthermore, insofar as they are intrinsically effective, legitimacy becomes a progressively less important factor of their effectiveness—at the end of this series lies resort, first to various types of coercion, eventually to the use of force as the most intrinsically effective of all means of coercion.[16]

I should like now to attempt to place both money and power in the context of a more general paradigm, which is an analytical classification of ways in which, in the processes of social interaction, the actions of one unit in a system can intentionally be oriented to bringing about a change in what the actions of one or more other units would otherwise have been—thus all fitting into the context of Dahl's conception of power. It is convenient to state this in terms of the convention of speaking of the acting unit of reference—individual or collective—as *ego*, and the object on which he attempts to "operate" as *alter*. We may then classify the alternatives open to ego in terms of two dichotomous variables. On the one hand ego may attempt to gain his end from alter either by using

[15] There is a certain element of generality in physical force as a negative sanction, which gives it a special place in power systems. This will be taken up later in the discussion.

[16] There are complications here deriving from the fact that power is associated with *negative* sanctions and hence that, in the face of severe resistance, their effectiveness is confined to deterrence.

some form of control over the situation in which alter is placed, actually or contingently to change it so as to increase the probability of alter acting in the way he wishes, or, alternatively, without attempting to change alter's situation, ego may attempt to change alter's intentions, i.e. he may manipulate symbols that are meaningful to alter to such a way that he tries to make alter "see" that what ego wants is a "good thing" for him (alter) to do.

The second variable, then, concerns the type of sanctions ego may employ in attempting to guarantee the attainment of his end from alter. The dichotomy here is between positive and negative sanctions. Thus through the situational channel a positive sanction is a change in alter's situation presumptively considered by alter as to his advantage, which is used as a means by ego of having an effect on alter's actions. A negative sanction then is an alteration in alter's situation to the latter's disadvantage. In the case of the intentional channel, the positive sanction is the expression of symbolic "reasons" why compliance with ego's wishes is "a good thing" independently of any further action on ego's part, from alter's point of view, i.e. would be felt by him to be "personally advantageous," whereas the negative sanction is presenting reasons why non-compliance with ego's wishes should be felt by alter to be harmful to interests in which he had a significant personal investment, and should therefore be avoided. I should like to call the four types of "strategy" open to ego respectively (1) for the situational channel, positive sanction case, "inducement"; (2) situational channel, negative sanction, "coercion"; (3) intentional channel, positive sanction, "persuasion"; and (4) intentional channel, negative sanction, "activation of commitments"; as shown in the following table:

		Channel	
		Situational	*Intentional*
Sanction type	*Positive*	1 Inducement	3 Persuasion
	Negative	2 Coercion	4 Activation of Commitments

A further complication now needs to be introduced. We think of a sanction as an intentional act on ego's part, expected by him to change his relation to alter from what it would otherwise have been. As a means of bringing about a change in alter's action, it can operate most obviously where the actual imposition of the sanction is made contingent on a future decision by alter. Thus a process of inducement will operate in two stages, first contingent offer on ego's part that, if alter will "comply" with his wishes, ego will "reward" him by the contingently promised situational change. If then alter in fact does comply, ego will perform the sanctioning act. In the case of coercion the first stage is a contingent threat that, unless alter decides to comply, ego will impose the negative sanction. If, however, alter complies, then nothing further happens, but, if he decides on noncompliance, then ego must carry out his threat, or be in a position of "not meaning it." In the cases of the intentional channel ego's first-stage act is either to predict the occurrence, or to announce his own intention of doing something that affects alter's sentiments or interests. The element of contingency enters, in that ego "argues" to alter that if this happens, on the one hand alter should be expected to "see" that it would be a good thing for him to do what ego wants—the positive case—or that if he fails to do it it would imply an important "subjective cost" to alter. In the positive case, beyond "pointing out" if alter complies, ego is obligated to deliver the positive attitudinal sanction of approval. In the negative case, the corresponding attitudinal sanction of disapproval is implemented only for noncompliance.

It is hence clear that there is a basic asymmetry between the positive and negative sides of the sanction aspect of the paradigm. This is that, in the cases of inducement and persuasion, alter's compliance obligates ego to "deliver" his promised positive sanction, in the former case the promised advantages, in the latter his approval of alter's "good sense" in recognizing that the decision wished for by ego and accepted as "good" by alter, in fact turns out to be good from alter's point of view. In the negative cases, on the other hand, compliance on alter's part obligates ego, in the situational case, not to carry out his threat, in the intentional case by withholding disapproval to confirm to alter that his compliance did in fact spare him what to him, without ego's intervention, would have been the undesirable subjective consequences of his previous intentions, namely guilt over violations of his commitments.

Finally, alter's freedom of action in his decisions of compliance versus noncompliance is also a variable. This range has a lower limit at which the element of contingency disappears. That is, from ego's point of view, he may not say, if you do so and so, I will intervene, either by situational manipulations or by "arguments" in such and such a way, but he may simply perform an overt act and face alter with a *fait accompli*. In the case of inducement, a gift which is an object of value, and with respect to the acceptance of which alter is given no option, is the limiting case. With respect to coercion, compulsion, that is, simply imposing a disadvantageous alteration on alter's situation and then leaving it to alter to decide whether to "do something about it," is the limiting case.

The asymmetry just referred to appears here as well. As contingent it may be said that the primary meaning of negative sanctions is as means of prevention. If they are effective, no further action is required. The case of compulsion is that in which it is rendered impossible for alter to avoid the undesired action on ego's part. In the case of positive sanctions of course ego, for example in making a gift to alter, cuts himself off from benefiting from alter's performance which is presumptively advantageous to him, in the particular exchange.

Both, however, may be oriented to their effect on alter's action in future sequences of interaction. The object of compulsion may have been "taught a lesson" and hence be less disposed to noncompliance with ego's wishes in the future, as well as prevented from performance of a particular undesired act and the recipient of a gift may feel a "sense of obligation" to reciprocate in some form in the future.

So far this discussion has dealt with sanctioning acts in terms of their "intrinsic" significance both to ego and to alter. An offered inducement may thus be possession of a particular object of utility, a coercive threat, that of a particular feared loss, or other noxious experience. But just as, in the initial phase of a sequence, ego transmits his contingent intentions to alter symbolically through communication, so the sanction involved may also be symbolic, e.g. in place of possession of certain intrinsically valuable goods he may offer a sum of money. What we have called the generalized media of interaction then may be used as types of sanctions which may be analyzed in terms of the above paradigm. The factors of generalization and of legitimation of institutionalism, however, as discussed above, introduce certain complications which we must now take up with reference to power. There is a sense in which power may be regarded as the generalized medium of coercion in the above terms, but this formula at the very least requires very careful interpretation— indeed it will turn out by itself to be inadequate.

I spoke above of the "grounding" of the value of money in the commodity value of the monetary metal, and suggested that there is a corresponding relation of the "value," i.e. the effectiveness of power, to the intrinsic effectiveness of physical force as a means of coercion and, in the limiting case, compulsion.[17]

In interpreting this formula due account must be taken of the asymmetry just discussed. The special place of gold as a monetary base rests on such properties as its durability, high value in small bulk, etc., and high probability of acceptability in exchange, i.e. as means of inducement, in a very wide variety of conditions which are not dependent on an institutionalized order. Ego's primary aim in resorting to compulsion or coercion, however, is deterrence of unwanted action on alter's part.[18] Force, therefore, is in the first instance important as the "ultimate" deterrent. It is the means that, again independent of any institutionalized system of order, can be assumed to be "intrinsically" the most effec-

---

[17] I owe the insight into this parallel to Professor Karl Deutsch of Harvard University (personal discussion).

[18] "Sadistic" infliction of injury without instrumental significance to ego does not belong in this context.

tive in the context of deterrence, when means of effectiveness which *are* dependent on institutionalized order are insecure or fail. Therefore, the unit of an action system which commands control of physical force adequate to cope with any potential counter threats of force is more secure than any other in a Hobbesian state of nature.[19]

But just as a monetary system resting entirely on gold as the actual medium of exchange is a very primitive one that simply cannot mediate a complex system of market exchange, so a power system in which the only negative sanction is the threat of force is a very primitive one which cannot function to mediate a complex system of organizational coordination—it is far too "blunt" an instrument. Money cannot be only an intrinsically valuable entity if it is to serve as a generalized medium of inducement, but it must, as we have said, be institutionalized as a symbol; it must be legitimized, and must inspire "confidence" within the system —and must also within limits be deliberately managed. Similarly power cannot be only an intrinsically effective deterrent; if it is to be the generalized medium of mobilizing resources for effective collective action and for the fulfillment of commitments made by collectivities to those we have here called their constituents, it too must be both symbolically generalized and legitimized.

There is a direct connection between the concept of bindingness, as introduced above, and deterrence. To treat a commitment or any other form of expectation as binding is to attribute a special importance to its fulfillment. Where it is not a matter simply of maintenance of an established routine, but of undertaking new actions in changed circumstances, where the commitment is thus to undertake types of action contingent on circumstances as they develop, then the risk to be minimized is that such contingent commitments will not be carried out when the circumstances in question appear. Treating the expectation or obligation as binding is almost the same thing as saying that appropriate steps on the other side must be taken to prevent nonfulfillment, if possible. Willingness to impose negative sanctions is, seen in this light, simply the carrying out of the implications of treating commitments as binding, and the agent invoking them "meaning it" or being prepared to insist.

On the other hand, there are areas in interaction systems where there is a range of alternatives, choice among which is optional, in the light of the promised advantageousness, situational or "intentional," of one as compared to other choices. Positive sanctions as here conceived constitute a contingent increment of relative advantageousness, situational or intentional, of the alternative ego desires alter to choose.

---

[19] I have attempted to develop this line of analysis of the significance of force somewhat more fully in "Some Reflections of the Role of Force in Social Relations," first published in Harry Eckstein, ed., *The Problem of Internal War* (Princeton, N.J.: Princeton University Press, 1963), reprinted in my *Sociological Theory and Modern Society,* Chapter 9.

If, in these latter areas, a generalized, symbolic medium is to operate in place of intrinsic advantages, there must be an element of bindingness in the institutionalization of the medium itself—e.g. the fact that the money of a society is "legal tender" which must be accepted in the settlement of debts that have the status of contractual obligations under the law. In the case of money, I suggest that, for the typical acting unit in a market system, what specific undertakings he enters into is overwhelmingly optional in the above sense, but whether the money involved in the transactions is or is not "good" is not for him to judge, but his acceptance of it is binding. Essentially the same is true of the contractual obligations, typically linking monetary and intrinsic utilities, that he undertakes.

I would now like to suggest that what is in a certain sense the obverse holds true of power. Its "intrinsic" importance lies in its capacity to ensure that obligations are "really" binding, thus if necessary can be "enforced" by negative sanctions. But for power to function as a generalized medium in a complex system, that is, to mobilize resources effectively for collective action, it must be "legitimized," which in the present context means that in certain respects compliance, which is the common factor among our media, is not binding, to say nothing of being coerced, but is optional. The range within which there exists a continuous system of interlocking binding obligations is essentially that of the internal relations of an organized collectivity in our sense, and of the contractual obligations undertaken on its behalf at its boundaries.

The points at which the optional factors come to bear are, in the boundary relations of the collectivity, where factors of importance for collective functioning other than binding obligations are exchanged for such binding commitments on the part of the collectivity and *vice versa,* nonbinding outputs of the collectivity for binding commitments to it. These "optional" inputs, I have suggested above, are control of productivity of the economy at one boundary, influence through the relations between leadership and the public demands at the other.[20]

This is a point at which the dissociation of the concept of polity from exclusive relation to government becomes particularly important. In a sufficiently differentiated society, the boundary-relations of the great majority of its important units of collective organization (including some boundaries of government) are boundaries where the overwhelming majority of decisions of commitment are optional in the above sense, though once made, their fulfillment is binding. This, however, is only possible effectively within the range of a sufficiently stable, institutionalized normative order so that the requisite degrees of freedom are pro-

---

[20] Thus, if control of productivity operates through monetary funds, their possessor cannot "force," e.g., prospective employees to accept employment.

tected, e.g. in the fields of employment and of the promotion of interest-demands and decisions about political support.

This feature of the boundary relations of a particular political unit holds even for cases of local government, in that decisions of residence, employment, or acquisition of property within a particular jurisdiction involve the optional element, since in all these respects there is a relatively free choice among local jurisdictions, even though, once having chosen, the citizen is, for example, subject to the tax policies applying within it—and of course he cannot escape being subject to any local jurisdiction, but must choose among those available.

In the case of a "national" political organization, however, its territorial boundaries ordinarily coincide with a relative break in the normative order regulating social interaction.[21] Hence across such boundaries an ambiguity becomes involved in the exercise of power in our sense. On the one hand the invoking of binding obligations operates normally without explicit use of coercion within certain ranges where the two territorial collectivity systems have institutionalized their relations. Thus travelers in friendly foreign countries can ordinarily enjoy personal security and the amenities of the principal public accommodations, exchange of their money at "going" rates, etc. Where, on the other hand, the more general relations between national collectivities are at issue, the power system is especially vulnerable to the kind of insecurity of expectations that tends to be met by the explicit resort to threat of coercive sanctions. Such threats in turn, operating on both sides of a reciprocal relationship, readily enter into a vicious circle of resort to more and more "intrinsically" effective or drastic measures of coercion, at the end of which road lies physical force. In other words, the danger of war is endemic in uninstitutionalized relations between territorially organized collectivities.

There is thus an inherent relation between both the use and the control of force and the territorial basis of organization.[22] One central condition of the integration of a power system is that it should be effective within a territorial area, and a crucial condition of this effectiveness in turn is the monopoly of control of paramount force within the area. The critical point then, at which the institutional integration of power systems is most vulnerable to strain, and to degeneration into reciprocating threats of the use of force, is between territorially organized political systems. This, notoriously, is the weakest point in the normative order of human society today, as it has been almost from time immemorial.

[21] This, of course, is a relative difference. Some hazards increase the moment one steps outside his own home, police protection may be better in one local community than the next, and crossing a state boundary may mean a considerable difference in legal or actual rights.

[22] *Cf.* my paper "The Principal Structures of Community," *Nomos* 2 and *Structure and Process, op. cit.*, Chapter 8. See also J. W. Hurst, *Law and Social Process in the United States* (Ann Arbor: University of Michigan Law School, 1960).

In this connection it should be recognized that the possession, the mutual threat, and possible use of force is only in a most proximate sense the principal "cause" of war. The essential point is that the "bottleneck" of mutual regression to more and more primitive means of protecting or advancing collective interests is a "channel" into which all elements of tension between the collective units in question may flow. It is a question of the many levels at which such elements of tension may on the one hand build up, on the other be controlled, not of any simple and unequivocal conception of the "inherent" consequences of the possession and possible uses of organized force.

It should be clear that again there is a direct parallel with the economic case. A functioning market system requires integration of the monetary medium. It cannot be a system of N independent monetary units and agencies controlling them. This is the basis on which the main range of extension of a relatively integrated market system tends to coincide with the "politically organized society," as Roscoe Pound called it, over a territorial area. International transactions require special provisions not required for domestic.

The basic "management" of the monetary system must then be integrated with the institutionalization of political power. Just as the latter depends on an effective monopoly of institutionally organized force, so monetary stability depends on an effective monopoly of basic reserves protecting the monetary unit and, as we shall see later, on centralization of control over the credit system.

THE HIERARCHICAL ASPECTS
OF POWER SYSTEMS

A very critical question now arises, which may be stated in terms of a crucial difference between money and power. Money is a "measure of value," as the classical economists put it, in terms of a continuous linear variable. Objects of utility valued in money are more or less valuable than each other in numerically statable terms. Similarly, as medium of exchange, amounts of money differ in the same single dimension. One acting unit in a society has more money—or assets exchangeable for money—than another, less than, or the same.

Power involves a quite different dimension which may be formulated in terms of the conception that A may have power over B. Of course, in competitive bidding the holder of superior financial assets has an advantage in that, as economists say, the "marginal utility of money" is less to him than to his competitor with smaller assets. But his "bid" is no more binding on the potential exchange partner than is that of the less affluent bidder, since in "purchasing power" all dollars are "created free and equal." There may be auxiliary reasons why the purveyor may think it advisable to accept the bid of the more affluent bidder; these, however, are not strictly economic, but concern the interrelations between money and other media, and other bases of status in the system.

The connection between the value of effectiveness—as distinguished from utility—and bindingness, implies a conception in turn of the focussing of responsibility for decisions, and hence of authority for their implementation.[23] This implies a special form of inequality of power which in turn implies a priority system of commitments. The implications of having assumed binding commitments, on the fulfillment of which spokesmen for the collectivity are prepared to insist to the point of imposing serious negative sanctions for noncompliance, are of an order of seriousness such that matching the priority system in the commitments themselves there must be priorities in the matter of which decisions take precedence over others, and, back of that, of which decision-making agencies have the right to make decisions at what levels. Throughout this discussion the crucial question concerns bindingness. The reference is to the collectivity, and hence the strategic significance of the various "contributions" on the performance of which the effectiveness of its action depends. Effectiveness for the collectivity as a whole is dependent on hierarchical ordering of the relative strategic importance of these contributions, and hence of the conditions governing the imposition of binding obligations on the contributors.

Hence the power of A over B is, in its legitimized form, the "right" of A, as a decision-making unit involved in collective process, to make decisions that take precedence over those of B, in the interests of the effectiveness of the collective operation as a whole.

The right to use power, or negative sanctions on a barter basis or even compulsion to assert priority of a decision over others, I shall, following Barnard, call authority. Precedence in this sense can take different forms. The most serious ambiguity here seems to derive from the assumption that authority and its attendant power may be understood as implying opposition to the wishes of "lower-order" echelons which hence includes the prerogative of coercing or compelling compliance. Though this is implicit, it may be that the higher-order authority and power may imply the prerogative is primarily significant as "defining the situation" for the performance of the lower-order echelons. The higher "authority" may then make a decision which defines terms within which other units in the collectivity will be expected to act, and this expectation is treated as binding. Thus a ruling by the Commissioner of Internal Revenue may exclude certain tax exemptions which units under his jurisdiction have

23 As already noted, in this area, I think the analysis of Chester I. Barnard, in *The Functions of the Executive, op. cit.*, is so outstandingly clear and cogent that it deserves the status of a classic of political theory in my specific sense. See especially Chapter X.

thought taxpayers could claim. Such a decision need not activate an overt conflict between commissioner and taxpayer, but may rather "channel" the decisions of revenue agents and taxpayers with reference to performance of obligations.

There does not seem to be an essential theoretical difficulty involved in this "ambiguity." We can say that the primary function of superior authority is clearly to define the situation for the lower echelons of the collectivity. The problem of overcoming opposition in the form of dispositions to noncompliance then arises from the incomplete institutionalization of the power of the higher authority holder. Sources of this may well include overstepping of the bounds of his legitimate authority on the part of this agent. The concept of compliance clearly should not be limited to "obedience" by subordinates, but is just as importantly applicable to observance of the normative order by the high echelons of authority and power. The concept of constitutionalism is the critical one at this level, namely, that even the highest authority is bound, in the strict sense of the concept bindingness used here, by the terms of the normative order under which he operates, e.g. holds office. Hence binding obligations can clearly be "invoked" by lower-order against higher-order agencies as well as *vice versa*.

This of course implies the relatively firm institutionalization of the normative order itself. Within the framework of a highly differentiated polity it implies, in addition to constitutionalism itself, a procedural system for the granting of high political authority, even in private, to say nothing of public organizations, and a legal framework within which such authority is legitimized. This in turn includes another order of procedural institutions within which the question of the legality of actual uses of power can be tested.

POWER AND AUTHORITY

The institutionalization of the normative order just referred to thus comes to focus in the concept of authority. Authority is essentially the institutional code within which the use of power as medium is organized and legitimized. It stands to power essentially as property, as an institution, does to money. Property is a bundle of rights of possession, including above all that of alienation, but also at various levels of control and use. In a highly differentiated institutional system, property rights are focussed on the valuation of utility, i.e. the economic significance of the objects, e.g. for consumption or as factors of production, and this factor comes to be differentiated from authority. Thus, in European feudalism the "landlord" had both property rights in the land, and political jurisdiction over persons acting on the same land. In modern legal systems these components are differentiated from each other so the landowner is no longer the landlord: this function is taken over mainly by local political authority.

Precisely with greater differentiation the focus of the institution becomes more generalized, and while specific objects of possession of course continue to be highly important, the most important object of property comes to be monetary assets, and specific objects are valued as assets, i.e., in terms of potentials of marketability. Today we can say that rights to money assets, the ways in which these can be legitimately acquired and disposed of, the ways in which the interests of other parties must be protected, have come to constitute the core of the institution of property.[24]

Authority, then, is the aspect of a status in a system of social organization, namely its collective aspect, by virtue of which the incumbent is put in a position legitimately to make decisions that are binding, not only on himself but on the collectivity as a whole and hence its other member-units, in the sense that so far as their implications impinge on their respective roles and statuses, they are bound to act in accordance with these implications. This includes the right to insist on such action though, because of the general division of labor, the holder of authority very often is not himself in a position to "enforce" his decisions, but must be dependent on specialized agencies for this.

If, then, authority be conceived as the institutional counterpart of power, the main difference lies in the fact that authority is not a circulating medium. Sometimes, speaking loosely, we suggest that someone "gives away his property." He can give away property rights in specific possessions but not the institution of property. Similarly, the incumbent of an office can relinquish authority by resigning, but this is very different from abolishing the authority of the office. Property as institution is a code defining rights in objects of possession, in the first instance physical objects, then "symbolic" objects, including cultural objects such as "ideas" insofar as they are valuable in monetary terms, and of course including money itself, whoever possesses them. Authority, similarly, is a set of rights in status in a collectivity, precisely in the collectivity as actor, including most especially rights to acquire and use power in that status.

The institutional stability, which is essential to the conception of a code, then for property inheres in the institutional structure of the market. At a higher level the institution of property includes rights, not only to use and dispose of particular objects of value, but to participate in the system of market transactions.

[24] Two particularly important manifestations of this monetization of property are, first, the general legal understanding that executors of estates are not obligated to retain the exact physical inventory intact pending full settlement, but may sell various items—their fiduciary obligation is focussed on the money value of the estate. Similarly, in the law of contract increasing option has been given to compensate with money damages in lieu of the specific "performance" originally contracted for.

It is, then, essentially the institutionalized code defining rights of participation in the power system which I should like to think of as authority. It is this conception which gives us the basis for the essential distinction between the internal and the external aspects of power relative to a particular collectivity. The collectivity is, by our conception, the definition of the range within which a system of institutionalized rights to hold and use power can be closed. This is to say, the implications of an authoritative decision made at one point in the system can be made genuinely binding at all the other relevant points through the relevant processes of feed-back.

The hierarchical priority system of authority and power, with which this discussion started, by this criterion can only be binding within a given particular collective system. In this sense, then, a hierarchy of authority—as distinguished from the sheer differences of power or other coercive capacities—must be internal to a collectively organized system in this sense. This will include authority to bind the collectivity in its relations to its environment, to persons, and to other collectivities. But bindingness, legitimized and enforced through the agency of this particular collectivity, cannot be extended beyond its boundaries. If it exists at all it must be by virtue of an institutionalized normative order that transcends the particular collectivity, through contractual arrangements with others, or through other types of mutually binding obligation.

POWER, INFLUENCE, EQUALIZATION, AND SOLIDARITY

It is on this basis that it may be held that at the boundaries of the collectivity the closed system of priorities is breached by "free" exercise, at the constituency or integrative boundary, of influence. Status in the collectivity gives authority to settle the terms on which power will be exchanged with influence over this boundary. The wielder of influence from outside on the collectivity is not bound in advance to any particular terms, and it is of the essence of use of power in the "foreign relations" of the collectivity that authority is a right, within certain limits of discretion, to spend power in exchange for influence. This in turn can, through the offer of accepting leadership responsibility in exchange for political support, replenish the expenditure of power by a corresponding input.

By this reasoning influence should be capable of altering the priority system within the collectivity. This is what I interpret policy decision as a category of the use of power as a medium to be: the process of altering priorities in such a way that the new pattern comes to be binding on the collectivity. Similarly, the franchise must be regarded as the institutionalization of a marginal, interpenetrating status, between the main collectivity and its environment of solidary groupings in the larger system.

It is the institutionalization of a marginal authority, the use of which is confined to the function of selection among candidates for leadership responsibility. In the governmental case, this is the inclusion in a common collectivity system of both the operative agencies of government and the "constituencies" on which leadership is dependent, a grant not only in a given instance of power to the latter but to a status of authority with respect to the one crucial function of selection of leadership and granting them the authority of office.

In interpreting this discussion it is essential to keep in mind that a society consists, from the present point of view, not in one collectivity, but in a ramified system of collectivities. Because, however, of the basic imperatives of effective collective action already discussed, these must, in addition to the pluralistic cross-cutting that goes with functional differentiation, also have the aspect of a "Chinese box" relation. There must be somewhere a paramount focus of collective authority, and with it of the control of power—though it is crucial that this need not be the top of the total system of normative control, which may for example be religious. The complex of territoriality and the monopoly of force are central to this, because the closed system of enforceable bindingness can always be breached by the intervention of force.[25]

The bindingness of normative orders other than those upheld by the paramount territorial collectivity must be defined within limits institutionalized in relation to it. So far as such collectivities are not "agencies" of the state, in this sense, their spheres of "jurisdiction" must be defined in terms of a normative system, a body of law, which is binding both on government and on the nongovernmental collectivity units, though in the "last analysis" it will, within an institutionalized order, either have to be enforced by government, or contrariwise by revolutionary action against government.

Since independent control of serious, socially organized force cannot be given to "private" collectivities, their ultimate negative sanctions tend to be expulsion from membership, though many other types of sanction may be highly important.

Considerations such as these thus do not in any way eliminate or weaken the importance of hierarchical priorities within a collective decision-system itself. The strict "line" structure of such authority is, however, greatly modified by the interpretation of other systems with the political, notably, for our purposes, the importance of technical competence. The qualifications of the importance of hierarchy apply in principle at the boundaries of the particular collective system—analytically consi-

[25] Since this system is the territorially organized collectivity, the state with its government, these considerations underlie the critical importance of foreign relations in the sense of the relations to other territorially organized, force-controlling collectivities, since, once internal control of force is effectively institutionalized, the danger of this kind of breach comes from the outside in this specific sense of outside. The point is cogently made by Raymond Aron.

dered—rather than internally to it. These I would interpret as defining the limits of authority. There are two main contexts in which norms of equality may be expected to modify the concrete expectations of hierarchical decision-systems, namely, on the one hand, the context of influence over the right to assume power, or decision-making authority, and, on the other hand, the context of access of opportunity for status as a contributing unit in the specific political system in question.

It is essential here to recall that I have treated power as a circulating medium, moving back and forth over the boundaries of the polity. The "real" outputs of the political process, and the factors in its effectiveness —in the sense corresponding to the real outputs and factors of economic production—are not in my sense "forms" of power but, in the most important cases, of financial control of economic resources, of money, and of influence, in the meaning of the category of influence, defined as a generalized mechanism of persuasion. These are very essential elements in the total political process, but it is just as important to distinguish them from power as it is to distinguish financially valuable outputs and factors of production from money itself. They may, in certain circumstances, be exchangeable for power, but this is a very different thing from being forms of power.

The circulation of power between polity and integrative system I conceive to consist in binding policy decisions on the one hand, which is a primary factor in the integrative process, and political support on the other, which is a primary output of the integrative process. Support is exchanged, by a "public" or constituency, for the assumption of leadership responsibility, through the process of persuading those in a position to give binding support that it is advisable to do so in the particular instance—through the use of influence or some less generalized means of persuasion. In the other political "market" vis-à-vis the integrative system, policy decisions are given in response to interest-demands in the sense of the above discussion. This is to say that interest groups, which, it is most important to note as a concept says nothing about the moral quality of the particular interest, attempt to persuade those who hold authority in the relevant collectivity, i.e. are in a position to make binding decisions, that they should indeed commit the collectivity to the policies the influence-wielders want. In our terms this is to persuade the decision makers to use and hence "spend" some of their power for the purpose in hand. The spending of power is to be thought of, just as the spending of money, as essentially consisting in the sacrifice of alternative decisions which are precluded by the commitments undertaken under a policy. A member of the collectivity we conceive as noted to have authority to "spend" power through making binding decisions through which those outside acquire claims against the collectivity. Its authority, however, is inalienable; it can only be exercised, not "spent."

It has been suggested that policies must be hierarchically ordered in a priority system and that the power to decide among policies must have a corresponding hierarchical ordering since such decisions bind the collectivity and its constituent units. The imperative of hierarchy does not, however, apply to the other "market" of the power system in this direction, that involving the relations between leadership and political support. Here, on the contrary, it is a critically important fact that in the largest-scale and most highly differentiated systems, namely the leadership systems of the most "advanced" national societies, the power element has been systematically equalized through the device of the franchise, so that the universal adult franchise has been evolved in all the Western democracies.[26] Equality of the franchise which, since the consequences of its exercise are very strictly binding,[27] I classify as in fact a form of power, has been part of a larger complex of its institutionalization, which includes in addition the principle of universality—its extension to all responsible adult citizens in good standing, and the secrecy of the ballot, which serves to differentiate this context of political action from other contexts of involvement, and protect it against pressures, not only from hierarchical superiors, but, as Rokkan points out, from status-peers as well.

Of course the same basic principle of one member, one vote, is institutionalized in a vast number of voluntary associations, including many that are subassociations of wider collectivities, such as faculties in a university, or boards and committees. Thus the difference between a chairman or presiding officer, and an executive head is clearly marked with respect to formal authority, whatever it may be with respect to influence, by the principle that a chairman, like any other member, has only one vote. Many collectivities are in this sense "truncated" associations, e.g. in cases where fiduciary boards are self-recruiting. Nevertheless the importance of this principle of equality of power through the franchise is so great empirically that the question of how it is grounded in the structure of social systems is a crucial one.

It derives, I think, from what I should call the universalistic component in patterns of normative order. It is the value-principle that discrimination among units of a system must be grounded in intrinsically valued differences among them, which are, for both persons and collectivities, capacities to contribute to valued societal processes. Differences of power in decision-making that mobilizes commitments, both outward in relation to the environment of the collectivity and internally, to the assignment of tasks to its members, are ideally grounded in the intrinsic conditions of effectiveness. Similarly, differences on the basis of

---

[26] See, on this process, Stein Rokkan, "Mass Suffrage, Secret Voting, and Political Participation," *European Journal of Sociology*, 2 (1961), 132–152.

[27] I.e., the aggregate of votes, evaluated by the electoral rules, determines the incumbency of office.

technical competence to fulfill essential roles are grounded in the strategic conditions of effective contribution.

These considerations do not, however, apply to the functions of the choice of leadership, where this choice has been freed from ascriptive bases of right, e.g. through kinship status or some imputed "charismatic" superiority, as in such a case as "white supremacy." There is a persistent pressure of the sufficiently highly valued functions or outcomes, and under this pressure there seems to have been a continual, though uneven, process of erosion of discriminations in this critical field of the distribution of power.

It may be suggested that the principle of universalistic normative organization which is immediately superordinate to that of political democracy in the sense of the universal equal franchise, is the principle of equality before the law; in the case of the American Constitution, the principle of equal protection of the laws. I have emphasized that a constitutional framework is essential to advanced collective organization, given, of course, levels of scale and complexity which preclude purely "informal" and traditional normative regulation. The principle in effect puts the burden of proof on the side of imposing discriminations, either in access to rights or in imposition of obligations, on the side that such discriminations are to be justified only by differences in sufficiently highly valued exigencies of operation of the system.

The principle of equality, both at the level of application of the law and of the political franchise, is clearly related to a conception of the status of membership. Not all living adults have equal rights to influence the affairs of all collectivities everywhere in the world, nor does an American have equal rights with a citizen of a quite different society within its territory. Membership is in fact the application to the individual unit of the concept of boundary of a social system that has the property of solidarity, in Durkheim's sense. The equal franchise is a prerogative of members, and of course the criteria of membership can be very differently institutionalized under different circumstances.

There is an important sense in which the double interchange system under consideration here, which I have called the "support" system linking the polity with the integrative aspect of the society, is precisely the system in which power is most directly controlled, both in relation to more particularized interest-elements that seek relatively particularized policies—which, of course, includes wanting to prevent certain potential actions—and in relation to the more general "tone" given to the directionality of collective action by the character of the leadership elements that assume responsibility and that, in exchange, are invested, in the type case by the electoral process, with authority to carry out their responsibilities. One central feature of this control is coming to terms with the hierarchical elements inherent in power systems in the aspects just discussed. Certain value systems may, of course, reinforce hierarchy, but it would be my view that a universalistically oriented value system inherently tends to counteract the spread of hierarchical patterns with respect to power beyond the range felt to be functionally necessary for effectiveness.[28]

There is, however, a crucial link between the equality of the franchise and the hierarchical structure of authority within collectivities, namely the all-or-none character of the electoral process. Every voter has an equal vote in electing to an office, but in most cases only one candidate is in fact elected—the authority of office is not divided among candidates in proportion to the numbers of votes they received, but is concentrated in the successful candidate, even though the margin be very narrow, as in the U.S. presidential election of 1960. There are, of course, considerable possible variations in electoral rules, but this basic principle is as central as is that of the equality of the franchise. This principle seems to be the obverse of the hierarchy of authority.

The hierarchical character of power systems has above been sharply contrasted with the linear quantitative character of wealth and monetary assets. This has in turn been related to the fundamental difference between the exigencies of effectiveness in collective action, and the exigencies of utility in providing for the requirements of satisfying the "wants" of units. In order to place the foregoing discussion of the relations between power and influence in a comparable theoretical context, it is necessary to formulate the value-standard which is paramount in regulating the integrative function which corresponds to utility and effectiveness in the economic and political functions respectively.

This is, with little doubt, the famous concept of solidarity as formulated by Durkheim.[29] The two essential points of reference for present purposes concern the two main aspects of membership, as outlined above, the first of which concerns claims on executive authority for policy decisions which integrate the total collective interest on the one hand, the "partial" interest of a subgroup on the other. The second concerns integration of rights to a "voice" in collective affairs with the exigencies of effective leadership and the corresponding responsibility.

[28] Of course where conditions are sufficiently simple, or where there is sufficient anxiety about the hierarchal implications of power, the egalitarian element may penetrate far into the political decision-making system itself, with, e.g. insistence that policy-decisions, both external and internal in reference, be made by majority vote of all members, or even under a unanimity rule. The respects in which such a system—which of course realistically often involves a sharply hierarchical stratification of influence—is incompatible with effectiveness in many spheres, can be said to be relatively clear, especially for *large* collectivities.

[29] It is the central concept of *The Division of Labor in Society*. For my own relatively recent understanding of its significance, see "Durkheim's Contribution to the Theory of Integration of Social Systems," in Kurt Wolff, ed., *Émile Durkheim, 1858–1917* (Columbus, Ohio: State University Press, 1960), pp. 118–153, reprinted in Talcott Parsons, *Sociological Theory and Modern Society* (N.Y: The Free Press, 1968).

The principle is the "grounding" of a collective system in a consensus in the sense of the above discussion, namely an "acceptance" on the part of its members of their belonging together, in the sense of sharing, over a certain range, common interests—interests that are defined both by type and by consideration of time. Time becomes relevant because of the uncertainty factor in all human action, and hence the fact that neither benefits nor burdens can be precisely predicted and planned for in advance; hence an effective collectivity must be prepared to absorb unexpected burdens, and to balance this, to carry out some sort of just distribution of benefits which are unexpected and/or are not attributable to the earned agency of any particular subunit.

Solidarity may then be thought of as the implementation of common values by definition of the requisite collective systems in which they are to be actualized. Collective action as such we have defined as political function. The famous problem of order, however, cannot be solved without a common normative system. Solidarity is the principle by virtue of which the commitment to norms, which is "based" in turn on values, is articulated with the formation of collectivities that are capable of effective collective action. Whereas, in the economic direction, the "problem" of effective action is coping with the scarcity of available resources, including trying to facilitate their mobility, in the integrative direction it is orderly solution of competing claims, on the one hand to receive benefits—or minimize losses—deriving from memberships, on the other to influence the processes by which collective action operates. This clearly involves some institutionalization of the subordination of unit-interest to the collective in cases where the two are in conflict, actual or potential, and hence the justification of unit interests as compatible with the more extensive collective interest. A social system then possesses solidarity in proportion as its members are committed to common interests through which discrete unit interests can be integrated and the justification of conflict resolution and subordination can be defined and implemented. It defines, not the modes of implementation of these common interests through effective agency, but the standards by which such agency should be guided and the rights of various constituent elements to have a voice in the interpretation of these standards.

POWER AND
EQUALITY OF OPPORTUNITY

We may now turn to the second major boundary of the polity, at which another order of modifications of the internal hierarchy of authority comes to focus. This is the boundary vis-à-vis the economy where the "political" interest is to secure control of productivity and services, and the economic interest lies in the collective control of fluid resources and in what we may call opportunity for effectiveness. I shall not attempt here to discuss the whole interchange complex, but will confine myself to the crucial problem of the way that here also the hierarchical structure of power can, under certain conditions, be modified in an egalitarian direction.

Productivity of the economy is in principle allocable among collective (in our sense political) claimants to its control as facilities, in linear quantitative terms. This linear quantification is achieved through the medium of money, either allocation of funds with liberty to expend them at will, or at least monetary evaluation of more specific facilities.

In a sufficiently developed system, services must be evaluated in monetary terms also, both from the point of view of rational budgeting and of the monetary cost of their employment. In terms of their utilization, however, services are "packages" of performance-capacity, which are qualitatively distinct and of unequal value as contributions to collective effectiveness. Their evaluation as facilities must hence involve an estimate of strategic significance that matches the general priority scale that has been established to regulate the internal functioning of the collectivity.

Services, however, constitute a resource to be acquired from outside the collectivity, as Weber puts it through a "formally free" contract of employment. The contracts thus made are binding on both sides, by virtue of a normative system transcending the particular collectivity, though the obligation must articulate with the internal normative order, including its hierarchical aspect. But the purveyors of service are not, in advance, bound by this internal priority system and hence an exchange, which is here interpreted to operate in the first instance as between strategic significance expressed as power-potential, and the monetary value of the service, must be arrived at.

Quite clearly, when the purveyor of service has once entered into such a contract, he is bound by the aspect of its terms that articulates the service into this internal system, including the level of authority he exercises and its implications for his power position in the collectivity. If the collectivity is making in any sense a rational arrangement, this must be tailored to an estimate of the level of the value of his strategic contribution, hence his performance-capacity.

Since, however, the boundary interchange is not integral to the internal system of bindingness, the hierarchical imperatives do not apply to the opportunity aspect of this interchange on the extra-political side. This is to say that the same order of pressures of a higher-order universalistic normative system can operate here that we suggested operated to bring about equality in the franchise. Again the principle is that no particularistic discriminations are to be legitimized which are not grounded in essential functional exigencies of the system of reference.

In the case of the franchise there seems to be no inherent stopping place short of complete equality, qualified only by the minimum consideration of competence attached to fully responsible membership—excluding only minors, "defectives," through retardation and mental illness, and those morally disqualified through crime. In the service case, on the other hand, given commitments to optimum performance which in the present context can be taken for granted, the limit to the equating of universalism and equality lies in the concept of competence. Hence the principle arrived at is the famous one of equality of opportunity, by which there is equalization of access to opportunity for contribution, but selection on criteria of differential competence, both quantitative and qualitative.

Whereas the equalization of the franchise is a control on differential power "from above" in the hierarchy of control and operates mainly through the selection of leadership, equality of opportunity is (in the corresponding sense) a control from below, and operates to check particularistic tendencies which would tend to exclude sources of service which are qualified by competence to contribute, and/or to check tendencies to retain services which are inferior to those available in competition with them.

It is the combination of these two foci of universalization, the equalitarianism of upper rights to control through the franchise, and of rights to participate through service on the basis of competence, which account for the extent to which the "cumulative advantage,"[30] which might seem to be inherent in the hierarchical internal structure of power systems, often in fact fails either to materialize at all, or to be as strong as expected.

Long and complex as it is, the above discussion may be summed up as an attempted solution of the second of the three main problems with which this paper began, namely that of the relation between the coercive and the consensual aspects of the phenomenon of power. The answer is first premised on the conception of power as a specific but generalizd medium of the functioning of social relationships in complex, differentiated systems of social interaction.

Power is secondly specifically associated with the bindingness of obligations to performance within a range of circumstances which may arise in a varying and changing situation. The obligations concerned are hence in some important degree generalized so that particularities under them are contingent on circumstances. The bindingness of obligations implies that they stand on a level of seriousness such that the invoking agent, ego, may be put in the position of asserting that, since he "means it," alter must comply; he is prepared to insist on compliance. Partly then as a

---

[30] *Cf.* C. Wright Mills, *The Power Elite* (New York: Oxford University Press, 1956) and my commentary in *Structure and Process in Modern Societies, op. cit.*, Chapter 6. [Reprinted as Chapter 8 in the present volume: ed.]

symbolic expression of this seriousness of "meaning it" and partly as an instrument of deterrence of noncompliance,[31] this insistence is associated with command of negative situational sanctions the application of which is frequently contingent on noncompliance, and in certain cases deterrence is achieved by compulsion. We would not speak of power where situational negative sanctions or compulsion are in no circumstances attached to non-compliance in cases where a legitimate agent insists on compliance.

Thirdly, however, power is here conceived as a generalized medium of mobilizing commitments or obligation for effective collective action. As such it ordinarily does not itself possess intrinsic effectiveness, but symbolizes effectiveness and hence the bindingness of the relevant obligations to contribute to it. The operative validity of the meaningfulness of the symbolization is not a function of any one single variable but, we argue, of two primary ones. One of these is the willingness to insist upon compliance, or at least to deter noncompliance, a line of reasoning which leads to the understanding of willingness to resort to negative sanctions, the nature of which will vary, as a function of the seriousness of the question, on the dimension of their progressively more drastic nature—in the last analysis, force.

The other variable concerns the collective reference and hence the justification[32] of invoking the obligations in question in the situation. This aspect concerns the dependence of power on the institutionalization of authority and hence the rights of collective agents to mobilize performances and define them as binding obligations. This justification inherently rests on some sort of consensus among the members of the collectivity of reference, if not more broadly, with respect to a system of norms under which authority and power are legitimized on a basis wider than this particular collectivity by the values of the system. More specifically, authority is the institutionalized code within which the "language of power" is meaningful and, therefore, its use will be accepted in the requisite community, which is in the first instance the community of collective organization in our sense.

Seen in this light, the threat of coercive measures or of compulsion, without legitimation or justification, should not properly be called the use of power at all, but is the limiting case where power, losing its symbolic character, merges into an intrinsic instrumentality of securing compliance with wishes, rather than obligations. The monetary parallel is the use of a monetary metal as an instrument of barter where as a commodity it ceases to be an institutional medium of exchange at all.

[31] Cf. Durkheim's famous essay, "Deux lois de l'évolution pénale," L'Année Sociologique, 4 (1899–1900): 65–95.

[32] Cf. my paper "On The Concept of Influence," op. cit., for a discussion of the concept of justification and its distinction from legitimation. [Reprinted as Chapter 15 in the present volume: ed.]

In the history of thought there has been a very close connection between emphasis on the coercive element in power systems and on the hierarchical aspect of the structure of systems of authority and power. The above discussion has, I hope, helped to dissociate them by showing that this hierarchical aspect, important as it is, is only part of the structure of power systems. The view advanced is that it is an inherent aspect of the internal structure of collectivities. No collectivity, even the nation, however, stands alone as a total society, since it is integrated with norms and values; subcollectivities can even less be claimed to be societies. The collectivity aspect of total social structure may in a particular case be dominant over others, but always in principle it impinges on at least two sorts of boundary-problems, namely, that involved in its "support" system, and that involved in the mobilization of services as sources of contribution to its functioning.

In both these cases, we have argued, quite different principles are operative from that of the hierarchy of authority, namely, the equality of franchise on the one hand, equality of opportunity on the other. In both cases I envisage an interchange of power, though not of authority, over the boundary of the polity, and in neither case can the principle governing the allocation of power through this interchange be considered to be hierarchical in the line authority sense. The empirical problems here are, as elsewhere, formidable, but I definitely argue that it is illegitimate to hold that, from serious consideration of the role of power as a generalized medium, it can be inferred that there is a general trend to hierarchization, in the total empirical social systems involved.[33]

THE ZERO-SUM PROBLEM

We are now in a position to take up the last of the three main problems with which the discussion started, namely whether power is a zero-sum phenomenon in the sense that, in a system, a gain in power by a unit A is in the nature of the case the cause of a corresponding loss of power by other units, $B, C, D. . . .$ The parallel with money on which we have been insisting throughout should give us clues to the answer, which clearly is, under certain circumstances, yes, but by no means under all circumstances.

In the monetary case it is obvious that in budgeting the use of a fixed income, allocation to one use must be at the expense of alternative uses. The question is whether parallel limitations apply to an economy con-

[33] Failure to see this seems to me to be a major source of the utopian strain in Marxist theory, expressed above all by the expectation of the "withering away of the state." There is perhaps a parallel to the confusion connected for many centuries with the Aristotelian doctrine of the "sterility" of money.

ceived as a total system. For long this seemed to many economists to be the case; this was the main burden of the old "quantity theory of money." The most obvious political parallel is that of the hierarchy of authority within a particular collectivity. It would seem to be obvious that, if A, who has occupied a position of substantial power, is demoted, and B takes his place, A loses power and B gains it, the total in the system remaining the same. Many political theorists, like Lasswell and C. Wright Mills, generalized this to political systems as a whole.[34]

The most important and obvious point at which the zero-sum doctrine breaks down for money is that of credit-creation through commercial banking. This case is so important as a model that a brief discussion here is in order. Depositors, that is, entrust their money funds to a bank, not only for safe keeping, but as available to the bank for lending. In so doing, however, they do not relinquish any property rights in these funds. The funds are repayable by the bank in full on demand, the only normal restrictions being with respect to banking hours. The bank, however, uses part of the balances on deposit with it to make loans at interest, pursuant to which it not only makes the money available to the borrower, but in most cases assumes binding obligations not to demand repayment except on agreed terms, which in general leave the borrower undisturbed control for a stipulated period—or obligates him to specified installments of amortization. In other words, the same dollars come to do "double duty," to be treated as possessions by the depositors, who retain their property rights, and also by the banker who preempts the rights to loan them, as if they were "his." In any case there is a corresponding net addition to the circulating medium, measured by the quantity of new bank deposits created by the loans outstanding.[35]

Perhaps the best way to describe what happens is to say that there has occurred a differentiation in the functions of money and hence there are two ways of using it in the place of one. The ordinary deposit is a reserve for meeting current expenses, whether "private" or "business," which is mainly important with respect to the time element of the degrees of freedom mentioned above. From the point of view of the depositor the bank is a convenience, giving him safekeeping, the privilege of writing checks rather than using cash, etc., at a cost which is low because the bank earns interest through its loaning operations. From the point of view of the borrower, on the other hand, the bank is a source of otherwise unavailable funds, ideally, in the economist's sense, for investment, for financing operations promising future increments of economic productivity, which would not otherwise have been feasible.

[34] H. D. Lasswell and A. Kaplan, *Power and Society* (New Haven: Yale University Press, 1950) and Mills, *The Power Elite, op. cit.*

[35] Whether this be interpreted as net addition to the medium, or as increase in the velocity of circulation of the "slow" deposit funds, is indifferent, because its economic effects are the same.

The possibility of this "miracle of loaves and fishes" of course rests on an empirical uniformity, namely that depositors do in fact, under normal circumstances, keep sufficient balances on hand—though they are not required to—so that it is safe for the bank to have substantial amounts out on loan at any given time. Underlying this basic uniformity is the fact that an individual bank also will ordinarily have access to "reserves," e.g. assets which, though earning interest, are sufficiently liquid to be realized on short notice, and in the last analysis such resources as those of a federal reserve system. The individual bank, and with it its depositors, is thus ordinarily relatively secure.

We all know, however, that this is true only so long as the system operates smoothly. A particular bank can meet unusual demands for withdrawal of deposits, but if this unusual demand spreads to a whole banking system, the result may be a crisis, which only collective action can solve. Quite clearly the expectation that all depositors should be paid, all at once, in "real" money, e.g. even "cash," to say nothing of monetary metal, cannot be fulfilled. Any monetary system in which bank credit plays an important part is in the nature of the case normally "insolvent" by that standard.

Back of these considerations, it may be said, lies an important relation between bindingness and "confidence," which is in certain respects parallel to that between coercion and consensus in relation to power, indeed one which, through the element of bindingness, involves a direct articulation between money and power. How is this parallel to be defined and how does the articulation operate?

First, the banking operation depends on mutual confidence or trust, in that depositors entrust their funds to the bank, knowing, if they stop to think about it, that the bank will have a volume of loans outstanding that makes it impossible to repay all deposits at once. It is well known with what hesitation, historically, many classes have been brought to trust banks at all in this simple sense—the classical case of the French peasant's insistence on putting his savings in cash under the mattress is sufficient illustration. The other side of the coin, however, is the bank's trust that its depositors will not panic to the point of in fact demanding the complete fulfillment of their legal rights.

The banker here assumes binding obligations in two directions, the honoring of both of which depends on this trust. On the one hand he has loaned money on contract which he cannot recover on demand, on the other he is legally bound to repay deposits on demand. But by making loans on binding contractual terms he is enabled to create money, which is purchasing power in the literal sense that, as noted above, the status of the monetary unit is politically guaranteed—e.g., through its position as "legal tender"—and hence the newly created dollars are "as good as" any other dollars. Hence I suggest that what makes them good in this sense is the input of power in the form of the bindingness of the contractual obligation assumed by the banker—I should classify this as opportunity for effectiveness. The bank, as collectivity, thus enjoys a "power position" by virtue of which it can give its borrowers effective control of certain types of opportunity.

It is, however, critically important that in general this grant of power is not unconditional. First, it is power in its form of direct convertibility with money, and second, within that framework, the condition is that, per unit of time, there should be a surplus of money generated; the borrower can and must return more money than he received, the difference being "interest." Money, however, is a measure of productivity, and hence we may say that increasing the quantity of money in circulation is economically "functional" only if it leads after a sequence of operations over a period of time to a corresponding increase in productivity—if it does not the consequence is inflationary. The process is known as investment, and the standard of a good investment is the expected increment of productivity which, measured in money terms, is profitability. The organizational question of allocation of responsibility for decisions and payments should, of course, not be too directly identified with the present level of analytical argument.

It may help round out this picture if the concept of investment is related to that of "circular flow" in Schumpeter's sense.[36] The conception is that the routine functioning of economic processes is organized about the relation between producing and consuming units, we may say firms and households. So long as a series of parametric constants such as the state of demand and the coefficients of cost of production hold, this is a process in equilibrium through which money mediates the requisite decisions oriented to fixed reference points. This is precisely the case to which the zero-sum concept applies. On the one hand, a fixed quantity and "velocity of circulation" of the monetary medium is an essential condition of the stability of this equilibrium, whereas on the other hand, there is no place for banking operations which, through credit expansion, would change the parametric conditions.

These decisions are governed by the standard of solvency, in the sense that both producing and consuming units are normally expected to recoup their monetary expenditures, on the one hand for factors of production, on the other for consumers' goods, from monetary proceeds, on the producing side, sale of output, on the consuming, sale of factors of production, notably labor. Solvency, then, is a balance between monetary cost and receipts. Investment is also governed by the standard of solvency, but over a longer time period, long enough to carry out the opera-

[36] Joseph Schumpeter, *The Theory of Economic Development* (Cambridge: Harvard University Press, 1955), translated by Redvers Opie.

tions necessary to bring about an increase of productivity matching the monetary obligations assumed.

There is here a crucial relation between the time-extension of the investment process and use of power to make loan contracts binding. Only if the extension of control of resources through loans creates obligations can the recipients of the loans in turn assume further obligations and expect others to assume them.

The essential principle here is that, in the sense of the hierarchy of control, a higher-order medium is used as a source of leverage to break into the "circle" of the Schumpeterian flow, giving the recipients of this power effective control of a share of fluid resources in order to divert them from the established routine channels to new uses. It is difficult to see how this could work systematically if the element of bindingness were absent either from loan contracts or from the acceptance-status of the monetary medium.

One further element of the monetary complex needs to be mentioned here. In the case of investment there is the element of time, and hence the uncertainty that projected operations aiming at increase in productivity will in fact produce either this increase or financial proceeds sufficient to repay loans plus interest in accordance with contract. In the case of the particular borrower-lender relationship this can be handled on an individual contract-solvency basis with a legally determined basis of sharing profits and/or losses. For the system, however, it creates the possibility of inflation, namely that the net effect of credit-extension may not be increase in productivity but decline in the value of the monetary unit. Furthermore, once a system involves an important component of credit, the opposite disturbance, namely deflation with a re-arrangement of the meaning of the whole network of financial and credit expectations and relationships, is also a possibility. This suggests that there is, in a ramified credit economy, a set of mechanisms which, independently of particular circular flow and credit-extension and re-payment transactions, regulates the total volume of credit, rate of interest, and price-level relations in the economy.

ZERO-SUM: THE CASE OF POWER

Let us now attempt to work out the parallel, and articulating, analysis for power systems. There is, I suggest, a circular flow operating between polity and economy in the interchange between factors in political effectiveness—in this case a share in control of the productivity of the economy—and an output to the economy in the form of the kind of control of resources which a loan for investment provides—though of course there are various other forms. This circular flow is controlled by the medium of power in the sense that the output of binding obligations, in particular through the commitment to perform services, broadly balances the offer of opportunity for effective performance.

The suggestion is that it is a condition of the stability of this circulation system that the inputs and outputs of power on each side should balance. This is another way of saying that it is ideally formulated as a zero-sum system, so far as power is concerned, though because it includes the investment process, the same is not true for the involvement of monetary funds in the interchanges. The political circular flow system then is conceived as the locus of the "routine" mobilization of performance expectations either through invoking obligations under old contractual— and in some cases, e.g. citizenship, ascriptive—relations, or through a stable rate of assumption of new contractual obligations, which is balanced by the liquidation, typically through fulfillment, of old ones. The balance applies to the system, of course, not to particular units.

Corresponding to utility as the value-pattern governing economic function I have put forward effectiveness as that governing political function. If it is important to distinguish utility, as the category of value to which increments are made by the combinatorial process of economic production, from solvency as the standard of satisfactory performance in handling money as the medium of economic process, then we need to distinguish effectiveness as the political value category, from a corresponding standard for the satisfactory handling of power. The best available term for this standard seems to be the success of collective goal-attainment. Where the polity is sufficiently differentiated so that power has become genuinely a generalized medium we can say that collective units are expected to be successful in the sense that the binding obligations they undertake, in order to maintain and create opportunities for effectiveness, is balanced by the input of equally binding commitments to perform service, either within the collectivity in some status of employment, or for the collectivity on a contractual basis.

The unit of productive decision-making is, however, in a sense corresponding to that applying to the household for the economic case, also expected to be successful in the sense that its expenditure of power, through not only the output of services but their commitment to utilization by particular collectivities, is balanced by an input of opportunity which is dependent on collective organization, that is, a unit in a position to undertake to provide opportunities which are binding on the unit.

In the light of this discussion it becomes clear that the business firm is in its aspect as collectivity in our technical sense, the case where the two standards of success and solvency coincide. The firm uses its power income primarily to maintain or increase its productivity and, as a measure of this, its money income. A surplus of power will therefore in general be exchanged for enhancement of its control of economic productivity. For a collectivity specialized in political function, the primary criterion of success would be given in its power position, relative, that is, to other collectivities. Here there is the special problem of the meaning of the term power position. I interpret it here as relative to other collectivities in a competitive system, not as a position in an internal hierarchy of power. This distinction is, of course, particularly important for a pluralistic power system where government is a functionally specialized subsystem of the collectivity structure, not an approximation to the totality of that structure.[37] In somewhat corresponding fashion a collectivity specialized in integrative function would measure its success in terms of its "level of influence"—for example, as a political interest-group in the usual sense, its capacity to influence public policy decisions. A consequence of this reasoning is that such an influence group would be disposed to "give away" power, in the sense of trading it for an increment of influence. This could take the form of assuring political support, without barter-like conditions, to leadership elements that seemed to be likely to be able to exercise the kind of influence in question.

Is there, then, a political equivalent of the banking phenomenon, a way in which the circular flow of power comes to be broken through so as to bring about net additions to the amount of power in the system? The trend of the analytical argument indicates that there must be, and that its focus lies in the support system, that is, the area of interchange between power and influence, between polity and integrative system.

First I suggest that, particularly conspicuous in the case of democratic electoral systems, political support should be conceived as a generalized grant of power which, if it leads to electoral success, puts elected leadership in a position analogous to that of the banker. The "deposits" of power made by constituents are revocable, if not at will, at the next election—a condition analogous to regularity of banking hours. In some cases election is tied to barterlike conditions of expectation of carrying out certain specific measures favored by the strategically crucial voters and only these. But particularly in a system that is pluralistic not only with reference to the composition of political support, but also to issues, such a leadership element acquires freedom to make certain types of binding decision, binding in the nature of the case on elements of the collectivity other than those whose "interest" is directly served. This freedom may be conceived to be confined to the circular flow level, which would be to say that the input of power through the channel of political support should be exactly balanced by the output through policy decisions, to interest groups that have specifically demanded these decisions.

There is, however, another component of the freedom of elected leadership which is crucial here. This is the freedom to use influence—

---

[37] If very carefully interpreted, perhaps the old term "sovereignty" could be used to designate this standard somewhat more definitely than success.

for example through the "prestige" of office as distinguished from its specified powers—to embark on new ventures in the "equation" of power and influence. This is to use influence to create additions to the total supply of power. How can this be conceived to work?

One important point is that the relation between the media involved with respect to positive and negative sanctions is the obverse of the case of creating money through banking. There it was the use of power embodied in the binding character of loan contracts that "made the difference." Here it is the optional capacity to exert influence through persuasion. This process seems to operate through the function of leadership which, by way of the involvements it possesses with various aspects of the constituency structure of the collectivity, generates and structures new "demands" in the specific sense of demands for policy decision.

Such demands, then, may be conceived, in the case of the deciders, to justify an increased output of power. This in turn is made possible by the generality of the mandate of political support, the fact that it is not given on a barter basis in exchange for specific policy decisions, but once the "equation" of power and influence has been established through election, it is a mandate to do, within constitutional limits, what seems best, in the governmental case "in the public interest." Collective leadership may then be conceived as the bankers or "brokers" who can mobilize the binding commitments of their constituents in such a way that the totality of commitments made by the collectivity as a whole can be enhanced. This enhancement must, however, be justified through the mobilization of influence; it must, that is, both be felt to be in accordance with valid norms and apply to situations that "call for" handling at the level of binding collective commitments.

The critical problem of justification is, in one direction, that of consensus, of its bearing on the value-principle of solidarity as we have outlined this above. The standard, therefore, that corresponds to the value principle of solidarity is consensus, in the sense in which that concept has been used above.

The problem, then, is that of a basis for breaking through the circular stability of a zero-sum power system. The crucial point is that this can only happen if the collectivity and its members are ready to assume new binding obligations over and above those previously in force. The crucial need is to justify this extension and to transform the "sentiment" that something ought to be done into a commitment to implement the sentiment by positive action, including coercive sanctions if necessary. The crucial agency of this process seems to be leadership, precisely conceived as possessing a component analytically independent of the routine power position of office, which defines the leader as the mobilizer of justifications for policies that would not be undertaken under the circular flow assumptions.

It may be suggested that the parallel to credit creation holds with respect to time-extension as well as in other respects. The increments of effectiveness that are necessary to implement new binding policies that constitute an addition to the total burden on the collectivity cannot simply be willed into being; they require organizational changes through recombinations of the factors of effectiveness, development of new agencies, procurement of personnel, new norms, and even changes in bases of legitimation. Hence leadership cannot justifiably be held responsible for effective implementation immediately, and conversely, the sources of political support must be willing to trust their leadership in the sense of not demanding immediate—by the time of the next election —"pay-off" of the power-value of their votes in their decisions dictated by their own interests.[38]

It is perhaps legitimate to call the responsibility assumed in this connection specifically leadership responsibility and distinguish it in these terms from administrative responsibility that focuses on the routine functions. In any case I should like to conceive this process of power enhancement as strictly parallel to economic investment, in the further sense that the pay-off should be an increment to the level of collective success in the sense outlined above, that is, enhanced effectiveness of collective action in valued areas that could not have been expected without risk-taking on the part of leadership in a sense parallel to entrepreneurial investment.

The operation of both governmental and nongovernmental collectivities is full of illustrations of the kind of phenomenon I have in mind, though because this type of formal analysis is somewhat unfamiliar, it is difficult to pin them down exactly. It has, for example, often been pointed out that the relation of executive responsibility to constituency-interests is very different in domestic and in foreign affairs. I suggest that the element of "political banking" in the field of foreign affairs is particularly large and that the sanction of approval of policy decisions, where it occurs, cannot infallibly be translated into votes, certainly not in the short run. Similar considerations are very frequently involved in what may be called "developmental" ventures, which cannot be expected to be "backed" by currently well-structured interests in the same sense as maintenance of current functions. The case of support of research and training is a good one since the "community of scholars" is not a very

---

[38] Perhaps this is an unusually clear case of the relativity of the formal legal sense of the bindingness of commitments. Thus the populistic component in democratic government often ties both executive and legislative branches rather rigidly in what they can formally promise. However, there are many *de facto* obligations assumed by Government which are very nearly binding. Thus legally Congress could withdraw the totality of funds recently granted to universities for the support of scientific research and training, the formal appropriations being made year by year. Universities, however, plan very much in the expectation of maintenance of these funds and this maintenance is clearly something like a *de facto* obligation of Congress.

strong "pressure group" in the sense of capacity directly to influence large blocks of votes.

It would follow from these considerations that there is, in developed polities, a relatively "free-floating" element in the power system which is analogous to a credit-system. Such an element should then be subject to fluctuation on a dimension of inflation-deflation, and be in need of controls for the system as a whole, at a level above that of the activities of particular units.

The analogue of inflation seems to me to touch the credibility of the assertion of the bindingness of obligations assumed. Power, as a symbolic medium, is like money in that it is itself "worthless," but is accepted in the expectation that it can later be "cashed in," this time in the activation of binding obligations. If, however, "power-credit" has been extended too far, without the necessary organizational basis for fulfillment of expectations having been laid, then attempting to invoke the obligations will result in less than a full level of performance, inhibited by various sorts of resistance. In a collectivity undergoing disintegration the same formal office may be "worth less" than it otherwise would have been because of attrition of its basis of effectiveness. The same considerations hold when it is a case of overextension of new power-expectations without adequate provision for making them effective.

It goes without saying that a power-system in which this creditlike element is prominent is in a state analogous to the "insolvency" of a monetary system that includes an important element of actual credit, namely, its commitments cannot be fulfilled all at once, even if those to whom they have been made have formally valid rights to such fulfillment. Only a strict zero-sum power system could fulfill this condition of "liquidity." Perhaps the conservatism of political ideologies makes it even more difficult to accept the legitimacy of such a situation—it is all too easy to define it as "dishonest"—than in the corresponding economic case.

There is, however, a fine line between solid, responsible and constructive political leadership which in fact commits the collectivity beyond its capacities for instantaneous fulfillment of all obligations, and reckless overextendedness, just as there is a fine line between responsible banking and "wild-catting."

Furthermore, under unusual pressures, even highly responsible leadership can be put in situations where a "deflationary" spiral sets in, in a pattern analogous to that of a financial panic. I interpret, for instance, McCarthyism as such a deflationary spiral in the political field. The focus of the commitments in which the widest extension had taken place was in the international field—the United States had very rapidly come into the position of bearing the largest share of responsibility for maintenance of world political order against an expansionist Communist movement. The "loss of China" was in certain quarters a particularly traumatic experience, and the Korean war a highly charged symbol of the costs of the new stewardship.

A pluralistic political system like the American always has a large body of latent claims on the loyalty of its citizens to their government, not only for the "right sentiments" but for "sacrifices," but equally these are expected to be invoked only in genuine emergencies. The McCarthy definition of the situation was, however, that virtually anyone in a position of significant responsibility should not only recognize the "in case" priority—not necessarily by our basic values the highest—of national loyalty, but should explicitly renounce all other loyalties that might conceivably compete with that to the nation, including those to kith and kin. This was in effect a demand to liquidate all other commitments in favor of the national, a demand which in the nature of the case could not be met without disastrous consequences in many different directions. It tended to "deflate" the power system by undermining the essential basis of trust on which the influence of many elements bearing formal and informal leadership responsibilities, and which in turn sustained "power-credit," necessarily rested. Perhaps the most striking case was the allegation of communist infiltration and hence widespread "disloyalty" in the army, which was exploited to try to force the army leadership to put the commitment of all associated personnel, including e.g. research scientists, in completely "liquid" form. Two features of the McCarthy movement particularly mark it as a deflationary spiral, first, the vicious circle of spreading involvement with the casting of suspicion on wider and wider circles of otherwise presumptively loyal elements in the society and, secondly, the surprisingly abrupt end of the spiral once the "bubble was pricked" and "confidence restored," events associated particularly with the public reaction to McCarthy's performance in the televised army hearings, and of Senator Flanders' protest on the floor of the Senate.[39]

The focus of the McCarthy disturbance may be said to have been in the influence system, in the relation between integrative and pattern-maintenance functions in the society. The primary deflationary effect was on the "credit" elements of pluralistic loyalties. This, in turn, would make leadership elements, not only in government but private groups, much less willing to take risks in claiming loyalties that might compete with those to government. Since, however, in the hierarchy of control the influence system is superordinate to the power system, deflation in the former is necessarily propagated to the latter. This takes in the first instance the form of a rush to withdraw political support—which it will be remembered is here treated as a form of power—from leadership elements

---

[39] I have dealt with some aspects of the McCarthy episode in "Social Strains in America," *Structure and Process, op. cit.* [Reprinted as Chapter 7 in the present volume: ed.] The inherent impossibility of the demand for "absolute security" in a pluralistic system is very cogently shown by Edward Shils in *The Torment of Secrecy* (New York: The Free Press, 1956), especially in Chapter VI.

which could in any sense be suspected of "disloyalty." The extreme, perhaps, was the slogan propagated by McCarthy and played with by more responsible Republican leaders like Thomas E. Dewey, of "twenty years of treason," which impugned the loyalty of the Democratic Party as a whole. The effect was, by depriving opposition leadership of influence, to make it unsafe even to consider granting them power.

The breaking through of the zero-sum limitations of more elementary power systems opens the way to altogether new levels of collective effectiveness, but also, in the nature of the case, involves new levels of risk and uncertainty. I have already dealt briefly with this problem at the level of the particular collectivity and its extension of commitments. The problem, of course, is compounded for a system of collectivities because of the risk not only of particular failures, but of generalized inflationary and deflationary disturbances. There are, as we have noted, mechanisms of control that operate to regulate investment, and similarly extension of the commitments of particular collectivities, both of which have to do with the attempt to ensure responsibility, on the one hand for solvency over the long run, on the other for success of the larger "strategy" of extension. It is reasonable to suppose that beyond these, there must be mechanisms operating at the level of the system as a whole in both contexts.

In the monetary case it was the complex of central banking, credit management and their relations to governmental finance which has been seen to be the focus of these highest-level controls. In the case of power it is, of course, the first crucial point that there was to be some relatively paramount apex of control of the power and authority system, which we think of as in some sense the "sovereign" state.[40] This has mainly to do with the relations between what we have called justification and legitimacy, in relation to government as the highest-order tightly integrated collectivity structure—so far. This is the central focus of Weber's famous analysis of authority, but his analysis is in need of considerable extension in our sense. It seems, among other things, that he posed an unduly sharp alternative between charismatic and "routine" cases, particularly the rational-legal version of the latter. In particular it would be my view that very substantial possibilities of regulated extension of power-commitments exist within the framework of certain types of "legal" authority,

---

[40] In saying this I am very far from maintaining that "absolute" sovereignty is an essential condition of that minimal integration of political systems. On the contrary, first, it is far from absolute internally, precisely because of the pluralistic character of most modern political systems and because of the openness of their boundaries in the integrative economic and other directions. Externally the relation of the territorial unit to norms and values transcending it is crucial, and steadily becoming more so. See my paper "Polarization of the World and International Order" in Quincy Wright, William M. Evan, and Morton Deutsch, eds., *Preventing World War III* (New York: Simon and Schuster, 1962), pp. 310–331, reprinted in *Sociological Theory and Modern Society.*

especially where they are aspects of a political system that is pluralistic in general terms. These problems, however, cannot further be explored at the end of what is already a very long paper.

CONCLUSION

This paper has been designed as a general theoretical attack on the ancient problem on the nature of political power and its place, not only in political systems, narrowly conceived, but in the structure and processes of societies generally. The main point of reference for the attack has been the conception that the discussion of the problem in the main traditions of political thought have not been couched at a sufficiently rigorously analytical level, but have tended to treat the nation, the state, or the lower-level collectively organized "group," as the empirical object of reference, and to attempt to analyze its functioning without further basic analytical breakdown. The most conspicuous manifestation of this tendency has been the treatment of power.

The present paper takes a radically different position, cutting across the traditional lines. It takes its departure from the position of economic theory and, by inference, the asymmetry between it and the traditional political theory,[41] which has treated one as the theory of an analytically defined functional system of society—the economy—and the other as a concrete sub-structure, usually identified with government. Gradually the possibility has opened out both of the extension of the analytical model of economic theory to the political field and of the direct articulation of political with economic theory within the logical framework of the theory of the social system as a whole, so that the *polity* could be conceived as a functional subsystem of the society in all its theoretical fundamentals parallel to the economy.

This perspective necessarily concentrated attention on the place of money in the conception of the economy. More than that, it became increasingly clear that money was essentially a "symbolic" phenomenon and hence that its analysis required a frame of reference closer to that of linguistics than of technology, i.e. it is not the intrinsic properties of gold which account for the value of money under a gold standard any more than it is the intrinsic properties of the sounds symbolized as "book" which account for the valuation of physically fixed dissertations in linguistic form. This is the perspective from which the conception of power as a *generalized symbolic medium* operating in the processes of social inter-action has been set forth.

This paper has not included a survey of the empirical evidence bearing on its ramified field of problems, but my strong conviction is not only

[41] I myself once accepted this. Cf. *The Social System* (New York: The Free Press, 1951), Chapter V, pp. 161–163.

that the line of analysis adopted is consistent with the broad lines of the available empirical evidence, but that it has already shown that it can illuminate a range of empirical problems that were not well understood in terms of the more conventional theoretical positions—e.g. the reasons for the general egalitarian pressure in the evolution of the political franchise, or the nature of McCarthyism as a process of political deflationary spiral.

It does not seem necessary here to recapitulate the main outline of the argument. I may conclude with the three main points with which I began. I submit, first, that the analytical path entered upon here makes it possible to treat power in conceptually specific and precise terms and thus gets away from the theoretical diffuseness called to attention, in terms of which it has been necessary to include such a very wide variety of problematical phenomena as "forms" of power. Secondly, I think it can advance a valid claim to present a resolution of the old dilemma as to whether (in the older terms) power is "essentially" a phenomenon of coercion or of consensus. It is both, precisely because it is a phenomenon which integrates a plurality of factors and outputs of political effectiveness, and is not to be identified with any one of them. Finally, light has been thrown on the famous zero-sum problem, and a definite position taken that, though under certain specific assumptions the zero-sum condition holds, these are not constitutive of power systems in general, but under different conditions systematic "extension" of power spheres, without sacrifice of the power of other units, is just as important a case.

These claims are put forward in full awareness that on one level there is an inherent arbitrariness in them, namely that I have defined power and a number of related concepts in my own way, which is different from many, if not most, of the definitions current in political theory. If theory were a matter only of the arbitrary choice of definitions and assumptions and reasoning from there, it might be permissible to leave the question at that and say simply, this is only one more personal "point of view." Any claim that it is more than that rests on the conception that the scientific understanding of societies is arrived at through a gradually developing organon of theoretical analysis and empirical interpretation and verification. My most important contention is that the line of analysis presented here is a further development of a main line of theoretical analysis of the social system as a whole, and of verified interpretation of the empirical evidence presented to that body of theory. This body of theory must ultimately be judged by its outcomes both in theoretical generality and consistency, over the whole range of social system theory, and by its empirical validity, again on levels that include not only conventionally "political" references, but their empirical interrelations with all other aspects of the modern complex society looked at as a whole.

TECHNICAL NOTE

The above analysis has been presented in wholly discursive terms. Many decisions about categorization and detailed steps of analysis were, however, referred to a formalized paradigm of the principal structural components and process categories and relations of a society considered as a social system. For the benefit of readers with more technical interests in social system theory it has seemed advisable to present a very brief outline of the most directly relevant parts of the general paradigm here, with a brief elucidation of its relevance to the above discussion.[42]

The structural reference points are essentially two, namely first that at a sufficiently high level of differentiation of a society, economy, polity and integrative system become empirically distinct in terms of the primacy of function of structural units, e.g., there is an important structural difference between a private business firm, an administrative agency of government, and a court of law. Secondly, every such unit is involved in plural interchange relations with other units with respect to most of its functional requirements from its situation—i.e. for factor inputs—and the conditions of making its contributions to other units in the "division of labor"—i.e., disposal of "product" outputs. This order of differentiation requires *double* interchanges between all the structural components belonging to each category-pair, e.g. firms and households, firms and political agencies (not necessarily governmental, it should be remembered) etc. The double interchange situation precludes mediation of processes in terms either of ascriptive expectations or barter arrangements, or a combination of the two. It necessitates the development of generalized symbolic media, of which we have treated money, power, and influence as cases.

At a sufficiently high level of generalized development the "governing" interchanges (in the sense of cybernetic hierarchy) take place between the media which are anchored in the various functional subsystems —as power is anchored in the polity. These media in turn serve as instrumentalities of gaining control of "lower-order" resources which are necessary for fulfillment of expectations. Thus the expenditure of money for "goods" is not, at the system or "aggregate" level (as analyzed by Keynes), acquisition of the possession of particular commodities, but

---

[42] The paradigm itself is still incomplete, and even in its present state has not been published as a whole. The first beginning statement dealing with process was made by Parsons and Smelser in *Economy and Society*, esp. Chapter II, and has been further developed in certain respects in Smelser's two subsequent books (*Social Change in the Industrial Revolution*, and *Theory of Collective Behavior*). In my own case certain aspects, which now need further revision, were published in the article "Pattern Variables Revisited" (*American Sociological Review*, August, 1960, and in *Sociological Theory and Modern Society*, Chapter 7). Early and partial versions of the application to political subject-matter are found in my contributions to Roland Young, ed., *Approaches to the Study of Politics*, and Burdick and Brodbeck, eds., *American Voting Behavior*. [Reprinted as Chapter 9 in the present volume: ed.]

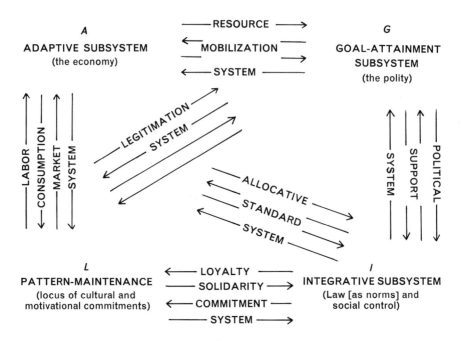

FIGURE I. *Format of the Societal Interchange System*

consists in the generalized expectation of availability of goods on "satis-factory" market terms. This is the primary output of the economy to consumers. Similarly, when we speak of control of productivity as a factor of effectiveness, it is not managerial control of particular plants which is meant, but control of a share of general productivity of the economy through market mechanisms, without specification of particulars.

The paradigm of interchange between general media of communication is presented in Figures 1 and 2. Figure 1 simply designates the format in which this part of the paradigm is conceived. The assumptions of this format are three, none of which can be grounded or justified within the limits of the present exposition. These are (1) that the patterns of differentiation of a social system can be analyzed in terms of four primary functional categories, each of which is the focus of a primary functional subsystem of the society. As noted in the body of the essay, economy and polity are conceived to be such subsystems; (2) The primary interchange processes through which these subsystems are integrated with each other operate through generalized symbolic media of the type that I have assumed money and power to be,[43] and (3) at the level of

---

[43] There is a very crucial problem area which concerns the nature of the interchanges between a society as a system in our sense and its environment. This set of problems unfortunately cannot be entered into here.

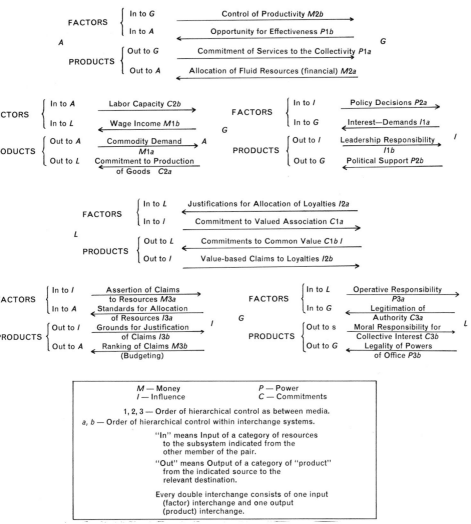

FIGURE 3. *The Media as Sanctions*

differentiation of interest here, each interchange system is a double interchange, implying both the "alienation" of resources and products from their system of origin and the transcending of the barter level of exchange. Under these assumptions, all Figure 1 does is to portray a system of six double interchanges between each logically given pair among the four primary functional subsystems of a society. For convenience tentative names are given to each of these six double interchange systems.

Figure 2, then, places each of the six interchange systems on a horizontal axis, simply because they are easier to read that way. It adds to Figure 1 only by introducing names of categories, directions of flow and designations as to medium (money, power, etc.) for each of the four places in each of the six interchange systems, thus presenting twenty-four categories, each of the four basic media appearing in four "forms."

Among the six interchange sets, power as a medium is involved, by our analysis, in only three, namely the interchanges of the polity (G) with each of the other three. These are the system of "resource mobilization" *vis-à-vis* the economy, the support system that involves the input of political support and the output of decisions *vis-à-vis* the integrative system and the system of legitimation (as I have called it) *vis-à-vis* the value aspect of the pattern-maintenance system. The last of these three is a special case which does not involve power as a medium, but rather the structure of the code governing authority as defining the institutionalized uses of power, hence the legitimation of authority. Primary attention can thus be given to the other two.

The categories included in the A-G (economy-polity, or resource mobilization) interchange can be described as "forms" of power and of money (or wealth) respectively. They will be seen to be the categories which have been used in the appropriate parts of the discursive exposition of the body of the paper. The double interchange here, as in the classic economy—or labor-consumption case, involves first one factor-interchange, namely, control of productivity as factor of effectiveness exchanged for opportunity for effectiveness (in the particular case of capital, as a factor of production). Productivity is a monetary factor because it is a pool of resources controlled through monetary funds—which of course in turn can be exchanged for the particular facilities needed, notably goods and services. Opportunity, however, is a form of power in the sense discussed.

The second part of the double interchange is one of "product" outputs. This takes place between commitment of services to organization—typically through employment—which I have interpreted to be a form of power, and the allocation of fluid resources to the purveyors of service as facilities essential to the performance of their obligations—typically the control of budgeted funds, though often generalization does not extend as high as this. Thus fluid resources in the ideal type case take the form of money funds.[44]

The second primary interchange system, which for convenience I shall call the support system, is that between polity and integrative system (*G-I*), which latter involves the associational aspect of group structure and solidarity in relation to the system of norms (legal and informal)—as distinguished from values. The basic difference lies in the fact that power here is interchanged not with money but with influence, and that whereas *vis-à-vis* money it was the "controlling" medium, *vis-à-vis* influence it is controlled. This difference is symbolized by the placing of the power categories here in the outside positions, whereas in the *A-G* case they were placed inside (as the monetary categories were in *L-A*).

The relevant factor interchange here is between policy decisions as a "factor of solidarity" and interest-demands as a factor of effectiveness, in the senses in which these concepts were used above. Essentially we may say that interest-demands "define the situation" for political decision-making—which of course is by no means to say that demands in their initial form are or should be simply "granted" without modifications. Like other factors they are typically transformed in the course of the political process. Correspondingly policy decisions are a factor in solidarity in that they constitute commitments for collective action on which "interested parties" within limits can count.

The interchange of "product" outputs, then, consists of leadership responsibility as output of the polity (a form of influence, note, *not* of power), and political support as an output of the "associational" system—in the governmental case, e.g., the electorate, which is a source of the political "income" of power. It will, of course, be noted that the units involved in any particular case of these two interchanges typically are not the same—thus party leaders may bid for support, whereas administrative officials make certain policy decisions. This type of "split" (carried out to varying degrees) is characteristic of any highly differentiated system.

Figure 3 attempts to look at the generalized media from the point of view not only of their hierarchical ordering, but of the relation between the code and message components, and the position of the latter as sanctions controlling on the one hand factors essential to the various functional subsystems, on the other hand product outputs from these subsystems. The rows are arranged from top to bottom in terms of the

---

[44] The process of investment, which I conceive to be one very important special case of the operation of this interchange system, seems to work in such a way that the power component of a loan is a grant of opportunity, through which an increment of otherwise unavailable control of productivity is gained. The recipient of this "grant" is then, through committing (individual or collective) services, in a position to utilize these resources for increasing future economic productivity in some way. This is a special case, because the resources might be used in some other way, e.g. for relieving distress or for scientific research.

familiar hierarchy of control—each row designating one of the four media. The columns, on the other hand, designate components into which each medium needs to be broken down if some of the basic conditions of its operation in mediating interaction are to be understood.

In the body of the paper I have discussed the reasons for which it seems necessary to distinguish two components in the code aspect of each medium, namely what have been called the relevant value principle on the one hand, the "coordinative standard" on the other. The most famous concept of utility seems to be the relevant value principle, whereas that of solvency is the coordinative standard. Utility is the basic "measure" of value in the economic sense, whereas the imperative to maintain solvency is a category of norm for the guidance of units in economic action. For the political case I have adopted the concept of effectiveness in Barnard's sense as the parallel to the economist's utility. Success, for the unit in question, notably the collective ease, seems to be the best available term for the corresponding coordinative standard. (Possibly, used with proper qualifications, the term sovereignty might be still more appropriate for this standard.)

At the other most important direct boundary of the polity, solidarity in Durkheim's sense seems to be the value-principle of integration that is parallel to utility and effectiveness, whereas the very important (to political theory) concept of *consensus* seems adequately to formulate the relevant integrative coordinative standard. Since they are not directly involved in the interchange systems of immediate concern here, I merely call attention to the designation of the value-principle of the pattern-maintenance system as *integrity* and the corresponding coordinative standard as *pattern-consistency*.

The A and G columns of Figure 3 then designate contexts of operation of each of the four media as sanctions, but arranged not by interchange system as in Figure 2, but by control of factor inputs and product outputs respectively. Thus money, though not itself a factor of production, "controls," i.e. buys, labor and capital as the primary factors, in the A-L and the A-G interchange systems respectively, whereas for "consuming" systems money buys outputs of the economy, namely goods (in A-L) and services (in A-G) respectively.

The involvement of power is conceived to be parallel. On the one hand it "commands" the two primary mobile factors of effectiveness, namely control of productivity (in G-A) and interest-demands (in G-I) (as justified in terms of appeal to norms). On the other hand the "consumers" or beneficiaries of the outputs from the process can use power to command these outputs in the form of fluid resources (e.g. through budget allocation in G-A) and of leadership responsibility for valued goals (in G-I).

It will be noted that in Figure 3, negative and positive sanction types

COMPONENTS OF MEDIA AND INTERCHANGE RECIPROCALS / MEDIA IN HIERARCHY OF CONTROL	CODES		MESSAGES (SANCTIONS)		TYPES OF SANCTION AND OF EFFECT
	VALUE-PRINCIPLE	COORDINATION STANDARD	FACTORS CONTROLLED	PRODUCTS CONTROLLED	
L			SOURCE	DESTINATION	
COMMITMENTS	INTEGRITY	PATTERN—CONSISTENCY	WAGES A / JUSTIFICATION OF LOYALTIES I	CONSUMERS' DEMAND A / CLAIMS TO LOYALTIES I	NEGATIVE—INTENTIONAL (activation of commitments)
I					
INFLUENCE	SOLIDARITY	CONSENSUS	COMMITMENTS TO VALUED ASSOCIATION L / POLICY DECISIONS G	COMMITMENT TO COMMON VALUES L / POLITICAL SUPPORT G	POSITIVE—INTENTIONAL (persuasion)
G					
POWER	EFFECTIVENESS	SUCCESS	INTEREST—DEMANDS I / CONTROL OF PRODUCTIVITY A	LEADERSHIP RESPONSIBILITY I / CONTROL OF FLUID RESOURCES A	NEGATIVE—SITUATIONAL (securing compliance)
A					
MONEY	UTILITY	SOLVENCY	CAPITAL G / LABOR L	COMMITMENT OF SERVICES G / EXPECTATION OF GOODS L	POSITIVE-SITUATIONAL (inducement)

FIGURE 2. *The Categories of Social Structure*

alternate in the hierarchy of control. Power, as the medium depending on negative situational sanctions, is "sandwiched" between money (below it) with its positive situational sanctions and influence (above it) with its positive intentional sanctions.

Returning to Figure 2, power is also involved in the legitimation system (L-G), but this time as code, as aspect of authority. This may be conceived as a mechanism for linking the principles and standard in the L and G rows. What is called the assumption of operative responsibility (P_3a), which is treated as a "factor of integrity" is responsibility for *success* in the implementation of the value-principles, not only of collective effectiveness, but of integrity of the paramount societal value-pattern. It may be said that the legitimation of authority (C_3a) "imposes" the responsibility to attempt such success. Legality of the power of office on the other hand (P_3c), as a category of output to the polity, is an application of the standard of pattern-consistency. At the various relevant levels action may and should be taken consistent with the value-commitments. In exchange for legal authorization to take such action, the responsible office-holder must accept moral responsibility for his use of power and his decisions of interpretation (C_3b).

Chapter *15*

On the Concept of
Influence

*i*t may plausibly be held that the development of research technology in the
field of opinion and attitude study has outrun the development of theory.
The intention of the present paper is to help to redress the balance by
essaying a contribution in the theoretical area to try to bring to bear on
the opinion field a more generalized conceptual scheme that has been
worked out mainly in other connections.

First, let me state the main context of problems within the field on
which I would like to concentrate. The first step beyond immediate description and classification of opinions is, of course, to attempt some
analysis of determining factors, to answer such questions as why or
under what conditions certain opinions are held or changed. It is within
this area, rather than that of categories suitable for description and
classification, that I wish to operate. To narrow the field still further, it
is a question of whether anything can be said about *generalized* kinds of
process or mechanism through the operation of which such determination, notably of change of opinions, comes about. It is as such a generalized mechanism by which attitudes or opinions are determined that I
would like to conceive "influence," for the purposes of this paper.[1]

[1] It is taken for granted here that there is no formal standardization of terminology in this field,

Reprinted from Public Opinion Quarterly (*Spring 1963*). *Also in* Sociological Theory and Modern
Society, *Chapter 11*.

A further step in specification is to restrict my consideration to the problem of the operation of generalized mechanisms in the process of social interaction in its intentional forms. Thus, if a person's opinion has been changed by his experience of a natural event, such as a hurricane, or even by social events that could not conceivably be understood as intentionally oriented to having an effect on his opinions, such as a business depression, I shall not speak of these as "influence" in the present sense—similarly with the famous example of the alleged relation between a judge's legal opinions and the state of his digestion. Influence is a way of having an effect on the attitudes and opinions of others through intentional (though not necessarily rational) action—the effect may or may not be to change the opinion or to prevent a possible change.

GENERAL MECHANISMS OF SOCIAL INTERACTION: THE CASE OF MONEY

What, then, is meant by a generalized mechanism operating in social interaction? There are various ways of approaching this question. Language is perhaps the prototype and can serve as a major point of reference. Having an effect on the action of others, thus possibly "influencing" them, through linguistic communication, is to present them with "symbolic" experiences in place of the concrete things or objects to which the symbols refer, which they "mean." Thus, a sign, "Beware the dog," may induce caution without the passer-by's actually seeing or hearing a dog. "Intrinsically," the language symbols do not have any caution-inducing properties, the black marks on the signboard have never bitten anyone, nor have they even barked.

In the well-known formulation of Jacobsen and Halle,[2] a language must be understood to involve two aspects: on the one hand, the use of language is a process of emitting and transmitting messages, combinations of linguistic components that have specific reference to particular situations; on the other hand, language is a *code* in terms of which the particular symbols constituting any particular message "have meaning." In these terms, a message can be meaningful and hence understood only by those who "know the language," that is, the code, and accept its "conventions."

Language, as that concept is generally understood, is not an isolated

[2] Roman Jakobson and Morris Halle, *Fundamentals of Language* (The Hague: Mouton & Co., 1956).

and that, hence, there is inevitably an element of arbitrariness involved in giving technical meaning to a term in such general usage as "influence." I make no apology for doing this, since in the social sciences the only alternative in this and many other cases is coining neologisms, the objections to which are overwhelming.

phenomenon. In the field of social interaction, many mechanisms have properties so similar to those of language that it is not too much to say that they *are* specialized languages. Mathematical and artistic symbol systems are cases in point, but one that is both well known and lies close to our concern is money. Hence, for my purposes, I would like to say not merely that money resembles language, but that it *is* a very specialized language, i.e. a generalized medium of communication through the use of symbols given meaning within a code.[3]

I shall therefore treat influence as a generalized medium which in turn I interpret to mean a specialized language. I should like now to attempt, using money, because of its familiarity, as an illustration, to outline a paradigm of such a generalized medium, preliminary to stating the principal properties of influence as another such medium.

Seen in this light, money is a symbolic "embodiment" of economic *value*, of what economists in a technical sense call "utility." Just as the *word* "dog" can neither bark nor bite, yet "signifies" the animal that can, so a dollar has no intrinsic utility, yet signifies commodities that do, in the special sense that it can in certain circumstances be substituted for them, and can evoke control of relations with them in the special kind of process of social interaction we call economic exchange. This means that holders of objects of utility will, on occasion, be willing to relinquish control over them for money, and, conversely, holders of money will be able to acquire, by use of the money (its "expenditure"), control over objects of utility.[4]

The economic value called utility, however, is the basis of a type of *interest* in objects in the situation of action. It defines an aspect of their actual or potential meaning, under which rubric I wish to include not only what they "are" but what they "do," if they are actors, and what can be done *with* them, such as "consuming" them in the economist's sense, if they are commodities, or "utilizing their services," if they are persons. For symbolization to take place, it is necessary for the basis of this interest to be defined with sufficient clarity and specificity, just as the category of object "dog" must be adequately defined if the linguistic symbol is to designate it unambiguously. In the case of money, this involves a very high level of generalization, since the variety of objects of

[3] This perspective on money as a language is strongly suggested by the usage of the classical economists (e.g. Adam Smith, Ricardo, and J. S. Mill), when they spoke of the dual nature of money, first, as "medium of exchange" (message transmission) and, second, as a "measure of value" (code).

[4] It is important to note that the linguistic parallel holds here. The experience of an encounter with a ferocious dog can be "converted" into words, in that, for example, the person frightened can tell another about it in the absence of the dog and evoke in him appropriate reactions. Conversely, in our example above, linguistic warning can evoke an attitude set appropriate to dealing with such an animal in the absence of direct experience of the dog. The linguistic symbols do not have the properties either of dangerousness or of capacity to cope with danger, but they can *mediate* the action process by "orienting" an actor to danger.

utility is immense; furthermore, it means a very strict quantification on a linear scale.

In addition to the relevant category of value for human actors on the one hand, the basis of interest in objects in their situation on the other, there are two further indispensable references in the conceptualization of a generalized symbolic mechanism. One of these is to the "definition of the situation," that is the categorization of objects in the situation with reference to their bearing on the type of interest in question. In the economic-monetary case, the situation consists in "objects of utility," that is, those in which actors may have an economic basis of interest. Implementation of the interest consists in acquiring control over such objects to the extent that this is a condition of "utilizing" them. The "way" of acquiring such control is through exchange, which, if money is involved, may be called "market" exchange.[5]

In the case of money as a symbol, one of its meanings is clearly in the field of "procurement," of the opportunities of using it to gain access to and control over objects of utility. The first component of the situation needing definition, then, consists in the manifold objects that not only have utility but are available within the exchange system; thus certain objects of potential utility, such as full control of other human beings by owning them as chattels, are excluded in our property system. The second component concerns sources of supply, namely, units in the interaction system which, on the one hand, have control of such objects and, on the other, may be presumed to be willing to relinquish such control in exchange for other utilities, including especially money. The third component concerns the conditions on which terms of exchange can be settled, the most important one being the institutionalization of the offer of specific sums of money as a way of inducing transfer of control. And, finally, the fourth component concerns the question of the time relations involved in bringing the two ends of a chain of exchange of utilities together, for example the relinquishment of control over labor services to an employer, and the acquisition of control over consumer's goods.

By contrast with the two "pre-monetary" modes of exchange mentioned above—ascriptive and barter exchange—money introduces altogether new degrees of freedom in all four of these respects. Thus, unlike the holder of a specific commodity in surplus—relative to his own wants—who wants to barter it for another commodity, the holder of money is not bound to find a specific partner who has what he wants and wants what he has. He has the whole range of the "market system" open with respect both to the items for which he wants to spend his funds and to

[5] There are two modes of exchange that involve levels of differentiation of the interest in utility short of what I am here calling the "market" level, namely, ascriptive exchange, the case of obligatory gifts, well known to anthropologists (cf. Marcel Mauss, *The Gift* (New York: The Free Press, 1954)), and the case of barter. Both lack the involvement of a generalized medium that specifically symbolizes utility, namely, money.

the sources from which he might wish to purchase each item—so long as the market for the item is not monopolized. Exceedingly important, he is not bound to any particular time, since money, unlike virtually all commodities, does not intrinsically deteriorate through time and has minimal, if any, costs of storage. Finally, he has much greater freedom to accept or reject terms, and to negotiate them.

These freedoms, like all freedoms, are bought at a price. Money, being a symbol, is "intrinsically" worthless. Hence, in relinquishing control of objects of "real" utility for money, one risks never gaining an equivalent in return and being "stuck" with the symbol; similarly, if one relies on a sign rather than on actually seeing a dog, one risks being fooled, either by being alerted when there is no danger at all, or by being prepared to deal with a dog when in fact a tiger is lurking in the neighborhood.

There have doubtless been heroic figures in the history of market exchange who have risked everything on a conception of the sheer *value* of money without the existence of any institutionally established normative framework of rules according to which such a medium should be used. It seems clear, however, that, without such a framework, a *system* of market exchanges in which participants will regularly put major interests into monetary assets that, in our sense, are "intrinsically" worthless can hardly be expected to function. The most elementary of these rules is the condition of reciprocity in the acceptability of money. This may be formulated as follows: He who urges money on others in exchange for "real assets" must be willing in turn to accept money from others in exchange for his assets. Only mutual acceptability can make money a functioning medium rather than simply a way of getting something for nothing. From this central point, the network of norms that we ordinarily think of as the institutions of property and contract can be worked out. This is the fourth of the basic components of the complex that constitutes a generalized medium.

If a symbol or category of symbols is to function as a generalized medium in mediating the processes of social interaction, there must therefore be, I have contended, specific definition and institutional acceptance in four basic respects: (1) a category of *value*, of respects in which needs of the acting units are at stake; (2) a category of *interest*, of properties of objects in the situation of action that are important in the light of these values; (3) a *definition of the situation*, of the features of the actual situation that can be "exploited" in the implementation of the interest; and (4) a *normative framework* of rules discriminating between legitimate and illegitimate modes of action in pursuit of the interest in question. Only with institutionalization in all four respects can the risks inherently involved in accepting the "symbolic" in lieu of the "real" be expected to be widely assumed by whole categories of acting units.

WAYS OF GETTING RESULTS
IN INTERACTION

Because it is highly institutionalized and hence familiar, and because the conditions of its functioning have been very thoroughly analysed by professional economists, I have used money as the example in terms of which to elucidate the nature and conditions of a generalized medium in the sense of this paper. In approaching a fuller analysis of the primary object of our concern, influence, a next step is to attempt to place both it and money in the context of a wider family of mechanisms. It is my view that money belongs in such a family, of which another well known member is power, in the broadly political sense. These mechanisms operate in social interaction in a way that is both much more specific and more generalized than communication through language. Furthermore, they have in common the imperative mood, i.e. they are ways of "getting results" rather than only of conveying information. They face the object with a decision, calling for a response such as the acceptance or rejection of a monetary offer.

These considerations indicate the approach. Such mechanisms are ways of structuring *intentional* attempts to bring about results by eliciting the response of other actors to approaches, suggestions, etc. In the case of money, it is a matter of offers; in the case of power, of communicating decisions that activate obligations; in the case of influence, of giving reasons or "justifications" for a suggested line of action. How can these various modes of getting results be classified?

My suggestion is that there is a very simple paradigm of modes by which one acting unit—let us call him "ego"—can attempt to get results by bringing to bear on another unit, which we may call "alter," some kind of *communicative operation*: call it "pressure" if that term is understood in a nonpejorative sense.[6] It can be stated in terms of two variables, the cross-classification of which can then yield a fourfold typology. The first variable is whether ego attempts to work through potential control over the *situation* in which alter is placed, and must act, or through an attempt to have an effect on alter's *intentions*, independently of changes in his situation. Let us call this the "channel" variable. Thus an offer in economic exchange operates situationally, in that it offers control either of an object of utility or of money, which in turn is exchangeable for control of such an object.

Offers are contingent—they say that, *if* alter will do something ego wants done, ego in turn will do something that is situationally advan-

---

[6] The closest approach to this paradigm with which I am familiar from the literature is Herbert C. Kelman, "Processes of Opinion Change," *Public Opinion Quarterly*, Vol. 25 (1961), pp. 57–78.

tageous to alter. There is, however, the limiting case in which ego confers a situational advantage on alter without giving him any option —this would be the pure case of the gift. This element of contingency, varying to the limit of no option, applies throughout the present typology.

The second variable concerns the nature of the contingent *consequences* for alter of ego's intervention in his action-complex, that is, in one aspect, the kind of decision with which alter is faced. So far as the element of contingency is involved, this concerns whether the *sanctions* contingently imposed by ego are positive or negative in their significance to alter, that is, constitute advantages or disadvantages to him. Thus, in the case of economic exchange, ego *promises* that if alter will do what he wants, he in turn will do something which alter presumably wants, that is defined as advantageous. Giving him money or control of an object of utility are prototypical cases. On the other hand, ego may attempt to get alter to do something by saying, in effect, "You must, should, or ought to do so and so." Alter may then say, "But what if I choose not to?" If ego takes this approach and "means it," he must contend that in some sense the consequences of alter's choosing noncompliance (if he can "do anything about it") will be disadvantageous to alter. If the channel is situational, this will put him in the position of having to *threaten*, contingent on noncompliance, to do something disadvantageous to alter. On the other hand, he may give alter reasons why noncompliance will, independent of ego's intervention in the situation, prove to be unacceptable, so that *intentional* noncompliance cannot make sense to alter. Here the negative sanction would be internal or intentional, and not situational so far as alter is concerned.

The limiting case where alter is given no option is, in the situational-negative combination, compulsion: ego simply structures the situation so alter *must* comply.

Cross-classification of these two variables for the case of contingency yields the set of four types shown in our table: (1) Inducement is ego's attempt to get a favorable decision from alter by an offer of situational advantages contingent on ego's compliance with his suggestions. (2) Deterrence is ego's corresponding attempt to get compliance by invoking commitments in such a way that noncompliance exposes alter to a contingent threat of suffering a situational disadvantage.[7] (3) Activation of commitments is ego's attempt to get compliance by offering reasons why it would, from alter's own point of view, be "wrong" for him to refuse to act as ego wished. And, finally, (4) persuasion is ego's attempt to get compliance by offering reasons why it would, from alter's own

---

[7] This case, as well as the setting in which it fits, is much more fully discussed in my paper, "On the Concept of Political Power," *Proceedings of the American Philosophical Society,* Philadelphia, 1963. [Reprinted as the preceding chapter in the present volume: ed.] Generally, this is a companion piece to the present paper.

point of view, independent of situation advantages, "be a good thing" for him to act as ego wished.

		CHANNEL	
		Situational	*Intentional*
SANCTION	*Positive*	Inducement	Persuasion
	Negative	Deterrence	Activation of Commitments

I should now like to suggest that this simple paradigm of modes of gaining ends in social interaction is matched by a paradigm of generalized media by which, in the appropriately structured type of interaction system, an enhanced capacity to gain such ends is made possible, provided the risks of acceptance of such a medium in the requisite situation are assumed. Seen in these terms, money should be regarded as a generalized medium of inducement, and influence as a generalized medium of persuasion. I shall try presently to elucidate further what the latter conception implies, but it will be useful first to put it in the context, not only of a comparison with money, but of this still more general classification of media.

Money and influence may be conceived to operate as positive sanctions in the above sense, money through the situational, influence through the intentional, channel. The negative medium corresponding to money on the situational side is then power in the political sense; on the intentional side, the negative medium corresponding to influence is generalization of commitments. The relation between the two pairs requires some elucidation.

Inducement and persuasion are ways of eliciting positively desired responses. Imposition of sanction and response correspond here. Deterrence, on the other hand, is intended to establish an inverse relation between sanctioned act and desired response. The purely negative side is the withholding of sanction in case of "compliance." What ego desires, however, is precisely compliance, the performance of obligation. He imposes sanctions only if "forced to."

It is hence not appropriate to define power simply as a generalized medium of deterrence, but rather of mobilizing the performance of binding obligations, with the conditional implication of the imposition of negative sanctions—in the situational case, "punishment"—in case of noncompliance. The intention of ego, however, is not to punish but to secure performance. Hence we may speak of power as generalized capacity to secure performance of binding obligations in the interest of effective collective action (goal attainment). Parallel to this, on the intentional side (so far as alter is concerned), we may speak of the generalization of commitments as the capacity, through appeal to a subjective sense of obligation, to motivate fulfillment of relevant obligations without reference to any threat of *situational* sanctions (thus differentiating it from power). In this case, however, tendencies to noncompliance will be met with evaluative expressions on ego's part (disapproval of noncompliance) that are calculated to help activate alter's sense of obligation and threaten him with guilt feelings if he fails to comply.[8] We may then insert the four generalized media in the paradigm of sanctions, as follows:

			CHANNEL	
			Situational	*Intentional*
		MODE	Inducement	Persuasion
	Positive			
		MEDIUM	Money	Influence
SANCTION				
		MODE	Deterrence	Activation of Commitments
	Negative			
		MEDIUM	Power	Generalization of Commitments

Note: For readers familiar with the more general paradigm of the analysis of action on which various associates and I have worked for some years, it may be of interest to note that I conceive inducement and money to have primarily adaptive functions in the social system; deterrence and power, primarily goal-attainment functions; persuasion and influence, primarily integrative functions; and, finally, activation of commitments and the generalized commitments so activated, primarily pattern-maintenance functions.

Let us now attempt to get somewhat closer to the analysis of influence by calling attention to another aspect of the generalized media as mechanisms operating within the social system. This is the sense in which they bridge the gap between normative and factual aspects of the system in which they operate. This is to say that, from the point of view of the acting unit, whether it be individual or collectivity, there is one "direction" in which the medium serves as a means of furthering its interests, and this includes the structuring of conditions under which, in various contingencies, its interest is more or less secure. On the other hand, what from the acting unit's point of view are certain norms or rules to which it is subject in furthering its interest are, from the point of view of the system, a set of conditions under which process in it can be carried on stably, without disturbance to its integration and other essential functions.

In the case of money, the rock bottom of security for the unit is the possession of the proper quantity and combination of concrete objects of utility to the unit itself, namely, full "economic self-sufficiency" in terms of "real assets." The next level is possession of objects, such as gold, diamonds, land, that can be exchanged in almost any contingency and

---

[8] Ego can implement this threat through use of the *attitudinal* sanction of *disapproval*, and in the case of compliance, by using influence he can reward alter with his *approval*.

the value of which is not subject to deterioration. Institutionalized money has the advantage of a far wider usefulness in exchange than such goods but the disadvantage of vulnerability to disturbances in the system. Money, however, as we have insisted, is a symbol, the "meaning" of which (in this case, its economic value) is a function of its mutual acceptability. In one direction, this acceptability is well-known to depend on its convertibility into objects of rock-bottom economic security, notably the monetary metal. Convertibility, however, is one thing, but frequent insistence on actual conversion is quite another.

The point is very simply that the insistence on actual conversion can be met only by measures that destroy the very degrees of freedom that make money an advantageous mechanism from the point of view *both* of the unit and of the system.[9] The maintenance of the degrees of freedom, however, is dependent on minimum levels of compliance with the norms of the economic complex with respect to the fulfillment of contractual obligations and the rights and obligations of property. It is by this path that we come to the conception that, while in one context the value of money rests on its "backing" by convertibility into a secure utility, for example metal, in another and probably more important context, it rests on the effective functioning of a ramified system of monetary exchanges and markets. This, in turn, is one major set of factors in the productivity of the economy of which these markets are a central part. No economist would suppose that such productivity can be created simply by adding to the supply of monetary gold.

I suggest that this duality of reference is characteristic not only of money as a mechanism, but of the whole set with which we are concerned—indeed, more broadly, of language, law, and various others. For the case of power, the basis of unit security corresponding to economic "real assets" consists in possession of effective means of *enforcing* compliance (that is, fulfillment of wishes or performance of obligations) through implementing coercive threats or exerting compulsion. In this context, it is well known that physical force occupies a special place, a place which, it may be suggested, is parallel to monetary metal in the economic case. This is above all because force is the deterrent sanction par excellence. In turn, the most important aspect of this deterrence is very generally blocking channels of communication; for example, the most important feature of imprisonment is preventing the prisoner from communicating with others except in ways and through channels his custodians can control.

But just as possession of stocks of monetary gold cannot create a highly productive economy, so command of physical force alone cannot guarantee the effective fulfillment of ramified systems of binding obli-

---

[9] The most important reason concerns the role of banking and credit, the bearing of which on the functioning of influence will be taken up later.

gations. The latter is dependent on such factors as the institutionalization of a system of norms in the fields of authority, and the legitimation of the power of leadership elements. The mutuality of the institutionalization of authority, on the one hand, and the acceptance of the legitimacy of its exercise, on the other, is the parallel of the mutual acceptability of "worthless" money in exchange. Clearly, the functioning of a *system* of power is preeminently dependent on the effective implementation of this normative structure. The analogue of economic productivity here may be said to be the *effectiveness of collective organization.*

INFLUENCE AS A
SYMBOLIC MEDIUM OF PERSUASION

Let us now attempt to apply this line of argument to the field of influence. There is a sense in which all four of the mechanisms under consideration here depend on the institutionalization of attitudes of trust. In the economic case, the actor relinquishes his interests (in commodities or labor) to the market and the question is on what basis he can have confidence or trust that he will receive "fair value" in return for what he has relinquished. We have argued that there are two distinct foci of the problem of trust, namely, the convertibility of money into "real assets" and confidence in the functioning of the "system," which for the actor means the fulfillment of his more or less legitimate expectations from actual and potential exchange partners. Similarly, in the case of power, an actor may relinquish his coercive self-sufficiency: he cannot then defend himself adequately with his own strong right arm alone. In entrusting his security to a power *system,* there is on the one hand his possible identification with actual control of coercive means (in the last analysis, force), on the other his confidence that his expectations will be effectively fulfilled through agencies beyond his personal control, because the power *system* is effective.

In order to fit influence into this system, it is necessary to ask what influence symbolizes. In the case of money, it symbolizes utility; in the case of power, effectiveness of collective action.[10] An answer seems to be given in our paradigm of interactive performance—sanction types. Influence is a means of *persuasion.* It is bringing about a decision on alter's part to act in a certain way because it is felt to be a "good thing" *for him,* on the one hand independently of contingent or otherwise imposed changes in his situation, on the other hand for positive reasons, not because of the obligations he would violate through noncompliance.

It then seems that, to correspond to the intrinsic "want-satisfiers,"

[10] For reasons of space, no further attempt is made here to ground this statement. Cf. my paper on political power, *op. cit.*

which the economist calls "goods and services," there should be a category of intrinsic "persuaders." The most obvious member of this category is "facts" from which alter can "drawn his own conclusions." Ego, that is, can persuade by giving alter information which, given his situation and intentions, will lead him to make certain types of decisions.[11] It seems probable that information is indeed the proper parallel to commodities, with a special kind of information—the announcement of firm intentions of action on the part of significant others—the parallel to services.[12] Influence as a symbol, however, cannot be either of these, but must be more generalized relative to both.

The crucial thing to look for seems to be a symbolic act or component of action on ego's part which communicates a generalized intention on the basis of which trust in more specific intentions is requested and expected. This may operate in the realm of information. Here there must be some basis on which alter considers ego to be a trustworthy source of information and "believes" him even though he is not in a position to verify the information independently—or does not want to take the trouble. It can also operate in the realm of ego's intentions, and this is indeed a crucial matter; for example, agreeing to a contract is essentially an announcement of intentions that can perhaps be fulfilled only by a long series of performances over an extended period of time.

The monetary metal is not "just" one among many commodities; it is one with certain properties that favor security and maximum exchangeability. Similarly with force as an instrument of coercion-compulsion. Is there, then, any comparable "intrinsic" source of persuasion that has a special likelihood of inspiring trust? If, in answering this question, we remember that we are dealing specifically with social interaction, it seems reasonable to suggest that the most favorable condition under which alter will trust ego's efforts to persuade him (independent of specific facts or "inherently" trustworthy intentions) will be when the two stand in a mutual relation of fundamental diffuse solidarity, when they belong together in a collectivity on such a basis that, so long as the tie holds, ego *could not* have an interest in trying to deceive alter. We may then suggest that common belongingness in a *Gemeinschaft* type of

[11] To take an extreme example, a middle-aged man might stubbornly refuse to make a will because of a kind of phantasy of immortality. If, however, a physician informed him that because of incurable cancer he had only a few months to live, this might well be enough to persuade him to make the will. This treatment of information and intentions as the primary types of intrinsic persuaders has recently been modified.

[12] For many purposes, economists have bracketed "goods and services" together as the two ultimate "want-satisfiers." For certain purposes of economic sociology, however, the distinction is vital, particularly because the concept of services constitutes one perspective on labor as a factor of production. (Cf. Talcott Parsons and Neil J. Smelser, *Economy and Society* (New York: The Free Press, 1956), p. 157, for a preliminary discussion of the importance of the distinction.)

solidarity is the primary "basis" of mutual influence, and is for influence systems the equivalent of gold for monetary and force for power systems.

This, however, can be only the security *base*. Just as a ramified monetary system cannot operate with an exclusively metallic medium, so a ramified influence system would be stultified if only close *Gemeinschaft* associates ever trusted each other beyond completely concrete levels of information and binding intentions. The degrees of freedom associated with the market are here matched by those of "communication" systems, e.g., freedom of the press and the like. Like any other interchange system, the stability of a free communication system is dependent on regulation by a set of institutionalized norms corresponding to those of property and contract. These have to do with the conditions normatively regulating types of association of people with each other, the kinds of obligations assumed in making assertions and giving opinions, and the kinds of obligations involved in statements of intention. Thus, the very fundamental principle of freedom of association may be said to be the normative principle in this sphere that corresponds to freedom of contract in the sphere of market organization; in both cases, of course, the freedoms are far from absolute, being subject to such restrictions as are imposed by the interests of third parties.

What then, can be said in general about the nature of these normative references? In the case of money, the reference, within the range of freedom of contract, is to value equivalences in the utility sense. Money functions here as the measure of value, and price is a statement of the assessed value of an exchangeable item. In the case of power, the reference is to authorization, in the sense that a unit with power is, within the given limits, authorized to make decisions that bind not only himself but certain categories of others and the relevant collectivity as a whole. Thus, the vote is an exercise of power, and, subject to the electoral rules, the aggregate of votes in an election will determine bindingly the incumbency of office.

In the case of influence, I suggest that the corresponding conception should be the normative justification of generalized statements about information or intention (*not* their empirical validation). The user of influence is under pressure to justify his statements, which are intended to have an effect on alter's action, by making them correspond to norms that are regarded as binding on both.[13] With reference to items of information, justification is necessary, since influence is a symbolic medium. The function of justification is not actually to verify the items, but to provide the basis for the communicators' *right* to state them without

---

[13] The term "justification" here refers to the level of norms. It seems useful to distinguish it from "legitimation," by which I would mean reference to the level of values. Cf. Talcott Parsons, Part II of General Introduction, in Parsons, E. Shils, K. Naegele, J. Pitts, editors, *Theories of Society* (New York: The Free Press, 1961), Vol. I, pp. 43–44.

alter's needing to verify them; for example, ego may be a technically competent "authority" in the field. With reference to intentions, justification may be regulated by various aspects of status that are regularly invoked to indicate that such intentions should prove trustworthy when stated by persons in the category in question.[14] A very important category of the justification of influence is what is ordinarily meant by "reputation." The same statement will carry more "weight" if made by someone with a high reputation for competence, for reliability, for good judgement, etc., than by someone without this reputation or with a reputation for unreliability. The common component may be called "fiduciary responsibility." A unit wields influence in proportion as, in the relevant context, its unverified declarations of information and intention are believed to be responsibly made. This is the "reputational" parallel to financial credit standing.

Put in familiar sociological terms, the associational base of influence might be regarded as primarily particularistic. The question is *who* the wielder is in terms of his collectivity memberships. The normative reference, however, is primarily universalistic. It is not what he is saying, which is a "content" matter, but what "right" he has to expect to be taken seriously, over and above the intrinsic cogency of what he says.

I spoke above of influence as "based" on *Gemeinschaft* solidarity, on the elementary, diffuse kind of belonging-togetherness of which, in a society like ours, the family is the prototypical case. The relevance of associatedness in collectivities is not, however, exhausted by this limiting case. Indeed, we may say that at many levels being "one of us" is a factor enhancing influence, whether it be membership in a local community, an occupational or professional group, or any one of many others. For this reason, nonmembers of groups must exercise special care in matters concerning the affairs of the group, lest they be felt to be "interfering." An obvious case is a foreigner speaking about a nation's domestic politics, especially one holding an official position at home. If this is true, then, conversely, attempting to influence is to a degree an attempt to establish a common bond of solidarity, on occasion even to bring the object of influence into common membership in a collectivity. Thus, being subject to mutual influence is to constitute a "we" in the sense that the parties have opinions and attitudes in common by virtue of which they "stand together" relative to those differing from them. There are, of course, various other conditions for establishing a full collectivity besides openness to mutual influence among its members, but we can certainly say that this is a necessary, if not sufficient, condition of a stable collectivity.

There is a very clear relation between this point and the findings of the study *Voting*, by Berelson, Lazarsfeld and McPhee, concerning the

[14] This, it should be noted, is independent of the assumption of formally binding obligation.

importance for voting behavior of the solidary group structures in which individuals are involved, starting with their families, but going on to occupations and ethnic, religious, and other groupings.[15] The broad presumption seems to be that a person will tend to vote with others whom he defines as "my kind of people" and that it is the "cross-pressured" groups which are most likely to break away from this tendency—cross-pressuring being itself a consequence of the increasing role pluralism of a complex society. Indeed, this finding was one of the most important points on which it seemed to me possible to relate empirical studies of voting behavior to the broad scheme of analysis of social interaction that has been the point of departure of the present essay.[16]

TYPES OF INFLUENCE

We may now approach the problem of classification of types or modes of influence. Here is it essential to bear in mind that the influence system is not a closed system. On the one hand, of course, it is used to get consent to particular attitudes and opinions that are to influence what particular commodities and services are to money. In this sense, we may think of influence as a "circulating" medium. To get consent, an "opinion leader" must expend some of his influence. He must therefore carefully husband it by choosing the occasions on which to intervene and the appropriate mode of intervention. The classic type of thriftless expenditure is illustrated by the nursery story about the repetition of the cry, "Wolf! Wolf!" so that when the wolf actually came, the warning was not believed. This is to say that by wasting his influence, the author of the cry had lost his influence, that is, his capacity to convince.

The circulating character of influence as a medium can be brought out more clearly if we break it down into types, since in each context it is easier to identify the nature of the flow in both ways than if it is treated on the more general level. I should like to suggest the following tentative classification: (1) "political" influence, (2) "fiduciary" influence, (3) influence through appeal to differential loyalties, and (4) influence oriented to the interpretation of norms. The fact that, in order to characterize the last two types, it is necessary to resort to cumbrous phrases rather than succinct single-word designations indicates clearly that the subject is rather undeveloped and needs elucidation. An important guide line for interpreting the first three types lies in the convertibility of each with one of the other three types of generalized media we have discussed.

---

[15] B. Berelson, P. Lazarsfeld, and W. McPhee, *Voting* (Chicago: University of Chicago Press, 1954).

[16] Cf. Talcott Parsons, "'Voting' and the Equilibrium of the American Political System," in Eugene Burdick and Arthur J. Brodbeck, editors, *American Voting Behavior* (New York: The Free Press, 1959). [Reprinted as Chapter 9 in the present volume: ed.]

1. When speaking of political influence, I mean it in an analytical sense, but one in which there is a directly significant relation between influence and power. The prototypical structural context is that of the democratic association, whether it be in the field of government at any one of several levels, or of private associations. The democratic association is characterized by a structure of offices the incumbents of which are authorized to take certain decisions binding on the collectivity as a whole and, hence, on its members in their respective capacities.[17] Such authorization is for action defined within constitutional norms, and there are also constitutional procedures by which incumbents of office are chosen, summed up as election and appointment.

The making of decisions binding on a collectivity I interpret to be an exercise of power, which includes the exercise of the franchise in the electoral procedure, since it is the aggregate of votes which determines who is elected to office. But both in seeking election and in office, officers and candidates are continually using other ways of getting the results they want besides the use of power in a strict sense. They are, of course, giving information and announcing intentions, in the detailed sense. They may well be offering inducements, making coercive threats outside the context of the power of office, and activating their own and others' commitments. But they are, above all, operating with influence, in our technical sense.

There are, as I conceive it, two main contexts in which this is the case. Because associations are typically differentiated on the axis of leadership-followership, we may use this axis here. One focus of influence, then, is the establishment of leadership position or reputation, either as incumbent of office or as explicit or implicit candidate, so that, for the followership in question, there will be a basis of trust going beyond the direct exercise of power, the giving of specific information and the like, and also beyond the manipulation of inducements, informal threats, etc. A leader, I suggest, must try to establish a basis on which he is trusted by a "constituency," in the symbolic sense of this discussion, so that when he "takes a position," he can count on a following "going along with him" on it, or even actively working for its implementation according to their respective capacities and roles. We often put this by saying that a leader "takes responsibility" for such positions. In any case, I would treat the concept of leadership as focusing on the use of influence, and the concept of office, on the use of power.

The other context is the obverse, that of the processes by which units not in a leadership position in the relevant respects can have and use influence oriented to having an effect on leadership. This is by and large

[17] Of course, for this analysis to be relevant, the association in question need not be "fully" democratic, but this problem of ranges in degrees of democracy need not concern the present very limited discussion.

the well-known field of "interest groups," very broadly in the sense of parts of the constituencies of parties and officeholders. The influence may be used in electoral processes, trying to establish terms on which electoral support—a form of power—will be given. Or, it may play on incumbents of office by trying to influence their decisions of policy. In either case, it is the use of a basis of presumptive "trust" and, hence, "right to speak" to try to swing a balance in favor of what the influencer advocates—or opposes—relative to alternatives, whether these be candidates or policies.

Political influence, then, we would conceive as influence operating in the context of the goal-functioning of collectivities, as generalized persuasion without power—i.e., independent of the use of power or direct threat,[18]—used, on the one hand, by units either exercising or bidding for leadership position and, on the other, by nonleaders seeking to have an effect on the decisions and orientations of leaders. Though political influence is analytically independent of power, we conceive the two to be closely interconnected. Very generally, leaders expect a major share of their influence to be translated into binding support, particularly through the franchise, and constituents in turn expect an important part of theirs to be translated into binding decisions congenial to them. But the independence of influence from power means that the influence system is an open one. To tie it to power in direct, matching terms would be to reduce the power-influence relation to a barter basis, and thus destroy the element of symbolic generalization we have treated as essential.

2. The second type of influence suggested has been called "fiduciary." The relevant context here is not the effective determination of an attainment of collective goals, but the allocation of resources in a system where both collectivities and their goals are plural and the justification of each among the plural goals is problematical. The interests in control of resources and in attainment of goals are the classical instances of the operation of "interests" in social systems. In a more or less pluralistic system, the allocation of resources must, however, be subject to normative control; distribution must be justified by reference to norms more general than the mere desirability to the unit in question of getting what it wants. Furthermore, resources constitute, from the point of view of goal attainment, the principal opportunity factor that conditionally controls prospects of success. Hence, influence bearing on the allocation of resources is a particularly important field of trust.

There is a relation to money in this case which is in certain respects parallel to that to power in the case of political influence. This derives

---

[18] Incumbents of office, though they have power, are often very careful when pleading for certain measures to make clear that they will not directly bring their power to bear in the particular case. A good example is when officeholders who are adherents of a particular party lend their influence to strictly nonpartisan causes. Thus a state governor who is a good Republican may plead for *all* the people, regardless of party, to contribute generously to the Red Cross campaign.

from the fact that, in a society in which the economy is highly differentiated relative to other elements of the social structure, money becomes the most important allocative mechanism, not only over commodities, but over human services. Hence, the focus of the fiduciary function is in the allocation of funds, because the possessor of funds is in turn in a position to claim, through market channels, control over the indicated share of "real" resources.

The interchanges we have in mind here do not constitute the use of money as a circulating medium, but rather as a measure of value. On the monetary side, an example is setting up a budget. The various interests that expect to share in a budget "assert their claims," and the budget-making agency reaches some kind of allocative ranking of these claims. This is the expression of need and of "right" in monetary terms. But both claims and accession of right in turn are subject to standards of justification, in our technical sense. These are never assertions of value as such, because the agency, dealing as it does with scarce and allocable resources, must always consider situational exigency and competing claims. It operates, that is, at the level of norms, not of values. Those who assert claims may concretely, of course, use power to gain them; they may use inducements—in the extreme case, bribery—or various other means. But a special role is played by influence. A good example would be, in budgetary negotiations, the assertion of a highly qualified and trustworthy technical expert that to fulfill expectations he must have a certain specific minimum of resources at his disposal—an assertion that a budgetary officer, not himself an expert in the field, will find it difficult to contest. On the other hand, decisions of allocation in turn must be justified by reference to agreed standards of proper priority in claims. Such standards, of course, are likely to be made most explicit where there is an unaccustomed stringency of resources and hence sacrifices must be justified. Just as the budgetary officer is often unable to judge the needs of the technical expert, so the latter, operating only in one specialized sector of the system, is not qualified to judge the urgency of the claims competing with his own. Hence the necessity for mutual influence to operate to cover this gap.

The case of a budget is the neatest case, because the relevant system is more or less closed by unitary organizational control of the resources and by power, in the strict sense, to make the allocative decisions binding. The same basic principles, however, apply in processes of allocation through free market channels. The economist's ideal of free competition is here the limiting case in which influence as an independent factor disappears. Here, then, it is in two areas that influence is most obviously operative. One is the establishment of norms by which the allocative process is regulated, as through tax legislation and the like; the other is through such modifications of "pure" market process as the involvement of voluntary contributions in allocations. The very term "fiduciary" is also most generally used for cases where certain "interested parties" cannot be expected to protect their interests without help, for example, administration of the property interests of minors by "trustees," i.e. people who can be trusted to apply acceptable standards even though their actions are not dictated by personal financial interest.

3. The third category has been called "influence through appeal to differential loyalties." Whereas in the political influence case the differentiation on the axis of leadership was the central structural focus, and in the fiduciary influence case it was the problem of allocation of scarce resources, in this case it is the pluralistic structure of memberships in society. This operates at the level both of individuals in roles and of collectivities. The more highly differentiated the society is structurally, the more every concrete unit is a responsible member of a plurality of collectivities.[19] He is therefore in a position of having to balance the claims of these plural collectivities on his loyalties, i.e. a class of his normative commitments.

For the individual, particularly the adult male, the most important case is normally the relation between kinship and occupation, since for most men it is essential to participate in both, and in modern societies they are structurally independent of each other. Generally, in a reasonably stable situation, the broad lines of allocation of obligation are institutionally settled, but there are always areas of indeterminacy and of shift in the light of changing circumstances. Moreover, our society is rapidly changing, and one of the principal aspects of such change is the rise of new collectivities, and hence loyalties to them, and the decline of old ones. A large part of the population is thus faced with decisions about whether to take on new commitments or to sacrifice old ones, or both, or to shift balances among loyalties.

The commitments we have in mind are grounded in institutionalized values, which can, for purposes of analysis, be presumed to be shared by members of a society. But it is in the nature of a differentiated society that there is an important difference between asserting, however sincerely, the desirability of a value and, on the other hand, taking personal responsibility for its implementation, since the capacities and opportunities of units for effective contribution are inherently limited, and, moreover, some kinds of attempt would infringe the prerogatives of other units. It is with this problem that the present type of influence is concerned. It is a matter of the justification of assuming particular responsibilities in particular collectivity and subcollectivity contexts.

A person, then, will be faced by manifold demands for commitment through participation in collectivities, and will often be put in a position

---

[19] For the collectivity as unit the relevant membership is that in more inclusive collectivities; e.g., a department is a subcollectivity in a university faculty.

of having to justify the allocative decisions he makes. The normative structure (of "commitments") governing such processes then involves, on the one hand, appeals to common values and, on the other, assertion of norms governing the practical decisions of allocation of commitment among plural loyalties. The categories of influence, then, are, first, the plea that an actor ought, as a practical matter, to undertake such and such a collective responsibility (not merely that it is desirable that the function be effectively performed independently of *his* commitment; that is an assertion of its value), and second, the assertion of the norms it is held should govern such decisions, again at the level of practical allocation.

In one sense, this, like the last category of influence, concerns the allocation of "resources." But what I am here referring to as loyalties are not the same kind of resource as money and power, or the concrete utilities and modes of effectiveness controlled by them. From the point of view of the unit, the question is not with what means he will implement his commitments, but *whether he will undertake the commitment in the first place.* It is not, given that he "intends" to do something, a question of *how* he is to accomplish it, but rather whether he *ought*—in our sense of justification—to undertake it at all. Commitments in this sense surely constitute a societal resource, but, in the analysis of unit action, they concern the "orientational" side, not the situational side, of the action paradigm.[20]

As noted earlier in this paper, I consider generalized commitments to constitute a symbolic medium operating on the interaction process in the same basic sense that money, power, and influence do. Any promise by which the actor forecloses certain alternatives may be regarded as a *particular* commitment. By invoking a *generalized* commitment, however, the actor is enabled to command a series of more particular commitments, to be in a position to "activate" them in response to appropriate circumstances, as we have said above. A good example is securing the acceptance of a job offer. Commitment to the job by the prospective employee then entails a commitment to perform a complex series of more particular acts as occasion arises, including commitment to accept certain types of authority within the organization.

Being grounded in values, generalized commitments in some sense involve the "honor" of the actors concerned, the more so the more generalized they are. They therefore cannot in general be altered lightly. Nevertheless, in a pluralistic and changing society, complete rigidity of commitments would introduce an intolerable rigidity into its structure. Commitments must therefore involve priority scales of seriousness, i.e. be referred to general standards, and there must be norms defining

[20] Cf. Talcott Parsons, "Pattern Variables Revisited," *American Sociological Review,* Vol. 25 (1960), pp. 467–483 and *Sociological Theory and Modern Society,* Chapter 7, for an elucidation of this essential distinction.

the situations in which particular commitments may be changed, not only new ones assumed but also old ones abandoned, even where this means the breaking of promises made and accepted in good faith. A good example here is the general norm that even in occupations where rules of tenure bind the employing organization, incumbents of such positions are generally considered entitled to resign subject only to giving "reasonable" notice. The category of influence with which we are now concerned operates in this range of flexibility of commitments and concerns the relation between the justification for change and the more generalized loyalties to fulfillment of commitments made.

4. The three types of influence so far discussed deal with the relations of the normative or integrative system to the other primary functional subsystems of the society, namely, what I should call the "polity," the "economy," and the "pattern maintenance" (in a structural aspect, the value maintenance) systems respectively.[21] The fourth and final type, which was referred to as influence oriented to the interpretation of norms, is internal to the integrative system. Here the prototype is the process of interpretation of legal norms in the appellate phase of the judicial process.

Since norms mediate between value commitments and particular interests and situational exigencies, they are, in formulation, in need of continual adjustment to the variations at these levels. Futhermore, since their primary function in the social system is integrative, the problem of consistency is a particularly important one. Hence, in a complex system of normative regulation, the interpretive function is highly important. A category of influence is organized about it of which the best example is the influence involved in the reputations of judges and lawyers. As in so many other fields, substantive arguments, i.e. particular justifications, of course play a central part. But there is the same need for symbolic generalization here as in the other fields. Another type of example of interpretive influence would be in the field of exegesis of ethical norms, which plays such an important part in many religious traditions.

This has been an exceedingly sketchy and tentative attempt to review a typology of the different contexts of the operation of influence. All, I think, are fields in which the general themes of the above analysis can be illustrated in sufficiently well-known terms to carry conviction of the reality and importance of the phenomena here called "influence." Let me reiterate that the critical common fact is a mechanism of persuasion that is generalized beyond appeal to particular facts, particular intentions, particular obligations and commitments, particular normative rules. The

[21] This refers to a generalized paradigm of analysis in terms of four functional categories, elaborated more fully, for example, in the General Introduction to *Theories of Society* and in "Pattern Variables Revisited," as cited.

general suggestion is that, in the absence of a ramified system of influence in this sense, there would either be a much more pervasive atmosphere of distrust than in fact obtains, or the level of trust could be raised only by introducing more rigid specification as to who could be trusted in what specific ways, which would greatly limit the ranges of flexibility so important to a complex society.

IS INFLUENCE A FIXED QUANTITY IN A SOCIAL SYSTEM?

One further major topic is so essential to the general understanding of symbolic media that the discussion would be seriously incomplete without a brief treatment of it. It concerns a problem that has been particularly prominent in the history of the analysis of money and power, but the technical analysis of influence has been so primitive that it has scarcely arisen in that connection. It may be put in terms of the question whether any or all of these media are in general subject to a "zero-sum" condition of their operation.

At certain levels and in certain contexts it is obvious that this condition does hold. For a unit with fixed money income, increase of expenditure for one purpose must be balanced by reduction for one or more others. Similarly in power systems, electoral rules mean that a vote cast for one candidate must be denied to others, and persons in authority must choose between mutually incompatible alternatives in making many decisions. Important as this is, it is not, however, the whole story.

The most familiar case in the monetary field in which the zero-sum conception fails to apply is the creation of a credit through banking. Money in one aspect is the most important object of property rights. Depositors in a bank in one sense "lend" their property to the bank. But, unlike most contracts of lease, they do not, even for a term, relinquish any of their rights: the main feature of a deposit is that it is repayable on demand, subject only to rules such as those regulating banking hours.

The bank, however, does not simply act as custodian for its depositors' funds. It lends a certain proportion to borrowers on contractual terms that enable the latter to "spend" them so long as they are presumptively in a position to repay at the term of the loan, and of course pay interest and any other charges. This means that *the same dollars* are functioning double as circulating media, so that the bank loans outstanding constitute a net addition to the quantity of the circulating medium.

This commonplace of economics has a very important implication. Clearly, an operating bank is in *one* important sense always formally "insolvent," in that its deposits are held on demand whereas its loans are on term. If all the depositors demand repayment at the same time, the bank cannot meet its obligations without outside resources. It usually keeps sufficient cash—and other resources—on hand to meet expected rates of withdrawal, with a margin of safety, but if it were completely "liquid," it would cease to be a bank. Financial panics are, precisely, occasions on which an abnormal rate of demand puts the bank in a difficult if not impossible position, in the extreme case forcing its "failure."

The question arises whether there are, with respect to the other media, phenomena analogous to those of banking and credit in the monetary field. The dominant opinion in the field of analysis of power seems to have been that there are not,[22] but this position has been questioned. The most appropriate context seems to be the relation between the grant of power of leadership in the democratic association and the use of that power by leadership.

Elected leaders may be said to be the recipients of a grant of power through the exercise of the franchise. This grant is, moreover, typically and in principle revocable, if not on demand, then at the end of a stated terms of office, when the voter can transfer his support to a rival candidate. It could be argued, then, that this is a "deposit" of power, which is at the disposal of the depositors for the "purchase" of political benefits through the decisions made by the incumbents of office somewhere in the system, not necessarily this particular office. This would make it a "circulating" system where the amounts of power balanced.

It may be suggested, however, that this is only part of the story. Some of the power acquired through election to offices may be "invested" in collective enterprises that are not direct responses to the interest-demands of constituents, and this power in turn may be utilized by agencies other than constituents. Since power is in certain circumstances convertible into money, for example through taxation, it may be suggested that some of the use of tax funds, as in the support of scientific training and research, is a process of "investment" by officeholders—in both the executive and the legislative branches—that puts the funds at the disposal of scientists and educational institutions. If the electorate, like the bank's depositors, should demand immediate and strict accounting of power, the system would, like a good bank, turn out to be "insolvent" in the sense that these commitments could not be liquidated all at once. Often, however, politicians can shrewdly estimate the latitude it is safe to assume in making commitments other than those specifically demanded by the constituents on whom they are dependent. Politically organized collectivities, including government, can probably serve as agents of creative social change mainly by virtue of this type of mechanism, namely, the creation of increments of new power, since

[22] For example, this seems to be the position of Harold D. Lasswell and Abraham Kaplan, *Power and Society* (New Haven: Yale University Press, 1950).

generating direct constituency demands for these changes may involve much more serious difficulties.

It would seem logical that the same reasoning should apply to influence. The case in which the zero-sum concept should particularly apply is political influence, because, on the economic analogy, this is a kind of "circular flow" situation in which the process of eliciting collective decisions in a ramified system is mediated.[23] The economic parallel lies in the markets for consumers' goods and for labor.

In the field of influence, the analogy with banking and credit seems most obvious in connection with the allocation of loyalties. The postulate on which our whole analysis in this area is based is that it applies most clearly to a highly pluralistic social system in which the allocation of loyalties cannot be wholly based on direct assessment of the importance of the intrinsic issues involved, but that commitments are widely made in response to influence. If the quantity of influence is not fixed, but is expansible along the lines suggested by monetary credit, then it becomes possible for influence to operate as a mechanism by which a given capacity for power and commitments (in our technical sense) can be reallocated, in that the influence to command such commitments can be more or less directly and deliberately put in the hands of certain agencies.

My suggestion is that the principal way in which this is done in a society like the American is through voluntary associations that, unlike government even in its "democratic" aspect, are not primarily concerned with political functions—again our technical sense. The "joiners" of such associations are analogous to depositors. They have, as we often put it, "lent their names" to the association and its leadership. But such an association often does more than simply collect increments of influence; it creates the effect of adding to the total amount of influence in circulation. This can occur in proportion as leadership exercises *independent* judgment in how to use the "name," not of individual members but of the association, to encourage commitments which they consider to be desirable, generally in quarters outside the membership itself.

Such associations may thus be considered to be a kind of "influence bank." Like money banks, they are formally "insolvent." Hence, if their members call for strict accounting—"You shall not use the name of the association without explicit consent of all the membership to the detailed implications"—this, of course, destroys the freedom of action of leaders, and leads to a deflation of "influence credit." The effect of this in turn is to deprive many agencies, dependent on the "backing" of such influence purveyors, of the basis on which they can "afford" to make important commitments. In more ordinary circumstances, however, leaders

---

[23] For the concept of circular flow, cf. J. A. Schumpeter, *The Theory of Economic Development* (Cambridge, Mass.: Harvard University Press, 1934), Chapter 1.

of such associations operate on a judgement of the acceptable margins of their independence. They do, in fact, make commitments of the association's name beyond the level of explicit authorization—though not of realistic expectation of "justification"—by the membership. In so doing, they add to the net amount of influence circulating in the system and have an effect on the distribution commitments in the society in the direction of promoting the "causes" they hold to be desirable.

It should be clear from the above argument that phenomena analogous to deflation and inflation in the economic case should be found in the fields of power and influence as well. We have already indicated the direction that deflationary trends would take in these fields. In the field of power it is toward progressively increasing reliance on strict authority and coercive sanctions, culminating in the threat and use of physical force. In the field of influence it is toward undermining the basis of trust in reputations and fiduciary responsibility through increasing questioning of broader loyalties and rising insistence on narrow in-groupism.[24]

Inflationary process, on the other hand, is, for influence, the extension of claims to authoritative diagnoses of situations that cannot be validated with solid information and, on the other hand, the declaration of praiseworthy intentions that will not be backed by actual commitments when occasion arises. Unfortunately, there is no space here to develop these themes as they deserve.

It should go without saying that this essay has been very tentative indeed. It cannot claim to be more than the barest approach to the very complicated problems of this area. I hope, however, that it can serve as a useful basis not only for discussion but for the stimulation of serious research.

[24] McCarthyism was a classic instance of a deflationary episode entering in the influence field, which at its culmination approached panic proportions: the demand for "absolute loyalty" was analogous to the demand for a return to the gold standard in the financial area. Cf. E. A. Shils, *The Torment of Secrecy,* and "Social Strains in America." [Reprinted as Chapter 7 in the present volume: ed.]

Postscript to
Chapter 15

Some of the difficulties in the treatment of influence in the above chapter have, in the absence of opportunity for a full reworking of the subject, stimulated me to try to help the reader by adding a brief postscript.

It seems to me that there is one main point at which the original discussion is positively wrong. If influence, like money and power, is to be treated as a generalized medium of interchange, it must possess the equivalent of the economists' attribution to money of "value in exchange" *as distinguished from* "value in use." If, as I have argued, it is a medium of persuasion, there must be categories of "intrinsic persuaders"—parallel to "want satisfiers"—which its use can command in exchange, but which do not themselves constitute influence in the present sense. For the economy, these are proverbially "goods and services." In the article, two categories of intrinsic persuaders were suggested, namely *information* and *declarations of intentions*.

The first part of this note will discuss the status of the category of intentions, showing that one type of such intentions is in fact an intrinsic persuader, namely, what we have been calling value-commitments. Two other categories of intrinsic persuaders, namely, political support for the leadership of collectivities and the ranking of claims to fluid resources, stand on a somewhat different footing. The first is, however, a special class of intentions and not intentions in general. In formal terms, all three are *product* outputs of the integrative system to each of the other three primary subsystems respectively (cf. Figure 2 of Technical Note to Chapter 14). The problem of the status of information is different, and we will next try to clarify that important point.

The second main part of this note will be concerned with two important extensions of the analysis of influence beyond the level reached in the original paper. The first of these concerns the relation of the influence mechanism to the functioning of plural systems of interpenetrating solidary groupings, as distinguished from its operation within a single such collective system. This extension will be seen to link up with reference group theory.

The second extension will consist of an approach to the problem of defining and analyzing the quantitative dimension of influence systems, a task which was not attempted at all in the original paper. It will become evident that this will require a rather careful discrimination between influence and the problem of its quantification on the one hand, and money, power, and commitments, on the other. The thesis will be put forward that the main focus of the quantification of influence lies in the rank ordering of priorities among the functions performed by the different units or subsystems of the system of reference, including, of course, the plural interpenetrating network of such subsystems referred to above.

The problem raised by the concept of intentions has, I think, been substantially clarified by the treatment of value-commitments in Chapter 16, which was written well after Chapter 15. Here the problem is essentially to interpret "intentions" on the proper level, as involving the specification of value-commitments to the level that is requisite for operative practicality in particular situations. The prototype is the validation of the persuasiveness of an exertion of influence by its eliciting a "commitment"—on the part of an individual or a collectivity—to act, in the future of course, in the manner the user of influence has suggested. This, essentially, is to say that not *any* declaration of intentions falls in the relevant category, but only those that can be held to constitute commitments in the technical sense of Chapter 16. The major criterion is acceptance of the onus of moral blame if the commitments are not fulfilled, unless nonfulfillment is adequately justified by reference to incompatibility with higher obligations. Otherwise "good intentions" may constitute the material with which, proverbially, "the road to hell is paved."

Commitments are not, of course, as such, the ultimate "desirables" from the point of view of actors involved in the process of persuasion, but constitute "packages" of components which are presumptively relevant to the affected decisions and the implementation of their consequences. The persuader, through the use of his influence, "receives" certain commitments which he, in turn, can "use." What this means may perhaps be elucidated by the example of the use of influence to bridge the "competence gap" in medical practice. In a very simple instance a patient may be "advised" to undergo a certain operation, and, when he "accepts" that advice, i.e., makes a commitment, the surgeon may then proceed to plan for the actual operation with a high probability that the patient will "go through with it." In a more complicated case, the patient may be advised to follow a rather complicated regimen in dealing with a continuing health problem. In accepting the advice he makes a commitment to perform a variety of acts in differing circumstances and extending over time. This, of course, is normally reciprocated by the physician's commitment to continue to supervise the regimen. The "initial" commitment, however, is the primary lever by which the persuader, the physician, exercises continuing control over his patient's behavior, for instance by reminding him, directly or indirectly, of what "he promised." In the formal terms stated in Figure 2 of Chapter 14, the interchange we have in mind is between the integrative and the pattern-maintenance systems. The relevant "form" of commitment is "commitment to common values," i.e., to the affirmation of the value base, in the promotion of the patient's health, of the relation of physician and patient, which implies sensitivity to the former's advice. Of course, it should not be assumed that the two do not influence each other; i.e., the physician seeks the patient's commitment to accept his advice, and vice versa the patient seeks the physician's commitment to do his best in the interest of the former's health. The mutual specified commitments are made meaningful by virtue of the more general commitment on both sides to the valuation of health.

The input of commitments to the integrative system, formulated as commitment to valued association, is the factor in promoting solidarity that stands highest in the cybernetic scale, in this sense superordinate to solidarity itself. In this respect its role is parallel to that of power in a credit system, making access to otherwise unavailable economic resources possible for the increase of productivity through investment. Contrary, however, to what was said in the body of the paper, we do not now consider it to be the "security base" of influence as a generalized medium. This question will be taken up again below.

Information as a possible "intrinsic persuader" stands at a farther remove from the primary status of "intrinsic persuader" than does "intention" in the sense in which that concept was used in Chapter 15. If the relation is symmetrical to that in the L-I interchange, then the relevant input should be a form of political power, specifically, political support. If this is the case, it would be stretching a point to call this also a form of "intentions." The difference from commitments to common values most relevant here, however, lies in the fact that political support is, as a form of power, as we argued in Chapter 14, *binding on a collectivity*, whereas value-commitments are "internally" binding on an acting unit, but not specifically linked to concrete collective measures. An act of political support may, however, be initiated by a declaration of intention to act, and then consummated by voting. Hence *both* of the two principal categories of intrinsic persuaders are at least in part forms of the "declaration of intention."

Information stands at quite a different level, in that it is a component in all the interchange processes of the social system. It is not itself, in isolation from other components, a medium of interchange. Thus the information that a commitment has been, or is likely to be, made is crucial to the persuasive capacity of the commitment, and similarly with an act of political support. The same is true of the "basis" of influence because, in the previous example, the information *that* it is the considered, responsible opinion of a reputable physician that patient X *ought* to undergo a given operation is a crucial factor in X's decision whether or not to make the commitment. The information on the basis of which the physician forms *his* opinion, of course, lies on a different level, usually, because of the competence gap, only partially accessible to the patient. Thus, other things equal, given items of information may be the decisive factors in persuading a given alter to be influenced by a given ego, in the paradigm set forth above. But, on both sides of the commitment-power relation, information is a component of the "package" which is intrinsically persuasive in our technical sense, not a "type" of such package, to say nothing of the only such type.

Where an item of information is sufficient to persuade, it is often backed up by the exercise of influence. The common pattern is that when ego says to alter "did you know that . . . ?" he is more likely to be believed if, in the absense of alter's capacity to check easily on his own, ego has influence in his relation to alter, on the bases we have reviewed.

One of the reasons why the treatment of information as an intrinsic persuader was so seductively plausible seems to be that it does indeed have a further very important place in influence systems. The important point is that commitment to solidarity (valued association) is not, as we have noted, the security base of influence systems, but rather certain types of knowledge which, for present purposes, can be treated as forms of information. This plays a role in such systems parallel to gold in monetary systems and force in power systems. It stands at the limit of the symbolic character of the medium, the point where, in the case of gold, it is its *commodity* value, i.e., value in use, which is the main consideration, because the special properties of gold make it almost always acceptable in exchange, except where especially critical wants are involved—e.g., a "diet of gold" would not be very nourishing. Similarly the use of force is the "ultimate" instrument of coercion which can "enforce" binding decisions, but, like gold, it has certain critical limitations, notably being an ultimate preventive but not necessarily the ultimate "positive motivator" to compliance. Similarly, a kind of knowledge or information may in certain limiting circumstances be sufficient to persuade, and is more secure than the mere "opinion" of the user of influence. Its limitation is that it cannot cross the various gaps over which persuasion is important —such as the "competence gap" we used for illustration above. Hence a system of persuasion reduced to the circulation of solidly verifiable information would enormously deflate the functioning of influence as a medium.

We may now turn to the two primary directions of extension of the analysis of influence beyond the levels reached in Chapter 15 which, as noted, I should like briefly to comment upon in this postscript, though it will not be possible to develop them in detail. One of these concerns the nature of the systems of solidary, associational groupings within which the influence medium operates. For the most part, the discussion of Chapter 15 is focused on its operation within a single solidary collectivity. The implications even of this reference, if fully followed up, would certainly lead far. They become, however, much more salient when they are considered in the context of a "pluralistic" system of such interpenetrating groupings, which, with multiple participation, from the point of view of the unit, notably the individual, becomes a *reference group* system.

By interpenetration, I mean here that the same individuals and collective units are members of two or more such solidary groupings; thus an employed individual is both a family member and a member of the employing organization, as well of course of various others. Within limits, then, influence, like the other media, should be conceived to be *transferable* from one solidary grouping to another, in a manner somewhat similar to that in which wage income is transferable from the employing organization to the family household.

Here the unit, individual or collective, with common membership, acts as a "node" through which influence may flow from one group to the other. For the individual case, we may think of the process operating in some manner wherein the "prestige" of an individual in one collectivity makes it easier for him to persuade the members of the other along the lines of his wishes. The phenomenon of the "corporation wife," much discussed a decade ago, is a case in point. The company, through her husband's position in it, may exert influence on her to participate beyond the limits which would otherwise obtain, though in turn such "marginal" persons may have perceptible influence on the operations of the company.

The suggestion is that there is, in the field in which influence operates, a problem analogous to that of the "extent of the market," as this has been emphasized in economics at least since Adam Smith, and that this extent of the market is bound up with an aspect of the "division of labor," especially in Durkheim's sense, namely, the involvement of the "influence system" with a range of differentiated solidary groupings. It is in this context of its relation to structural pluralism that the high significance of influence as a mechanism of integration of social systems is above all to be seen. This view in a general way permeates a good deal of the discussion in the various papers included in Part III of this volume.

Explicit introduction of the pluralistic set of references for the analysis of influence systems makes two problems particularly salient. These include not only the question of quantification, referred to above, but also that of the nature of the institutional code in terms of which influence is legitimately exercised, in the sense parallel to that in which property is the institutional code underlying monetary evaluation, and authority that of the "right" to use power. It is clear that such a code must be more general than its involvement in any single collective system.

I would like to suggest that what I, among many others, have called the *system* of stratification in a society is the core, at least, of that code.[1] It concerns essentially the criteria by which units in a social system are given a *generalized* status rank, one which transcends specificity of function or situation. The relative rank position of a given unit then, individual or collective, may be called his or its *prestige*. A position of prestige, which is inherently relative, i.e., having a place in a rank order, is the status-base from which the unit functions as a node, in the above sense, in the processes of circulation of influence, including not only "exerting" influence, but coming to be in a position to do so through receiving an "income" of influence, as through the recognition of particular achievements, or through acquiring prestigeful membership statuses, or indeed offices.

A particularly obvious illustration is that when an individual assumes, by election or appointment, a high office in the political sense, public or private, he not only acquires a higher than otherwise level of control of power, but whatever influence he may previously have commanded is enhanced by the combination with enhanced power. Thus the recent election of Richard Nixon to the Presidency of the United States will enormously increase the power at his disposal, but also substantially enhance the level of his influence in many sectors of the society. This latter consequence I would formulate, or rather label, by saying that his prestige had increased.

This familiar phenomenon points to the theoretical problem of the *quantitative* dimension of influence as a medium, which was hardly opened up in the discussion of influence in Chapter 15. There is little doubt about what is meant when it is said that X has more money than Y, since money as a quantity varies on a linear continuum defined in terms of a formally established unit, the "currency" unit. It is, however, important that what is meant is not "having," e.g., in some storage facility, more "dollars" in the sense of cash, but having control of "assets" of monetary value, many of which, such as equity securities, rest their value on "expectations" as much as anything else.

Similarly, within a defined organization context, it is not difficult, on the basis presented in Chapter 14, to define what is meant by saying that

---

[1] This concept was set forth in my early essay on the theory of stratification, and further developed in the later "revised" approach. Both essays are reprinted in the 1954 edition of my *Essays in Sociological Theory*, as Chapters IV and XIX respectively.

X has more power than Y. In a fully institutionalized sense I would say that, within a single collective organization, it means that X occupies an office which stands higher in a given hierarchy of authority than that of Y. The criterion is that, in case of a conflict of views, X's decision will prevail, from the point of view of bindingness on the collectivity, over Y's.[2] Where, finally, different systems of collective organization are involved, it is power in the more inclusive and superordinated collective system which, other things equal, prevails over that in subsystems or less inclusive ones. Federalism and the separation of powers place barriers to the full transferability of power among units in this case, as does clear differentiation among private units of organization. Thus there is ordinarily no clear relation of relative authority of office between the president of a university in a local community and the top executive of a business firm with roughly comparable relative "importance" in that community. Their primary relations to each other is *not*, in our terms, one of relative power.

The question, what do we mean by saying that X has more *influence* than Y? should be placed in this context, by *distinguishing* the meaning of greater influence from that of "more power" or greater wealth. It is, specifically, how is it that X has more persuasive capacity than Y, independently of either's direct control of "intrinsic persuaders," including as we have just reviewed, unit commitments and political support? The answer to this question is not simple, and is deeply involved in and with the theory of social stratification. When dealing with the hierarchical aspect the suggestion is that we should speak of a "prestige hierarchy." The question necessarily arises of whether this is not identical with the scale of superiority of wealth, i.e. command of assets convertible into money, or of power, command of capacity to bind collective organizations.

The answer is clearly *no*. The generation of influence is a function of *factors* deriving from both the economy and the polity; hence both wealth and power are *related* to level of influence. But influence is also a function of the input of factors *other* than those of wealth or power, separately or taken together, namely, in strict social system terms, commitment to values and loyalty to solidary groupings. *Neither* commitments to values nor loyalty, to say nothing of both taken together, varies as a simple dependent variable relative to wealth or power or both. In our reference system, the structure of solidary groupings is partially dependent on, but also partially independent of, the structure of collectivities with economic and political primacy, though of course it interpenetrates with both.

Simple examples from contemporary society concern the influence of

<hr/>

[2] In a limited way this pattern extends to the market situation. In a buyers' competition for acquisition of an asset, often the offer of the highest bidder will prevail. This may legitimately be considered to be a use of "economic power," i.e. the use of superior financial resources—or willingness to commit such resources as are available in *this* context—to *prevail over* a competitor within the same system. Here money is used as an "instrument of power." The allocation of resources is made binding by virtue of the institution of contract.

spokesmen of the churches and of ethnic groups as such. In the former case, the Catholic church, for example, is not particularly rich, nor does its membership, in spite of the Kennedy clan, comprise generally the most affluent sector of the population, nor, in the famous words of Stalin, does it command many "divisions." Its influence is, I should say, well out of proportion to its wealth and power. A somewhat similar argument might be set forth about universities: though they consume a major share of wealth, they are not, on the whole, wealthy "in their own right"; on the contrary they are heavily subsidized, and they have to "go begging," e.g., to state legislatures, and hence do not command the power to allocate financial resources to themselves, again "in their own right." They are, however, highly influential as units of modern society.

In this connection the pluralism of the solidary systems in which influence operates again becomes particularly important. The version of the "division of labor" in Durkheim's sociological sense which is relevant means that, through the extended "influence market" involving many interpenetrating groups, access both to factors of influence, such as commitment to valued association, and to "intrinsic persuaders," such as political support, is far wider than it otherwise would be. Indeed it seems justified to set forth the hypothesis that the quantitative dimension of influence should be defined by the *scope* of the interpenetrating channels within which influence can be exercised on the one hand and from which it can be drawn on the other. This suggests that he who has the highest prestige among a set is he who can exert his influence in the widest range of different collective subsystems, and who can draw on the resources of such a range—which in both cases involve varying *proportions* of the factors and products. This proposition will require much firmer grounding and exploration of its implications but it seems to be a reasonable basis of approach to the essential problem of definition of the quantitative dimension.

These considerations reinforce the view that prestige is relatively independent from, though of course interdependent with, both wealth—the distribution of economically valuable assets—and power—the distribution of authority, and indeed of value-commitments. This independence rests, I think, on two main bases. One of these is the *scope* of the system of interprenetrating solidary groupings just discussed within which the influence of the position is effectively operative. The famous sociological distinction between "locals" and "cosmopolitans" is relevant to this point.

The second, however, is the place which the solidary groupings of reference occupy with reference to the various subsystems of the value system institutionalized in the larger societal system, and the priorities of relative importance which are involved with or "built into" this value system. Thus I think it can be said that in the American value system there has occurred in the last generation a substantial shift in the relative position of the subvalues of "economic rationality" in favor of those of "cognitive rationality" and of "distributive justice." This shift in turn has altered the balance of legitimation in the sense of less stress on the importance of economic productivity as the primary function of a sub-system of the society, in favor of stress on that of the inclusion of "min-ority groups" and of education and research as functionally urgent. This is a *relative* shift, but not for that reason unimportant.

We assume, of course, that relative "distinction" in achievement, of whatever the relevant type, is always a factor in prestige. Thus a Carnegie or a Rockefeller was a hero of productivity, an Einstein or any one of the list of Nobel Prize winners, of the advancement of knowledge. But given this, and the factor of scope, influence depends on the relative valuation of the *functions* in the larger system of the solidary groupings we are talking about. From this point of view prestige, and the influence which clusters in prestigeful units of the social structure, may be thought of as capacity to determine—subject always to conditions—*the allocation of functions* in the social system, including the rise in opportunity for the performance of some functions and the relative fall in salience of others.

In a relatively stable society, the tendency is probably for influence and power to be empirically somewhat more closely correlated than is the case for a changing society, though nonetheless analytically distinct. It is probably the case that the current salience of such problems as that of the status of influence, as distinguished from power, is in part a product of the fact that contemporary society is, in fact, rapidly changing.

Chapter 16

On the Concept of Value-Commitments

CULTURE, VALUES AND COMMITMENTS

*I*n this paper, I will take up a long-standing commitment (!) to "round out" the analytical scheme for the four generalized symbolic media of interchange that operate within *societal* systems, as distinguished from the general action system and from the other three primary subsystems of action. The three societal media besides value-commitments are money, political power, and influence. I have never written a paper specifically on money, but have discussed it extensively as the theoretical model for the analysis of all these media. Specific papers have been devoted to the concept of power and influence, though the latter, especially, leaves a great deal to be desired.[1]

The present paper will neither discuss the background of the conception of generalized symbolic media in social systems and other action systems

---

[1] Though originally published in different places, these two papers comprise Chapters 10 and 11 in my recent volume of essays, *Sociological Theory and Modern Society* (New York: The Free Press, 1967). They comprise Chapters 15 and 16 above in the present volume. A major reason for not yet revising the paper on influence is that the concept has been extensively amplified in a current study of the American academic profession, and it seems better to report these developments in connection with that study. The present discussion of commitments has benefited greatly from them, however.

Reprinted from Sociological Inquiry *38 (Spring): 135–160 No. 2*

nor review the major features of the other media, except where they seem directly relevant to the exposition.[2] However, I will proceed from the available knowledge of the other three media, along with the addition of certain other considerations. The most important of these other considerations concerns cultural systems, their nature, and their role in social systems.

This paper is thus an attempt to link two principal aspects of the theory of social systems, both of which have concerned the author over a long period. One concerns the problem of the conceptualization of values at the level of their relevance to social systems, and the ways in which values can be understood to enter into concrete social processes, especially from the point of view of what here will be called their implementation. Special concern will be with the conditions of effective implementation in concrete types of situation. The other primary reference is, as noted, to the role of generalized symbolic media as primary aspects of the determination of *process* in social systems. The best known example of such a medium, money, has happened to operate at a level relatively remote from the primary zones to the incidence of values in the structure and processes of societies. Hence, the connections of present concern have been relatively neglected.

First it is necessary to clarify *the relevant conception of values* as a structural component of social systems and as a factor in the determination of process. There seem to be, in the literature of social science, two main approaches to the problem of conceptualization. One of these, which I reject, is what I like to call the "Chicago" approach, which I think originated in the work of Thomas and Znaniecki.[3] This takes its departure from the dichotomy of "attitudes" and "values." In this formulation attitudes are properties or characteristics of *actors*, while values pertain to the *objects* to which the actors are oriented. The crucial difficulty with this concept lies in its identification of the distinction with the actor-object (or situation) dichotomy as *concretely* conceived. It has more recently been most conspicuously followed by political scientists who stand in the "Chicago" tradition, notably Lasswell and Easton.

I should like to contrast this with a view that derives, I think, mainly on the one hand from Max Weber, and on the other from American anthropology, especially Clyde Kluckhohn. This is the view that a value is not a category of concrete object or a property of one but is, to use the anthropological word, a "pattern." It is at the same time a component of the structure of the *culture,* which concrete social objects are not, and a factor in the *regulation* of the interaction of actors and objects in the social processes, which is always in some sense one of interaction. The

[2] The reader may find such discussion in my other two papers on the societal media.
[3] Cf. Herbert Blumer, "An Appraisal of Thomas and Znaniecki's *The Polish Peasant in Europe and America*" (New York: A Social Science Research Council Monograph, 1939).

"mechanisms" by which values operate as empirical factors in social process and constitute structural components of social systems involve the phenomena of institutionalization[4] and internalization in the personality of the individual.

I therefore accept the first part of Kluckhohn's well-known definition of *values as conceptions of the desirable*.[5] The cultural reference is given in the key term "conceptions," whereas the distinctiveness of values, as distinguished, e.g., from "existential ideas" or expressive symbols, is given in the term desir*able*, which Kluckhohn is very careful to distinguish from only desir*ed*.

Values, then, are "patterns" at the cultural level which can, by institutionalization, become determinants—of course, never alone—of empirical social processes. They can do so by involvement with the units of social systems in their "roles" *both* as actors and as objects, which is *always* true of every unit in a social system, indeed any action system.

The question then arises of *what aspects of values are of special sociological significance*. Here, not a disagreement with, but an addition to, Kluckhohn's analysis becomes essential. *Evaluation* is a process by which certain modes of *relation* between actors and objects are established. The special case of values and the process of evaluation with which this analysis is concerned is that in which the system of reference is the same on *both* sides of the evaluative relationship. This is the case where the units participating in a social system—at some point acting human individuals—evaluate the social system in which they themselves participate, i.e., take such a system as object to them. *The values that come to be constituitive of the structure of a societal system are*, then, the conceptions of the desirable *type of society* held by the members of the society of reference and applied to the particular society of which they are members.[6] The same applies to other types of social systems.

A value-*pattern* then defines a *direction* of choice, and consequent commitment to action. Perhaps "selection" is the better term, since we do not wish to imply any particular psychological mechanism. In principle, a value-pattern may be relevant to the orientation of a class of actors to the whole of the "human condition." When we speak of societal values in the sense just stated, however, we speak of the specification of the pattern to a certain defined scope of commitment within the human condition,

---

[4] Leon H. Mayhew, *Law and Equal Opportunity* (Cambridge: Harvard University Press, 1968)' Chapter I.

[5] Clyde Kluckhohn, "Values and Value-Orientations in the Theory of Action: An Exploration in Definition and Classification" in T. Parsons and E. A. Shils, editors, *Toward A General Theory of Action* (Cambridge: Harvard University Press, 1951).

[6] On various occasions I have said a good deal about the place of values in social systems. Perhaps the most nearly complete statements so far published are in Part II of the "General Introduction" to *Theories of Society* (New York: The Free Press, 1961), and my article with Winston White, "The Link Between Character and Society," which is included in my collection, *Social Structure and Personality* (New York: The Free Press, 1964).

namely that of conception of the desirable type of society—or other social system—on the part of acting units that are members of that society. *This excludes*, therefore, conceptions of desirable types of personalities, organisms, physical objects, and other cultural objects, except insofar as these inherently interprenetrate with the particular social systems of reference.

Our master conception under that of value-pattern here is that of *commitment*. Regardless of what other value-commitments an acting unit may have, our concern is with his or its commitments to implement value-patterns in his capacity as a member of one or more social systems. The *level of generality* of his commitment in this context then defines the *scope* of the evaluated system within which the commitment may be said to be operative. Though there are complications for other modes of system reference, the most important range of variation is from system to sub-system. In each case, there are two dimensions of specification. One concerns the macroscopic-microscopic range applying to progressively smaller segments of the same functionally defined system. The second concerns relations to functionally differentiated subsystems.

COMMITMENTS AND
THE FOUR-FUNCTIONS SCHEME

It is in the latter context that differentiated subvalues articulate with the generalized symbolic media of interchange. This articulation is structured within each of four primary functional subsystems of a society, which are defined analytically, not concretely. As shown in the left-hand column of figure 3 in Chapter 14, page 403,[7] the processes of each of the functional subsystems are conceived to be "governed" in the cybernetic sense of the term by a characteristic value-principle that provides functional specification.

In the case of the economy, as the primary adaptive subsystem of a society, we have called the relevant value-principle *utility*, in the sense of economic theory. Production is in one aspect a process of value-implementation: it is the use of combinations of the factors of production to increase the utility of goods and services available in the economy as a

---

[7] The theory of cybernetics was first developed by Norbert Wiener in *Cybernetics* (Cambridge: The M.I.T. Press, 1948, second edition, 1961) and was applied to social problems in his *The Human Use of Human Beings* (Garden City: Anchor Books, 1954). A good introductory statement for the social scientist will be found in Karl W. Deutsch, *The Nerves of Government* (New York: The Free Press, 1963). The theory gives an analytical account of the conditions under which systems high in energy but low in information can be controlled by systems with the obverse characteristics: low in energy but high in information. The thermostat, controlling the energy-output of a heating system, is a simple example—the relevant information is a registered discrepancy between actual space temperature and the temperature for which the thermostat has been set.

system and, through its outputs, for "consumption." Money, in one of its classical roles, is a measure of utility. This measure is used to coordinate producing units with each other and with interchanging units outside the economy through the standard of *solvency*, which in its full application means the expectation that, over requisite time periods, the money costs of economic operations can be met by the money proceeds of these operations i.e., the sale of products. Finally, the articulation between commitment to enhancement of the value-principle of utility and the concrete allocation of resources and distribution of productive output involves the use of money as a medium of exchange for the purchase of factors of production and the sale of outputs which are generally classed as "goods and services."

The polity we conceive as a second primary functional subsystem of a society, that concerned with collective goal-attainment, not only as applied to government but any type of collectivity. The relevant value-principle we designate as *effectiveness*.[8] This is conceived as contribution to the functioning of the system of reference, the meaning of such contribution being defined in terms of the implementation of the values institutionalized in the system. The old term *success* has then been chosen to designate the coordinative standard by which such contribution is evaluated.[9] This is to say that any goal-oriented collectivity is subject to a standard of success which is parallel to that of solvency in the economic case. In the case of collectivities with primary functions other than political it may be necessary for them to be "subsidized" by an extra infusion of the factors of effectiveness, parallel to the financial subsidization of collectivities other than firms.

Power then, is the generalized symbolic medium that focuses in the political context. I define it as *generalized capacity to activate collective obligations of member units in the interest in the implementation of goal-oriented decisions binding on the collectivity of reference*. Power in this sense may be a measure of effectiveness, both for the collectivity as a whole and for its decision-making organs. Through differential evaluation of success it serves as a standard for the allocation of resources, and operatively it accomplishes this function by serving as a generalized medium of interchange.

Finally, a few words may be said about influence. The functional subsystem of reference is the integrative system, which, at the level of the

---

[8] Using that term in the sense given it by Barnard. Cf. Chester I. Barnard, *The Functions of the Executive* (Cambridge, Harvard University Press, 1938).

[9] This is clearly an unusual usage of the term which most frequently is applied to the performances of individuals. Using it in the present way registers a conviction, which has grown for a long time, that the relevant agency of goal-oriented contribution to the functioning of a social system is always collective. The case of purely "solo" contribution is the limiting case which may be designated as that of a one-member collectivity. See my paper "Some Theoretical Considerations Bearing on the Field of Medical Sociology," Chapter 12 in *Social Structure and Personality* (New York: The Free Press, 1964).

society as a whole, can appropriately be called the *societal community*. Its governing value-principle I have called *solidarity*, in Durkheim's sense, with special reference to maintaining the complementarity of units making qualitatively differentiated functional contributions to the society as a system. Solidarity is a state of "cohesion" of a social system which includes both resistance to centrifugal forces, such as "factionalism," which tend to divide and fragment it, and the promotion of positive coordination among the segmented and differentiated parts.

Influence or prestige may be treated in one of its functions as a measure of contribution to the level of solidarity in such a system. It measures successful combination of factors of solidarity, such as commitments to valued associational ties and securing solidarity-promoting collective decisions. There is, we maintain, a quantitative dimension of influence, but it is ordinal rank-ordering, not a cardinal order on a numerical continuum.

Influence, then, can also be used to coordinate units with each other in producing consensus, which becomes the primary standard of successful contribution to solidarity. It is important to note here that new consensus is continually needed because new situations, the effects of which are usually partly divisive, are continually arising. Thus, insofar as the legitimacy of the legal system is accepted, decisions in courts of law produce new consensus in that *both* parties to a litigation usually accept the decision of the court and, as it were, go on from there. Again, the articulation between commitment to enhance solidarity and the processes of concrete mobilization of relevant resources involves the use of influence as a medium of interchange, especially as means of securing what we have technically called commitments to valued association and the collective commitments resulting from legitimate policy decisions.

When we come to the role of values in the fourth of the main functional subsystems, the "Pattern-Maintenance" system, a somewhat special set of problems arises. The reason is that the primary functions of this subsystem concern the maintenance of the effective cybernetic control of the value-pattern itself, which is by no means incompatible with a great deal of concrete social change—quite the contrary. The problem here, however, is not specification to "lower" levels of generality, either more microscopic or differentiated in one direction, but the *integrity* of the pattern itself. Hence, we have designated integrity as the appropriate subsystem value principle. It is not, in the same sense that applies to the other three primary subsystems, a problem of values guiding the process of their implementation in the usual sense, but rather of maintaining the commitment that is the central normative *condition* of the process of implementation.

We are here dealing with a type of social system in which the level of differentiation is high: otherwise, we would not bother to designate the complex differences among several functionally differentiated subsystems of the society. The problem of maintaining integrity in the present sense is, therefore, not only a matter of choosing between right and wrong in a particular situation. It concerns rather the maintenance of integrity of commitment to the pattern over a wide range of different actual and potential decisions, in differing situations, with differing consequences and levels of predictability of such consequences. It is necessary, if this is to be possible, to combine adherence to a standard of pattern-consistency or "congruence" with flexibility in openness to exploitation of diverse opportunities for authentic implementation of relevant values and rejection of false possibilities.

If evidence of integrity is to go beyond primitive levels in the differentiation of social systems—such as the conviction that either maintenance of integrity is, to quote Stanner, a "one possibility thing" or a simple choice between the absolutely good and the absolutely bad—there must be standards of *quantitative* generalization of the more general value of integrity in the obligation to implement commitments. As suggested above, we can speak of *value-generalization* as this dimension. This is to say that implementation, in accord with the value of maintenance of integrity, will be enhanced in proportion as the maintenance of integrity is held to be compatible with a wide *scope* of action areas and opportunities in which both segmented and differentiated implementive activities can be legitimized. It seems likely that the conception of scope, as advanced here, is subject to the logic of ordinal ranking, and that this is the primary basis of its articulation with influence systems.

This, in turn, suggests its articulation with another variable which we may call that of *intensity* of commitment. This expression itself suggests, in the context of our previous discussion, that the problem of intensity concerns priority relations among different, more specified commitments within the same value pattern. In a sense parallel to that relevant to economic production, we may say that a combination of the predilections of the unit of reference, including its capacities, with the opportunities open to it in addition to the more generalized commitment to the implementation of a value-pattern, is necessary to determine in what line and direction the most important implementive effort will take place for particular units and classes of them.

Given a level of generality of commitment, then, there is need for some mechanism by which more specific commitments will be pursued with greater intensity than others that are, within the manifold, equally legitimate in a basic sense. It is for this reason that, in the title of this paper, we have spoken of commitments in the plural. We infer that the features of the system just sketched mean that there is a need for a quantitative measure of commitment, which we suggest is given in the dimension of scope in terms of level of generality. There is also need for a coordinative standard, which we have suggested is given in the imperative of pattern consistency or congruence. But beyond these, there is also need for a generalized medium through which not only can more detailed commitments be allocated along lines of specification and still be held to be in conformity with the imperative of integrity, but such commitments may be used in exchange for non-value factors necessary for their implementation, and may also be legitimized as in accord with the general requirement of integrity. It is in this context that we wish to analyze the sense in which value-commitments may be treated as a generalized medium of societal interchange in the same class with money, power, and influence.

COMMITMENTS AS A
GENERALIZED SYMBOLIC MEDIUM

Within this framework, we shall proceed to treat commitments to values as a *generalized symbolic medium*, in a sense parallel to the treatment of the other three media, and show how they in fact function in this way. The first desideratum is clarity and consistency about the criterion that a symbolic medium does *not* have intrinsic efficacy. Thus, in the sense of the classical economists, money does not have "value in use" but only "value in exchange." Power, in my conception, is not "intrinsically effective" for attaining collective goals, e.g., through coercion; it is effective only through communications that "activate" obligations to contribute to collective processes through compliance with collective decisions. Influence is not an "intrinsic persuader," like giving relevant information, but consists of appeals for certain types of action in the interest of an integral unit-collective solidarity. As we move away from the relatively familiar case of money, it becomes more difficult to adhere consistently to this criterion. Nevertheless, I consider it most essential, theoretically. If we confine our discussion of the implementation of value commitments to "barter" or ascriptive processes, the *whole* opportunity for new theoretical contribution will be lost.

Any symbolic medium (money is particularly good for illustration because it is so familiar) is a facilitator of, and guide to, the combination of resources in the interest of bringing an action *system* closer to congruence with a set of normative expectations that, as noted, root ultimately in the value-system. In the economy, it is the factors of production that undergo combination as evaluated in money terms to define the *cost* of production and the monetary value of output in terms of actual or prospective market proceeds. It is, thus, that money becomes an evaluative medium, as well as one of exchange, for judging the "rationality" of production policies that may be implemented through the combination of factors. Factors of production, in turn, have to be "translated" into terms relevant to the technological processes that can minimize costs and maximize the value of outputs.[10] I contend that the same basic logic applies wherever generalized media in the present sense are involved. We have also emphasized that commitments occupy a special place, in that they operate in the functional reference of pattern-maintenance. From this derives the value-principle of maintaining the integrity of the pattern, as we have called it. This focus of stabilization,[11] however, needs to be integrated with understanding of the flexibility characteristic of a generalized medium of interchange.

The relation between the value-content of the general pattern-maintenance subsystem and of the particular pattern-maintenance sectors of the four societal subsystems involves *specification* of the value-pattern to a lower level of generality. Such specification constitutes one step in the processes of value-implementation. Though the typical unit committed to economic production is presumptively faithful in its commitment to the general value system, it is also freed from responsibility for the implementation of the latter with respect to the *other* (non-economic) societal functions. In the process of implementation, it becomes subject both to imperatives of combination with factors different from those required by social units in other functional subsystems and to different standards for the elevation of performance. From this point of view, the specification of a generalized value-pattern can be conceived as an inverted tree with branches proliferating at each stage of specification. In general, we may surmise, it follows a pattern of fourfold division at each main stage. Combinatorial considerations, then, determine the patterning of cross-links between the various branches at the various levels. For example, economic resources are needed to implement the values of cognitive rationality in scientific research.[12]

Let us now consider the criteria that are distinctive of commitments as a generalized medium—and the ways in which they relate it to the other media. The best starting point is a paradigm that interrelates various types of attempts to determine the action of others, i.e. that treats the sanction

---

[10] Cf. Talcott Parsons and Neil J. Smelser, *Economy and Society* (New York: The Free Press, 1956).

[11] Because of the evolutionary continuity between the genetic component in the structure of organisms and the cultural component in the structure of action systems, the core of this stabilizing—and "reproducing"—function lies in the *code* aspects of the symbolic system that comprises the core of cultural systems. Symbolic codes are by no means immune to change, but, like genes, they change more slowly and are generally more difficult to change. They also change by different processes than do the other components of action. We consider value-patterns to be elements of the codes which "program" the patterning of action.

[12] I would contend, therefore, that the logic of the process of implementing value-commitments is essentially the same "value-added" logic that is applicable to the process of economic production. Smelser especially has set this argument forth very clearly in his *Social Change in the Industrial Revolution* (Chicago: University of Chicago Press, 1959), and his *Theory of Collective Behavior* (New York: The Free Press, 1963).

system.[13] It is repeated below, in a version somewhat modified from previous presentations:

SANCTION	*CHANNEL*	
TYPES	*Situational*	*Intentional*
Positive	*Inducement:* through offer of advantage, contingent on agreement, backed by "enforceability" e.g., of contracts.	*Persuasion:* through information or declaration of intentions, backed by status-prestige.
Negative	*Activation of collective commitments,* backed by contingent coercion.	*Activation of value-commitments,* backed by moral sanctions.

FIGURE 1. *Paradigm of Sanctions*

This fourfold classification concerns the alternatives open to any acting unit, conventionally designated as *ego* (though it may be a collectivity), that is seeking to bring about an act (or prevent an undesired one) on the part of another unit, *alter*. It involves two dichotomized axes: (1) whether ego's presumptive conditional output is advantageous or disadvantageous to alter, what I call the difference between positive and negative sanctions; (2) whether the advantage or disadvantage involves a prospective or conditional change in *alter's* action *situation*, independent of his intentions, or concerns his intentions, namely the definition of his goals, specified values, etc., independent of his situation. The four generalized media fit in as follows: money is a generalized medium of *inducement*, the offering of contingent situational advantages; power is a generalized medium of *activating obligations* to comply with collectively binding decisions, with contingent coercive sanctions—situational disadvantages to alter—being attached to non-compliance; influence is a generalized medium of *persuasion* that operates through appeals to alter's definition of what he "really wants" and in the legitimate cases, integrates his own best interest with the interest of a collective system in which he and ego both hold membership.

Commitments constitute a generalized medium for the *activation* of obligations, which are presumptively *morally binding* by virtue of values which ego and alter share. The sanctions attached to nonimplementation of the values are, as in the case of power, negative; but they are also "internal" in that they consist, for the individual, in guilt (or possibly shame) and, for the collectivity, in some kind of internal reordering, such as dismissal of an official responsible for a decision unacceptable on value grounds.

I conceive the very central concept of *bindingness* to be common to power and commitments, as comprising the basis for the relevance of

---

[13] This paradigm has been used previously in the papers on power and influence. See *Sociological Theory and Modern Society*, pp. 310 and 363. [See also the Postscript to Chapter 15 of the present volume: ed.]

negative sanctions. Bindingness implies a presumptive "duty" to act in the expected manner, including refraining from doing "wrong" things. Failure or, still worse, deliberate refusal so to act should, therefore, be in some sense "punished." The difference between the power-related and the commitment-related forms of bindingness lies in the source of the sanctions and, *hence*, the locus of responsibility.

Both presume, prior to any act by ego that "activates" alter's obligation, that there has existed a controlling generalized level of obligation. As a member of a collectivity, one in some sense accepts the legitimacy of its normative order and its "duly constituted" authorities; when collectively binding decisions are made—whether by single officers or by a vote of the total membership is indifferent for our purposes—this generalized obligation is "translated" into a specific obligation binding alter to comply with whatever implications are salient to his situation. A tax bill voted by a legislature imposes an obligation on the "good citizen" to pay what he owes according to the terms of the law. A membership vote imposes on the losing minority an obligation to comply with the decision of the majority. Here the specification is from generalized collective obligation, through decision-making by collectively legitimate "authority," to the particular obligation of units or classes of units. Since responsibility for the decisions rests with particular agencies of the collectivity, they, perhaps along with special agencies entrusted with "enforcement," must take the responsibility for ensuring compliance. Hence, the sanctions cannot in general be self-imposed by the units upon which particularized obligations fall, e.g., the responsibility for ensuring tax payment cannot rest solely on those who owe the tax.

In the case of value-commitments, we assume that there is a generalized obligation that is regarded as "morally" binding.[14] Commitment at this level does not, however, prescribe a detailed course of action for fulfilling the obligation when the unit is confronted with the imperative of imple-

---

[14] There is a problem of analytical elaboration which I shall not take space to work through here, but of which the reader should be aware. This concerns the analytical distinction between the cultural and the societal levels of the value components of action systems. Where it is important to stress this distinction, it is appropriate to use the term *moral* to designate the cultural level, which in the cybernetic sense provides the highest-order normative patterning involved in action as a whole. The moral components are located in the integrative subsystem of culture and integrate the relations of the religious system to society, personality, and organism.

Societal values, then, constitute the zone of interpenetration between the moral system and the society as the system, in an ideal-type sense, of their *institutionalization*. In their cultural reference, they are "moral," though they do not exhaust the category of being moral; in particular, both "purely" cultural commitments and "personal" commitments, independently of societal involvement, have the quality of moral bindingness. Only at a few points in the present exposition, however, is it necessary to refer to these broader references of the category moral. In dealing with commitments as a societal medium of interchange, we refer to commitments to societally institutionalized values. In an analytically parallel sense, among the many possibilities for the technologically "efficient" production of physical goods, utility in the economic sense confines technological relevance to involvement in institutionalized contexts of "want-satisfaction," as the older economists put it.

menting its value-commitments in a concrete situation. Thus, as a social scientist, I consider myself as firmly committed to the values of cognitive rationality as most of my colleagues. However, this commitment alone does *not* tell me what to say in evaluating the contribution of a complicated book in a review. It must be specified to the proper level and combined with other components, such as empirical and theoretical competence in the particular subject matter, concern for the particular readership, etc. But the *responsibility* for making these decisions rests, in this case, with the particular reviewer. The *American Sociological Review* is an "official" journal of the American Sociological Association, but the Association neither "writes" the book reviews by majority vote of its members nor takes corporate responsibility for the specific content of the reviews. Selection of reviewers is a responsibility delegated to the book review editor; the author of the review takes, within very broad limits, sole responsibility for its content, including the *integrity* of its adherence to the value-commitments presumptively shared by members of the Association.

For such reasons, the primary sanctions that back value-commitments must be internal to the responsible unit. Where the implementation of value-commitments is at issue, and insofar as this is the case, we speak of the responsibility as moral. A unit may then be legitimately criticized or "blamed" from outside, but it cannot in the usual sense be "punished." Of course, a reputation for laxity in implementing value commitments may readily lead to, and hence be a factor in, future loss of professional opportunities. However, when an editor directly disciplines an author for a lapse of integrity, such as plagiarizing a colleague's work, the case enters the power system, not the commitment system.

FLEXIBILITY IN THE ALLOCATION OF COMMITMENTS

We must next discuss the basis of flexibility in the *allocation* of value-commitments. The particular uses of physical land, as distinguished from its total supply, can be determined by price, in that rights to its use in specific ways can be purchased, subject to normative regulation. The same principle applies to the value component of land,[15] in that commitments to implement economic rationality in particular lines of production under particular circumstances can also be "purchased," for example by employment or by prospect of profit.

It may simplify matters to illustrate in terms of the general activism of the American value-pattern.[16] In this value system, moral obligation generally emphasizes commitment not only to the desirability of a particu-

---

[15] Cf. Parsons and Smelser, *Economy and Society*, p. 25.
[16] Cf. Parsons and White, *op. cit.*

lar situation but also to its actual implementation so far as that is possible. Most directly, this stresses specification from general value-commitments to the acceptance of obligations to attempt to achieve particular *goals*, individual or collective. The process of goal-attainment, however, must take account of the *exigencies* of particular situations, such as uncontrollable conditions that preclude some kinds of desirable action and scarce means that, if used for one goal, cannot be used for others.

One crucial exigency lies in the combination of two others. First, moral obligation rests at the *unit* level, which, by definition, is only a part of the primary system of reference.[17] Secondly, the *capacities* of any such unit are, relative to environmental exigencies, inherently limited; a unit cannot, while having any realistic chance of success, assume responsibility for implementing *in toto* the value commitments of the system as a whole. In order to make them realistically compatible with the exigencies of successful implementation, therefore, it must *limit* its commitments in either or both of two directions: (1) specification of *level* of responsibility within the hierarchy of segmentation of structure; and (2) specialization of functional "role" in the division of labor, making a *partial* contribution to the more general implementation process.

In the first case, an obvious model for comparison is the hierarchy of bureaucratic authority and responsibility. In that context, the higher an incumbent's level of authority in a collective system, the broader the *scope* of matters for which he can be held responsible, and the greater the share of power he must control if he is to discharge his responsibility. Authority—and with it responsibility—is then "parcelled out" to progressively lower echelons according to the exigencies of successful goal-attainment. In the political case, this often involves progressively smaller territorial subunits, but possibly units established on other bases. In manufacturing, it may concern particular parts of the finished product, as distinguished from larger "assemblies." Authority and power must be "delegated" to the lower echelons because only there can requisite levels of control be attained over situational exigencies; e.g., the top executive cannot personally supervise all the detailed operations that contribute to successful collective goal-attainment.

The implementation of commitments is similar, yet subtly different. In the ideal-type case, generally, commitment to a highly general value-pattern is shared by all units of the social system in which it is institutionalized. However, it does not follow that the level of commitment to *implementation* is equal among all units, at least not in the sense of their taking equal responsibility for all modes of implementation. A *stratification of responsi-*

[17] There is an inherent relativity of system reference here. What is a unit at one level is generally a system at another. There are value-commitments on the part of total societies, hence an imperative of definition of the exigencies of implementation *for* the total society. The present discussion is couched mainly at the level of the society as system, concerned with the commitments held to be binding on its units, subcollectivities, and individuals-in-roles.

bility in the direction of segmentation focuses about the phenomenon often called "moral leadership." Because of the close connection between the moral level of value-institutionalization and religion, the primary moral leadership of many societies has been grounded in religious bodies, especially their "professional" elements, such as priesthoods. With the kinds of differentiation associated with secularization, however, political movements have often played a significant part in moral leadership. There has sometimes been a "moral elite," the members of which have collectively assumed such leadership.

The predestined "Saints" of early Calvinism and the Communist Party have in some respects been similar elites of moral leadership, both treating political power as on the whole an *instrument* for implementing their moral commitments. There are empirical questions of how far moral leadership rests in sharply differentiated statuses and groups and of how far it is shared by those who hold political power. Weber, among many others, emphasized the tension between moral leadership and political power.

The "division of labor" context, which comprises both the economists' and Durkheim's senses of the term, operates somewhat differently. Relative to the most general level of the value system, commitment *to implementation* here also becomes "partial," rather than "total," in its involvement of responsibility. In this case, responsibility is partial in relation not only to a *level* of implementation, but also to a differentiated *kind* of implementation. For example, responsibility for efficient economic production, whether high or low, is not the same as responsibility for contributing to the advancement of knowledge; both are responsibilities for one aspect of value-implementation. In the metaphor of the inverted tree, an implementation-obligation may be located not only at a certain remove from the undifferentiated "basic" trunk, but also on a specific branch.

If we clearly recognize the importance of the distinction between these two modes of restriction of the scope of implementation-responsibility— as well as the generalization that the more highly differentiated the society, the more refined its differentiations on *both* axes—we face two major problems about the nature of commitments as a "circulating" medium of social interaction. The first concerns the nature of the "exigencies" of successful implementation, hence the "resources" which it requires and the conditions of access to them. We view this problem from the point of view of the unit responsible for implementing commitments of a given kind and at a given level. The second problem concerns the relation of the allocation of commitments to the integration of the system, one aspect of which concerns its relation to allocation of the other types of social resources, notably economic (through financial media), political (through authority and power), and solidary-communal (through prestige and influence).

On the first problem, the most important principle is that successful implementation of *any* value-commitment generally involves *all* of the factors of successful action, so that access to them to some degree constitutes meeting "necessary exigencies." Insofar as we are speaking of social system functioning, this applies particularly to the factors of social process, both at the "intrinsic" level and at the symbolic medium level. Back of the social components, however, stand those of the rest of the action system, physical environment, behavioral organism, motivational structure of personality, and cultural system.

Of course, the *combinations* of these factors vary with levels of responsibility and kinds of responsibility. It seems that the lower the level of responsibility, the greater the *relative* importance of factors lower in the hierarchy of cybernetic control. Thus, physical and organic resources have the greatest relevant importance at the lowest cybernetic levels.[18] This holds essentially because the lower the level of the subsystem, the greater the extent to which the "control functions" have been performed in superordinate systems—especially in that the obligations of the lower ones are relatively strictly defined, as well as the scope of their freedom of action with respect to their assigned functions. If value-commitments provide the highest-order control among the generalized symbolic media within the social system, it follows that physical and organic considerations weigh particularly heavily on the lower cybernetic levels, followed by the economic level, the great salience of which was a social index of societal "upgrading" in the 19th century.

The American value-system structures a very special problem concerning the status of factors that are *analytically* political. The activistic component of the value system exerts "normative pressure" toward effectiveness of implementation, including a tendency to value immediacy of "results." Hence there is a bent toward "politicizing" definitions of responsibilities which can easily conflict with respect for the higher-order factors that center on the influence and value-commitment systems, independent of particular goal-orientations as such, whether for the polity as a whole or for its various subsystems. The American cult of "success," extending from the individual in his occupational role, through operative organizations such as firms, to anxiety about how the society is "doing" as a whole, is in part a consequence of this. Precisely, because of the openness of the problem of the desirable pattern of *allocation* of commitments, however, there is always the question of how far such "politicization" may lead to "overcommitment" to particular goals, collective or individual, thereby constricting freedom to reallocate in the light of changing

[18] This proposition is not negated by the case of technology. The direction of technological processes does not require the responsible executive to manipulate the main physical facilities personally; he directs the manipulators in what, when, and perhaps how they should work. Similarly, a commanding general does not fire guns or pilot bombers but gives "orders" to those who do.

circumstances and interpretations of the basic value-responsibilities themselves. This may in part explain the American sensitivity to Communism,
which may seem to stand for an approach to the total politicization of
the societal system as a whole.[19]

Of course, the *qualitative* differentiation of a social system into functionally distinct sybsystems also has an hierarchical aspect, since the different
functional categories are interrelated through the cybernetic hierarchy.
Thus, political function takes precedence over economic, integrative over
political, and pattern-maintenance over integrative. In evaluating these
relationships, however, one must remember that, at appropriate levels
of distinction, *all* of the functional categories are involved in *every* subsystem. I have often suggested that higher education and research have in
recent decades become increasingly important in the structure and processes of modern societies, perhaps especially in America. In social system
terms, higher education is located mainly in the pattern-maintenance
subsystem, the primary zone of society's interpenetration with the cultural
system. Its chief value-principle, which we call cognitive rationality,[20]
stands cybernetically higher, among the differentiated subsystems of
the general value system, than either economic or political rationality,
though, being the value of a primary functional subsystem, it does not
involve the same *order* of functional significance for the society.

For reasons such as the above, it is essential to think in terms of value-
systems; complex action systems cannot be "governed" by a single undifferentiated value, nor by discrete, unrelated, particular values conceived
in terms of the "culture traits" concept, as used by the "historical"
anthropologists. The elements of such a system are differentiated by levels
of specification and responsibility for implementation and by type of
subvalue according to both the function performed by the relevant societal
subsystem and the exigencies of implementation involved. Nevertheless,
values are integrated into a system in terms of the "congruence" of the
pattern prescribed by the different types and levels, so that we can legitimately speak of an overall system-pattern of values—although its degree
of institutionalization is always an empirically open question.

At every level and for every subtype, however, the obligation of implementation necessitates that the value-commitment be combined with the

---

[19] The above argument has been deliberately focused upon social system terms. We suggest
that "level" of commitment, concerning the relative significance of the commitment component in the factor-system of the society as a whole, is a function of the status of units in the
hierarchy of control. In one sense, this is an assertion that "intensity" of commitment is likely
to be a function of the unit's position in the hierarchy. It is *not* a psychological generalization,
couched in terms of the personalities of individuals. The usual pattern of variation should be
postulated here: persons in the requisite statuses are *more or less* intensively committed, as
personality systems, to the implementation of the value patterns institutionalized in their
respective statuses.

[20] Cognitive rationality is discussed briefly in Talcott Parsons and Gerald M. Platt, "Some
Considerations on the American Academic Profession" *Minerva*, Fall, 1968.

other factors involved in coping with the exigencies of successful implementation. That is, for any subsystem or system as a whole value-commitment can be only one of the determinants of action. Those who are inclined toward positions of value-absolutism often tend to regard the giving of attention to these other factors as "compromising" the value-commitment. Although such compromising is undoubtedly a common and important phenomenon, it is hardly realistic to hold that all combination with other factors constitutes compromise. How far the integrity of a value commitment has, and has not, been upheld in a given case can only be judged in light of the nature of the exigencies, the alternative modes of coping with them, and the moral "imperative" of the commitment itself. Moreover, the cost of implementing the commitment is a relevant factor in all such judgments, from the view points of both the implementing unit and the wider systems involved.

Probably all such value-implementing processes should be regarded in the first instance as goal-oriented—as having, analytically, political primacy. In what is authentically Weber's sense, I think, the value-system *legitimizes* such implementive action, including the necessary combinatorial relations with other than value factors. In our interchange paradigm (see figure 3, Chapter 14, page 403) the output of legitimation from the pattern-maintenance system to the polity comprises the performance of this function by the value system. Its complexity should not be underestimated. Even if the overall value-pattern is stable, structural changes occur continually and at many different levels in all parts of a society. Relative to subvalues, exigencies are continually undergoing change, thereby necessitating reevaluation of the legitimacy of different modes of coping with them. Indeed, structural changes in some parts of the system create new exigencies for other parts, by changing their situations.

It is *the combination of this differentiated and specified complexity with the exposure to change*—much of which is unpredictable in advance—*that makes commitments as a generalized symbolic medium essential* to the functioning of a society. Only in a simple and highly traditionalized society can even approximate implementation-obligations be specified concretely in advance.[21] To do so would require the complete ascription of commitments. But even allocating commitments by some kind of *ad hoc* agreements of legitimation among the parties immediately concerned (a rough equivalent of barter in the economic sphere) would be exceedingly awkward and uncertain.

The generalized medium permits the unit to have the freedom to make its own decisions of legitimacy. The unit is presumed to possess sufficient

---

[21] This specification also goes very far in so-called "legalistic" systems of ethics, such as the Talmudic tradition in orthodox Judaism, and much of Islamic Law. The implementation of such a detailed system of obligations is possible only in highly restricted social circumstances, and even then the cultural safety-valve of casuistry has to be given a good deal of scope.

commitment at generalized levels so that the steps of specification for which it assumes responsibility will on the whole proceed in accord with the relevant value-pattern. This presumption must cover the unit's judgments about the legitimacy of meeting non-value exigencies and of spending resources in order to acquire non-value factors for effective implementation.

When we speak of *an ego activating an alter's commitments*, we mean that, through symbolic communication, ego helps alter "define the situation" for alter's exercise of his moral freedom in the above sense. This can be done either by "admonition" in advance of action or by criticism after it. Generalized commitments, however, are also exchangeable for other desirables, notably money, power, and influence, and, through them, more concrete resources in the form of rewards or facilities. The use of commitments as sanctions implies that moral approval is a reward and disapproval a punishment, so long as ego and alter share values such that ego's approval or disapproval tends to "activate" alter's internal sanction system. Of course, certain qualifications must be made if ego and/or alter are collectivities rather than individual persons.

Each of the generalized media is subject to *scarcity imperatives*; a "stock" of medium will be depleted by some form of "spending" and its acquisition must be "paid for" by incurring some kind of cost. Moreover, the "income" of a medium can be enhanced by the indirect effects of judicious "spending," much as businesses can increase their future income through investing funds in productive operations. What kinds of processes fit these categories for the case of commitments?

Commitments as medium should be defined as *generalized capacity and credible promises to effect the implementation of values*. Its code component is what we mean by *moral authority* in its societal reference. Its messages are essentially assertions of commitment to the relevant value pattern which may take the form of elements implicit in acts pointing toward implementation, such as promises, which we often explicitly call commitments, to undertake certain specified obligations.

Here it is important that nonfulfillment of a commitment in this sense requires specific grounds of justification; an actor wishing to be relieved of a commitment carries the burden of proving that its fulfillment is in conflict with a higher-order obligation involving the same values. Making such promises is one form of the "spending" of free commitments.

We have strongly suggested that the primary negative sanctions are internal to the actor assuming the obligations. As in all such cases, however, such sanctions can be "activated" through communication with others. Thus we may speak of "admonition" as an expression of anxiety that a commitment will be violated, and moral disapproval as after the fact "punishment" by others. These sanctions are parallel to actual sanctions of coercion and compulsion in power systems. They constitute part of the "security base" of the medium, rather than parts of the functioning medium itself.

Moral authority is acquired through a reputation for integrity of commitment, individual or collective. To be *effective*, however, it must be judiciously used, a matter which involves maintaining a fine balance between tolerance and severity, scrupulousness and pragmatism. We have suggested that freedom to make one's *own* judgments about the legitimacy of more detailed implementive action is a crucial dimension of the generalization of value-commitments in a social system. Being too ready to admonish or condemn can institute an infringement of alter's freedom in this respect, and, since such freedom is itself valued, diminish ego's reputation for integrity. Yet, being too "easy-going" and failing to condemn too many dubious actions may also undermine such reputation. The equivalent of economic solvency consists essentially in the maintenance of this balance so that one's moral judgment will ordinarily be respected.

Before attempting to delineate the principal subclasses of specified commitment that operate to mediate interchanges in the social system, it will be well to try to make clear *how we conceive the "circulation" of value-commitments to take place*, in a sense that is parallel to the circulation of money in a market system.

Each of the generalized media has a primary *anchorage* in one of the primary sub-systems, e.g., money in the economy. With a sufficiently high level of differentiation, however, the relations of the primary system of reference to its "neighbouring" systems must be *mediated* on a generalized level. The classical instance is the circulation of money between firms and households—the latter *not* being primarily units of the economy, but of the pattern-maintenance subsystem. The money income of households is in the first instance the product of the output of labor commitment to the economy. In turn it is "returned" to the economy through consumers' spending, a relationship made famous by the Keynesian analysis. Similar considerations apply to the capital markets and those for "services" as distinguished from labor and goods.[22]

We have argued that commitments, in proportion to their level of generalization, have to be allocated among contexts of specification. Since, furthermore, implementation requires combination with non-value factors, those in possession of high "stocks" of commitment may use them to secure control of these other factors. Just as firms pay wages to secure control of labor as a factor of production so, we may

---

[22] These relationships constitute a major focus of difficulty in defining the boundaries of functional subsystems. Thus many economists would include the "household" in the analytical sense in the economy on the ground that it is overwhelmingly involved in monetary interchanges. Similarly such a political theorist as David Easton tends to include what I call the "societal community" in the political system because of its involvement with interchanges of power.

suggest, in one particularly important context holders of value-commitments "pay" for the privilege of association with others in the implementation of their commitments. This means that they "give" commitments to the association of reference, which become "assets" to that
association, both collectively and for its members individually. The
association is in a stronger position for the implementation of the values
held in common by its members, by virtue of the fact that those who join
it have "given" their commitments to it. For the "joiners" then, the
commitments have been "spent" in the sense that they have in a degree
relinquished control of them. They have come to be bound by obligations
of loyalty to the associational collectivity that they have joined.

In general, however, these obligations are not absolute. In a social
system characterized by pluralism, from the roles of individuals through
many levels of collective organization, loyalties must be balanced within
a manifold of claims. This is to say that, in becoming committed, e.g., to
an association, a member unit does not "spend" its *whole* stock of commitments, but reserves some of it for other channels in which commitment
may take place, including other associational solidarities.

The "back flow" of commitments, e.g., from integrative to pattern-
maintenance subsystems, takes the form of the demonstration, in the
course of collective action, of the integrity of the association's commitment
to the values in question. In such a situation, however, "in unity there is
strength," in that the assembled commitments of a plurality of associated
units have a greater impact than if they were implemented only unit-wise
with the possibility of fragmentation and dissipation of effect.

Of course, another implication of the parallel with money and the
economy lies in the fact that in the kind of "double interchange"
we are postulating, the units on the two sides of a system of particular
transactions are generally not the same. Just as households secure their
"real" income from many firms, most of which are quite distinct from
the employers of their members, so value-implementing units secure their
"backflow" of commitments on the one hand, their "income" of influence
or power on the other from units of the system that are quite distinct.
It is *the mediation of integration within such a system of differentiation that
is the primary function of commitments as a generalized medium.* The alternative
to such generalization is the functional equivalent of barter.

COMMITMENTS AND
THE INTERCHANGE PARADIGM

The earning of moral respect is a function not only of exchange of commitments, but also of what the unit does in other spheres of his action
in respect to their interdependence with value-components. Our interchange paradigm (see figure 3, Chapter 14, page 403) suggests that there

are three such spheres of primary importance to the pattern-maintenance subsystem of society. We have already discussed one, namely, that involving the legitimation of goal-oriented action, which in social systems is presumptively collective action that is analytically political. In this interchange system, the "income" of commitment capacity comes primarily from taking what we call "operative" responsibility for actual implementation, including the effective utilization of non-value factors. The output from the polity to the pattern-maintenance system of "moral responsibility for the collective interest" comprises the obverse aspect of the sharing of values by ego and alter.

The second primary interchange involving commitments is the familiar one in which, ideal-typically, households and firms constitute the interchanging units.[23] The output of commitments from households we call *labor*; that of firms, *goods*. Both of these concepts require elucidation for present purposes. In dealing with generalized media at the social system level, we clearly do *not* refer to goods as physical objects, nor to labor as the physical performances of the behavioral organism. Rather, we refer to mechanisms by which such objects and processes are controlled, in a sense that includes their allocation.

As a category of output from the economy, "goods" constitutes a commitment to *produce* in the economic sense. The appropriate subvalue pattern is economic rationality. Commitment to its implementation (classically delineated by Weber as the "spirit of capitalism") carries the obligation to undertake its "rational" combination with the other factors of production and to supervise the technological procedures that are appropriate in terms of the specified control system constituted by rational combinations. Success in production, then, is measured in terms of the *utility* of the goods or commodities produced, a matter precisely of the *sharing* of the value of economic rationality by firm and household. At a series of levels of specification, then, firms are committed, first to production generally, then to production of particular commodities, then to distribution in particular markets, etc. At each level, however, the commitment (which, as factor of production, we classify as "land") must be combined with the other factors of production. The success of these economic combinations is then measured by the standard of "solvency," i.e. by the capacity of the producing unit to meet, over appropriate time periods, *all* the monetary costs of its operations from the money proceeds of its sales.[24] In modern societies, households as well as

---

[23] This interchange is discussed more extensively, but somewhat differently, in Parsons and Smelser, *op. cit.*

[24] In modern societies, units with other than economic primacy are expected to be solvent in a modified sense. While money income is expected to balance expenditures, not all (sometimes not any) of the income is expected to come from the financial proceeds of operations. In the case of such a private, nonprofit unit as a university, much of the income consists of gifts, grants, etc., rather than students' tuition payments, for example.

firms are expected "normally" to be solvent in this sense, i.e., to "support" their standard of living by the money earnings or other financial assets of the members. The household is the *only* type of societal unit, other than firms, to which this expectation applies. Of course, incapacity to meet this requirement does not, as in the case of the firm, normally create a presumption that the household should be liquidated; the normal reaction is to find ways of subsidizing it, e.g., through relief.

As an output from households, labor should be regarded as a commitment to implement the value of economic rationality through contribution to production. Since labor is only one factor of production, a sufficiently differentiated economy must institutionalize the "alienation" of labor, for normally one cannot successfully implement the labor commitment in organizational contexts totally controlled by oneself or by those with whom one associates on a *Gemeinschaft* basis, such as members of one's household. In general, one requires a political component operating through an employing organization, an input of capital, and the like. In this sense, the *differentiation* of labor as a factor from the diffuse matrix of primordial solidarities is a principal hallmark of modern social organization.

Analytically speaking, labor is a factor of production in the economic sense, while "service"—which economic theory has traditionally bracketed with goods—is to be regarded as an *output* of the process of production. In service, the commitment to labor has *already been combined* with the other economic factors, in the interest of effective implementation. Analytically, we categorize the output of service as *power* in the political sense, not as commitments.[25] Its primary direct link with commitments is structured through the L-G interchange, involving the acceptance of moral responsibility for collective interest and operative responsibility in a collective system. An *indirect* link through the economy, via L-A and A-G, is essential at high levels of differentiation, however.

The matter of primary interest here is "employment" in an "organization." In a sufficiently differentiated system, such employment is *always* economic in the sense of taking place through a "labor market." In modern societies, quantitatively by far the largest employers are firms—a socialist economy is not basically different in this respect. Hence the market has a double incidence, defining criteria both for the allocation of services and for the solvency of the employing firm. The individual in occupational role, however, need not accept complete economic primacy in the utilization of his services. He has, above all, two choices bearing on this. The first concerns the L-G interchange and the order of operational responsibility that he assumes. A research scientist employed in a commercial laboratory, for example, may take virtually no responsibility

[25] Cf. "On the Concept of Political Power," *op. cit.*

for the firm's solvency.[26] The second concerns the *type* of collectivity in which he seeks employment. The academic profession, for example, has its own special type of "labor market," but its employing organizations are not firms in the ideal type sense. These choices constitute further steps in the process of implementing the value system. They modify the primacy of economic rationality with components, respectively, of political rationality and of "associational" loyalty. While economic rationality has to govern all the various submarkets for services, each is partially insulated from the others, and one primary factor in its insulation is the greater commitment of its participants to its distinctive subvalues. Thus an academic man should have a higher commitment to cognitive than to economic rationality; he should tend not to compete directly in the most general markets for economically valuable services, but should restrict his competition to the "academic market place." Too gross discrepancies of financial reward, however, would tend to weaken or break down these insulating mechanisms.

The third interchange operates between the pattern-maintenance system and the societal community, the integrative system. Here, commitments are specified to a context of "valued association"; in terms of combinatorial logic, this involves the acceptance of the normatively-primary *social* (as distinguished from political and economic) conditions of effective value-implementation. The individual unit no longer "goes it alone" but adopts associational status, which gives him expectations of solidarity with fellow-members of the community or collectivity in question. Favorable combinations of associational relations can greatly enhance capacity to implement successfully, since solidarity and the concomitant influence-potential can realistically control power and economic resources, as well as reassure. Status in an appropriate collectivity constitutes what, from the viewpoint of the participating unit, is the primary societal "base of operations" from which further combinatorial stages of implementation can be undertaken. Indeed, unless this base is relatively secure, capacities for successful implementation are likely to be gravely impaired. Although it is the *shared* value-commitments of its members that above all create the possibility of such a security base, these value-commitments do not implement themselves. Hence, solidary association is the first further condition of successful implementation, even though there must, beyond that, be provision for effective collective goal-attainment and the mobilization of generalized resources.

Thus, as noted, value-commitment to an associational collectivity "buys" loyalty, i.e. "support" of endeavors toward value implementation in a general, nonpolitical sense. But at this point there arises a particularly important problem, which is accentuated in modern societies, namely

---

[26] Cf. the chapters on formal organizations in my *Structure and Process in Modern Societies* (New York: The Free Press, 1960).

pluralism. We have stressed that commitments focus at the *unit* level in the structure of social systems, from various collectivities to the individual-in-role. The more highly differentiated a social system, however, the more any unit's "memberships" become pluralized. For the individual this is commonplace; for example, one may belong to a family household, an employing organization, various neighborhood groups, a religious association, a political party, various associations promoting "good causes," etc. The same principle applies to collectivities. Thus, Harvard University is a "member" of the local communities of Cambridge and metropolitan Boston, the Commonwealth of Massachusetts, the United States and, in some sense, "world society." It is also "involved" in—or "with"—innumerable other associations, such as different levels of government, the complicated world of the organization of scholarly interests, the readership of the publications of its faculty members, etc.

Thus an individual's or subcollectivity's problem of optimizing the implementation of its value-commitments can not be solved by its joining *the* single appropriate association. Generally no one valued association is adequate from the unit point of view, so that collective involvement becomes a matter of the complex interrelation of associational ties. From the unit viewpoint, the elements of such a complex comprise *reference groups* in the usual social-psychological sense. Such groups vary on several dimensions. One is that of inclusiveness; the national societal community, in which the individual is a citizen, is far more inclusive than his employing organization, even if the latter is the Federal Government. A second dimension concerns the types of qualitatively different interests that "motivate" participation; an individual usually has a high vested interest in both his familial and his occupational role involvements, but they are typically very different from each other. Third, the participations may be systematically interrelated within a single value-oriented subsystem. Thus an academic professional is generally a member at least of two primary cross-cutting categories of collectivity, namely his "employer" (college or university, at each of two primary levels of inclusiveness, department and faculty) and his "discipline" on a national or international basis, generally involving formal associational memberships. Quite clearly, the unit must *allocate* its commitments among these various contexts of participation, perhaps including aspired but unattained associational memberships.

The problem is complicated by the fact, noted above, that the exigencies that govern the value-implementive effectiveness of commitments cannot be assumed to be stable. In a sense directly analogous with a firm's need continually to adjust to changing market conditions, the value-implementing unit must stand ready to adapt the allocation of its commitments to changes in the exigencies of implementation. In the academic profession, for example, a readiness to consider offers of new appointments in other universities need not be a function *only* of seeking personal advantage, such as higher salary, but may involve better *opportunity* to implement one's academic value commitments. To put loyalty to one's current university too highly above readiness to utilize such opportunities might imply relative weakness in commitment to the relevant values.[27]

INFLATION AND DEFLATION
OF COMMITMENTS

The foregoing considerations clearly indicate that commitments as a generalized medium must be treated as flexible. However, this flexibility is, in the ideal type case, not at all incompatible with stability at the higher levels of generality and aggregations. Such stability is, nevertheless, complicated by the familiar problem of deflation-inflation that affects the functioning of all generalized media. The inflationary case involves what is frequently called *over-commitment*, at least in the value-implementation context. It occurs when a unit has made so many, so diverse, and such "serious" commitments that its capacity to implement them effectively must reasonably be called into question. Overcommitment is subject to admonition about the prospects for actual implementation or to criticism for failure to "come through" with legitimately expected implementive measures. The cogency of admonition and criticism may then undermine "confidence" in the integrity of the committed unit, with the consequence that trust in its future commitments, or even those already in force, will be lessened.

The deflationary tendency is a disposition toward unwillingness to "honor" the commitments that units are willing to make. Hence, it comes to involve some restriction of the degrees of freedom that a unit may enjoy in the sphere of value implementation, especially by shifting responsibility from the unit to some outside agency, e.g., the "law." The rationale is to impose stringent external controls to guard against being "let down" by failure to implement. Major movements in this direction, however, have the familiar consequence of purchasing "security" at the expense of benefits which may accrue from greater freedom for autonomous responsibility.

We have stressed the importance of the *complexity* of value systems.

---

[27] In a society in which there is very widespread readiness to impute guidance by crass "self-interest," it is important to stress this point. Where self-interest and opportunity for value-implementation affect a decision in the same direction, there is a certain disposition to say that "of course" it was the self-interested element that made the difference. It is furthermore important that, where value-commitments are genuinely internalized, it is concretely to the self-interest of an individual to give high priority to their implementation; failure to do so would be "paid for" in terms of guilt as well as possible loss of reputation. The frequent use of the expression "prostituting" of talents is indicative of this context.

While this is most salient at the societal level, the foci of our concern here, the values of societal systems and subsystems, comprise only part of still larger normative systems, which involve most centrally the cultural system, but also very importantly the personalities and behavioral organisms of individuals. All of these systems interpenetrate with the societal components of values. Furthermore, the value system is differentiated on the higher-lower axis of cybernetic order on the macroscopic-microscopic range, and in qualitative terms, defined by function in the social system and in the general system of action.

Deflation of commitments may come to focus at any level in the hierarchy or in any qualitative "branch" of the functional "tree." However, the common feature of all deflation is what we may call value *absolutism*. It is the assertion of sharp limitations on implementive flexibility, restricting the obligation to the most immediate, often most drastic, steps for implementing the pattern at the particular level of reference. Legitimation is thereby withdrawn from otherwise open ranges of flexibility with respect to more remote means of implementation or other subvalues within a larger system.[28] The test of "real" commitment then tends to become the extent to which the acting unit makes direct implementation of the value-focus salient at the time its overwhelmingly primary, if not sole, concern. As in any deflationary process, the deflated units, in seeking the security of an indubitably "real" commitment, are cut off from wider systems having more extensive degrees of both freedom and solidarity. They are forced to "go it alone" and, since the sanctions for nonfulfillment of commitments are negative, they are exposed to processes of "escalation," for example, reciprocal increases in severity of condemnation for noncompliance, often bringing about the generalization of conflict, and readiness to use force. This results, in turn, in *exclusion* from the moral community of elements previously treated as legitimate.

In cybernetic terms, the highest level of commitment is the religious. For this reason, "fundamentalism" seems to be an appropriate prototype of deflationary pressure on the commitment system, presuming the current usage of this term to connote a reaction *against* what is usually called the "liberalization" of religion.[29] It attempts to restrict the tendering of broad degrees of freedom to elements that are, by the strictest possible test,

[28] Weber formulated this as *Gesinnungsethik* (which I translated as "ethic of absolute value") and contrasted it with *Verantwortungsethik*, the "ethic of responsibility." The latter stresses freedom to choose from a wider range of alternatives, but also responsibility for the consequences of such choice. See *The Sociology of Religion* (Boston: The Beacon Press, 1963).

[29] The term "moral absolutism" may be used instead of "fundamentalism" if it is felt that the latter term seems too restrictive in its connotations to stand for what must be understood to be a very general phenomenon. I am generalizing the usage of the term "fundamentalism" only because I take the contemporary fundamentalist religious movements to be striking and relatively well understood instances of the more general phenomenon. We should take great care, of course, not to establish an ethnocentric framework for the analysis of other cases of the deflation of commitments by uncritical usage of the term.

"sound," like the gold of monetary systems or the security of superior force in political systems.

From this point of view the "secularization" of modern society, regarded as the outcome of vast processes of differentiation, institutionalizes degrees of freedom in the implementation of religious commitments that are incompatible with fundamentalist versions of Protestantism—or of Catholicism or Judaism, for that matter. Thus, groups that have historically been defined as religious, which reject the main patterns of secularization and define them as "loss of faith," are fundamentalist in the strict sense.

However, the focus of fundamentalism may not be on religion in the analytical sense, but on tenets about the organization of society or "personal" morality, the other most important contemporary focus. From this point of view, the sharp ideological dispute between socialist and capitalist commitments constitutes a "deflationary" movement within the development of Western society and its commitment system. Each side claims the absolute moral legitimacy of its own commitments, thereby justifying, in the extreme case, "war," if only of the "cold" variety, against the other. Fortunately, from my point of view (but then I am neither a committed capitalist nor a committed socialist), we have been experiencing a certain loosening of these fundamentalist rigidities, and new degrees of freedom are now beginning to appear.

From a certain point of view, existentialism and the related "neo-anarchist" currents may be seen as a fundamentalist pattern of what Durkheim called the "cult of the individual." This orientation would test the authenticity of the individual's commitment to his moral freedom by requiring him to abjure all commitments to what we have called "valued association." The new "love" cult (focusing about the "Hippie" movement) seems to restrict allowable association to "primordial" *Gemeinschaft* solidarities or certain substitutes for them, thereby declaring all assocation within the universalistic-impersonal structures of modern society illegitimate.

The history of complex societies is clearly permeated with fundamentalist movements in the commitment system. While high degrees of symbolic generalization and attendant freedom of choice have been achieved, there have been severe conflicts and great costs—even now they rest in many respects on precarious ground. It is not surprising that the "secular religions" of our own day are experiencing repeated waves of commitment deflation. This is not unrelated to the revival—how serious is very difficult to judge—of calls for security to be gained by deflation of the other generalized media. Thus, President de Gaulle is urging the restoration of the traditional unqualified gold standard in the monetary sphere. The warranting of national security sheerly by superiority of physical force is by no means without advocates, despite the nature of modern weaponry. Indeed, the note sounded by de Gaulle, for the case of French Canada, that ethnicity is so basic to national solidarity as to constitute by itself a valid claim to sovereign independence, is a fundamentalism of the integrative sphere.

The interpretation of the causes and probable consequences of such deflationary movements will provide a useful transition to the question of the application of the zero-sum problem to the medium of commitments. This problem involves the generalization to the field of commitments of the logic underlying explanation of the phenomena of credit creation in the monetary field and the corresponding phenomena in the fields of power and influence. We suggest that through the operation of what is perhaps most appropriately called "moral leadership" there exists a type of mechanism that cannot only allocate existing value-commitments, but add to their quantity in the system, quantity being conceived as a resultant of the combination of level of generality and intensity in the above senses.

In the economic case, there is a striking asymmetry between the rights retained, in the case of ordinary banking, by depositors and the obligations assumed by the bank. Depositors, that is to say, do not relinquish any of their property rights in the funds deposited, as is made clear by their right to withdraw their deposits in "cash" in full on demand. Banks, on the other hand, lend "other people's money" on a contractual basis, whereby the crucial feature of the contract is the assumption of a legal obligation *not* to demand repayment before the expiration of the term of the loan.

It is well known that, in the sense of being in a position to "honor" all of its formal obligations, if all its depositors insist in payment in full immediately, every functioning bank is "insolvent." It is only on the basis of the expectation that this will not happen, that the bank is justified in "betting" that its loan contracts can be liquidated in an orderly sequence without its being faced by an imperious demand for repayment by depositors at a rate far above the "normal." This expectation is, of course, generally backed by a system of "reserve" mechanisms.

In the case of commitments, we have tried to make clear that there is a high premium on maintaining their "liquidity," i.e., the openness of alternatives of allocation. The primary condition of this is, as with all the media, *trust*, this time in the integrity of the commitments. This applies first to those who "deposit" them, including acts of "entrusting" their liquidity to some other agency, and second, to those who accept this latter trust. The "commitment banker" to whom freedom of action in implementing commitments is entrusted, is always an agency possessing some kind of moral authority; this is what was meant by the reference to moral leadership above. More obvious examples would be religious bodies to which members of the more general public look for guidance. Various "lay" bodies, and individuals, however, also possess moral authority in this sense, and thus trust in the integrity of an academic institution in its commitment to academic freedom, or trust in a political party.

"Depositing" of commitments in this case means that on the one hand decisions of allocation may be, for the time being, held in abeyance; the "income" of commitments need not be "spent" at the same rate and rhythm at which it is received. On the other hand, protection of integrity need not be on the sole responsibility of the "depositing" unit, but it may associate itself with fellow-depositors in trusting the integrity of a collective or collectively trusted agency. This agency, then, may make use of this trust by taking action to extend the range of commitments, especially to higher levels of generalization, beyond that ventured by any of the unit depositors as such or independently of any direct collective authorization by them. As in the case of routine commercial banking, this special freedom of the bank may be used in relatively routine ways to iron out the exigencies of fluctuation in the situations of various units in the market system through loans to "tide them over" such exigencies. Bank loans, however, may go beyond that in being extended to genuine economic innovators as new "investment." Such funds may then be utilized to re-organize the productive system in some special way to bring about an increase in its total productivity. A new increase in the total monetary circulating medium is an essential condition of this. If the increase of productivity is sufficient and occurs within a requisite time period, the effect will not be inflationary.

I should like to suggest that institutions possessing marked "moral authority" in societies, may on the one hand function as relatively "custodial" guardians of unit commitments, but that on occasion they may engage in the innovative extension of commitments with the consequence of reorganizing the value-institutionalization system.

COMMITMENT "BANKING" AND CHARISMA

Probably the most generalized formulation of the role of the "commitment banker" in sociological thought is Weber's concept of charismatic leadership.[30] The charismatic leader imposes compliance with his "demands" as a *moral duty*, not as enhancement of self-interest. However, he typically emphasizes that these demands are not for the fulfillment of routinely established obligations, but for something new. Weber repeatedly quoted from the Gospels, "it is written, but *I say unto you*."

Although Weber's analysis was concerned mainly with religious systems, he did not explicitly exclude political or even economic leader-

[30] Max Weber, *The Sociology of Religion, op. cit.*, and *Theory of Social and Economic Organization* (New York: Oxford, 1947).

ship from the charismatic type. This raises very complex questions of system-reference for the analysis of the actual functioning of any of the generalized media. Our primary concern is with the social system, but its interdependence with the rest of the action system must not be overlooked.

In terms of the general action system, the raising of "moral" issues in a social context places the focus at a high level in the general cybernetic scale. The paradigm for the general action system indicates that this is due to a special relation between the cultural and personality system, one which may well help account for the connection between charisma and "personal" qualities.[31] The implication is that the individual as a personality must bear the primary focus of moral responsibility for the *implementation* of cultural values. In this context, the individual's involvement with "valued association" is in the first instance instrumental, especially in "defining the situation" for implementative action. Hence, "deflationary" pressures, whether affecting individuals or collectivities, tend to restrict the possible impact of any "charismatic" influences within an already legitimized framework, which does not itself open opportunities for charismatic innovation in the value-commitment sphere.

One of the more difficult problems in interpreting Weber's conception of charismatic "breakthrough" concerns the degree of "totality" of the break.[32] Since such movements tend to be involved with severe conflict, and since both proponents and opponents tend toward value absolutism, there is a tendency to emphasize this totalism—perhaps also because dramatic cases are especially visible. The generality of totalistically divisive forces may be questioned, however. In the light of historical evidence, for example, the basic continuity in terms of values between Christianity and the culture of Israel, on the one hand, and of Hellenism, on the other hand, must certainly be accepted. Somewhat similarly, Marxism-Leninism is clearly an outgrowth of the main currents of Western culture in the 19th century. Of course, the formation of both movements involved very general elements of innovation which are *not* to be denied herewith.

If breaks were as drastically radical as ideologists often hold them to be, it is difficult to see how their movements could avoid occasioning, almost immediate "runs" on the "commitment banking" system, so that commitment-creation through the charismatic type of process would be impossible. I suggest that very often such movements constitute "extensions" of the system's previous state of value-commitment and that, although their legitimacy is often vociferously questioned from more or less fundamentalist perspectives, the line of distinction between legitimacy and illegitimacy is seldom free of ambiguity. Thus "capitalist" values do not

[31] See the discussion of charisma in my *Structure of Social Action,* (New York: McGraw-Hill, 1937) pp. 662 ff. Also *Max Weber on Charisma and Institution Building,* S.N. Eisenstadt (ed.) (Chicago: University of Chicago Press, 1968).
[32] Cf. my introduction to Weber, *The Sociology of Religion, op. cit.*

readily concede that "exploitation" is good or prevalent; the "Peoples' Democratic Republics" share some meanings of the word "democracy" with the democratic societies of the "free" world. Elements of the "left" within the non-socialist societies emphasize aspects of common commitment with the socialists, maintaining that their differences lie in judgment of the best methods of implementation, not basic value commitments. At least some of the "commitment depositors" do not immediately withdraw their commitments in fright about the "unsoundness" of the banking agent, the charismatic innovator, but lend, often indirectly and passively, all-important support. If the first flashes of a charismatic movement immediately polarized the attitudes of individuals at the commitment level, the result would almost certainly be quick suppression of the movement.

The element of continuity also indicates an answer to the question of whether such movements always inflate value-commitments—as well as the standard of their not doing so, if they do not. The answer lies, I think, in the conception of the *institutionalization* of value innovations. A charismatic commitment-expansion will be noninflationary insofar as it represents a first step in a process of institutionalization. It must lead to the establishment, in structures congruent with the new level of value-commitments, of viable patterns of both valued association and command of "operative" resources, notably in the form of organizational effectiveness and mobilizable resources, particularly economic ones. Inflationary consequences would ensue if the charismatic movement generated formidable new commitments on the part of large and important population elements, but did not give rise to effective implementive procedures that could eventually, in Weber's term, be "routinized" on a sufficient scale. Deflation would ensue where such stringent conditions were imposed at various steps of implementation, that either no charismatic expansion could occur or its early stages were opposed so sharply as to induce withdrawal. In *both* cases, of course, the relation of the charismatic process to the "normal" commitment system is vital. In a system which has strong expectations of institutional provision for innovation, failure of success, in either form, is profoundly disturbing.

SOME SOURCES AND CONSEQUENCES OF DEDIFFERENTIATION

Here we encounter a second application of the concept of the *intensification* of commitments. A "loan" of commitment-capacity, once acquired through the charismatic process, will tend to be legitimized, not in every context in which commitments operate, but wherever a felt need can be combined with opportunity. The process is parallel to the acquisition of new capital resources by developing industries.

The pressures deriving from sponsorship of, or identification with, a set of commitments that stand in at least partial conflict with the established system seem to produce two major tendencies. First, the commitment element comes to be stressed relative to other factors in the innovating subsystem. Second, because it must be partial and specialized, the innovating subsystem very often becomes the focus of a process of *dedifferentiation* relative to the historical background. Thus the allocation of commitments tends to concentrate sharply in the field of innovation commitment. Responsibilities focusing in other "normally" obligatory areas may be neglected or, if the tension rises sufficiently, explicitly repudiated to the point of being declared specifically illegitimate. Thus a very large sector of common Western liberal socio-political values were repudiated by the Communist movement, especially in its Stalinist phase. The values of free speech, orderly procedure in reaching collective decisions, and many other aspects of "civil liberties" have been downgraded. Indeed, for the elite "cadres," most of the values concerning the private life of the individual have been sacrificed.[33] Such "sacrifices" have often been interpreted as signs of the sincerity of the commitment, with the fundamentalist implication that those who share the values, but insist on retaining a broader pattern for allocating rights, are "enemies" of the innovative movement.[34]

The consequences of such processes of dedifferentiation—in this case in the direction of *Gesinnungsethik*, with increasing unconcern for the exigencies of broadly differentiated implementation—depends on the mode of articulation, or lack of it, with the previously established system of institutionalization of values. Perhaps four main alternatives may be specified.

First, a movement may be so "deviant" that it cannot articulate with the bases of evaluative support in sufficient quantity, with the probable consequence that it will be eliminated through the negative process of sociological "natural selection." This has been the fate of many "exotic" sectarian movements, whether at strictly religious or other levels.

The second possibility is that the movement might offer a sufficiently "mild" challenge that, despite tensions and resistances, the society can "absorb" it without major structural changes. Very considerable advances of scientific knowledge in particular fields, including even rather major technological applications, probably fit this category. Among the difficult questions of degree in such cases are those that concern articulation with broader innovative movements. Thus the first great synthesis of modern physical science did not in itself "revolutionize" 17th century society; it

[33] Paul Hollander, "The New Man and His Enemies: A Study of the Stalinist Conceptions of Good and Evil Personified," unpublished Ph.D. dissertation, Princeton University, 1963.

[34] The withdrawal of the Christian religious orders, by their vows of celibacy, poverty, and obedience, from the "normal" commitments of the life of the Christian laity, is another prime example of this process of dedifferentiation.

was part of a very broad movement that included a variety of other components, at legal, political, and economic levels.

This type of innovation would probably not usually be called charismatic. It certainly need not involve a major convulsion of the social system as a whole. We should remember, however, that the disturbance occasioned by major innovations is relative to the system reference. What for a small-scale subsystem of a society is a major disturbance may hardly cause a ripple far beyond its boundaries. The most important point to make is that, not only does the innovative process leading to what we have called "progressive" social change occur by processes that do not always entail major social conflicts, but that, in all probability, commitment creation plays a major part in these as well as in the more dramatically charismatic cases. A good illustration would be the establishment of the American university system in the last third of the nineteenth century which, compared to the great industrial changes, the rural-urban tensions of the period, and the reinsulation of the post-Reconstruction South, did not occasion prominent social conflicts, though some within the educational system itself. Yet, this process was one of the principal aspects of the educational revolution which has already had profound consequences for the society.

The third alternative maximizes the potentials of conflict between the established and innovative sectors by creating and exacerbating conflict and/or by exploiting conflict which is already present. The Marxian theory of the basis of the "proletarian" revolution in the structured class conflict of "capitalist" society may stand as its prototype. Such a movement may bring about "schism" of the previous system, which term itself suggests the example of the division of Christianity between the Eastern and Western Churches, which came to formal break only in the late Middle Ages. This example also indicates that the lines of division are often closely related to preexisting, underlying structural and cultural differences. In the Christian case the line fell between the territories of the Eastern and Western halves of the Roman Empire, with each church conducting large-scale missionary proselytization to the north of its main bases. The Communist movement has also divided on an East-West axis, broadly between the more fully "industrialized" societies and those to the East of the European center, which are in "need" of more basic economic development. The more "revolutionary" alternative may now make the "road back" to reintegration exceedingly difficult. It seems that complete "conquest" of one side by the other, whether peaceful or violent, is quite rare, once such division has become really deepseated. Perhaps the Reformation offers a typical example in that the present "ecumenical" trend is toward religious pluralism within a socio-cultural structure that in some sense synthesizes the two main patterns of implementation of Western "Christian" value-commitments, the Protestant and Catholic.

The Reformation illustrates the fourth main possibility for charismatic innovation, the institutionalization of a new level of *value-generalization*. This may make it possible, institutionally as well as culturally, to include within the emergent system *both* the "established" commitment system and the new charismatically introduced modes of commitment. A critical aspect of practically all "progressive" evolution in social systems, it amounts to "insight" that the two positions share common "value-premises." If due account is taken of the various exigencies to which the different "sectors" of the broad system are subject, and if mutual tolerance of implementive action related to these exigencies is institutionalized, then it is possible for *common* commitments at the most general level to coexist along with *differentiation* of implementive commitments at lower levels. Thus, in a religiously pluralistic society like the United States, there is a *moral* basis of consensus on fundamental societal value-commitments combined with a broad pluralism at the strictly religious level—though of course there is not an indefinite range of religious variation.[35]

It seems that the higher the level of generalization of a value-system, the broader the range, in terms both of level and of qualitative type, of the subvalues that can and *must* be legitimized in terms of it. However, this also means that the higher the level of generalization, the greater the scope for fundamentalist revolts against current patterns and levels of implementation, in the name of value-absolutism at various levels and in reference to various particular concerns. These circumstances seem to define a primary aspect of the unease and conflict-riddenness of our time. The great question with which this paper can be brought to a close is, I think, more empirical than theoretical. It concerns the *balance* among the alternative responses to value-innovation. Our second possibility was the relatively "innocuous" one of smooth institutionalization. Leaving that aside, we must ask which is most important: (1) fundamentalist regression to more primitive levels, (2) schismatic revolutionary outcomes, which will tend to maximize conflict, or (3) institutionalization of new levels of generality in value systems? Sociology has a grave responsibility to help clarify the understanding of what is going on and of what lies at stake in the balance among these possibilities.

---

[35] Notably, the great public issue of the moment, the war in Viet Nam, which is very strongly felt to be a moral issue, does not seem to involve the religious subgroups of American society in *any* structured way. There is no specifically Catholic, Jewish, or even Protestant position on the war.

Chapter 17

Polity and Society: Some General Considerations

*t*he approach to the problem of theory in the political field that has gradually unfolded in the various essays comprising this volume has come to
focus on a rather strictly *analytical* conception of the nature and role of
that theory. There has been a self-conscious attempt, especially in the first
two chapters of Part IV (13 and 14), to treat "political theory" as theory
of the "polity" as nearly parallel as possible with the relation of economic
theory to the concept of economy. This in turn has implied that both
should be treated as parts of a more general theory of social systems
which in addition to economy and polity must include a parallel treatment of the societal community and the "pattern-maintenance" system.
Though the program of development of such a theoretical scheme for
the polity has not been carried very far, it has, I think, gone far enough
to show the high fruitfulness of pursuing this path. Indeed, a modest
further extension will be attempted in this chapter.

This analytical conception of the scope of political theory will seem to
many political scientists to impose an undue restriction on the definition
of their concerns. As we noted in the brief introductory statement, there
is a parallel here to the sense of restriction that many economists felt
when the conception of "political economy" gradually gave way to that
of "economics." I have even suggested there that the emergence of the
conception of "political sociology" is a kind of recognition of the recent
process of differentiation of theoretical schemes. In an older tradition the

This essay appears here for the first time.

term "politics" would presumably have been used to cover this area as well, without qualifications. In that tradition there would be little concern about what bearing "sociology" might have on the problems.

DUALITY OF THE CATEGORY "POLITICAL"

The category "political," I think, shares with that of "economic" and indeed of "social" a certain duality of reference which sometimes leads to ambiguity. Thus we may ask: Was not the Great Depression an "economic" phenomenon? And was not McCarthyism a "political" phenomenon? The whole tenor of the New Deal, however, made coping with the Great Depression and its consequences as much a political as an economic problem. I have suggested, further, that the primary roots of McCarthyism lay in strains in the societal community, not in the polity as that concept has here been defined with analytical strictness. Yet certainly it deeply involved the processes of government. My general view is that the depression presented problems of political economy par excellence, and McCarthyism, of political sociology. To illustrate from other types of society, Stalin's policy of the collectivization of agriculture in the early 1930's was ostensibly a set of measures toward the goal of economic development. It had, however, profound repercussions on the Soviet political system, certainly constituting one major factor underlying the great purges a few years later. Again, in the essays in Part II, especially Chapter 3, I have argued that strains in the German societal community, accentuated by the pressures engendered by military defeat in World War I and subsequent Allied policies, had much to do with the political explosion of the Nazi movement.

The primary link between the two references of the concept "political" lies, I think, in the conception of collective system goal-attainment. This has been defined as the tendency of an action system to change the relation between the system itself and certain features of its environment in the direction of fuller meeting of one or more functional needs of the system, which is roughly equivalent to lessening of "tension" between system and environment in the relevant respects. Full "attainment" of a system goal would then constitute an equilibrium point at which striving for such attainment would cease.

It follows from this conception that a goal attainment "problem," for the social system, i.e., in our analytical sense a "political" problem, can arise *wherever* this type of tension appears in the system-environment relationship. It may involve any of the internal parts of the system, as well as any features of its environment. In terms of "content," therefore, the political function is completely nonspecific. Here it should be remembered that, as set forth in Part I, we conceive the environment of a social system to include not only the physical environment and other social systems —such as "nations"—but also the organisms and personalities of its members, and the relevant cultural systems. Thus such "problems" as that of the health of its population, or of the level of their motivation to role performance, may be political problems for a society, as may be the improvement of the level of knowledge through research.

This does not imply, however, that the theory of the polity is simply a synonym for the total theory of social systems, since the "point of view" from which these variant "content" problems are approached when they are defined as political problems has a constant *analytical* reference. This, I hope, has been clearly defined as involving a goal or set of goals that are meaningful and important for the system to seek to attain, and the mobilization of its *collective* resources to that end, including the imposition of binding obligations on its members, whether individuals or sub-collectivities.

For the American governmental system a particularly good statement of one aspect of this relationship, coming from a sociological source, was the phenomenon, discussed in Chapter 9, of issues coming to what Berelson, Lazarsfeld, and McPhee called the "gateway." This meant that many potential issues, as occasions for governmental action, remain "latent" for long periods and only with certain shifts in balances of forces become the kind of "live" political issues that executive and legislative agencies will actively seek to deal with. Thus, of course, in a number of phases, the issue of political—as distinguished from legal—responsibility for the civil and other rights of Negro Americans has gone through a complicated process before, first, the governmental action issuing in the Civil Rights Acts of 1964 and 1965 became possible, and the closely related "war on poverty," with its important bearing upon the problems of the northern urban Negro.[1] Another major issue recently coming to the "gateway" has been that of the responsibility of the federal government for the support of education.

It is, I think, correct to say that for a large proportion of political scientists their discipline has been "problem-oriented" in the above sense, namely, that it dealt with any subject matter with which "political agencies" became concerned, the latter concept being overwhelmingly governmental in reference. But since economics and sociology, to say nothing of other disciplines, deal with many of the same concrete subject matters, the problem of defining the disciplinary division of labor still remains. For the case under discussion, as for others, I should say that the principle of the division of labor between disciplines as such not only should be analytical, but that it should deal with differentiated structures and pro-

---

[1] Cf. my Introduction to *The Negro American*, Parsons and Clark, Eds., Boston: Houghton Mifflin Co., 1966, entitled "Why 'Freedom Now,' Not Yesterday?"

cessual mechanisms, which are not substantively specific, but are "available" and suitable for performing certain functions with respect to a wide range of subject matters. Thus the *problem* of coping with mass unemployment in the great depression was largely economic, but the agencies of doing so were largely political. The problem of the status of the Negro American is, I feel, at least to a high degree, integrative, but political agency is fundamental in attempts to cope with it.

The idea of agency in this sense is the core of the concept of the "political aspect" put forward in Chapter 13, and developed a little further now. It centers on the conception of collective action which is sufficiently focused to need the conception of collective goal orientation to define its directionality. Insofar, then, as within a social system there is differentiation of structures and mechanisms around the function of collective action, not only do these differentiated structures and mechanisms have relatively definable properties that distinguish them from those with predominantly different functions in the social system, such as economic or integrative, but, once the lines of differentiation can be conceptualized and empirically analyzed, the problems of the *interrelations* between the political subsystem and the others become crucial. It is a cardinal tenet of the theory set forth here that functionally differentiated subsystems are *always* open systems, engaged in continuous and functionally vital interchanges with environing systems, and *not only* (though often) through the processes of political goal-attainment as such.

In the traditions of political science, and to a lesser extent of its neighboring disciplines, there is of course a very rich body of codified knowledge of the wide variety of structural forms of what we are calling political agencies, and of course of a wide variety of processes by which they operate internally and are related through interchange to other systems, the environments of the polity. If, of course, the polity is seen in our technical sense as a subsystem of the society, it should open the way to further codification on all levels, since, for example, structural classifications that are used in sociology could be more systematically related to those used in political science. A good example of such disciplinary articulation and very likely interpenetration would of course be the rather widespread use made by political scientists of Max Weber's typology of authority, to be referred to later. Another extremely important field is that of social stratification as it bears on political organization and the distribution of power.

THE THEORETICAL SALIENCE OF
THE CONCEPT OF POWER

It seems, however, that the most strategic point of reference for theoretical advance, including analysis of the relations of the polity to its environments, should lie in the concept of power, seen not only in its more narrowly political context, but in that of its involvement in the relations of the polity to the other primary functional subsystems of the society. This is one point at which the conception of political power as a generalized symbolic medium of societal interchange may turn out to be especially fruitful. This is a particularly important area in which systematically ordered relationships can be established; indeed, a substantial beginning in that direction has already occurred. The key here lies in the relations between power as a medium and the other media, each anchored in another primary subsystem, with which power stands in interchange relations.

This began with what in a certain sense was an analysis of the "sociology of money" with a view to generalizing the conception of a symbolic "medium" to cases other than the monetary. This, of course, necessitated establishing "categorial" relationships between money and the other media, notably power, but it would not have been very fruitful to stop there. It was essential to try to establish the ways in which each medium, in its involvement in interchanges over the boundaries of its "home" subsystem, articulated with each of the other three media.

If certain of the premises of the analysis are granted, then some highly specific conclusions follow. These premises above all are, first, that for a society there are *four*—and only four—primary functional subsystems and, second, that, if each of these is sufficiently highly differentiated internally and the four are sufficiently differentiated from each other, there will be a generalized symbolic medium anchored in each of the four subsystems. Then each subsystem will have an open boundary with each of the other three, over which interchange presumptively involves, or in some sense is "mediated by," its "home medium."

If this be granted, then a typology of "political problems" in the above sense should be derivable from the primacy relations of the processes centering on each of these open boundaries of the polity respectively, and the various combinations in which the importance of such boundary interchanges may stand. There is a sense in which the relations vis-à-vis each of the other three primary subsystems of the society constitute an "inner circle" of political problems, and those vis-à-vis the other subsystems of the general action system, the physical environment and other societies, constitute a kind of "outer circle."

Three very broad areas of political problems can, in this sense, be simply read off the general paradigm of societal interchanges.[2] These have very generally been understood as political problems in the narrower sense, but it follows from the present argument that they should be treated as boundary problems involving relations between political theory in an analytical sense and neighboring analytical theoretical disciplines.

[2] See Talcott Parsons, *Sociological Theory and Modern Society* (New York: The Fress Press, 1967) p. 350. [Reprinted as Chapter 14 in the present volume: ed.]

Instead of looking now at the total interchange relation between polity and neighboring subsystems, it may be useful to look first at the polity as the "consumer" of the "product" outputs of the other three systems, and then as the utilizer of factors inputs from each of them and the three in combination. The three categories of product input to the polity in the first place are *all* forms of its "income" of power. They are, according to the paradigm, political support (from I), commitment or allocation of services to the collectivity (from A), and legality of powers of office (from L). It is quite clear that every political "leadership group," if we may focus on that aspect, must be very much concerned with all three problems and with their coordination with each other, just as every economy—e.g. in some sense centrally "controlled" as by monetary policies—must be concerned with maintaining the volume of consumers' spending, the input of capital funds, and the maintenance of claims to a share of financial resources.

Political support may be structurally ascribed, of course, as in the case of the older style of "legitimist" monarchies where the population were "subjects" of the king. Once, however, this ascriptive basis is gone, definitive measures may have to be taken that are directed to the mobilization of support, often in competition with other leadership groups that are trying to supplant a group "in power"—in modern "democratic" régimes, with a constitutional right to attempt to do so or, of course, attempts to supplant the incumbents by unconstitutional means. Political support in our technical sense is an input of power to the polity, and above all its leadership component, but an input from "outside," i.e., from the societal community. In a parallel way consumers' spending is an input to the economy from outside, in an analytical sense from "households" that are not themselves primarily economic in function in the society. The politically significant parallel to what Keynes called "saving" is the withholding by constituents of support that can potentially be given to political leadership, possibly "hoarding" it, possibly "investing" it in directions other than the support of current and possibly "routine" leadership.

The distinction, basic to modern "democratic" political organization in private collectivities as well as in government, between the status of elective and of appointive office, and in the broad "policy" field the subordination of the latter to the former, is built into the interchange paradigm. The power of elective office is, we have suggested, drawn from members of the societal community in their capacity as composing the "constituencies" of candidates for and incumbents of elective office. The power input that is distinctive of appointive office, however, falls in the category we have called "allocation of services to the collectivity." This allocation[3] of course is contingent on the decision of appointing authority,

---

[3] The paradigm set forth in Chapter 14 uses the term "commitment" at this point. It does not, however, designate a category of commitments in the more technical sense of Chapter 16, so wherever feasible I have substituted the term "allocation."

but the appointing authority does not perform the actual services of, for example, an administrative organization. The usual way of looking at it has been to say that the appointing authority "delegates" its power to appointive officers of the organization. This aspect we have conceptualized as giving to them "opportunity for effectiveness." But this power *output* from the polity would not contribute to collective effectiveness were it not balanced by the availability, from the pool of "manpower" of the society, of a sufficiently large and competent contingent to commit[4] their services, through appointment.

We thus conceive this to be a *double* interchange between persons acting in their "political" capacity in our analytical sense, and persons acting in the capacity of "members of the labor force," i.e., qualified to perform economically valuable services for which they may legitimately be financially remunerated, and offering such services, if acceptable contractual terms can be arranged with employing agencies. Thus the flow of power to the "labor force," though presenting opportunity for effectiveness, need not impinge exclusively on the same population elements as those responding to such opportunity through commitment of their own services. In the political science literature, this has often been put[5] as presenting to political organization the "problem" of *mobilization* of adequate manpower to meet its obligations in the society or to attain its collective goals.[6]

As an output of the economy, services are in the first instance to be

---

[4] In the case of an actual "contract of employment" there is a *component* of commitments in our technical sense, but this is not a "form of power."

[5] Cf. Karl Deutsch, "Social Mobilization and Political Development," *American Political Science Review*, Vol. 55 (September 1961), pp. 493–514, and S. N. Eisenstadt, *Modernization: Protest and Change* (Englewood Cliffs, N.J.: Prentice-Hall, 1966).

[6] Since we define *service* as an input of power from the economy to the polity, and *product* as an output of the economy, to avoid confusion a distinction is necessary between service in this sense and labor as a factor of production, as dealt with in economic theory. The older economic theorists generally bracketed "goods and services" together as the primary outputs of the productive process, destined for "consumption." With the theoretical developments following from *Economy and Society*, however, it became increasingly necessary to discriminate them as, in the case of goods, an input to the household (L), and of services, to the polity (G). This theoretical decision was grounded in the view that *all* direct functional "contribution" in a societal system involves collective performance (cf. *Social Structure and Personality*, Chapter 12), and hence the contribution of persons in roles is directly to a unit of the polity, and only through it to the society.

Labor as a factor of production, on the other hand, is conceived as the "real" output (i.e. nonmonetary) of the household to the economy. Essentially it is conceived as a *commitment* (in the technical sense) of capacity for instrumental performance to productive function in the economic sense. However, this commitment of "labor capacity," as we have called it, is not utilizable; literally it does not possess *utility* until it has been *combined* with the other factors of production. It emerges from this combinatorial process as a product with utility that can be acquired on the "labor market" by organizations seeking collective goals. Later on we shall present a typology of such organizations, of which the firm is one. Unfortunately current terminology, including the prevalent usage of economists, does not stress the analytical distinction between labor and service, which is essential to the clarification of this complex set of relationships.

evaluated in economic terms. Commitment of services to particular "employments," however, we treat as an input of power from the economy to the polity. This input may be valued in strict political terms for its contribution to the effectiveness of collective goal-oriented action. The problem then arises of the nature of the goal-orientations of the collectivities in question. If they are governmental, we would expect a coincidence between the power input and the primary function, in the society, of the collectivity itself. In modern societies, however, a very large proportion of services is devoted to the function of economic production; in this case the political function of the collectivity, usually called a "firm," is secondary to its economic function. The power input through allocation of services is then "diverted" from "purely political" use to economic uses.

Essentially the same considerations apply where the functions of collectivities are primarily integrative or cultural in the sense of pattern maintenance. A good example here is the educational system, and the related function of research, where the manpower committed to such functions is withdrawn from the primarily political function context and "diverted" to another. This diversion may be regarded analytically, as parallel to the diversion of "consumers" income from return to the economy via the "circular flow"[7] to savings and then into the channel of investment. This diversion may or may not acquire its meaning from a societal "need" to improve over the long run the political effectiveness of the society, or its level of integration, or even its cultural levels. The power input may simply be "hoarded" and withdrawn from any effect on societal processes. This would be the case, for example, when qualified members of the labor force simply refuse to accept "opportunities for effectiveness" and remain passive so far as contributions to collective goal-attainment are concerned. Similarly, in the European Middle Ages, the allocation of such a large fraction of manpower to the Church, both in the secular priesthood and in the religious orders, was predominantly not for "political" reasons in the functional sense at a *societal* level.

It is here important to note, however, that the category "opportunity for effectiveness" is not exhausted by its function as a mechanism for mobilizing services for, in the analytical sense, political functions. The famous investment function in the economy is also dependent on this category of mechanism. The essential point is that banks, and some other agencies, make political decisions to make funds available to productive units—in the economic sense—usually on "loan," but with binding commitments to allow the borrower to control the funds for the stated period of the loan contract. This is a case of power as a medium controlling a transfer of control of monetary assets from a "fluid" if not a "consumption" status to use for presumptive increase of economic productivity.

---

[7] Cf. Joseph A. Schumpeter, *The Theory of Economic Development* (translated by Redvers Opie, Cambridge: Harvard Economic Studies Series, Vol. XLVI, 1934).

We have suggested that, other things equal, the authority and hence power of elective office is or should be superordinate to that of appointive office, where the distribution of power by the elective process is legitimated, which it by no means is in all cases. The third primary source of income of power to the polity is in the form of the category we have called "legality of the powers of office." The structure of modern political systems, especially at the most differentiated governmental level, suggests strongly that this source is primarily "constitutional." The constitution of government or of a private organization must itself of course be legitimated in our terms by value-commitments. Some aspects of legality are literally given in constitutionally defined terms. Insofar as this is a variable component, however, the most important agency of variation seems to be judicial decision or its equivalent. Among other things, in the American system, the courts, eventually the U.S. Supreme Court, have a dual function. On the one hand, they "interpret" the Constitution to the other components of government, federal, state, and local, and to the general "citizenry" in a wide range of private capacities, defining the rights and obligations of many private collectivities. In this capacity, they are "spellers-out" of the presumed value-consensus that underlies the legitimation both of government and of "private" rights.

The Constitution itself, however, is by no means only an assertion of value-commitments. It states many rather specific *norms* concerning the conduct of government itself and the relations of its various agencies to units in the private sector. Both as interpreters of constitutional "tradition" and as deciders of "cases" brought to them, the courts serve to *link* the constitutional specifications of value-commitments with the range of norms that regulate highly differentiated unit performances, both governmental and nongovernmental.

A common case of at least partial functional equivalence in premodern societies is that where the religious institutions perform not only a function of cultural legitimation, but the principal norm-defining functions for the polity. This, for example, was eminently true of the traditional Chinese Empire, but a particularly interesting set of cases is provided by the Islamic Empires, especially perhaps the Ottoman Empire at its height.[8] Here what Lybyer calls the "religious institution" was at the same time court and church, and there was no differentiation between religious law and secular "political" law—as indeed was also the case for classical Judaism.

This input to the political system is of a qualitatively different character from the other two, namely political support and commitment to services. It concerns the "structure of authority" rather than the *amount* of power. To elucidate this difference, it should be remembered that a generalized

[8] Cf. my volume, *Societies: Evolutionary and Comparative Perspectives* (Englewood Cliffs, N.J.: Prentice-Hall, 1966), Chapter 5, pp. 82 ff., and A. Lybyer, *The Government of the Ottoman Empire in the Time of Suleiman the Magnificent* (Cambridge, Mass., 1913).

symbolic medium of interchange has two primary components, which have been most clearly distinguished in linguistics under the heading of the distinction between *message* and *code*.[9] A code is a normative structure, often described as a set of rules, within which messages, e.g., linguistic utterances, may be formulated with the prospect of being "understood" by the recipients of communications, under the assumption that both sender and receiver "know" and utilize the same code. I suggest that the term authority can appropriately be used to designate the code in terms of which the use of power is the class of messages that have meaning within the code. The use of power, as capacity to *bind* a collectivity and its members, is meaningful within the code of authority in the sense that the unit promulgating "policy decisions" can expect compliance only if it is acting within the scope of its authority. Thus the inputs to the polity from the pattern-maintenance system must include both a code of "legitimation" and a mode of "implementing" that code through defining what we are here calling more specific "powers" of office.

It follows from this that the "amount of power" going with any particular position of authority—in the case of the individual, his "office" —is a function of the scope of discretion given in the definition of the legal powers of the office or, for a collectivity, such as a legislature, the "constitutional" scope of its powers. It is, however, also a function of the capacity of the incumbents of or candidates for office to mobilize political support and for the political collectivity to mobilize commitments to service. In the background of all three is the problem of the status of the collectivity, including its political "régime"—as distinguished, for example, from "government of the day"—in terms of legitimacy. Hence there is no presumption that the legal powers of office alone provide the resources necessary to "govern effectively," i.e., to attain collective goals as defined in the political process. Loss of basic legitimacy, of political support, or of access to sufficient and properly qualified manpower may all be factors in preventing politically effective performance.

This loss of legitimacy, of support, and of access to manpower has operated in premodern, "nonconstitutional" systems by other mechanisms. Thus in the Chinese Empire, the approaching end of a dynasty was usually marked by a conviction that it had lost the "mandate of Heaven." In the support context,/coups d'état and revolutions could displace "governments" or "régimes" without benefit of constitutional procedure. Finally, in the "service" sector a very common process has been ascriptive "traditionaliza-tion" of the status of manpower, as happened on a massive scale in the process of "feudalization" following the decline of the Western Roman Empire, and in somewhat different form, as a major aspect of Byzantine decline.[10]

[9] Cf. Roman Jakobson and Morris Halle, *Fundamentals of Language* (The Hague: Mouton, 1956).
[10] On all of this, cf. S. N. Eisenstadt, *The Political Systems of Empires* (New York: The Free, Press 1963).

With reference to the base concept of valuation of collective effectiveness and its place in turn in the more general value system, the three inputs of power to the polity reviewed above all produce outputs of other primary subsystems of the society, and constitute mechanisms by which the political function and the level of its performance are evaluated, and therefore the goals and procedures of politically important units of the society are further specified. The legality of powers of office essentially defines the *procedural code* within which political functions in our sense may and should be undertaken, including very importantly the limits on the legitimate use of authority and power.[11]

The power input from the societal community through the support system then may be regarded as one of the mechanisms that has to do with determination of the collective goals that shall be given salience. The central mechanism, in a differentiated system, is the choice among the proposals of competing leadership elements that is expressed through the electoral process, a function, as we shall see, also of "interest-demands." Where the system is pluralistic, and in the absence of acute crisis situations, this will not be confined to supporting a single goal-orientation, but rather a "direction" of goal-striving that implies some kind of a priority relation among more particular collective goals. It is in this context that the first order typology of political "problems" should be focused, e.g., on "governments" or "administrations" rather than régimes[12] that stress the relative importance of economic productivity, societal order, distributive justice, or cultural concerns domestically, and determine a broad orientation to problems of foreign relations, and the way in which this fits with domestic concerns.

The input of allocation of services to the collectivity concerns the level of means to collective effectiveness rather than the goals it serves. The most massive instance of it operates through the allocation of manpower in the labor market, which is one side of the phenomenon of individual choice of occupation and employment. The differential availability of manpower for different types of collective goals, including those of government, but involving the whole range available in a pluralistic society, constitutes a vital factor in the feasibility of any given class of

---

[11] It should always be kept in mind that the above considerations apply to private as well as to governmental collectivities.

[12] There is danger of terminological confusion here. I have no desire to attempt to impose usage but we need to distinguish at least three levels. They are (1) the "constitutionally" established set of offices: power, procedures that essentially define "authority structure" —in government or private collectivities. For this level the term "régime" seems most appropriate. (2) The "leadership" component which, *within* such a framework, exercises the paramount *power* position in the collective system. In British terminology, this is the "government" (of the day); in American, the "administration." (3) The predominantly implementive "apparatus," sometimes called the "bureaucracy." We often speak of it as having "administrative" functions. It is often more solidly established than is a "government" and sometimes even a "régime."

subcollectivity performing a set of functions in the society. One currently salient example is the problem of motivating young men to accept military service through the mechanism of the draft, which of course is not a case of "normal" occupational choice, but still a direction of allocation of manpower requiring the commitment of services. The capacity of a collective subsystem to perform certain functions effectively is thus dependent on its ability to attract services from those who, in economic terms—if the economic inducement is not crosscut, as in the case of the draft, by politically imposed compulsion—are in a position to choose among various alternatives for commitment of their services.

A Constitution like the American leaves some room, through the process of amendment, for "orderly" change in constitutional provisions. This deliberately cumbersome process probably should be classified with judicial decision as a factor in the variability of inputs of legality of powers of office. Constitutional change, however, which does not observe the procedural norms of the amendment process or the powers of the courts, is the governmental definition of "revolution." It leads to a break, not only with "legality" but with the "legitimacy," not only of the "administration" but of the "régime."[13] Since a revolutionary change in this sense in general grounds *its* legitimacy in some combination of the institutionalized value system—which the going regime allegedly violates—and of still higher-order values, it of course claims the right to control, not only the inputs of legality to the polity, but obviously the categories subordinate to this, namely, political support and commitment of services. For a revolutionary regime, however, securing the necessary inputs of power to "solve" these two sets of problems may not be very easy. Thus the fifty-year history of the Soviet regime involves major struggles that may be interpreted to involve, first, questions of legitimacy and legality—e.g., the "de-Stalinization" crisis which culminated in the removal of Stalin's body from the Red Square mausoleum, which is surely the most sacred monument of *Soviet* Russia. There have further been many discussions of "socialist legality." On policy levels, of course, controversies have been endless, but the accusation against Khrushchev of having committed the régime to "hare-brained schemes" will serve as an example. Finally, such a régime has had to resort on a major scale to requisition of manpower and even today has many difficulties, perhaps especially with respect to the role of the "intellectuals."

The above considerations enable us to say something more definite than before about the quantitative aspect of the variability of power. The central principle, as for all the media, including money, is a combination of position in a cybernetic hierarchy on the one hand with effectiveness of the cybernetic controls of the necessary inputs on the other.

[13] At lower levels of collective organization and in different constitutional systems, further distinctions would have to be made.

Thus, within any given system of political organization in our sense, there is a hierarchy of authority with respect to the making and implementing of decisions that bind the collectivity in question. The higher in this hierarchy an instance—which may be collective, including even a total electorate—stands, the greater presumptively is its power. Second, a complex pluralistic society involves a network of collectivities which both interpenetrate and stand in relations of broader inclusion of each other, culminating in the "central" government, the existence of which is a primary criterion of a society as distinguished from other types of social system (cf. Chapters 1 and 2). We may formulate this component in the concept "amount of power" as the *scope* of authority, i.e., the range of affairs over which the individual office incumbent or collective authority has the "legal" right to make decisions at his or its discretion. Obviously the President and Congress of the United States have by this criterion more power than any other agencies in this society, except the total electorate.

Beyond this, however, the question arises of how effectively such a position of authority is used to secure an "income" of power, i.e., inputs of political support and of services, the latter of course being highly dependent on financial resources. In systems of elective office, of course, and beyond that in revolutionary situations, political support is the principal means of attaining the authority of office, but the power controlled in the form of such support need not be a constant through a period of incumbency, nor may the command of services, depending as these do on financial resources, but also, for example, appeals to loyalty.

It would follow, as noted, that the individual or agency has more power in proportion to the scope of authority, in combination with that, the amount of political support that can be commanded or "counted upon," and the allocation of services that can be counted upon, but with support taking cybernetic precedence over services, as authority does over support.

The measure of "command" of these two variable classes of power is the effectiveness with which "appeals" evoke responses that are proportional to the expectations built into the authority structure and the conditions of attaining positions in it. In the case of political support it is above all the use of influence in the form of "taking leadership responsibility" that is the crucial factor. If the level of influence declines, it should be expected to diminish capacity to command political support.

It was said above that these principles apply to the quantification of *all* the generalized media, including money. This represents a change from earlier views, when the fact that money varied on a linear continuum seemed to make it the most "perfectly quantitative" medium, and direct the search toward as nearly comparable features of the others as possible.[14]

---

[14] On some principal modes of quantification. cf. S. S. Stevens, "Measurement, Statistics, and the Schemapiric View," *Science*, Vol. 16, pp. 849–856.

There is obviously no generalized unit of power comparable to a currency unit, so power seemed only "partly quantifiable."

My suggestion now is that property rights constitute the cybernetically superordinate focus of money, comparable to scope of authority (formulated in the interchange paradigm as the *I-A* product input to *A*, "standards for the allocation of resources"). These, then, should be in a position to control the monetary inputs, namely the allocation of fluid resources and consumers' spending (demand for goods) in that order of cybernetic precedence. Linear measurability in terms of money then seems to be a special empirical advantage of the monetary system which derives from factors other than its status as a generalized medium.

Support and services as well as "legalities" are inputs from *outside* the polity. Like other genuine components of the power system, they may on occasion be used outside the institutionalized framework of legitimized collective authority. Personal and group assumption of binding commitments, including willingness to use coercive sanctions to enforce "demands," may be and often are made. Within a collectivity such as a revolutionary party, we may speak of this bindingness as a case of power, but only *within* the collectivity of reference. Its use of coercion, threats, and various modes of "confrontation" on units of its environment is then parallel to the use of coercion or threats of it by governments in relation to other governments or their "nationals." Though this is in part a semantic problem, I think there are substantial advantages in not following very common usage in calling such use of "pressure" as the exercise of power in a technical sense, but confining the latter concept to the use of decision-making and implementive authority *within* organized collective systems that are to some significant degree integrated, and in institutionalized interchanges with their environments.[15]

The product-inputs of power to the polity from its neighboring subsystems thus constitute a mechanism for evaluating past and prospective political performance of collective agencies. The other class of inputs has a different order of functional significance. This, of course, is the input of "factors" to each subsystem, which category is of course modeled on that of the "factors of production" as this conception has developed in the history of economic theory. First it is necessary to *insist* on the importance of the distinction between factor and product inputs, as well as outputs.

We have been operating with a paradigm of *double* interchanges between the members of each of the six pairs of primary functional subsystems of a society, the original model for which was the labor-consumption interchange between economy and "household" as representative of the pattern-maintenance system. It was the level of differentiation, i.e., the "division of labor" in Adam Smith's sense, that accounted for the necessity of the

---

[15] From the author's personal point of view this constitutes an explicit change of opinion. Cf. *The Social System*, (New York: The Free Press, 1951, Chapter IV) for my earlier view.

double interchange and hence the involvement of a generalized symbolic medium, in this case money. Further analysis showed that, again to use this case for illustration, one interchange concerned the "disposal" by one subsystem, the economy, of its products, namely goods, to house-holds, the other the acquisition, by the economy, of labor as a factor of production. There had to be two interchanges, because the sources of goods available to a household in a system with high division of labor, could not closely correspond with the sources of "wage" income through the commitment of labor capacity *in the individual case*, though their aggregate quantities had to balance as a condition of system equilibrium.

It has been a "finding" of the generalization of this, the economists' familiar paradigm, that, from the perspective of any *one* primary subsystem, all three of the *product* inputs from the others took the form of the gener-alized medium anchored in that subsystem, e.g. for the economy, "com-modity demand," "allocation of fluid resources," and "ranking of claims to resources" are all monetary categories; for the polity "commitment (or better allocation) of services," "political support," and "legality of powers of office" are all forms of power.

Factor inputs, on the other hand, are *never* in the form of the medium anchored in the subsystem of reference, but consist, from each of the other three subsystems respectively, of inputs of *each* of the other three general-ized media, which in turn control the "intrinsic effectors." Thus, for the economy we interpret labor to be a form of commitments, capital, of power, and "organization," of influence. Similarly, for the polity, control of productivity is monetary, interest-demands operate through influence, and legitimation of authority is a form of value-commitments.

THE FACTORS OF COLLECTIVE EFFECTIVENESS

In the case of the polity it is not at all surprising to social science common sense that the input we classify as a "factor of effectiveness" from the economy is called "control of productivity." There *is* indeed a basic need for the effective functioning of all collective systems in advanced societies, for financial resources that constitute a claim on the product-ivity of the economy. This is perhaps particularly salient in our type of society, for the case of the "private, nonprofit" sector, which can neither rely on market proceeds of sales nor on the compulsory taxing power of government for its monetary income.

Control of productivity here is very close to being in the position of holding and being capable of implementing property rights, but at the level of monetarily mobilizable resources rather than "possession" of goods or "claims" to services. The category is independent of the source of these rights, the three primary sources being purchase, through market channels, requisitioning, for example through the taxing power of government, or voluntary contribution. Inheritance is perhaps a comparable fourth source, with a pattern-maintenance reference. This category should of course be broadened beyond the kinship nexus, especially to cover continuity of the corporate property rights of collectivities independent of the persons or subcollectivities that are at any given moment the incumbents of offices.

Legitimation of authority as a factor of collective effectiveness is also, since Weber, relatively unproblematical. It also belongs with legality of powers in the code category. It is not, however, the most general value-pattern as such, but its specification, not only to the polity, which we formulate as the *L*-component, the valuation of effectiveness, but further specification to the still more specific contexts in which operative authority is relevant. In this connection it is important to remember that it is a category under the generalized medium we have called value-commitments and that, therefore, the analysis presented in Chapter 16 applies here. Furthermore, it is important to note that we extend the concept of authority, and with it power, to *all* membership statuses in organized collectivities. Thus the franchise must be conceived to be authentic power, though the vote of one member is only a very little power. Such a member in turn has the authority to cast his vote under the given procedural rules, and of course to have it "counted" according to said rules.

It is essential to the conception of circulation of a medium beyond the boundaries of its "home" subsystem that the relevant "codes" should be institutionalized, not only in the home subsystem itself, but in the others involved in the interchange of the medium. Thus, in spite of the fact that family households are noneconomic in their functional primacies, it is entirely clear that they are typically property holders, and legitimate claimants to monetary income through market interchanges. Similarly, though the voter is, in a governmental reference, *qua* role, a member of the societal community rather than the political system, he is unquestionably a holder of authority with its appropriate access to circulating power.

It is perhaps a little more difficult to see that the unit of the economy which is the recipient of outputs of "opportunity for effectiveness" must be in a similar position, in that it must possess some order of legitimate authority to offer such opportunity beyond the boundary of the polity with collectively binding consequences. In this case the primary value-reference is equality of opportunity, whereas in that of the franchise it is equality of membership rights.

Legitimation, therefore, is a mechanism of *allocation* of authority to different subcollectivities and statuses within them, by virtue of which they are "put in a position" to acquire and use power. It is a case of the specification of value-commitments. From this point of view, for example, both membership in the labor force, i.e., capacity to provide services (cf. above) and ownership of property (control of productivity) are the bases of membership statuses that involve a component of authority. Weber was, accordingly, basically correct in giving such prominence to the legitimation of authority in his treatment of the subject. Of the three primary mobile factors of effectiveness in our technical sense, legitimation stands highest in the order of cybernetic control. Hence variations in its organization will have strong repercussions with respect to the two of lower cybernetic order.

The relatively nonmobile factor, namely, "valuation of collective effectiveness," also needs a word of comment; it is the "land" factor of the polity. This refers, I take it, to the *constitutional* level of collective commitment as that concept has already been briefly discussed. It concerns not only commitment to collective effectiveness in a generalized sense, but also the allocation of such commitments among a variety of collectivities in the society. Government, of course, will have to occupy a prominent place, but the nature and extent of its primacy over other collectivities may vary widely. Our own is a rather highly decentralized and pluralistic governmental system and one that leaves wide scope for the use of authority and power in private collectivities. Beyond this the L-factor defines limits on the legitimate use of authority and power in the name of a variety of "freedoms" of the general Bill of Rights type. The general principle is that the basic allocations of authority on the one hand, and of rights against authority on the other, belong in the pattern-maintenance category; they are "not negotiable." If, on the other hand, they are "negotiable," that is, subject to reallocation by ordinary political and other procedures, they belong in the categories of legitimation and legality of powers.

The generalized commitment system is, of course, by no means immutable. In the present case it may be changed by revolution, or by what may be called a process of "revolutionary drift" without violent breaks. But this is different from processes of reallocation by specification in the course of adjusting to shifting exigencies. The creation of a new administrative agency by act of Congress, with authority to use governmental power for certain collective goals, of course within certain limits, is a type case of such reallocation by specification.

The above considerations perhaps provide an adequate setting for bringing up the interpretation of our view that the factor of effectiveness, which is the input from the societal community consists in "interest demands," as we have called them, rather than political support, which is a product input. The rationale for this contention rests squarely on the importance of differentiation between societal community and polity. One primary goal-orientation of a political unit is to earn a sufficient input of interest demands from its "constituencies" by its output of leadership responsibility and policy decisions. It is, however, enabled to "pay" for them by its income of political support. The "control" of both political support and interest demands lies outside the political agency in the constituency; it is "their" demands that count. Such an agency, above all, is concerned with authenticating the goals it strives for as "truly" those of the collectivity, and needs clear definition of the interests involved, with respect both to their urgency and to their character and limits vis-à-vis others. It is important here that the two primary cases of "demand" are expressed in terms of media other than power or value-commitments. The demand for commodities, the type case of economic demand, is expressed in terms of money offers. That for leadership responsibility and policy decision is expressed in terms of influence, an attempt to persuade without resort either to inducements or to coercive or moral sanctions.

We have, however, tried to show, in Chapter 15, that influence as a medium operates by combining or synthesizing the interest of the unit with an appeal to its justification because its "satisfaction" would *also* presumptively contribute to the collective interest, which in the broadest integrative terms is defined as "solidarity." This is parallel to the money value of a commodity output of the economy creating a presumption that its production is not *only* technologically efficient, but also economically justified in terms of the use of scarce resources to enhance the satisfaction of consumer "wants."

It has often been said that in relation to "pluralistic" political theory the outcome of the political decision process is a result simply of a "play of interests" which is directly parallel to the competitive market. The outcome is said to be "compromise," which has no presumptive relation to any general interest other than the mitigation of destructive conflict.

The degree to which this is indeed the case in any given instance is a legitimate empirical question. Theoretically, however, the effectiveness of an attempt to use influence is a function of the extent to which it can be justified—using that term in a technical sense—in terms of a common interest shared within the solidary collective system of reference. This justification is a product input to the integrative system from that of pattern-maintenance, thus itself a form of influence, which is one source of the "income of influence" of which "interest-demands" constitute a part that is a factor output to the polity. Thus we assert that *one*—but no tthe only—source of capacity to make effective interest-demands is capacity to "justify" such demands in terms of common interests, through the input labeled "value-based claims to loyalties."

This factor-output from the societal community to the polity, namely, interest-demands, then is conceived to be the primary basis on which leadership elements of the polity are put in a position, through the use of their influence, to appeal for political support (cf. Chapter 9), which includes the "backing" of their own policy decisions by "gambling" that they will not cost them exorbitantly in loss of support.

Thus we conclude that knowing constituents' wants, as well as partly "shaping" them through leadership initiative, and willingness to offer certain types of collective decisions in return for the "assertion" of such constituent wants, is a crucial factor in political effectiveness. As such, however, it must be combined, with some approach to "optimization," with the other factors—the commitment to collective organization in the first place, the legitimacy of the authority claimed by the decision-makers, and the control of productivity necessary to ensure the resources essential to effective implementation.

From this analysis it is perfectly clear that it is neither desirable nor realistically possible for political leadership, in governmental or other collectivities, to attempt to "satisfy" all demands or wishes of its constituents. Given scarcity of resources it is indeed realistically impossible. At the same time there is always the problem of justification. Some demands are directly illegitimate and should be rejected on that ground. Among those that establish some order of legitimation there is then very much a problem of priorities, which should be settled in terms of standards of justification.

Here the analogy of the economy is helpful. In some sense consumers' wants are insatiable. Even the most productive economy does not seek to satisfy all conceivable wants of all of its consumers. The regulatory mechanisms of money demand and price for particular goods intervene to select, or sometimes their place is taken by rationing. However that may be, there must be a selection among consumer wants. Similarly in the case of the polity, there must be a selection between what constituents actually or latently assert that decision-making agencies should do—not necessarily serving only the "self-interest" of the advocates—and what responsible political leadership in our sense can in fact decide to do. Hence the concept "demands"—which I have taken from Easton—should be thought of as parallel to "effective demand" in the sense of economics. It is bidding, from the constituency side, for desired policy decisions, which have a component of realistic hope that "authority," i.e., in our terms, leadership components, will in fact "grant" them. The process, however, is one of adjustment among plural factors in both sides, and hence in some sense always a "compromise." On the "interest" side, however, it is important to keep in mind that what we have called justification is *one* major factor in exerting the influence necessary to bring about desired decisions and, on the policy decision side, the legitimacy of authority and the powers of office are essential ingredients, along with the need to keep or select political support. To say that "in the last analysis" it is the need for political support that "motivates" such decisions is unacceptable, as are all similar statements about multifactoral systems.

In political processes, generally speaking, power and the command of it constitute mechanisms which, by priority of cybernetic control, take precedence over the "factors of effectiveness" as these have just been reviewed. Power, including the authority component, after all is defined as the capacity to command the factors of effectiveness, as well as to "satisfy" the wishes of constituents.

This statement may raise a question of cybernetic hierarchy, because two of the three categories of factor-input we have reviewed, namely, value-commitments and influence, are media that as such stand higher in the cybernetic hierarchy than does power. The apparent paradox is to be explained in terms of the scope of institutionally defined "rights" of the co-optation of the medium in question for the particular functions of the receiving subsystem. Thus the value-commitments that legitimate authority are *specified* to the level of the valuation of collective effectiveness, which by no means need be the highest in the broader hierarchy of sub-value priorities, indeed in the American system most certainly is not the highest. But it is only within the range of the valuation of effectiveness so far as it does not interfere with other subvalues that political authority can be said to be legitimized. The main significance of the Bill of Rights is to define limits to the use of authority that can claim legitimacy and hence to the capacity of power to "control" the relevant value-commitments. By strong contrast, the Soviet system places a far higher premium on the collective effectiveness of the society in "building socialism," with the implication that it is justified to sacrifice many "private rights" to this collective goal. Parallel considerations are involved in the use of influence in the form of interest-demands. Especially in a pluralistic system, such demands have to be *justified*, as we have suggested, in a double context, namely that if they are to be implemented by political action, they are in a collective as well as a unit interest and, second, that they are not modes of action that ought to be kept outside the analytically defined political sphere altogether, as in the case of "purely" moral obligations.

I should now like to carry the implications of the above analysis of products and factors involved in the polity and its contiguous subsystems to the level of their bearing on the variability of structural types of collectivities. This analysis, in turn, will be divided into two sections. The first will deal with those collectivities that have political primacy at the societal level, whereas the second will deal with types having primacy of other functions.

The first set of types raises a problem that is the political parallel of a famous problem of economic analysis. This is the problem of the relation between the "substantive" function of the collectivity and its function of self-maintenance with respect to the input-output balances of the principal medium of interchange with which it is involved. In the economic case it is the old question of whether the "primary" function of the firm is to produce goods and thereby "satisfy wants," or to "make money". It should be clear, of course, that in most contexts the question of primacy is not meaningful. The salience of the medium-balance is a function of the institutionalization both of the medium itself, and of its relations to certain types of structural differentiation and organization of the system, in the economic case the market. Incapacity to remain "solvent" in this sense raises the question of whether the substantive function is sufficiently important to warrant subsidy, in this case of money.

In the political case the two functions are substantive collective goal attainment on the one hand, and maintaining an input-output balance of power on the other. In a "fully differentiated" political system there should be, ideally, the same order of coincidence between these two functions that there is in a "normal" market situation between the financial exigencies of firms and their "productive" functions. There are, however, many cases in which they do not coincide, hence the question of subsidy of power must be raised as an alternative to some kind of "liquidation." Perhaps the Weimar Republic of Germany in the 1920's and early 30's, and the French Fourth Republic could be cited as familiar examples of insufficiency in the generation of an *income* of power.

"Purely political" collectivities, in our view, must be governmental, i.e. they must be central governments—including of course constituency membership—of "politically organized" societies, or segmental sub-divisions of such political systems, like state and local governments in our own society. All other collectivities within a society, but also across societies—such as churches—should have primacy of function *other* than political. They will hence have a "political aspect" but this will be subject to the primacy of such other functions as economic production, associative solidarity, or cultural development. As we noted at the beginning of this chapter, a government in this sense may undertake in "content" terms to solve *any* problem of interest to the collective system; it is not restricted to a particular concrete subject-matter.

Our typology of collectivities, however, must also take into account the extent to which and ways in which the political component is differentiated from others. Indeed these levels of differentiation, more than any other considerations, define which categories of power input, and of course also factor inputs from other subsystems, can be considered to be predominant in different systems. Generally, the most fully differentiated system is to be regarded as that in which all three of the principal interchange systems are relatively "free" from constraints other than the mutuality of the functional "interests" of the polity on the one hand, each of the other primary functional subsystems on the other.

Pursuing the theme of levels of differentiation, however, a first primary distinction must be made between the case where government, in our analytical sense, is so highly "embedded" in nonpolitical structures and exigencies that it cannot be said to be a differentiated system. Because of its place in the cybernetic hierarchy, we think that the legitimation system (*L-G*) is likely to be the focus of the first evolutionary developing differentiation, so that primarily political "authority" comes to be differentiated from value-based, usually "religious" authority. The situation where differentiation on this axis has not yet taken place, we take to be the essential criterion of what Weber called *traditional* authority. Here there is no "problem" of the legitimation of governmental authority independent of that of the institutionalized social order in general, nor does collective effectiveness have independent status as a *specified* value-pattern. Above all, the individual or other agency that holds the highest position of prestige in the societal community also and *ipso facto* holds the top governmental authority. Both authority and prestige are generally grounded in a religious level of legitimation.

A first step in differentiation, from our point of view, occurs when there is structural differentiation between the leadership elements of government and whatever is the important legitimizing agency. Perhaps the best-known case is that of the legitimation of the "state" in the Western Mediaeval tradition by the Church, symbolized by the coronation of Charlemagne by the Pope in 800 A.D. This, of course, constitutes a state of the *differentiation* of Church and State, but by no means their "separation" in the modern sense.[16] A much less complete example is the differentiation, mentioned above, between the "religious institution" and civil government in some of the Islamic societies.

The obvious consequence is that civil authority comes to be bound, as the "price" of its legitimation, by some kind of "constitutional" framework over the establishment and validation of which it does not alone have constitutive authority.

This phase of differentiation, however, can occur without any significant development of the mobility of either the power or the factor inputs from the other subsystems, namely the economy and the societal community. These can remain predominantly ascribed, as was on the whole true for Western Mediaeval society, though of course the problem of what resources and loyalties are ascribed to predominantly political authority, and what to the legitimating agency, remains a difficult question that has been a primary source of realistic conflict. Hence in the Middle Ages the "problem of church and state" was a dominant one. The "relative neutralization" of both categories is a condition of the next steps of differentiation in which we are interested.

The most important subtype under Weber's category of traditional authority is the "patrimonial," where there is substantial disposability of manpower, but on the basis of particularistic ties to the "chief" or other

---

[16] Cf. Talcott Parsons, "Christianity", *International Encyclopedia of the Social Sciences*, David L. Sills, ed. (New York: The Macmillan Company and The Free Press, 1968).

authority element. There is, in the later sense, no "labor market" and no system of more or less "technical" qualifications for appointment. The early modern monarchies took steps beyond "Mediaevalism" in this direction through the establishment of professional services, both civil and military, so that a much more mobile input of power to government through this channel became possible.[17] Very broadly, it is the combination of a constitutional rather than a purely traditional basis of legitimation, on the one hand, with the development of an *occupational* service system, on the other, that defines the *Rechtsstaat*, to use the German term, which above all characterized the predemocratic phase of Western governmental development after the decline of Feudalism.

It has been, however, a major characteristic of this system that the input of power through what we have called the *support* system remained ascribed. This was true at the top through the institution of monarchy, and for the mass of the population through the definition of their status as "loyal subjects." The *top* leadership, in Weber's term the "nonbureaucratic head of the bureaucracy," was thus ascribed and it was assumed that his political support would not be put in question short of a revolutionary overturn.

Here it is notable that next to the legitimation system itself, the support system stands high in the cybernetic hierarchy, that is, higher than the resource mobilization system. It seems reasonable to suggest that it is less threatening to relinquish "control," on the part of monarchs and their close particularistic associates, of the service sector than of the support sector. This, of course, does not mean that all control vanished, but still civil servants had to be appointed on terms that were only partly prescribed by their monarchical employers. The support problem, however, could be much more threatening, in that mobility in this sphere could jeopardize the basic political leadership position of monarchy itself.

A still further phase of differentiation, then, has concerned that of the support system from its previous ascribed matrix in the general status of membership in the societal community which carried with it the obligation to support the *going* political authority. This occurred through gradual extension of the franchise, as organization of the *power* to choose top political leadership, from various elite groups to include finally the whole adult population not specifically disqualified, as for instance by mental

---

[17] It is an important fact that, for the European states in this category, it seemed to be easier to "bureaucratize" civil services than their military counterparts. This fact is of course connected with the role of aristocracy, with its historical connections with feudalism—it is surely significant that it has long remained appropriate to speak of a type of person who was "an officer and a gentleman" but much less so "an official and a gentleman." In the Western world only in the present century have officers' corps come to be extensively "bureaucratized." On the side of the common soldier, a system much more like the patrimonial was very persistent. The modern conscript army on a *national* basis is different from the semi-ascribed obligations of peasantries to fight in their "lords'" wars.

incompetence.[18] Understandably, in the historical circumstances, there was a more moderate version of this extension in the form of "constitutional monarchy" whereby that of "chief of government" was made contingent on electoral support, either of the electorate as a whole or of a majority in an elected Parliament.

The more radical alternative is of course "Republicanism," where the formal headship of the political system itself becomes contingent on political support. The American (but recently even French) type of "Presidential" system broadly fits this rubric. There is surely a connection between the playing down of written constitutions in constitutional monarchies—the monarchical institution itself is in a sense a constitution —and the emphasis on them in Republics. It is, for example, rather difficult for contemporaries to appreciate the horror with which "Republicanism" was regarded, even in the more "liberal" régimes that were moving in constitutional directions. Republicanism is, however, the "logical" end of the line in the process of differentiation we have been outlining.

With appropriate modifications, considerations of the above type apply to rather different kinds of governmental systems. A notable example would be the small-scale "collegial" type which has been found in the more or less independent "city state" from the Italian Renaissance through a good deal of early modern history in Europe. This has usually been a kind of aristocratic regime with an essentially hereditary "patriciate" in the primary position of authority, but with considerable modifications. This type was indeed, in European conditions, a stimulus toward the "Republican" pattern, though by no means necessarily in its most democratic form.

On the more macroscopic level, however, it should be emphasized that, once the process of differentiation that we have sketched reaches virtual completion, so that there is a relatively clearly defined sphere for the values of political effectiveness, and a set of open interchanges between the polity and all three of the other primary subsystems, there is still a crucial set of problems which concern the relative primacies among these aspects of the system.

We can start with the problem of the primacy accorded to the valuation of political effectiveness as such. This valuation clearly seems to stand highest in those cases where a collective "mission" defined in cultural terms is highly prominent. Such earlier cases as ancient Israel and Islam, and such recent ones as the Communist societies, but also those of ascetic Protestant background come to mind. Within the modern world, perhaps the Latin Catholic cases most remote from the main "modern" complex,

[18] In some respects the most comprehensive statement so far available is the Introduction by Lipset and Rokkan to their volume on *Party Systems and Voter Alignments* (New York: The Free Press, 1967). On the development of the franchise, cf. Stein Rokkan, "Mass Suffrage, Secret Voting, and Political Participation," *European Journal of Sociology*, Vol. 2, 1961, pp. 132–52.

such as Southern Italy and several Latin American societies, are farthest removed.

This order of value-primacy has a strong tendency to press the régime away from the consitutional focus to combine societal and political legitimation in a single "package." This "dedifferentiation" seems to have occurred, relative to the institutional developments of the time, in the Calvinistic movements where independent institutionalization of contingent support was suppressed in favor of the rule of the "predestined Saints" and again in the Communist movements with the rule of the "historically predestined" Party. A more "pluralistic" emphasis, probably going back to the value system, can, however, legitimate constitutional rights independent of the government of the day and thereby reinforce the independent contingency of political support. On still another front, the institutional complex that Weber, without derogatory overtones, called the "formally free labor market," creates presumptions that the service inputs to the polity will have independently contingent significance. If a régime presses in the direction of effectiveness, its dependence on competent and loyal service is heightened, and the "problem" of maintaining ascriptive claims to such service may become acute. Conversely, within limits a relatively low "pressure" in favor of effectiveness may make it easier to "tolerate" contingency of support and hence a relative democratization of the system.

The relatively "full" modern type of democratic political organization therefore seems to be dependent on several conditions. The first is that the urgency of the *societal* sense of mission, or that of the group who claim to speak for it, is not so intense that differentiation between legitimating agency and politically operative agency is precluded. From this point of view constitutionalism is in part a function of the mitigation of the highest levels of value-committed tensions. Secondly, however, it depends on freedom of the governmental agencies that are, by whatever processes, given responsibility for the implementation of major collective goal-commitments to have relatively open opportunity in the mobilization of resources to carry out their task—resources which above all include financial support and the availability, through the labor market, of adequate and competent persons to perform the essential service functions. Third, of course, such "policy"-deciding leadership must be in a position not only to count on ascriptive support, but to feel that they are in a position, in the political system as a whole or the relevant sectors of it, to count on the "voluntary" support of sufficiently extended constituencies.

The cases of "dedifferentiation" just cited bring us back around to the problem of the role of charisma in political systems. This, I think it is correct to say (cf. Chapter 16), always gives primacy to value-considerations, either for the polity itself, or for the broader societal system that is conceived to have a "mission" that is in part politically defined. The effect, then, is to tie legitimation very tightly to the obligation to implement the mission—e.g. build a "Holy Community" or "Communism"—and to define the other modes of participation even more strictly in terms of ascription to this mission, e.g. to require unquestioned political support to charismatically legitimated leadership, and to recognize the obligation of putting resources, including service, at the disposal of the "cause."

"Routinization" of charisma consists in the mitigation of the stringency of this primacy of the valuational component. The very "secularization" of government in the form that we understand as the "separation of church and state" is a major step of routinization in this sense. Beyond that, recognizing that the contingency of political support is also legitimate, and that resources may be allocated to private rather than governmental concerns, that hence government must "pay"—in more than monetary senses—for the resources it uses, are further steps in routinization in Weber's sense.

Again, as Weber noted, one possibility of routinization is "retraditionalization," which need not, however, simply restore the precharismatic situation; it may be profoundly altered, but will still have the characteristics of a traditional system. The more important alternative, however, is routinization in the "rational-legal" direction, as Weber called it. Types two through four in the schematic classification to be presented presently are built about this conception and represent steps of differentiation from pure traditional or charismatic undifferentiatedness, introducing "pluralistic" flexibility into successive interchange relationships in which the polity is involved.

The bearing of the dynamic relations between traditionalism, charisma, and routinization in the rational-legal direction on the processes of structural change in political systems should be evident. This particularly concerns the potential of charismatic movements for breaking through the zero-sum limitations of many political systems. It will not, however, be possible here to go beyond the level of discussion of that problem that was attempted in the last main section of Chapter 16.

It will thus be evident that this typology is a modification of Weber's famous one, and that it rests on the interpretation previously stated[19] that the three types of his original classification do not lie on the same level, but stand in different relations to social change. On these assumptions the typology can be summed up, roughly, in terms of the following five categories:

1. *The Traditional Type*, where ascribed legitimation of authority is associated with ascription *both* of political support *and* of access to services.
2. *The "Mediaeval" State*. Here constitutional legitimation is at

[19] Cf. "Authority, Legitimation and Political Action," in *Structure and Process in Modern Society*, Chapter 5.

least partly contingent on the consent of a legitimizing agency independent of government, e.g. a church. This shades into

3. The early modern *Rechtsstaat*, to borrow the familiar German term. This is also likely to be a "bureaucratic" monarchy, where not only the contingency of legitimation obtains, as above, but also services are organized through a "labor market," eligibility and access being on universalistic bases. All citizens, however, are ascribed to support as "loyal subjects" of the sovereign.

4. The *modern "Democratic" state*, where not only are services more or less bureaucratized, but there is a clear differentiation between "regime" and "government" or "administration," and hence change of the latter need not involve "constitutional" levels of institutionalization. Being "in power" in the latter sense, is contingent on command of sufficient political support.

5. *Charismatic Types*. Here the source of nontraditional legitimation from outside the polity is so dominant that it subordinates other factors. It usually defines a "régime" that is directly controlled by the agency of charismatic legitimation, generally a minority. It claims, however, "plebiscitary" support from its membership, but without opening the door to loyal opposition. The Puritan elect of Calvinistic polities and the modern Communist Parties are prototypical cases.[29]

NONGOVERNMENTAL COLLECTIVITY TYPES

If the above is at least the beginning of a typology of governmental institutional forms, which leans on Weber but attempts to carry the analysis of differentiation beyond him, then a next step is to consider ways in which the "political aspect" is structured in cases where the primary

[20] The above analysis will, I hope, give the reader a somewhat better perspective on the developing theoretical significance of the more empirical materials that were discussed in the essays in Parts II and III. The typology of governmental collectivity organization that has emerged has clearly an evolutionary cast to it. The taking of major steps in an evolutionary process of structural change seems always to be fraught with severe conflicts and disturbances. The Fascist movements, with which Part II was primarily concerned, seem to stand out as in the first instance manifestations of such disturbances. They were initially successful, and if continuing too long, threatened to consolidate what may be called *regressive* effects in the evolutionary sense. That, by and large, the Fascist movements have not become firmly consolidated in Western society I take, therefore, to be evidence of the continuing vitality of these societies. There have, of course, been important "fascistoid" phenomena in other societies, of which a major example was McCarthyism in the United States.

Very broadly, disturbances with a more "left" ideological orientation seem to me, on balance, to have a quite different meaning, even though full consolidation of some of them may have powerful "diversionary" if not permanently dominant effects in the societies in which the movements gain control. The most obvious example of this century, of course, is the Communist movement, the full assessment of which still leaves many unsolved questions. Much more or less "radical" ferment outside Communism raises somewhat comparable problems. Some kind of bifurcation of effect of "radicalisms" on a regressive-progressive axis, however, seems to be inherent in the kind of change modern societies have been undergoing. For adequate understanding of such processes, however, far more detailed and analytically sophisticated *comparative* knowledge than this book has been able to review will be necessary.

functions of the collectivities in question are not governmental. This, among other things, means that, in differentiated societies, the coercive sanctions that "back up" the use of power must generally stop short of the autonomous use of force because of the governmental monopoly of the organized use of force.

Perhaps the most obvious case to take up first is that of the firm in a market economy. First, it may be remarked again that a government is, in ideal type, autonomous with respect to power, without the necessity of being "subsidized." This is to say that its inputs of power from environing subsystems, in the form of political support, allocation of services, and legality should suffice to cover its "expenditures" of power through the issue of policy decisions, the offer of opportunity for effectiveness, and the assumption of collective responsibility. A government should generate this power for its effective handling of collective goal-interests, and its expenditures for the acquisition of factors of effectiveness should, with the usual reservations for fluctuations over time, through the process of circulation, generate a sufficient income of power to effect a balance all through the governmental system's own operations.

Similar considerations apply to the firm, but here the critical medium is money, not power. The standard of satisfactory performance is solvency, in the sense that the firm should, from its own operations, namely, sale of products, "earn" sufficient money income to cover its expenses, including, of course, in differentiated economies, the acquisition of the factors of production. Among the factors of production, however, is a category of power which we have called opportunity for effectiveness. Where this has been involved in the above discussion we have stressed its relation to the "manpower" element involved with service. In the reverse direction, however, this is the category that includes the mode of control of economic assets that economic theorists call capital, which is the use of *power* to change the allocation of economic resources in the direction of investment. This factor input to the economy and the corresponding service input to the polity constitute the most important direct power relations between economy and polity.

It is a notable fact that in modern economies the organization of firms has been conspicuously nondemocratic;[21] thus the many experiments in so-called "producers' cooperation" have not eventuated in major structural patterns. The line authority pattern, evolving in some connections from the "patriarchalism" of the family firm, has been greatly modified, to be sure, from one direction by trade unionism, and from another by the new involvement of technical services at professional levels, but neither of these has led to the situation of paramount authority being placed in the hands of an electorate, the "members" of the firm.

[21] I deliberately do not say *un*democratic, since this might imply that democratic standards *should* prevail.

In the socialist versions, of course, the "people" ultimately control economic enterprise, but not the workers in the particular firm. In the "capitalist" version, to be sure, there has been the extension of property rights to the governmental authority of stockholders over the firm. At most, however, this has been a "pseudo-democracy," since the principle has not been one member, one vote, but one share—i.e., money quantity— one vote. In fact, of course, the "rights" of stockholders actually to determine collective policy, or even leadership, have been progressively attentuated. Hence stockholding is much less a mechanism of the government of firms than, on the one hand, of capital-procurement, and on the other, of establishing, through the market standing of securities, a prestige position for the firm. For the larger firms the present tendency seems to be toward a system of fiduciary boards—occupying the position Weber referred to as the "nonbureaucratic" top of a bureaucratic structure —which have many resemblances to the boards that exist in the private nonprofit sector.

The basic reasons for this broad trend seem to be the following: First, there is a strong stress on efficiency of production, including minimization of cost relative to value of output, which in political terms is a form of collective effectiveness. In this connection there has emerged, in the more recent period, an immense set of available resources based on science and technology. Second, there is, with all its difficulties, a rather special regulatory mechanism in the discipline of the market and the associated cost-accounting standards of solvency. Third, this is supplemented by a complex system of legal and governmental regulation. On a more theoretical level, "democratic" production would contravene the important principles often called "consumer sovereignty."

Though it has been strenuously contested for more than a century, we may say, I think, that the legitimacy of economic production has become strongly established and that its private enterprise form is not widely challenged in a basic sense outside the socialist societies. This issue, though, however acute it has been, seems to be on the whole distinct from that of the role of the "political" constituencies of economic enterprise. Here the conspicuous fact has been, as noted, the weakness of the pressure to the democratization of firms. This, I think, is essentially a matter of the predominance of interests in consumption, including the efficiency of provision for it, combined of course with national security and prestige, which in turn is a function of efficiency, as opposed to participation in the "government" of firms. There is a certain parallel between the political neutrality of "employees" of firms—political of course as understood with reference to the firm's own affairs—and that of civil servants with respect to the policy levels of government in general.

Almost the sharpest possible contrast is provided by the "purely voluntary" private association, though there are considerable compli-

cations in this field as well. The ideal type of voluntary association would
be one in which there was the functional parallel to far-reaching "consumer sovereignty" in an economic case. In our technical terms this would
mean the sovereignty of constituency interest demands and something
like a maximization of the contingency of political support for leadership.
One would say that in such associations there is a strong feeling that it is
undesirable to have too large an "apparatus" of persons in appointive
office, lest they gain too much power and influence relative to the elected
officers and the electorate, and that even elective leaders should not be permitted much security of power.

In the case of governments in complex societies, the enormous scope
and seriousness of their functions precludes any great minimization of the
"apparatus" component, even in part aside from the role of military
forces. Moreover, the size of electorates as well as their diversity in many
respects also precludes much "direct democracy," at least with respect
to the determination of decisions that involve the system as a whole
rather than small segments of it. Various kinds of "decentralization" are,
of course, practiced and others advocated in this area. Selection of the
highest leadership through elective systems that present relatively
structured alternatives seems to be the most effective way yet evolved to
give some genuine constituency choice and at the same time meet certain
conditions of relative stability and effectiveness (cf. Chapter 9).

Even in the case of private associations, a large size of membership seems
to necessitate a certain degree of centralization of "control," both through
the development of appointive *apparati* and through some kind of consolidation of the position of established "political" i.e., ideally elective—
leaders. Trade unions constitute a very familiar example, but the same can
be said of political parties and of some of the larger professional associations.

There have of course been various more or less legendary examples of
effectively working "pure democracy," notably perhaps the citizen body
of the Greek *polis*, in its best period, and the early New England Town
Meeting. Even in these small-scale governmental cases it should, however,
be remembered that the citizens were a minority of the population of the
polis—in fifth-century Athens voting adult males numbered not much more
than ten thousand out of about one hundred and fifty thousand—and that
in the New England town a very prominent part was played by a self-
appointed elite of the presumptive "elect," who were clearly a minority
and enforced restrictions on the franchise. Indeed the purest egalitarianism
seems to be confined to essentially "sectarian" groups in a state of charismatic "effervescence," and small "very private" associational groups.

From this set of circumstances, perhaps especially sharply dramatized
by Robert Michels in his conception of the "iron law of oligarchy,"
it should not be inferred that the principle of equality, as institutionalized

in social systems generally or associational structures in particular, is un-important. Quite the contrary is the case, and I should regard the equality complex as one of the few most important structural constitutions of modern society. Its stabler forms of institutionalization can be seen to cluster about the three principal interchange boundary relations of the polity. In the "constitutional-legality" context (*L-G*) it concerns the "equality of rights" in the sense, familiar to Americans, of the rights written into the Bill of Rights, and not only interpreted, but extended by the courts. In the context of the opportunity for effectiveness and of service (*A-G*) it concerns the very basic pattern of "equality of opportun-ity." Finally, in the context of what we have called the "support system" (*G-I*) it concerns the pattern of equality of "ultimate" or residual rights in the determination of collective decisions, most fully institutionalized in procedures for the selection of leadership.[22]

The ideal type of voluntary association should be thought of as regulated by a standard parallel to that of solvency for the firm and self-sufficiency in effective power for the governmental unit. This standard essentially is the attainment and/or maintenance of maximum solidarity through consensus. The ideally democratic government minimizes the use of power, especially at the electoral level. The electoral component is ideally a voluntary association superimposed on a power system, and many forms of idealism, certainly very many of them utopian, have hoped for the total elimination of the association's involvement with power. In associations, however, that do not have the heavy responsibilities of governments, it may be possible to minimize the factor of power, though seldom of money, but the latter may be acquired almost entirely by voluntary contribu-tion.[23]

Clearly what we have just called solidarity through consensus, in sufficiently extensive and differentiated associations, is partly brought about through operation of the influence mechanism, since what we have called "intrinsic persuaders" are not likely to suffice. This, however, is not enough. The level of solidarity attained within a given solidary group-ing must then be integrated with that attained by other such groupings within the societal community and perhaps beyond. In pluralistic systems this of course poses problems. Partial solidarities are often attained at the expense of wider ones, as in such cases as ethnic, religious, or other "interest" groups. The primary integrative problem of pluralistic societies,

[22] These are the three primary components of the citizenship complex as delineated by T. H. Marshall, *Class, Citizenship and Social Development* (Garden City, N.Y.: Doubleday, 1964).
[23] A kind of limiting point, noted in Chapter 13 above, is that so many such associations depend on membership dues for their financial means, and, when members sometimes refuse to pay, an acute question arises of whether they may be permitted to continue to enjoy the rights of membership and still not contribute financially. In most cases, I think, long-standing deliberate refusal to pay dues is treated as adequate ground for expulsion, which is certainly a case of use of power complete with coercive sanctions.

then, is the integration of the many partial solidarities in a system, which not only minimizes internal conflict but provides mutually reinforcing complementary interest-structures. The achievement of this with a minimum of subsidization, especially of influence, is a measure of the integration of a social system.

The acquisition of necessary financial resources through voluntary contribution is not to be regarded as subsidization in this sense. The case of power is somewhat more complex, but it seems to be a sound principle that the use of power is not only not incompatible with the pattern of voluntary association, but is essential to it, in that such associations, as social systems, must have collective goals and must therefore be in a position to come to some collectively binding decisions and implement them effectively. This in general implies a differentiation of the association on a leadership axis, with more power going to leadership elements than to the average member. It is, however, ideally possible for the necessary power to be acquired by the goal-attaining subsystem through the support system by voluntary political support. The measure of subsidization then would seem to lie in the intervention of coercive elements beyond those strictly self-imposed virtually by consensus of the whole membership. The coercive sanctions backing the law of the state may serve as an external source of power-subsidy to voluntary associations in the sense that law sets limits of variation in the structure and policies of such associations, which must be "respected." Further subsidization occurs through governmental "regulation" which goes beyond the setting of legal limits to give specific agencies of government power to make decisions affecting the functioning of the association, e.g., with reference to tax obligations.

There is also a problem of subsidization of voluntary associations from the pattern-maintenance system. This essentially consists in the involvement in it of value-commitments at a further level of specification than is true of commitment to the most general values of the society. There is a possible ambiguity of the word *voluntary* in this connection. From the point of view of the individual, especially vis-à-vis coercive political authority, value-commitment is by definition voluntary. Yet (in Chapter 16) we have argued that the agents of value-commitments assume *obligations* and do not accept memberships simply because it "pleases them" to belong. To quote the late Clyde Kluckhohn, the realm of values is that of the desir*able*, not merely of the desir*ed*.

A subsidy of value-commitments, in this sense, is present when the negative (internal) sanctions of moral obligation tend to be invoked to counter any possible or suspected threats of disloyalty. So far as it is possible to acquire the necessary inputs of value-commitments—at the level and of the type of specification appropriate to the function of the association—without *special* appeal to the activation of moral obligations, the association may be said to be maintaining its solidarity without commitment-subsidy.

Perhaps the most obvious historic case of such commitment-subsidy in the societal sphere is the role of formally established churches. The development within "liberal" Protestantism of the conception of the "visible" church as a voluntary association may be construed as a case of withdrawal of such subsidy—as well as that of state-provided financial support—so that churches were much more "on their own" as voluntary associations. A parallel set of problems concerns what we call the "professional complex" in modern society, which may now be discussed briefly. It is a kind of secularized case of the religious phenomenon.

It belongs in the broader context of the equality complex which is, in general, a particularly important context of many modern societies, perhaps especially the American, and there are certain respects in which its significance centers on the role of associational structures. It is perhaps particularly useful to regard it as a counterweight to the "bureaucratic" tendencies that have been so widely held to be the dominant trends of modern societal development. There is unfortunately a certain tendency, which is not sociologically tenable, to regard virtually all structures that deviate from the ideal type of "pure" egalitarian democracy as bureaucratic.

Of course the "contractual" structure, above all but not exclusively prominent in the economic sphere, is a sociological relative of the association; though in many respects different, it is clearly not primarily "bureaucratic." Similar things can be said about communication systems in modern society (cf. Chapter 10). But even apart from the vast proliferation of voluntary associations in other fields, perhaps notably trade unions and political parties, a highly important and characteristic case is to be found in the "professional complex," which is far more prominent in modern society than it ever has been before.

The ideal type of the democratic association, including that of the politically organized society as a whole, is built on the principle that all full members are basically equal, as expressed in the principles of equal freedom to communicate (hence attempt to persuade) and equality of the franchise on the basis of one member, one vote. Such functionaries of the association who are not ordinary members, or their elected representatives, then function in a quite different role, as "employees" who ideally have no voice in policy except perhaps as voting members.

THE PROFESSIONAL COMPLEX
AS A SPECIAL CASE

With respect to constitutive qualifications, members of collectivities in the professional complex are not basically all of one category, but essentially of two.[24] They are, that is, professionals and lay "clients," which includes recipients of service in the role of patient and student and even, as I have recently argued, of research subject.[25] There, are of course, many inequalities within the professional contingent, not only differentiation among fields of competence, but also with respect to levels of competence, and more intangibly of professional integrity, and on the client level, of varieties of objective, of interest, and of course of capacity to utilize the benefits of professional service.

There is at least a substantial difference between the client role in the above generalized sense and that of "customer" or consumer with respect to the economic market. In spite of the strictures on this formula, a particularly easy way to state the difference is to say that the standard of *caveat emptor* cannot legitimately be applied to professional service. Even though, of course, the client, e.g., the student, is positively encouraged to be critical of his teacher's offerings, the latter still stands in a *fiduciary* relation to the student. This relation is grounded in two primary factors, namely, *competence* in relatively technical subject matter, which cannot be fully shared by the student *before* he has undergone the learning process, and in the *integrity* to the standards of his profession. The seller of an economically valuable item need not be especially competent in this sense, nor need he be characterized by integrity that goes beyond "common honesty" in his dealings with customers.

The fiduciary component of the professional relationship implies that the client enjoys an important type of *membership* status in the collective system that performs the relevant set of functions. Membership is, however, stratified on the essential axis of competence and its attendant commitment to the culturally anchored *values* involved. The competence of professions obviously varies widely, though it also varies for clients, especially for students, e.g., as a function of duration of involvement. Commitment may also be presumed to be shared, but typically to stand on a higher level for the professional than for the client.

From the point of view of our political interchange paradigm, the professional system seems to present a peculiar set of paradoxes. It has been a temptation, for this writer as well as many others, to treat the professional-client relationship as simply a special case of the seller-buyer relation,[26] modified above all because it is a service rather than a commodity that is being purveyed. It is, however, equally plausible to treat the client as employer of a service, who, for example, "hires" his physician or his teacher to cure or instruct him.

[24] Where complex collective affairs are concerned a third, which in the university context we call "administration," is also involved.

[25] Cf. Talcott Parsons, "Human Experimentation and the Professional Complex," *Daedalus*, Spring 1969, forthcoming.

[26] Cf. *Social Structure and Personality*, Chapter 12, and Talcott Parsons and Gerald M. Platt, "Considerations on the American Academic System," *Minerva*, Vol. VI, No. 4, Spring 1968.

Insofar, however, as professional and client are defined to be fellow-members of an associational collectivity, the further question arises of how far that collectivity should ideally be "democratic" *across* the professional-client line. In the nature of the case, even if the professionals were treated as full "members" rather than "just" employees, in such situations clients greatly outnumber professionals, so that the primary governing power would, by such a definition, belong in the former's hands. I do not know of any situation where collectivities of patients are claiming, *qua* patients, the right to govern specific health-care institutions—e.g., a specific hospital, though this has a certain connection with the patterns of consumers' cooperation—but there is the currently very prominent case of students claiming equal rights with faculties, member for member, in the government of universities.

In my opinion, this claim is as unjustified as would be either of the other suggested ones, namely, that clients should be treated "merely" as customers of the purveyors of professional service, or that professional practitioners should be treated as simple "employees" of their clients. The solution of this set of apparent paradoxes lies, I think, in consideration of the fourth functional reference of such a system, namely, the pattern-maintenance boundary that articulates with the cultural system. It is perhaps permissible to discuss this with reference to the academic system, more specifically the university, because it is in a sense the "purest" organizational example of what I have called the professional complex.

Put in our formal terms, the essential reason why it is not justified to treat the client in a professional organization as customer, as employee, or as democratically equal "member" or associate, is that the professional complex is anchored in the primacy of *cultural* standards and that these impinge on the organization of social systems through the pattern-maintenance subsystem. This is to say that a special role is played by value-commitments and the need of such a system to maintain its position of "solvency" with respect to such commitments, in the case of the professional complex to the subvalues we call *cognitive rationality*.

The cybernetically paramount input of commitments into such a system is the assumption of "moral responsibility" for implementation of the values of the collectivity as a product output of the operative collective system. Here the client role, unlike that of citizen in a democratic association, cannot be the focus of the same order of assumption of equal responsibility as that of the full professional. The second is a rather special case of the commitment to "production" (of "goods") to this particular enterprise, in which the commitment of the professional to "produce"—health service or knowledge—is prominent. The third order of primacy is the product output from the integrative system to the professional complex, as a "latency" subsystem, namely the commitment to (the implementation of) the common values institutionalized in a particular collective context in the system. This also suggests an inequality of loyalty.

The expectation from all members of an input of commitment to common values clearly implies an order of membership status that is not parallel to that of the customer of the business firm, because this set of commitments in turn "governs" the allocation of collective loyalties of participants. To put it excessively schematically, there is no loyalty to a particular commercial source of supply comparable to the expected loyalty to alma mater. This expectation of loyalty, like the corresponding one of power for the voter, projects a "code" component of membership on participants in such a pattern-maintenance subsystem.

We will pursue this discussion with special reference to the "core" structures of the modern professional complex, namely the academic, and come back to the formal problems at the end of the discussion.

THE MODERN UNIVERSITY

Insofar as an academic system comes to be collectively organized, and is not confined to purely individualistic practitioner-client service relations, the difference of status with respect both to competence and to level of commitment to the specifically relevant values thus implies that it will be a *stratified* collective system. The core subcollectivity is the faculty, which has come to be institutionalized predominantly as a "collegial" body. This is a collectivity that functions, so far as its *self*-government is concerned, as a democratic association, as a company of equals on the principle of one member, one vote. Its members have, however, demonstrated a special level of commitment to academic values by embarking on an academic *career* so that, not only is the status of a member at any given time that of incumbency of a "full time job," but there is on the average a nearly permanent commitment over the "working" sector of the life cycle. There is a special kind of institutionalization of the implications of this commitment in assertion of the "rights" of full academic professionals to the status of tenure which, interestingly, is not shared by either of the other two major internal components of the academic collective structure, namely, administrative officers and students.

Admission to full membership status in a faculty is by a process of "election" strongly conditioned by standards of competence, which in turn is related to evaluation of candidates' past achievement and estimates of probable future achievement. A faculty as such is very definitely a corporate entity, usually defined as above all concerned with and having jurisdiction over matters of "educational policy," and within subdivisions of learning of course this is eminently true of its most important subdivision, the department.

Students as such cannot, in the nature of this type of social system, be "full members" of the central faculty collectivity, though they should, and in many respects do, enjoy an important type of different membership in the *wider* collectivity that comprises the university as a whole. This membership status is symbolized by the fact that of course students also are "elected" through "admission" procedures—as customers are not—but on the basis of standards and qualifications different from those governing the election of faculty members. It would then seem to be justified to say that, while students do not have "rights" to full equality with faculty members, certainly within the spheres of special faculty concern, they do have certain rights of influence and political participation of three principal types. One concerns matters affecting the university community as a whole. The second sphere is that concerning the special interests of students as a subcommunity within the academic community, and the third, certain matters concerning student-faculty and student-administration relationships. I am not, however, suggesting that such rights should always take the form of the democratic franchise as the ultimate forum of decision. The argument against this view rests essentially on the special *responsibility* that faculties and administrations must take for the effective implementation of academic values. That there is both a realistic trend toward and a justified need for greater student participation in academic political processes seems, however, to be beyond doubt. The desirable forms and the limits of such justified participation, however, are far from clear.

A particularly important feature of the teacher-student relation (as of all professional-client relations) that differentiates it clearly from both the officeholder-citizen relation in government and the parent-child relation is what I have called its functional specificity. It is limited in content by the relatively specific subject matter of the teaching process, the more so the higher the level of education involved. It is on this basis that competence is a critical focus of professional status as it is not one of eligibility for elective office, or indeed for parenthood. The responsibility and integrity of the teacher are focused about the acceptable use of his competence which, in the particular area, is institutionally by definition greater than that of the average student. But *outside* this area there is no presumption of special authority. This consideration explains why the prerogatives of faculties focus on matters of educational policy, but this, along with contributions to knowledge, is the *core* function of an institution of higher education. It also explains why this nonspecific problem-orientation of governments, discussed at the beginning of this chapter, does not apply to universities.

The third principal component of a university, usually called the "administration," is often divided into two subsectors, one or more "governing boards" that play a primarily fiduciary role, and a set of appointed "officers" who play primarily executive-administrative roles.

Both are functionally necessary because of a series of well-known exigencies of the government of large and complex collectivities. Faculties, first, have become so large as to be cumbrous as decision-making bodies, except in rather general policy contexts, and second, the exigencies of their members' own primary functions of teaching and research, in many different substantive fields, are so demanding that a modern university presumably could not function effectively by a system of "pure" faculty self-government, to say nothing of faculty-student self government. There must be a component, and a major one, specialized in the functions of "keeping the organization going" and in some respects guiding its development.

As compared both to faculties and to student bodies, administrations are characterized by relatively high investment with power. This is particularly evident in their very high responsibility for and control over the basic financial affairs of the university—although there are pluralistic elements here in the importance of relatively independent sources of support for particular enterprises within the university—the "research entrepreneur" with direct relations to a governmental fund-granting agency illustrates one type of such independence.

The power of administrations is partially at least balanced by the commitments and competence of faculties and the influence that is largely a product of these factors and which, by our paradigm, should be "manifested" both in value-based claims to loyalties, i.e., to the academic enterprise on the basis of common membership and in interest-demands as a factor input to the academic power system. As political leadership, then, administrations function as at least partly responsible to their faculties as constituencies and beyond that to the wider academic communities which in some respects include students. On the other side, however, there is a wider system-reference in that they mediate the relations of the university to a societally "higher" source of both legitimation and authority. In the case of public institutions it is that of the governmental units, state and municipal for the most part, that establish and finance them, in that of the private category, a now perhaps somewhat anomalous proprietary status of governing boards which, however, in both cases should be construed as mainly channels for the input of value-commitments from the societal community.

In the history of American academic organization, of course, faculties have rather strongly asserted their rights against trustees and administrations, the institution of tenure having much to do with this assertion, though it by no means rests only on "bargaining power," but also on *legitimation* of faculty status and security through commitment to the common values of cognitive rationality. There is, however, a case to be made for the view that, with the enormous growth of the academic system in the last generation, the balance may have been tipped unduly far in the direction of administration power more than counterbalancing faculty influence and value-commitments in determining total outcomes.

A particularly important mechanism of integration of course has been the *interpenetration* of faculties and administrations. As far as individual personnel is concerned, it starts with presidents, who with few exceptions, have been drawn from the academic profession, though they usually cannot continue actively to teach and investigate. Such exceptions as General Eisenhower's brief presidency of Columbia University have not been conspicuously successful. Below the president the tendency is to bifurcate, so that academic vice-presidents and deans are usually academic men, whereas comptrollers, financial vice-presidents, etc., usually are not. The academic qualification usually applies not only to "policy" deans but also to "deans of students." Finally, department chairmen are generally drawn from the regular membership and typically serve for limited periods. Somewhat similar things can be said about joint administration-faculty committees which are modes of interpenetration as well. They serve not only as channels for the transfer and exertion of influence, but also channels through which power is distributed. Through such channels, as well as through the more formal ones of faculty and department "action," a certain equalization can take place.

To return to the student situation, it is clear that both on the level of commitment and its relation to influence, and that of institutionalized power, students have been traditionally of substantially lower standing than either of the other two principal components. Given a general atmosphere in which there is a strong movement to improve students' relative status, it is expectable, in one set of terms, that there should be extensive probing of the efficacy of two channels of effective action. One, of course, is the assertion of broadened claims of access to collective decision-making power through the channel of status in the democratic association. The extreme in this direction, of course, is the attempt to define the university as a democratic association *in toto* in which everyone with *any* membership status must be treated as the equal of every other member.[27] The other channel, intensively resorted to by the radical minorities, is the use of "confrontation" tactics that threaten the normal academic processes with disruptions of varying degrees of severity as a means of coercing changes in favor of "student power." In the "logic" of the weak student situation, resort to the power of numbers, in which they obviously excel, and to collective coercion, is not to be wondered at. The parallel to industrial labor relations in situations of tension is obvious and apposite. It seems no more likely, however, that "student power" in the present sense will be able to take over and organize the modern system of higher education than could "union power" do so for the industrial system. Here, of course, it should be noted that where "socialism" has prevailed, the "workers" have always been, in any literal sense, a minority of the constituency from which socialist parties, notably the Communist, have sought political

[27] Cf. *The New York Times*, December 28, 1968, on the University of Florence.

support and have never directly achieved control. In particular, as noted above, there is *no* case of a national economy in which the actual workers in particular plants have, as democratic associations, gained effective long-run operating control of the enterprises and maintained or enhanced their efficiency. It seems to be in the "logic" again of the educational system that the corresponding order of student control would not work, and indeed will not prove politically viable as a program very widely or for very long.

What, then, are we to make of institutions of higher education as socio-political systems? To treat them as "pure democratic associations," including students as "fully equal" members, would negate the special functions of faculties and administrations and undermine the basis for their acceptance of responsibility for those functions. It would further undermine the institutionalization of responsibility for promoting the interests of higher education in the wider society that is highly involved now in the roles of governing boards and administrations. It would "politicize" the university probably in a double sense. If it came to focus on the particular institution it would make all leadership elements dependent on contingent support, which in turn would be dependent on satisfaction of interest-demands on the part of persons not, on the average, sufficiently highly committed to academic values, or sufficiently competent to support faculty commitments, or adequate to evaluate faculty perform-ance. If, on the other hand, the focus were on the academic "system" as a whole, it would presumably have to be linked up with the national political system in such a way that the universities, probably under student leadership, would become virtually a political party.[28] Such a party might or might not fit into the present type of political system, it might well become a revolutionary party, as is clearly envisaged now by a group of student radicals. Faculties would, however, clearly have to "go along" with this politization and in the process, from the present point of view, lose much of their academic freedom.

Exclusion of students from any significant membership status, on the other hand, would tend to reduce them to the status of "customers" of the academic enterprise, who might well "shop around" for better deals, but not, in any more significant sense, participate in it. Among other considerations, I doubt that the fully "adult" components of the academic system, i.e., faculties and administrations, could maintain their position if they lost student support, not only in the sense that students might actively combat the "academic establishment" and attempt to depose it, but that they should "withdraw" into the role of purely self-interest "customers." A somewhat more remote possibility, of course, is reversion,

---

[28] Possibly parallel to a religious party and hence equally unlikely to be viable under American conditions. Cf. Chapter 9. There is also a parallel to labor or socialist parties based on trade union organization.

on the part of governing boards and administrations, to the older pattern of treating even faculties simply as classes of "employees," to be hired and fired at the discretion of the "management."

The illustrations we have been reviewing in the last few pages constitute clearly an oversimplification of the actual academic system. The liberal arts college involves, clearly differentiated from each other, the three structural components of faculty, students, and administration, the latter, for many purposes being divisible into governing boards and appointed officers of administration. The "full" university, however, is much more complex. First, its teaching functions and student bodies are divided, within the "core" arts and sciences sector, into undergraduate and graduate divisions, and this core sector is differentiated from the "ring" of professional schools that are now usually present. If the simpler model was "pluralistic," this is pluralism compounded.

On a previous occasion I have suggested[29] that the model that combines both federalism and the separation of powers comes closer to the mark than any of the others that we have reviewed. The federal element applies to the fact that it is a diversified system, composed of many autonomous units that are not administratively coordinated into a single system as, for example, has long been the case for French universities. In this context, the autonomy of the particular university, or "state" system of higher education, or indeed faculty within a university is comparable to a case of "states' rights." There is, at the same time, however, a level of "federal"—but nongovernmental—coordination and problems. There are common standards, and a nationwide "academic marketplace" for personnel. There are some nationwide sanctions, such as distribution of federal funds, on the one hand, and distribution of individual and institutional honors, on the other, e.g., election to the National Academy of Sciences, and the "ratings" of the distinction of universities relative to each other.

The national system is, however, pluralistic, in something like the separation-of-powers sense, though of course far from being exactly like it. In pursuing this theme let us remember that we are not dealing with a primarily political system, but with one grounded in *cultural* commitments, hence at the social system level, the pattern-maintenance system. This suggests that the primary prestige status, and at certain levels, control, would not be expected to accrue to the "elective" component, but rather to the analogue of the constitutional, and "spelling this out," the judicial, process.

Perhaps we can approach this question a little more clearly if we raise that of the sense in which a type of collective system at the social level with pattern-maintenance functions is subject to standards of performance parallel to that of "solvency" for firms, and an input-output power

[29] Cf. "The Academic System: A Sociologist's View," *The Public Interest*, Fall, 1968.

balance for governments, and what the state of affairs in this respect is for the American academic system. We suggest that the relevant standard, which has very tentatively been called "patern consistency" (technical note to Chapter 14, Figure 3) is to be implemented by the collective unit's capacity to balance its input-output "acounts" in terms of value-commitments, as these have been analyzed in Chapter 16. The obverse question is how far such a system is, in relevant respects, subject to "subsidy" in order to keep going, or is even allowed or forced to "liquidate" by reason of the equivalent of insolvency.

In its relations to the economy, an academic system is clearly dependent on *economic* subsidy. But the availability of the necessary subsidies in this connection may or may not be secured through being able to count on a sufficient input of commitments to divert the requisite shares of productive capacity to this mode of "consumption," as economists call it, from increase of production and from other, more usual modes of consumption. Realistically this diversion is controlled through monetary channels in the two primary forms of economic subsidy from public funds, mainly derived from taxation, and from voluntary contributions. Probably the considerable component of "payment" by students and their families for educational services (tuition, etc.) should be regarded more as a contribution than as a "price" for the services rendered. The crucial point here is that, in a division of labor in the Durkheimian sense, a unit like a university cannot be *economically* self-sufficient or solvent, but it may, under certain circumstances, be valuationally self-sufficient, which I would interpret in the present context to mean it could legitimately *count* on the necessary economic subsidies.

The second main context where the problem arises is that of the relation between values and loyalties, or of commitments and influence. In terms of solidarity, especially within the broader, pluralistic system of involvements, the input of influence to *this particular* specified sector of the value-system, as implemented through justification of loyalties to academic collectivities, cannot be taken for granted. In terms of collective loyalties also, the academic system must be "subsidized." The question is that of the adequacy of the "income" of value-commitments in the form of commitment to common values which it receives and with which it can "purchase" the necessary influence. Beyond the need for subsidy, if the academic system is to grow, it must receive the equivalent of creation of new capital resources for the economy by *more* loyalty to academic collectivities—"bought" by commitments to the specified academic values—than would be necessary to maintain a given level of academic functioning on a "circular flow" basis.

The third context of product input is the *G-L* relationship. Here the necessary input is acceptance of *operative* responsibility. This interchange, as we have suggested, helps to define the "code" by which the more detailed and situation-oriented interchanges just reviewed are regulated. It is through a *specified* focus of moral responsibility that more operative commitments to the specified values and allocation of economic resources to such enterprises as the academic are legitimated. These commitments, in turn, are essential to securing the necessary economic support, collective loyalty, and operative responsibility in the direct process of implementation.

To take a very schematic excursion into more empirical interpretation, and with due respect to far more complex interdependencies than have been analyzed here, it seems to be possible from the vantage point just gained to understand somewhat better the rather special focus of strain, in not only the American but other academic systems, on the student status.

Formally it is a question of capacity of the system to command the inputs of value-commitment from its neighboring systems that are necessary for its effective functioning and growth; if not, what possible sources of subsidy are available? There seems, at least, to be an actual or threatened deficit of input of value-commitments in two of the three main categories, namely, assumption of moral responsibility for implementation of the values of cognitive rationality as such, and commitment to the implementation of such values in the context of academic organization.

Here it is particularly important to note that the necessary input is one of value-commitments *specified* to the subcategory of cognitive rationality. Faculties and, to some extent, members of administrations may be considered to be on the whole more highly socialized with reference to commitment to these specific values than are students, especially undergraduates. The deficit, then, is not in value-commitments in general, but commitments at the requisite *level of differentiation and specification* from others (cf. Chapter 16). Broadly speaking, dissident students are highly moralistic, but tend to "politicize" their value-commitments by making the moral responsibility in question responsibility, not for the implementation of academic values as such, but for a set of more general societal-political values, broadly of a "radical" character, with which, however, the academic values are linked.

The second main context of deficit of commitment-input is that involved with the procurement of loyalty to academic associations. Here the pattern is similar to the above, namely, the relative unwillingness to make commitments to this particular *type* of "valued association" with sufficiently high priority relative to others. The tendency therefore is, as so frequently, to wish to "have one's cake and eat it," namely, to redefine the association itself in the direction of lowering if not eliminating the primacy of more purely academic values, a shift in the direction of what Daniel Bell calls conceiving the university to be a microcosm of the total society, rather than a specifically differentiated subsystem.[30] Again this tendency is

[30] Cf. Daniel Bell, "Columbia and the New Left," *The Public Interest*, No. 13 (Fall 1968).

considerably stronger among students than faculties because the former do not have the kind of career-commitments and socialization for them that faculty members usually do. Again the main pattern does not seem to be one of relatively "frivolous" concern for personal hedonistic interests. The moral component is salient. But it tends to take the form of a relatively dedifferentiated commitment to values of egalitarian social welfare, rather than a more differentiated one to cognitive values.

The vast recent increase in the size of student bodies certainly bears on the situation just sketched, because vastly greater resources of the requisite type of value-commitment, as well as other categories of input, have come to be needed to make such a hugely enlarged academic system function.

If we are correct that the focus of the problem for the highly salient case of student dissent lies in deficits of sufficiently differentiated and specified value-commitments, then it is easier to see that similar difficulties are to be found on the side of administrations and, probably to a lesser degree, of faculties themselves. Here the deviation from an academic ideal type of differentiation is probably more than anything else a function not of the older political conservatism of trustees so much as of the success of the academic enterprise and some of the conditions on which it has depended, namely support of science by the Federal Government—for the U.S. case. There has been, that is, an insufficiently clear differentiation between the relatively "pure" intellectual disciplines and interest in many of their fields of application, notably military fields for the natural sciences. This is presumably the primary reason why opposition to the war in Vietnam has had such powerful repercussions not only *in*, but *on* the universities. Faculties become involved, unevenly of course, by virtue of the interests of their members in such support for their work, and the powerful appeals to national interest and solidarity that underlie these interests.

There is, hence, at least a partial "symmetry" between the "deviation" of dissident student orientations from the principal norms clustering about the primacy of cognitive rationality, and deviations in which administrations and to a lesser degree faculties have also become involved.

When we speak of academic collective organization as closer to the model of the separation of powers than to that of the pure democratic association, I hope the above brief review of technical input-needs of the system makes clear that we emphatically do *not* treat it as a governmental body, but one anchored in the functions of implementing a differentiated subset of cultural values in a differentiated sector of the structure of modern society. It therefore belongs neither in the range of governmental types that were briefly sketched above, nor the other nongovernmental types such as the firm, the market system, the predominantly "bureaucratic" type of organization, or the "pure" voluntary association. It belongs to a distinctive type, unlike any of these others, with a "political aspect" that is fused with and importantly subordinated to others.

In a book devoted mainly to the relations of political and sociological theory, the justification for including such a relatively long discussion of academic organization in part lies in the importance of making as clear as possible that political theory in the *analytical* sense, which has dominated the approach to it in this book, should not be treated as a *general* theory of social structure. Academic organization, of course, has its political aspect, as does every other form, private as well as governmental. But it requires the mobilization of other disciplines in order to give anything like a satisfactory account of this in the "problem" sense present—"politically"—salient sector of modern societies.

CONCLUSION

The most general theoretical conclusion I should like to leave with the reader of this book is the great strategic significance of the concept of power as a point of focus for the theoretical organization of political subject matters. In this respect, of course, it is not the specificities of power as a phenomenon, but this combined with the fact that it belongs to a family of generalized symbolic media of societal interchange that is decisive. It may sound strange for a noneconomist, and a sociologist at that, to be "lecturing" political scientists about the theoretical virtues of monetary theory, but this is indeed the main key to the significance of this idea.

Economists, especially starting with Keynes, have indeed worked out a theory of money that constitutes, for economics, the major theoretical advance to that we refer. Economists, however, have notably confined their concern to their own field and have not, to my knowledge, even suggested that monetary theory could be regarded as a special case of a much wider body of theoretical possibilities. If there is any special merit in the "sociological" perspective of this book, I should like to see it attached to the idea of the feasibility of *generalization* of the monetary case to all of the *four* generalized media of a highly differentiated societal system.

This "sociological" perspective, however, came to be highly dependent in turn on a political one, in the sense that the first step in generalization beyond the monetary case virtually had to be to the political one. As noted in Chapter 14, power was by far the most likely current theoretical concept in the political field to fit in this context. However, a survey of the literature on power was decidedly discouraging as to the possibility of finding any sort of consensus on its definition as a symbolic medium. In the circumstances it was necessary to resort to rather drastic modifications of the positions taken by all the main current theoretical schools among political scientists on the subject of power.

The most serious obstacle was the almost unanimous assumption that power should be regarded as an "intrinsic effector"—following the great tradition of Hobbes—thus eliminating consideration of the most crucial single property of a generalized symbolic medium given for money in the tradition of the classical economics and ever since that money has "value in exchange" but *not* "value in use." But if power were to be conceived as a medium, then the instruments of coercion, so central to political theory, could not be treated as they almost unanimously have been, as "forms of power," any more than intrinsically valuable commodities could be treated as "forms of money."

Once, however, the symbolic medium concept of power was clearly defined, it became possible to resolve several of the prominent dilemmas that have plagued discussions of power for a long time. Three of them were discussed in the opening pages of Chapter 14, but may be recalled here because they are so centrally important to our general analysis. The first is the problem of delineating the *scope* of inclusion under the concept power. If all "intrinsic effectors" were to be included, then—as was quite explicit in Hobbes' famous definition, literally—*anything* with instrumental significance for the attainment of human goals must be treated as a "form of power." A concept of such diffuseness is unlikely to be very helpful analytically. My answer was the radical one of excluding intrinsic effectors altogether.

Second, by tying the concept of power to the *collective* setting and using institutionalized *bindingness* as a primary criterion—in addition, of course, to the symbolic nature of power—it was possible to avoid the old dilemma as to whether "in the last analysis" the basis of power is coercive or consensual. The identification of the use of physical force as a "security base" for a power system parallel to the monetary metal in the case of money helped greatly to clarify this context. This position, however, it must be made clear, meant the sacrifice of some types of generality, notably the use of power to explain phenomena in uninstitutionalized relational systems. These, it has been contended, must be handled in other ways. As noted, this position constituted a major change of opinion on my own part.

The third problem was called that of the implicit zero-sum assumption in the work of most theorists of power. Since this could not be the case for money—although in the history of economics such assumptions have been common—if it had to be accepted, this alone would nearly destroy the prospects of treating power as a generalized symbolic medium. I feel confident of having demonstrated, on the basis set forth, that such an assumption is unwarranted and, indeed, that dropping it opens the door to some of the most important potentials for theoretical political analysis. I shall return to some of these presently.

Chapter 14 did not make fully explicit still a fourth basic problem of the use of the power concept, namely, the tendency to treat power as inherently hierarchical. Indeed, Dahl includes the phrase "power *over*" without comment in his formal definition of power.[31] A common consequence of this assumption has been to hold that power and equality are inherently antithetical, and that, therefore, patterns of equality could gain in social systems only at the *expense* of their power potential. Durkheim, in his contention that "organic solidarity" through the division of labor was not antithetical to the growth of political organization and hence of the power of the state, achieved a partial insight into the complex that has been generalized here. One of its first "payoffs" is the conception that the franchise held by an individual citizen or member is in fact a "form of power," though only a small amount. The pattern of the democratic franchise, one citizen, one vote, is not a *negation* of the role of power in governmental systems, but a *special way* of organizing it. The assumption of the inherently hierarchical character of power, which can be compared to Aristotle's famous but equally erroneous view of the sterility of money, has underlain much of the utopian stance of modern political thought and has been pernicious in creating a false dilemma.

On the more general level the theoretical reorientation that focuses on the redefined concept of power presented here implies bringing political theory to a new level of analytical generality, which in turn of course entails higher levels of abstractness in certain contexts, though through the gain in specificity of theoretical focus it makes possible a much sharper definition of many empirical problems. One of the first fruits, indeed a major stimulus to the reorientation, has been the conception of the polity not as a concrete collectivity, but as a *functionally* defined system, in the same analytical sense as is true of the economy. This position implies immediate abandonment of the conception of political theory as the "theory of government," as this has been held by so many political scientists. Government is the concrete structural system in societies that have the highest level of political primacy of function, with structural and processual implications accordingly. But *all* forms of collective organization have a "political aspect," as it was put in Chapter 13, as indeed they also have an economic aspect.

Opting for the analytical-functional view of the polity in place of the concrete collectivity view is directly connected with another critical point, namely, treatment of the polity or political system as inherently an *open* system in the general sense in which this is true of all living systems and certainly of all systems of action. This is to say, as we stressed in Part I, that all such systems are involved in complex and continuing interchanges with their environments, and of course, at action levels, these interchanges involve and are in part regulated by generalized symbolic media.

This is to say that the boundaries of an analytically defined functional subsystem *cannot* legitimately be defined as the limits of the circulation of the generalized medium which, as we have put it, is "anchored" in that

[31] Cf. Robert Dahl, "The Concept of Power," *Behavioral Scientist*, Vol. II (July 1957).

system. By such a definition the economy would have to include all of government, all households, and all of the "private nonprofit" sector, as well as the aggregate of business firms—in other words almost the whole society. The alternative view, adopted here, is of course that the medium of reference circulates *over* the boundaries of its home system and into those of its "neighbors," and of course, vice-versa, the media anchored in these systems circulate in, for example, the polity.

For this reason it is imperative to treat the media as a "family," and hence to attempt *systematically* to work out their similarities and differences, and their relations to each other. Only with such theoretical resources can we hope to work out theoretically determinate accounts of their interchanges both with each other and with the various classes of "intrinsic effectors."[32]

If, as I suggested at the beginning of this conclusion, it was imperative to work out a system of media, it had to include a political case, and this was likely to be the one that most illuminated certain problems of the relations between polity and economy. But equally, it was imperative not to stop with a political case, but to go all the way "around the clock" of the four-function paradigm. This has proved to be a slow and difficult process, but at least an outline can now be said to be complete, and its completion improves not only the newly developed sectors but the scheme as a whole. Thus I feel on much solider ground now in the analysis of power because of having made considerable progress in the complementary analyses of influence and of value-commitments, and the relation of all three to each other and to money.

It is only with the highly sophisticated development of monetary theory that it has become possible to carry out at all accurate analyses of the processes of equilibration and disequilibration, and also growth and structural change, of a total economy. The corresponding possibilities should be opening up for political theory and for theoretical sociology, but so far only certain foundations for them have been laid and only some general approaches can be formulated.

In Chapter 14, for instance, I went to considerable pains to try to show empirically as well as theoretically that the creation of new power in a sense parallel to the creation of new money (credit) through banking operations could and *did* occur in political systems, especially involving the functions of leadership. I took similar pains for the other two media in Chapters 15 and 16. Establishing this point is in my view essential if *any* serious theoretical progress is to be made, but at best it is only a beginning.

[32] This is the main basis on which I feel justified in criticizing the "theoretical isolationism" of so much of economics, with its assumption (usually implicit) that money is a totally unique phenomenon. To me, a deleterious consequence of such isolation has been the tendency of some economists to stretch the concept "commodity" to include *everything* for which money is exchangeable, in other words to treat all nonmonetary entities involved in markets as belonging to a single residual category.

When generalized, this leads to the proposition that the "amount" of any of the media operating in the system of reference is a variable, not a constant, and is dependent on operations directly involving it. Its "value," however, is a function, not only of its "supply" but also of its relation to intrinsic effectors and to other media, *both* within the system itself *and* in its environing systems. The medium itself, its status and its "value," become the focus of complex processes of mutual adjustment among many factors and variables on both sides, but with a built-in duality of deviation from some sort of "steady" or "equilibrium" state (which of course may be "moving" rather than "static"). For the economic case these two directions of "deviation" have acquired the standard labels of "inflation" and "deflation."

If the general conception of the four media is in any way correct, there seems to be every reason to generalize this major focus of economic analysis to all of them. It is this kind of development that, I think, indicates the direction for far greater generality and analytical precision in the theoretical operations of both political science and sociology than they have heretofore attained.

There is a particularly important relevance of these considerations to the problems of growth and structural change. Credit creation has been proved by economic analysis to be a powerful agent of economic growth, though of course it has by no means been implemented only by banks, but often by governmental units or private "magnates." Credit creation, however, is also a ready source of inflationary forces, and hence of danger to economic stability. Therefore in some sense collective risk is part of the price of growth potential. Conversely, of course, every functioning bank is in a technical sense "insolvent" and the assertion of rights to immediate fulfillment of all legitimate claims against it—e.g., to the return of deposits—can readily precipitate a deflationary process that is just as much a threat to economic stability as is the inflationary deviation.

This frame of reference inherently raises the problems of defining, for the system as a whole, including its environments, the conditions under which the various alternative trends are likely to develop, thereby immensely sharpening empirical problem foci of theoretical relevance. It is our conviction, then, that this theoretical precision can in fact be generalized to the political system, the societal community, and the "main-tenance" system, and eventually to societies taken as a whole.[33]

This appears to me to be the most important *single* direction for theo-retical work that, on the basis of the contents of the present volume, a sociologist can commend to theoretically minded political scientists. It

---

[33] Work on these problems, especially for the polity and the societal community, is in fact going on, of course in other centers, but specifically by Mr. Mark Gould, in collaboration with the author. It is not far enough along, however, to merit presentation at this time. I am indebted to Mr. Gould for many helpful criticisms of the first draft of this Chapter and suggestions for its revision.

clearly is not the only one, and there are perhaps others of equal merit. On such issues only one final comment may be made, namely, about the relations of macroanalyses and microanalyses.

This, of course, has been the focus of a continual oscillation of interests and alleged legitimacy within the sciences. In early modern physics, surely the macrotheories from Copernicus to Newton gained the grand prizes, though not without very important contributions from terrestrial mechanics. Much later, in biology it is probably correct to say that the Darwinian synthesis made a crucial contribution without which, microbiology, which has today become so salient, would not have developed so fully. Some no doubt would say that, because Darwin's genetics was virtually nonexistent, to say nothing of his biochemistry, he ought not to have tried to generalize about biological phenomena at all. Yet ... ?

Contemporary social science seems to be involved in another version of the old macro-micro argument. There are those, like George Homans, who contend that a full clarification of the "elementary forms" of social behavior is the most solid foundation on which to build social science theory and perhaps that everything else should wait. Contrary to this has been the immense flowering, in both political science and sociology, of macroscopic work, extending conspicuously into the comparative and evolutionary fields.

I do not think that there is an ultimate conflict between these two emphases. Perhaps, however, for political science, in its increasingly intimate relations with sociology, the macroemphasis presents, in the present state of development of the social sciences as a whole, a special opportunity for major theoretical advance. This is not to the exclusion of the contributions of the microemphasis, but suggests that undue neglect of this opportunity might result in serious retardation of the scientific potentials of our fields.

Bibliography of
Talcott Parsons

1928
"Capitalism" in Recent German Literature: Sombart and Weber, I.
Journal of Political Economy 36:641–661.

1929
"Capitalism" in Recent German Literature: Sombart and Weber, II.
Journal of Political Economy 37:31–51.

1930
Translation of Max Weber, *The Protestant Ethic and the Spirit of Capitalism*.
London: Allen and Unwin; and New York: Scribners; xi + 292 pp.

1931
Wants and Activities in Marshall.
Quarterly Journal of Economics 46:101–140.

1932
Economics and Sociology: Marshall in Relation to the Thought of His Time.
Quarterly Journal of Economics 46:316–347.

1933
Malthus.
Encyclopedia of the Social Sciences 10:68–69.
Pareto.
Encyclopedia of the Social Sciences 11:576–578.

1934

Some Reflections on "The Nature and Significance of Economics."
Quarterly Journal of Economics 48:511–545.
Society.
Encyclopedia of the Social Sciences 14:225–231.
Sociological Elements in Economic Thought, I.
Quarterly Journal of Economics 49:414–453.

1935

Sociological Elements in Economic Thought, II.
Quarterly Journal of Economics 49:645–667.
The Place of Ultimate Values in Sociological Theory.
International Journal of Ethics 45:282–316.
H. M. Robertson on Max Weber and His School.
Journal of Political Economy 43:688–696.

1936

Pareto's Central Analytical Scheme.
Journal of Social Philosophy 1:244–262.
On Certain Sociological Elements in Professor Taussig's Thought.
Jacob Viner (ed.), *Explorations in Economics: Notes and Essays Contributed in Honor of F. W. Taussig*, New York: McGraw-Hill (xii + 539 pp.), pp. 352–379.

1937

The Structure of Social Action.
New York: McGraw-Hill; xii + 617 pp. Reprinted by The Free Press, New York, 1949.
Education and the Professions.
International Journal of Ethics 47:365–369.

1938

The Role of Theory in Social Research.
American Sociological Review 3:13–20. (An address delivered before the Annual Institute of the Society for Social Research, at the University of Chicago, Summer, 1937.)
The Role of Ideas in Social Action. (Also in *Essays in Sociological Theory.*)
American Sociological Review 3:653–664. (Written for a meeting on the problem of ideologies at the American Sociological Society's annual meeting, Atlantic City, N.J., December, 1937.)

1939

The Professions and Social Structure. (Also in *Essays in Sociological Theory.*)
Social Forces 17:457–467. (Written to be read at the annual meeting

of the American Sociological Society in Detroit, December, 1938.)
Comte.

Journal of Unified Science 9:77–83.

1940

Analytical Approach to the Theory of Social Stratification. (Also in
Essays in Sociological Theory.)

American Journal of Sociology 45:841–862.

Motivation of Economic Activities. (Also in *Essays in Sociological
Theory*.)

Canadian Journal of Economics and Political Science 6:187–203.

(Originally given as a public lecture at the University of Toronto
and also published in *Human Relations in Administration: The
Sociology of Organization*, Robert Dubin (ed.), 1951.)

1942

Max Weber and the Contemporary Political Crisis.

Review of Politics 4:61–76, 155–172.

The Sociology of Modern Anti-Semitism.

J. Graeber and Stuart Henderson Britt (eds.), *Jews in a Gentile
World*, New York: Macmillan, 1942 (x+436 pp.), pp. 101–122.

Age and Sex in the Social Structure of the United States. (Also in
Essays in Sociological Theory.)

American Sociological Review 7:604–616. (Read at the annual meeting
of the American Sociological Society in New York, December,
1941, and republished in several places, notably Logan Wilson and
William Kolb, *Sociological Analysis*, and Clyde Kluckhohn and
Henry A. Murray, *Personality in Nature, Society and Culture*, 1st and
2nd editions.)

Propaganda and Social Control. (Also in *Essays in Sociological Theory*.)

Psychiatry 5:551–572.

Democracy and the Social Structure in Pre-Nazi Germany. (Only in
revised edition, 1954, of *Essays in Sociological Theory*.)

Journal of Legal and Political Sociology 1:96–114.

Some Sociological Aspects of the Fascist Movements. (Also in *Essays
in Sociological Theory*, revised edition, 1954 only.)

Social Forces 21:138–147. (Written as the presidential address to
the Eastern Sociological Society at its 1942 meeting.)

1943

The Kinship System of the Contemporary United States. (Also in
Essays in Sociological Theory.)

American Anthropologist 45:22–38.

1944

The Theoretical Development of the Sociology of Religion. (Also in
Essays in Sociological Theory.)

Journal of the History of Ideas 5:176–190. (Originally written to be read at the Conference on Methods in Science and Philosophy in New York, November, 1942.) Reprinted in *Ideas in Cultural Perspective*, Philip Wiener and Aaron Noland (eds.), New Brunswick, N.J.: Rutgers University Press, 1962.

1945

The Present Position and Prospects of Systematic Theory in Sociology. (Also in *Essays in Sociological Theory*.)
George Gurvitch and Wilbert E. Moore (eds.), *Twentieth Century Sociology*, A Symposium; New York: Philosophical Library.

The Problem of Controlled Institutional Change: An Essay on Applied Social Science. (Also in *Essays in Sociological Theory*.)
Psychiatry 8:79–101. (Prepared as an appendix to the report of the Conference on Germany after World War II.)

Racial and Religious Differences as Factors in Group Tensions. Louis Finkelstein *et al.* (eds.), *Unity and Difference in the Modern World*, A Symposium; New York: The Conference on Science, Philosophy and Religion in Their Relation to the Democratic Way of Life, Inc.

1946

The Science Legislation and the Role of the Social Sciences.
American Sociological Review 11:653–666.

Population and Social Structure (of Japan). (Also in *Essays in Sociological Theory*, revised edition, 1954 only.)   .
Douglas G. Haring (ed.), *Japan's Prospect*, Cambridge: Harvard University Press (xiv + 474 pp.), pp. 87–114. (This book was published by the staff of the Harvard School for Overseas Administration.)

Certain Primary Sources and Patterns of Aggression in the Social Structure of the Western World. (Also in *Essays in Sociological Theory*.)
Psychiatry 10:167–181. (Prepared for the Conference on Science, Philosophy, and Religion at its September, 1946 meeting in Chicago, and also published in the volume issued by the Conference.)

Some Aspects of the Relations Between Social Science and Ethics.
Social Science 22:23–217. (Read at the Annual Meeting of the American Association for the Advancement of Science in Boston, December, 1946.)

Science Legislation and the Social Sciences.
Political Science Quarterly, Vol. LXII, No. 2, June, 1947. *Bulletin of Atomic Scientists*, January, 1947.

Max Weber: The Theory of Social and Economic Organization.
Talcott Parsons, editor, and translator with A. M. Henderson;

Oxford University Press. Introduction by Talcott Parsons. (Also in *Essays in Sociological Theory*, first edition, 1949, only.) Reprinted by The Free Press, New York, 1957.

1948

Sociology, 1941–46.
  Co-author with Bernard Barber. *American Journal of Sociology* 53: 245–257.
The Position of Sociological Theory. (Also in *Essays in Sociological Theory*, first edition, 1949, only.)

1949

Essays in Sociological Theory Pure and Applied.
  New York: The Free Press; xiii + 366 pp.
The Rise and Decline of Economic Man.
  Journal of General Education 4:47–53.
Social Classes and Class Conflict in the Light of Recent Sociological Theory. (Also in *Essays in Sociological Theory*, revised edition, 1954, only.)
  American Economic Review 39:16–26. (Read at the meeting of the American Economic Association in December, 1948.)

1950

The Prospects of Sociological Theory. (Also in *Essays in Sociological Theory*, revised edition, 1954, only.)
  American Sociological Review 15:3–16. (Presidential address read before the meeting of the American Sociological Society in New York City, December, 1949.)
Psychoanalysis and the Social Structure. (Also in *Essays in Sociological Theory*, revised edition, 1954, only.)
  The Psychoanalytic Quarterly 19:371–384. (The substance of this paper was presented at the meeting of the American Psychoanalytic Association, Washington, D.C., May, 1948.)
The Social Environment of the Educational Process.
  Centennial, Washington, D.C., American Association for the Advancement of Science, pp. 36–40. (Read at the AAAS Centennial Celebration, September, 1948.)

1951

The Social System.
  New York: The Free Press; xii + 575 pp.
Toward a General Theory of Action.
  Editor and contributor with Edward A. Shils and others. Cambridge: Harvard University Press; xiii + 506 pp. Reprinted, Harper Torch-books, 1962.
Graduate Training in Social Relations at Harvard.
  Journal of General Education 5:149–157.

Illness and the Role of the Physician: A Sociological Perspective. *American Journal of Orthopsychiatry* 21:452–460. (Presented at the 1951 annual meeting of the American Orthopsychiatric Association in Detroit.) Reprinted in Clyde Kluckhohn, Henry A. Murray, and David M. Schneider, *Personality in Nature, Society, and Culture*, 2nd ed., New York: Knopf, 1953.

1952

The Superego and the Theory of Social Systems. (Also in *Social Structure and Personality*, 1964.)
Psychiatry 15:15–25. (The substance of this paper was read at the meeting of the Psychoanalytic Section of the American Psychiatric Association, May, 1951, in Cincinnati.) Reprinted in Parsons, Bales, and Shils, *Working Papers in the Theory of Action*, New York: The Free Press, 1953 and 1967.

Religious Perspectives in College Teaching: Sociology and Social Psychology.
Hoxie N. Fairchild (ed.), *Religious Perspectives in College Teaching*, New York: The Ronald Press Company (viii+460 pp.), pp. 286–337.

A Sociologist Looks at the Legal Profession. (Also in *Essays in Sociological Theory*, revised edition, 1954, only.)
Conference on the Profession of Law and Legal Education, Conference Series Number II, The Law School, University of Chicago, pp. 49–63. (This paper was presented at the first symposium on the occasion of the Fiftieth Anniversary Celebration of the University of Chicago Law School, December, 1952.)

1953

Working Papers in the Theory of Action.
In collaboration with Robert F. Bales and Edward A. Shils. New York: The Free Press; 269 pp. Re-issued, 1967.

Psychoanalysis and Social Science with Special Reference to the Oedipus Problem.
Franz Alexander and Helen Ross (eds.), *Twenty Years of Psychoanalysis*, New York: W. W. Norton and Company, Inc., pp. 186–215. (The substance of this paper was read at the Twentieth Anniversary Celebration of the Institute for Psychoanalysis, in Chicago, October, 1952.)

A Revised Analytical Approach to the Theory of Social Stratification. (Also in *Essays in Sociological Theory*, revised edition, 1954, only.)
Reinhard Bendix and Seymour M. Lipset (eds.), *Class, Status, and Power: A Reader in Social Stratification*, New York: The Free Press, pp. 92–129.

Illness, Therapy and the Modern Urban American Family.
Co-author with Renée Fox. *Journal of Social Issues* 8:31–44.
Reprinted in E. Gartly Jaco (ed.), *Patients, Physicians, and Illness*,
New York: The Free Press, 1958.
Some Comments on the State of the General Theory of Action.
American Sociological Review, Vol. 18, No. 6 (December, 1953), pp.
618–631.

1954

The Father Symbol: An Appraisal in the Light of Psychoanalytic and
Sociological Theory. (Also in *Social Structure and Personality*, 1964.)
Bryson, Finkelstein, MacIver, and McKeon (eds.), *Symbols and
Values: An Initial Study*, thirteenth Symposium of the Conference
on Science, Philosophy and Religion, New York: Harper & Row,
pp. 523–544. (The substance of this paper was read at the meeting
of the American Psychological Association in September, 1952, in
Washington, D.C.)
Essays in Sociological Theory (revised edition).
New York: The Free Press; 459 pp.
Psychology and Sociology.
John P. Gillin (ed.), *For A Science of Social Man*, New York:
Macmillan, pp. 67–102.
The Incest Taboo in Relation to Social Structure and the Socialization
of the Child. (Also in *Social Structure and Personality*, 1964.)
British Journal of Sociology, Vol. V, No. 2 (June, 1954), pp. 101–117.

1955

Family, Socialization and Interaction Process.
With Robert F. Bales, James Olds, Morris Zelditch, and Philip E.
Slater, New York: The Free Press; xi + 422 pp.
Éléments pour une théorie de l'action.
With an introduction by François Bourricaud. Paris: Plon.
A Sociological Approach to the Theory of Organizations. (Also in
Structure and Process in Modern Society, 1960.)
Administrative Science Quarterly, I (June, 1956), pp. 63–85; II
(September, 1956), pp. 225–239.
A Sociological Model for Economic Development.
Co-author with Neil J. Smelser. *Explorations in Entrepreneurial
History*, Cambridge: Harvard University Press.

1957

The Distribution of Power in American Society. (Also in *Structure
and Process in Modern Society*, 1960.)
World Politics, X (October, 1957), pp. 123–143.

Malinowski and the Theory of Social Systems.
> Raymond Firth (ed.), *Man and Culture*, London: Routledge and Kegan Paul.

Man in His Social Environment—As Viewed by Modern Social Science. *Centennial Review of Arts and Science*, Michigan State University, Winter, 1957, pp. 50–69.

The Mental Hospital as a Type of Organization.
> Milton Greenblatt, Daniel J. Levinson, and Richard H. Williams (eds.), *The Patient and the Mental Hospital*, New York: The Free Press.

Réflexions sur les Organisations Réligieuses aux États-Unis.
> *Archives de Sociologie Des Religions*, January–June, pp. 21–36.

Sociologia di dittatura.
> Bologna: Il Molino.

1958

Authority, Legitimation, and Political Action. (Also in *Structure and Process in Modern Society*, 1960.)
> C. J. Friedrich (ed.), *Authority*, Cambridge: Harvard University Press.

The Definitions of Health and Illness in the Light of American Values and Social Structure. (Also in *Social Structure and Personality*, 1964.)
> E. Gartly Jaco (ed.), *Patients, Physicians, and Illness*, New York: The Free Press.

Social Structure and the Development of Personality. (Also in *Social Structure and Personality*, 1964.)
> *Psychiatry*, November, 1958, pp. 321–340.

General Theory in Sociology.
> Robert K. Merton, Leonard Broom, and Leonard S. Cottrell, Jr., (eds.), *Sociology Today*, New York: Basic Books.

Some Ingredients of a General Theory of Formal Organization. (Also in *Structure and Process in Modern Society*, 1960.)
> Andrew W. Halpin (ed.), *Administrative Theory in Education*, Chicago: Midwest Administration Center, University of Chicago.

Some Reflections on the Institutional Framework of Economic Development. (Also in *Structure and Process in Modern Society*, 1960.)
> *The Challenge of Development: A Symposium*, Jerusalem: The Hebrew University.

Some Trends of Change in American Society: Their Bearing on Medical Education. (Also in *Structure and Process in Modern Society*, 1960.)
> *Journal of the American Medical Association*, May, 1958, pp. 31–36.

The Pattern of Religious Organization in the United States. (Also in *Structure and Process in Modern Society*, 1960.)
> *Daedalus*, Summer, 1958, pp. 65–85.

The Concepts of Culture and of Social System.
Co-author with A. L. Kroeber, *American Sociological Review*, October, 1958, p. 582.

1959

An Approach to Psychological Theory in Terms of the Theory of Action.
Sigmund Koch (ed.), *Psychology: A Study of a Science*, Vol. III, New York: McGraw-Hill, pp. 612–711.

The Principal Structures of Community: A Sociological View.
(Also in *Structure and Process in Modern Society*, 1960.)
C. J. Friedrich (ed.), *Community*, New York: The Liberal Arts Press.

"Voting" and the Equilibrium of the American Political System.
Eugene Burdick and Arthur Brodbeck (eds.), *American Voting Behavior*, New York: The Free Press.

Durkeim's Contribution to the Theory of Integration of Social Systems. (Also in *Sociological Theory and Modern Society*.)
Kurt H. Wolff (ed.), *Emile Durkheim, 1858–1917*: A Collection of Essays, with Translations and a Bibliography, Columbus, Ohio: Ohio State University Press.

Implications of the Study.
(On Marjorie Fiske's "Book Selection and Retention in California Public and School Libraries.") *The Climate of Book Selection*, a symposium of the University of California School of Librarianship. Berkeley: University of California Press.

Some Problems Confronting Sociology as a Profession.
American Sociological Review, August, 1959.

The School Class as a Social System.
(Also in *Social Structure and Personality*, 1964.)
Harvard Educational Review, Fall, 1959. Reprinted in A. H. Halsey, Jean Floud, and Arnold C. Anderson (eds.), *Education, Economy and Society*, New York: The Free Press, 1961.

An Approach to the Sociology of Knowledge.
Proceedings, Fourth World Congress of Sociology at Milan, Italy, September, 1959, Vol. IV.

1960

Mental Illness and "Spiritual Malaise": The Roles of the Psychiatrist and of the Minister of Religion.
Hans Hofmann (ed.), The Ministry and Mental Health, New York: Association Press. (Also in *Social Structure and Personality*, 1964.)

Structure and Process in Modern Societies.
(A collection of essays.) New York: The Free Press; 334 pp.

In memoriam
"Clyde Kluckhohn 1905–1960," *American Sociological Review*, December, 1960.

The Mass Media and the Structure of American Society.
Co-author with Winston White, *Journal of Social Issues*, Vol. XVI, No. 3, 1960.

Pattern Variables Revisited: A Response to Professor Dubin's Stimulus.
American Sociological Review, August, 1960.

Toward a Healthy Maturity.
Journal of Health and Human Behavior, Fall, 1960. (Also in *Social Structure and Personality*, 1964.)

Social Structure and Political Orientation.
World Politics, October, 1960. (A review of S. M. Lipset, *Political Man*, and William Kornhauser, *The Politics of Mass Society*.)

Review of
Max Weber: An Intellectual Portrait, by Reinhard Bendix, *American Sociological Review*, October, 1960.

1961

Theories of Society.
Co-editor with Edward Shils, Kaspar D. Naegele, and Jesse R. Pitts. 2 Vols., New York: The Free Press.

Some Principal Characteristics of Industrial Societies.
C. E. Black (ed.), *The Transformation of Russian Society Since 1861*, Cambridge: Harvard University Press. (Also in *Structure and Process in Modern Society*, 1960.)

The Link Between Character and Society.
Co-author with Winston White, Seymour Lipset, and Leo Lowenthal (eds.), *Culture and Social Character*, New York: The Free Press. (Also in *Social Structure and Personality*, 1964.)

The Contribution of Psychoanalysis to the Social Sciences.
Science and Psychoanalysis, 1961, Vol. IV.

The Cultural Background of American Religious Organization.
The Proceedings of the Conference on Science, Philosophy and Religion, 1960.

The Point of View of the Author.
The Social Theories of Talcott Parsons, Max Black (ed.), Englewood Cliffs, N.J.: Prentice-Hall.

The Problem of International Community.
International Politics and Foreign Policy, James N. Rosenau (ed.), New York: The Free Press.

Polarization of the World and International Order.
Preventing World War III, Quincy Wright, William M. Evan, and Morton Deutsch (eds.), New York: Simon and Schuster, 1962. (Also in *Berkeley Journal of Sociology*, 1961.)

Youth in the Context of American Society.
Daedalus, Winter, 1961. Reprinted in *Youth: Change and Challenge*,

Erik H. Erikson (ed.), New York: Basic Books, 1963. (Also in *Social Structure and Personality*, 1964.)

Some Considerations on the Theory of Social Change.
Rural Sociology, Vol. 26, No. 3, September, 1961.

A Sociologist's View.
Values and Ideals of American Youth, Eli Ginzberg (ed.), New York: Columbia University Press.

Comment on
Llewellyn Gross, "Preface to a Metatheoretical Framework for Sociology," *American Journal of Sociology*, September, 1961.

In memoriam
"Alfred L. Kroeber, 1876–1960," *American Journal of Sociology*, Vol. LXVI, No. 6, May, 1961.

Comment on
William Kolb, "Images of Man and the Sociology of Religion," *Journal for the Scientific Study of Religion*, October, 1961.

Discussion of Trends Revealed by the 1960 Census of Population.
Proceedings of the Section on Social Statistics, American Statistical Association, 1961.

1962

Foreword
to *Herbert Spencer: The Study of Sociology*, University of Michigan Press, Ann Arbor Paperback Series.

In memoriam
"Clyde Kluckhohn, 1905–1960" (with Evon Z. Vogt), *American Anthropologist*, February, 1962. Reprinted as Introduction to a new edition of Kluckhohn's *Navajo Witchcraft*, Boston: Beacon Press, 1962.

Comment on
Dennis Wrong, "The Oversocialized Conception of Man," *Psychoanalysis and Psychoanalytic Review*, Summer, 1962.

Review of
Hurst, *Law and Social Process*, for *Journal of the History of Ideas*, October–December, 1962.

The Aging in American Society.
Law and Contemporary Problems, Winter, 1962.

The Law and Social Control.
Law and Sociology, William M. Evan (ed.), New York: The Free Press.

In memoriam
"Richard Henry Tawney, 1880–1962," *American Sociological Review*, December, 1962.

Review of
Paul Diesing, *Reason in Society*, in *Industrial and Labor Relations*

Review, July, 1963.
La struttura dell' azione sociale.
> Introduzione di Granfranco Poggi. Bologna: Il Molino. (Italian translation of *The Structure of Social Action*.)

1963

Introduction
> to Max Weber, *The Sociology of Religion* (translated by Ephraim Fischoff from *Wirtschaft und Gesellschaft*), Boston: Beacon Press, 1963.

Social Strains in America: A Postscript (1962).
> *The Radical Right*, Daniel Bell (ed.), Garden City, N.Y.: Doubleday.

Christianity and Modern Industrial Society.
> *Sociological Theory, Values, and Sociocultural Change: Essays in Honor of Pitirim A. Sorokin*, Edward A. Tiryakian (ed.), New York: The Free Press.

Social Change and Medical Organization in the United States.
> *Annals* of the American Academy of Political and Social Science, March, 1963.

On the Concept of Influence, with rejoinder to comments.
> *Public Opinion Quarterly*, Spring, 1963.

On the Concept of Political Power.
> Proceedings of the American Philosophical Society, Vol. 107, No. 3 (June, 1963). (*Influence* and *Power* also reprinted in *Sociological Theory and Modern Society*.)

Death in American Society.
> *The American Behavioral Scientist*, May, 1963.

1964

Some Theoretical Considerations Bearing on the Field of Medical Sociology.
> Written for a symposium that did not appear. Was published as Chapter 12 in *Social Structure and Personality*, 1964.

Social Structure and Personality.
> (A collection of essays.) New York: The Free Press.

The Ideas of Systems, Causal Explanation and Cybernetic Control in Social Science.
> *Cause and Effect*, Daniel Lerner (ed.), New York: The Free Press, 1965. (Presented at the 4th Hayden Colloquium, Massachusetts Institute of Technology, 1964.)

Evolutionary Universals in Society.
> *American Sociological Review*, June, 1964.

Max Weber, 1864–1964.
> *American Sociological Review*, April, 1964.

Sociological Theory.
Encyclopedia Britannica, 1965.
Some Reflections on the Place of Force in Social Process.
Internal War: Basic Problems and Approaches, Harry Eckstein (ed.), New York: The Free Press.
Levels of Organization and the Mediation of Social Interaction.
Sociological Inquiry, Spring, 1964.
Die Juengsten Entwicklungen in der Strukturell-Funktionalem Theorie.
Koelner Zeitschrift fuer Soziologie und Sozialpsychologie, 1964, 16, I, pp. 30-49. English version in Haring *Festschrift*.
Youth in the Context of American Society.
Man in a World at Work, Henry Borow (ed.), Boston: Houghton Mifflin. (Slightly modified version of an article previously written for *Daedalus*, 1961.)
Unity and Diversity in the Modern Intellectual Disciplines: The Role of the Social Sciences.
Daedalus, Winter, 1965, pp. 39-65.
Evaluation and Objectivity in the Social Sciences: An Interpretation of Max Weber's Contributions.
(An address delivered at the Weber Centennial, April, 1964.) Published in German with discussion in *Max Weber und die Soziologie Heute*, Otto Stammer (ed.), Tubingen: Mohr, 1965. English version published in the *International Journal of the Social Sciences*, 1965. (Also in *Sociological Theory and Modern Society*.)
Beitrage zur soziologischen Theorie.
Editor and translator, Dietrich Ruschmeyer; Luchterhand Verlag GmbH.

1965

An American's Impression of Sociology in the Soviet Union.
American Sociological Review, Vol. 30, No. 1, February, 1965.
Full Citizenship for the Negro American?
Daedalus, November, 1965. Reprinted in *The Negro American*, Parsons and Clark (eds.), 1966.

1966

Societies: Evolutionary and Comparative Perspectives.
Foundations of Modern Sociology Series, Alex Inkeles (general editor), Englewood Cliffs, N.J.: Prentice-Hall.
The Political Aspect of Social Structure and Process.
Varieties of Political Theory, David Easton (ed.), Englewood Cliffs, N.J.: Prentice-Hall.
The Negro American.
Co-author with Kenneth Clark. Boston: Houghton Mifflin.

Die Bedeutung der Polarisierung fuer das Sozialsystem: Die Hautfarbe als Polarisierungsproblem.
Militanter Humanismus, Alphons Silbermann (ed.), Frankfurt am Main: S. Fischer Verlag.

1967

The Nature of American Pluralism.
Religion and Public Education, Theodore Sizer (ed.), Boston: Houghton Mifflin, 1967.
Social Science and Theology.
America and the Future of Theology, William A. Beardslee (ed.), Philadelphia: The Westminster Press, 1967.
Sociological Theory and Modern Society.
New York: The Free Press, 1967.
Death in American Society.
Co-author with Victor M. Lidz. *Essays in Self-Destruction*, Edwin Shneidman (ed.), New York: Science House, 1967.
Comment on
Kenneth Boulding, "An Economist Looks at the Future of Sociology," *et al.*, Vol. 1, No. 2, Winter, 1967.

1968 and forthcoming.

Components and Types of Formal Organization.
Comparative Administrative Theory, Preston P. LeBreton (ed.), Seattle: University of Washington Press, 1968.
Comment on
Sir Eric Ashby, "The Future of the Nineteenth Century Idea of a University," *Minerva*, Spring, 1968.
American Sociology.
(A collection of essays edited by Talcott Parsons.) New York: Basic Books, 1968.
"Commentary" on
Clifford Geertz, "Religion as a Cultural System," Donald R. Cutler (ed.), *The Religious Situation: 1968*, Boston: Beacon Press, 1968.
Christianity.
Emile Durkheim.
Interaction: Social Interaction.
Vilfredo Pareto: Contributions to Economics.
Professions.
Systems Analysis: Social Systems.
Utilitarians: Sociological Thought.
International Encyclopedia of the Social Sciences, David L. Sills (ed.), New York: The Macmillan Company and The Free Press, 1968.

The Position of Identity in the General Theory of Action.
The Self in Social Interaction, Chad Gordon and Kenneth J. Gergen (eds.), New York: John Wiley and Sons, 1968.

The American Academic Profession: A Pilot Study.
Co-author with Gerald M. Platt. Cambridge: multilith, 1968.

The Academic System: A Sociologist's View.
The Public Interest, No. 13 (special issue), Fall, 1968.

On the Concept of Value-Commitments.
Sociological Inquiry, Vol. 38, No. 2, Spring, 1968.

Cooley and the Problem of Internalization.
Cooley and Sociological Analysis, Albert J. Reiss, Jr. (ed.), Ann Arbor: University of Michigan Press, 1968.

Sociocultural Pressures and Expectations.
(A paper presented to the American Psychiatric Association.) *Psychiatric Research Reports,* February, 1968.

Order as a Sociological Problem.
The Concept of Order. Paul G. Kuntz (ed.), Seattle: University of Washington Press, 1968.

The Problem of Polarization on the Axis of Color.
Color and Race, John Hope Franklin (ed.), Boston: Houghton Mifflin and Company, 1968.

Considerations on the American Academic System.
Co-author with Gerald M. Platt. *Minerva,* Vol. VI, No. 4, Summer, 1968.

Law and Sociology: A Promising Courtship?
The Path of the Law from 1967; Harvard Law School Sesquicentennial Papers, Arthur E. Sutherland (ed.), Cambridge: Harvard University Press, 1968.

The Disciplines as a Differentiating Force.
Co-author with Norman Storer. *The Foundations of Access to Knowledge,* Edward B. Montgomery (ed.), Syracuse, N.Y.: Syracuse University Division of Summer Sessions, 1968.

The System of Modern Societies.
Englewood Cliffs, N.J.: Prentice-Hall, forthcoming, 1969. Companion volume to *Societies: Evolutionary and Comparative Perspectives,* cited above.

Facilitating Technological Innovation in Society.
Purposive Systems, Proceedings of the First Annual Symposium of the American Society for Cybernetics. New York: Spartan Books, forthcoming.

Clyde Kluckhohn's Contribution to the Integration of the Social Sciences.
Essays in Anthropology, Evon Vogt and John Fischer (eds.), forthcoming.

Readings on Premodern Societies.
> Co-editor with Victor M. Lidz. Englewood Cliffs, N.J.: Prentice-Hall, forthcoming.

Kinship and the Associational Aspects of Social Structure.
> *Kinship and Culture*, Francis L. K. Hsu (ed.), Chicago: Aldine Press, forthcoming.

Higher Education as a Theoretical Focus.
> *Institutions and Social Exchange: The Sociologies of Talcott Parsons and George C. Homans*, Richard Simpson and Herman Turk (eds.), Indianapolis: Bobbs-Merrill, forthcoming.

Some Problems of General Theory in Sociology.
> *Theoretical Sociology: Perspectives and Developments*, John C. McKinney and Edward A. Tiryakian (eds.), New York: Appleton-Century-Crofts, forthcoming.

Some Afterthoughts on Gemeinschaft and Gesellschaft.
> To appear in a volume on Toennies edited by Werner J. Cahnman in the Heritage of Sociology Series, Chicago: University of Chicago Press.

Research with Human Subjects and the Professional Complex.
> *Daedalus*, Spring, 1969.

Higher Education and the Character of the American Age Structure.
> Co-author with Gerald M. Platt. *Aging and Society*, Matilda White Riley et al. (eds.), New York: Russell Sage Foundation, forthcoming.

Index